REPORTING
LIVE

LESLEY STAHL

Simon & Schuster

SIMON & SCHUSTER
Rockefeller Center
1230 Avenue of the Americas
New York, NY 10020

Copyright © 1999 by Lesley R. Stahl
All rights reserved,
including the right of reproduction
in whole or in part in any form.
SIMON & SCHUSTER and colophon are
registered trademarks of Simon & Schuster Inc.
Designed by Edith Fowler
Manufactured in the United States of America

10 9 8 7 6 5 4 3 2 1

Library of Congress Cataloging-in-Publication Data
Stahl, Lesley.
    Reporting live / Lesley Stahl.
        p.   cm.
    Includes index.
    1. Stahl, Lesley.   2. Reporters and reporting—
United States.   3. United States—Politics and
government—1945–1989.   4. United States—
Politics and government—1989– 5. Women
television journalists—United States—Biography.
I. Title.
PN4874.S63A3   1999
070'.92—dc21   98-43481   CIP
ISBN 0-684-82930-4

A leatherbound signed first edition of this book has
been published by Easton Press.

To Aaron and Taylor
Dolly and Lou

CONTENTS

PART ONE

NIXON
AND
WATERGATE

I WAS BORN on my 30th birthday. Everything up till then was prenatal. By 30 I knew two things for sure. One was that I wanted to be a journalist, which would mean, in the environment of the early 1970s, surmounting my femaleness and my blondness.

I was right about the profession. From my first story, journalism has been a drug. I love it, every aspect, just as I knew I would. But it turned out I wasn't as much of a natural as I thought I'd be. I had to plug away. There are two kinds of reporters. There are those like the late Charles Kuralt who wrote so well he could spin a good story out of one or two bits of information. And there's the other kind, door kickers like me. My reports have to have lots of hard facts.

The other thing I knew for sure was that I wanted to be like my father—not in his success at business, but in his character. He was patient, always respectful, gentle. I figured that in this matter too there'd be a lot of overcoming to be done.

By 1972 I was on the path toward goal one. I was an on-air reporter at Channel 5 in Boston.

I'D BEEN IN BOSTON for two years, enough time to finish decorating my apartment, which overlooked the Charles River—I could see the steeples at Harvard and the crew teams practicing early in the morning—and enough time to get snarled up in a going-nowhere romance. My boyfriend Amos was a sleek Cary Grant type. There was a time when his handsome face would live in my eyes all day long, even at work. My mother, Dolly, didn't appreciate him and—what a surprise—she wouldn't let me forget why. The why was that I was living "The Ballad of the Sad Café"; Amos had another girlfriend. She knew about me and I about her, yet we both clung to him for nearly two years. "He's agonized about this," I told Dolly. "Oh, sure," she said.

It was early April 1972. The Equal Employment Opportunity Act had just passed a month earlier, and the Federal Communications Commission had recently included women in its affirmative action program for television broadcasting. In other words, the television networks were scouring the country for women and blacks with any news experience at all. A friend in New York had called to tell me about a memo floating around CBS News mandating that "the next reporter we hire will be a woman."

I applied to all three networks, sending them each an audition tape, a "pitch reel" of my five best stories on Channel 5. I included a Thanksgiving feature about a group of hardy Bostonians living the way the Pilgrims had in the nonelectric, nonheated 17th century. They had ground up some wheat to make bread the old-fashioned way and offered me a piece. I took a bite, made a face, and almost heaved it up on camera. That story attracted Bill Small, CBS's bureau chief in Washington, where I would have thought there was little need for a comedienne. But he invited me for an audition.

Small at 45 was a gentle bulldog, known for his firm control of his bureau. He was a large man with a cherubic face and a voice so soft you had to lean in to hear him. After a brief chat, he handed me two fat rolls of wire copy and said, "Here, read these. Then let's see if you can write up a few radio pieces."

I worked hard on those radio scripts, because CBS had the premiere news department and I wanted to work there. The anchorman, Walter Cronkite — "Uncle Walter" — was number one in the ratings, and his team, his horsemen, were inspired by the legacy of Edward R. Murrow, who, in creating television journalism, had insisted on the highest standards of reporting.

Without grading my radio reports, Small sent me off, saying, "We'll be in touch." I was back in my apartment in Boston a few days later when the phone rang. Amos was there trying to distract me, so I said, "Shut up! It's Small."

"Excuse me," said Small, the inaudible. He had heard me say "Shut up." It was a movie. I was living a movie. "How soon can you get here?" That's how he started the conversation.

"Well, I have to pack up my apartment here, find a place to live in Washington, which I know nothing about. I think I could do it in, say, two weeks."

"If you can't start tomorrow," he said, "forget it." Small's reputation was that he was tougher than Walter Burns in the play *The Front Page*. But with all his gruffness, he had won the affection of the reporters in the bureau (as he would mine), because he simply would not tolerate attempts by the administration in power to chill him or his reporters. He stood up for his people, defending them from attacks either from outside the company or from his superiors at CBS, who were called, in those days, "those assholes in New York."

I said good-bye to Boston, to Amos (and the girlfriend), and started at CBS News in Washington the next day. My mother was ecstatic.

It was springtime. And my career was about to begin.

THIS WAS A TIME of prosperity and accomplishment for the CBS Washington Bureau. We had 21 reporters and correspondents (today there are nine), more than the other networks in numbers and quality. William Paley, who founded CBS, came close to pampering his News Division. We were his spoiled children, so money was rarely a factor in decision making. Experts were hired, boats rented, planes chartered. Physically, however, the Washington Bureau was a slum. The newsroom looked like a boneyard for old newspapers and coffee cups with floating cigarette butts.

I felt like Alice with everything oversized. On the left was a row of booths where editors were slumped over Moviola machines, cutting strands of film by hand with razor blades and splicing them together with narrow strips of Scotch tape. Along the back wall I gawked at a row of offices with no doors that looked like the windows at Saks Fifth Avenue. The occupants were always on view, onstage. And what occupants! There in one row was the reason CBS News was known as the crown jewel. On the far right was Dan Rather, 40, then covering the Nixon White House. He was fearless, and I wanted to be just like him. Next came Dan Schorr, 55, CBS's famous investigative reporter, known for breaking stories and creating controversy about himself. To his left was the State Department correspondent, Marvin Kalb, 41, a foreign policy expert with a special interest in the Soviet Union. Next was Roger Mudd, 44, the best writer in the bureau, who covered Capitol Hill with a delicious sauciness. He was a giant of a man with hands the size of shovels. Last was the office of George Herman, 52, a refined man who moderated *Face the Nation*, the Sunday interview program, and managed to float above the feuding that entangled all the others in that upscale neighborhood.

In the middle of the newsroom was "the desk." Actually, it was an island of desks where Bill Galbraith, the assignment editor, ruled over a litter of assistants and radio editors with an authoritarianism expressed, incongruously, in a disturbing whine. It was made clear to me almost immediately that this "heart of the newsroom" had little use for the women and minorities raked in by affirmative action. I was introduced to the two other "affirmative action babies" in what became known as the Class of '72. Connie Chung, 25, loved to tell self-deprecating jokes about being Chinese, about how Bill Small had hired her because, she'd say, "I do his shirts with extra starch!" The other in our threesome was Bernie Shaw, 31, a handsome black man with a mild, let's-be-friends manner.

In the beginning we had to scrounge around every day for a place to sit. Not that we expected to have our own open-faced offices in the newsroom or even an office in the back where the less famous correspondents worked: Marvin Kalb's brother Bernie, Nelson Benton, Phil Jones, Bob Pierpoint, Bob Schieffer. But the space we got was, well, inconvenient. We were each given a desk in a narrow corridor in the back. I don't recall that there were any chairs, which was just as well, because if we had sat at the desks, our knees would have hit our chins. They were second-graders' desks, useful only as a reminder of our status there.

After several weeks doing radio, my first TV report on *The CBS*

13

Evening News with Walter Cronkite was about a hijacking at Dulles Airport. It was brief, a minute long, and voiced over, meaning you never saw me on camera. But as was the custom for such debuts, everyone in the newsroom gave me a standing ovation, even Marvin Kalb and Roger Mudd. It was the best day of my life.

A few weeks later I reported on a promising new cancer treatment. (Over the next 20 years, I would go on to cover at least a dozen more supposedly promising cancer treatments.) This one was called BCG, and I did appear in the piece in my first network on-camera stand-up. I was so proud. I couldn't wait to hear from my cheerleader-critic mother. But she didn't call. This was curious since she called at every turn, even when she heard me on radio. (By then I had learned the bureau motto: "Fuck radio." Which was the attitude one was expected to adopt when working on a television story.)

When I called home, my dad had that she's-mad-at-you voice. What had I done this time? Dolly grabbed the phone. I could tell we wouldn't be talking to each other for days. "Forty million Americans saw you tonight. One of them is my future son-in-law, but he's never going to call you for a date," she said, "because you wore your glasses."

I managed to finish my third story for the *Evening News* early enough to hang around the newsroom, making friends and getting to know the other reporters. I was chatting with Fred Graham, our Justice Department correspondent, when John Armstrong, one of the television producers, hollered out, "Stahl! For Chrissake, where is she? Stahl!" I could tell I had done something very wrong. When he found me, he was livid. "You smiled. You smiled in the stand-up. Thank God there's still time for you to redo it. Kid, never, ever, ever smile. Ever." I was to be purged of all signs of humanity; the only display of personality allowed was a grimace. I don't think this core curriculum in TV comportment was taught with such vigor to the men. Women had to be trained especially hard to come across as authoritative.

As I worked on projecting a commanding presence, Dolly was waging a guerrilla war against my glasses. "Don't you think there's a reason Walter doesn't wear *his* glasses on television?" she would argue. "Don't you think Barbara Walters — she's so smart — has looked into this? *She* doesn't wear glasses on television."

My mother and I were fighting two different wars. She told me often enough that "good-looking people do better in life, and you'd better not forget it." She was always harping on me about my hair: "You need to go in to New York and get Kenneth to style it. That's where Jackie Kennedy goes." About my makeup: "Can't you find something to hide those circles under your eyes?" My clothes: "Where on earth did you pick up that little number? Get rid of it." It wasn't that I disagreed with my mother. It was just that her formula for success, being beautiful, had the effect of making people think I was brainless.

I knew my colleagues saw me as a lightweight, unqualified to join the Super Bowl champs of TV news. I had to find ways to convey my seriousness, to send out signals that I was resolute and earnest, not what the wrapping said I was. So I wore my glasses and worked round the clock.

I also promised myself I would never blame my setbacks on sexism. If thoughts like "It's just 'cause I'm a woman" crept into my head, I sat on them. I told myself, "Lesley, work harder. If you're good, they'll have to use you." And I assumed that Bill Small hadn't hired me because he wanted me to fail. If you were one of "Small's people" (Dan Rather, Marvin Kalb, and Bob Schieffer), you were under a special cloak of protection, and he promoted you. I had to become part of that club.

I wondered if I ever would. One day Small came by and read over my shoulder in the newsroom: "Congress, resting on its collective elbow . . ." Making sure everyone saw, he ripped the paper out of the typewriter carriage, crumpled it, and made a perfect hook shot into the wastebasket. "C'mon," he sniffed. Twelve thousand capillaries exploded in my stomach. *He's going to fire me. I can't write. He knows it. I've been found out. I want to die.*

I felt that way constantly in those days. One reason was that my very presence seemed to inspire resentment among several of the camera crews. Most of the cameramen were veterans in their 50s and 60s, and their attitude toward the new hires — two women and a black man — was not exactly welcoming. They acted as though we had cut in line, hadn't paid our dues, didn't belong in the precious orbit of the CBS Washington Bureau. How do I know they resented our being there? Because they wanted me to know.

In those days there was a clear distinction between the reporters and the crews. The crews were generally older and far more conservative politically. Reporters, for the most part, had come to oppose the Vietnam War; the crews had not. Reporters, for the most part, had come to dislike Richard Nixon; the crews had not. Reporters, for the most part, had come to see the national goal of racial and gender equality as a worthy one; the crews had not.

When I first got to Washington, the 1972 presidential election campaign was under way. One afternoon I was sent to cover a rally sponsored by Nixon's Committee for the Re-election of the President (CREEP) and discovered that far from the advertised spontaneous gathering of D.C. workers, most of those assembled were Republican stalwarts bused in from the suburbs.

15

"Get me some pictures of those buses over there," I said.

"What kind of stupid idea is that?" growled the cameraman in front of a crowd. An urge to weep became a recurring problem. If I got it in the office, I would hold it in until I could get to the ladies' room, where I'd duck into one of the stalls and sob—no noise, of course. But out on a story, there was no hiding place. Often in the crew cars, I'd be locked up with these tormentors for hours, staring into their looks of contempt. I can still hear one cameraman as he argued into his walkie-talkie, "Do I *have* to work with her?" making sure I overheard. Of course, they did have to work with me and I with them.

One day I was sent to Arlington National Cemetery to cover a ceremony at John Kennedy's grave. When the cameraman saw that I was the reporter on the story, he picked up his heavy camera cases and hurled them one by one into the trunk of his car, creating a series of explosions. Everyone around the grave site looked up in terror. The bullyragging was toughening me up.

I found an apartment in the Watergate complex, moved all my stuff from Boston, and didn't miss a day of work. Amos came to visit, though less and less often, but that was all right because I worked all the time. I was determined to show everybody I could do this: the crews; Bill Small, who had given me this opportunity; and David Brinkley. When I had worked at NBC News in the late 1960s, I'd asked his advice about a producer's job in London. Brinkley had told me I was not going to make it in journalism. "You're a pretty blonde," he'd said. "You should stay in New York and have fun." I decided I'd show him.

JUNE 1972. Most of the reporters in our bureau were on the road, covering the presidential campaign. Thus, I was sent out to cover the arrest of some men who had broken into one of the buildings in the Watergate complex. That CBS let me, the newest hire, hold on to Watergate as an assignment was a measure of how unimportant the story seemed: just "a third-rate burglary," in the words of Nixon's press secretary, Ron Ziegler.

It was considered so unnewsworthy that I was the only television reporter covering the early court appearances. When the five Watergate burglars asked the judge for a bail reduction, I got my first scoop. Unlike my competitors, I was able to identify them. That time the cameraman listened when I said, "Roll! That's them!" And so CBS was the only network to get pictures of the burglars. I was a hero at the bureau.

The judge asked one of the men, James McCord, what he did for a living. "Security consultant," he said. "Who have you worked for?" the judge asked. "The CIA." He said it so softly, I had to ask the people around me, "What did he say? Not the CIA?"

With each surprise, I would race to a phone in the hallway and call in to the CBS Radio desk to offer a piece, often breathlessly: "These guys are from Cuba" or "They were carrying around phony passports!" or "They had money in consecutively numbered hundred-dollar bills." While I was sensing an earthquake of a story, the editors in the bureau tended to rely more on *The New York Times* than on the new kid. And the *Times* thought the Richter scale number on Watergate was so low, it wasn't even covering the story. So while I recorded piece after piece over the phone, I learned years later that they had rarely been used on the air.

Within a few weeks the case moved up to the federal court, where still the only other people in the press section were from the Washington *Star* and *The Washington Post*. I had a rule against flirting in the office, but technically this wasn't the office, so when the preppie-looking guy introduced himself — "Hi, I'm Bob Woodward with the *Post*" — I made sure he knew I wanted to be friends. He called me for a date later that day. And so I began to forget about Amos.

It was clear why so many sources confided in Bob Woodward. He had a protective personality, a way of making you feel you could trust him. He was also driven, acting as if he were making up for lost time. I was like that too. In fact, we were at the same place in our careers: little-known rookies with no track records.

Everyone I knew in Washington was obsessed with their work, but Bob's tenacity bordered on clinical compulsion, which was why he was such a good reporter. He never left any doubt about his list of priorities: I came after Watergate, Carl Bernstein, and the entire staff at *The Washington Post*, including the pressmen.

It seemed odd that such opposite characters as Bob and Carl could form a partnership — until you got to know them. Together they were the complete journalist. Bob was the persistent, kick-the-door-down type who would make the 100th phone call and pursue without letup. Carl, more of a loosey-goosey creative person, was an elegant writer. They were the real Oscar and Felix. Bob, always punctual and meticulously thorough, was a man of straight lines. Carl's lines wiggled. He was undisciplined, inventive. Bob was methodical, Carl intuitive.

Once when I called Bob, Carl got on the phone and barked at me, "The only reason you go out with Bob is because you're trying to get him to share his sources." Was I wrong to be insulted? The truth was that Bob told me next to nothing. I didn't even know there was a Deep Throat, though I was aware he was interviewing some guy in a garage as well as White House secretaries late at night. Several times when I thought the Watergate story was dying — "Bob, this story has no legs" — he'd encourage me to stick with it. "You must hang on to this," he would say. "Trust me."

Late in the summer of 1972 "Woodstein," as the *Post* team was known, began writing stories about secret "hush money" flowing from the

Nixon campaign to the burglars. But Watergate was not registering with the public.

One reason was that newspapers around the country were reluctant to follow the lead of two young *Washington Post* reporters who rarely revealed their sources. It was often the case that local papers ran denials of Woodstein's reports without ever having run the original story. But CBS saw the significance, so Cronkite often repeated Woodstein's exclusives. One problem for me was that this was a story without pictures. Up to that time there was an axiom in television that for the most part, if it wasn't visual, we couldn't cover it.

But that changed right before the election. Walter Cronkite, as managing editor of the *Evening News*, decided to put together a Watergate primer, pictures or not. Producer Stanhope Gould was put in charge. In his late 30s, he looked like no other CBS producer. Most of them wore tweed jackets and narrow Ivy League ties; Gould, with his dusty jeans and stringy ponytail, radiated "counterculture." But he was smart and imaginative, just the man to solve the no-pictures problem.

He set up shop in the Washington bureau, and I was called in to help. Relying heavily on Woodstein's reporting, Gould wrote a script and designed a package of graphics to explain as clearly and simply as possible what we knew about the scandal up to that point. Cronkite was the narrator. While the piece was pointed and cleverly illustrated, its most important message was its length: 14 minutes, well over half the broadcast. That by itself would be a signal that CBS News considered Watergate momentous and pressing. There was a debate in New York about making it shorter, but Cronkite wanted to air the entire package and put his personal prestige behind it.

The first time I met Walter Cronkite, I was surprised at how young he looked in person. I had always heard that television makes you look ten years older; it put 20 years on Cronkite. I liked him right away, but then, most people did. Convivial and unpretentious, he is of that rare breed who wear the cloak of fame comfortably.

He was our leader in the true sense. If he as much as breathed that we in the bureau had been second best on a story, we'd pour ashes on our heads for a week. Once Cronkite thought a story had merit, CBS would pounce on it with full energy, as with the space launches. And in the unusual case when he took a stand on an issue, it had enormous influence. In 1968, when Walter declared on the *Evening News* that it was time for the United States to get out of the war in Vietnam,[1] Lyndon Johnson said, "If I've lost Walter Cronkite, I've lost Mr. Average Citizen." Now Cronkite was taking a stand on Watergate.

His 14-minute story ran on Friday, October 27, 11 days before the election. There was great excitement in the bureau. We all knew that allotting so much time to reporting the charges of wrongdoing would incite the wrath of the Nixon White House and campaign. A large group gathered in the newsroom to watch. When the Watergate piece ran, we all applauded, because it was powerful and brave, and I was filled with pride. Cronkite and Gould set to work immediately on part two, a 14-minute follow-up about the Nixon campaign's money laundering. What we didn't know was that over the weekend White House aide Charles Colson called CBS Chairman Bill Paley at home. (Colson was famous for his comment that he would drive a truck over his grandmother for Richard Nixon.) When he spoke to Paley, he was in high dudgeon, accusing CBS News not only of irresponsibility but of being in the pocket of Nixon's Democratic opponent, George McGovern.[2]

I had swallowed the CBS promise that there was an unbreachable wall between management and the News Division, that reporters were insulated from corporate pressure. The wall, if it had ever existed, crumbled like old newspapers. On Monday Paley all but ordered the president of CBS News, Richard Salant, to kill part two.

Putting his job on the line, Salant refused, though he did instruct the *Evening News* to trim down the time. Some say he stood up to Paley and preserved a hard-hitting Watergate report, but Stanhope Gould felt that Salant had caved in to corporate pressure, and was furious. He stomped around accusing our bosses of cowardice and timidity, but the deadline pressure impinged and he was forced to cut part two nearly in half. Even in that truncated form, it was two to three times longer than most pieces. This report implicated the White House chief of staff, H. R. Haldeman, and former Attorney General John Mitchell, then chairman of Nixon's reelection campaign. The final stroke was Cronkite's conclusion that the White House denials about Watergate were not convincing. Yet eight days later Nixon won the election by a landslide. When the economy is healthy, as it was in 1972, the public is reluctant to change leaders, even in the midst of a scandal.

I watched our CBS election coverage at home with Woodward, who was stunned by the results. He had been certain the CBS pieces would turn the tide.

JANUARY, 1973. My assignment on Inauguration Day was to ride in the wire service car in the parade down Pennsylvania Avenue. We were several cars behind the president's armored limousine, I in the backseat, my cameraman right behind us taking pictures, perched dangerously on the tailgate of a station wagon. The soundman held him in place — his only security against a sudden stop of the motorcade.

While I took notes, Helen Thomas of UPI was in the front seat on an open phone line, dictating a running commentary. Of course, the baton had already been passed from AP and UPI to CBS and NBC. We were the real wire services, since the parade was on live TV. As we inched along, I had a queasy feeling that this was what it must have been like moments before Kennedy was shot in Dallas.

But Kennedy's crowds had been welcoming. Helen was describing one angry disruption after the next: antiwar protests and chantings ("Four more years of death!"), obscenities, flag burnings, smoke bombs, and even eggs and fruit hurled at Nixon's limo.

And then the denouement. Despite the lesson of Dallas, Nixon threw open the sunroof, stood up with Pat, and waved defiantly. He had won a landslide victory. He should have been on top of the world. But even that day he threw down the gauntlet.

BOB AND I decided to go to New York together for a weekend. I assumed we were there to take a break from Watergate, go to the art galleries, take in Greenwich Village, try out the new "in" restaurant. But Bob wanted to work. First he insisted we try to find John Mitchell's wife, Martha, who had taken to calling reporters late at night with on-the-record jibes at Nixon. When we couldn't find her, Bob wanted to sit in the hotel room and read.

When the weekend was over, so were we. I had made it through without one display of emotion. My self-discipline at work was leaching into my personal life.

AS THE WATERGATE STORY got bigger, I got bigfooted. CBS made Dan Schorr the primary Watergate correspondent. I became his backup. His number two. His slave. And I was eager to learn from the master. My job was to gather up information and feed it all to Dan for his reports on television. That left only radio for me, though he often insisted that radio was part of his franchise as well. Dan and I covered the first trial of the Watergate burglars together. It was supposed to start in November but was postponed for two months because the presiding judge, John J. Sirica, had a pinched nerve. "Maximum John" Sirica was liked by the press because he had a fondness for us that was unusual for a conservative Republican. As chief judge, he made the decision to set up a spacious newsroom, so we were able to transmit our stories from inside the courthouse. And he imposed no restrictions outside the building, which meant we could chase after the various witnesses to get pictures of them as they came to testify, even big-deal White House officials.

I was a regular. I lived at the court, chasing after suspects as they came in to plea-bargain or staking out the grand jury. One day I was in hot pursuit of Donald Segretti, who had run a Nixon campaign dirty-tricks operation. Months later, he would tell me that he and I had stood shoulder to shoulder in the courthouse elevator that day as I studied the only picture I had of him, a grainy newspaper photo. He said he had gotten off on the sixth floor; there had been not a flicker of recognition on my part.

I often sat on the floor outside the prosecutor's office with my main competitor, ABC's hyperkinetic Sam Donaldson, long-lost brother of Mr. Spock on *Star Trek*. He was fun to be with and so competitive that he put my drive into warp speed. From time to time the judge would invite small groups of us in for a chat. "I can't tell you fellas and gals anything about the case, ya know what I mean," he would say. And then he'd tell us stories about his boxing career and his friend Jack Dempsey.

As the trial progressed, Sirica grew increasingly impatient with the prosecutor, Earl Silbert, who one day pointed to defendant G. Gordon Liddy, general counsel on Nixon's reelection committee, and declared, "He's the mastermind." Liddy was the only one of the seven men on trial who talked to the press. During the breaks he would lean over the bar in the front of the courtroom and boast about his exploits. Once, he told us that he liked to hold his hand in a candle flame, just for fun.

Sirica wasn't buying Silbert's theory about Liddy. "He kept needling the prosecutor," I reported. "What about the higher-ups?" Sirica would ask. "Aren't you going to ask about the higher-ups?" I questioned the propriety of a judge second-guessing a prosecutor like that in open court, but Sirica went even further. To the chagrin of the defense team and the prosecutor, to the amazement of the press, the judge began cross-examining. "Isn't it true that you have been under great pressure to plead guilty?" he asked one of the burglars, Bernard Barker. "I want to know where the money comes from. There were hundred-dollar bills floating around like coupons." It was incredible.

When the defendant replied that he had gotten the money "in the mail in a blank envelope," Sirica shot back, "I'm sorry, I don't believe you." When the defense lawyers protested the judge's intrusions, he responded, "I don't think we should sit up here like nincompoops. The function of a trial is to search for the truth."

With each judicial intervention, I would bound out of the courtroom, race down the corridor — not so easy in my spike heels — then down three flights of stairs to the pressroom, where a microphone with an open line to CBS had been installed for the trial. On rare occasions the news was dramatic enough for a bulletin: "This is a CBS News instant report," I'd pant. "I'm Lesley Stahl, reporting from the U.S. District Court in Washington, where Judge Sirica has just accused one of the Watergate defendants of lying." It read well, but because I had just run a sprint, I sounded as if I were in distress, in which case I was reprimanded. But there was no way I could be on the air first and not sound out of breath.

When I complained to a friend that I was at a gender disadvantage, she said, "Well, then, wear sneakers." Which was bitchy, since I loved my high heels and she knew it.

Five of the Watergate defendants pleaded guilty; James McCord and G. Gordon Liddy were convicted of conspiracy, burglary, and illegal wiretapping. Sirica postponed the sentencing for three months to squeeze them into breaking their silence. He signaled that he would be lenient if they "spoke freely." He squeezed so hard, legal scholars complained that the judge was crossing the line. But it worked. On March 23, 1973, the day of sentencing, Sirica read a letter in court from defendant James McCord revealing that indeed there had been higher-ups and that perjury had been committed at the trial. Dan Schorr was out of town, so I got to tell the country that the lid was about to blow off the Watergate cover-up.

RIGHT AROUND THAT TIME I met Senator Bob Dole, then chairman of the Republican Party. Recently divorced, he too lived in the Watergate complex. One night when we were both in the lobby picking up our mail, he asked me out.

I found him funny, attractive, and marvelous company, even though, as he admitted, he never read books — "only newspapers and the *Congressional Record.*" But who needs book smarts when you have an acerbic tongue? He had an amiable way of forgetting I was a reporter, jabbing slyly at his fellow pols.

At dinner, he would ask me to cut his meat; he couldn't because his right arm had been injured beyond use during World War II. He told me that before the war he had assumed that he'd be able to ride out his life on his good looks, but then in Italy, as he was trying to rescue his radioman, he had been hit by machine-gun fire. "Everything, everything was shattered," he said. "I had nothing left. I had never studied much in high school. Without my looks and my body, I felt there was nothing I could do. When I was finally able to get up out of bed and look at myself in a mirror, I wanted to die." He said he had had to build a whole new person. This was a man who had suffered and overcome, and while I was sure there was bitterness there, he showed me none of it.

While we swapped stories about ourselves, we also discussed the topic that was consuming all of Washington: Had Nixon known ahead of time about the Watergate break-in and/or the cover-up? Dole told me he wanted to ask Nixon face-to-face, but he was having trouble getting in to see him. "Haldeman and [John D.] Ehrlichman [Nixon's close aides] have built a wall around the president." He was perplexed: "I'm chairman of the Republican National Committee, and I have no way to get in to see him. They're keeping me away. They've decided to cut me out."

"How do you know it isn't Nixon himself?" I asked.

" 'Cause I know."

"Oh, come on," I said, "it has to be Nixon who for one reason or another doesn't want to confront you. They're only following his orders. How could you possibly think they run him?"

If Haldeman and Ehrlichman were controlling Bob Dole's access, then they were the ones who were running the Watergate cover-up. I could see him fighting the inevitable conclusion that Nixon was involved.

THE STAKEOUT is an opportunity for reporters to relinquish their dignity by loitering around someone's office or house waiting to ask a question the target wants to avoid. The stakeout became a prime tool of news gathering once "Woodstein" had guided the Watergate story into the Nixon White House. After that it was hard to reach anyone close to the president, so CBS decided to intercept the principals at their homes before they left for work in the morning. I was one of the instruments through which CBS practiced this degrading form of journalism, chosen because I was too new to say no. I became a stakeout queen.

There was a time in 1973 when I, at the home of one or another of the Watergate suspects every morning, caught many of them in their pajamas as they opened their doors to pick up *The Washington Post*: Mitchell, Haldeman, Ehrlichman. The assignment desk would tell me, "Be there before the sun comes up." It was dirty work, especially when wives came running after you in their bathrobes, hollering, "Get off my lawn!" One day I was sent to stake out Jeb Magruder, deputy director of the Nixon campaign. I asked his children as they walked to school if their dad was still home. Gail Magruder tore out of their house and chewed my face off. She was right.

One morning the desk called to send me to the home of Justice William O. Douglas. "Stake out a Supreme Court justice?" I asked. "What has *he* done?"

"We just want pictures of him jogging for a profile Fred Graham's doing," said the deskman.

"But it's hailing out," I said, "and he's 75 years old."

"If you knew more about this town, kid," the assignment editor said condescendingly, "you'd realize that Douglas is a great outdoorsman and if he doesn't jog per se, he'll be out there walking his dog. So get there . . . before the sun comes up."

The crew was just delighted to be sitting in the dark at 5:30 A.M. in front of Douglas's house with the pitter-patter of hail on the car roof. They blamed me.

There was no sign of activity around the Douglas house at 5:30 or 6:30. In fact, nothing happened till 9:30 (you had to have an iron bladder to be a good staker-outer), when Justice Harry A. Blackmun pulled up in a limousine—they were carpooling—that went right up the driveway. Mrs. Douglas, who was much younger than her husband, held the outdoorsman tightly around his waist as he made a shaky trip across the icy pavement. The crew and I waited at the base of the driveway. The justice lowered the electric window. "Good morning, sir. We're here to get pictures of you jogging."

"Are you crazy?" asked Douglas. "I'm 75, and it's hailing!"

Failure never discouraged the assignment editors, and every now and then a stakeout paid off. I got an interview with Jeb Magruder the morning he was fingered by Woodward and Bernstein as a central Watergate player. Even if an official refused to talk, I often got pictures—manna in my world.

I usually drove back to the bureau with the crew unless my pictures or interviews were "hot" and it was possible I could get them onto the *Morning News*. Then I would reach the assignment editor, Galbraith, on a walkie-talkie and he would send a courier to pick me up. The couriers —CBS had a stable of them—were good-ole-boy motorcycle cowboys (and one cowgirl). If we were on deadline, Galbraith would scream over a radio, "Get up on the sidewalk! Do what you have to do, but get that stuff in here *now!*" I, in a dress, would sit sidesaddle on a Harley-Davidson hog and worry about my hair.

MARCH 1973. As the Watergate story pierced the White House wall, President Nixon tried to plead "executive privilege" to keep his counsel, John Dean, from testifying before Congress. I was dispatched to the White House to be Dan Rather's helper for a day. Just after Dan left for lunch, an unexpected announcement came over the loudspeaker system: "The president will be in the pressroom momentarily to take questions." There was pandemonium as the crews raced their cameras into position.

By the time Nixon walked into the briefing room, there was a crush. I found a place to stand along the side. When I saw him, I wondered, as I had so many times before: How did such an awkward, uncomfortable man ever get elected president of the United States? An election is a popularity contest: he seemed to lack the grace and simple likability you'd think would be a basic requirement. It was through sheer doggedness and tenacity that he had made his great comeback from his narrow defeat by John F. Kennedy in 1960.

I had never asked a president a question, so I felt brave raising my hand like the veteran reporters, but Nixon ignored me. So I waved my hand and pumped my hand and flapped until finally he saw me. I could tell he was curious about this new face with the long blond hair. So he called on me. It was the first question that day about Watergate, and he

24

was not pleased. I asked if he would allow his White House counsel, John Dean, to appear before Congress to answer questions about the scandal. "Would you object to that?" I asked.

"Of course," he said dismissively.

With my heart racing, I got up the gumption to follow up. "Why?" I asked, trying to keep my voice firm.

"Well, because it's executive privilege. . . . No president could ever agree to allow the counsel to the president to go down and testify before a committee." This he said as if the question was absurdly stupid. Had I asked a dumb question? I was filled with self-doubt.

Although Nixon rarely appeared in the pressroom, he did again a week later on March 15, 1973, and there I was, my second assignment at the White House. This time Nixon noticed me right away, and even though my hand was not waving around — it wasn't even raised — he turned to me and, well, apologized for the put-down. He was discussing executive privilege: "I answered that question rather abruptly, you recall, the last time I was asked by one of the ladies of the press here." He looked straight at me. "I did not mean to be abrupt, I simply meant to be firm." I blushed for 30 minutes at least.

THE SENATE HEARINGS on Watergate got under way on May 17. I was progressing, cultivating sources, breaking a few stories. I was still tethered to Dan Schorr, but even as his number two, I was glad to be covering the biggest story in the world.

The Senate Caucus Room has towering, 50-foot Corinthian columns, mahogany and pink marble walls, a coffered ceiling, and pendulous chandeliers. It says: this is where important business takes place. Mary McCarthy, writing for the London *Observer*, sat next to Norman Mailer, movie stars made cameo appearances, and people all over Washington fought to get a VIP seat for a day. To me it was home.

I sat up front in the press section at a long table next to Mary McGrory of the Washington *Star*, a veteran who wrote better than any of the other 250 reporters in that room. In between witnesses, she and I talked about politics and clothes. She told me she resented the young women who had gotten their jobs through affirmative action. I squirmed.

I figured out who on the committee leaked and who didn't. By then most of the press corps had adopted "Woodstein's" style of quoting anonymous sources, and there were plenty of those to go around. One source, highly placed, keyed in on me, giving me one scoop after the next, leaking the secrets the committee investigators were learning from interviews with various witnesses.

Why do people in government leak? Sometimes it's because they hope that publicizing information about an issue will help build support

25

for whichever side they're on. Sometimes they're merely settling a score, getting even. In the case of my Senate source, I think, to be honest about it, that he thought I would be grateful. One night he visited me at home. It was the only time a source was ever that brazen with me. "How about a hug? Let's have a kiss," he said, but without forcing himself on me. No favors, period, though I tried to be as diplomatic as I could. Dolly had taught me that the surest way to create an enemy is to embarrass him. Luckily, I did not lose him as a source.

Another Senate source on the Republican side passed a big story my way. I transmitted it to Schorr for his *Evening News* piece, as I was expected to, and he reported it on the air that night. When I went back to the office, I was surprised that no one said, "Great get, Stahl." I had begun to bridle at my role as Schorr's factotum. I had assumed he would be my mentor, but unfortunately, he wasn't teaching. While he seemed proud to parade the young blonde around as his protégée, he acted as though I were a threat. But as long as my bosses knew when I had brought home the bacon, it was tolerable. So that night I said something: "Hey, what about my story?" I was told that Schorr had gotten that one on his own. That was too much to take. Instead of tears, out came ferocity and temper. Before I could control it, there it was, a loud, very loud growl: "I will *never* give him a story again."

Schorr responded by telling me I was finished at CBS. And his producer, John Armstrong, said he was reporting me to Small, who was out of town.

All weekend I ground my teeth and worried that my career was over. On Monday I went to see Small: "You must hear my side of this. I hope you haven't formed any opinions about me not being a team player without hearing me out." Small was inscrutable. All he said was "You need a haircut." (Dolly was instructing me to keep my hair long.) "But, Mr. Small, I have my version of what happened."

"I was beginning to think you would never stand up to that SOB," he said. "I was beginning to think I was wrong about you. Now that you've shown me a little spine, I think you're ready to go out and report on your own."

From that day on I was the official *Morning News* correspondent covering the Senate hearings, and if I could come up with my own story, I would get on the *Evening News*.

I worked even harder than before, cultivating a Senate source who was so consistently reliable, he made me famous. One day he called with one of his best tips: Rose Mary Woods, the president's personal secretary, had been deliberately evading the U.S. marshals who were trying to serve her with a subpoena. They had tried so many times that they were now in the process of "surrounding the White House with a ring of marshals to catch her when she leaves to go home," he told me.

"You've got to be kidding!" Not only would this be a hell of a scoop, but we'd get pictures to boot. He said, "You're the only one who knows. This is very hush-hush." At CBS we had rules to live by, and one was that we had to disclose our sources to at least one producer. In my case it was the top producer in Washington for the *Evening News,* Ed Fouhy, a young, charismatic ex-marine everyone in the bureau wanted to follow into battle. If his bosses in New York asked, "Do you feel safe with this story?" he could say, "The source is golden" or "I have to be honest, the source is shaky."

No one called my source "Deep Throat," but "Lesley's guy" was golden. He had an impeccable record for accuracy. So there was no question we would react to his tip with all our resources. Crews were pulled away from stakeouts and out of hearings. It was pretty late in the day, around five o'clock, so the dispatching of crews to all the gates of the White House put a strain on the bureau, but it was done. Bob Pierpoint, the seasoned correspondent who was Rather's backup at the White House, was asked to walk outside and locate the marshals for the crews.

I started writing a script. My piece was number one in the lineup. I'd be the lead. At 5:30 Pierpoint called me. "Hey," he said with an edge, "I just ran all around the White House [an arduous hike, the equivalent of about 12 city blocks] and didn't see a single marshal. What a cocka-mamy story, Lesley."

I called "my guy." He made some calls himself and got right back. "They should be there," he assured me. By 6:15, with only 15 minutes to air, I nearly panicked. I called Terry Lenzner, the chief investigator of the Senate Watergate Committee, and his lieutenant, Scott Armstrong. "You have to tell me about these marshals," I insisted. "I'm about to go on the air and say they're surrounding the White House. If it's not true, it would be irresponsible of you not to tell me." We reporters use various lines to cajole officials into confirming or denying stories. I hadn't called Lenzner earlier because I was convinced we'd see the marshals.

Lenzner and Armstrong said they'd call me back, which they didn't do till 6:25, by which time I'd had to kill the story. "There are no mar-shals," they told me. "We were trying to catch your source . . . and now we have."

They had suspected "my guy," had set a trap with the phony Rose Mary Woods story, and had snagged him. Though he wasn't fired, his leaking slowed to a dribble. But I had other sources. I had become a reporter.

☐

27

THERE WAS A STRONG current of idealism in the press corps in those days. At least I thought what I was doing involved a public service. It was a high calling—I say this in all seriousness—that of helping cleanse the system peacefully.

Every day I read every word written about Watergate in sources ranging from *The Washington Post* to the *Detroit Free Press* to *Women's Wear Daily* to *Time* and *Newsweek* to the AP and UPI wires. Part of the daily ritual among the reporters in the hearing room was complimenting one another's work. Great embarrassment came with not knowing about the most obscure scoop in the smallest publication.

Every reporter there wanted to provide a piece of the puzzle and make a mark on what was clearly historic, as well as to catch up with Woodward and Bernstein. So the competition was intense. But we became friends too. The hearing room became a village, one I loved inhabiting. Someone would write a poem or a joke about a witness, and as in high school it would be passed from one table to the next and then up to the senators. Reporters consulted one another constantly, swapping theories about the case; we hung out together and, as time went on, had parties. I threw several myself, once sending out subpoenas as invitations. In this sense, we were similar to a press corps on a presidential campaign. But here we were covering the *un*-making of a president.

At lunch breaks I'd seek out staff members and Senate aides, I'd call lawyers of upcoming witnesses, anyone I could find to tell me what to expect in the afternoon. CBS had a radio recording booth in the Senate press gallery, where I'd go to make my calls. This was Roger Mudd's turf, though I didn't grasp at first how much he thought of it as his private domain. During one lunch hour he was in the booth working on a script. I joined him to wait for one of my sources to call me back and had to hold on to the table because I could actually feel Mudd willing me out of the room, the force of his unhappiness at my being there was so great. I was determined to stay, so Mudd sprang up out of his chair, threw open the door, and said, "I can't work in here. You're wearing too much perfume!"

I came to know all the senators on the committee. Chairman Sam Ervin became the second Watergate hero, after the unlikely John Sirica. Like the judge, Ervin at 76 had lived long enough to have perspective. With his wispy white hair, Ervin was a paunchier and jowlier Spencer Tracy who charmed with his wit and coyness, as when he'd protest in a slow southern cadence, "I'm just a simple country lawyer." This was a simple country lawyer from Harvard Law School who wowed everyone with his mixture of country homilies and off-the-top-of-his-head quotations from the Bible and Shakespeare.

When Nixon invoked executive privilege to prevent his aides from

28

testifying under oath before the committee, Ervin exploded, "Divine right went out with the American Revolution and doesn't belong to White House aides. 'What meat do they eat that makes them grow so great.' . . . That is not executive privilege. It is executive poppycock. . . . I'm not going to let anybody come down at night like Nicodemus and whisper something in my ear that no one else can hear." We reporters dived for our reference books.

The vice chairman, Republican Howard Baker, could have been his son. Another southerner, Baker was so good-looking that *Women's Wear Daily* added him to its "stud list" alongside Robert Redford. His repeated question about the president became a mantra: "What did he know and when did he know it?"

The committee's game plan was to start with low-level Nixon campaign aides and build to the major players. So it wasn't until the 19th witness, Jeb Magruder, that the spotlight hit the White House. Starting on June 14, Magruder incriminated just about everyone close to the president. The hearing room was in a frenzy, we at the press tables abandoning our detached composure and giving in to the excitement that we, the chosen ones, were there as the noose tightened around the presidential neck.

You can't imagine the electricity in that room, day after day, week after week, as we careened from tragedy out of Aeschylus to depravity out of Elmore Leonard, from a sense of doom for the presidency to a feeling of outrage at the corruption. And there was a constant punctuation of raucous hilarity as one witness after the next came out with code names and expressions you couldn't believe were bandied about the White House. Not telling the truth was "modified limited hangout"; John Mitchell was the "big enchilada"; there were "black bag jobs" and documents that were "deep-sixed." Secret operations run by shadowy characters had names such as Gemstone and Sandwedge; campaign dirty tricks were called Sedan Chair.

It wasn't just the reporters in the room who were obsessed with the drama; much of the public was glued to the hearings broadcast by the three television networks during the day on a rotating schedule. One day CBS would air them, the next day NBC, then ABC. Woodward and Bernstein had broken a blizzard of stories and would win a Pulitzer for the *Post*; yet it was television that changed public opinion. When the hearings started, Nixon's so-called silent majority refused to believe he was involved in the cover-up. He had an impressive approval rating of 69 percent. One month into the hearings, 67 percent thought he had been involved.

Three nights a week, CBS did a 30-minute sum-up of the hearings. Bill Small asked if I thought I was ready to join some of the senior correspondents in a roundtable discussion on the shows. I lied and said I was ready. But my two male partners (not always the same) argued so much with each other, I rarely got a word in. Night after night I'd be introduced, but except for a few scattered bleats from me — "I disagr—" "Don't you thi—"—I was drowned out. Finally the bosses explained that telegrams and phone calls were pouring in complaining that the men were being rude to the girl. The bosses said, "If she doesn't talk tonight, no more roundtable."

That night our moderator in New York, John Hart, asked a mischievous opening question about "the gossip" about John Ehrlichman.[3] I said to myself: Why should I, the woman, answer a question about gossip? Let the men do that; I'll take the next question. But naturally the men, Dan Rather and Dan Schorr, waited for my response until the silence became excruciating. Finally Schorr said, "Well, if you want to start with 'gossip,' I'd better turn this over to the woman."

I wanted to punch him. Instead, I gibbered incomprehensibly, not parsing, not tracking. When I wound down, Schorr made my humiliation complete. "Well, let's fill in a couple of facts here," he said, "before we go off on our wild gossip."

Mercifully the show ended. I raced upstairs and called home. "Daddy," I said, "they threw me the ball, and I dropped it. Help me write a letter of resignation. I can never show my face around here or anywhere ever again."

Being a dad, he said, "Don't be ridiculous. You were, in a word, magnificent. Smarter than those two. What thoughts! What ideas you had! And you looked good too."

"Dad, if you can't be honest with me — because I know how dreadful I was — put Mother on the phone."

There was a pause. "Mother can't talk right now," he said. "She's too upset."

Eventually my mother called me and did her magic, bucking me up and sending me back into battle.

THE STAR of the hearings was to be John Dean, but the committee agreed to postpone his appearance one week because Soviet leader Leonid Brezhnev was in town for a summit meeting with Nixon. That week I went to Dean's house in Alexandria, Virginia, early every morning, hoping to get a picture or get off a question. Sam Donaldson was usually there too. By then Sam had taken to calling Nixon "the felon," which he would bellow out at every opportunity. But he didn't get a chance to bellow at Dean, who stayed hidden inside.

Sam and I were bumping into each other constantly. He was ABC's chief staker-outer. We both got word one day that the newly named special prosecutor, Archibald Cox, was at a meeting in one of the Senate office buildings where camera crews were not allowed to shoot except in designated areas. Abiding by the rules, I went searching for Cox without my crew. The daring Donaldson said to himself: what a silly rule. As Cox appeared, so did Sam — with crew. "What's this?" I asked. "A camera?" As I hurled myself in front of the ABC camera lens, one of Sam's colleagues put his two arms under my armpits, picked me up, and removed me from the area. Sam got an interview with Cox. I did not.

A certain, shall we say, rambunctiousness was becoming my trademark. So was my persistence. One afternoon I drove to Dean's house and knocked on his front door. "Who's there?" It was his voice! I said who it was, got down on my hands and knees, opened the mail slot in his door, and begged him for a quote. He got down on his hands and knees too and peeked at me through the slit. And what was my big coup? All he told me was that he'd gotten a close-cropped haircut and planned to wear his glasses when he testified. A soul mate! He wanted to convey a sense of soberness. Like me.

Dean, 33, testified for a full week near the end of June. There was a lot of designing for television, even in those days: not only did he wear his glasses, he made sure that his pretty wife, Maureen, was positioned right behind him so the camera often had a shot of the two of them together, softening his icy image as he testified. The whole country watched as Dean, in a six-hour opening statement, plunged his sword deep into the president. He testified that Nixon — at the heart of the Watergate cover-up — had discussed paying the burglars hush money, and he revealed the existence of the president's "enemies list." I wrote a script for the *Evening News* about 20 people Nixon had targeted with, among other things, IRS audits. Dan Schorr was on the list and loved it. To be on Nixon's list of political and journalistic enemies was a badge of honor.

I began to realize that the personality flaws of presidents can determine history as much as their ideas. Nixon's cramped, untrusting view of life had set not only his own course but the country's as well. His paranoia had thrown us all into crisis, his abiding insecurities infecting us with a cynicism about government that we have not yet fully overcome.

It was the dead of summer, and the writer Aaron Latham was sent by *New York* magazine to the hearings for the first time, meaning he had to compete with those of us who'd been sitting there since May. After a full day he concluded that his notebook had not one scrap of an original observation, impression, or quotation. He panicked. A friend of his told him, "If you want sidebar material, call Lesley Stahl." It was true that I had notebooks full of unused gossip and funny asides that were too frothy for CBS. When Aaron called and offered to buy me dinner, I said he could pick me up in the CBS newsroom.

In walked six feet, four and a half inches of well-formed, well-proportioned, well-put-together Texas gorgeous with a bashful smile of straight teeth. And he wore a natty brown corduroy jacket with leather elbow patches and cowboy boots. If his reddish-brown beard hadn't been scraggly, I would have found him too perfect. What also took the edge off the dazzle of his looks was his modesty and shyness. He was fetching beyond words.

He took me to a pizza joint. He told me afterward that he had seen me on television talking about John Mitchell and it had made him nervous about making conversation and asking me questions. Halfway through dinner he relaxed, realizing he didn't have to ask me questions. I had so many Watergate stories, I chattered nonstop. He filled up two notebooks.

I then invited him up to my apartment to see the Watergate subpoena I had sent out as a party invitation. He was positive that I was his, that he was going to score. But I handed him the subpoena and said good night. Finding himself unexpectedly *outside* my apartment, he was — how can I put this? — enraptured.

His boss at *New York*, Clay Felker, liked Aaron's article so much, he asked him to return to Washington every two weeks to write a Watergate column. So he wooed me. We had dinner every other week and became good friends.

I COVERED Ehrlichman's and Haldeman's testimony before the Senate committee. Ehrlichman, 48, in his half glasses, was pugnacious; Haldeman, 46, in his out-of-date crew cut, was mild-mannered. Even though they had both been forced out of their jobs at the White House, they denied everything and protected the president.

The most startling of all the testimony came on July 16. Senator Ervin announced a surprise witness, Alexander Butterfield, who supervised internal security at the White House. On the stand for a mere 30 minutes, he revealed an Oval Office taping system. After the initial shock of his testimony, the hearing room exploded with chatter as we all came to realize that there might be evidence on tape that would either clear the president or nail him. As it turned out, what brought the president down in the Watergate bugging scandal was that Richard Nixon had bugged himself!

I WAS DRENCHED, my hair matted down by a double layer of scarves. I had spent much of the day shivering in the rain, staking out sources for other correspondents' pieces. Back in the office, my colleague Marya McLaughlin looked as wet and miserable as I did.

"You know, Marya," I said, "I hate to scream *sexism*. In fact, I've made it my personal resolution not to, but when I look at you and me and then I notice that the he-men around here are all warm in their Harris tweeds with every dry hair combed, I have to wonder."

"I've done a study of this," said Marya. She was our in-house Dorothy Parker; it was always a big mistake not to be there when she got going. "When Galbraith asks Roger Mudd to go stand out in the rain, what does he say?" she asked.

"What?"

"He says 'No!' with such a boom and resonance that Galbraith jumps under his desk. So then he goes to Ed Bradley and says, 'Go stand in the rain.' And Bradley says nothing for a while, then in a simmer he hisses, 'Get yourself another dude.' And Galbraith's hair sizzles. So he comes to you, and what do you say? You pout and stamp your foot and whine in a high pitch, 'I don't wanna.' "

Schorr was still my senior partner, but I was coming up with stories for the *Evening News*. My biggest coup was in July 1973, when my producer said, "Lesley, wouldn't it be great if you could find out what John Mitchell's going to say when he testifies at the Ervin hearings?" It was always easier to find something out when you had a specific question. So I went up to the Senate, knocked on doors, asked, "What will Mitchell say?," and managed to nag several sources into submission. That night I reported, "CBS News has learned that Mitchell will acknowledge he knew about hush-money payoffs."

Most days I didn't have a clear question, so I'd just troll or make dozens of calls, asking hundreds of questions. I wanted to make sure that if someone got the urge to leak, I'd be there to catch the drip. Often I'd make a call just to get help on what questions to ask. If I couldn't get through to one of the principals or their lawyers, I'd ask for a secretary or junior assistant, hoping he or she would be flattered and eager to show off. If I picked up any information at all from one conversation, I would drop it into my next call to sound as if I knew more than I did. Or I'd throw out wild propositions, bat around theories, just to test reactions. "I hear Dean is asking for no jail time," I once told a lawyer.

"That'll never happen."

Next call: "I heard Dean's talking about less than a year in jail."

"You're not far off."

It was late July 1973. When the special prosecutor, Archibald Cox, issued subpoenas for nine of Nixon's tapes, the White House balked. Schorr, Rather, and I were on the air in one of our roundtables. By this time, they were asking me about more than the day's gossip. Schorr said that the polls showing that the public didn't think Nixon was telling the

33

truth weren't necessarily definitive or significant. I tried to respond: "Dan —" but Rather interrupted. Then I said, "Right —" and as usual Schorr jumped in: "Polls show what people think at a given time and —"

"They're pretty important in a democracy," said Rather, disagreeing.

Schorr came back, "But at any given time the people may be wrong, and they may wake up to it, so that he —"

I actually interrupted: "But doesn't public opinion affect how these senators will react in that hearing room?" It wasn't a large point, but I felt I had hit a passing shot down the line that Schorr couldn't return.

After each show I would call home for my parents' affirmation. I needed their assurances that I hadn't been as hesitant and garbled as I feared. Because I didn't have an office, I would make these almost nightly calls from the newsroom, so I was often overheard. I'm sure that while I was seen as toughening up in some ways, this unwinding with my parents exposed my self-doubts.

I WENT to a dinner party with Jerry Landauer of *The Wall Street Journal* on Saturday night, October 25. There were two topics of conversation. The first was the sudden resignation of Vice President Spiro Agnew, who had taken bribes when he was governor of Maryland and even as vice president. Nixon had looked on Agnew as his "insurance policy" in the belief that the Democrats, who controlled Congress, would hesitate to impeach him if it meant that Agnew would become president. Nixon had miscalculated, and now he was so weak, the Democrats all but demanded he choose Congressman Gerald Ford to replace Agnew. Ford was a Republican the Democrats could live with.

Topic two was Nixon's latest stiffing of the special prosecutor. Resisting Cox's subpoena for the nine tapes, he had offered a trick play: he would release "summaries" of the tapes that would be authenticated by Mississippi Senator John Stennis.

"Look," said Landauer, "Nixon knows that Stennis is 72 and will probably miss any discrepancies between the summaries and the actual recordings. It's a cunning but transparent ruse." In return for "the Stennis compromise" Nixon wanted Cox to cease any further attempts to get the tapes. Cox turned down the offer almost immediately.

Around eight o'clock one of the guests, also a reporter, got a call and without explanation left. Life in journalism is a running tournament. In a friendly setting, you're scheming to beat the pants off the guy you're seated next to, even if he's your date. There was no question that the man who left had gotten a hot tip, so suddenly the dinner party was transformed into Aqueduct and we were all horses at the gate. I called the desk.

"Know anything?" I asked Galbraith.

34

"White House announcement in 20 minutes," he said.

I panicked. What if Galbraith didn't ask me to come in? I'd be totally humiliated at this party. "I'll be right there," I said and hung up before he could object. I told everyone about the announcement and apologized to the hostess and my date, explaining, "The office needs me."

I got to the bureau in time to catch the president's press secretary, Ron Ziegler, announcing on television that both Attorney General Elliot Richardson and his deputy, William Ruckelshaus, had refused Nixon's order to fire Archibald Cox and had resigned.[4] Heightening the atmosphere of crisis, the White House dispatched fully armed FBI agents to occupy the attorney general's office. I got on the phone in the newsroom and called my sources for comments on what became known as the Saturday Night Massacre. Everyone was appalled: here was Nixon, the man under investigation, quashing the investigation. Calls for his resignation streamed into Congress as the airwaves bristled with disconcerting questions: Was the president abrogating the Constitution? Was this tantamount to a coup d'état? Would he send in the army next?

Nixon's approval rating plunged to an arctic 27 percent. At a news conference in late November in southern California, he declared, "I am not a crook" and again tried to blame the press, calling the TV news coverage of him "outrageous, vicious, distorted." When my CBS colleague Bob Pierpoint asked what specifically about the coverage made him angry, he said he wasn't angry. "You see, one can only be angry with those he respects." Nixon had long loathed the press, but there was an added hostility when it came to television, since by the early 1970s broadcast news and the presidency were two of the country's most powerful institutions and they were vying for control of the public agenda.

Meanwhile, the mockery of the man was merciless. Cartoonists were exaggerating his five o'clock shadow, drawing him as a twisted, evil spirit. Stand-up comics lampooned his uncoordinated gesticulations and unspontaneous smiles. Novelist Philip Roth wrote *Our Gang* about President Trick E. Dixon, who held high-level briefings in full football gear and was eventually drowned in a Baggie after an operation to remove the sweat gland from his upper lip.

Nixon finally agreed to turn over the nine subpoenaed tapes to Judge Sirica for a ruling on claims of executive privilege. I was back in Sirica's courtroom for a hearing on the matter when the White House revealed the existence of an 18-minute gap on one of the tapes. The gap — more precisely, a buzz — occurred in the middle of a conversation between Nixon and Haldeman three days after the Watergate break-in. The White House said that the president's personal secretary, Rose Mary Woods, had accidentally erased the 18 minutes by pressing the "Record" button on the tape machine when she meant to push the "Stop" button. Sirica hauled the woman into court, where she tried to explain how she could have made the mistake. It was hard not to laugh as she demonstrated a stretch and a swivel, a twist to answer the phone, and a press of the wrong button, all at the same time.

Nixon's new chief of staff, Alexander Haig, was summoned to testify. He told Sirica a different story: that "some sinister force" had erased the tape. Playing to us in the press gallery, Sirica asked Haig if he knew who that sinister force might be. We laughed again at the judge's obvious reference to the president.

In December, when the Ervin committee issued its own subpoena for 40 tapes, Haig went to Capitol Hill to try to negotiate a compromise. I was tipped off by a source about the secret meeting with the committee staff, so when "the general" — as Haig was known — emerged, I rushed forward, thrust a microphone into his face, and asked, "Did you make a deal?"

Since elaborate measures had been taken to sneak him out of the Senate, he was surprised to see me, but not so much that he answered. "Will the president agree to turn over *any* of the tapes?" I pressed. At that a uniformed guard with the Capitol Hill police rushed forward, picked me up, and carried me off. Haig was escorted to his waiting limousine as I was being deposited several yards away in a heap on the grass. I was muttering, "Gestapo tactics," but I wasn't hurt, not even a little. Still, I stormed off with an exaggerated limp as Haig's car passed by.

When I got to the bureau, I got a call from Haig. "Lesley, are you all right?" he asked. "I was appalled at the way that guard treated you and just want you to know I had nothing to do with it. The White House had no part in it. And if you want, I will personally file a complaint."

I assured him I was fine. "I don't even have a scratch as evidence. But as long as I have you on the phone — " I asked Haig for any comment at all about the tapes, the negotiations, or the president's state of mind. No surprise, he had to get right off.

In February 1974 the House of Representatives approved an investigation by the House Judiciary Committee into the possibility of impeaching the president. I'd wake up every morning wondering: How can he take the pressure? How is Mrs. Nixon holding up? On the night of February 14 the desk ordered me to "move, move now" to Trader Vic's on K Street, four blocks from the White House. It was Pat Nixon's birthday, and the president was taking her out to their favorite restaurant. The maître d' had called CBS.

Nixon had bunkered himself inside the White House — he hadn't held a news conference for four months — and his disappearance from public view was feeding rumors that he was degenerating into madness. This would be the first chance in weeks for any newsperson to see him.

There was only one other reporter there, the indomitable Helen Thomas of UPI. Of all the reporters on the White House beat, Helen had the biggest heart and asked the toughest questions. She and I joined forces. The maître d' gave us a table with a clear view of the president, Mrs. Nixon, and their friend Bebe Rebozo. We ordered spareribs and drinks that came in the oversized glasses with the paper umbrellas. We watched, wrote down what they ate, and congratulated ourselves on our scoop.

Thomas and I had a plan: when the Nixons emerged, we'd be right outside, in a perfect position to get off a few questions. But when we opened the door to leave, we were met by a swarm of cameras, microphones, and reporters jostling and shoving. The Nixons were right behind us, so Helen and I were run over and pushed to the back of the pack, out of hearing range. So much for our scoop.

But we were not so hapless after all. Mrs. Nixon was also jostled to the back. It was a raw night, and there she stood, shivering in her brown cloth coat, looking frail, her eyes sad.

The other reporters surrounded Mr. Nixon and shouted out one accusing Watergate question after the next. In those days it was not unusual for the Secret Service to allow reporters in close to the president; in fact, we were seen as a shield, a layer of protection. (That changed in 1981, after Ronald Reagan was shot by someone standing with the press.)

Mrs. Nixon turned to Helen and me and said, "Isn't he wonderful. Just look at him. Can you imagine with all his troubles, all the pressure he's under, he took the time to take me out." Her eyes teared up. All I could think was: Look what he's put you through; this is the least he could do. I was once told by a Nixon adviser that at the many dinners he had attended at the White House, he had never once seen Nixon address his wife, or even look at her.

In March I organized a birthday party for Judge Sirica. We got a cake and candles, lured him into the pressroom, and together — print reporters, newscasters, cameramen, radio techs, other judges, prosecutors, and courthouse secretaries — we all yelled, "Surprise!" He loved it.

It seemed that it was Sirica and the courts, Ervin and the Congress, and the press on one side, Nixon on the other. But the president kept singling out the media. We were portrayed as working in cahoots with the liberal Democrats, out to get him for political reasons, which was nonsense. Reporters are equal opportunity stalkers when an open wound is exposed. But the attacks, especially on CBS, struck a chord with conservatives. That's why the White House began prodding owners of affiliated stations — usually Republicans — to lean on CBS News to tame our Watergate coverage. They did, but to no avail.

TV Guide ran a two-page article about me covering Watergate, and I began to get requests to give speeches. I was new at perching on stools up on stages, pontificating about the goings-on in Washington. Television work is antiseptic; there's hardly a give-and-take with the camera. So I enjoyed the interaction, especially in the question-and-answer period. It gave me a chance to sense the mood of the country.

On the night of April 29 I was speaking to 300 students and townspeople at Bowling Green State University in Ohio. Together we watched Nixon on TV, projected onto a large screen behind me, as he announced that he would not comply with the subpoenas for more tapes but instead would release 1,200 pages of edited transcripts. Some of the students laughed and jeered at Nixon. In *Amusing Ourselves to Death* Neil Postman wrote that Nixon's problem was "not that he lied, but that on television he *looked* like a liar" (my emphasis).[5]

I took questions and felt the force of the antimedia emotion among Nixon's supporters. When I said I thought impeachment was possible because of the Saturday Night Massacre and the president's dilatory tactics over the tapes, a woman shouted at me in fury, "You're out to get the president!"

Never, in all my years in Washington, would the press face as much hostility as we did during Watergate. Nixon whipped up some of the animosity, but there was a natural resentment toward the messengers of a story the public did not want to hear about a president they had reelected in a landslide. There was a desire among some of the CBS affiliates to have Dan Rather, one of Watergate's toughest messengers, removed from his job as White House correspondent, but Bill Small and news president Dick Salant backed him and withstood the pressure.

I flew back to Washington and volunteered to cancel my vacation. With his usual light touch Galbraith said, "No, go. We won't be needing you." I was crushed.

Then I found out that CBS was planning a prime-time special the next night in which Nixon's edited transcripts would be read aloud. Haldeman, Ehrlichman, Dean, Nixon, and the others would each be played by a CBS News correspondent. When I wasn't given a part, I went to the producer, Bill Crawford, to complain. "But they're all men," he said.

"So what?" I protested. "This is acting. It really doesn't matter who reads the parts."

"Of course it does," he said.

"But I've covered this story from the beginning. Don't you think it's unfair to cut me out of a big special just because I'm a woman?"

"Sorry, Toots," he said. I smoldered.

A year later, when several correspondents who had never covered Watergate won Emmys for the show, I burned again.

I needed a vacation, so when Aaron Latham asked me if I wanted to go to Bermuda with him, it sounded like a good idea. By then he had become my best friend. When I was sad or happy or lonely or when I'd heard a good one, he was the one I called. We began to plan.

When my dad asked me, "Who's this Erin you're going to Bermuda with? Is she a new friend?" I told him about Aaron.

"But have you slept with him?"

"Dad!"

"I'm serious."

"If you must know, I haven't."

"Well, then," he said, "you're not going."

"Excuse me? I'm not going?"

"No, because it's inevitable that you'll get down there, have some bad experience with him, and call me. Well, sister, I'm not coming to pick you up in far-off places."

If my mother had said that, I'd have been on the next plane to Bermuda. But this was Lou, my dad. So I thought over what he said and decided he was right. You don't go to a romantic island with a "friend." I went instead to a tennis camp, alone.

My first night there Aaron, who'd stayed in Washington, called and said I was nuts to have left town. There were Watergate parties every night where reporters dissected the Nixon transcripts. They were punctuated with "expletive deleted," which added to a sense that Nixon's Oval Office conversations were sordid and that the office itself was full of malice. Aaron said, "The whole town's alive with excitement. You have to come back — now."

It was early May. I flew home, took one look at Aaron, and realized I adored him and never wanted to be without him again. He was the smartest man I ever knew and the wisest, the best read, the funniest; and he was as good to me as my dad was to my mother. We hugged our first hug. He moved in that night.

WASHINGTON WAS SWALLOWED UP by the Nixon tapes. I went to a dinner party, where a group of us, including Ethel Kennedy, sat in a circle and read the transcripts aloud. Though Nixon had obviously cleansed them, his dark side showed through in the passages where he and his inner circle cussed and plotted wicked wrongdoings like a bunch of gangsters.

39

The impression was so damning, a Niagara of calls for his resignation drowned out whatever support was left him even within his own party. The Senate minority leader, Hugh Scott of Pennsylvania, called the transcripts "shabby" and "disgusting." Nixon would have been better off taking the Fifth.

On May 10 I went back to Sirica's court to hear another argument about the subpoenaed tapes. Afterward we chased the president's lawyer, James St. Clair, with our cameras. He said, "Nixon will not resign . . . under any known circumstances." St. Clair usually had an open, Hey-look-at-me!-I'm-hot-stuff smile. But that day he was fidgety and impatient.

The front of the federal courthouse was a war zone. When a designated reporter, acting as lookout, spotted anyone important in the Watergate case, such as St. Clair, he would shout, "He's here!," which had the same effect as a general giving the order "Charge!" A phalanx of crews would surge forward, their microphones extended on long boom poles looking for all the world like bayonets. At first I hung back. Jumping into pitched battle held little charm for me, especially in my heels. But I soon realized that if I wanted to be treated as one of the boys, I would have to join the scrum, so I learned to ram and butt and poke and shove my way up to the front so I could ask questions or, more important, get my face on film. This was combat, and woe to any target of our attack who didn't do the prudent thing, which was to stop and answer a few questions. One day Mrs. Ehrlichman was whacked on the head by one of the 20-pound cameras. It was a serious blow and should have given us pause.

Through May and June the House Judiciary Committee proceeded with its impeachment investigation, while revelations about dirty tricks, laundered money, and cover-ups seemed to come like a boxer's combination, one punch after the next.[6] Then on July 24, the Supreme Court voted to uphold the special prosecutor's subpoena for 64 more tapes. The decision was 8–0, with Chief Justice Warren Burger recusing himself.

The impeachment debate started in prime time that very night. I was in the hearing room looking for off-lead stories. By then it was known that the president had undermined the FBI and the Justice Department in an effort to punish his political opponents and then cover it up. According to the Gallup Poll, Nixon's popularity had sunk to 24 percent. Watergate was, of course, the reason for the drop, but presidents mired in scandal have often been cushioned by a buoyant economy. Nixon was not lucky. Inflation was at 12 percent; the Arab oil embargo had produced long lines at gas stations; consumer confidence was low. He had no cushion.

I sat in the press section in the Impeachment Committee hearing room, moved by the speeches and impressed especially with the poetry of

Congresswoman Barbara Jordan of Texas. She said that she, as a black, was determined to uphold the Constitution, which she *had* felt left out of. "But through the process of amendment, interpretation, and court decision, I have finally been included in 'We, the people.'" And I was amused by Congressman Bill Cohen of Maine blowing kisses to his wife, Diane.

As the proceedings moved forward, the ugly partisanship that marked the first few days faded as the seriousness of the process took hold. After six days of agonized debate, the committee voted, several Republicans crossing over to answer "Aye," in a solemn roll call to recommend impeachment of the president for obstructing justice, for abusing his presidential powers, and for contempt of Congress. When it was over, Barbara Jordan left the room in tears.[7]

On August 5 I was sent on an early stakeout to the home of John Rhodes, the House minority leader. When I rang the bell, his wife thought I was an Avon lady and invited me in. When I told her who I really was, she said her husband had laryngitis.

Later that day on Capitol Hill I could feel tension, but I couldn't find out what was going on. I went from office to office, learning of secret powwows but gathering little hard information. Together with Sam Donaldson I hopped onto the subway under the House office buildings; we both knew something big was happening.

We met up with a group of reporters staking out Minority Leader Rhodes's office. Dan Thomassen of Scripps Howard rushed over to tell us about a statement Nixon had just released at the White House. No wonder there were so many secret meetings all over the Hill. Nixon was making public a transcript of a meeting six days after the Watergate break-in during which he had instructed Haldeman to have the CIA say falsely that the break-in had been one of their secret operations. The tape was the "smoking gun" evidence of Nixon's early involvement in the cover-up.

The reporters said, "I knew it" or "Holy shit" over and over. One of my colleagues repeated Senator Howard Baker's mantra, "What did the president know, and when did he know it?" As it turned out, he had known everything about the cover-up from the very beginning.

Nixon's lawyer, St. Clair, was briefing the Republican leaders. When he emerged, he said, "Hi there," a greeting to the Watergate reporters who had crowded around him for months. "Are you going to resign because the president lied to you?" someone asked.

"No comment."

I followed him outside, where cameras were waiting. The crush for position was as violent as ever. I got a poke in the ribs as a reporter I didn't recognize tried to elbow me out of the way. It was one thing when the "primitives" (what the newspapermen called the cameramen) shoved me aside; they had to get a clear shot. But there was a code among the reporters: we were as civil to each other as possible given the circumstances. I didn't take it as a compliment that this stranger treated me as just another guy. What I thought was: Who is this galoot violating the rules? Who does he think he is? I dealt with it by chopping *my* elbow into *his* gut. It was as powerful a wallop as I could muster, delivered with a ferocious grimace. I know this because NBC captured it on film and ran it on the John Chancellor *Nightly News*. Dolly called me, horrified. Bill Small loved it. I was one of the boys.

As the day wore on, it became clear that if Nixon didn't resign, the House would impeach him by a wide margin. "He won't get ten votes," I was told by a head counter. All day long Republicans met in little cells, plotting ways to get Nixon to leave office before they had to vote. Meanwhile, Peter Rodino, chairman of the Judiciary Committee, which conducted the impeachment hearings, was refusing GOP requests to speed up his proceedings. The Democrats wanted the drama to last as long as possible: if they could drag this out until November, they'd blitz the election.

The next day I was sent back to the courthouse. A batch of tapes arrived in a silver-gray suitcase with Secret Service escort. In court St. Clair was subdued. I was so used to him fighting each and every motion, challenging every word the prosecutor uttered, that this new man was hard to watch. He went so far as to say, "Anything that's reasonable we'll be pleased to do." To each demand he said, "We can work it out." They had given up.

August 8. For the second time in my CBS career, I was assigned to cover the Wholesale Price Index. Now, on the day I was sure Richard Nixon would resign, I was at the godforsaken Labor Department. This is how correspondents become paranoid.

After my radio spot on wholesale prices, I was sent to cover Betty Ford, the presumed next first lady. I joined a posse of women reporters — in the rain, naturally. I felt I couldn't complain. Since I'd been at CBS, there had been only a few times I'd been sent to cover a "woman's" story. Before my time that's what most women reporters had done most of the time.

Once it became clear that Nixon was about to resign, all the networks moved their mobile trucks into place at Ford's residence. Cables were laid down, live cameras put into position, and a bank of microphones placed on the path to the Fords' front door. Then the Secret Service came along and moved us women down the block.

Meanwhile, Aaron was at the White House. I called him on a mobile phone so he could tell me about the great drama in the pressroom, which had been sealed off. "They've locked us in!" Aaron said. "Everyone's running around yelling, 'Coup, coup!' We can't leave." Only later did we learn that it was because Nixon had wanted to walk around the Rose Garden one last time.

When Gerald Ford came outside to speak to the American people and CBS Radio came to me for "color," I had to admit I was a block away and couldn't see a thing. The radio anchorman, Neil Strawser, watching television in the studio, had a far better view of "the scene."

I listened to the resignation speech on radio. Nixon started by acknowledging, "I no longer have a strong enough political base in the Congress" to continue. In an unsatisfying phrase in the passive tense he said, "I regret deeply any injuries that may have been done." That was it. No "I'm to blame," no "Forgive me" or "I'm sorry." The country needed to hear him admit that his denials had been lies, that his attacks on his enemies and the press were part of the cover-up he had engineered. He accepted zero responsibility. There was no honor in his speech.

The next day, Nixon's last as president, he made his farewell address to his staff and cabinet on television. Mrs. Nixon and their daughters, Tricia and Julie, stood with him, glassy-eyed but composed. What it must have taken to hold themselves together there in the glare — these three women who had been dragged into his disgrace. Nixon's speech was compelling because you kept thinking he was going to break down or go berserk. He talked of his father as "sort of a little man" and of his mother as "a saint." The most revealing, the most naked part of the speech came at the end: "Never be petty; always remember, others may hate you, but those who hate you don't win unless you hate them, and then you destroy yourself." Did he understand himself that well?

Nixon boarded *Marine One,* the presidential helicopter, on the South Lawn of the White House, turned back, waved, and was gone. And so was Watergate.

WATERGATE CHANGED JOURNALISM forever. It introduced an era of reporting through anonymous sources. It ushered in a swarm-around-'em mentality where reporters and cameramen hounded people; it was undignified, lacked decorum, and reduced our standing with the public. From Watergate on, nearly every government utterance would be subject to skeptical scrutiny. The assumption would be: government officials skirt the truth. Presidents had been protected by newsmen: Franklin D. Roosevelt's wheelchair and John Kennedy's women had gone unreported. Watergate brought an end to the protections; thereafter, presidents would view the press as a squad in a perpetual adversarial crouch, always ready to pounce.

There had never been a news story quite like it, and, because the press had been so prominent, it glamorized journalism as a profession, turning some reporters into celebrities. Lost in all the myth-making was the fact that the courts and Congress had played the crucial role, not the press. Sirica and Ervin were the heroes, but, as a friend once said to me, "Robert Redford didn't play either of them in the movies." One could argue that people inside the Nixon administration who leaked stories — the still secret Deep Throat and many others — were more significant than Woodward and Bernstein and all the other reporters. But the impression was left that the press had single-handedly driven the president from office, which gave us a dangerous aura of invincible power.

One of the repercussions of the scandal was the worst possible from Nixon's point of view: CBS News was enhanced. We had had our share of scoops, but our real contribution was in turning Watergate into a national story. Giant audiences learned about the cover-up and the dirty tricks, about the tapes battle, the Senate hearings, and the impeachment proceedings, through the eyes of CBS and the other networks.

This was a time when more than 40 million citizens were watching the same event, interpreted the same way night after night. That was the number of people who watched the Cronkite news. Television had surpassed newspapers, magazines, and radio as the major source of news in the country. A Roper survey found that the public trusted television by two to one over any other medium for credibility.[8] You could feel our growing strength.

I was living with Aaron. Nixon, who had filled our lives, was gone; he was all we had thought about for two years. Now there was a big hole. It was like the empty-nest syndrome. What would we have in common now? What would we talk about?

What saved our relationship, of all things, was a diet, the Bob Woodward Cabbage Soup Diet. The first day, all we could eat was fruit and all the cabbage soup we wanted. Whenever we ran out of things to discuss, we'd bring up how many pears we had eaten and how bad the cabbage soup was smelling up the apartment.

Day two was vegetables and all the cabbage soup we wanted. We were beginning to find other things to discuss, though we were still in Nixon withdrawal.

The third day was half fruit, half veggies, and lots of cabbage soup. After two weeks I had lost eight pounds, Aaron ten, and we had bridged the gap.

When I was in high school, I read *The Fountainhead* and *Atlas Shrugged* by Ayn Rand and decided I was a libertarian nonconformist who lived by my own rules. But here I was in the mid-1970s doing what Ayn Rand

44

would have denounced and exactly what the feminists of the time were railing against. I was adapting myself to someone else's standards, to whatever the men who hired me wanted me to be. I wore curlers to bed and sprayed my hair so much, I even called myself "helmet head." And I worked as hard as I could to project an image of malelike authority. Only when it came to my clothes was I true to myself. I have a taste for bright colors, frills, eyelets, and flounces. No one said a word to me about camera clothes, so I just wore what I liked, the most feminine outfits and highest heels I could find.

At the same time feminists were burning the "tools of oppression" — curlers, *Cosmopolitans*, eyelash curlers, and girdles — much as Vietnam War protesters had burned their draft cards. Curlers. Was I oppressed?

Whenever I talk about the women's movement, I have more than a twinge of guilt because it did so much for me while I, a reporter, sat on the sidelines neither marching nor protesting. I never even went to a consciousness-raising group, which is close to admitting I wasn't alive in the early 1970s.

While the women's movement was pushing for equal work and equal pay, I was working at Channel 5 in Boston and seeing a psychiatrist two mornings a week. I went because I was unable to extricate myself from Amos. But Bernie the shrink was far more interested in women in the workplace. While I wanted to explore the hypotenuse of my triangulated love affair, Bernie asked me how I was getting along with my boss. "Just fine," I said, "except he's always injecting sexual innuendo into our conversations."

"Then you must be encouraging it," Bernie said.

"Oh, no. I'm not the least bit interested in him. He's the one who's always making these asides about how I look."

Bernie asked me to remember precisely my conversations with the news director, Bob Caulfield. And sure enough, when he forbade me to wear pants to the office — when the other women could — I'd ask with a smile, "Why me?"

"Because that's the rule — for you," Caulfield would challenge me the way a boy dunks a girl's braids into an inkwell. I would put on a display of mock anger. The little argument would blossom into a game of verbal footsie.

So embedded was this flirtatious reflex that even after Bernie helped me understand my role as a come-on, I still couldn't change. So he put me through a reconditioning course, explaining that if I wanted a career, I would have to send off unmistakable signals to every man I worked with or reported on that my work wasn't a game to me. Bernie got down to elementary lessons: "When he says, 'No pants in the office,' you say, 'Okay' and walk out. End of discussion. Get the cuteness out of your voice. Don't take the bait. Be serious." By the time I stopped my visits with Bernie, my instinct to flirt in the office had been cured.

I WAS AMBIVALENT about covering the women's movement, as were most of the women reporters I knew. This was an issue we wanted to report on yet one we were afraid would typecast us. Ed Bradley told me that, being black, he felt the same way about civil rights. "I was very conflicted," he said. "When I was assigned to a black story, I'd complain, 'You can't do that to me.' But these were the very stories I was interested in. If I didn't go, they wouldn't be covered at all. Yet you had to be careful it wasn't a slot they put you into." I felt exactly the same about the "women's beat."

By 1973 the women at *Newsweek* were suing over sex discrimination; 50 women filed a claim against NBC News. CBS management had moved to forestall a similar action by, among other things, hiring five women reporters and making sure we got airtime: Sylvia Chase, who had been a radio producer in Los Angeles; Michele Clark, a black TV reporter from Chicago; Connie Chung; Marya McLaughlin; and me. Other women were hired as producers.

Sylvia Chase helped organize a committee to go to the president of CBS, Arthur Taylor, with demands for more changes in how women at the network were treated. "Lesley, will you join us?" she asked. I thought it over. I knew that the women's agenda items were taken by many men as personal assaults on them. "I can't," I said. "I'm afraid if I do Mr. Small will kill me." What a coward. Women like Sylvia who confront and make waves are often punished, while the rest of us ride on their backs. I know I owe them. But I saw an inner contradiction in going to bat for "women" just as I was downplaying my own womanliness in my attempts to join the testosterone club. Some of my friends have told me they went to great lengths to de-emphasize and conceal all curves, protrusions, and other brands of femaleness, dressing in the Western equivalent of a chador. One said, "I adopted the affect of a librarian." This I never did.

Barbara Walters told me that when she had coanchored the *Today* show in the 1970s, she'd had to fight to do serious stories and interviews: "I got letters from women saying, 'Hang in there. What you're doing is good for all of us.' " She said, "I did it for me. But I think it helped them too." I also told myself that succeeding at becoming a woman of authority on television would in itself help other women. By telegraphing an image of a woman with some power and heft, I rationalized I could help the cause.

46   THERE WERE RULES of the road for men and women in social settings, but we were improvising a new etiquette in the office as we moved along.

These were days of great confusion for everyone. Could the producer hold the door for me? He didn't know; neither did I. If I interviewed an acquaintance, could we social-kiss in greeting? He didn't know; neither did I. Was I a news*man*? Was Pat Schroeder a congress*man*? Everyone was touchy about the rights and wrongs, even if we didn't know exactly what they were.

The issues then concerned equal pay, promotions, and maternity leave. I had equal pay because I was a member of AFTRA, a union. Sexual harassment hadn't hit the radar screen. Yet I can remember going to Capitol Hill and being warned by the other women reporters to stay away from certain senators. The idea that our bosses or any man "had no right" hadn't dawned on us. We relied on our ability to run faster (we were generally younger); complaining about advances was seen as futile or, worse, self-destructive.

As it turned out, the meeting between the women's committee and CBS President Taylor went well. By mid-1974 salaries for women at CBS were improved, a new maternity benefits program was put into place, and there were several new shows by and about women on the air. Some women thought these were great victories; most others said they weren't enough.

I WANTED TO BE a political reporter. In 1974 I became one when CBS sent me to cover the congressional campaigns in the West. I put together a report on the Senate race in Colorado, in which Gary Hart, who had been George McGovern's campaign manager, was the Democrat. One day he asked if I'd like to ride with him and his wife, Lee, to the next event. I sat in the backseat of what we'd call today a subcompact while Gary shut his wife up every time she tried to join in the conversation. "You don't know what you're talking about," he snipped. "Why don't you just be quiet?" And "Hush." And of course, "Shut up." I wanted to tell *him* to shut up; I wanted to reach out and touch Lee, but all I did was ask my questions and pretend to ignore his angry belittling of her. To me, one of the lessons of Watergate was that the press hadn't done enough reporting on personal character. As I sat in that backseat, I wished I had film of Gary Hart browbeating his wife.

After covering the western campaigns, I went to New York for election night. I was going to be one of the desk anchors, announcing the winners of races in the West for governor, senator, and congressman. As the first CBS woman to do this, I felt a lot of pressure, and I confided in CBS News President Richard Salant that I was scared. He told me that was silly and took me on a tour of the election night set to prove it. The carpenters were still working on a large drum with seats marked off for each of the anchors.

"It's quite cozy," said Salant. "All of you are in a friendly circle. Nothing to make you nervous." We walked around the drum. "This is where Walter sits." He pointed to a desk with the name "CRONKITE" on it. "And here's Dan's seat." It said "RATHER." Mike's place said "WALLACE" and Roger's said "MUDD." "And here's yours," said Salant. It said "FEMALE." He blushed.

I STUDIED HARD for election night, cataloguing interesting facts about all the candidates and anecdotes about the campaigns, gathering solid intelligence about why X or Y won or lost his race. When Walter and Betsy Cronkite invited Aaron and me to dinner, I was suspicious. "He's going to ask me to give him all my good information, and I'm going to have to," I told Aaron. "He wants to suck me dry of all my research," which I had committed to five-by-eight-inch index cards.

I was dead wrong. Walter and Betsy lived in a brownstone on the East Side of Manhattan. Two other couples were already there. "No shoptalk, Lesley," Walter said. "Tonight, just fun." Up to then I had known "Uncle Walter" the way the audience knew him, as the epitome of rectitude. He was like the preacher in town, the man everyone looked up to for his integrity and good judgment. But just as the camera showed Walter from his waist up, it captured only part of his personality. What I saw that night was the other side: the worldly, hilarious, even ribald Uncle Walter.

He was sitting on an ottoman in the middle of his den telling stories: about the war, courting Betsy, living in Europe. He played all the roles in the stories, imitating women, Germans, Frenchmen, and people we knew. And his jokes were earthy. Betsy laughed as hard as the rest of us, even though I'm sure she had heard them all before. She was puckish and as sophisticated and full of fun as Walter. My favorite Betsy Cronkite line was "I could never have an affair; I couldn't hold my stomach in that long!"

I think Walter invited us to lighten me up. Around midnight he announced he was about to tell a party-ending joke, one so raunchy that he was right, it cleared the room. Aaron and I had a wonderful time. I have loved Walter ever since.

FINALLY TUESDAY night came. I wore a bright red dress with double-strand, opera-length pearls that jangled against the microphone and drove the director, Artie Bloom, crazy. I was given my own hairdresser, who jumped up after each of my reports to recomb. When he'd finish, I'd call home, right there on the set: "Mum! How'd I do?" I'm still teased about that to this day.

The outcome of the 1974 election was breathtaking. The Republicans were sacked and pillaged as the voters punished them for Watergate, President Ford's pardon of Nixon, and double-digit inflation. Forty-three new Democrats were voted into the House, three into the Senate, and four into governor's chairs.

I was convinced that my appearance on the show had propelled me into instant fame, certain I would be unable to go to a restaurant without being spotted and hounded. Just walking down the street would become a race against the paparazzi.

The day after the election I put on a scarf to hide my hair and a pair of sunglasses, which I see now would only draw attention in the chill of November. Aaron and I went for a walk down Fifth Avenue. He was slouching, worried that my new public stature would alter the equation of our well-balanced relationship. We walked from Bergdorf Goodman at 58th Street down to Doubleday at 56th. Not one person noticed me. I took off the shades. Still no one. By the time I got to St. Patrick's Cathedral my scarf was off and I was staring at passersby, all but begging them to recognize me. We walked all the way to 42nd Street. Aaron wasn't slouching anymore.

I went back to Washington to be a general assignment correspondent. Gerald Ford was president. It was a boring time. We all missed the Trick.

I WAS IN LOVE with my boyfriend, and with our life. We'd been living together in Washington for nearly a year and a half, though Aaron kept his apartment in New York. With a Texan you expect ten-gallon gasconade and swagger, but he was more like my New England father (what a surprise!) and brother, reserved and laconic. One reason Aaron became such a successful reporter was that he's a man who does not abhor the vacuum of silence. He can ask a question, then wait patiently for an answer—however long it takes.

I had friends who warned me that Aaron and I came from worlds too far apart ever to be compatible: he from a small farming town, population 1,350, in the *Last Picture Show* part of Texas, I from an upscale suburb in the *Rabbit, Run* part of Massachusetts. But we never thought we were that unlike. He was the only man I ever met who called his parents as often as I called mine.

While he was shy with most people, with me he was funny and brilliant, impressing me with his memory of poems and scenes from hundreds of books. Because he had insomnia, he stayed up reading deep into the night, going through one author's entire repertoire before moving on to the next. His favorite author was F. Scott Fitzgerald, which was

49

curious since he looks like Fitzgerald's literary rival, Ernest Hemingway. Aaron turned his Ph.D. thesis at Princeton into his first book, *Crazy Sundays: F. Scott Fitzgerald in Hollywood.*

His boss at *New York* magazine, Clay Felker, was creating the New Journalism, which borrowed the techniques of fiction, and Aaron was one of his favorite writers. Among Aaron's more famous articles were his reconstructions of the Saturday Night Massacre, the investigation of Spiro Agnew, and his "Evening in the Nude" with Gay Talese (July 1973). That one caused such a stir in New York that both Gay's wife, Nan, and Gay's friend David Halberstam stopped talking to Aaron, although Gay never did.

That article was followed by a profile of Sally Quinn (July 1973), the *Washington Post* style writer who was about to coanchor *The CBS Morning News* with Hughes Rudd. Sally was delightfully brassy, but her humor and sarcasm didn't translate well into print; there her quotes seemed more bawdy than funny. Bottom line: once again Aaron had an old friend who wasn't talking to him. The problem for me was that Sally was my friend as well. She asked me to dinner one night and urged me to break up with Aaron. Of course I didn't, which meant that I too lost her friendship.

The Talese and Quinn pieces came out back-to-back. Together they produced such a ferocious reaction that Aaron was shell-shocked and switched to covering the intelligence community. His article on James Jesus Angleton, the weird, conspiratorial head of counterintelligence at the CIA, became a novel, *Orchids for Mother*, one of the best books ever written about the inner workings of the Agency.

IT WAS LATE 1975. As one of President Ford's early official acts a year earlier, he had pardoned Richard Nixon, freeing him from any criminal or civil liability. While this was unpopular, Ford had also offered clemency to Vietnam draft dodgers and military deserters, enabling them to "wipe the slate clean." The two acts together had had a healing effect on the nation. Throughout the Vietnam-Watergate decade a culture of protest had polarized the country. Ford's pardons brought on a season of peace.

As a general assignment reporter, I was covering a different story every day, which meant I was never allowed to concentrate long enough even to scratch the surface of an issue. One day I was sent to a Pentagon briefing about the War in Vietnam. It was all about ARVN and KIAs; it was S and D and sappers.[9] Had I slipped into a briefing in Urdu? I got so lost, I had to read the wires later to understand what I'd heard.

Occasionally I went out to lunch with my colleagues. One day at Provençal near the bureau, producer Don Bowers, correspondents Bob

Schieffer and Phil Jones, and I were chewing over the topic *du jour*, Dan Schorr's claiming that he was not getting on the air very much because he had been too tough during Watergate. CBS headquarters, he contended, was silencing him, which we all found absurd. "He's been giving speeches charging that CBS corporate officers are interfering with the news," said Bowers.

"Why don't they fire him?" I asked, then answered myself: "I remember him once telling me, 'Executives come and go, but we people on the air *are* CBS. They can't fire us.' "

His theory was about to be tested. In early 1976 Schorr, 59, was leaked a copy of a secret report on specific misdeeds of the cloak-and-dagger set at the CIA, a report compiled by a special House investigating committee headed by Representative Otis Pike of New York. Schorr's pieces on the *Evening* and *Morning News* made a big splash, but after just a few news cycles, the producers in New York felt they had exhausted the "Pike Papers" and told Schorr no more stories. He thought his scoop was as significant as the leak of the Pentagon Papers in 1971 and went railing about the office, incensed at the "poor judgment" of his bosses. He wanted CBS to put together a prime-time hour on his exclusive. Not long after, on February 16, Don Bowers pulled me aside in the newsroom: "There's something you need to know."

He was so uncharacteristically somber, I got scared. "What?"

"You've seen *The Village Voice*, haven't you?" He held up a copy with a screaming tabloidlike headline: "What the Government Doesn't Want You to Know About the Pike Papers." The *Voice* had published the secret Pike Papers from beginning to end, just as *The New York Times* had printed the Pentagon Papers — with an introduction by Aaron Latham.

"What I need to warn you about," said Bowers, "is that Dan Schorr is telling people you stole his copy of the report and gave it to your boyfriend."

I was flabbergasted. I knew Schorr disliked me, but accusing me of stealing? It was insane, in fact, because I knew that Schorr himself had handed the Pike Papers to *The Village Voice*. But I didn't tell Bowers, because that would be divulging Aaron's source, which I felt I couldn't do, even to protect myself from slander.

Within minutes the *Evening News* researcher, Susan Zirinsky, pulled me into an empty office and closed the door. "Dan Schorr told me this morning that he thinks you rifled through his desk, found the Pike Papers, Xeroxed them and gave them to Aaron. And he's told Sandy [Sandy Socolow, the new bureau chief], and all the big guys in New York are right now debating what to do about you."

"You mean they believe him?" I asked.

"I think so."

I looked Susan in the eye. "I didn't do it." I felt like David Janssen in *The Fugitive*. I realized I had to do something, but marching into the bureau chief's office and merely issuing a denial would not be enough, and I couldn't tell him Schorr himself had photocopied the report and leaked it.

The name David Shapiro came to mind. Not only was he one of Socolow's best friends, he was one of the best criminal lawyers in town. I had met him when he had represented Chuck Colson, one of the Watergate defendants. "Can I come see you right away?" I asked Shapiro on the phone. "I'm in trouble."

I walked around the corner to his office and told him everything. Shapiro, who looks and even acts like the actor Ed Asner, picked up the phone and called Socolow. "I'm representing Lesley Stahl," he said without any introduction. "We understand she is under suspicion of stealing. If this accusation goes one step further, if any hint of such a charge becomes public, we will sue CBS like it's never been sued. And just for the record, she didn't do it." And he hung up.

"Now listen to me," he said. "You are to keep your mouth shut. You are to say nothing about this. Don't go blabbing around the office. Don't start denigrating Schorr. I know this will be hard, but this is the best advice I can give you. You are under, as they say in court, a gag order."

I went back to work and followed his instructions, though it was hard to concentrate. I spent most of my time trying to find Aaron so I could ask him, if push came to shove, would he clear my name? I realized that by passing the report on to another news organization Schorr had violated the terms of his contract with CBS and that he was trying to weasel his way out of admitting what he had done. What baffled me was why he didn't think Aaron would come to my rescue.

The next day *The Washington Post* ran a front-page story by Larry Stern saying that Schorr himself had leaked the report. I was off the hook. Then, on February 23, CBS suspended Schorr. The House Ethics Committee had launched an investigation into the leak of the Pike Papers with Schorr as its prime witness. CBS said it would be unseemly for him to continue working while he was the subject of a congressional hearing. That was the public explanation; I was told he had been suspended because of his lying about me.

Aaron was a wreck. He was called to testify at the Ethics Committee hearings, which were being televised. Worried about Aaron landing in jail, his lawyer, Ted Kheel, wanted him to say he had no idea who had leaked the report to Schorr. But Aaron wanted to strike a blow for the First Amendment, so when he was asked if he knew Schorr's source, Aaron said, "Well, I have some trouble personally answering questions about sources at all."

"On what grounds?"

"The First Amendment protection of sources."

I was watching on television. I could tell that Aaron was nervous. He was asked why he thought he had the right to publish a classified document. "We thought," Aaron said, "we were doing the country a service."

Congressman James Quillen of Tennessee asked, "And what country do you think that you provided a service for in publishing the report?" I clutched my stomach.

"I believe the United States of America," said Aaron. "We showed that we could investigate our own wrongdoing. . . . I believe that this is why the First Amendment was written, to give the press that authority."

When Schorr testified later that day, he also gave a stirring defense of a reporter's right to protect his sources. He was so ringing in defending the First Amendment that the CBS brass feared a public backlash if he were not reinstated. But his returning to work in the Washington Bureau would have been an affront not just to me but to the bureau chief as well, because Schorr had claimed that it was Socolow who first suggested I might have stolen the papers. Socolow called Schorr a liar.

In mid-September the Ethics Committee dropped its investigation of Schorr (and Aaron), so it was time for CBS to decide whether to bring him back. As part of his rehabilitation, Schorr submitted to a Mike Wallace interview on *60 Minutes*. I watched at home.

"You denied to CBS management that you supplied the Pike Papers to *The Village Voice*," said Mike.

"That's not exactly right, that I denied. I—I dissembled."

"You permitted your colleague, Lesley Stahl, to be implicated as the person who had leaked the Pike Papers."

"For a few hours," Schorr said, "until I realized how silly that was and stopped it." He had "stopped it" only after *The Washington Post* had fingered him as the leaker. I watched with fury as he persisted in minimizing the act of accusing a colleague of theft, calling the episode "office gossip . . . basically trivia."

"Well, I think that's in the eye of the beholder," said Mike. "Certainly in—in Lesley Stahl's mind it wasn't trivial."

"Lesley Stahl knows less about it than anybody, but she's never asked me about it." (Eric Sevareid, the CBS commentator, had advised me, "Never talk to Schorr until he apologizes fully and unequivocally." Sounded right to me.)

"But if Lesley Stahl is implicated," said Mike, "why don't you—gentleman, honorable, straightforward—call Lesley on the phone or walk into Lesley's office and say, 'Lesley, I made a mistake. It was a stupid thing to do. I panicked for a moment.'"

"Well, I *didn't* make a mistake," Schorr blustered. "That's *your* version. I've told you that I didn't make a mistake. I didn't try to implicate Lesley."

The next day Schorr resigned from CBS. When asked if he would have offered Schorr his old job back, Dick Salant said, "Dan spared me having to make a decision."

Several weeks later Mickey Bazelon, the wife of the chief judge of the U.S. Court of Appeals in Washington, phoned me. "Dan wants to call you," she said.

"Well, why doesn't he?"

"He's afraid you'll hang up on him."

"Please."

"He asked me to call you to make sure you'd hear him out."

"What is this?" I asked. "He's *afraid* to call me?" Mickey was a friend whom Schorr knew I could not refuse. If she asked me a favor, I would have to say yes. And she asked: "Talk to him as a favor to me."

Remembering Sevareid's advice, I said, "Mickey, if he's calling to apologize, of course I'll take the call, but tell him that."

A few days later, he called: "Lesley, I just want you to know that I'm sorry if I caused you any pain."

"Is that an apology, Dan?" I asked.

"Well, I just want you to know how badly I feel that you may have been embarrassed or made to feel uncomfortable."

CBS moved me into Schorr's old office in the front row.

"You don't have to carry my suitcase!" I said, smiling at Scoop. It was the fall of 1975, and I was covering my first presidential candidate, Henry "Scoop" Jackson, 62, the Washington State "senator from Boeing," as he liked to call himself, the "candidate of the old-time bosses," as others called him. Despite his staff's admonitions that he not schlepp the CBS lady's luggage around, he had once again gotten to my bag before I could. "I *want* to carry this," he insisted. "A woman shouldn't have to lift heavy suitcases."

Roger Mudd had teased me about being assigned to Scoop. "There is no way you'll be able to stay awake," he said. "This man is duller than a mashed-potato sandwich." But I thought the assignment was a plum since Jackson had a serious shot at winning the Democratic nomination. I boarded his campaign bus with an open mind and a heavy suitcase and realized quickly that Roger Mudd was right. Jackson—a little man with short arms and a long, doleful face—was boring. Yet in his stolid Norwegian way he was as decent and honest a politician as ever there was.

Aaron, who often joined me on the Jackson campaign, was surprised that the television reporters didn't go out drinking every night with Scoop's staff. With newspaper deadlines as late as 11 o'clock, campaign

54

press secretaries routinely scheduled late-night spinning sessions over beers in the bar. But my deadline was early in the afternoon. Those were the days before satellite feeds; I had to leave time for the film to be flown to New York for processing and editing. So either I had all the information in hand by midday or there was no story. But instead of my having to adjust, the campaign did. To get the TV exposure, they paid the network reporters special attention, making sure we had everything we needed by noon.

Jackson started out with great promise, winning the Massachusetts primary on March 2. But the public was weary of Scoop's Cold War hot rhetoric; they wanted a soft-spoken, gentler leader. Enter the drawling Jimmy Carter, former governor of Georgia. He clobbered Jackson in Florida.[10]

Scoop began grumbling about Carter. He disliked the Southern Baptist peanut farmer with a raw repugnance. "I just don't trust a man who wears his religion on his sleeve like that," he told me.

GOD PUT JOB through the trials of Hell, including boils, but Job never had to convert from film to videotape overnight. While some of the local stations had made the switch to videotape, the networks hadn't. CBS would go first, and I was chosen to be one of a handful out on the campaign trail to be a test pilot. Why me? We moved cold turkey from what we knew how to do into the world of the unknown. Overnight my crew and I became people learning how to play the piano and give a concert at the same time.

We called the new system ENG, short for electronic news gathering. By eliminating the time for film processing, we were told, we would knock three hours off our deadlines and theoretically have more time to gather news. But we smacked hard into the law of unintended consequences. Every one of the dozens of new buttons to push and switches to flick created an opportunity for a glitch. There were endless, infuriating malfunctions: the color would die, the tape would get snarled, or the speed would be off. The misnamed Minicams came in two pieces. The portable video camera was the Japanese-made Ikigami HL-33. HL stood for Handy Looky, but we called them Ickies. They weighed 12 pounds, which doesn't seem like much, except that the cameraman (usually a converted film man) also had to wear a cumbersome backpack with the electronics and power supply, including bulky 20-pound batteries that were supposed to last an hour but never did. Altogether, he was dragging around at least 45 pounds. Making life even more difficult, the cameraman was tethered with a ten-foot umbilical cord to his soundman, who was now carrying his own 50 to 60 pounds of equipment, mainly a Sony tape recorder with a maddening habit of breaking down. With film, there had been three-man crews; now just two had to carry heavier equipment plus lights and a tripod and cope with adjusting to the new technology all at the same time.

But when the minicameras worked, we could be live and up to the minute. If something terrible happened, such as a president being shot, you could put the pictures on television unedited as soon as you could dash to a microwave facility. Videotape revolutionized the TV news business by compressing the time it took to get pictures onto the network. That time became almost instantaneous, meaning that in a crisis so did the time for our news judgments. In the days of film, if an event happened late, we didn't file a report until the next day. But now our time to reflect on the events we covered, to put them into context and figure out what was important and what was not, was disappearing. This was obviously a momentous change, but little thought was given to the consequences. We didn't have time to think.

A lot of our time was spent adjusting to the new contraptions. During one of Scoop Jackson's speeches in New York the Sony recorder ate the entire tape cassette. There was no retrieving either picture or sound. I was frantic. During Scoop's walk through Harlem, the battery died just as he met up with Congressman Charlie Rangel. One afternoon my producer back in the office in New York came unhinged when he was editing my piece. One of the disadvantages of the new editing console was that you couldn't view anything in reverse. The editor had to sneak up on the desired portion of the tape, but because the machine was so inaccurate, he was usually off by several frames, meaning he'd end up with the end of the previous word. So Senator Jackson would say, "umpMy policies will . . ." or "enI pledge to. . . ." Often the edit wouldn't take and the whole process would have to be repeated. We weren't just test pilots, we were crash-test dummies. Yet no matter how much we complained, there was no turning back. It *had* to work, because CBS had already invested in all the equipment.

JACKSON WAS DOING WELL in New York, where he spent 80 percent of his time in union halls and synagogues. I think we visited every Jewish group in the state. But he was having trouble attracting large audiences in the northern industrial states and was falling further and further behind Carter in the national polls. What happened in Wausau, Wisconsin, seemed to say it all. Jackson's DC-3 flew in just as Carter's 727 was loading up to leave. The gate area in Wausau was so small that Carter's jet couldn't taxi because Scoop's plane was blocking its route out. After summitlike negotiations between the campaigns, the Jackson staff and press corps were all made to get off our old flying machine and push it out of the way, as if it were a jalopy that had run out of gas. We said it was a metaphor for the state of Scoop's campaign.

Jackson won New York, but then he lost Wisconsin and was left nearly out of money. Three days after he lost the Pennsylvania primary on April 27, I had my first major scoop on the campaign trail. When I found out that Jackson had canceled his radio ads in Indiana, I got on the phone and plumbed all the people on the campaign I'd been cultivating. That night, I broke the story that Jackson had decided to call it quits. I led the Cronkite show by saying, "Jackson determined that he did not have and could not raise sufficient money to run the kind of campaign needed to beat Jimmy Carter."

Several weeks later, as a measure of our affection, a group of reporters from the Jackson plane threw him a party in New York. Scoop and I remained friends until he died on September 1, 1983, at the age of 71.

As I HAD, the other CBS correspondents came off the campaign trail one by one as their candidates dropped out. By early June, Jimmy Carter was the only one left standing.

In the 1960s and 1970s the way to judge who was up and who was down in network news was to watch the national political conventions. Floor correspondents, those lucky few assigned to roam the range of the convention delegations, were the A team, the first string, and I was disappointed when I wasn't chosen to be one in 1976. Instead I was named "relief correspondent," a new animal that CBS created to keep its hungry younger reporters in the game. Conventions were as much a vehicle for the networks to showcase their stars as they were political events. Since CBS had so many stars, it had to create a second tier. Four of us juniors were each assigned to relieve one of the starters when they got tired or had to relieve themselves. Ed Bradley was paired with Rather, Dick Threlkeld with Mudd, Betty Ann Bowser with Wallace, and I with Mort Dean.

The Democrats held their convention in July at Madison Square Garden in New York City. The problem for the Carter forces was building some interest in the event, since the Georgian with the soft, soothing manner had the nomination sewn up. There was no suspense, leaving the press and the pols to use the event to promote each other in an affair of incestuous collusion.

And so the convention was all television, a fully produced, stage-managed, four-part miniseries, Monday through Thursday in prime time. The most visible sights in the hall were the network anchor booths lit up in bright colors high up in the skyboxes like eagle aeries. Many of the delegates had no view of the podium because of the giant camera platform in the middle of the floor. Even the seating of the delegates was determined by camera angles, with the big states and key people such as Mayor Richard Daley of Chicago placed within easy camera range.

My preconvention assignment was to cover the Platform Committee and report on the CBS delegates' poll, which showed that the delegates were more liberal than the party as a whole but included fewer women and blacks than in 1972. This was a crowd that could be controlled.

Each day, in the late afternoon, CBS held strategy meetings with the four seniors and four juniors. We tried to agree on themes we could develop during the all-night broadcast, what issues to explore. At one of the meetings, Rather was proposing an idea when, to everyone's discomfort, Roger Mudd started repeating what Dan was saying word for word, the way a child does in that irritating echo game. Rather shrugged it off and went on with his proposal, but Mudd escalated his taunt into outright heckling. I stopped breathing. So did everyone else in the room. Mudd had let his competition with Rather for anchorman — which of the two would succeed Cronkite — grow into a serious feud that made us all uncomfortable. Finally, Mort Dean asked Roger to calm down so we could finish our business. I wondered what would have been said if a woman had acted like that.

For me to go out onto the floor, Mort Dean, who had covered the space shots for CBS, had to come off. That first night, as Mort left to start our coverage he said, "Lesley, remember those urine tubes the astronauts had? I'm wearing one of them. I won't have to come off the floor to go to the bathroom for a week!"

But the floor producer, Don Hewitt, whose regular job was producing *60 Minutes*, made sure there was a rotation, so about an hour and a half into the broadcast, around 9:30, he buzzed me: "Get ready, kid, your turn is coming up." Like any benchwarmer called into the game, I suited up. I had to wear a big, bulky headband that was both a radio receiver and a transmission unit. A cup fit over my left ear so I could hear the CBS program and get directions from Hewitt. Connected to the headband was a minimicrophone that arced across my right cheek so I could broadcast from the floor. All of this posed an engineering puzzle because I did not want my hair flattened down. I looped clumps of hair over the headband as fast as I could, building a little teased house around it. Deep down I must have thought I *was* my hair. As I dressed for the floor, I thought of knights preparing for a joust. My squire, a CBS engineer, strapped a thick, heavy belt around my waist with pockets for the batteries and transmitter. It felt as unwieldy as armor. And he handed me my lance, a thin, wandlike microphone.

I forgot how hulky I looked the minute I walked onto the floor at Madison Square Garden, which was packed with more than 3,000 delegates from 50 states. It was claustrophobic like the subway at five o'clock, but here everyone knew everyone else. There was a cousins'-club feel with people who hadn't seen each other in four years air-kissing and gossiping and trying to impress the roving reporters with hot tips. I kept searching for ways to get on the air. As I wandered, I did have to laugh at the inanities — a man from Saskatchewan wearing a wedding cake hat, a mother from Albuquerque breast-feeding her infant, a Vermont delegate blowing a kazoo. Conventions are nutty, adolescent fun. But at this one, news was in short supply. Because the convention was so tightly controlled, the heavyweights of TV journalism — Dan, Peter, Tom, Mike, Roger — were reduced to interviewing "personalities" who did little more than spout the party line.

I was able to get to the Illinois sector, beep Don Hewitt on my intercom, and pitch an interview with Mayor Daley. "Sure, kid," he said. "Find camera C." Daley made me think of Snow White's Grumpy as I escorted him to a small clearing so camera C would have a clean shot of us. There I stood next to history, next to the man credited with winning the 1960 election for Jack Kennedy and losing 1968 for Hubert Humphrey by instigating the violence outside the Democratic National Convention in Chicago. "Your candidate for vice president is Adlai Stevenson Jr.?" I asked.

"That's right," said Grumpy.

"People here are saying you're the only one left supporting him."

"Well, I never leave 'em once I support 'em."

That was it for news out of Daley. I was then sent up into the VIP section to find Jimmy Carter's mother, Miss Lillian, a feisty woman of 77 with proud, deep lines in her face and a yeasty sense of humor. "I understand, Mrs. Carter, you are about to become a journalist," I said. "Is that true?"

"Well, don't get afraid. I don't want your job," said the first-mother-to-be.

"What do you think you're going to write about for your column tomorrow?"

"I'll tell all about you interviewing me up here."

After that penetrating interview, I was sent to find the youngest of the Carter women, eight-year-old Amy, the candidate's daughter. "Amy, Amy? Hi. I'm Lesley Stahl from CBS. Can you tell us what your impressions are of this convention? Do you think it's exciting?"

"Yes."

"Do you have any advice for the young people of America who are watching tonight?"

"No."

"You don't?"

59

"No."

"Well, looking out over the crowd — can you sort of turn around and look out? Do you think that when you grow up that you'd like to run for president some day yourself?

"No."

"Definitely not?"

"No."

"You know, Amy, one big question all America is waiting to have answered is: What have you done with your lemonade stand while you're up here in New York?"

"It's still in Plains."

"Who's operating it?"

"Nobody. Not now."

"Okay. Thank you very much. Walter."

Now, that's a tough day at the office. Several months later, after the election, when Rosalynn Carter took Amy to her new school in Washington, I overheard Amy ask her mother, "Now that we won, do I have to be nice to the press anymore?"

ON THURSDAY, the final night, I was out on the floor standing in a crush when the lights went out for a campaign-produced film on Jimmy Carter. When the lights came up, Carter was not at the podium, as everyone expected, but walking across the floor. TV screens were filled with one visual message: here comes a man of the people, a Washington outsider — just what the country wanted after Watergate.

That night Carter seemed to have everything we would soon be complaining he lacked: the gift of inspiring, the ability to motivate and bring us together. He exuded leadership and strength. Was that a mantle he borrowed for the night like Cinderella's ball gown? Or did the made-for-television production create an illusion? A few days later a Louis Harris poll showed Carter 30 points ahead of Gerald Ford.

ONE MONTH LATER we did it all over again in Kansas City, where the Republicans held their convention at the Kemper Arena, a big open space with wide aisles. After Madison Square Garden it felt like a Texas cattle ranch. There was a bubble of excitement over Ronald Reagan's challenge to the incumbent president, Gerald Ford. But again the convention was more about television than about selecting a standard bearer for a political party.

This was the year of the role switch. Disciplined Democrats, recalcitrant Republicans. In Kansas City, every time Reagan's name was mentioned, a tumultuous, out-of-control, horn-tooting demonstration would break out. These free-for-alls lasted so long, both Ford's nomination and his acceptance speech were pushed right out of prime time.

When Ford did speak, he said, "The American people are going to say . . . 'Jerry, you've done a good job. Keep right on doing it.' "

It was the best speech he ever gave, interrupted by 69 bursts of applause. But then he made a mistake. He invited Ronald Reagan up to the podium, and as Reagan spoke, with his perfect actor's pitch and timing, Gerald Ford lost his luster, right there on national television. Ford left his convention farther behind than any president in the history of modern polling.

When I left Kansas City I asked myself: If there had been no television coverage, would there have even been conventions? No, there'd be no need anymore, now that the outcomes were decided well in advance, in the primaries.

ONCE THE POST-CONVENTION CAMPAIGN started in 1976, videotape changed the rhythm of our coverage. Network correspondents broke away from the campaigns later and later in the day. Editing equipment would be set up ahead of time at the local TV station or, if there wasn't one, in a school or an airport from which our story would be edited and then fed to New York over phone circuits. A quiet place to record voice-overs had to be found, more often than not in a closet or bathroom. As Carter and Ford caught on to the new deadlines, they figured out that the later they issued their big, make-news statements, the less time we would have to analyze, check their facts, or find opposing views.

I wasn't assigned to Ford or Carter, so I spent most of the fall covering the issues and strategies. On one of our campaign specials, I explained that President Ford's strategy was to whip up uncertainty and fear about "Carter, the unknown, Carter, the inexperienced."

Sometimes a technology change makes a real substantive difference. Now, with videotape, which was less expensive than film, the crews began rolling on everything the candidates said and did. Once everything was recorded, the press began catching the discrepancies and inconsistencies, the errors of fact, the gaffes and goofs. Gerald Ford, who had played football in college, had been known until then as the athlete president; during the campaign he became the bumbling president. We kept catching him on tape tripping and bumping his head and slipping down stairs. It was distorting and unfair, but it was inevitable. Yet as the campaign progressed, President Ford began creeping up in the polls, his harping on Jimmy Carter's lack of experience having taken root. By election day, Carter's 30-point lead had melted like soap in a hot shower.

There have been election nights where the networks knew who won

61

as early as four in the afternoon from our exit polling, but in 1976 we had no clue when we went on the air at 7 P.M. One of my problems as anchor of the West Desk was that voting in the Rockies and on the Pacific coast continued until 11 or 12 o'clock Eastern Time, and our rule was not to call the outcome of a race until the polls in that state closed. So I was barely seen in prime time.

Even without the airtime, I was in heaven, up there in the clouds with Eric Sevareid, Bill Moyers, Mudd, Rather, Wallace, and Cronkite. As returns tumbled in from the eastern states, I worked the phones. Not only did I stay in touch with my contacts in the western states, I called and got calls from friends and sources in the Carter and Ford campaigns who wanted to know CBS's latest data. "What do you have on Texas?" they'd ask. I could punch up any state on my computer and read a whole array of constantly updated polling numbers: how the union vote was going in Illinois or the black vote in New York or the elderly vote nation-wide.

The story line of our coverage was that Gerald Ford had all but closed the 30-point gap with Jimmy Carter and that this was a razor-close, nose-to-nose race. Ford was a solid favorite in my territory, except for California.

I finally popped up at ten to report that Ford had won Colorado and would have to win a solid West to offset the near-solid South for Carter. Bill Moyers followed me, pointing out, "There are simply more Democrats than Republicans [by two to one]. Somebody said Republicans sleep in twin beds, which is why there are probably more Democrats than there are Republicans."

Rather was armed with his usual colloquialisms. "If Gerald Ford cannot carry four states in the Midwest," he said, "it's turn-out-the-lights for him. . . . You can pour water on the fire and call in the dogs because the hunt will be over."

Eleven P.M.: "The Rockies are coming in," I said with energy. "This is the area of the country that Ronald Reagan carried in the primaries. Tonight it's Ford who's winning them." We had no idea who would win; my instincts told me that Ford would pull it out.

One A.M.: Rather said, "In Ohio it's dead even, not a peanut shell of difference between them at the moment." I said, "We have four cliff-hangers in the West: California, New Mexico, Washington, and Hawaii." I was getting my turn more and more often; in the western zone, they were still in prime time.

Three A.M.: Walter said that UPI had declared Carter the winner, but "we're being hypercautious." At 3:30 NBC and ABC called the race for Carter. At CBS he was still five electoral votes shy. Walter asked what the biggest surprise of the night was. I said, "That I'm able to give you results that still matter."

Finally, at 3:50, Walter said that Jimmy Carter would be the third Baptist, the seventh farmer or rancher, and the 11th whose mother had lived to see him elected president of the United States. We went off the air at 5 A.M. with me saying, "We still see no trend in California."

It was thought that Carter won because of his masterful use of television imagery, but in the immediate aftermath of the election I was struck by how much ground he had actually lost over the course of the campaign. One reason was that he had refused to accept help from the old-time Democratic politicians and constituencies such as labor. They were insulted by not being asked and by their perception that he saw them all as scoundrels. Carter's unwillingness to include the old guard in his victory might have helped with his Mr. Clean image in the campaign, but it would hurt him once in office.

Aaron wrote an article for *New York* magazine saying that each president comes to office having been shaped by a formative historical experience. For Dwight Eisenhower and John Kennedy, it had been World War II, which had taught them to expect to win and made them optimists; Lyndon Johnson's had been the Alamo, where the Texans had been massacred. That's probably why he had turned the White House into a fortress surrounded by enemies. Aaron quoted James Schlesinger — Nixon's CIA director, Ford's secretary of defense, and Carter's soon-to-be secretary of energy — as saying that Jimmy Carter's formative experience had been the Civil War. And so he would expect to lose and also to be good at it.

AARON WANTED CHILDREN; I didn't. I was so happy with him, I was afraid this would drive him off, but I didn't think I'd be a good mother. Besides, Dolly had been telling me for years, "Never have children, they'll ruin your life." Thanks, Mum. She pounded into me the idea that I had to have a career, which was the real route to happiness. I bought into her prescription for my life wholeheartedly. But I was coming up on my 35th birthday. At the time it was firmly established that 35 was the end of the child-bearing years, but I felt no pressure to change my life plan, which did not involve a family. But then, right before my birthday, I got a three-page letter from Dolly.

"Dear Only Daughter," she began, "I've made so many mistakes." She laid out an argument free of sentimentality on why I should have a baby — right away. Never once was the word "grandmother" mentioned. Her first point was that we are all animals. "What do you think we were put here for anyway if not to procreate? It is the very purpose of life." The second point came from a study she had read. "People (men and women) with children go much farther in their careers," she explained. "Do you realize that if you never have a child, you always see yourself as a child. Only a parent can take charge." Finally, she argued, women without children are "unfulfilled and feel cheated. I know I've been on your back a long while not to have children. Intuitively I knew I was right, but now I don't want my kid to have regrets."

She went on to say that Aaron would be a wonderful father and that I would not have to give up my career: "I am getting old, but I'm still young enough to pitch in and help you. If you take two weeks off for delivery or even one extra week, I can't see where your future can do anything but become enhanced. Don't wait until I'm too old to help you. Please. M."

PART TWO

JIMMY AND ROSALYNN CARTER

H

OW MUCH of my life my mother controlled was unclear to me. I knew I had the career she had encouraged. And I looked the way she wanted me to—probably because she had bought my clothes until I was 30. On the rare occasion when she saw me in something I had picked out myself, she'd treat me as if I'd besmirched the family name. When she was angry at me, I'd get so distraught I could barely breathe, at 35. I thought all mother-daughter relationships were like ours and was fascinated but disbelieving when my friends told me that ours was, well, unusual. When anyone suggested that Dolly was my Svengali, I'd laugh; don't be silly. Until I got pregnant.

I had always felt I wouldn't be a good mother. I was too single-minded about my career, too absorbed with my independence (I never saw being under my mother's spell as a form of dependence), and too impatient. Of course, I said those things at a time when my mother was instructing me not to have children.

Then Clay Felker weighed in. Aaron and I had dinner with him before we headed off on a late-night flight to Greece for a vacation. Clay had the appearance of a good-looking baby with pink skin, and when you were with him, as with a child, you felt an obligation to perform. Like other great editors he was a sponge, blotting up information from other people; a listener more than an entertainer. I loved his company because, unlike most men, he actually elicited the views of women. The three of us were at a choice table at Elaine's, Clay distracted by the buzz in the room until I told him about my mother's letter. He grabbed my shoulders. "The biggest mistake of my life," he said, shaking me, "is not having had a child. Listen to your mother."

A few hours later our plane took off for Athens. "You know that Clay and your mother are right," Aaron said. "We should have a child." I loved this man; I wanted to be with him forever. But a child? What happened next is open to argument. Aaron swears I asked him, "If I did get pregnant, would you marry me?" I have no recollection of this, and if pressed I will swear I never said it. And yet it appears that within a few days, poof! A little angel was on the way. I think it happened the night we met Cokie and Steve Roberts (he was the *New York Times*' correspondent in Athens) with their two gorgeous children, Becca and Lee. Or maybe it was a whisper from the Oracle at Delphi. Whatever magic brought this on, I didn't realize my condition because it was impossible. I had taken every precaution.

Two months later, when I fainted in Senator Ted Kennedy's office, I didn't know why. As I say, it was impossible. One night—I was more than three months along—Aaron asked where I wanted to have dinner. "That restaurant that begins with P," I said.

67

"Which one is that?" he asked innocently.

As Aaron told me later, I snapped. I went racing through the apartment, ranting about the letter P. When I calmed down, Aaron said, "There aren't many explanations for what's wrong with you." That's when he said that the place that began with P was "pregnant" — which, I assured him, was ridiculous.

First thing the next morning I went to the doctor. I was in my office around three o'clock when he called to say, "It's positive." I was so surprised, I ran to my sanctuary, the ladies' room, and locked myself in a stall. How could this have happened? Was it that I had deep down wanted Aaron's baby? Or did I simply do whatever Dolly told me to?

Aaron was ecstatic. And after the initial shock, so was I.

Two weeks later I was writing a story on how Medicare patients in New York City and Beverly Hills pay more for gallbladder and cataract operations than do the elderly in rural Nebraska or Findlay, Ohio. When I finished, I did the forbidden and slipped away at 4:30 in the afternoon. The rule was that correspondents with stories in the broadcast didn't leave. The *Evening News* had two editions: one at 6:30, the other at 7:00. If we made a mistake, we were expected to correct it for "the second feed." We might also be asked to cut time out of pieces at the last minute to make room for late-breaking news. I told Rita Braver, my producer that night, that I had to do something very important and asked her not to tell anyone I was gone.

Wearing an old blue dress and a new pair of shoes, I borrowed a necklace from a friend in the office, Joan Barone, and sneaked out to elope. Aaron and I met in Judge David Bazelon's chambers and got married at five. The only ones there were my brother, Jeff; his wife, Paula, who was our photographer; Aaron's college friend Tom Plate, who was our best man; and my friend Mickey Bazelon, the judge's wife. When Aaron couldn't get the ring onto my finger, I broke into one of those out-of-control laughing jags, the kind where you feel the heat and perspiration in your chest because you realize you can't stop and you're a flip side away from crying. The judge, bless him, said, "The most important thing in a marriage is that you can laugh together." This made everyone laugh and helped me out of my last-minute panic. We finished early enough for me to get back to CBS before the show went on the air. Rita later told me she'd thought I had gone across town to ABC for an interview about jumping networks.

It turned out that eloping was a mistake. When I called to tell my parents, instead of feeling triumphant as I thought she would, Dolly went silent with anger because I hadn't invited her. I had hurt my mother, which was certainly not my intention. She refused to talk to me till the baby was born.

68

Two days after our wedding, I flew to New York to meet Aaron. I had been teasing him that there was something unnatural when a wife has never seen her husband's face: he still had the scruffy reddish beard he'd had the day we'd met. When I got to his apartment in New York, I walked right past him. Who was that man? He was wearing Aaron's corduroy jacket. I ran back. He'd shaved. I burst into tears. First uncontrolled laughing, now crying: this pregnancy business wasn't for sissies. I had married a stranger. None of his features were in the right place. It was as if Picasso had had a go at him: his nose too close to his chin, his lower lip too big, his head off-kilter. I called my mother for comfort, but she hung up on me. Poor Aaron. He was only giving me the wedding present he thought I wanted. He never shaved again.

The last thing Aaron needed was a crank for a wife. Only a few weeks before, Rupert Murdoch had managed to wrest control of *New York* magazine away from Clay Felker in a hostile takeover. Murdoch had befriended Clay and then betrayed him, taking off with his magazine, his only child. Aaron and most of the other writers and editors walked out in solidarity with Clay, but this act of principle left Aaron with a pregnant wife and no job. Thus started his career as a freelancer. He peddled story ideas to *Esquire* and *Playboy*. He was feeling insecure, but under pressure he became more prolific than ever and made more money than ever.

I missed Dolly in those months, but then being in her deep-freeze lockout meant I didn't have any fights with her. I had read about birth defects that occur because the mother has an emotional upheaval during pregnancy, so I decided the incident over Aaron's beard would be the last time I'd allow anything to upset me. Maintaining an atmosphere of sublime tranquillity for my child became my first priority. I decided to remain sunny and cheerful. Everyone in the office seemed to conspire with me; they were all so solicitous of the pregnant lady, especially the cameramen. I was a novelty, one of the first women at CBS News to try anything so revolutionary. I was certainly the first on-air reporter to do so.

I kept working as my body began protruding in every direction. I felt like one of those pink elephants in *Fantasia* — a big hulk daringly bobbing around on a pair of incongruously dainty toe shoes. I can still hear my click-clacking heels in the halls of Congress as my bulging body ran in a swaying motion after an escaping senator. I was assigned to a series of investigations on Capitol Hill: Koreagate, Saccharinegate (did it cause cancer?), a look at why the Food and Drug Administration had no authority over cigarettes either as a food or as a drug. Nothing changes.

I thought I was beautiful. "You really do have that glow," people would say, and I believed it until June 17, the fifth anniversary of the Watergate break-in. CBS had been shooting me tighter and tighter. Every month my close-ups got closer. The last thing the bosses wanted was to show a pregnant lady on television. What a prudish lot we Americans were in the 1970s. In many places pregnant teachers were still being forced to stop teaching. But that night my report for the Cronkite show ended with me in an underground garage, talking about Deep Throat. I walked into frame from behind a pillar, exposing a full-body profile. I hadn't seen myself from that angle: not adorably plump but huge. A bloated, ungainly, abdominous, protruberant cow.

Aaron was working on an article for *Esquire* about the Republican Senate candidate in Virginia, John Warner, and his wife, Elizabeth Taylor. They had invited Aaron to lunch at their Georgetown home and asked if I wanted to come. Well, who wouldn't? Warner, who had been secretary of the navy, was dashing. I thought as he opened the door that he could play the president in a movie. He was wearing a navy jumpsuit, and he pulled Aaron aside to tell him in a guy-to-guy whisper that he loved wearing jumpsuits "'cause your balls can roam free."

As he led us into the living room, Warner hollered up the stairs, "Elizabeth, hurry up. They're here. Lesley's seven months pregnant, and she's thinner than you are."

When Taylor finally made her entrance, I'm sure she read the word "aghast" on my face. How had Cleopatra spread that much? How could anyone that fat still be so blaringly beautiful? She was wearing a buff-colored muumuu that did little to conceal the tubby midriff. Nothing hid the double chins. But her face, crowned with a ratted nest of black hair and bejeweled with those glittering eyes, was as gorgeous as in the movies.

What surprised me was how smart she was, and how funny. Curled up on the couch in Warner's arm like his little girl, she told us with great humor how she'd met him on a blind date — "I thought he was dishy" — and how she'd bought a blue cornfield by van Gogh. But her good humor turned dark when Aaron asked if she were a Republican like her husband. She hissed like Maggie in *Cat on a Hot Tin Roof*, "I will be when *he* comes out for the Equal Rights Amendment. And not until!"

With that, Warner jumped up and ran in a circle, then out the door. Ms. Taylor leaned into the little microphone on the side of Aaron's running tape recorder and repeated a famous John Mitchell line about Kay Graham of *The Washington Post* from Watergate days: "If you print that, Aaron, I'll get my tit caught in a wringer."

WHILE THE *Evening News* tried to hide my pregnancy, Don Hewitt asked if I'd do a summer relief piece for *60 Minutes*. I jumped at it, of course, but unfortunately the subject was "Whither Puerto Rico?" There I was in San Juan in July with *60 Minutes* shooting my belly in all its glory. Hewitt understood the showbiz value of the unusual on television: a working girl in her eighth month.

I worked right up to August 13, when my water broke.

Aaron and I had been going to Lamaze classes, so when we found ourselves in a pool of water in the middle of the night, we knew just what to do. We got out our class notes and followed them precisely. I showered and packed an overnight bag while the "coach" made himself a sandwich in case he was tied up at the hospital for hours. Aaron put down a layer of mayonnaise, then a slab of meat, then a layer of mayo and a tomato, then more mayo and lettuce and even more mayo and a slice of Muenster.

When we got to George Washington Hospital, I thought I was in labor and that I was handling myself with remarkable fortitude, given my nonexistent tolerance for pain. But after 18 hours, I was informed I had not tripped over into real labor, so it was time to induce. As a young intern began administering Pitocin, Aaron decided it was time for his sandwich, which he bit into just as I had my first full-blown labor pang. Everything happened in one piercing moment: I let out a scream at the very minute Aaron bit into his sandwich, which produced an explosion of billowy mayonnaise all over his beard. He was so rattled by my savage shriek that he began rubbing my back and panting in the hope I would do the same. Forget that. All the while he clutched his sandwich because he didn't know what to do with it.

I had interviewed several obstetricians, settling on the one who said he'd give me painkillers the earliest. So I called him on his pledge and got an epidural almost immediately. But then the doctor handed the stethoscope to Aaron — this was peculiar — and asked, "Do you think the baby's heart is skipping beats?" Just then I went into shock. I was raced into the operating room for an emergency cesarean, leaving Aaron behind. "We can name her Taylor," he said as I was wheeled off, gray and scared. Taylor was my choice, Tara his.

Taylor was born pink and, as cesarean babies generally are, perfectly shaped. Everyone agreed that she looked just like Aaron, even Dolly, who — having forgiven me the minute I went into labor — had rushed to Washington.

For the week we were in the hospital, Aaron and I would stare at Taylor for ten, 15 minutes, saying nothing. We were like swooning lovers. She barely cried, and we thought we had the sweetest baby ever born. Then we took her home, and we noticed a change. It was hard to miss. Our daughter cried. She cried all the time. Our little angel had colic. Some of the pressure was relieved when Dr. Ross, the pediatrician, said he believed in treating the mother as well as the baby and recommended drugs. After a few weeks of colic, we relented and began giving Taylor drops to stop the paroxysms of pain.

By then I was back at work. I've often been asked how I did it, how I worked full-time with a baby. At the time I just improvised. I find it hard to remember many of the logistical details, but generally I was able to "do it" because of two factors in my own circumstances. First — and I'm not going to dance around this — was money: I had enough to pay for a reliable nanny. Yet even with that, like all mothers who work, I lived with a constant, insidious anxiety. This perpetual gnawing became so ingrained, I didn't realize it wasn't a natural part of me until Taylor went off to college 18 years later.

I had the working mother's typical worries but not the typical guilt, and that's because of factor number two: Dolly. Most of my working-mother friends say their mothers sent them signals of disapproval, sometimes subtle, sometimes not, that said in one way or another, "How could you leave that baby?" Dolly told me the opposite. She said that not only could I work full-time and raise Taylor, I *should* do both. I'd be happier, therefore I'd have a happier child. Dolly didn't come to Washington regularly to change Taylor's diapers, as she had once promised, but she gave me something more valuable: she found our nanny for us. Irene, originally from Germany — "I was a war bride," she explained — was now divorced and in her 50s, with iron gray hair and a sturdy construction.

I took a ridiculously short maternity leave, just three weeks, and never dreamed of asking for any slack. I was so afraid CBS would treat me differently, give me less to do and less challenging assignments, that I felt I had to prove I was just as available as ever. But I had a problem: my hormones were raging. I was like a lioness with new cubs, ready to pounce at the slightest hint of trouble. I cried and struck out at all manner of imagined slights and insults. I was in no shape for the office. But there I was, insecure but holding on tenaciously. I was also buxom as hell.

After a few weeks I was asked if I wanted to coanchor the *Morning News*.[1] This was not the first time. In 1972 there had been pressure on CBS management to hire a woman anchor, and Bill Small asked if I wanted the morning job. I said no; I knew I wasn't ready. Women were being pushed along too quickly. The Peter Principle holds that executives are promoted up the corporate ladder until they reach their level of incompetence, where they remain until they retire or leave. I coined the phrase "The Peggy Principle." Because companies were so eager to prove they were "equal opportunity employers," young women were being promoted immediately to their level of incompetence.

This time I said yes. Not only did I think I could handle the job, I realized the schedule would get me home in the afternoons to be with Taylor. I also wanted to work with Hughes Rudd, a wonderful, unusual television personality from Waco, Texas, with a gravelly voice and sardonic wit. He called to tell me how enthusiastic he was about our teaming

72

up, making me feel he'd been waiting to work with me his whole life. No wonder everyone at CBS News loved him.

I started on October 3, 1977. Taylor was six weeks old.

The first show was straightforward. Hughes led off reading an item about skyjackers in Syria, then I followed with a story about President Carter raising taxes on imported oil. Back and forth we went — he in New York, I in Washington — for an hour, from 7 to 8 A.M. I wrote a closing essay about a survey of the Harvard Law School Class of '62. Only ten percent said their favorite form of relaxation was sex. "There may be no connection, Hughes," I said, "between this and another survey that showed Harvard lawyers get prematurely old." Hughes called afterward to encourage me.

Five days after I started, Hughes was told he was being taken off the show. We were both stunned. He joked cavalierly, "I've been ditched, bumped, dumped," but he admitted to me that what he really was was hurt. He loved the show; it was his. He said "they" had told him the reasons were that he was overpowering Lesley Stahl and that he was too gruff for the morning. I don't know one person who agreed with that. I never got an explanation.[2]

Hughes's replacement was Richard Threlkeld, good-looking and one of the best writers among the younger correspondents. Our publicity photo made us look as though we were starring in a sitcom: a happy couple, Mr. and Mrs. Jones.

I wasn't doing a great job as anchor. I often stumbled over words. "President Kimmy Jarter . . ." When I'd try to correct myself, I would do it awkwardly. "Oh, no! Let me do that again. President . . ." My frustration would come through. Bill Small, by then the number two man at CBS News in New York, called one day to say, "Look, if you make a mistake, just move on. Don't stop to correct it." That made me more nervous.

I had jumped into the unknown of live broadcasting, never imagining that the rip cords wouldn't work. I had built a reputation as a sedulous, grind-it-out-on-the-ground reporter. As I was so often told, I'd earned my spurs. I had been chosen because of that, not because I registered high on the warm-quotient meter. That became obvious.

My greatest enemy was the TelePrompTer. Eventually a genius invented a machine that reflects words right across the eye of the camera, making it possible to read and look directly out at the same time. But in 1977 the prompter consisted of a roll of paper that scrolled several inches above the eye of the camera. If you were an expert like Walter Cronkite, you figured out a way to read and give the appearance of making eye contact with the audience. I, on the other hand, had an annoying habit of darting my eyes back and forth between the copy and the camera. Even with my big, round glasses, this was distracting.

Even harder than that was smiling. First the bosses make you inca-pacitate every smile muscle in your face, then they make you an an-chorman and complain that you're not warm enough: smile more. But I just couldn't get the hang of looking into the glass-eyed camera-monster and giving it a sincere grin. After a few weeks Dolly came up with the name of a television teacher, Dorothy Sarnoff, and sent me to New York for a smile lesson. Dorothy set up a video camera, got me laughing and smiling into it, then taught me how to reproduce my own smile on call, like Pavlov's dog.

Only one producer, Paul Liebler, came in early with me, and his job was to organize the taped pieces. I was left by myself to write my copy, which I rarely finished before I had to go to makeup. So there I was, struggling nearly every morning to finish writing the show in the commercial breaks. It was hard to admit I was having trouble. I worried that if I complained they would think, "What did you expect? She's a girl." But the job was daunting, I was sinking, and I finally asked for help.

Four months after I started, the cavalry arrived in the shape of Terry Martin, a radio producer sent to Washington to be "Lesley's person." Terry — sharp and quick, shrewd and gruff, impatient and irreverent — was an answered prayer. He came in at 3:30 A.M. with me, and we'd sit there together reading *The Washington Post* and the wires or taking notes as someone in New York dictated stories from *The New York Times* over the phone. Terry and I would decide which items I should write up and tell, then he'd become a tiger with the producers in New York, arguing for more time for me. It was a daily skirmish. Sometimes I'd jump on the line and, never one to dance around when I was under deadline pressure, say, "How can you give me 20 seconds for a story about Carter taking heat over the Panama Canal treaties when you're allotting 40 seconds for the shortage of lipstick in Moldavia?"[3]

The argument always came down to the same question: how much of the show should be spent on government issues. It was a perpetual clash between New York and Washington: "Gee, Lesley, that budget story is so complicated." Whether it was the *Morning News* or the Cronkite show, New York was always trying to shift the fulcrum away from the capital into the heartland.

When I had worked for the *Evening News,* I had spent my days in an electronic Turkish bazaar. Walter Cronkite and his producers were the buyers and CBS reporters around the world, the rug merchants — barter-ing, negotiating, hyping, doing whatever it took to sell their stories and make the deal.

74 Cronkite and his team picked over the goods. After discarding some submissions, they began to bargain: Can Schieffer hold his Carter piece

to a minute? Can Mudd shave off his last paragraph on Tip O'Neill? Can David Dick do his tornado in Georgia in two? Can Drinkwater's profile of Jerry Brown hold till tomorrow? This went on all day, as more submissions poured in. Eventually they would end up with about nine pieces, having based their decisions on that thing elusive and hard to define, "news judgment," and on the limitations imposed by our resources. Where CBS deployed its reporters and cameras made certain judgments all but inevitable. In 1977 four reporters were assigned to the White House every day. That's why every now and then you'd see a story that said, in effect, "The president did nothing today." Correspondents covered the Pentagon and the State Department full-time, but there was no permanent presence at the Department of Health, Education and Welfare.

Another limitation on news decisions is time. A news broadcast is not expandable as a newspaper is. In those days the Cronkite show, given the commercials, ran a total of just 22½ minutes. (Today it's down to 21 minutes.)[4] Each story had to be lean. The average piece ran a minute and a half, a frustrating restraint. One morning Ray Brady was asked to expound on the impact of steel prices on the economy in 75 seconds; Marya McLaughlin explained college tuition tax credits in a minute, 20.

I thought that if a woman moved up to a decision-making position on one of the shows, there would be more stories on social issues, health, the arts, education. So there I was, an anchor, running the bazaar myself, choosing what stories to put on from Washington, and I ended up making the same kinds of decisions as the men. I led with what the president wanted to do about taxes and went into great detail on plans for the neutron bomb and MX missile.

Along with writing and reading items on the *Morning News,* I did some long pieces: a tour of the new National Gallery of Art with the architect, I. M. Pei; an investigation of disposable diapers; and a farewell tribute to Eric Sevareid when he retired.[5] Nixon once explained why Sevareid was the one newsman he would never attack: "We were scared to," he said. "He looked and dressed exactly like God."

In my interview I asked Sevareid, "What do you hope television news will look like in the future?"

"I think we have to find a way to make room for the word as well as the picture, because there are a lot of things you can't do with a camera. You can't take a picture of an idea."

WITH TERRY MARTIN on the scene, I was able to slip into a routine. I never acclimated to getting up at 2:30 in the morning, though there was a compensation: I could get home in the early afternoon and play with Taylor. Her colic cleared up right on schedule at three months, and she became the world's easiest, cheeriest baby. At seven months, she would light up when I got home, so that if I had any worries at the office, they would fade away the minute I opened the door and saw her beaming face.

Aaron, then full-time with *Esquire* (which Clay Felker had bought in late 1977), worked at home, which made a big difference in my life. He had an office that was off-limits to everyone else in the apartment, yet I knew that if something happened with Taylor, he was right there. He would emerge from his office around five, as though he were coming home from a day downtown. We'd have dinner together early, and then I'd go to bed. Most of my countrymen went to sleep with Johnny Carson; I went to sleep with Walter Cronkite.

IT WASN'T LONG before our coverage of President Jimmy Carter on the *Morning News* reflected the country's verdict: that he was failing as president. He had won the campaign by attacking Washington insiders and by use of populist symbols (as when he carried his own bags), but once he was in office both backfired on him. He started off by "depomping" the presidency, cutting back on the use of White House limousines, silencing the Marine Corps band at his official functions (no more "Ruffles and Flourishes" when the president entered a room); and wearing an unassuming, common-man beige cardigan on national television.

These little pantomimes were meant to announce his message: I am not Richard Nixon. It was well received at first, but soon the one-of-us image transposed into a he-lacks-presidential-stature image. Some of the blame had to go to the inexperienced staff of young southerners he brought with him to the White House, especially his 33-year-old chief political adviser, Hamilton Jordan. In March 1978 *Esquire* published a profile, "Hamilton Jordan: A Slob in the White House," written by Aaron. As he was researching the article, Aaron would amuse me with the stories he was hearing. Ham had lived in his green Corvair when he went to the University of Georgia. Ham was such a slob that he would throw his dirty clothes and half-eaten burgers into one big pile in the back seat . . . until he got mice. Aaron reported Ham's confession: "I'm a sloppy son of a bitch. That hasn't changed. I'm terribly disorganized."

Aaron started the piece with Jordan in his office, answering a congressman's letter. "Let's misspell his name *again*," he told his secretary. The portrait of arrogance, pettiness, and sloppiness helped explain the insufficiencies of the Carter White House. It also guaranteed that Aaron would never again get an interview at the White House.

CARTER RECOVERED some public confidence at the end of 1978, when he pulled off his greatest foreign policy achievement, the Camp David Accords, which led to peace between Egypt and Israel. The accords grew out of a grueling 13-day meeting at Camp David with Anwar Sadat of Egypt, Menachem Begin of Israel, and President Carter. When it was over on September 19, I interviewed Prime Minister Begin, the onetime terrorist, on the *Morning News*. Right before we got our cue, he pinched my cheek and said *"Shayne mayd'l,"* Yiddish for "Pretty girl." I squirmed as I wondered what Roger Mudd would have done if some prime minister hand-squeezed his cheek.

In addition to calling on Israel to return the Sinai to Egypt, the accords created something called "Palestinian autonomy." "What's the difference between autonomy and sovereignty?" I asked Begin.

"Ha, ha! Well, you have to look into the encyclopedia, my friend." He beamed. "The difference is very simple. Sovereignty means a state, a government with a parliament, et cetera, and with all the attributes of independence. Not so autonomy."

When I asked what it was like being sequestered for so long at Camp David, he said it had became tedious. "I said to Professor [Zbigniew] Brzezinski [Carter's national security adviser], 'This is a concentration camp deluxe.' He told me that 'you have got experience. Perhaps you started already to dig a tunnel.' There came a moment when we all felt we must bring it to an end."

The Camp David Accords succeeded because Jimmy Carter midwifed them, massaging and cajoling. It brought his presidency back to life.

I HAD BECOME addicted to the stress of holding down a full-time job and taking care of a year-old baby. When we went on vacation, I found I couldn't unwind and, in fact, began inventing stressful situations to simulate the atmosphere at work. I'd contrive phony deadlines, such as going shopping 15 minutes before I'd have to meet a friend or starting dinner 30 minutes before the guests were due. *The New York Times'* Science section ran an article explaining that people who live under constant deadlines and urgency (emergency room doctors, stockbrokers, daily reporters, mothers) secrete a mildly addictive chemical related to adrenaline that we actually crave whenever we relax, and it said there was nothing unhealthy about benign activities that help pump out the chemical. From then on I accepted my hyperactivity and Aaron agreed to stop with the irritating "Why don't you relax?"

He had written an article for *Esquire* called "The Ballad of the Urban Cowboy" about oil workers in Houston and their favorite hangout, Gilley's, a ten-gallon Texas honky-tonk with a huge dance floor and a bucking mechanical bull. We were in Nantucket for two weeks "relaxing" when half of Hollywood began calling. Twenty different producers and studios wanted to make a movie of "Urban Cowboy," and they were all wooing my husband. Eventually there was an auction, and Irving Azoff, manager of the Eagles and other rock groups, came up with the highest bid. He immediately sold "Urban Cowboy" to Barry Diller at Paramount.

More exciting, Taylor began to walk.

THERE WAS an assumption in those days, often stated as a rule of thumb, that no woman could survive as a newsperson on television past the age of 40. The presumption was that wrinkles, jowls, and paunches, acceptable on a man, would not be tolerated on a Charlotte Kuralt or an Erica Sevareid by the viewers or our male bosses. I was 36 and thinking: How does anyone know how long we'll survive? There haven't been enough of us to test the rule.

One woman over 40 who was thriving was Rosalynn Carter, age 51. With her sweet, flannelly voice and sturdy backbone, she was dubbed the Steel Magnolia. Even so, it was assumed that femininity and toughness could not coexist in the same person.

But as I saw during a series of interviews, the first lady was indeed a compelling combination of fragility and force. We taped her promoting her mental health projects, as well as her daily routine at the White House, including a morning in the solarium on the top floor of the family quarters, where she got down on her hands and knees to play with her grandson, James Earl Carter IV. We also shot a few of her self-improvement lessons: taking Spanish with Mrs. Cyrus Vance and violin with Amy. Here was a woman at the summit who still considered herself a work in progress; I thought: still working overtime to make sure no one calls her a hick from Plains.

A part-time shampoo girl in Plains when she was young, Rosalynn had overcome an insecurity so intense that she often vomited before speaking in public. Now *Newsweek* was calling her "a one-woman Kitchen Cabinet." Never before had a president's wife participated so fully in her husband's administration, from sitting in on Cabinet meetings, to telling the speechwriters how to rewrite the speeches, to acting as witness and observer at Camp David. Other first ladies might have been as influential, but they had been more discreet about it. "I have influence. And I know it," she told *The New York Times*.[6] If you're going to break patterns, especially if you're a woman, you have to expect to be reproached for it, and, of course, Mrs. Carter was scolded for meddling in affairs of state: "Who elected her?"

My friend Linda Wertheimer, who was covering Capitol Hill for National Public Radio, used to joke about how men saw us strong gals as "uppity women," defined as any female who asserted herself or sat in a chair assumed to belong to a man—chairs at Cabinet meetings or news-anchor desks or in Wall Street boardrooms. Linda, who was often the only woman at the press table on Capitol Hill, says, "The way they would let you know you were second class was, someone would say, 'I heard a great story last night, but I can't tell it because Linda's here.'" How many times I had been in just that spot. "What do you do? Do you say: 'I love dirty jokes, let me tell you one' and thereby convert into one of them? The choice was, either you grossed them out or you deprived them of having a good time. Either way, you lost." This was their way of running her off, but of course, she stayed, the "intruder," day after day. Linda says we had to forgive them. The guys saw us as a threat to a traditional way of working. And we were. In the end we did change the rules, not to mention the luncheon chatter.

But in 1978 men were still trying to buck the tide, the personification of which was the unlikely Rosalynn Carter. My read was that she was more magnolia than steel. I thought that until our last day with her, when we shot a lengthy interview in the Green Room on the first floor of the White House, with its green Turkish Hereke rug and walls of green watered silk. I asked about Jimmy's first year as governor of Georgia. "There were so many things I wanted to do," she said, "and it was all new and different to me, and I just got very distressed about how I could handle all of it."[7]

A thought lodged in my mind: She'd had a nervous breakdown. "And I think in that kind of situation you finally realize that you can't solve all your problems by yourself, that you have to have some help." That's when she'd been born again. "I think I just finally realized I had to turn my life over to God. . . . I just kind of said, 'I can't do it by myself anymore, Lord. Do with me what you will.'"

I asked the next question that came into my head, which was if she thought her turning to God was a substitute for going to a psychiatrist. That's when I saw the steel. She pierced me with a cold glower. The interview was over.

RICHARD SALANT, our beloved CBS News president, was forced to retire at the mandatory age of 65. He was replaced by Bill Leonard, a former CBS correspondent who was married to Mike Wallace's ex-wife (and Chris Wallace's mother), Kappy. He was a short, solid man who looked something like Spencer Tracy and had the same aura of moral authority. He also had a wicked sense of humor. There weren't many things a new president could do to put his mark on the news division. He wasn't going to tinker with the *Evening News,* the most watched news show, or replace Cronkite, the most respected man in America. The only thing he could change was the *Morning News.* And so Threlkeld and I began hearing rumors, which soon turned up in gossip columns: "Stahl and Threlkeld on their way out." I was told it wasn't true, but the rumors persisted.

Finally, on December 1, 1978, CBS announced that Dick and I were being replaced by our White House correspondent, Bob Schieffer. I wasn't sorry I wouldn't be getting up in the middle of the night anymore, but I didn't think I had fully mastered the job. Besides, *they* were taking me out of the game; it wasn't my decision.

Threlkeld and I anchored the *Morning News* as lame ducks for five weeks, worried about our next assignments. I was imagining the worst when, one afternoon, Bill Leonard called me at home and made a proposal: "How would you like to be the next White House correspondent?" I accepted instantly, without thinking. I didn't ask about the travel, the days and nights away from home. I only asked, "Are you serious?" To me the White House was the pinnacle. When I hung up, I turned to Taylor, who was playing with her stuffed animals and my lipstick. I read her some pop-up books and began to shake with fear.

I called Aaron at Paramount Studios. He was writing the screenplay for *Urban Cowboy.* "We'll work it out," he said. "Don't worry."

I called Dolly. "I don't know if I can do it. I'm scared."

My cheerleader said, "You can do it, and Dad and I will take Taylor whenever you want."

AARON AND I were at a black-tie Christmas party with a mix of congressional leaders, White House officials, and reporters, all thrown together, all engaged in the one-topic shoptalk of your typical Washington parties, what one wag called Beltway halitosis. At 9 P.M. we stopped to watch President Carter on television announce the United States' recognition of China and the breaking of diplomatic relations with Taiwan. Carl Bernstein said, "The U.S. just told the Taiwanese they are all officially boat people!"

"I start at the White House in February," I told Jody Powell, the president's 35-year-old press secretary.

"Everything will work out," he drawled, "if y'all just trust me completely." He walked off.

A few days later Bob Woodward called to warn me that "the Big Three at the White House" were not pleased that I was coming over there and that there had been "some attempt to get CBS to change its mind about the assignment."

"Who are the Big Three?" I asked. They were Ham Jordan, Jody Powell, and the president himself.

Bob said, "They think you're a hatchet man from your Watergate reporting, but more important, they hold Aaron's *Esquire* piece about Ham against you."

80   "Come on," I said, "that's absurd."

"No, it's the truth, and if I were you I'd spend my first two months doing nothing but straight substantive reporting."

The next day I was summoned to New York to meet with the new number two man at CBS News, Bud Benjamin, a 50ish, big-hearted man, and his new number two, John Lane. Bud got right to it: he felt he was going out on a limb with me. "There are important people at CBS who aren't convinced you can handle the White House." Even while the room was spinning, I was thinking: What about *building* my confidence? Is this the way big-time coaches send in their rookie quarterbacks?

John Lane asked about Taylor: "Is your head going to be able to take all this? Will you feel you're not giving enough to your child?" I said I wouldn't be taking the job if I hadn't thought it through — which was not exactly the truth. What was this how-could-you-leave-your-child guilt trip, anyway? I wondered if they were bowing to pressure from the White House and trying to convince me *not* to take this job.

"Have you heard that Carter and Company are holding Aaron's *Esquire* piece against me?" I asked. Yes, it was true, but no White House, they said, was going to tell CBS News who it could or could not assign to cover the president. This declaration made the purpose of the meeting all the more confusing.

Finally we discussed the Bob Pierpoint problem. They were asking him to be number two at the White House, in other words, my backup, even though he was more qualified than I — he'd been a White House correspondent since 1957. I was conscious of a rumble in the bureau about my being chosen "because of her blond appeal."

It was no secret that Pierpoint was upset. But Bud said that Bob had assured him he wouldn't deliberately try to trip me up. I was wading into a drowning pool, my colleague resentful, the White House opposed, my baby yanking on my sleeve.

That meeting didn't make sense to me until recently, when Pierpoint told me that he had wanted to resign. "I've had enough of training new people. I want out," he told our bosses. But then Cronkite called him and said, "We need you at the White House very badly. Lesley doesn't know the beat, and we need all the help we can get. If you'll stay," Bob quotes Walter as saying, "we'll give you a big raise. Please, Bob, do this as a favor to me."

"They rewrote my contract," Bob said. "I got a 40 percent hike." My God, they damn near bribed him to stay.

ON THE SHUTTLE back to Washington I sat with Gloria Steinem, a friend of Aaron's from their days together at *New York* magazine. She was furious at Jimmy Carter because he had just fired former Congresswoman Bella

Abzug from the position of chairman of his National Advisory Committee on Women. Gloria said that she and other feminists were flying to Washington as a show of support. It would not be their first nor their last anti-Carter protest. The president was offended by their off-and-on support. Hadn't he and Rosalynn campaigned to win passage of the Equal Rights Amendment, the highest priority of the women's movement? If "with friends like these who needs enemies" applied anywhere, he felt it was here.

When he had met with his committee on women, he'd brought his resentment in with him, starting off by scolding them for being too confrontational. In response, Bella Abzug, more or less proving his point, had wagged her finger at him and in effect told him off. Imagine being that insolent to the president of the United States. You had to wonder if it was a measure of Bella's impertinence or Jimmy Carter's vulnerability. Either way, before the day was out she'd been told to pack her bags.

I'm sure the president felt good about dumping her like that, but the move was shortsighted. Further alienating the powerful women's organizations, a major force in the Democratic Party, could only hurt him. But Carter had no touch for making allies. While most pols project a kind of avid inclusiveness, this president practiced a self-defeating exclusiveness. In fact, he had a habit of making enemies of the very people he needed the most.

For example, Scoop Jackson. Ever since the campaign, he and I had gotten together every few months. We'd become Washington friends. At one of our lunches in the Senate dining room, we discussed my new assignment. "The quintessential Jimmy Carter story," he told me, "involves Tip O'Neill," the speaker of the House. Apparently Carter had refused Tip's request for extra tickets to the Inauguration for his family. "Day one, and he strikes out at the guy at the top." Scoop rolled his eyes. "People around here like to blame Carter's staff, but it's him." And then he told me that he had gone to see Carter in the Oval Office "to make peace."

"I offered him my loyalty," said Scoop. This was not easy for Jackson, a proud man who probably felt he deserved the job far more than this peanut farmer did. Jackson was chairman of the Senate Energy Committee at a time when oil shortages and energy conservation were at the top of the national agenda. "I offered him access to my staff," he told me, "and all the smart people I'd met around the country on the energy issue. I said 'Mr. President, I'd like to put them at your disposal.'" Now, maybe this offended Carter; maybe he sensed a degree of condescension. But Scoop thought he was being obliging and considerate.

82   "And what do you think the president said after all that?" he asked me. "He turned those cold eyes of his on me and said, 'I won't need your

help.'" Here the president had a Senate bull pledging fealty, offering himself as an ally, and Jimmy Carter spurned him. He humiliated him. And he ensured that the would-be confederate would never again go out of his way to help him.

I WENT to get my credentials as a permanent member of the White House press corps. After having my picture taken for a laminated pass, a badge I would wear around my neck at all times, I spent the day with Bob Schieffer, the outgoing CBS White House correspondent, to get the feel of the place. He told me how demanding the job was: "You're totally out of control of your life."

Bob and I, my old Watergate stakeout partner Sam Donaldson, UPI's Helen Thomas, and many other White House regulars stood outside in the biting cold, huddled around what was called "the stakeout position," an area where reporters and cameramen were allowed to lollygag as we waited for people who were meeting with the president. As we waited, the fellas asked Judy Woodruff, the NBC White House correspondent, and me to stand back-to-back to see who was taller. It was a weigh-in for what the men saw as the inevitable catfight between the two network ladies.

The pressroom was really two rooms. One was a small theater for the briefings; the other, an area with booths for the wire services and TV networks and two rows of cubbyholes where the major newspapers and magazines had phones and desks where their reporters could park for a few hours a day. Most of them showed up for the daily briefing and then left. Those of us who worked for the wires and networks used our booths as full-time offices. I would rarely go in to the CBS bureau.

We were a short walk from the Oval Office in our own little precinct within the White House, encased in the tomblike CBS booth, which was painted a cheerful shade of khaki and so incommodious that every time we turned the doorknob, as Woody Allen had said of his first apartment, we rearranged the furniture. It was four feet wide with a long table for three correspondents and a radio technician. In the back there was a small, soundproofed room for recording our TV tracks and radio spots. Four of us spent eight to ten claustrophobic hours a day in that telephone booth, overhearing one another's phone conversations and bumping elbows as we typed our scripts.

Our next-door neighbor, Sam Donaldson, had invented a new way to cover the leader of the Free World: shouting. Sam had a bong of a voice with a built-in echo, much like Big Ben. When he bonged at the president, the walls quivered and the president more often than not responded, providing all of us that thing most precious to television correspondents, a sound bite. I took a few stabs at the Donaldson bellow method of reporting but discovered that when I shouted, my voice rose into an irritating caterwaul rather than a resounding command. It was clear I was going to have to find some other way to distinguish myself at the White House.

Sam told me, "Jody [Powell] is the *only* source in the White House." I wasn't sure if he was being a pal or trying to throw me off the scent. But Schieffer seemed to bear out Sam's tip by spending the afternoon trying to get Powell on the phone. I can only assume that Sam had more success. He had a nifty little scoop that night: Carter had invited Richard Nixon to the White House to meet Chinese leader Deng Xiaoping.

I went back to the White House the next day as an observer at Powell's daily briefing. Most of the questions were about the invitation to the yet-to-be-rehabilitated Nixon. "It was the decent, proper thing to do," said Jody with a ya-wanna-make-somethin'-of-it inflection. It seemed to me that Powell spent more time attacking the reporters than answering questions. About a story in *The New York Times* he said, "There was never a more absurd example of damn-the-facts, full-speed-ahead journalism." And that was his warm-up. Jody often answered a question at his briefings by saying, "That's simplistic" or "Damn, what a dumb question." There was nothing defensive about this cat.

I started getting calls warning me that Jody and Hamilton Jordan would probably take reprisals against me because of Aaron's piece. A *Time* reporter said, "A whole slew of Ham loyalists will never deal with you, never return your calls." So I went to see Bob Strauss, former chairman of the Democratic Party and soon to be chairman of Carter's reelection campaign. He looked a little like Orson Welles. "Do you think Ham will ever talk to me?" I asked.

"Doubt it," he said, suggesting I soften him up by doing an early piece on how there was no backbiting in this White House, how even after two years one group was not "telling on" another.

I said, "Ham blaming me for Aaron's article is just like Carter being blamed for what Billy says and does." The president's brother, Billy, was a beer-guzzling good ole boy who often embarrassed the White House. Strauss said that was an apt analogy and that he'd pass it on to Jordan, but he let me know how unfair he thought Aaron's piece was. "Are you happily married?" he asked.

"Very."

Strauss said I should stay married till Aaron was a multimillionaire, then sue the shirt off his back. His eyes flashed as he said he'd represent me for free . . . and made me swear I'd tell Aaron.

84 THE WHITE HOUSE CORRESPONDENT I wanted to emulate was Dan Rather, crisp and tough. I wanted to stand up to bullying and ferret out

dishonesty. When Dan had left the White House in 1974, he had gone to *CBS Reports* as anchor, then, in 1975, to *60 Minutes.* When I called him for advice about covering the White House, he suggested lunch, so I flew to New York and met him at Alfredo's on Central Park South, a favorite CBS hangout. He spoke to me the way he delivered his on-air pieces: in bullets. These are the notes I took.

#1. Hours to reach sources: 7:30–9:30 am, 7:30–11 pm.

#2. Work the Hill and the Pentagon. People in the agencies are more likely to talk to a WH correspondent than the reporter on their beat . . . less traceable.

#3. Be the cutting edge. Tell when what the WH is spoon-feeding you is nonsense. Emphasize when they're spouting PR. Write scripts about what they *do* say and what they *don't* say. When you don't buy the line they're selling, convey that to the public.

#4. Said he'd picked up rumblings at CBS that my writing is not very strong. The vultures [my word] are already saying I'm slow and won't meet the deadlines.

I thanked Dan. We had been friends in Washington; I considered him an ally.

I SPENT several more days at the White House as an observer, trying many times to get together with Jody Powell, but he avoided me. I did catch a glimpse of the president jogging around the Rose Garden in his white shorts and red jacket. Sam, alone, was monitoring. I sat in a briefing for the State of the Union Address, the theme of which was "New Foundations." Sam ran around trumpeting, "Carter's speech is about underwear!"

I went home in a state of apprehension, sure I would never catch on to the intricacies of covering the White House. It seemed impenetrable. I could feel the weight of the responsibility I was taking on. And I ached about not having enough time with Taylor. She usually fell asleep at 7:30. On a normal night, I'd just be walking in the door.

I finally got in to see Powell. I'd been warned by the other women covering the White House that he had trouble dealing with us. Until the mid-1970s, like every other power center in the country, the White House press corps had been a white man's brotherhood. I was the ninth woman in that first wave to cover the president's side of the White House for mainstream magazines and networks.[8] Most of us were in our 30s, the same age as the Carter aides. Actually, I was three years older than Jody.

Powell sat behind that famous press secretary's desk, crescent-shaped so reporters could crowd around in a semicircle. He drank several iced teas, snorted nose spray, and smoked incessantly, smashing out his butts in a large, overflowing ashtray. I liked him — his open, doughy face, his fidgeting, his machine-gun wit, and the seriousness with which he took his duties. I wanted him to like me, but he made it clear that the rumors I'd heard were true.

I asked if I'd have any trouble at the White House, said I'd heard I would, and wanted to find out why and clear the air.

He stared at me for a while, then, stuttering as he often did, he said, "Look, Lesley, er — uh — we know you're against us. We know what you think about us and that you're, um, on the other side." Other side of what? I wondered until he mentioned, "We know you're from Massachusetts." Ah. Ted Kennedy. He accused me of being unfair to the president on the *Morning News*. "You seem to delight in zinging him."

I was dumbfounded. I barely knew Ted Kennedy and was not antagonistic to Jimmy Carter. Like most everyone I knew, I thought he was not the most effective president we'd ever had, but on the other hand, I respected his diligence and his integrity. Either Jody was trying to chill me or he really did see me, as he seemed to be saying, as an enemy.

I said I hoped he would be fair with me. He said he would.

As I thought about it that night, I decided that part of my problem was that I wasn't southern. When the president or his Georgia inner circle were criticized as incompetent (Hamilton Jordan was widely known as Hannibal Jerkin), they'd circle the wagons and blame it on "southern-hating northerners," which to them included the media. The Georgians succumbed to a tyranny of trivial resentments against the Washington establishment and the press.[9]

I MET Representative Les Aspin of Wisconsin for lunch in the congressional dining room on January 25, 1979. I had met him in 1968, when he was running Lyndon Johnson's reelection campaign for the Wisconsin primary and I, then a researcher with NBC News, was writing a handbook on Wisconsin for the Election Unit.

Les slurped the Hill's famous navy bean soup and I ate a grilled cheese sandwich as he told me how inept the White House staff was. And then he leaned in and passed on a knockdown delicious story: The task force at the State Department charged with planning Deng Xiaoping's state visit had been given two mandates by the White House: first, Deng could not go to California; second, he could not go to Massachusetts. The reason: there were to be no pictures of him with either Jerry Brown or Ted Kennedy, both potential Carter rivals in the upcoming 1980 campaign.

"There's more," said Les. Carter was refusing to invite Ted Kennedy to the state dinner for Deng. Kennedy, one of the first senators to call for recognition of China, had met Deng on a recent trip to Peking. He belonged at the dinner and had specifically asked to be included. When he wasn't, he'd gotten Secretary of State Cyrus Vance to intercede. Les explained that Vance himself had called Hamilton Jordan to say "This is ridiculous and counterproductive," but to no avail.

Les shrugged. Why were the Georgians deliberately antagonizing Teddy? "Sure," he said, "there are loads of liberals out there who want Kennedy to run against Carter, but this White House seems to be begging him to run. Doesn't make any sense."

After lunch I pitched the story to Cronkite's producers in New York and they liked it, so I set about trying to get it confirmed. A press aide at the State Department called me back: no comment. Kennedy's press secretary, Tom Southwick, said it was true that the senator had not been invited to the state dinner and urged me to pursue the story.

Jody was unavailable, so I told the story to his assistant, Rex Granum, and asked for a comment. Within an hour Southwick called. "Thanks," he said. "You got Kennedy invited!"

A few minutes later Jody came by the CBS booth and confirmed the Kennedy invitation part of the story, saying, "We finally decided to invite him 'cause otherwise it might look petty."

The Cronkite show said it wasn't interested after all, and I told Jody so. But then at 6:15 the Cronkites changed their minds. I rushed to comb my hair, slap on lipstick, and dash out into the cold to do my first stand-up on the White House lawn.

> STAHL: It was easier for the White House to invite former President Richard Nixon to attend the state dinner for Deng Xiaoping than it was to invite Democratic Senator Edward Kennedy.

The wind was blowing so hard, my hair stood straight up like a whale's spout, meaning I had to redo the stand-up. I finally succeeded on take six and ran inside to watch. I had decided to take off my glasses — a new me. After all those years, Dolly won.

It seemed like a good day of reporting, but that was deceiving for two reasons. First, I had broken a cardinal rule: never blindside the press secretary. The last Jody had heard from me, I was not in our broadcast. Second, this story would solidify the notion that I was in Kennedy's pocket.

THE NEXT MONDAY was my first official day as CBS's chief White House correspondent, and my first official story was historic: the first visit of a chairman of the Chinese Communist Party to the United States. When Deng arrived, I stood up on some scaffolding to watch. Unlike the other reporters, who had seen the full-honors welcoming ceremony before, I was electrified by the pageantry, especially the fife-and-drum corps in their red Revolutionary greatcoats, white overalls, black tricorn hats, and white wigs, marching and tootling "Yankee Doodle Dandy." There was an unexpected tumult when two protesters who had managed to sneak into the press section began shouting and heckling. They were hauled away by the Secret Service as Deng was enchanting the audience, even in Chinese.

I worked hard on my script, in which I included a paragraph about Deng's foreign policy. My producer, Lane Venardos, excised that part, explaining that that was Marvin Kalb's bailiwick—a turf war on my first day.

> STAHL: The journey from Ping-Pong diplomacy to full normalization of relations between China and the U.S. was climaxed at the White House this morning with this handshake beween President Carter and Deng Xiaoping.

I went on to say that the anti-Deng protesters "threw the president off his stride," causing him to stutter through his remarks: "Mister Prim—Pri—Mister Pr—Vice Premier."

After the broadcast I went in to the CBS bureau. "Call for Stahl," someone blared out. It was Jody Powell. "Hey," I said. But instead of a friendly response, I was hit with a tirade: "The president wasn't sputtering and stuttering and stumbling!" He yelled at full throttle for a good ten minutes, calling me names: "The most irresponsible, unfair, over the top—"

"Well, Jody, it's always nice to have your views on my work," I said, praying that he wouldn't hear my choking up.

I had already been warned that Jody tended to overreact to even mild criticism of Carter. I'd been told that he saw Carter as a father figure and therefore took any negative slant in a story personally, as if reporters were attacking his dad. I confided in Bob Pierpoint, who told me that after one of his pieces Jody had called him at a dinner party and blasted him for twenty minutes. Bob said he had just listened until Jody tuckered out.

The next day, Tuesday, I woke up sicker than I'd ever been. I had laryngitis and diarrhea and stayed out the rest of the week, wondering if everyone thought it was psychosomatic.

JIMMY CARTER had a thin, unintimidating voice and an unimposing stature. He was not magisterial like FDR, nor did he inspire fear as LBJ had. In fact, the key to Carter was the word "small." His mind tended to fix on the small parts of issues, and as his first secretary of health, education, and welfare, Joseph Califano, once told me, "He didn't trust anything large like labor, business, big education; he didn't trust them enough to use them to get things done." And he especially disliked big shots. I had seen this myself when I had been one of his questioners on *Face the Nation* in 1975. He had hung around after the show for the cocktail party, where the guest and reporters usually talked informally. But Carter had spent his time chatting up the bartender.

After covering the Carter White House for a short time, I began to focus on Jody's word, petty. I was curious how a man so steeped in the turn-the-other-cheek New Testament as Jimmy Carter could cold-shoulder a Senate powerhouse or leave Senator Kennedy off a dinner-party guest list. Penny-ante stuff, unbecoming a man of power. It reminded me of how teenage girls get back at one another, and I thought that maybe I could cover the place with a special understanding after all.

FEBRUARY 12, 1979. I was edgy. It was my first news conference as White House correspondent. The bosses would be watching, so I spent all morning thinking up questions. I had questions on the Ayatollah Khomeini in Iran and on double-digit inflation at home in case the president called on me early, and a second tier about the CIA and health policy for later in the news conference. I had 20 in all, just in case other reporters asked my questions before the president called on me, which he surely would since he *always* called on the three network correspondents. I sat in the front row, jumped up, pointed, and shouted, "Mr. President, Mr. President!" like everyone else. While Carter turned icy eyes on me several times, he rebuffed me.

I kept thinking that the White House would be so much smarter if it wooed me. More than 40 million people watched the Cronkite show every night. I had been cautioned that beat reporters often got too chummy with their "jailers." That was one problem I was not going to have to confront. I was not even given the usual private introduction to the president that was a routine formality for new correspondents with major news organizations.

In his news conference Carter held out the hand of friendship to Iran and its new rulers, especially Khomeini. An hour later Jody held one of his shirtsleeve, catch-as-catch-can briefings in a hallway, refining the president's remarks. One of the treacheries of covering Jody Powell was that he often held ad hoc, impromptu sessions and if you happened not to get wind of them, you were in trouble. Well, I didn't get wind — I suspected because Jody didn't want me to. Ralph Harris, the Reuters correspondent, was kind enough to fill me in. When I rewrote my script to reflect Jody's revisions about Iran, Sandy Socolow, who was now the executive producer of the Cronkite show, called: "I'm sick and tired of Jody Powell editing this show every night. I've had it with him explaining after the fact what the president *meant* to say. If Jimmy Carter said something, he said it, period."

The next day, I got my first leak. I was trying to find out the state of U.S. intelligence in Iran and reached someone on the National Security Council staff who was willing to tell me it didn't exist. We used to rely solely on the shah's police, SAVAK, he told me. "Now our intelligence is almost nonexistent."

I was slow writing my script and had to ask Lane Venardos, my producer, for help. He was a large man with a stand-up comic's sense of humor. This was not the last time he would come to my rescue. I already had a reputation at CBS for being late. I raced out to the microwave position on the snowy lawn to do the stand-up. The wind was biting. It was 6:25, and I muffed it. It was Judy Woodruff's turn; in those days only one transmission at a time was possible, so those of us at the three networks had to go in shifts. She recorded her stand-up at 6:29; then it was my turn again at 6:31, after the show had begun. That's late.

Aaron called from Los Angeles: "You shouldn't wear your beaver coat. You should go out and get a simple cloth one." I was too cold out there, I thought, to give up my fur.

IN THESE EARLY WEEKS I was overwhelmed by the number of issues I had to be up on and was often lost in the briefings. I felt swamped. The White House was more than just another stakeout. I watched my boothmate Pierpoint handle the job with ease (we often did two pieces from the White House) and thought: I'll never get there.

I found that the deadline pressures meant there was no time for polite discourse. There were no amenities about my scripts. I never heard "Gee, we love it, especially the way you said that thing about Carter's slumping entrance." I never heard "Lesley, we have a little problem with time in the broadcast tonight, so we'd really appreciate it if you could find ten seconds to cut." It was just "Cut ten seconds. *Do it.*"

I had to get up early to read three papers from front to back, clipping and underlining obsessively, and to wash my hair and spray it into a cap of cement so I wouldn't have to think about it again all day. During the day I phoned smart people constantly and checked the wires, huge tubes of paper that I'd unfurl as I read. I lived in perpetual vigilance.

Which didn't help on my first presidential trip abroad. I sat with Judy Woodruff on the "writers' plane" to Mexico on Valentine's Day. The camera crews and radio techs had their own, which we called the "zoo plane" or "Visigoth country." They were boys without their Ritalin.

All the events on foreign trips were covered by assigned "pools," small groups of reporters who went to events on a rotating system. Except that television was so powerful and important — we were such gorillas —

that three network correspondents got into every pool. The responsibility of the magazine and newspaper reporters in the pool was to write up reports for all their colleagues who were left behind in the newsroom, usually set up in the ballroom of the press hotel. It was possible for a reporter to go on a presidential trip and never once leave the hotel.

Carter's first event in Mexico City was a luncheon, but it ran so late I had to leave the pool and go to our jerry-built edit room, where Venardos and a videotape editor were screening tapes and getting ready to record my script about how even the president of Mexico lectured this president of the United States. Everyone, it seemed, pushed him around.

If I had seen the pool report of the lunch written by Eleanor Clift of *Newsweek*, I would surely have included what Jimmy Carter said in his toast about diarrhea. According to Eleanor, Rosalynn had "covered her face with her hands in embarrassment" as the president told his "tale of Montezuma's Revenge" on his earlier visit to Mexico. Audience reaction, she wrote, consisted of "several people rolling their eyes in disgust."

None of this was in my script because I never saw Eleanor's report. No one had told me there was any such thing as a pool report. And Pierpoint, who was supposed to be my safety net, was not on the trip. I offered no excuses when New York called to complain after they watched Sam's piece. I just suffered inside. I'd messed up.

I WROTE several pieces about the battering the president was taking, including one about "those critics on all sides now who say his foreign policy is impotent and ill defined." [10] The perception of Carter as weak and ineffectual was hardening. Tom Shales, in *The Washington Post*, said he came across as a combination Mr. Rogers and John the Baptist.

The criticism wasn't confined to foreign issues. On February 28, 1979, half of the Congressional Black Caucus refused Carter's invitation to the White House; those who did go came out to the stakeout position and blasted his proposed budget cuts. Several said they wouldn't support him for reelection.

Here were key players in the Democratic Party at odds with their own president not only because he rejected their liberal policies but also because they felt they didn't owe him. The outsider president was now being punished for running against the insiders. But for Carter, playing the outsider game was more than a political miscalculation; it was an imperative. Perhaps it came from a southerner's insecurity, but he just had to prove he could do the job *on his own*. He seemed compelled to demonstrate that he and the young southerners he had brought with him weren't the yahoos the columnists were saying they were. He would show them. And he would show the press, which, like so many of his predecessors, he had come to see as an army arrayed against him.

91

□

NIGHT AFTER NIGHT I got on the air with pieces that didn't have as much information as Sam's and Judy's. They seemed to have sources I could never find, insiders who provided them insights and trenchant quotes. Each day I made more and more phone calls — sometimes as many as 30. But still I wasn't getting as close to officials in the loop as my competitors were. I thought I would never figure it out.

This all came to a head when Israeli Prime Minister Begin came to Washington in early March to discuss the collapsing Camp David Accords. On the last day of his visit, March 5, around lunchtime, NBC went on the air with a bulletin: "NBC News has learned" — the dreaded words — "that President Carter has decided to go himself to the Middle East." He was going to both Jerusalem and Cairo to try to save the accords. This was a huge story. My phone rang. "Lesley!" Lane was yelling. "Can we go with it too?"

I said I'd get it confirmed and get right back to him. Jody Powell wouldn't take my call. Zbigniew Brzezinski, the national security adviser, had his own press team, which was usually accessible and helpful, but they too were unavailable. I couldn't reach a single high-level person. Five minutes went by, and ABC was on the air. I was in terror, and Bob Pierpoint was off. AP's bells began ringing . . . and UPI's . . . and still I couldn't get anyone to help me. I finally told my office to go on the air and say, "The Associated Press is reporting that . . ."

Humiliation and ruin — a fireable offense. I was sure CBS would yank me out of the White House. At least the story broke in the middle of the day. I was able to come back with a strong script for the *Evening News*, but the feeling of defeat was hard to shake.

I would later come to realize that Jody's harsh treatment of me was becoming a badge of honor — at least within the halls of CBS. As long as he made it clear I was persona non grata at the White House, my job was secure because my bosses lived by a set of commandments, and number one was that no government official could interfere with the network's internal decisions, especially who covered what.

The next morning, Sam pulled me aside. There was something he wanted me to know. "Day after day," he said, "Jody Powell has Judy Woodruff and me up to his office for a private one-on-two background briefing. He's deliberately cutting you out."

How stupid I'd been. Of course! Jody, the only source.

"I'm telling you," said Sam, "because one day he'll get mad at me and have you and Judy in and cut *me* out. Now, if he were leaking great scoops to me alone, I'd never say a word. But this ganging up on one of us is wrong; I don't think it's fair." You don't get menschier than that.

"I know what you're doing, Jody," I said when I finally got a private appointment with him. "I know about your daily sessions with Sam and Judy." I thought he would try to deny it, but he just stared. "It doesn't make any sense," I said. "CBS reaches more people than either of the other two networks. All you're doing is depriving my audience of the message you're trying to put out. You're only spiting yourself. And besides, you told me you'd treat me fairly."

"You're right."

"What?"

He said he would stop singling me out. And he did. As far as I know, Jody was evenhanded from that day on. That doesn't mean he did me any special favors. He didn't. Never. Not once.

SAM HAD an endearing way of gallivanting around the pressroom, flapping his script in the air and howling, "I'm nailing him tonight!" or "There's blood in the water, we've got him now!" or "He'll never survive *this* one!" Sam describes these rantings as "mock ferocity." When we weren't busy trying to keep up with him, most of the reporters got a big kick out of Sam. To know him was (and is) to love him.

The year 1979 was the peak of network news power. Something like 120 million viewers tuned in to the three networks every night. There really wasn't much else to watch. We were so predominant and influential that our deadline at 6:30 Eastern Time became the deadline of the entire federal government. The daily rhythm at the White House was synchronized with our rhythm. And so even though Jody and the other officials were unhappy with me, they pampered me at the same time.

Along with the ABC and NBC correspondents, I was fussed over, no question about it. We had our own reserved seats in the front row of the pressroom for Jody's briefings and the president's news conferences. We always got first-class seats on the press plane, and choice positions were saved for our crews on the camera platforms. White House officials consulted our bureau chiefs regularly to see if their plans met with our approval.

Whenever the president wanted to deliver a speech on television, the press secretary had to request time with each network separately. If CBS thought the speech was too political or not important enough to relinquish airtime to, we'd turn it down, and the White House would go crackers — ineffectually.

The political writer Richard Reeves believes that there's a fixed amount of power in the world, so that when a president is weak, for instance, the press is emboldened. Which is what happened in 1979. Carter was weak, and CBS, with Walter Cronkite number one for 12 unbroken years, was at the crest. Cronkite was so much an institution (in Sweden a news anchor was called a "cronkiter") that he began not only influencing policy but making it. In 1977 *The New York Times* had called it "Cronkite Diplomacy" when Egypt's Anwar Sadat told Walter in a TV interview that he was willing to meet with Israel's Menachem Begin without any preconditions. Within hours Cronkite had Begin on the air, inviting Sadat to Jerusalem.

CARTER LEFT for Egypt on March 7 at 6:30 P.M., so the takeoff would lead the *Evening News*, live. I reported from Andrews Air Force Base that the president was aware the "mission is a gamble." I was one of the pool reporters on *Air Force One*, which sounded like a treat to me. I should have known better the minute Sam told me I would *love* it. As always, there were four pool reporters: this time Helen Thomas of UPI, Frank Cormier of AP, Bernie Gwertzman of *The New York Times*, and me. We sat cramped, in fact folded up, around a table for the entire 13 hours. The president had a cabin with a real bed, so he could sleep and get off the plane refreshed. For me sleeping was out of the question since Gwertzman, a portly man (I flew sitting backward), snored and kicked all night long.

We never saw Carter during the flight. The minute we landed in Cairo at 7 A.M. local time, I went right into a pool, following Carter to a meeting with Sadat at his residence. This would be a five-hour stakeout in the humidity of Cairo, during which we would communicate with our crews and producers by walkie-talkie. We were in a hive of electronic voices, spreading morsels of intelligence about Carter's facial expressions and asking questions such as "When the hell is lunch arriving?" Finally we were blessed with news: a short statement, Sadat explaining that Carter's proposals for peace "had too many problems." Unlike most presidential trips abroad, this one had been put together too quickly for the usual meticulous scripting. There was no prepackaged final communiqué, and therefore no guarantee of a smiling final photo and handshake. Carter was taking a huge risk.

After a full day of pool assignments, the real work began. We went to private briefings at our hotel with "senior government officials" in "deep backgrounders," where the progress of the talks was explained as long as we agreed not to reveal the identity of the briefers. These sessions were usually held one hour before our "feed time," 1:30 A.M. local time, when our reports were sent to New York by satellite. The networks each fed three or four pieces a night in rotation, through one outlet in one small sliver of time. Just as you unwound from the deadline pressure, you were desperate for sleep, but what you did was shower and get ready for your first pool of the morning. Before long both we in the press and the staffers we dealt with were fatigued, irritable, and short-tempered.

On the third day we flew to Jerusalem, where Carter's motorcade from the airport was pelted with eggs. It dawned on me that presidents rarely visit open democracies such as this one. And so when Carter pleaded with the Israeli parliament, the Knesset, to "seize this precious opportunity" for peace, he got a cool reception. When Begin spoke, he was heckled.

That was the day we were supposed to leave for home. We had a baggage call for 10 A.M., so all the reporters and camera crews checked out of the hotel, dragging our suitcases down to the pressroom, where Billy Dale of the White House Travel Office made sure they were taken out to the airport and put onto the press plane. But the departure time kept slipping and we couldn't find out why, until finally at 10 P.M. Jody Powell announced that our baggage was being returned to the hotel; we would spend one more night, even though, he admitted, "I see very little possibility that these issues are going to be resolved."

It was decided that Pierpoint would do an analysis of how the talks had fallen apart and I would write a humorous piece about our wandering luggage.

It was close to midnight when Jody Powell's secretary, Carolyn Shields, invited me to Jody's room: "He wants to see you." I found this very peculiar. His room? I had begun to think I was suffering from "Stockholm Syndrome," in which you come to love your captor. That's what he was, and I was his prisoner, since clearly he had the power to make me look like either a genius or a fool. He was, after all, the only source. The invitation was a pleasant change, but there was no way I was going to allow anything untoward to happen in his room. As I made my way along the corridors of the King David Hotel, I rehearsed ways of letting him down gently.

Carolyn answered the door. Jody had a grand suite. When I turned a corner and entered the living room, I had to laugh at my vanity. There were Sam and Judy! This was one of Powell's background sessions to make sure we got the story right.

He told us that Secretary of State Vance and Israeli Foreign Minister Moshe Dayan were holding a late-night meeting to see if the peace plan could be salvaged but that he wasn't optimistic. In fact, he was pretty glum: "To say [the peace mission] is hanging by a thread is putting too optimistic an interpretation [on things]." He did add, though, "You never know."

We dashed off, I to give Pierpoint a fill for his story. We at CBS were pretty strong that night about the collapse of the talks. Walter led the show: "All indications now are that President Carter's high-stakes gamble in the Middle East has failed." And Pierpoint continued in the same vein, leaving himself an out along the lines of Jody's "You never know."

After our broadcast I was approached by an Israeli official, who told me that the Americans were painting a far too gloomy picture in an effort to apply pressure on Begin to make concessions. "It's psychological warfare," he accused.

Yeah, but . . . it worked. The next morning the American briefers told us the peace process was back on track. As Carter and the rest of the White House press corps went back to Cairo to consummate the agreement, I stayed behind to report that the Israelis were furious at U.S. briefers, who had "deliberately overplayed the gloom and doom" and "distorted the facts."

Bob Pierpoint and several other reporters were steaming at Jody, believing that he had deliberately deceived us. But rather than apologize for leading us in the wrong direction, Powell attacked CBS for our "arrogant" coverage, singling out my piece as a way of expressing CBS's pique at him on the air.

No wonder Jody was put out with us. Jimmy Carter had pulled off a miracle. Through stubbornness and persistence, he engineered the first peace agreement between Israel and an Arab state by investing his personal capital in it. Some of my colleagues agreed with Jody that any kind of critical story that first night was off base. Carter deserved at least one news cycle of undiluted praise for his historic and personal accomplishment.

There's no explaining it, but even those news organizations that gave Carter his due that first day were soon focusing on how many billions of dollars the peace process would cost the U.S. taxpayer. Once again he got very little reward for his accomplishment and virtually no bounce in the polls.

SADAT AND BEGIN came to Washington to sign the peace treaty in late March. I covered the event standing on a towering scaffolding set up on the North Lawn of the White House. The signing took place there because a giant tent covered the South Lawn, which was usually used for such ceremonies. That night 1,340 guests attended a sit-down state dinner (with 110 kosher meals) in the tent. Just about every reporter who had been on the Middle East shuttle trip was invited except . . . guess who?

Well, that was all right. I told myself I didn't really care. I was embarked on a journey into self-control. It was something I had decided was absolutely necessary — both for this job and for Taylor, who was now two. Whenever I walked in the door, she would run down the hall and hurl herself into my arms. There was never love like that. And yet I had chewed her little head off one day when I had come home and found huge red and green crayon marks all over the walls. Aaron came out to see who Taylor had murdered. He told me coolly, "Either change or pretend to change, I don't care which." When I told Aaron he was right

96

as usual and that I felt bad, he hugged me and calmed me. He seemed to love me in spite of it all.

I worked on mastering my temper and deadening that reflex of tearing up whenever I got particularly angry. Little did I realize that I would do such a good job of containing my emotions that one day I would have trouble finding them. Self-control can become an insidious habit. For some mysterious reason, the television camera is particularly sensitive to this bottling up. It doesn't like it; it registers as unauthentic.

Aaron was spending more and more time in Los Angeles and Houston working on *Urban Cowboy*. After he finished the screenplay, he glued himself to the director, Jim Bridges, managing to become his right hand during the making of the movie. I joined Aaron one weekend in Houston when John Travolta was in town to look over Gilley's honky-tonk. Paramount was wooing him as the lead. I met John at a dinner at the Palm and found him good-natured and surprisingly vulnerable. He told me that Amy Carter had invited him to have dinner with her at the White House on her birthday. He was her present.

After our dinner at the Palm, our party of close to 20 piled into a motorcade of limousines and drove off to Dew Westbrook's apartment. Dew was the real-life oil-worker, mechanical-bull cowboy Travolta would play if he agreed. Aaron, Jim Bridges, Irving Azoff, John Travolta, and three or four of John's "people," plus seven or eight folks from Paramount and I, all crammed into Dew's subcompact living room. Dew made no move to turn off or even turn down the TV, so we had our little visit with *The Rockford Files* on the whole time. We weren't there two minutes when Dew told Travolta, "You're disco. You'd never go over as a cowboy. Now, that's nothin' against you."

The Hollywood suits scattered, Jim looked like Munch's painting *The Scream*, and Aaron, who had suggested this encounter, was trying to dissolve into the wallpaper. Only Travolta seemed unfazed.

We left quickly and all went on to Gilley's, where John danced and Aaron rode the mechanical bull. As Travolta left, he gave every one a thumbs-up. The next day he expressed his only concern: "How bad will I get hurt riding the bull?"

There was then a search for Sissy, the female lead. I thought Sissy Spacek would be perfect, but Aaron said that when Debra Winger auditioned, he came face-to-face with the Sissy he had created and talked Bridges into hiring her.

THERE WAS NOTHING but headaches for Jimmy Carter from the intensifying energy squeeze brought on by the Arab oil embargo. "Peace in the Middle East," said a White House source, "doesn't help one damn bit with inflation," which was running in the double digits. To deal with the oil crisis, Carter presented a new set of energy proposals in a televised speech: new conservation measures and new taxes on oil companies to offset any windfall profits. But he hadn't laid the groundwork. Scoop, whom he had already alienated, and Tip and the rest were blindsided. Carter kept doing good things badly. He liked the exercise of making decisions, of examining, studying, analyzing until he commanded even the most arcane intricacies of an issue. Then he'd come up with a well-conceived solution to a policy problem. He seemed to assume that was all there was to it, that once he presented his decision, everyone else would see the wisdom of his choices. He never caught on that selling and bargaining were necessities of his job.

Carter's preference for studying policy papers to thrashing things out with people was one of his cramping foibles. He disparaged the wheedling and arm-twisting that make Washington work. A White House official described an Oval Office meeting Carter had with a New York congressman to win his pivotal vote on the windfall profits tax. After the president made his pitch on the merits, the congressman replied, "They're closing the post office in my district." Everyone understood that if Carter came up with a mere $50,000 to keep the post office open, he'd win the crucial vote. But to his aides' horror, Carter came back with another dry speech on the oil tax. The congressman walked out and voted against the president.

The majority leader of the House, Jim Wright, said that Carter didn't think politics was a clean profession: "Jimmy Carter makes *me* feel dirty."

CARTER WAS ONE of the most accessible presidents. He held 59 full-fledged news conferences, many more brief ones, and countless interviews. His aides will tell you today that this was a mistake, that he was overexposed and it hurt his image. While I generally disagree, there was an undisciplined air about his approachability. A photo opportunity in, say, the Oval Office was bedlam. We'd wait outside until the doors opened, at which time we'd all rush in together, jostling for position — cameras, microphones, reporters — as if someone were giving away free tickets to the Super Bowl. There was no guarantee that any of the networks would get a decent picture or clear sound, so everyone pushed and grunted their way to the front of the pack.

It was even worse when the president traveled. The problem was that Carter was so prone to answer questions thrown at him on the spot that it was risky to leave his side. So we all swarmed in and formed a writhing cocoon around him. He was accessible and we appreciated that, but on television it looked like mayhem and added to a sense that no one was in control.

On foreign trips there was more restraint. In June 1979 we went to

Vienna for the president's first and only summit with Soviet leader Leonid Brezhnev, a meeting Carter had been seeking ever since taking office. Jody Powell wisecracked, "The Reds and the Rednecks were going to square off!" Actually, they were going to sign the SALT II arms control treaty.

The leaders met first in an anteroom of Vienna's gilded Hofburg decorated with flying putti. I was in the pool, standing in a forest of still photographers from around the world. President Carter arrived right on time. But Brezhnev didn't. As Carter cooled his heels, we in the international press gallery just stared in silence as POTUS—President of the United States—spent a long five minutes wilting. Brezhnev finally arrived, shuffling, halting, and unsteady. That his health was failing was obvious, and yet he held his substantial body proudly erect and towered over Carter, who was, by then, so ill at ease that he seemed to shrink before our eyes.

Embarrassing television pictures are like a time-release poison, since they are played over and over and in the repetition can come to be defining. One such picture was shot as the summit in Vienna was ending. After the two leaders signed the SALT II treaty Carter, on an apparent impulse, drew the enfeebled Brezhnev to him in an emotional embrace and then, to everyone's astonishment—gasps rose in the gallery—he kissed the Bolshevik on the left cheek.

As happened repeatedly with Carter, he was unable to profit from the successful summit. The buss on the cheek fed the notion that he was shrinking. Constriction was becoming an affair of state. The president was dwindling in size, partly from his vigorous jogging, mainly from an impression that he was overwhelmed by his job. Reporters took to calling him the Little Peanut; cartoonists drew him as a little kid in a big chair, then eventually as nothing more than a row of protruding teeth.

Then OPEC, the Arab oil cartel, announced another price hike, increasing oil prices tenfold over 1973. There could not have been worse news for Jimmy Carter. "Was God," asked *Newsweek*, "out to get his devoted servant?" On July 5 he canceled his planned television speech on the energy crisis. I reported that the president had given no explanation before disappearing to Camp David "very mysteriously." Thus began one of the odder episodes of the Carter presidency.

For several days the only people who saw him at Camp David were his wife and a few close aides. My producers in New York said I would have to deal with the spreading rumors that the president was sliding off the edge. So I went on the air: "In response to reporters' questions, the White House said the president is not suffering from nervous exhaustion." Jody was not pleased with me—again. But from that night on we got reports of how physically and mentally fit the president was.

It was an intuition, but I felt it strongly, that Carter was collapsing from the frightening realization that he was failing. After a week of near solitude, he invited a select group of aides up to see him, a decision that wrought resentment among the staff members who were not invited. This produced agreeable repercussions for me as those left behind began returning my calls and giving me quotes — unattributable, of course — such as "A bunker mentality has set in up at Camp David." My 20 calls a day were paying off at last.

During the next week Carter invited a stream of governors, congressmen, and economists up to his retreat to solicit their ideas on solving the country's problems. Mrs. Carter took notes, and so did the president, each on a yellow pad. Still we had no pictures, no direct word from the president, who, it seemed, had vanished at the height of a national crisis, conveying an impression that the captain of the ship was at his wit's end.

Meanwhile, the grousing about who had been invited up to the mountain and who had not resulted in Cabinet officers and other appointees complaining, which was nothing short of delightful for a reporter. One night I said from the White House lawn that a top official was calling the Camp David retreat "a little drama produced out of desperation."

When Carter finally descended from the mountain, he went right on national television. His pollster Patrick Caddell had converted the Carters to his theory that the faltering poll ratings were due not to a failure of leadership but to pessimism in the country, and he wrote a speech to reflect that. In a July 10 memo to the president, Carter's media adviser, Gerald Rafshoon, predicted that if Carter gave that speech it would be a "disaster." He wrote that people "don't want to hear you whine" about their problems. "We must look carefully," he advised, "at each negative comment about America. We'd hear them thrown back ad nauseam during a campaign."[11] But the first lady disagreed.

As Carter flagged, Rosalynn became his anchor. There were those who took to calling her the "deputy president." On the margins of position papers and memos Carter would often scribble, "Ros. What think?" or "Have you shared this with Rosalynn? She needs to know this too." When asked about her influence at Camp David, she answered disingenuously, "I don't know that I had any. I sat in on the meetings, I listened with him and then we — uh — then he made the decisions."[12]

I listened to Carter's July 15 speech in the CBS studio with Roger Mudd and Bruce Morton. The beginning was an extended self-criticism, Carter quoting one of his visitors at Camp David as saying, "Mr. President, you're not leading this nation." After his mea culpa, he went on to give a thoughtful analysis of the state of the nation, describing a "crisis of spirit" in the country.

The initial reaction was positive. "Really an extraordinary speech," said the usually skeptical Roger Mudd. "A very strong one, very upbeat." He turned to me and asked if I thought it would be a turning point.

"It certainly was an attempt at that," I said. "And I did hear a new voice, Roger. . . . There was a little bit of a sermon to it, reaching for the moral tone he accomplished when he was winning primaries."

"A high point, wasn't it?" asked Roger.

"Absolutely."

I thought that the analysis of a gloomy national mood was right on the money. And instead of looking defeated, the president had managed to convey an air of confidence the public hadn't seen in him for months. His performance had been as important as the speech's content. Television imparts information in a way that creates a visceral response. Often we forget *what* a president says specifically about an issue, but the brain retains the visual signals and impressions. We absorb those TV blips as emotional imprints that last. Rafshoon said that people listen to presidential speeches the way they listen to rock music: "They may not know the words, but they receive the tone, the beat, the rhythm."

Carter jumped 11 points in the national polls.

The Deacon — his Secret Service code name — embarked on "a revivalist crusade," as I called it on the air, starting in Kansas City and Detroit. Things were going exceedingly well. Then, two days after the speech, he blew it.

ON JULY 17 the White House announced that the president had asked for the resignations of his entire 12-member Cabinet. It was called "a slaughter," "a purge." I reported, "One source said one reason for all this is just so the president can fire [Secretary of Energy] Schlesinger in a pack." Others said the one he was really after was Secretary of Health, Education and Welfare Joseph Califano. The impression: he was too timid to fire them one-on-one. The call for resignations, like the nearly two weeks up on the mountain, was unsettling. The dollar plunged, and Europeans, with their parliamentary systems, assumed that the Carter government had fallen.

The glow from his speech flickered out within a few days, and Rafshoon's prophecy took root. Everyone began deriding his speech as a whiny attempt to shift the blame from his own shortcomings to others'. It became known as the "malaise" speech, though Carter had never uttered that word.

BY NOW there was a detachment of officials and aides eager to spread disparaging stories about the president, and who better to leak to than me, the Georgia crowd's bête noire. I began to break stories and to hear inside accounts of the president's meanness. Time and again I was told about his brusqueness, his cold glance of disapproval, his judgmental aloofness. One aide said that before Carter would come in to the regular Tuesday leadership breakfast with congressional leaders, they would be carrying on the usual politicians' banter. Then the president would arrive. "Never hail fellow well met, never easy in the club," said the aide, "he'd act as if he'd had a bad night." He would cast his steely blues around the room and end the fun like a guillotine's blade. Carter, it was said, was like Lucy in the *Peanuts* comic strip, who said, "I love Mankind; it's people I can't stand."

I THOUGHT Jody Powell was a good press secretary. He never lied to me (not all the reporters on that beat say this); he was completely plugged in as one of the president's closest confidants; he made sure the press corps was educated on the issues; and he was funny. Jody would defuse hostilities with a joke or a wisecrack before they got out of hand.

But the more I admired him, the more he spread accusations that I had an agenda. He called my bosses a few times with the "She's biased against us" complaint. I would be called by those same bosses and told to keep up the good work. Without it ever being said in so many words, there was an attitude in our newsroom that good journalists hold the feet of pols in power to the fire: "Look, we were strenuous and leathery toward Nixon; we should be 'fair' by being just as rigorous when it comes to a Democrat." It was an ethic one breathed in the CBS air. The tougher I was, the more Sandy Socolow and my other bosses praised me. In fact, my copy was often stiffened. I was asked to toughen it up.

Some of my problems had to do with gender. With all their support of women's issues, a simmering sexism pervaded the Carter White House. I was treated differently. Sam Donaldson told me that it was my aggressiveness, "because women simply aren't supposed to bull their way in." It was around that time that Bob Strauss urged me — as a friend, he said — to ease up. It simply wasn't becoming, he advised, for a woman to be so negative. Sam and I could make the same point in our reports. Jody was philosophical about what Sam said, because that was part of the inherent adversarial relationship between the press and the presidency; but in his view, I crossed the line. Still, Jody and I dealt with each other cordially every day. Washington is a place of great accommodations.

IN THE END, the resignations of half the Cabinet secretaries were accepted.[13] And I began trying to find out who the new appointees would be. On the night of July 26, 1979, I broke the story — "CBS News has learned" — that Moon Landrieu, the former mayor of New Orleans, was Carter's choice for secretary of housing and urban development. NBC's

John Dancy told me I was wrong. I bolted for Jody's office. I had not run the story by him earlier, afraid he would tell Sam and deprive me of my exclusive. On the way, I passed the Rose Garden, peeked out, and saw the president walking along the colonnade with Moon, who had an overnight bag slung over his shoulder. A night in the Lincoln Bedroom? I concluded that I'd gotten the story right, which I had.

Judy Woodruff found out who the education secretary, a new post in the Cabinet, would be. Each evening Sam, Judy, and I stood near each other on the White House lawn to record our stand-ups in sequence. That night as I waited my turn, I overheard her. She saw me there; we even chatted. When I finished my report, I raced inside, made one phone call, and got her scoop confirmed by one of my new sources immediately — even before our broadcast started. What I should have done was sit with the information until Judy's piece aired — it was, after all, her story. But I called CBS, and Roger Mudd (substituting for Walter) was able to lead our show with the name of Shirley Hufstedler, actually beating Judy's report by a few seconds. She was livid. Soon everyone was mad at me for "stealing" her story.

I was surprised at the reaction. I told myself, "You didn't eavesdrop, you weren't being sneaky about it; Judy knew you were listening and never said, 'Please step away.'" I worried about losing Judy's friendship, but still my reaction was to tough it out and say I had done nothing wrong. And I believed that until I asked Pierpoint, whose judgment I had come to rely on. I knew Bob was a man of integrity and decency. So when he told me that what I had done was like cheating on an exam, I was stricken low. "You don't do that," he said like a father explaining, "I'm not mad at you, just disappointed." I never "overheard" anyone again, and if I did, I forgot what I heard. Fortunately, Judy and I are still friends.

In AUGUST Taylor and I went to visit Aaron in Houston to watch the filming of *Urban Cowboy*. I had never understood why Aaron hated CBS functions or coming with me to parties connected with my job. Now in Houston I got it. The cast and crew had their little inside jokes — not very funny ones — but at the drop of a punch line, Aaron and Debra Winger would make eye contact and break up laughing. Or Aaron and Jim Bridges would sink into shop-talk minutiae about the next day's shoot, leaving me with recovered memories of the wallflower I had been in seventh-grade dancing school.

In other words, Aaron and I had a huge fight. I returned home early and got ready for a trip down the Mississippi with the president in mid-August. Carter was taking a weeklong cruise on the *Delta Queen*, a four-deck, stern-paddle-wheel steamer, to gather support for his new energy conservation measures. We went 660 miles down the river from St.

Paul to St. Louis. The boat was scheduled to make four stops, but Carter got it to stop 47 times, driving the press crazy with his "Hi, I love you"s at every dinky little lock along the route.

He also drove the 15 other passengers crazy from day one with his jogger's thumping 22 laps around the decks at 6:30 in the morning. I wrote that in my script one night, but I also showed the large crowds along the banks. The White House was so pleased at the reception and the coverage that Powell joshed, "From now on we're only going to campaign on navigable rivers."

The press corps followed the Carters from the shore, but every night a small pool of five got to sleep on the boat. When it was my turn, we were summoned at sunset to the bow, where lawn chairs were arranged in a circle so that we could have a casual get-together with the president. He chatted with us for an hour until the sun went down, confiding that he dictated a diary — "I do it every day. It's amazing how detailed mine is." He told us he read two or three books a week and particularly liked potboilers. He had just finished *Gemini Contender* by Robert Ludlum. Asked how he found time to read so much, he told us that he, Rosalynn, and Amy all read at the table during meals. "And" — he flashed his famous smile — "I read in the bathroom!"

AARON AND I made up. I figured out that I was jealous of the movie. I thought he was smitten with Debra Winger and that the Hollywood gestalt had turned his head. He confessed that he had fallen in love with the movie business, that he wanted to make screenwriting his career, but he also made it clear that Taylor and I were home base.

I did my best to avoid going to Plains but was rarely successful. "Town" in Plains was like town in *Tobacco Road*: one row of stores, many owned by the Carters themselves. The largest industry after peanuts seemed to be worms. I got the impression that the Carters owned half of everything, including the land and the worms. Jimmy Carter was the scion of the most successful family in one of the country's smallest places, population 680. Plains mirrored a lot about the White House, which, it seemed, Carter had tried to mold into something familiar and manageable, an insular community with a closed circle of small-town boys.

Each time I was in Plains, Jimmy and Rosalynn walked down Main Street, going into and out of the shops, starting at the Plains Flower and Gift Shop, where Rosalynn's mother worked part-time, then continuing on to the Carter Peanut Warehouse and the Carter worm farm office. We in the national press would trail after them, scrawling down the "Howdy"s and "Howya doin' "s. On one such walk the president weighed himself at the Plains Primary Clinic: "I'm 151 with all my clothes on." He really was small! But in Plains he was king.

On Sunday, September 2, 1979, the Carters went to Sunday school at Maranatha Baptist, the 11 o'clock service at Plains Baptist, and lunch at Plains Methodist. I had never been to a Baptist Sunday school, and there I was, the pool reporter, when the president taught the class of a dozen adults. He chose a short passage from Exodus about Laws for Protecting the Male Hebrew Slave, "Thou shalt not raise a false report," which he analyzed for nearly 30 minutes. At the end he walked right up to me, pierced me with those cold blues, and said, "I hope you got something out of that."

BECAUSE OF Ted Kennedy's threat to Carter's nomination, the reelection campaigning started earlier than usual. Carter was preoccupied with the Kennedys, but to be fair, Richard Nixon and Lyndon Johnson had been just as obsessed with them—three dogged presidents driven to distraction by three brothers, Jack, Bobby, and Ted, one after the other.

By mid-1979 the youngest Kennedy, Teddy, "the crown prince," was beating Carter in the polls three-to-one; it was generally assumed he'd win the nomination in a walk. But I wasn't so sure after Carter spoke at the dedication of the John Fitzgerald Kennedy Library in Boston on October 20.

> STAHL: It was a delicate moment for President Jimmy Carter as he came on the stage and into the world of the Kennedys.

Caroline Kennedy introduced her brother, John, who read a poem. Senator Edward Kennedy was eloquent in describing the brother who had taught him to ride a bicycle and sail against the wind. But if it was a contest—and it unmistakably was—Carter, the underdog, bested them on the Kennedys' home court.

He did it by making the death of John Kennedy as much his "grievous, personal loss" as the Kennedys': "My president. I wept openly for the first time in more than ten years, for the first time since the day my own father died." Carter went on to quote Ted once saying he wasn't sure he ever wanted to be president. Carter turned to him with a "gotcha!" look and smiled. I laughed; everyone laughed. Carter owned the day.

You might be inclined to chalk that up as a good day for Jimmy Carter, but his luck would not turn so easily. Two weeks later, on November 4, nearly 3,000 Iranian "students" stormed the U.S. Embassy in Tehran and took 66 Americans hostage. They held 52 of them for 444 days.

The embassy takeover was precipitated by Carter's decision to allow the deposed shah of Iran to come to the United States for medical treatment of his lymphatic cancer. The Iranians threatened to kill the hostages or put them on trial as spies if the United States did not return the shah to Iran at once. Carter refused.

Over the next several weeks the networks fed the American people a diet of Iranian demonstrators chanting anti-American slogans and burning effigies of Jimmy Carter. Critics charged that our coverage intensified the crisis and prolonged the hostages' captivity. But in the beginning the White House encouraged our approach. Hodding Carter, the State Department spokesman, was instructed to express indignation at Iran at his daily televised briefings. Jody Powell also went on camera, stressing that the safety of the hostages was the first priority. And President Carter's ratings went up. And up. Thus variations on the statements were repeated every day, which meant that we, the networks, had not only pictures of chanting mobs in Tehran — "the black hats," as Hodding Carter put it — but also sound of the "white hats," the caring officials in the Carter administration. "We were shameless," says Hodding. "We designed a policy to keep the president in the center of the passion." Back then, he says, he agreed with the plan of feeding the beast (the press) and pumping up the story. There was no complaining in the beginning, when Cronkite ended every broadcast with an account of how long the hostages had been held.[14]

The ordeal was unifying the country behind the president. The more the Iranians attacked Carter and called him the Great Satan, the more his stature grew. Soon he canceled all travel, vowing not to leave the Rose Garden until all the hostages were released — better to "lead" by staying close to the Situation Room.

What Carter didn't grasp was that his strategy of keeping the story on the front burner and the front page would increase the value of the hostages to their captors. But in the short run he gained from the publicity, and so did we: more people than ever, over five million more, were watching network news. The country was riveted.

ON DECEMBER 4, Carter made a brief announcement at the White House that he would seek reelection. It was, as Walter Cronkite reported that night, the 31st day of the hostages' captivity. Before facing the cold outdoors, I memorized what I had written:

> STAHL: Strategists admit the crisis has worked a miracle on this campaign. It's made the president look presidential. For the most part it's quieted criticism from political opponents and drawn attention away from inflation.

Kennedy's and Carter's poll numbers flipped. The president's ratings had climbed 13 points since the hostages were seized,[15] so it was now Kennedy's campaign that was howling about press bias. If there is a press bias, it's not in favor of Democrats — just ask Jimmy Carter — but against the front-runner, which Kennedy had been. Whichever force has the most power, whether in a campaign or in the running of the government, usually faces the toughest scrutiny.

The president met with the families of the hostages. Once the public came to know the mothers and the wives, there were more and more calls for action. On December 8 Carter invited 12 radio reporters to breakfast, and CBS decided I should go. When the White House protested, my bosses argued, "She does radio too." The president told us he was trying to balance the public's thirst for tough retaliation with the need for patience lest the hostages be jeopardized. I thought, as I tried to eat and take notes at the same time, that Carter looked drawn and gray. He'd aged in the last month. One could feel the burden this man was carrying.

TWO DAYS AFTER Christmas, on the 53rd day of the hostage siege, the Soviet Union invaded Afghanistan. This from Brezhnev after that sweet hug and kiss. Now Carter was under tremendous pressure from all sides to retaliate against the Soviets. On January 4 Johanna McGeary, *Time*'s White House correspondent, and I had lunch in the CBS booth. We considered Carter's options and decided that the most logical action would be a grain embargo, even though that would anger farmers and hurt the president in the January Iowa caucuses against Kennedy and Jerry Brown. For years the Soviets had been buying millions of tons of wheat, corn, and soybeans from us.

I called a friend on the Hill, who said that one way to find out if the hunch was real was to see if cables were going out to our allies. I called several embassies and an official at the Agriculture Department. No one was in. In the meantime, I asked my new producer, Susan Zirinsky (the bureau researcher during Watergate), to gather pictures of wheat being harvested. At five the man from Agriculture called me back. "I hear there's about to be an embargo," I said, embellishing. "All I really need is a little background on how many tons are involved." He said he was surprised I'd found out — *yes!* Since I knew anyway, he said, he'd help me get it right.

Before I went on the air, someone from the British Embassy called me back and added a few details. I led the *Evening News* by announcing "a limited but stiff grain embargo on the Soviet Union." Clean kill. I was alone with it and the happiest kid in town.

ONE OF MY REPUBLICAN SOURCES on the Hill leaked me a story about Carter scrubbing a powerful underground nuclear test because, the source said, he was afraid of how the Russians would react. "That coward," he said. "He's chicken, Lesley. Scared silly of the Russians. He doesn't belong in that job."

A few days later Zbigniew Brzezinski, the president's hawkish national security adviser, confirmed the story right down to its code name.

"What I heard," I said, "was that the president canceled the test at the last minute out of fear of the Soviets."

Zbig laughed. "I can't tell you why it was canceled — that's classified — but I can assure you it had nothing to do with fear."

Zirinsky gathered pictures of nuclear rockets; I called experts for information on megatonnage and fallout. I was penciled in as the lead on January 11. Around two o'clock I called one of Brzezinski's lieutenants. As I went through the points in my story one by one, he said, "Not true," "No way," "Where did you get this? None of that is true, not a word."

"Don't play with me," I said. It was hard not to think that *all* White House officials lied *all* the time. "I already know the story is accurate; I'm just checking on my language."

"Well, I don't know how you *know* the story is accurate," he said sarcastically, "because it isn't."

"Brzezinski told me himself."

Five minutes later Powell summoned me to his office: "Let me be frank with you; Zbig got a little confused." Clearly, I thought, they're trying to steer me off a story that would embarrass the president.

Next thing I knew, I was in the basement of the White House, where an official on the National Security Council said he would give me the facts — off the record. That meant that I could not report any of it. I had no choice. At CBS we had already decided that with such a strong denial from Jody, we would have to hold back on the piece until I could check it out.

It turned out that both Brzezinski and my source had mixed up part of one test with another test, and apparently the code name applied to yet a third.

That night on a special about Iran and Afghanistan called "Hot War: Cold War — Crisis in the Near East," I reported what was left of my exclusive in one sentence: the administration was engaged in a top-to-bottom review of U.S.-Soviet relations, "including an assessment of the U.S. underground nuclear testing program." I did have a little "get": that the administration was considering boycotting the 1980 Olympic Games in Moscow. "Some officials say that would upset the Kremlin as much as the U.S. grain embargo, if not more."

CARTER HAD PLEDGED not to leave the White House until the hostages were free, so I began signing off, "Lesley Stahl, CBS News, with the Carter campaign at the White House." The president was able to run effectively that way, beating Kennedy in the Iowa caucuses in January 1980 and the New Hampshire primary in February. But then, with inflation roaring and a sense of paralysis over the hostage situation, his weakness issue revived and his poll numbers drooped. Four months into the hostage crisis I reported that despite the "pledge," the president was rethinking the Rose Garden strategy.

By then the White House was trying to undo its media policy. Hodding Carter at State was told, "Knock it off. No more daily fix, no more beating up on the Iranians. No more comments." Hodding later told me that the damnedest thing had happened: "As I retreated, everyone retreated." After months of saturation coverage, the number of stories was way down. The *Evening News* ran only nine stories on the crisis in the entire month of August. Hodding says he remembers thinking, "My God! We're controlling the spigot." Still, there was growing frustration over the stalemate. This was an administration that couldn't sit patiently; it was always reacting to the press and to pressure. One official told me, "We're tactical. We respond to every stimulus that comes along." This, I felt, was a function of the average age of the people around Carter. Hamilton, Jody, and the others, most of them in their mid-30s, were too young to have acquired patience, and Carter was too inexperienced to realize "this too shall pass." So throughout his presidency, the lights in the White House often burned past midnight, as everything, it seemed, blew up into a crisis and a struggle. This is one insidious way a president affects the national temperament. Carter was making us all edgy.

When he finally succumbed to the pressure for action, it was a catastrophe. On April 25 we learned that a secret operation to rescue the hostages had ended in disaster at a desert staging area 200 miles from Tehran. Several of the helicopters failed because of a fierce desert dust storm; then, in retreat, one of the helicopters crashed into a C-130 transport plane, leaving eight crewmen dead amid a tangle of fiery helicopter debris.

When pictures of Iranians dancing around the bodies were televised, the American people, already outraged about the hostages, were both infuriated and dispirited. The incident came to symbolize a country that was no longer master of its destiny, and Carter had become the personification of the country's loss of control.

The failed rescue mission revived the blanket television coverage. Administration officials were enraged when we took up Iran's offer to let us interview the hostages on television. If we interviewed an ayatollah supporter, we were accused of providing a platform for terrorists; officials pleaded with us that we were shoring up the ayatollah's support and leading the "students" to believe that time was on their side. I got a real tongue-lashing when Mike Wallace interviewed the ayatollah himself on

60 *Minutes* and called him by his title, "imam." "When you interview a man like the ayatollah," a White House official said, "he'll be inclined to be as macho as possible. But that only boxes him in, prevents him from compromising. We know you have a right to air these interviews," I was told. "We're asking you to exercise your discretion for a common interest, which is the fate of the hostages."

TV pictures are, by the nature of the medium, "hot"; they spark emotional responses. There is no question that the pictures from Tehran and the intensity of our coverage narrowed the president's options. The public saw the American hostages blindfolded and bound and paraded through crowds shouting, "Death to America!" It was difficult to balance our responsibilities: to give the public all the information we had, not to censor ourselves, and yet not to inflame, not to do harm. There was a strong belief at CBS that if we erred, it should be on the side of full disclosure. Reporters do hold back in all kinds of situations: in kidnappings, police raids, military actions. But usually when we're urged by an administration to be "patriotic," it's a bad idea. We remember that John Kennedy said he wished *The New York Times* had ignored him when he asked them not to report on the Bay of Pigs invasion ahead of time.

In late May, on the 200th day of the hostage captivity, I said on air, "Ever since the failed rescue mission, the White House has done everything it could to bury the hostage story, keep it off the *Evening News*. . . . Administration officials now think the best tactic is to make the Iranians think their captives are no longer valuable, and so the president is deemphasizing the issue. Another reason: as one official put it, 'Why should he keep reminding the people of a six-month foreign policy failure?' " Powell thought that was unfair.

I TOOK A FEW DAYS OFF and flew to Los Angeles with Taylor to see Aaron. He was working with Jim Bridges in the editing room on the final cut of *Urban Cowboy*. Our relationship, recovered, had plunged back into unhappy phone conversations in which we accused each other of selfishness and indifference. But there I was, hoping for a rapprochement. Instead, we had a blowout on the second day. "It isn't that I don't love you; I don't *like* you," I said in a quiet rage. Aaron retorted, "Well, I don't like you either." It hurt more than I'd expected.

"I'm leaving here, and I'm leaving you," I said. I called the airlines for a reservation, called a cab, and, with Taylor under my left arm, began hurling clothes into my suitcase with my right.

"You can leave as far as I'm concerned," Aaron said in his soft voice. "I won't miss you. But I know that in two years you'll be in a similar room, packing in a similar way, walking out on the next guy, and then, two years after that, on the next one, and one day you'll look back and say, 'What do I have to show for the last ten years?' "

I kept throwing my clothes and Taylor's into the suitcase in one big jumble. "But," Aaron went on, "you could stay and work this out with me. And in ten years you'll look back and say, 'I preserved this family.' And that will be the thing you will be the most proud of, no matter what else you do with your life."

I stopped cold, frozen by the clarity of what he had said about me. There aren't many times in your life you hear a truth so piercing. He didn't accuse me of putting myself and my wishes ahead of Taylor's, he didn't say, "How dare you presume to deprive me of my daughter?" There was no attack, just a simple assessment of my future.

When the cab came, he sent it away. We talked. We cried. And we agreed to try. Now it's 19 years later, and it is the thing I am most proud of.

THERE IS SIMPLY nothing more fun for a reporter who likes politics than the political conventions, so this time I lobbied to be one of the floor correspondents. And it worked. I was one of CBS's senior horsemen in 1980.

The Republicans went first, from July 14 to July 17 in Detroit. Ronald Reagan had swept most of the caucuses and primaries; his nomination on the first ballot was a formality. The only drama, the only uncertainty, was whom he would pick as his running mate.

Still dealing with his right-wing image, Reagan needed a moderate to balance the ticket, someone who could help unify the Republican Party. He approached former president Gerald Ford, who said he would consider the offer if the vice president's duties were expanded. As negotiations ensued, the Reagan forces encouraged a Ford-for-veep demonstration on the floor, and this drove our coverage on the third day. Cronkite interviewed a coy Ford about the prospects of a "copresidency."

We were expecting an annoucement of the Ford choice when an aimless pro-Reagan demonstration broke out and lasted without explanation until 11:55, when Walter said, "Lesley Stahl has more on why this demonstration is being prolonged. Lesley?"

I'd been planning a report on the demonstration, but just as Walter was introducing me, one of Reagan's floor captains rushed up behind me and said, "Here's a little present just for you. It's Bush!" He said he didn't want to be interviewed, but this was solid. With that, Walter threw it to me.

"Walter, I am just being told by a high lieutenant that the choice is *Bush!* I am being told that the choice is George Bush!" I looked over at my source for reassurance. "He's telling me I can go with it. I'm being told for sure. Apparently the deal with Ford fell through. A couple of senators were just called off the floor into the trailer, and somebody came running out, came running up to me, one of the top lieutenants from the trailer. He says that Reagan is here to tell the convention it's Bush. . . . He just came running over to me, shouted at me, said, 'Go with it. It's absolutely true!' "

This after Walter had ridden the it's-Jerry-Ford story for five straight hours. It had come out of nowhere, and Cronkite was rattled by it.

WALTER: Lesley Stahl. That's the most amazing piece of news we've heard since we heard it was Ford. Now, hold on just a second. Who told you that?
STAHL: Walter, a top Reagan lieutenant. They're coming all around me to tell me it's not Ford. They're yelling "Bush" all around me!
WALTER: Well, they better bring the adrenaline up here to the anchor booth.

My heart was wild; I had just broken the only story at the whole convention. I was anything but the cool, composed correspondent delivering the facts in a stentorian voice. I was excited, and you could tell.

THE DEMOCRATIC NATIONAL CONVENTION in mid-August at Madison Square Garden in New York City was not the triumphant launch Jimmy Carter needed. Though he had the nomination sewn up, he had not made peace with Ted Kennedy, who was refusing to concede. Even Carter's acceptance speech was a letdown. I reported from the podium, "What struck us up here was the lack of fire in the audience while the president was speaking. It was a good speech, but it wasn't uplifting." Then, as Carter accepted the nomination, Kennedy went to the platform but refused to join hands and raise them with Carter in the traditional gesture of unity. The closing TV image was one of a divided party.

On the last night one of Carter's White House officials, Ann Wexler, and I had a conversation on the floor about TV coverage. She seemed to be assuming the press was anti-Reagan. "If you think the press is going to take sides and tilt toward Carter," I said, "if you're counting on this, you're making a big mistake." Ann told me later that that's exactly what she had thought, and that I had run a chill through her.

REAGAN RAN AGAINST CARTER'S proposition that there was a "crisis of confidence" in America. His optimism was appealing, and so was he. The actor-candidate jumped off the TV screen. The public's reaction to him reminded me of a song Sancho Panza sings in *Man of La Mancha* about

112

how he can't help himself, he just simply likes Don Quixote. As Carter campaign operative Bob Beckel told me, Reagan was "the Secretariat of politicians, a Thoroughbred on the hustings. I watched that guy campaign and said, 'Jesus.'"

President Carter's biggest problem was the economy. Elections usually come down to what the pollsters call pocketbook issues, which Reagan was able to exploit by using the "Misery Index" — a combination of the rates of inflation and unemployment — which Carter had come up with to run against Ford. "In 1976," Reagan would say, "Carter's Misery Index was 12.5 percent. Today, after three and a half years of Carter failures, the Misery Index has grown to 20.3 percent. By the very standard Jimmy Carter used to define failure, he has failed." [16]

Carter's team had welcomed the prospect of running against Ronald Reagan, whom they saw as a right-wing extremist the American people would never accept. By the fall of 1980, with the president's approval rating hovering around a wobbly 37 percent, the only thing holding the Carter candidacy together was whatever fear of Reagan he could drum up. Carter warned that it was too risky to leave the serious business of leadership in the hands of a cowboy actor. Confrontation in the nuclear age, he said, "is not just another shoot-out at the O.K. Corral."

Rather than bring up his own performance in office, Carter took to pouncing on Reagan's gaffes and emphasizing his intellectual shortcomings. Reagan gave Carter plenty of ammunition, expressing doubts about evolution and blaming trees, not cars, for smog. But his popularity ratings improved, so Carter descended to nastiness. His portrayal of Reagan as a "mad bomber" and a racist produced the "meanness issue." At a briefing on October 8 Jody Powell was asked:

> REPORTER: Why do you think James Reston today calls your man's campaign vicious and personal? Why do you think *The Washington Post* wrote a lead editorial accusing your man of meanness? These people are not Reagan supporters. Are they all wrong?

Within a few months Carter's image had flipped from that of an ineffectual but decent religious man to a vindictive villain.

I got my own dose of criticism. Bill Safire wrote a column in *The New York Times* about attractive young women reporters — "svelte stand-up savants" who believed that "their youth and appearance damaged their credibility as journalists." To remedy that, these young women "took on a hard cast of cynicism by emulating the likes of Dan Rather, Dan Schorr, and Sam Donaldson in their combativeness." Other men, he said, had to become more cynical to compete with the "brainy, gimlet-eyed knockouts." [17] I resented the suggestion that women couldn't simply be tough because we were tough, that in that category we had to be derivative. When I confronted Safire, he just smiled. I decided to take it as a compliment and move on.

THAT FALL I chased Carter all over the country. In those days TV traveled like the *QE2*. We had a huge contingent on the Carter plane: two two-man camera crews, two TV correspondents, two producers (one for *Evening News*, one for *Morning News*), a video editor, a radio correspondent and technician, and a lighting man. Today that's been pared back to one crew, one producer, and one correspondent.

Wherever we went, we hired cars and drivers and couriers who sped our tapes from campaign sites to edit rooms. We chartered helicopters as if we were hailing cabs. If we had to stay behind to edit a story, CBS, NBC, and ABC would charter a small jet for us to catch up. I spent more time with Sam and Judy and my producers than with my family.

A new inflation report came out 11 days before the election showing the cost-of-living increase jumping to 12 percent. Our economics correspondent, Ray Brady, reported that food prices were up because of the summer drought, car prices were up, mortgage rates were up. It was the worst possible news for Carter as he campaigned in New Jersey. That night I reported "a growing feeling that the outcome of the race rests on the debate next week and whether or not the hostages are released before November fourth." It was, as Walter Cronkite said that night, the 356th day of their captivity.

October 28, the night of the sole Carter-Reagan debate, in Cleveland, I said on the *Evening News*: "History will record that on the morning of the big presidential debate of 1980 the Democratic incumbent, having just recovered from a bout of laryngitis, went jogging in a freezing rainstorm just after dawn."

Several of Carter's aides had urged him not to debate. His negative strategy of scaring the public about Reagan had seemed to hold some promise. The week before the debate CBS News polls had them in a statistical dead heat. If Reagan could convince the public that he wasn't the sort of person to start a war, all would be lost. But that's pretty much what Reagan did with his low-key, reassuring tone of voice. Not only did he defuse the warmonger issue by asserting that military force should be used only as a "last resort," whenever Carter came after him, he replied with a mocking sigh, "There you go again!" He made the president seem whiny.

And Reagan didn't make a mistake, but Carter did. He confided that he'd turned to his daughter, Amy, to discuss arms control. In their sum-ups Reagan scored again, asking the catchy and memorable question "Are you better off than you were four years ago?" People were looking for an excuse to vote against Jimmy Carter. It was all over.

114

In a postdebate discussion Walter asked, "Lesley, what do you think tomorrow President Carter will regret most?"

"Having mentioned Amy as a person who talks to him about nuclear policy." "Ask Amy" signs began popping up. Reagan said, "I know he touched our hearts, all of us, the other night. I remember when Patty and Ron were little tiny kids, we used to talk about nuclear power!" Johnny Carson quipped, "We've got to make a choice. Who do you want running our nation for the next four years? Nancy or Amy?"

The Reaganites had worried about an "October surprise," a last-minute breakthrough in Carter's negotiations with Iran. Just before the election, there was a glimmer of hope and Carter raced back to the White House for one final attempt. But there was no deal when we went on the air on November 4, election night.

I was in New York along with Dan Rather, Bob Schieffer, and Harry Reasoner, bathed in 275 overhead lights, 180,000 watts of brilliance. It was Walter Cronkite's last election night as anchorman. Returns and exit-poll numbers flowed in from around the country into our Teletype machines and 75 computer terminals. An announcer boomed out instructions that no one was to applaud or react in any way once we went on the air.

My first report was on a poll showing that Carter's repeated attacks on Reagan as a warmonger had backfired in the West, where most of the voters remembered him as the easygoing governor of California. The number one issue in the West was inflation, which was working against the president all over the country.

By 11 o'clock in the East it was clear that Reagan was swamping Carter. Walter asked us why the polls over the weekend had shown a much closer race. The CBS News poll on Sunday had had Carter at 40 percent, Reagan at 41 percent. I said it was the hostages. "There was this last-minute breakthrough [in the negotiations], but Carter didn't seem to be able to do anything about it. He looked impotent once again, reminding us that the hostage standoff was over a year old and he was incapable of moving on it."

Jimmy Carter simply lacked the temperament for strong presidential leadership. He demonstrated that fine moral character — virtuous uprightness, godliness, marital fidelity — is not necessarily the prescription for effective governance. And his presidency poses the question: Can a POTUS who hates politics succeed? The answer is no. Because of his aversion to the necessary trimming and trading, the protoplasm of governing, he was unable to sell many of his ideas even at a time when his party controlled both houses of Congress. He simply wouldn't do what was necessary to marshal support for the policies he had so diligently devised. 115

And then, when he did succeed, he couldn't seem to translate his victories into support. He got no credit for saving the hostages' lives. (Every one of them would come out alive.) That was only one of his many unappreciated accomplishments. Carter started the smart-bomb program by launching the cruise missile and the stealth bomber technology; he put Pershing missiles in Europe to intimidate the Soviets; he took on the pro-Israel lobby—which was gutsy for a Democrat—by selling AWACS and F-15 fighters to Egypt and Saudi Arabia. And he prepositioned the U.S. military in the Persian Gulf because he saw that any Middle East peace would have to be secured by the United States. In other words, he gave Ronald Reagan the leverage to bring the Soviets to their knees and George Bush the ability to fight Iraq in the Gulf War. But while he was president, he rarely got the credit he deserved.

Reagan won by a landslide, 51 to 41 percent. Carter conceded an hour before the polls closed on the West Coast. The Carter campaign's assessment that Reagan wouldn't appeal to the mainstream was essentially correct. He won not with the traditional center but with a coalition of conservative southern Democrats, blue-collar workers, and the hard Right. This was also the first appearance of the "gender gap." A majority of women voted for Reagan, but by a smaller percentage than men did. That women would vote differently from men was a new phenomenon.

I recall James Schlesinger's prediction that Carter would expect to lose and then be magnificent in defeat. Which probably explains why he became such an inspiring ex-president.

PART THREE

RONALD AND NANCY REAGAN

R UMBLAGE" SHOULD BE A WORD. Rumblage: vicious gossip reported to the target of the rumor, as in "I thought you should know what everyone's saying about you." In my case it was that my bosses were about to pluck me out of the White House.

Newspapers and magazines such as *Time* and *Newsweek* usually change their White House reporters when a new president comes to town; the networks do so some of the time. So I was worried about my future anyway. Then came the rumblage that I would be replaced by Bill Plante, who had covered the Reagan campaign. There was no doubt that he'd have better sources in the new Reagan administration.

The rumblage seeped through me like mad cow disease. I brooded at night: "You idiot, it's your own fault. Why do you still panic on deadline? Don't you think they see that?" Or "Why do *all* your scripts have to come in late?" My gut churned, my teeth ground. "I know they want me out of there," I told Aaron.

"Why don't you just ask them?"

I was afraid. When I asked presidents tough questions, I wore the protective shield of CBS News; before my own bosses I'd be naked. But not knowing was worse. So in early December I flew to New York and asked pitifully, "Can I keep my job?"

"Of course, of course," said Bud Benjamin, smiling and oh so puzzled by the question. And Ed Fouhy, my old mentor from the Watergate years and by then an executive in New York, told me they were happy with my work and yes, everyone wanted me to stay on at the White House as chief correspondent. What a dark monster, the imagination. I was a cripple gone to Lourdes, instantly cured.

Within a few days I was assigned to cover the Reagan transition. By then the Reagans were back in California at their ranch-style home in Pacific Palisades near Beverly Hills. Like Reagan himself, what made the house was its presentation: a winding driveway to the top of a hill with a great view of the ocean — when it wasn't smoggy. Each network rented its own house on the Reagans' street, and every day I sat outside, staking out the president-elect.

There was a sameness to the days and nights. I would hang around the neighborhood, waiting for a signal from the Secret Service, which came at roughly 2 P.M. every day. "Presidential movement" they'd tell us without the slightest insinuation of humor. We'd jump in our cars, fall in behind the motorcade after it careened down Reagan's driveway, and speed off in a snaky line into Beverly Hills.

Day one, Reagan went to his meat locker. We scurried out of our cars — cameramen lugging their equipment — to shout a question at the soon-to-be leader of the Free World as he paid a visit to his butcher. He came out 30 minutes later with a bundle and a sweet excuse about why he couldn't answer our questions. By the time the day's activity was over it was 4 P.M., past my deadline in the East.

Day two was the same except that the presidential movement ended at Drucker the barber's for a haircut. Day three, it was Frank Mariani, the tailor. This is POTUS-to-be? With these little errands? I couldn't figure it out at first, but soon came to realize that I was witnessing the routine of an actor out of work. I always wondered: What *do* they do between movies anyway? But just *one* errand a day?

It was my first insight into this POTUS. The actor's rhythms were so ingrained in this man that he abided by them 16 years after his last movie. The actor in him wasn't just an advantage he had in communicating or a gift he shared with great leaders such as Winston Churchill, FDR, and Henry V. For Reagan, being an actor was a defining quality, a key to the man if not his core.

In 1981 there was an assumption, a collective wisdom that the presidency had become a dinosaur. Jimmy Carter had left us with the feeling that no one man could grapple with all the pressures and responsibilities. But it became clear early on that Reagan had innate potential for strong leadership. If Carter's take on the world was micro, every day for Reagan was a scene in an epic movie on the big screen. At six feet, one inch, and 185 pounds, he even loomed large. But mainly it was his sweeping view, as he'd displayed in the campaign. If Carter's perspective was farmer's plot, Reagan's was Cinemascope.

Yet it seemed inconceivable to me then that this laid-back actor who was content doing little more than running one errand a day could revive the institution of the presidency.

In early January Reagan announced that his press secretary would be James Brady, 36, a balding bear of a man — we even called him "Bear" — with a mollifying sense of humor. I liked him; we all liked him. When someone leaked a story that Nancy Reagan had objected to his appointment because he wasn't good-looking enough, the press corps grew to love him.

"I'm getting to be an irate husband at some of the things I'm reading [about Nancy]," said Reagan, with a smile on his face. It was my first Reagan news conference — my first close-up look — and all I could think was "He's irresistible." My view of him over the last year had been from inside the Carter White House, where Reagan had been demonized a hundred different ways every day. I was surprised at how simply likable he was.

Now he was making sweet little jokes — "Nancy thinks he's absolutely handsome" — smooth as peau de soie, defusing the Brady dustup. But as affable as Reagan was, he couldn't defuse all of Nancy's time bombs. She simply drew fire. Her adoring gaze seemed phony, and her Rodeo Drive tastes rankled. I had learned about the Reagans' affinity for the Hollywood value system during the transition by following them to parties. One night I staked them out at a Beverly Hills mansion where young valets parked Rolls-Royces and Bentleys on the lawn. It was a parody of the nouveau-riche life. If you had sold all the jewelry that walked in the front door, you could've fed Cleveland for a year.

I was enjoying the change, getting to know the Reagan players, when I was summoned to New York. Bud Benjamin told me he had decided after all that Bill Plante and I would share the White House beat. Share? If he had slapped me I would not have felt such pain. "What made you change your mind?" I asked.

"There was no change of mind. This was always in the cards."

"But you told me yourself I had the job, the job of chief correspondent, the same job I have now." I could not control my agitation.

"No, I didn't."

I turned to Ed Fouhy, my witness. But he said, "No, he didn't."

I left the office in an aching fog, bumping into my old White House producer Lane Venardos. He confided that, indeed, after they had told me I had the job they had asked Bill Plante to be my number two. He had refused, and that's when the sharing idea had come up. If they had said, "Lesley, we think you suck as White House correspondent, but we're going to let you stay there with Plante," I would have accepted it. If they'd said, "Lesley, we changed our minds," I would have gotten over it. But to tell me I hadn't heard what I'd heard was unbearable; it felt like a double cross. I got angry and stayed that way for a long time. In fact, I entered what I now call the "angry years." How many were there? I'm embarrassed to admit . . . ten long ones. A decade of rage.

I WAS BACK at the White House for Jimmy Carter's last full day as president, which began at 4:56 A.M. He came into the briefing room at that predawn hour to say, "We have now reached an agreement with Iran which will result, I believe, in the freedom of our American hostages." Carter wanted to greet the hostages in Germany while he was still president. But between 5 A.M. and 5 P.M., as during so many days before, nothing happened. I said on the air that night that White House officials believed that "the Iranians want to deprive 'The Great Satan' of his final wish."

CBS went on the air the next morning at 9 A.M. to cover Inauguration Day. I was in the briefing room reporting that even though Jimmy Carter would not be president when the hostages were freed, "he'll still fly to Wiesbaden to greet them. Mr. Reagan has asked him to be the official U.S. representative there."

At noon Ronald Reagan, 69, became the oldest man to take the oath of office as president of the United States. The cameras got a shot of Jimmy Carter on the podium with his eyes closed.

Two hours later Walter Cronkite reported that the planes carrying the 52 American hostages had cleared Iranian airspace; in his luncheon toast at 2:16 the new president announced, "The hostages are free!"

Carter's intimates are convinced that the Reagan camp had worked behind the scenes to delay the release of the hostages until Reagan was sworn in. Former Carter aide Peter Bourne writes in his biography of Jimmy Carter that Reagan's campaign manager William Casey (who later became CIA director) cut a deal with the Iranians to postpone the release in exchange for arms. This was never proved. But, Bourne writes, "Within days [of the Inauguration], the Reagan administration began shipping a long laundry list of military equipment to Iran." [1]

We were on the air all day reporting both stories: the Inauguration and the hostage release. "Walter," I said from the White House, "I wish I'd been on Air Force One with Carter [on his way home to Plains] to see his face as they told him that the hostages had cleared Iranian airspace."

Just then Reagan was visiting Tip O'Neill's office, where the speaker showed him the desk that had been used by Grover Cleveland. The new president noted that he had portrayed him in a movie. O'Neill reminded him that he'd played Grover Cleveland Alexander, the baseball player, not Grover Cleveland the president.

My role in the afternoon was as color commentator for the Inauguration parade, effusing over high school bands and palomino horses, and of course the reviewing stand where the handsome POTUS and his costar watched, beaming. Nancy wore a $3,000 red dress and coat by Adolfo with matching Jackie Kennedy pillbox hat.

We kept up our schizophrenic reporting for the rest of the day. At one point Walter said, "Lesley, we've just been advised that the planes carrying the American hostages have landed at Athens Airport. The hostages are tasting freedom for the first time since November 4, 1979."

THE WHITE HOUSE would be run by a troika: James Baker, a corporate lawyer–type conservative; Edwin Meese, representing the right wing; and pragmatist Michael Deaver, a public relations man. They liked to call the setup a board of directors, but it was more like a raging windstorm. Reagan's first-term White House would be a swirl of conflicting ambitions circling an eye that too often gave only sketchy guidance and paid little attention.

Ed Meese, 49, Reagan's chief of staff from his days as governor of California, ran the transition and had fully expected to be named chief of staff at the White House. But Nancy was warned that Cheerful Ed (whom she once described as "a jump-off-the-cliff-with-the-flag-flying conservative."[2]) wasn't up to the job. She persuaded her husband to pick Jim Baker, 50, a lawyer from Houston who had run not one but two campaigns against Ronald Reagan (Ford's and Bush's). Mrs. Reagan liked him anyway — Baker was handsome, after all — and so the organized and pragmatic Texan became chief of staff. Meese, who revealed that he often sat around listening to the police band on his radio, became the issues counselor — in other words, the keeper of the flame.

The third leg of the triumvirate was Deaver, 42, a former public relations man who had worked for Reagan when he was governor of California. Now he would be the guardian of the Reagan image and Nancy's man in the West Wing. This would be the first White House in history to have its media adviser at the very pinnacle of decision making and power. Actually, it wasn't a troika in the beginning. Ed Meese held most of the reins, overseeing not only the National Security Council but the Domestic Council and the Cabinet as well. But from day one he began losing influence to Baker, who accumulated authority like a power pickpocket. He won control over the Budget Office, which inevitably became the seat of policy making and exerted influence over the rest of the government through a cunning operation of press wooing and manipulation. Baker held two other cards — and they were big ones. One was Deaver, who usually sided with him in what became a decathalon of sibling rivalry between Baker and Meese. The other was Nancy Reagan, who would continually weigh in against Meese and the other Reaganites.[3]

Again the special training I'd had as a teenage girl allowed me to recognize the nest of jealousies and back stabbings. The Reagan White House was more riven with palace intrigue and machinations than anything else I'd ever seen. How enchanting of grown men. While many of the rivalries were personal, they were played out as ideological crusades, with the Meese side acting as protectors of holy dogmas against the Bakerite infidels. Reagan liked to deflect criticism about all the internal warfare with a joke: "Sometimes in our administration the right hand doesn't know what the far-right hand is doing."

What emerged from this trifurcated organization was something close to a Hollywood studio with a movie star at the heart, supported by an agent-lawyer, an accountant-manager, and a publicity director. Most movie stars don't read their contracts and don't see to their own finances; many don't even decide which films to accept or reject. And when it comes to the way they conduct their on-screen business, there's someone who tells them where to stand, what to say, and when to say it. There was even a head of the studio, a Lew Wasserman–Michael Eisner type, who *really* ran the place: Nancy.

As UNHAPPY as I was with my new arrangement, I got along with Bill Plante, a fastidious man with a sonorous voice who looked a little like the actor Robert Vaughn. Bill was one of the best-liked members of the press corps: decent and easygoing even when all six of his sons would call on the same day, a gourmet with a sense of humor. We were friends and became better friends, even though I was Oscar to his Felix. Bill Lysoled the booth every Thursday. After a while Jackie Adams joined us in the booth as the weekend reporter. When she, an African American, got a load of Bill's spritz-and-mop-up act, she said with a laugh, "I just love watching white folks clean!"

Bill and I decided to "share" by rotating every other week. When it was his turn to do the *Evening News* pieces, I did *Morning News*. And vice versa. It worked, though I stayed angry at my bosses. My father told me I was not handling myself well, and Aaron agreed with him. But Dolly, incensed over my demotion, goaded me to go see Bill Small — he was now president of NBC News — about jumping ship. Small had already lured Marvin and Bernie Kalb, as well as Roger Mudd, away from CBS. A friend said, "NBC's the exile place. That's where all the White Russians hang out." I made the call and began discussing a move to NBC.

TAYLOR WAS THREE and the most adorable little girl alive, with the bluest eyes and sunniest disposition. When we dropped her off at the Methodist Church Nursery School down the street her first day, all the other children were clinging to their mothers, screaming, "Don't leave me!" Not Taylor. She never looked back. She loved everything they did at school: painting, playing, and above all being with other children.

Aaron was the father of all fathers. Why is it that dads are the playmates, the fun ones? And moms, even those who work full-time, the disciplinarians? There was an upside to this division of labor: he did all the things with Taylor I hated, like taking her to the park.

By 1981 I had bonded with two other women at CBS News who had children. Joan Barone, producer of *Face the Nation* and one of my best friends, had adopted Sarah (my godchild), and Rita Braver, then CBS's legal correspondent, had Meredith. Rita lived in the same building we did, and Taylor and Meredith were devoted to each other. We three women, our husbands, and daughters, spent many a night with the diaper bags and bottles and bibs and swings and pacifiers.

124

Luckily for me, Carter had traveled very little in the last two years. I would be lucky again. Reagan didn't leave town much, preferring, I was told, to be home with "Mommy" every night. That's what he called Nancy. I told Aaron: Don't even think it.

REAGAN HELD his first formal presidential news conference on January 29. Before it started, Jim Brady told the assembled reporters that he expected us to conduct ourselves with decorum and dignity. "We are respectfully requesting that members of the press wishing to ask questions remain seated, raise their hands, and wait to be called upon." This would be a far cry — and I do mean far cry — from the way we had shouted and whooped at Jimmy Carter. My colleagues were sure it would never work. Phil Gailey of the Washington *Star* said, "It's like asking hogs not to root." Ted Knapp of Scripps Howard added, "I think this is the first true test of the Reagan presidency: not whether he can stand up to the Russians but whether he can get control of the animals at the press conference."

Well, he did. "It was the first laid-back California-mellow news conference Washington has ever seen," I said on the air. It started with Reagan, tall and trim, doing his John Wayne walk down a long, red-carpeted hallway into the East Room. What a picture! It said: This is a president.

He made some news. Setting a confrontational tone for U.S. relations with the Soviets, the new president said, "They reserve unto themselves the right to commit any crime, to lie, to cheat, in order to attain [their one-world government]." Such throw-down-the-gauntlet rhetoric hadn't been heard from an American president in years, and it wouldn't be popular.

But generally Reagan ducked the hard questions, explaining at least five times that he hadn't finished studying whichever issue was being asked about. And when he pointed to Judy Woodruff and then me, he called us both "young lady." It wasn't, we learned, that he didn't know our names. He simply couldn't tell us apart.

Questions about just how involved Reagan was in his own presidency bubbled up almost immediately. In a briefing on February 2, Deputy Press Secretary Larry Speakes was asked whether other people such as Ed Meese were really running the executive branch. "On the record, the president's role is superior."

"Then he's in charge?"

"Oh, yes."

Speakes was also cross-examined about a report called *The Imperial Media* written by Robert Entman for a conservative think tank in California. It was filled with recommendations on how Reagan could "tame" the press corps. Don't tell your press secretary everything, said the report.

The president "should not make a fetish of getting on television" and should inundate the press with facts and figures: "It could reduce the total value of reporting since dry data are often defined as unnewsworthy."

This hit like a cruise missile since many of the recommendations were being implemented. One day without warning or recourse, we were notified that the number of television reporters in the pool would be reduced from three (one for each network) to just one. Well, who did they think they were? This was clearly a call to arms, so we put up our dukes, refusing to send anyone to Reagan's photo opportunities. We thought if we deprived this White House of its life-support system — pictures on television — it would cave. Both sides dug in, but on the fourth day someone blinked — and it wasn't Reagan. It was NBC. "We need the video," said an executive there. By the next day we had all surrendered, and that's how the "tight pool" got tighter. And the Reagan press corps became less mighty than it had been when Carter was president.

Of course, the public loved it. They wanted a president who would stand up to powerful forces such as the press. The people were on his side. We should have known things would be different when Reagan got his Secret Service code name. Carter's had been Deacon; Reagan's was Rawhide.

There were so many ways the two presidents were different. Reagan seemed to love the little "household" chores and amenities Carter had found so odious, for instance, picture taking with congressmen and their important constituents. His many acts of courtesy and considerateness would make it difficult to cross him. He was Rawhide with a core of natural sweetness.

AROUND THAT TIME our radio tech, Lil Zimmerman, grew sullen. She was having her bathroom at home retiled, and right in the middle of the job, her contractor put the project on hold. The White House had called. Nancy Reagan wanted her bathroom retiled, and Lil's job would just have to wait.[4]

When the tile man returned to Lil's a few weeks later, he told her a fascinating story. One day while he was caulking away, Mrs. Reagan was getting ready to host a luncheon to promote volunteerism. Her cohost, Barbara Bush, showed up and horrified the first lady. The tile man reported that Nancy, aghast, had exclaimed, "You're wearing red!" That was *Nancy's* color. The tile man reported that Nancy sent Barbara home to change:

"And never wear red again as long as I live in this house."

When Lil finished the story, I saw visions of a nifty little scoop, but first I had to get the encounter confirmed, something I knew Nancy

Reagan would never do. So I called Mrs. Bush's office, but her press secretary stiffed me with a firm "No comment." I had no choice but to sit on the story for years; in fact, I never reported it, though I believe it to be true. I say that because the vice president's wife never wore red — she was partial to "Barbara blue" — until 1988, when George Bush ran for president. Then she wore red a lot.

ON FEBRUARY 5, Jim Brady escorted Sam Donaldson, Judy Woodruff, and me to the library in the lower level of the White House. We were to get a three-on-one interview with the president, but no cameras were to be allowed. Four armchairs were arranged in front of a roaring fire — nice touch. It was four in the afternoon, leaving us just enough time to put together a one-dimensional story about what the president said. No leeway to get reactions. Brady told us we'd have no more than 40 minutes.

With that, in walked Rawhide. My first impression: he was more wrinkled and frail than I'd realized. His face was ruddy and he stood straight and tall, but up close he didn't seem sturdy. The word "vulnerable" came to mind. Within a minute that voice, warm as cashmere, was apologizing to Judy and me for calling us "young ladies."

We asked about the budget, but Reagan talked in circles, curlicues, and mazes. Trying to pin him down on the inconsistencies of Reaganomics was like sawing into fog. We did not get a single quote that made sense.

"What's surprised you in this job?" Judy asked.

"My schedule has been so filled. I find myself pleading, 'When do I get time to be president?'" he said, and we laughed because he was so likable. "I miss spending time outdoors. At the White House you're a bird in a gilded cage."

REAGAN HAD MADE lowering taxes the main focus of his campaign. When candidate George Bush had called the plan "voodoo economics," Reagan and his supply-side sidekicks had argued that there would be such a burst of savings and business activity from the tax-cut stimulus, the government would be rolling in revenues and major cuts in government programs and services would be all but unnecessary.

It came as something of a surprise, then, when the president began talking of massive reductions in social programs. On February 3 he met with a group of mayors and then with members of the Congressional Black Caucus enraged over the planned cuts, but bedside manner counts in politics. Jimmy Carter's aloofness had hurt his programs; Ronald Reagan's sweetness helped his. I said that night, "He lullabyed them. The meeting seemed to have a subduing effect on these often fiery members of Congress."

127

None of the specific details of the budget cuts were made public. So the next day I worked the phones, calling as many congressmen as I could. Bingo! A Republican from the Midwest got on the phone himself and told me he had a book of the budget cuts Reagan planned to propose. "It's confidential," he said.

"Could I come see it?" I asked.

"Sure. I don't see why not."

So I went up to his office on the Hill and met with him privately. Then he and I together went to his Xerox machine and copied the entire book. I have no idea why he did that. I had never met him before.

My producer, Susan Zirinsky, had a reputation for wizardry. Unlike other producers, she seemed to thrive on my tardiness — good thing, because this one came in especially late. But Susan still managed to build a package of graphics to go with my script: that the biggest budget bites would come out of subsidies for the poor such as food stamps, child nutrition, job training, and unemployment benefits — 190 programs in all, including Medicaid. I also reported that even Social Security was on the chopping block. This was a healthy scoop and the first real sign that tax cuts would involve some serious pain.

Reagan became the mean stepfather of the government he'd been elected to oversee but that he held in contempt: he named antienvironmentalists to run the environmental programs and foes of civil rights to run those programs. It was cynical, as was the supply-side program, which had as a subsidiary goal the starving of Lyndon Johnson's Great Society programs into malnutrition by calling for nearly $50 billion in budget cuts. They were supposed to offset the more than $50 billion in tax cuts and a three-year, 27 percent rise in military spending, an increase so huge that experts questioned whether the Pentagon could spend it all. In an address to Congress on February 18 the president never hinted that "sacrifice" would be involved, though he did mention that the national debt had reached a trillion dollars: "That would be a stack of $1,000 bills 67 miles high."

The Democrats and many columnists swung wildly at the plan: this was just "trickle-down economics, welfare for the rich." Reagan ignored the criticisms and flew off to Santa Barbara for the first of many vacations at his ranch (he would spend 345 days of his presidency there), 688 acres in the Santa Ynez Mountains, 2,200 feet above the Pacific Ocean. His mornings would include horseback riding and chopping wood. Rawhide.

Reagan's well-spun image as a take-charge cowboy clashed with what we were hearing about his anything but take-charge style of decision making. In fact, the usual method was that his staff would simply reach a compromise so he wouldn't have to choose among various options. In big meetings he rarely asked questions, instead deviating from the subject under discussion with unrelated anecdotes. Once we learned that a national security decision paper had been okayed without Reagan ever being in the room. On February 26 Jim Brady had to answer for that at the daily briefing:

BRADY: The president was not physically present but—
REPORTER: Did he approve this? Did he say, "Do it this way"? or did Ed Meese say, "We'll do it this way"?
BRADY: He concurred with the final result.
REPORTER: After it had been taken?
BRADY: No, before it had been taken.
REPORTER: Is he a mere invisible participant?

Except for meeting with members of Congress to push his programs and working on his speeches, Reagan kept a healthy distance from the burdens of office. He'd come in after 9 A.M. I used to see him walking to the Oval Office along the colonnade that rims the Rose Garden. Reporters were allowed to stand next to the Secret Service agent guarding one of the doors, and I often got a smile and a wave as Reagan sauntered by. He left the office between five and six and on Wednesdays as early as three.

Did the public care about the lackadaisical approach? Not really. But misgivings about his policies were materializing. His plans to cut into social programs were unpopular. A Gallup Poll in February showed that he had a lower approval rating than most presidents did at that stage, lower even than Jimmy Carter's in the early months of his presidency. And Nancy wasn't helping, especially her "reimperializing" of the White House: the return of silver trumpets, mink coats, and white tie and tails.

With the falling approval ratings came an edginess. Mike Deaver began begging the president to stop answering reporters' questions on the run. But like Jimmy Carter, Reagan had an almost reflexive reaction to Sam Donaldson's shouting: he *had* to respond. That was part of his natural sense of courtesy and gentility. The problem was, he was gaffe prone. In our CBS polling we discovered that people were fully aware of Reagan's propensity for blunders, but they didn't care. They'd elected him for different reasons: to reassert a national spirit and sense of purpose. And after the brooding, pious Jimmy Carter, they wanted a president who could make them feel good.

But with his declining popularity, the White House tried to discourage his off-the-cuff responses to our questions. One danger zone was the South Lawn of the White House on Friday afternoons, when the Reagans would leave for Camp David. As he headed for his helicopter, the president would invariably stop to answer our questions.

Mike Deaver put up ropes to pen us in, but Reagan found ways to penetrate the barriers. Then one day as POTUS, the bee, headed toward the shouting flowers, a long, loud thunder drowned out our questions. Reagan, who was slightly deaf anyway, put his hand to his ear. "Can't hear you," he mouthed. We all screamed out in as loud a chorus as we could, but Deaver had found the answer. From that Friday on, he ordered the helicopter engines revved up just as the Reagans hit the lawn. Our honey-pot days were over.

MARCH 6. Walter Cronkite's last broadcast after 19 years as anchorman. When he said good-bye that night, I had a lump in my throat. "And that's the way it is," he said. "I'll be away on assignment, and Dan Rather will be sitting in here for the next few years. Good night." The end of Uncle Walter. *Esquire* called it "the death-of-God departure."[5]

Dan Rather, who had one of the highest Q-ratings (recognizability plus likability) in television news, had had offers from ABC and NBC. Roger Mudd, Walter's understudy for almost ten years, had lost out in the who-will-replace-Walter war because CBS didn't want to lose Dan. Besides, Dan had broader experience than Roger — stints at the White House, in London and Vietnam, and on *60 Minutes*. More than that, Dan was liked by the troops. He was one of the most generous men in the company.

Back in 1975 Aaron had been in Tehran writing a story about the shah's treatment of the Kurds when he disappeared. Clay Felker sent out search parties, I called the U.S. Embassy in Tehran, but we couldn't find him and began to fear the worst. Dan called me and said he had a pal in Iran who owed him a favor. Two days later the friend, Max McCarthy, found Aaron in a Tehran hospital under quarantine with a case of hepatitis. The point is, I never called Dan; he called me and then extended himself. Scores of people at CBS have similar stories to tell.

But as the new anchorman, Rather got off to a shaky start. If Walter was composed and unruffled, Dan was intense and barbed-wiry, and the public shied away. In his first week he lost 9 percent of the audience.

ONE MORNING as I was speeding through *The Washington Post*'s Style section I fell upon an item about a movie called *Eyewitness*, written by Steve Tesich, who had won an Oscar for *Breaking Away*. He was quoted as saying he'd been inspired by a crush on a reporter: "I developed this all-consuming fascination for Lesley Stahl." My eyebrows did a Groucho Marx. Me? Nothing like this had ever happened to me. "I used to see her on the screen," he said, "and wonder how far I would go in order to meet her." The movie starred Sigourney Weaver, who coincidentally had been Aaron's college girlfriend.

THE PROBLEMS with the Reagan presidency were forgotten on March 30. He addressed the building and construction trades unions of the AFL-CIO at the Hilton Hotel in Washington, telling them that crime in the streets had surged by 10 percent. After he left, I stayed behind for a few minutes, wandered out, and found a scene of choking fear: a man lying facedown, a narrow river of blood trickling from his head. What happened? I asked. "The president was shot at."

"The man?"

"That's Jim Brady."

Shaken, I ran inside, called the desk, and blurted out what I'd seen and heard. "We know," said Bill Galbraith. Our cameraman, Charlie Wilson, had rolled even as shots rang out around him. John Hinckley, the would-be assassin, had been standing in the press area.

As I made my way back to the White House, Dan Rather went on the air. For the first time in years, the country would have to get through a national trauma without Walter Cronkite. "President Reagan, according to the White House, is unscathed," said Dan. The president — I repeat for emphasis — was not hit."

A good 20 minutes after Dan and the other network anchors reported that the bullets had missed the president, Lyn Nofziger, Reagan's political counselor, announced that indeed the president had been hit — in the left side of his chest. "But he's all right."

Poor Dan. He was at the mercy of wire copy and rumors. "Well, this is a change," he said. "What you have had in the last minute, in the last few seconds, is a change. The president was struck or at least grazed, we don't know the extent of it."

This was rough, spontaneous television, covering a crisis while the White House was trying to play down any sense of real danger to the president's life. In his book *Bare Knuckles and Back Rooms: My Life in American Politics*, Ed Rollins wrote that Nofziger had called him at that point and said, "The guy's really in bad shape. They don't know if he's gonna make it or not." But the press and therefore the public were kept in the dark. We learned later that when Reagan had first arrived at the hospital, he had gone down on one knee and said, "I can't breathe." But everything we were told for the next several days was intended to minimize the gravity of the president's condition.

I was back at the White House in time for a four o'clock briefing by Brady's deputy, Larry Speakes, thrust so suddenly into the role of press secretary. He had been a press aide in the Nixon and Ford administrations but had had no relationship at all with Reagan.

"Larry, is the president in surgery?" I asked.

"I can't say, Lesley."

"We have confirmed reports," I told him. "So have other networks, so have the wires. Can't you help us?"

"As soon as we can confirm it, we will and —"

"Larry," I interrupted, "Reagan's brother, Neil, has been told that the president is in surgery right now, that he's already had blood transfusions. Is your information going to be that far behind what we're getting from other sources?"

"No, Lesley. We will do our very best to keep it up."

Down in the Situation Room, Cabinet secretaries and other top officials (Vice President Bush was on his way back from a trip to Austin) were watching Larry's performance, wringing their hands. When Speakes muffed a question about national security, Secretary of State Alexander Haig was so appalled he rushed to the Briefing Room, barged onto the podium and began blurting in his usual disjointed Haigspeak: "The president's condition as we know it — stable. Now undergoing surgery. And there are absolutely no alert measures that are necessary at this time or contemplated."

Some answers at last, I thought, looking up at Haig from my front-row seat. But he was trembling and perspiring. If his purpose was to convey a sense of calm authority, he was failing miserably. And he didn't make matters better when he declared, "As of now, I am in control here in the White House," because on television the secretary of state looked distinctly *out* of control. What the White House was working so hard to avoid, Haig's impetuosity had just created: a sense of crisis.

A little after five, Rather repeated a wire story that Jim Brady had died. He turned to me. "Lesley, can you confirm this report . . . that Jim Brady is dead?"

"Dan, I'm sorry. I cannot. We have been unable to confirm almost every report as you've been telling it to the American people today."

Ten minutes later Dan said the report of Brady's passing was confirmed and he asked for a moment of silence. It took another five minutes before Larry Speakes appeared in the briefing room to deny the reports. Rather was beside himself, and so was I.

"Lesley Stahl, you're at the White House," said Dan. "Did Larry Speakes say that the report about Jim Brady is untrue? Not true?"

"He said it is *not true*," I replied.

It was right around then that we began hearing about the president's quips and one-liners. We were told that when he had first seen Nancy at the hospital he had said, "Honey, I just forgot to duck." He was quoted as joking with the doctors in the operating room, "Please tell me you're Republicans!" These were meant to reassure the country that he was all right, a message reinforced by the hospital spokesman, Dr. Dennis O'Leary. "He was in no time in any serious danger." By contrast, O'Leary

132

sounded dire about Brady's brain injury. There was extensive damage of the right hemisphere of the brain, though there was some hope: he was responding to commands.

In a briefing the next morning Dr. O'Leary gave us more one-liners. "My favorite line," he said, was Reagan telling the nurses, " 'If I got this much attention in Hollywood, I'd never have left.' " The jokes became the heart and soul of the information we got, along with assurances that the president was perfectly able to make decisions. To prove it, Larry Speakes passed out a copy of the Dairy Price Support Bill, which the president had signed in the hospital early that morning.

The idea that all was well with this 70-year-old man who had just been shot in the left side of the chest was not believable, at least not to me. But most of the White House staff was as much in the dark as we were. David Gergen, director of communications, told me years later, "Even I didn't know how bad it was. It was 'incorrect' for us to ask. There was a real strong sense it would be read as an invasion of privacy. And anyway, we felt it was important to convey stability."

Larry Speakes was pelted with if-he's-in-such-good-shape-why-can't-we-see-him questions. In other words, prove it! Give us at least a photo. But Speakes said no.

STAHL: He doesn't look good?
SPEAKES: He looks very good.
STAHL: How can you say he looks good? You haven't seen him.
SPEAKES: I am told by the doctors.
Q: Does he still have the tubes in his nose? Is that why you didn't let the photographer in? Is he tired-looking?
SPEAKES: No, he's not tired-looking.
STAHL: There's a feeling that there's something you folks don't want us to see.

Speakes changed the subject, telling us that a second-grade class from Annandale, Virginia, had sent the president some drawings, including some of him in bed.

Q: They know more than we do, then. [laughter]
Q: Could you release those?

I did a story that night strongly suggesting that the White House was orchestrating a cover-up. What we didn't know was that the head of the studio had taken over. Nancy was in charge of all decisions, including one to hide from the public just how close the president had come to dying. Several days later, when the hue and cry for some evidence of the president's well-being became deafening, Nancy authorized the release

133

of one photograph, but not until all the tubes that were draining his chest had been removed.

Years later the president's daughter Maureen told me that when she arrived at the hospital a few days after the shooting, she found Nancy, her stepmother (whom Maureen had once called "the Dragon Lady"), all alone in the room adjacent to the president's, huddled in the corner of a couch listening to the nurses pound on Reagan's chest to get the phlegm up. "She looked so vulnerable and afraid. He was so much sicker than anyone realized," Maureen said, "and so I sat there with Nancy and we listened together, and I forgave her for all those years."

All doubts about Reagan's fitness vanished when he left the hospital, waving and shining his handsome smile. It was 12 days after the shooting. "What are you going to do when you get back to the White House?" one of my colleagues shouted. "Sit down!" said Reagan. His wit and the grace with which he handled what could easily have been a crisis were comforting, his courage admired. His poll numbers sprang up by 11 points, and he emerged with a new dimension of heroism and specialness.

Reagan, who had always been fatalistic, became convinced while in the hospital that there was a reason he had been spared. He told Mike Deaver, "I'm going to pay more attention to my own instincts," and Deaver told me that from that time on, Reagan was far more stubborn than he'd been about pursuing his own ideas.

I WAS DEVELOPING good sources inside the White House, benefiting from the feuding between Meese and Baker. I also kept in touch with my contacts in the bureaucracy who stayed on, administration after administration. On April 22, after a call to an old friend in the Agriculture Department, I was able to break another grain story: that Reagan was going to lift Carter's embargo against the Soviet Union in two days, on Friday.

The next day at the briefing, Larry Speakes denied my report: "The president has not made a decision on whether to lift the embargo. It is still under review."

After the briefing I met with Larry privately in his office and told him, "I'm 100 percent sure I was right."

He told me he had been instructed by Ed Meese to deny it. "What am I supposed to do? Meese is my boss."

"What you're supposed to do, Larry," I said, "is tell the truth."

The next day, Friday, the White House announced the lifting of the grain embargo.

Despite all the efforts to control the "imperial media," we network correspondents were still overindulged like a trio of only children. But now there was an interloper that would in time threaten our pampered status: CNN, the cable news company, with its new team at the White House. Ted Turner, CNN's founder and owner, took the three networks to court, charging that we were monopolizing the coverage of major news events by excluding his reporters from the press pools. But CNN was refusing to pay its share, a quarter of the pool costs. Still, Turner won. CNN joined the pool, doling out just 16 percent of the costs.

THE REAGANS went off for a second vacation at their ranch in Santa Barbara. Just eight weeks after being shot, the president was horseback riding and chopping wood again, and there was joy throughout the land.

The press was housed a good 45 minutes away, without any access to the ranch. So we began scouting the surrounding mountains in search of a lookout point for our cameras. We found a spot about two and a half miles away, but our pictures were so fuzzy and distant, the president was no more recognizable than an ant. To remedy that we brought in a high-powered lens from CBS Sports. I went on the air saying, "There's the president getting off his horse, removing the bridle, and heading for the barn." I had to say that because the pictures were still grainy and the president's horse was smaller than a Chihuahua.

Reagan's budget plans were drawing more and more criticism, especially his proposal to cut Social Security benefits for early retirees. The press reporting was unrelentingly negative. Many books have been written about how easy the press went on Reagan after he was shot, but that certainly did not apply to his economic program. I was hearing from my sources within the White House itself that the plan was flawed. On May 28 I did a story about how the deficit was creeping up $8 billion higher than projected. Asked "How much longer can you blame the Carter administration for the increasing deficit?" Speakes said, "Awhile longer."

It began to bother me that a man as ill informed as Ronald Reagan was setting the economic course for the country against the advice of so many of his own people. That was true of his foreign policy as well. My concerns were heightened at his third news conference on June 16. Asked about the Israelis' recent attack on an Iraqi nuclear reactor in which they had used U.S.-made jets, Reagan replied, "I can't answer that." On Israel's refusal to sign the Nuclear Nonproliferation Treaty? "I haven't given very much thought to that particular question there." Pakistan's refusal to sign the treaty? "I won't answer the last part of the question." Earlier in the week he had bumped into his own housing secretary at a reception for big-city mayors and said, "How are you, Mr. Mayor. How are things in your city?" There were quiet little suspicions among the reporters that Reagan, the course setter, was sinking into senility.

□

DESPITE the press's critical coverage of the supply side economic program, it passed easily. Reagan worked tirelessly, meeting with and cajoling scores upon scores of congressmen. But what pushed it over the top was the president's televised appeal for public support. There was an outpouring of affection for Reagan after his recovery; he had bonded with the American people in a way we reporters, who were too close in, hadn't grasped. Winning this, which he did by wide margins in both the House and Senate, was almost like Moses parting the waters, it was such an oceanic shift of forces. With a 25 percent cut in income taxes over three years, a massive increase in military spending, and a deep gash in spending on social programs, he produced an historic change of direction for the country, which had been on a course of liberal spending since FDR's New Deal.

In the campaign, when Reagan had said he would cut taxes, it had been taken as the usual come-on. But then he did it. Here was a politician who kept his promise. This in itself was historic and gave him the aura of a can-do, effective leader. Yet there seemed to be a carelessness about the exercise, a lack of concern with the bottom line. An air of irresponsibility would become a shadow trademark of the Reagan presidency. It would infect the national psyche.

DICK THRELKELD, my old *Morning News* partner, called to tell me he was leaving CBS to go to ABC News. While Bill Small at NBC was skimming off the cream of our veteran correspondents, Roone Arledge at ABC was raiding the crop of up-and-comers. He had already lured ten on-air correspondents from CBS, including Sylvia Chase and Jack Lawrence, and now Threlkeld, another star of the new generation. It had the effect of concentrating my bosses' minds on the possibility that I might leave as well. Somehow they found out I was talking to Bill Small.

Negotiations for a new contract began immediately, and I was offered a lot more money. I told Bud Benjamin that my unhappiness was not about money; it was about assignments. Why was I the only White House correspondent who never got to anchor a weekend newscast? When they asked me to substitute anchor on Schieffer's *Saturday News*, it only annoyed me. My dad said I was being unreasonable, Aaron told me my attitude was unseemly, but Dolly agreed that they were just throwing me scraps; it was an affront. They offered me more money. "Fellas," I said, "it's not about money." But they wouldn't believe me. They thought it was *always* about money and that I was just being a tough negotiator.

IF THE SHOOTING made Reagan a hero, his handling of the PATCO strike made him nearly invincible. On August 3 the 13,000 members of the

Professional Air Traffic Controllers walked off their jobs in the first nation-wide strike of federal employees in American history. It was an illegal action and Rawhide didn't flinch.

We in the media gathered in the Rose Garden, the perfect setting for the theater we were about to witness. The president started off gently by describing his fondness for unions from the days when he had been president of the Screen Actors Guild. He was accommodating; I was sure he was going to offer a compromise. But then he dropped his bomb: "They are in violation of the law, and if they do not report for work within 48 hours, they have forfeited their jobs and will be terminated. . . . There is just no other choice." In other words, pals, you're fired. Two days later, when Reagan made good on his threat, I said that he was decisive and that "he has managed to put the American people on his side, the strikers on the other side." The controllers predicted that the air system could not survive without them, but it did. Of course, Reagan had no way of knowing it would. He got lucky. It was only by the grace of God that a plane didn't crash.

The end result was that labor's already waning influence went into a further slide and Reagan looked like a strong leader willing to stand up for principle, a man of action. But this picture of strength and resolve would soon clash with another one: the sense that POTUS was detached came back like a stubborn infection, along with a feeling that he was neglectful of the responsibilities of office.

In early August Reagan was back in Santa Barbara for a monthlong vacation. The traveling press corps was invited up to his ranch to witness his signing — with 24 pens — the tax-cut and budget measures that constituted the heart of Reaganomics.[6] Taking pictures of the event wasn't so easy. Just as Reagan was signing, a heavy fog rolled in, cutting visibility to just a few feet: a metaphor, so it seemed, for the nebulous and uncertain plan he was initiating. The most revealing part of the event involved Reagan's dog. As he patted him, a reporter asked, "What's his name?" The president couldn't remember.

This was followed by a number of incidents that suggested that Ed Meese, not Reagan, was the man in charge. It started when navy F-14s got into a dogfight over the Gulf of Sidra and shot down two Libyan jets. Meese decided not to wake Reagan, so the president didn't learn of the confrontation for six hours and 24 minutes after it had been reported on the morning TV news broadcasts. I said on the air, "The commander in chief was the last to know."

A few days later, when reporters tried to ask Reagan about his plans for the MX missile, Meese interrupted to answer for him. That did it. Just three weeks after pulverizing PATCO, Ronald Reagan entered the Carter zone of ridicule. Johnny Carson barbecued him; Don Wright of the (now

137

defunct) *Miami News* drew Reagan in bed on the phone: "World War III? Six hours ago? No kidding? Well, gee, thanks for calling, Ed."

Newsweek ran a devastating article in its September 7 issue entitled "A Disengaged Presidency." It reported "displays of inattention and ignorance," of Reagan's reliance on "cue cards" when he dealt with congressmen and foreign leaders, and of his repeated inability to answer questions about issues. "He is easily bored, alternately joking and yawning through subjects that don't interest him. All he wants to do is tell stories about his movie days." The White House tried to discredit the piece—Jim Baker attributed the remarks to a few "dissatisfied staffers."[7] But it rang true to me.

I TOOK Taylor with me to Santa Barbara and threw her a birthday party on the beach with a clown and the entire press corps and their children. None of us ever complained about Reagan's penchant for long, lazy vacations.

The press was housed in the Santa Barbara Sheraton, a second-class hotel on the ocean. After Plains it seemed four-star. CBS took the same suite on the first floor each time we went, so the hotel constructed a platform bed for us to store much of our equipment under, including our phones. One night when we weren't in town, a guest called the front desk: "I'm going nuts. I swear, my bed is ringing!"

We were engaged in a lens war with ABC and NBC: Who would get the best pictures of the Reagan ranch? We had graduated from the sports camera to one that was used for space shots, but you still couldn't tell for sure that it was Reagan and not some other guy up on the horse. That's when our cameraman Greg Amadon went out, rented a huge motor-powered lens for $600 a week, and adapted a giant astronomer's reflector telescope onto it. It was cosmic, as big as Woody Allen's Orgasmatron. It was so big it took three jeeps to transport it up the rugged mountain road and two hours to set the damn thing up. Assembled, the camera looked like a mouse dangling off the end of a dragon.

But when we got the cassette, it was magical: Reagan—unmistakably! Riding, walking. Nancy in her bathrobe. Mrs. Reagan was convinced we could see into their bathroom. We assured the White House we couldn't, but she ordered all kinds of barriers and shades put up anyway. When Reagan saw the pictures, he wondered what the press would do if one day while we were taping he played a joke on us by grabbing his chest and falling off his horse!

138   I TOOK a week off from Santa Barbara to go to New York. My contract negotiations were heating up. Bill Small had offered me a job at NBC,

though he couldn't promise as visible an assignment as the White House. Yet I was still angry at CBS. I wanted my superiors there to admit they had lied to me. Instead they blandished me with prizes such as having me sit in as Rather's substitute when he went on vacation. One week in The Chair as anchorperson—a first for any woman at CBS.

When the week was up and I still refused to sign the contract, I was summoned to "Black Rock," CBS's headquarters in New York, for a private audience with the chairman, Bill Paley, an elegant man who was surprisingly easy to talk to. I spent an hour in his office discussing the president, pre-Columbian art, prime-time sitcoms, Europe during the war, his father's cigar business, my father's chemical business. When my time was up, he said, "Oh, by the way, I hope you stay with us." But I was still holding out.

THERE WAS GROWING CONSTERNATION on Wall Street at the prospect of out-of-control budget deficits. Interest rates went up, and Reagan responded by looking for an additional $13 billion to $16 billion in spending cuts. He turned, as he had before, to the so-called Boll Weevils, the conservative southern Democrats, as allies. "CBS News has learned," I said on September 14, that more cuts were planned "in food stamps, student loans, and unemployment compensation." Two days later I had another "CBS News has learned" when I reported that Reagan would propose a three-month deferral of Social Security cost-of-living allowance increases.

The Democrats came to life. They don't call Social Security a "sacred cow" for nothing. With his singular ability to act both tough and sweet, the president fired back with humor: "I've listened to those Chicken Littles who proclaim the sky is falling. But this concern about a plan not even in effect yet is nothing more than false labor. [laughter]" Truth is, the sky did fall—on Reagan; there was so much of a battering, he had to drop the idea of any change at all in Social Security benefits.

He would not, however, back off his proposed hikes in the defense budget. "The Soviet Union has the biggest buildup in history," he said. "[They] have not built a society, they've built an arsenal." The budget director, David Stockman, had pushed for a scaling back of the military spending increases, but he'd lost the battle with Defense Secretary Caspar Weinberger. Cap had outfoxed Stockman by showing up at a briefing for Reagan with a blown-up cartoon of three soldiers. According to Stockman's book *The Triumph of Politics: Why the Reagan Revolution Failed*, one was a wimpy soldier without a rifle labeled "Carter's budget." The second was a Woody Allen lookalike soldier with glasses and a tiny little rifle: Stockman's budget. Number three was "GI Joe himself" with an

M-60 machine gun. That was Weinberger's budget. "Did he think the White House was on Sesame Street?" asked Stockman. Must have been: Reagan decided there would be no cuts in the defense budget.

Then the Agriculture Department announced that in cutting the school lunch program it was reclassifying ketchup as a vegetable. What followed was the Democrats hurling everything they had at Reagan like the food fight in *Animal House*, contrasting the "shrinking school lunches" to the Pentagon's "all-you-can-eat budget increases."

Reagan held another news conference on October 1, his fourth. By this point, eight months in office, Carter had held 14. It was the first time Reagan called on me by name: "Lesley."

"Mr. President, what do you say to the single working mother whose eligibility for Medicaid and food stamps has been cut? What would you say to her about how she can no longer provide medical care for her children or feed them with food stamps?"

"I don't believe that we're actually doing that," Reagan said. "Where the cuts have come is around the periphery, and some may be hurt more than others."

Another reporter followed up asking if he was "sensitive enough to the symbolism of Republican mink coats, limousines, and thousand-dollar-a-plate china at the White House when ghetto kids are being told to eat ketchup as a vegetable."

The president denied that his administration was "a millionaire's parade." The ketchup plan was being shelved, he announced, and Nancy has "taken a bit of a bum rap. . . . I haven't counted any of the mink coats that have been around."

Protesters started following Reagan. He'd give a tough anticrime speech, and 200 demonstrators would show up, chanting about his slashing the budget for crime-fighting programs. It was like that wherever he went — protesters outside, hecklers inside. There's a sense today that Reagan was forever beloved, but in late 1981 he was often taunted and booed.

And so, as presidents will, he escaped on a foreign trip, this one to Cancún, Mexico, for a "North-South" meeting of rich and poor nations (and another vacation in the sun). I appeared on *The CBS Morning News* with its new coanchor, Diane Sawyer — the two of us outside on a balcony of the press hotel. We had talked many times about doing a show together — two blond women: it would be a first. And here we were in our tryout, discussing North-South economic disparities. Just as I was saying, "Ronald Reagan came here to listen, a good position for a man who doesn't understand the complex macroeconomic issues on the table," a gust of tropical wind hit our little balcony. Diane's hair began flapping and flying into her mouth, whirling up and sideways and then across her eyes. I just kept talking about how "all India and Bangladesh want is more U.S. aid, but Reagan is not in a giving mood." Not one hair on my cemented head moved.

That very day Nancy Reagan commented about a postcard of her dressed up as a queen. "Now, that's silly," she said. "I'd never wear a crown. It messes up your hair."

WHEN REAGAN RETURNED from Cancún, he went into a high-intensity offensive to win passage of his proposed sale to Saudi Arabia of sophisticated surveillance AWACS planes, along with improvements to the country's F-15 jet fighters. This was a fight, it was widely thought, he couldn't win since he was up against the powerful Jewish lobby. More than 220 members of the House signed a resolution opposing the sale because it was perceived as a possible threat to Israel. Before the AWACS battle, the president had been coasting for weeks, drifting, sliding, and showing little energy or oomph. What was this slump all about? Then it came to me: the actor's rhythm. Reagan had slid into his out-of-work mode; but now with AWACS he had a job to do and came to life for the performance. As actors do, he worked industriously on the project, doing whatever his "directors" told him to do: making phone calls and meeting personally with scores of senators to whom he would read off his index cards, then look up and tell a Hollywood story or two. After each meeting, he would mark an arrow with a line through it on his schedule, the way actors mark their scripts when they finish a scene.[8] And on October 28 he won on AWACS, the Senate voting his way, 52–48. This is what I said that night: "So once again the Congress . . . the city of Washington, and the rest of the country are all learning what they have learned so many times before: that it is always a mistake to underestimate Ronald Reagan."

Something interesting began appearing in the polls: criticisms of the president's policies were severed from evaluations of the man. While Reagan's issues were unpopular — his budget cuts were too deep, his anti-Soviet rhetoric too hot — a majority admired him personally. Words such as "resilient" and "consistent" were used. There was a disconnect between what he was doing and what he seemed to be.

Still, by November his overall approval rating slipped below 50 percent, mainly because the economy had sunk into recession. That produced a clamor for an easing of the budget cutting, but Reagan's spokesmen kept up a steady thumping of he's-standing-firm statements: "He's in no mood to compromise." "His feet are in cement on this."

EARLY ON NOVEMBER 10, the day of Reagan's fifth news conference, I trolled for question ideas. One of my sources asked if I had read the just-published Stockman article in The Atlantic. "It's dynamite," he said.

I had trouble finding a copy. Once I did, I raced through 24 pages of interviews that David Stockman had given over several months to William Greider, the assistant managing editor of *The Washington Post*. The budget director said that he had known as early as January that the president's program would produce out-of-sight deficits, and he admitted, in his own words, that supply-side theory was "a Trojan horse," new language for "trickle down." I thought about the abuse heaped on reporters for calling the program "tax cuts for the rich." Now the president's own budget director was conceding that we'd been right.

Reagan didn't call on me at the news conference, but I followed him out of the room, and with the camera on us I said, "Mr. President, your budget director says that your economic program . . . creates inflationary deficits."

"I'll ask him whether he said that."

I held up *The Atlantic* and asked if he'd seen the article. He hadn't.

When I got back to the booth Sandy Socolow, executive producer of the *Evening News*, called, irked. Why had I flashed the magazine all over television? "Now we won't be exclusive," he said.

"Damn," I said, "you're right."

My piece that night was definitely dynamite, and even though I had waved the magazine at the president, none of my competitors noticed. I got to break the Stockman betrayal to the country. Two days later, on November 12, he walked into the Briefing Room looking pale; I was sure he was a goner. He told us he had offered the president his resignation at a lunch that he said "was more in the nature of a visit to the woodshed after supper." But despite Reagan's anger at him, he had not accepted his resignation.

Five years later in his book, Stockman revealed what had really happened at that lunch. Reagan had told him, "You're a victim of sabotage by the press. They're trying to bring you down because of what you have helped us accomplish."[9] So much for the woodshed. The picture of a rebuking Reagan had been made up — like some movie.

The Meeseites wanted Stockman out. Mike Deaver and Nancy were for tossing him. But I was told by one of Reagan's top officials that it was Jim Baker who had come to his rescue "so he would own the budget director."

I WAS 39½ YEARS OLD. It had not been a particularly good year. The nines are never good. I was feeling the stress of the job — the incessant competition, constant dread that Sam knew something I didn't, the need to know something about every issue under the sun every day — all this and raise a child and maintain a marriage. I kept thinking I'd lost my freedom. The only upside was that for the first time in years, I didn't have to diet: my metabolism was running so fast, I ate anything I wanted and still lost weight. My favorite lunch was tuna on rye with tomato and extra mayo and a bag of chips, which I usually ate in the booth. Losing weight, though, did not appeal to the camera; I began to look drawn, and Dolly told me so — often: "You're haggard. You may have to do something about it."

"Like what?"

"A face-lift."

"But I'm *only* 39!"

In the meantime CBS News had a new president: Van Gordon Sauter came over from CBS Sports.[10] My only previous contact with him had been when he had sent me a message through Clay Felker that I shouldn't wear my fur coat on television. I had ignored the advice (as I had Aaron's). Right after his new job as my boss was announced, I went out and bought a lavender down coat that I wore for the next six years.

Sauter looked like a cross between Hemingway and the Schweppes man with his conscientiously groomed beard with flying buttresses. He was a man of considerable bulk who wore bow ties and, legend had it, had trafficked in eccentricity when he ran the CBS affiliate in Los Angeles, where he lived on a houseboat and walked around the office with a parrot on his shoulder. Now, in his new office in New York, I found a man with boundless enthusiasm and great charm, which he directed at me. Bill Paley had told Sauter he was sick about the exodus of his news stars. I was Van's first project.

Swigging on a can of Tab, he asked what I wanted. I recycled my complaint that every other White House correspondent had gotten to anchor a weekend newscast. He proposed a solution not uncommon to sports figures: "What if we write a window into your contract? We'll write that if you don't have your own show within a year and a half, then you can exercise an option to leave or renegotiate with us." By then I was looking for a way to save face myself, and this seemed fair. I accepted. It never hurts to help the new boss accomplish what his predecessor couldn't.

IN EARLY 1982, nothing was going right for the president. The "Reagan recession" was worsening and Rawhide's popularity fading. A president's ratings slump brings on a disease with three distinct symptoms: staff bickering, leak plugging, and press bashing, which, in this case, was accompanied by a welter of new rules. To cut down on the boss's gaffes, Mike Deaver proclaimed that there would be no more questions at photo ops.[11] It was one thing for Deaver to tell Reagan when to talk and when not to, another to tell the press. We decided we were entitled to as much freedom of speech as the next guy, so when the president held a photo session in the Oval Office with Chancellor Helmut Schmidt of Germany, the pooler asked a question about Poland and was thrown out. We kept at it and kept getting thrown out. When I posed a question as the pooler, Speakes glowered at me as if I were an insolent brat. Finally, the White House realized it couldn't gag the press, so the Deaver rule was scrapped, but it was not its last attempt to stifle us.

Plugging leaks and controlling photo ops weren't going to help Reagan's slump, because his problems were rooted in the economy, and the unemployment picture was darkening. I did a report on January 8 showing pictures of people on breadlines and families at soup kitchens.

These were Reagan's dog days. At another news conference on January 19, he responded to a question about 17 percent black unemployment by holding up the Help Wanted section of a Sunday newspaper: "Twenty-four full pages of . . . employers looking for employees," he said. Most of the openings were for computer operators, cellular immunologists, or the like. And to a question on whether he was planning to give more money to charity in order to set an example, he claimed that he tithed, meaning he gave a tenth. That night I was compelled, in the interest of accuracy, to point out that on his latest tax return, his charitable giving had been shown as 1.4 percent.

Later that month I got a tip from a lawyer who had worked in the Carter White House. "You ought to check on whether the first lady is taking gifts from Seventh Avenue and not reporting them. She's supposed to, ya know." He told me that many of Nancy's gorgeous designer clothes were "donations."

"You mean she's taking freebies?" I asked. If I'd been wearing a device to monitor my heart rate, I'm sure the dials would have been wagging wildly. He gave me a brief education on the ethics law that required high-ranking officials and their spouses to report any gifts worth more than $35 and loans exceeding $10,000.

While Zirinsky, my producer, gathered pictures of Nancy in Adolfo suits, Bill Blass dresses, and Galanos gowns, I worked the phones and got the story confirmed: Mrs. Reagan had accepted tens of thousands of dollars worth of high-fashion threads as loans and gifts and had not reported any of it. Over pictures of Nancy at the Inaugural Ball in her white-beaded, one-shoulder little Galanos number worth more than $10,000, I broke the story, closing with "What Mrs. Reagan doesn't need and doesn't want is another round of stories that portray her as a person preoccupied with her expensive tastes while the recession is deepening."

But that's just what she got. Newsweek noted that other first ladies hadn't joined "the free-for-all." Betty Ford paid wholesale; Rosalynn Carter paid retail.[12] Worse was the juxtaposition of Mrs. Reagan's clothes with reports of hungry people waiting in lines to get surplus government cheese. One reporter calculated that one of her designer handbags cost more than a year's supply of food stamps for a family of four. There was no letting up until Mrs. Reagan promised to stop taking the free clothes.[13]

If Nancy's wardrobe woes weren't enough, POTUS rescinded a 12-year-old IRS practice of denying tax-exempt status to Bob Jones University in South Carolina and other private schools that discriminated against blacks. Across the country editorials blasted him and black leaders accused him of giving aid and comfort to segregationists.

It had taken the country decades to reach a consensus that being outwardly racist was unacceptable. By 1980 even bigots held their tongues. But now the president himself was sending disturbing signals. This, along with his repeated stories about cheating "welfare queens" who bought T-bone steaks with food stamps, had me fearing that Reagan was giving license to the haters to speak up again.

FAR FROM CUTTING social programs to reduce the deficit, the Democrats were loading up appropriations bills with "pork" and special-interest favors, but that wasn't the big issue in early 1982. In mid-February the Congressional Budget Office said that the richer you were, the more you benefited from Reagan's 1981 tax cuts,[14] and that fed into the already festering "fairness issue." Republicans in Congress thought that Reagan's program, with its ever-deepening budget cuts and ever-rising deficit, was a heavy burden to carry into the fall elections. So a group of respected senators, egged on by the moderates on the White House staff, began trekking to the Oval Office to talk Reagan into taking remedial steps, such as increasing taxes. After one such meeting they came over to the stakeout position — Pete Domenici of New Mexico, Chairman of the Finance Committee Bob Dole, the president's pal Paul Laxalt of Nevada — shaking their heads: "He's locked in cement." Off to the side Domenici told me he was perplexed at Reagan's stubbornness and made it clear he thought that continuing along the same path was foolhardy.

My sources in the White House were telling me much the same. Baker, Stockman, and Deputy Chief of Staff Richard Darman were waging an undercover campaign to persuade Rawhide that his program needed some "readjustments," including higher taxes. A member of the administration who had come aboard directly from Wall Street told me that George Bush had gone in to argue Reagan out of his no-tax position "several times," as had "most of the Cabinet." My source said he himself had gone in four times, until Reagan "got angry and told me never to raise the issue again."

I found this confusing. If the president were so disengaged, so susceptible to the direction of others, how was he able to overrule such an army of brainpower? Clearly, when it came to cutting taxes, he was not just a priest but a fundamentalist with his belief rooted not in anything as worldly as statistics or bottom lines. For him it was a matter of faith, his concept of tax cutting closer to a *fatwa* than a worldly piece of legislation that could be easily undone. There was nothing religious about his staff, though. They inspired news stories about the dangers of runaway deficits, using us to pressure the president into raising taxes.

Meanwhile, with interest rates soaring, business leaders began sounding alarms over the deficit. And still Reagan refused to budge. He went into one of his high-energy phases, traveling around the country, picking on everyone who disagreed with Reaganomics: Republican leaders who were contradicting him publicly were "sob sisters"; the Dems were "born-again budget balancers." We in his traveling press corps, "the messengers of gloom and doom," got our own attack. "You can't turn on the evening news," Reagan told *The Daily Oklahoman*, "without seeing that they are going to interview someone else who has lost his job, or they're outside the factory that has laid off workers and so forth." He charged that our negative reporting was having a psychological effect that was prolonging the recession.

Two days later, on March 18, he apologized to the press, and I ran the bite in my piece:

> REAGAN: Presidents, even Thomas Jefferson, have their moods just like everyone else. . . . So I hope I didn't touch a nerve with any of the press because I think that most of the time the overwhelming majority of them are doing a fine job.
> STAHL: [White House] aides say the last thing the president needs now is a hostile press corps and a public that no longer finds him likable. Lesley Stahl, CBS News, the White House.

While many Republicans clawed away at the program, they were careful never to disparage "the old man," and even the Democrats avoided personal aspersions. That dam broke briefly when one of his own, Republican Senator Bob Packwood of Oregon, revealed that Reagan had an annoying habit of telling made-up anecdotes as if they were real. "We've got a $120 billion deficit coming," said Packwood, "and the president says, 'You know, a young man went into a grocery store, and he had an orange in one hand and a bottle of vodka in the other, and he paid for the orange with food stamps and he took the change and paid for the vodka. That's what's wrong.' And we just shake our heads."

This was just the kind of issue Sandy Socolow would have loved, so I put together a piece on Reagan's phony anecdotes, including the fact that they were becoming such an embarrassment that the White House had opened a new office of research to check on the accuracy of his

146

stories. But the story never ran. Socolow wasn't there any more. Sauter had replaced him with Howard Stringer, who rejected it. Stringer, at 40, was adored by me and everyone else at CBS News. A tall Welshman with curly hair, he was a prizewinning documentarian from *CBS Reports* who was warmly affectionate, coolly cosmopolitan, and wickedly funny. Along with Sauter, he was introducing a new sensibility to the News Division, preferring the magazine style with "breathing," which meant more picture and feature stories.

In 1981 Dan Rather's ratings had fallen off the cliff.[15] Sauter was trying to make Dan friendlier by having him smile more and soften his tone. None of it worked. But then one night Dan wore a V-neck sweater —and presto, he warmed up. So did the ratings. By the spring of 1982 Rather regained the lead and held on to it for 212 weeks. But I worried about the program's new direction.

Squeezed by rising production and satellite costs and competition from cable, network news saw its profits level off in the early 1980s. The dreaded words "austerity measures" were heard for the first time. For the most part, though, the White House remained a protected zone.

Bill Plante and I continued to work in harmony. We covered Reagan together for six years, and I can't remember having a single argument. If Bill had a temper, it flared only against inanimate objects. He took to throwing the walkie-talkies if they didn't work. He banged phones on the walls. He once tried to heave his typewriter. Otherwise Plante reminded me of my dad, the world's other nicest guy.

Why couldn't I be like them? I had an engine in me that never stopped chugging. It must have been the constant stress, subliminal guilt over Taylor, and residual resentment over my contract. Whatever it was, in those days I was the most tautly strung person I knew, including Donaldson, who was as incorrigible as ever. One afternoon he was at that colonnade door watching for the Gipper, when suddenly there he was. "Mr. President, do you know that 90 percent of men masturbate in the shower?"

"Why no, Sam, I didn't know that," said the leader of the free world, who then moseyed on home from the office. It was about five o'clock.

TAYLOR WAS FOUR; time to choose a school. Aaron had been the education reporter at *The Washington Post* in the early 1970s. He said the public schools were even more run-down and violent than I'd heard, so we decided we had no choice but to find a good private school.

After choosing the Sidwell Friends School, we had to submit our little girl to a battery of tests and an interview. We argued her into a dress and begged her to behave and concentrate. What a harrowing day. The interviewer came out to tell us she was impressed because Taylor had noticed the color of the socks she was wearing. On such colored threads hang destiny. Then Aaron and I were interviewed. This was far more of a strain than deadlines or prime-time news conferences. And when it was over, we had to wait weeks to see if she — if *we* — had been accepted . . . to preschool.

SPRINGTIME IN WASHINGTON is glorious: dogwoods blooming, tulips in all the parks. When I had first moved to Washington, a friend from Boston had asked me, "Are the leaves on the trees yet?" I didn't know. I hadn't looked. Ever after I made it a point. If Aaron didn't drive me to work, I would take the car and park it several blocks from the White House and walk along Lafayette Park. But now in the spring of 1982 I was walking past the homeless village that had sprung up there, across the street from the president's home.

Television news was making the fairness issue vivid and emotional with pictures of homeless families and out-of-work "Americans like us." Polls registered a widespread feeling that the president lacked compassion, that "he doesn't care about ordinary people."

Mike Deaver thought he could neutralize the issue with some countering vivid and emotional television. He decided to make little movies out on location about how much the president cared about people. In May he had Reagan visit a black family at their home in Maryland and a black high school in Chicago. The networks were his cinematographers.

Deaver picked a dairy farm in Pennsylvania, and off we all trudged — I, in my open-toed slingbacks and light blue suit, as a member of the traveling pool. When we got to the farm, Cal Marlin and Chuck Violet, the crew, had to scoot up a steep hill with all their gear because Deaver, as location scout, had decided that the best spot for picture taking — which was what this day was about — was the big barn on top of what seemed like a mountain. Cal couldn't race up ahead of Reagan if he had to carry his tripod, so I volunteered to lug it up for him. It had rained the night before. The hill was a vast seep of gunk and mud, and I was making *plup-plup-plup* sounds every time one of my Bruno Maglis sank into it. The backs of my legs were splatters of brown, and so was the hem of my light blue skirt.

"Oh shit," I puffed at David Gergen, who was climbing next to me. "This had better be nothing more than mud!" I was schlepping the tripod, which was much heavier than I'd imagined, and muttering at Jim Baker and Ed Rollins, "What idiot decided this was a good idea?" Reagan may have been the star of this production, but I was staging my own little drama. "Let me tell you fellas that the only thing that is going to redeem this hideous day is if one of you leak me a good story, because this sucks."

148

They laughed. When I got to the top, I said I would stand between Baker and Rollins and wait to be fed.

The barn reeked. Hay was clinging to that brown guck on my toes, and there was Rawhide, handsome, spotless, propped up on a bail of hay, twinkling because a newborn calf was being named Nancy. Please. He told the assembled group of farmers in their overalls (nice wardrobe touch), "We think we've got a well-balanced budget. But we also think that we are meeting the humane needs of those people who have to have help, and the figures reveal it."

There was no leak. No added tidbits. The only things I had to offer the *Evening News* were pictures of the president of the United States with some cows, telling farmers he cared. We couldn't resist the pictures. We ran the Deaver movie. Except for a shot of 1,000 demonstrators, he had all but written the script.

CHIEF OF STAFF Jim Baker finally talked Reagan into negotiating a budget compromise with the Democrats. Reagan went on television with a brawny statement about his commitment to cutting taxes but then signed a bill for fiscal 1983 that raised them. He was a wizard at having it both ways. Over the course of his presidency he would raise taxes 13 more times,[16] but each time he convinced everyone he'd never do such a thing. It seems that his rhetoric left a stronger imprint than his recurring signature on tax-hike measures.

JUNE 28. Around 4 P.M. the *Evening News'* producers met in the "fishbowl" in New York to decide on the lead. Their choices were: some exclusive combat footage of the war between Argentina and Great Britain over control of the Falkland Islands; Reagan's meeting with Israeli Prime Minister Begin on a day when the Israelis bombed Palestinian strongholds in Beirut; the birth of Prince Charles and Princess Diana's first child, Prince William.[17] In Cronkite's time it would certainly have been the Falklands or the Israelis. On the night of June 28 you could hear the snap, a loud unhinging in the Washington Bureau, when Dan Rather led off with the baby.

In Washington we had been getting reports from New York of Sauter's postmortems. Every night after the *Evening News* he would march into the fishbowl, often with a copy of the *National Enquirer* or *The Star* under his arm. "This is what real people care about," he'd say. He'd then put his feet up on the desk and critique the broadcast. These were long, excruciating sessions, we were told, in which the new boss found something wrong with every report: "Not relevant." "God, that piece on Medicare was *boring!*" or "If [Reporter X] can't write better than that, get him [or her] off the air." Washington pieces came in for particularly harsh goings-over. "Who gives a rat's ass about a hearing on the budget, anyway? If you want to do a story about the budget, go out to Peoria or Podunk and find me faces, get some real people." One time Sauter said, "If it ain't relevant to the heartland—don't even cover it." He seemed to believe, as Reagan did, that the American people hated Washington.

Those congressional hearings he found so infernally dull had been the meat and potatoes of the Cronkite show. We had regularly had five to six pieces from Washington on the air every night. By late 1982 we were down to two. The bureau was suffering from posttraumatic stress syndrome. A report from the State Department about U.S. attitudes toward the Israeli bombing of Lebanon would be dropped to make room for a "flock 'n' roll" story about some singing sheep.[18] Sauter, who had come out of local stations, was changing the very definition of what was network news; we felt he was downgrading us to some second-rate tabloid. We had thought of ourselves as chroniclers and analysts of daily events, television's counterpart of The New York Times. But if any of us complained, we were clumped into the dreary category of "yesterday's men." Sauter told Plante, "You all act like I'm pissing on the flame."

Part of Sauter's changes involved the look of the broadcast. Not only did he want more picture stories with emotional "moments," he called for sexier computerized graphics that zoomed and whirled, and asked the reporters to loosen up: Be more natural. Walk in the pieces, use your hands, turn, look down. These local-news mannerisms had been forbidden in the Cronkite era.

I wasn't opposed to all the changes. Howard Stringer was a first-rate journalist. He began emphasizing better writing with what we called the "Stringer paragraph" in which we were to explain "why you should care" about this story. And I didn't think it necessarily meant we were going "soft" just because we moved our focus out of Washington. Thank God Zirinsky was our White House producer. "They want the human element, they want emotion," she told me, "even in our pieces."

"So let's give it to them," I said. "Why not?"

Susan began a tireless search for "elements." If our story was about Reaganomics, she'd order up an interview and pictures at a soup kitchen. If the story was deepening unemployment, she'd find a way to incorporate footage of a plant closing and crying workers' spouses. She scoured the country every day for a "moment" for us to slide into the White House story.

But then the producers in New York began fiddling with my scripts "to improve my writing." I suspected what they were really up to was cleansing my copy of any hint of criticism of the president. One of the producers told me that Sauter thought my coverage was "knee-jerk" critical on Reaganomics. I argued, "This isn't bias. My sources are White House officials." But I was told, "Sometimes Sauter comes in here after the show ranting about you."

Joe Peyronnin, by then in charge of the *Evening News* in Washington, was the go-between. He would pass New York's complaints on to me: "They think you're zinging the president."

When the Carter White House had said that, my bosses had encouraged me to be "tougher." This was new.

"Do you think that?" I asked Joe.

"No, but they're the bosses."

These bosses were guiding me away from the kind of coverage I'd been trained to produce. So I fought back. And Joe, in the middle, tried to mediate. He was told that Sauter was "mad" because he didn't like my "tone." He thought my delivery was too hard-hitting. A shadow of a thought flew by: Was this some male problem with a strong woman?

Sauter was trying to steer the whole ship onto a friendlier course to mesh with the new sweatered Dan. The nice approach was working for Rather—why not for all of us? Sauter wanted a feel-good broadcast; it's the ratings, stupid.

ON JUNE 30, the fight for the Equal Rights Amendment was lost, three states short of ratification. Since Congress had passed the amendment in 1972, the women's movement had changed the workplace and family life. But ten years later there was a backlash, and Ronald Reagan was a big part of it. Under him the Justice Department declared that it would no longer ask employers to hire women on a preferential basis, and steps were taken to weaken Title IX, the program to upgrade women's sports in high school and college. Reagan even tried to blame the recession on women. "Part of the unemployment is not as much recession as it is the great increase in the people going into the job market," he said in April, "and ladies, I'm not picking on anyone, but because of the increase in women who are working today, the two-worker families and so forth." No wonder there was a backlash. If only women weren't working, there'd be jobs! Reagan was making feminism a dirty word.

Yet there were women astronauts, female cops, and a woman on the Supreme Court. We were everywhere men were; well, everywhere but at the top. We had even achieved a critical mass in network newsrooms. *Life* magazine marked the coming of age with a centerfold that opened up into a four-page spread on eight women network correspondents. ABC sent Sylvia Chase, Betsy Aaron (both had jumped ship from CBS), and Lynn Sherr; from NBC there were Jane Pauley and Jessica Savitch; the three from CBS were Diane Sawyer, Susan Spencer, and I. We were told to wear muted colors—no red, nothing bright—but had no other wardrobe instruction. I chose a silk blouse in soft mauve, one of my favorites because the collar didn't just have ruffles, it also had a bow — not quite Little Bo Beep but awfully close. Years later Sylvia said, "God, I hated what you wore." She was far more casual in a sporty blue-and-white-striped shirt with rolled-up sleeves and a vest, looking like an editor of a weekly newspaper in the Old West. Diane was the most glamorous, as usual, in a white sweater with a cowl neck and a long suede skirt. We didn't recognize her at first; she showed up in a black wig. "Diane," we jabbed, "you're so famous you go around in disguise?"

"No," she answered with a smile, "just thought I'd try to be different." We examined one another, got it and laughed. We were all blond. Every one of us.

The photo was taken by Annie Leibovitz the Great, who at first tried to strew us about on the floor over a map of the world. A few of us argued that it was undignified to be on our bellies, twisting about like *Vogue* models, so Annie moved on to Plan B, a layout of boxes arranged in different heights. She placed us so we were leaning or stretching our legs in one direction or another — she was very meticulous. There was something formal but relaxed at the same time about her picture, which I love and still keep on my office wall.

We all hung around that zany afternoon as long as we could. We loved being with one another because, as one of us said, "Hey, we're all the same person!" And we were, all trying to be nonchalant about the big-deal shoot, all pretending not to care how we looked. "Oh, do anything you want," we said to the makeup artists and hairdressers (I must have lost my mind!). We bantered; we one-upped: "But who among us is *really* blond?" We acknowledged that we all worked four times harder than the men, that we came in earlier and went home later, and that we had probably gotten our jobs *because* we were blond (real or otherwise). It got to the point where we laughed at everything everyone said. We definitely did not live up to the stateliness of the poses we had insisted on.

Throughout my 30s, my closest friends had been men. But now at 40, I was changing. Possibly because I had a child, more likely because I simply missed the comfort of being with people like me, I began to crave the company of women. A group of us in Washington started getting together for monthly lunches: Cokie Roberts, Linda Wertheimer, and Nina Totenberg, the brilliant trio that gave National Public Radio its reputation for standout reporting on Capitol Hill and in the Supreme Court (their corner of the NPR newsroom was known as "The Fallopian Jungle"); Dotty Lynch, director of polling at the Democratic National Committee; lawyer Nancy Dutton; congressional staffer Ann Smith; columnist and author Pat O'Brien; Judy Weinraub, editor of *The Washington*

Post's Home and Travel sections; Catherine Wyler, TV and film producer; and me. Since Washington was such a single-subject town, we set ground rules: politics and government were off the table. We would confine our topics to grooming (as in where to get your hair done), swapping fashion tips, decorating, raising children, recipes, dirty jokes, and gossip. We just wanted to be girls. As the years went by, we lived through one another's crises, including two divorces, two second marriages, and a firing.

One day in June at our favorite restaurant, Marrocco on 20th Street, Dotty Lynch, flushed and sad, dropped the bad news: the Democratic Party was eliminating her office. After commiserations and name-calling of the asshole who had done it to her, we set about "managing" the problem. By the end of lunch, each of us had an assignment of phone calls. By the end of the day, Dotty had more interviews lined up than she could handle; by the end of the week she had a new job as a consultant for the CBS News Election Unit. This was when we realized that not only had we women reached a critical mass, we were a mass with muscle.

Thereafter we were more like a family. Secrets were shared, troubles hashed out. I would never miss a lunch; none of us would. So much of my time over the previous ten years had been spent trying to be male-ish, this group was relief. I came to believe that women *need* the companionship of other women the way we need food and shelter.

AARON'S MOVIE, *Urban Cowboy*, with John Travolta and Debra Winger, opened, and I threw a party for my husband. Judge John Sirica came, as did Zbigniew Brzezinski in a ten-gallon hat. These were great times. The movie was a megahit. Country-western bars sprang up everywhere, some with their own mechanical bulls; Levi Strauss was reborn; and country music became popular all over the country. We saw a convergence of politics and popular culture. Aaron and I debated whether the craving for our old, romantic cowboy roots had made way for the election of Ronald Reagan, the cowboy actor, or whether Rawhide had created the craving? He tended to be a politician who stood still with his immutable beliefs, waiting for everyone else to catch up with him or drift back to him. He seemed to be there just as we were returning, as we do periodically, to our western myth.

Aaron was hot in Hollywood — and happy. Except that we were still living in Washington. He lost all interest in writing about government and politics. "This is such a one-industry small town," he would say. We both knew that if it were not for Taylor and me he'd have moved away. Instead he went to work for Jann Wenner at *Rolling Stone*, writing about such distinctly non-Washington types as Warren Beatty, Linda Ronstadt, Paul Newman, and John DeLorean. His career heart was in Hollywood. 153

☐

TELEVISION JOURNALISM is a team effort involving camera crews, editors, and especially producers. But we on-air reporters get all the credit. During my ten years at the White House, I worked with the best.[19] I relied on them every day for their pictures and sound, quick edits, and, in the case of producers, advice, support, hand-holding, and, more times than I like to admit, rescuing. Some in the business describe the collaborative relationship between a producer and a reporter as symbiotic, like that between Fred and Ginger, Rodgers and Hammerstein, bagels and cream cheese.

Which brings me to "Zee," aka Susan Zirinsky, the White House producer during most of the Reagan years and the leader of our "team." She's a shorter version of Natalie Wood who worked such long hours, I wondered if she *ever* slept. There were times when I'd find her at the office at 11 at night and think of slaves chained to the oars of a Roman ship. But all her obsessing was redeemed by her kind heart, her foul tongue, and her constant joking, often delivered when we were on the road over the walkie-talkies like punctuation marks. The funny banter took the edge off when Sergeant Zee was barking orders to the troops. "Marlin, do you read? Marlin, do you read?" she'd buzz the cameraman.

"I'm here."

"Protesters to your right. Hustle, Pumpkin."

Or to me: "News babe, shake a leg in those ridiculous heels."

Once when I lectured her about working too much, she wrote out everything she had to do to organize a Reagan trip: a two-day outing with one "RON"—remain overnight. It illustrated how we meshed as a team, and how much logistics and contingency planning it takes to organize a presidential trip.

Zee started arranging the trip over a week ahead of time when the White House Office of Advance called her with a heads-up: "August 2 and 3. The president's going to make a speech in Des Moines, then visit a hog and corn farm 50 miles west of the city in the late afternoon. Next day: Hartford." She began immediately, ordering telephones for every stop the president would make (she ordered dials, no push buttons; dials are cheaper) and booking places to edit in, preferably large hotel rooms. Next she hired motorcycle couriers to run videotape and, if necessary, correspondents around town, preferring off-duty cops since they would simplify the task of getting credentials from the Secret Service. To transmit our story from Des Moines to New York for the *Evening News*, we would share facilities with the other nets; it was simply too expensive to set up three separate feed units. So we rotated the "transmission pool" city by city. In Des Moines it was NBC's turn.

With our edit site at a downtown hotel, she decided to set up a microwave transmission facility from the farm to us in Des Moines. That way she and I could watch the event live on a TV monitor while our editor recorded it. As a backup, she hired a helicopter to fly the videotapes from the farm to Des Moines. A White House advance man told her that he could not allow three separate network helicopters to fly around a presidential event, but he agreed to one, so that too was pooled with the other nets. Once she chartered a chopper, she had to find a landing strip close to our edit hotel, finally convincing the Methodist Medical Center to let it land there.

With Jimmy Carter our trips were always early: wheels up at 6 A.M. But this is Reagan. We leave at a civilized ten o'clock. I had long since learned that the better way to travel is not on *Air Force One* but in first class on the press plane, in those days supplied by Pan Am. When we land I read Zee's "Trip Note," which orders me into the president's pool, so I jump into one of the press cars and join the motorcade behind Reagan's car, a decoy limo, a Secret Service van with armed agents, and staff cars. Behind us is an ominous ambulance.

Zee walkie-talkies me to see if Reagan answered any questions at the airport. "No," I tell her, "but there is a pool report. Speakes briefed on *Air Force One*." I read the salient paragraphs into the walkie-talkie so Jackie Adams can do a radio report.

At the president's speech in Des Moines, everything is going smoothly until cameraman Cal Marlin breaks into a sweat, turns gray, and collapses. We run frantically around the press platform, looking for the White House medic who always travels with us (the president's doctor comes along on all trips for him; there's a medic for the rest of us). He checks Cal out and calls for an ambulance. We're sure he's had a heart attack.

Zee keeps working, altering the battle plan. ABC agrees to help out — no hesitation, no problem. They loan us their lighting man to run our sound equipment. Zee sends Jim McClinchy, the *Morning News* producer, to the hospital with Cal, calls New York to get another crew credentialed and dispatched to Hartford for tomorrow, makes sure Bill Plante is in the pool to the farm, and then joins me to listen as I interview people in the audience. She tells me, "I brought some pictures of hogs and corn if you want to mention Reagan's farm policy."

Up in the edit room, I begin to write as pictures from the farm come in by microwave. We are most interested in Reagan's question-and-answer session with the farmers. It is now five o'clock Eastern Time, and my adrenaline is in overdrive.

"What's wrong? Goddamn it, don't tell me our friggin' equipment died. I'll kill myself." Zee is frenzied. We are suddenly hearing nothing from the farm. The pictures are perfect, but there's silence. The editor twitches his wires, he pushes his buttons. We are all going wild. Zee calls

155

the phone at the farm. Plante picks up and tells her, "The White House pulled the plug on our sound, they're not letting us get anywhere close with our mikes. We can't hear a thing, either the farmers' questions or Reagan's answers." They're that afraid of what he's saying? Guess so. Zee tells Plante to break out a tape cassette and get it to the chopper. At least it will have natural sound instead of the stony silence of the feed.

Since we can't take in the farm feed and edit at the same time, Zee waits to begin crash editing till 5:45 Eastern Time, dangerously late. I record a track on which I say, "While he's calling on the European allies to break their oil pipeline contracts with the Soviet Union, he was boasting to U.S. farmers about how he restored grain sales and the integrity of U.S. contracts." The editor slams in pictures of Reagan at the speech, then some Reagan sound: "The granary door is open, and the exchange will be cash on the barrelhead." I include a section about how the White House cut off our mikes at the farm. The courier bursts in at 6:20. He met the chopper and sped the farm cassette to us just in time to drop in one last shot. We make our feed to New York right on deadline at 6:30.

6:35. Cal calls from the hospital. It was food poisoning. He's fine.

Another day at the office. And as on most days, we were phosphorescing. We had gone to the brink and won. It was always cathartic, though not always as traumatic. We weren't cynical, we weren't nonchalant. We were alive and elated. We were a *Mission: Impossible* team that got the job done!

I call Taylor. She tells me I should come home. Aaron says he liked my piece and that everything's fine. And I call Dolly and Lou. My mother worries when I fly. I tell her I'm sleeping over in Des Moines so she can relax.

I decide to unwind by going out to dinner with a group of reporters, but Zee won't join us; she never unwinds. She stays in our edit room, cuts an 11 P.M. piece for CBS's local stations, and writes up a Trip Note for tomorrow in Hartford.

I get to the hotel around 11. The White House travel office has preregistered me, so all I have to do is ask for my key. My suitcase is already in my room. I call Aaron again, and we talk till I fall asleep.

Next morning we bus to the airport, watch Reagan take off, then race onto the Pan Am jet, which will do an interchange in the air, passing *Air Force One* so we can beat the president to Hartford and watch him land. Cal is weak but back with us. We ate eggs Benedict and read Zee's Trip Note for Hartford.

Zirinsky did what three producers do now.

156 OVER THE SUMMER of 1982 Reagan succumbed to the pragmatists again and agreed to raise corporate and excise taxes, though he was able to fend

off an attempt to scale back his income tax cuts. He was said to have told Tip O'Neill, "You may make me crap a pineapple, but you're not going to make me crap a cactus." The White House called the pineapple — which included new cigarette and telephone taxes — "revenue enhancements." Whatever they called them, the president was now fighting *for* a $98 billion, three-year tax *increase* bill with great vigor. In fact, he did battle with his own conservative allies, such as the sandpapery congressman from Georgia, Newt Gingrich, who tweaked Reagan in one of my pieces: "We need to continue the platform and the speeches that President Reagan was elected on." Not only did Reagan lobby the Republicans in the House, he appeared in the Rose Garden with Tip O'Neill to promote bipartisanship, and he made a televised plea for votes. And that's how the Tax Equity and Fiscal Responsibility Act (TEFRA) passed.

Reagan signed TEFRA, with its tax hike, on September 3, but there was no Rose Garden ceremony, no pictures of him with 24 pens, not even a notice in the pressroom. It was done in the dark of night while he was vacationing at his ranch. And he never mentioned it. He would remind audiences over and over that he had cut their income taxes by 25 percent, but somehow the signing of TEFRA never came up. The Gipper had become the Flipper, but nobody noticed.

I TOLD my mother everything — well, almost everything. So she was up to speed on the direction Van Sauter was moving in at CBS News. "Maybe you *are* a little stiff on the air," she said. "He could be right. Try to loosen up." Then one day she announced she had found me an acting teacher.

"Mother, you can't be serious. It's silly, and besides, I don't have the time."

"Number one, it isn't silly. You need someone to guide you, that's all. You work so hard on your reporting and writing, but you mustn't forget that you have to perform as well. And don't kid yourself, acting's part of what you do."

I didn't say a word.

"Well, it is," she argued. "Now, take down his name: Warren Robertson. Dad and I will come stay with Taylor while you go to New York. Find the time. You need this."

Why did I persist in going through the useless exercise of defying her? My protests grew weaker until one day I was in New York in Bermuda shorts, facedown on a carpeted floor, with Warren Robertson's knee in my back: "Take deep breaths and relax. Boy, are you tight."

I was taking private acting lessons, trying not to laugh at the absurdity, especially when Warren said something like "Think of something sad. Close your eyes and concentrate on a moment in your life when you were crestfallen, heartbroken." He told me to sit silently for several min-

157

utes thinking my most morose thoughts, after which I read one of my scripts, a straightforward 45 seconds on throw weight, in tears.

Next day, after the knee-in-the-back business: laughter. I dwelled on happy thoughts and read something dry in giggles. I did my best. Warren asked me to improvise sketches in which I was embarrassed or angry; I conducted mock interviews in which I feigned outrage or sympathy. I did a *tour d'horizon* of the world of emotions, learning, as if I didn't already know it, that on a scale of one to ten, my acting talent was in the .06 range. Though when my lessons ended I was able to laugh or cry on command.

That was the laboratory. Now I had to take the improved me into the real world, in my case that big white Hollywood studio on Pennsylvania Avenue, and what I found was that my emotions — so carefully girdled before — were now flabbily free and out of control. Crying on command would have been one thing; I cried ten times a day for no good reason. When I heard a joke — we heard a lot in that White House since Reagan loved them — I couldn't stop laughing. If Zirinsky said that New York wanted changes in my script, I'd scream; if Larry Speakes picked on anyone, anyone, in the briefing, I'd jump in and chide Larry as if he'd struck Taylor.

I was flipping, fussing, freaking, flying off — you name it — all of which were unacceptable for a White House correspondent. We were expected to be composed and collected. It took me more than a month to undo the damage of learning how to act. One thing that lingered: a new respect for Ronald Reagan.

THE WHITE HOUSE turned its attention to the congressional elections in the fall of 1982. They had layers of problems. For one thing, the economy had worsened. The president dealt with that by saying in so many words, "It ain't my fault." At his news conference on September 28 he was asked if any of the blame for the recession was his. "Yes," he said, "because for many years I was a Democrat."

I got a break from the routine of the White House in October, when CBS sent me out to cover the midterm elections. I was assigned the governors, and so, to get ready for election night, I went to look at the races in New York (Mario Cuomo versus Lew Lehrman), California (Tom Bradley versus George Deukmejian) and Texas (Mark White versus Bill Clements), as well as the big midwestern states, where unemployment had hit the hardest. The jobless rate, 10.4 percent, was the worst in 42 years, and Republicans were scared.

Election night, November 2. Rather led off our broadcast — "It's cardiac arrest time" — and set the tone: "This election is a nationwide referendum on Reaganomics and who's to blame for double-digit unemployment." My analyst, Bob Teeter, a Republican pollster with close ties to the White House, discouraged me from linking the governors' races to Reagan. I thought he was trying to protect the president, since my travels and instincts had told me that national Republican policies were central to the contests in the Midwest.

At 7:34 I said that the Democrat in Ohio, Richard Celeste, was winning two-to-one among blue-collar workers. "He ran emphasizing Reaganomics as a big issue. This race was clearly contaminated by the national issues." When I finished I swiveled around and bent over to ask my team how I'd done. Teeter was exasperated, and shaking his head in frustration.

We had sexy new computerized graphics that included a map of the nation that twirled into a three-dimensional box with red stripes for Republican and blue for the Democrats, then undulated into designs with demographic breakdowns. It was amazing.

A little after eight Rather said, "Lesley Stahl, we see some comeback winners tonight in these gubernatorial races."

"They're the liberals who are coming back, Dan, like Michael Dukakis. The Massachusetts voters threw him out four years ago. Now he's back, with a lot of help from Ted Kennedy."

A few minutes later Rather asked about Illinois, where the incumbent Republican governor, Jim Thompson, was battling Adlai Stevenson Jr. "Lesley Stahl, I'm stunned that the Thompson race is as close as it apparently is."

"It's a clear and obvious referendum on Reaganomics," I said, and Teeter buried his head in his hands.

In between appearances, I called Aaron and my parents. "Calling Mommy again, are we?" teased Mike Wallace, loudly. "How'd she say your hair looks?"

Around midnight I got a call from David Gergen, protesting our coverage. "You guys are far more negative than NBC or ABC."

"Is this a formal White House complaint?" I asked.

"No, no," he replied, backing off.

No wonder they were sensitive. That night, the Republicans got a drubbing. They lost 26 House seats and seven governorships. It was also a sour night for women who ran for major office: all of them (three Senate and two gubernatorial candidates) lost. And CBS lost the ratings. ABC won for the first time ever.

OVER THANKSGIVING in Santa Barbara, Larry Speakes confirmed that the president was considering a tax on unemployment benefits. This, Larry told us, "would make unemployment less attractive." No one could figure Reagan out. How could someone so sweet be so callous? How could someone so passive seem so strong? How could someone so detached and unaware be so effective?

Much of his personal appeal flowed from his ability to slough off or just forget unpleasantness; he was incorrigibly, alluringly sunny. As Steven Weisman, *The New York Times'* White House correspondent, wrote: ".No matter how grave things look, his attitude is invariably upbeat and reassuring. He seems to recognize that graciousness is the best policy politically. He does not hold grudges." There was also the memory of his passing tax and spending cuts in 1981, which lingered as a defining impression: people thought he could get things done and "make the government work."

But the economy was not bounding back as Reagan had predicted. The year ended with me saying from the White House lawn that there was "a sense of fatigue here, the kind of exhaustion that often comes out of defeat." The jobless rate had climbed to 10.8 percent, and the 1983 deficit was projected at $190 billion.

THE NATURE of the president's mind was a source of endless discussion and speculation in the press corps. Just as I would decide that he was vacant and mindless, someone like Richard Darman would assure me, "He's far more intelligent and involved than you guys in the press realize." There was always the caveat: "when he cares." But I kept hearing about Reagan doodling his way through national security briefings and sleeping through budget meetings, and meanwhile the gaffes and errors continued to trill off his tongue.

It was then that I got my own Deep Throat, a man who called me from St. Louis. "When I was in the military," he told me, "I saw an x-ray of Reagan's brain." He gave me his credentials and phone numbers; he seemed legitimate. He said Reagan had a rare disorder that accounted for his spaciness: parts of his brain weren't normal. "The x-rays still exist," he said, as he encouraged me to follow a trail he prescribed to get my hands on them. I made two dozen phone calls before giving up in frustration. When I told my friend Tom DeFrank at *Newsweek* the story one day, he asked if he could look into it. He also came up dry.

Internal warfare between the Reaganites who had the president's heart and the oh-my-God-we-have-to-fix-this-mess-ites was a recurring subject in editorials and columns as if Reagan weren't there. I did a story on January 6 about the presidency's midlife crisis in which I talked about "indecision and disarray" and quoted a frustrated official saying, "We don't even have a strategy for dealing with the deficits. No one's in charge." The president began getting mail about how his staff was pushing him around. In his answers, he often blamed the press. "Some in the media delight in trying to portray me as being manipulated and led around by

My parents, Dolly and Lou.

Below: CBS Washington Bureau chief Bill Small and Sylvia Westerman, executive producer of *Face the Nation.* That's me in the background. Small stood up for his people, defending them from attacks either from outside the company or from his superiors at CBS, who were called, in those days, "those assholes in New York."

Bottom: CBS's 1974 election coverage team: Roger Mudd, Walter Cronkite, Dan Rather, Mike Wallace, and "female."

1

2

3

President of CBS News Richard Salant. When CBS Chairman William Paley all but ordered Salant to kill a piece on Watergate in 1972, he refused.

With Ed Bradley in the CBS Washington Bureau in 1975.

4

5

With 1976 Democratic presidential candidate Scoop Jackson, who insisted on carrying my luggage when I was covering his campaign.

6

7

My father playing airplane with my daughter,
Taylor, in 1977. Dolly, who stopped talking to
me when Aaron and I eloped, forgave me the
minute I went into labor.

8

The publicity photo for the *Morning
News* with my coanchor, Hughes
Rudd. I started the job just weeks
after Taylor was born.

Hughes's replacement on the *Morning News* was Richard Threlkeld.
Our publicity photo made us look
as though we were starring in a sitcom as a happy couple, Mr. and
Mrs. Jones.

9

10

Jody Powell gave me this photo, taken during President Carter's *Delta Queen* trip down the Mississippi.

Carter's press secretary, Jody Powell *(left)*, and Carter's chief political adviser, Hamilton Jordan *(right)*, were not pleased when I was assigned to cover the White House.

11

Bob Pierpont and I covered the Carter White House together.

12

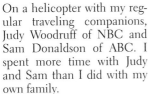

13

On a helicopter with my regular traveling companions, Judy Woodruff of NBC and Sam Donaldson of ABC. I spent more time with Judy and Sam than I did with my own family.

The 1980 CBS Democratic Convention coverage team, clockwise from top left: Susan Spencer, Ed Bradley, me, Mort Dean, Phil Jones, Dan Rather, Bob Schieffer, and Harry Reasoner.

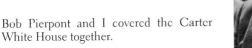

14

15 Election night 1980. Reagan won by a landslide. The election marked the first appearance of the "gender gap," women voting differently from men.

Below left: Reagan's troika—James Baker, Edwin Meese, and Michael Deaver.

Below right: Crammed into the CBS White House booth with Bill Plante *(middle)* and John Ferrugia. Bill looked a little like the actor Robert Vaughn and was one of the best-liked members of the press corps.

16   17

18

19

Above left: At three, Taylor was the most adorable little girl alive, with the bluest eyes and the sunniest disposition. Aaron was the father of all fathers.

Above right: Shortly after Reagan moved into the White House, Sam, Judy, and I were invited to a private meeting with the president. He told us, "I miss spending time outdoors. At the White House you're a bird in a gilded cage."

Larry Speakes became President Reagan's press secretary after James Brady was shot during the attempt on Reagan's life in 1981.

20

We were kept so far from the Reagan ranch in Santa Barbara that CBS brought in this 40,000-millimeter lens to keep tabs on the president.

21

22

Howard Stringer, Van Sauter, Lane Venardos, and Ed Joyce.

Howard Stringer with Dan Rather, who was wearing the V-neck sweater that pulled his ratings back up.

23

24

Above: As I approached 40, I began to crave the company of women. A group of us started having monthly lunches. *Clockwise from top left:* Ann Smith, Nancy Dutton, Linda Wertheimer, Patricia O'Brien, Nina Totenberg, Dotty Lynch, Cokie Roberts, Catherine Wyler, and Judy Weinraub. No shop talk was allowed: just gossip, fashion, children, and dirty jokes.

Right: "Zee," Susan Zirinsky, was the White House producer for the *Evening News* during most of the Reagan years. I wondered if she ever slept. But her obsessing was redeemed by her kind heart, her foul tongue, and her constant joking.

Senator Gary Hart appeared on *Face the Nation* shortly after the Iowa caucuses in 1984. He felt my questions about his changing his name were unfair and vowed never to appear on the show again. He won the New Hampshire primary two days later.

25

26

27

Joan Barone was my first producer on *Face.* She left in the spring of 1984 and succumbed to her cancer on March 10, 1985.

28

I told my bosses I wanted associate producer Karen Sughrue to replace Joan on *Face*. Karen and I went to Egypt to interview Hosni Mubarak. We are seated in his ornate palace in Cairo.

The infamous interview with Mubarak. Ed Joyce eventually forgave us for it.

29

Nancy Reagan ran the studio, and did so more as time went by.

30

With the CBS News team covering the 1984 Democratic Convention: Diane Sawyer, Ed Bradley, and Bob Schieffer.

Calling Mommy from the set on election night 1984.

The reason I was able to juggle my work and my child was Aaron's devotion to Taylor. He'd go with her to the dreaded park whenever she asked, and he always volunteered for field trips with her class. After a while, Tay signed him up without asking.

34

We worked for weeks convincing the Bushes to appear on *Face* together to launch the second Reagan-Bush administration. Mrs. Bush agreed to the interview because she wanted to apologize for seeming to call Geraldine Ferraro a bitch during the campaign, but her husband kept interrupting her.

Little-known Arkansas Governor Bill Clinton on *Face*, July 7, 1985.

35

Introducing Dolly to John Travolta at the premiere of *Perfect*.

36

I brought Aaron and Taylor to meet with President Reagan on my last day as White House correspondent. When we first got there, Reagan looked frail and didn't seem to know who I was. But as soon as Aaron mentioned Hollywood, the glaze in Reagan's eyes cleared and the color came to his cheeks.

37

When he was about to become prime minister of Israel, Yitzhak Shamir was my guest on *Face*. This was his first major American television interview. He was a straight shooter, no flourishes, no evasions. I liked the interview. He did too.

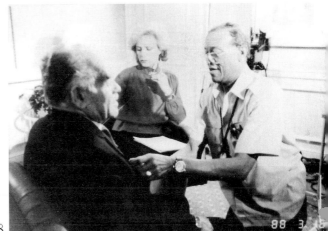

38

During Secretary of State George Shultz's appearance on *Face* in November 1986 about the sales of arms to Iran, it became clear that he wasn't going to fall on his sword for his president. He left the unmistakable impression that he did not approve of Reagan's actions.

39

40

In the spring of 1988, Bush's campaign manager, Lee Atwater, pictured here with Ed Bradley and Susan Zirinsky, was concerned that Reagan Democrats were shifting their support to Dukakis. Said Atwater, "If I can make Willie Horton a household name, we win the election."

41

My daughter the football player, #92.

I thought Dan Quayle comported himself well during this appearance on *Face*. But when I reviewed the videotape of a January 1989 interview, I saw what I had not seen in person: the Quayle freeze of fear.

4

43

Bush met more often with the press in his first 100 days than Reagan had in his last two years. He was so accessible that Tom Meyer of the *San Francisco Chronicle* drew this cartoon.

44

I was in the pool for one of Bush's impromptu get-togethers on the patio outside the Oval Office. I kept thinking: He's good-looking and he's not saying anything.

My brother, Jeff, and his son, Matthew, joined Aaron, Taylor, and me on our second safari. I thought I'd already had the best day of my life until we spent an hour with a family of gorillas in Rwanda.

45

46

With Charles Kuralt during our brief experience cohosting a series of nightly Persian Gulf specials. Charles was the best writer and reader in TV news, but with all his informality and warmth on the air, most people confronted a wall when they tried to get close to him.

47   My beautiful family, all grown up. Aaron was right, it's the thing I'm most proud of.

the nose," he wrote to Clymer Wright Jr. of Horton, Texas. "Clymer, I'm in charge. RR."[20]

On January 10, 1983, David Gergen announced at a briefing that White House officials would no longer be allowed to take reporters' calls without his permission.

> HELEN THOMAS: David, this happens in every White House at this point in time. When the press stories start turning bad, you all put out gag rules.
> GERGEN: I wouldn't call this gag rules. The president today in a meeting said, "I've had it up to my keister with these leaks."

The gag strategy didn't work very well not the least because the designation of David Gergen as leak watchdog was greeted as something of a joke. He was, after all, the administration's paramount leaker.

On January 14 Reagan himself came into the briefing room and tried to deal with the perception that he was abdicating his leadership role to his staff. But as Lou Cannon wrote in *The Washington Post* the next day, "His attempt to demonstrate that he is firmly in control and fully knowledgeable about the policies of his administration was marred by his reference to Paul Nitze, his chief arms negotiator, as 'Ed Nitze.' "

Deaver tried to alleviate the negative perceptions with his little movies: Reagan filling sandbags in Monroe, Louisiana, after a flood; Reagan visiting a black parochial school in the Chicago ghetto. We ran every frame; we were picture junkies. But the disarray persisted until finally Reagan tilted toward the pragmatists, conceding in his State of the Union Address in late January that "we who are in government must take the lead in restoring the economy." It was read as a retreat from supply-side theory, an acknowledgement that, yes, we do need the government to help solve our problems after all. The Democrats rejoiced.

When the question, How did Reagan maintain his reputation for consistency with all his concedings and retreatings? is asked, what happened next is revealing. He flew to Boston on a Deaver diversion to express in pictures his solidarity with the working class. He sipped beer with blue-collar workers at an Irish pub in Dorchester and toured a computer firm in predominantly black Roxbury. But when Reagan got to a meeting with executives at a bioengineering company, he let something slip: "I'll probably kick myself for having said this, but when are we going to have the courage to point out that the corporate tax is very hard to justify?" Getting rid of corporate taxes? If that wasn't Reaganomics, what was? And less than 20 hours after its alleged death knell.

The White House staff performed a deft act of circularity to undo this supposed misstatement. Larry Speakes was sent out to say that eliminating corporate taxes "is something that's not on the front burner, not on the back burner for that matter."

Outside by his helicopter, Reagan grinned: "Well, I said yesterday I'd kick myself for saying that. I have." With that he gave himself a little kick in the butt and walked off. With his Kabuki pantomime, he got to have it both ways. He had to eat his words, but he left the impression that he didn't want to.

When the 1984 budget was submitted, it was clear that the pragmatists had not won as much as we thought they had. The military budget actually went up; there were more cuts in food stamps and only modest tax increases. Long live Reaganomics.

I HAD ALWAYS dealt in a completely open and honest way with my producers. In fact, I took great pride in this. "I'm going to throw up," I'd say as my deadline closed in. "No one is returning my calls; I'm not sure I can get this done on time." I was a showcase of my insecurities, a layout of anxiety, an x-ray revealing my every fear.

When the office called Bill Plante, on the other hand, he was always the epitome of self-control. His voice would lower and calm: "All's well here. Nope, no problem. Just finishing up my script." He'd hang up and start mutilating his typewriter, busting the phone. He was just as panicked as I was, but he never let the office know, about which I was contemptuous. He was deceiving them, I told myself; I was aboveboard, forthright.

I didn't notice at first, but the producers began trusting Bill more than me and I suffered over it. Why? What am I doing wrong? Then the lightbulb: presentation counts. It's such a simple notion, one so obvious. Reagan was making the point every day. But it took me more than 12 years of my career to catch on. Why do men know that being cool instills confidence not just on camera; that it matters even with your colleagues, with the people who watch you make the sausage?

I recently discussed this with a psychiatrist, Anna Fells, who explained that Bill had quite naturally taken on the male role: in charge, in control. "You," she told me, "took on the female role: 'Oh, I need help.' Woman in distress."

At the time, it was a major epiphany for me. Confidence is something you impart by signals, and mine were obviously tentative. Now I had to add a new step to my list for the day: get Taylor off to school, and check on her when she gets home; read the papers and the magazines; place 100 phone calls and pray someone calls back; and now stifle my natural instinct — a habit, maybe even a need — of giving a running commentary on my emotional state. This was not so easily accomplished. I had to work on it. And as I did, I began to fear I was losing my femininity.

I began to wonder if, in my attempts to stifle my sexuality, all that was left of it were my dainty open-toed sling backs with those shy little pinkies poking out like eyes peering through a veil in Saudi Arabia. Dolly must have sensed as much. She sent me a picture of a pretty foot torn from a magazine with a note saying, "A nice smile and big boobs are not enough. Get a pedicure."

THE PRESIDENT had woman trouble; the "gender gap" that had first shown up in the 1980 campaign rebounded. So Reagan brought two women into his Cabinet: Elizabeth Dole as transportation secretary (it didn't hurt that she was married to an influential senator) and former Massachusetts Congresswoman Margaret Heckler as secretary of health and human services. But the appointments didn't help. Women were put off by Reagan's anti-Soviet rhetoric, by his budget cuts, and by his war on environmentalists, of whom he once said, "I don't think they'll be happy until the White House looks like a bird's nest." Cute, but unpopular.

His efforts to soothe women were hardly enhanced when 5,000 supporters of a nuclear weapons freeze flew into Washington from 47 states to lobby the government on March 8, 1983. The president, in Orlando, accused the freezeniks of "simpleminded appeasement" of the Soviets. He told a convention of evangelical Christians that the Soviet Union was "the focus of evil in the modern world." Flatly rejecting a nuclear freeze, he said, "I urge you to beware the temptation . . . to ignore the facts of history and the aggressive impulses of an evil empire."

I was standing with Zirinsky in the hall, both of us so boggled by the throwback Cold War exhortation, we ended up holding hands. If the president's intention was to shift attention away from the recession, he succeeded, though women were put off more than ever. This was raw meat; it was inflammatory when polls showed that the public wanted accommodation and arms control. It would become known as the "Darth Vader speech." And while historian Henry Steele Commager called it "the worst presidential speech in American history — and I've read them all," the boldness and resolve of that speech contributed greatly to the fall of Soviet communism.

Years later I filed a request at the Reagan Library for the speech and had to rethink my assumptions about Reagan's level of involvement in his presidency. His handwritten revisions are all over every page of the draft that was submitted by speechwriter Tony Dolan. On page one Reagan crossed out six lines and wrote the phrase "I believe in intercessionary prayer" in the margins along with a quote from Abraham Lincoln. He wrote out in longhand whole new pages 4 and 5 about illegitimacy and abortion, and on page 9 he scrawled in: "Unless and until it can be proven that the unborn child is not a living entity, then its right to life, liberty and the pursuit of happiness must be protected." Generally, he improved the speech, making it more colloquial, livelier. He was good at this. Yet, while he wrote the line "Let us pray for the salvation of all those who live in that totalitarian darkness," he was not the author of the term "the Evil Empire." Tony Dolan told me that while he wrote the phrase, "I certainly knew it was Reagan's thought," even though they had never discussed it. In fact, said Dolan, "this was a throwaway speech, not given much importance. The audience was a base group of core constituents and no one anticipated any foreign policy repercussions." When the speech vetters read the draft, they tried to edit out the Evil Empire language, but Dolan said, "Let the president decide." And so the lines remained intact.

I had been told that he rewrote many of his speeches, but I had such a fixed notion of him as a floater over the events of his presidency that I was startled when I actually saw the hard evidence. I called a friend who had worked for Reagan who said, "If you could get a pen or pencil in his hand, he'd engage. He seemed to think more sharply when he wrote out his thoughts." Another of his aides said, "He was always involved in the text. He fancied himself a speechwriter ever since 1964, when he wrote that famous address endorsing Goldwater." Reagan's level of engagement was a function of his interest in the subject. But with the speeches, I was told, he wasn't as involved as he had been. I asked, "Do you think there were signs of Alzheimer's back then?"

After a pause he said, "Looking back, I guess there were signs, but I never thought it the whole time I worked for him."

Speeches became far more central in the Reagan presidency than in most. They became an occasion for decision making, since the staff knew they were one of the few things Reagan would concentrate on. This was another way Jim Baker increased his influence, since through his number two, Dick Darman, he was in charge of the speeches. But the influence went only so far. The president gave the Darth Vader speech against the advice of both the pragmatists and his wife.[21]

Reagan's ideology grew directly out of what he saw as injustices during his career in Hollywood — and these resentments were embedded in his brain like the deep roots of a five-hundred-year-old tree (maybe that's what showed up on those x-rays!). His anti-Sovietism had been born when he was president of the Screen Actors Guild. It was then, he told Larry Barrett of *Time*, that he had discovered the Communists' "brutality," "cold-bloodedness," and "lack of morality," the very language of the Evil Empire speech.[22] His diatribe in Orlando was as much a reaction to Stalin's invasion of Hollywood in the 1950s as it was to Brezhnev's aggressive policies in the 1980s.

It was the same with Reagan's other lodestar, cutting taxes. In the early part of his career he was outraged by his 91 percent tax rate — so outraged that he became a lifelong bulldog on the subject, dragging the rest of us along with him.

IN A SPEECH on March 23, the president announced plans to develop a futuristic defense system that he said would blast incoming Soviet missiles out of the sky. Again, Reagan had rewritten key sections of the draft: "What if we could intercept and destroy strategic ballistic missiles before they reached our own soil or that of our allies? . . . Is it not worth every investment necessary to free the world from the threat of nuclear war? We know it is!"

"Star Wars" was considered unrealistic — Time called it "Reagan's video-game vision" and there was speculation that he had got the idea from Murder in the Air, one of his own movies in which his character, Lieutenant Brass Bancroft, deals with a death ray that can shoot down planes. But the Soviets seemed to believe in its possibility. And so, some contend, the prospect of having to spend billions to develop their own Strategic Defense Initiative (SDI) and/or reconfigure their existing forces to preserve an effective offensive capability is what eventually finished the job of bringing the Soviet Union to its knees. Of course, you could also argue that our own spending on such programs nearly brought us to our knees with the out-of-control deficits and national debt.

THE WINDOW CLAUSE in my contract was on my mind. It said I would anchor my own weekend newscast within 18 months. With the deadline just eight weeks away, I poked my head into Van Sauter's New York office one day and said offhandedly, "By the way, those 18 months are up in May."

"Glad you're here." He got up from his desk and moved around to greet me. "Come in." He seemed so happy to see me. "Sit down." He guided me to a couch, sat down beside me, and engaged me in a discussion of issues and movies and sports, dusted with a few "fucks" and "bastards." Van was often accused of having a child's attention span — he did flit from subject to subject, but I loved the man's range of interests. And I was flattered that he used profanity with me; I took it as an invitation to the club.

"I hope you remember about the weekend show," I said at last.

I was pretty softened up and off guard as he replied, shaking his head, "Lesley, Lesley, we're not going to give you a weekend show. We never were."

"What? But — but —" I sputtered, "I have it in writing."

"Oh, I know. I wrote that down so you wouldn't leave."

My mouth opened, but only sighs came out. I had no idea what to say. Sauter got up and went to the door. "I'm locking this," he said. "I'm

165

not letting you out of here until we find something else that will make you happy enough not to leave CBS." I was paralyzed — not by his cunning but by my own naïveté. What an idiot.

"What about *Face the Nation?*" he asked.

"No way. That's George Herman's show, and besides, I'm not interested."

He told me that he wanted to revamp the Sunday broadcast, "bring it into the 1980s," that George was closing in on 65 and would be replaced anyway. "What if we designed a new Sunday show for you? Give it a new name, new format, new look. I really think this would be good for you and good for us."

I balked, but the more he talked of "creating something new," my starch went limp. An hour after he had turned the key, we were batting ideas back and forth. He had seduced me with his enthusiasm, his willingness to experiment. And to be honest, I surrendered to the flattery of it all.

Before agreeing, though, I said I had to discuss it with Aaron, who thought I was crazy to have even a whiff of doubt: "Lesley, your own show. An interview show that you can shape and guide." When I called Van the next morning, I was more excited than I'd been in years. I agreed to take on the Sunday show without thinking through how I was going to handle what was essentially a second job.

About this business of Van's profanity: I was a sucker for anything that suggested an entrée into the Men's Fraternity. When Mike Deaver called and asked me to help him play a practical joke on Jim Baker, I was as happy as an African elephant in a mud hole. The idea was for me to write a CBS report on how Baker had fallen out of favor with the Reagans. If I produced it, Mike would persuade Jim it had actually run on the air.

I wrote a piece about a series of incidents that had caused the Reagans to lose confidence in the chief of staff. I used anonymous quotes from "White House aides" about Baker's "erratic behavior lately," along with the news that Reagan was considering asking Baker to resign. The clincher was my stand-up close: that Baker hadn't told anyone at the White House, but "CBS News has learned that the chief of staff has anorexia nervosa!"

The president, in on the gag, asked Jim and his wife, Susan, to represent him at a social event outside the White House at 6:45 P.M. At 6:35 Deaver called Baker's limo and said, "Better get back here, Jimbo, we've got trouble. Stahl just led the *Evening News* with a story saying the old man wants to dump you." Mike had edited my "report" into a tape of the *Evening News* and ran it for Jim and Susan. Deaver called me later, roaring with laughter. He said it was a great joke. Everyone loved it.

The next day Tom Wyman, the new chairman and CEO of CBS and my ultimate boss, called me at the White House booth. He had heard about my little prank and didn't think there was anything funny about it. He chewed me out for using CBS facilities, for spending my time — "which we pay you for" — on such frivolity, and besides, "It's inappropriate for you to be cavorting like that with the White House staff." He went on for a while like that till he broke down and said, "Baker's put me up to this; don't tell him I told you."

I adored the whole exercise. Not that I was ever one to play practical jokes; I just loved that they brought me in on their game. I was, for a rare split second, an insider.

How ironic that the Carter White House, which promoted the Equal Rights Amendment and other women's issues, was so unfriendly to women reporters, while the antifeminist (for the most part) Reagan team tended to treat us so fairly.

I DID AN *Evening News* report in April on the president's national security adviser, William Clark, in which I said that he had "risen to a position of almost unchallenged power in the White House. A conservative with little background in foreign policy, Clark has guided Mr. Reagan into increasingly harder-line positions." In my stand-up I said, "Now polls show a reemergence of the president's image as a warmonger."

Joe Peyronnin called at 6:32. "New York didn't like your close. We have to change it for the second feed."

"Why?" I felt my temper rise. "What didn't they like?" I demanded.

Joe said they hadn't liked my saying "warmonger." They wanted me to change the line to "Now polls show an erosion of confidence in the president's defense and foreign policy." After arguing for a few minutes, I gave in.

The "erosion of confidence" emboldened the Republican-controlled Senate Budget Committee to reject Reagan's request for a 10 percent increase in the Pentagon budget, and the president had to answer congressional charges that he was violating a law that prohibited aid to guerrilla groups trying to topple the government in Nicaragua.

TAYLOR WOULD CALL me every afternoon, unless I had arranged a play date for her. When I was growing up, I'd ride my bike home from school, change into pants (Dolly dressed me up for school), and go outside and play. My brother, Jeff, and I had a whole gang of friends our age who lived right on our street in Swampscott, Massachusetts. When it was time to come home for dinner, Dolly would stand at the front door, ring a bell, and call our names. Oh, God, was that embarrassing!

But the main thing was that Jeff and I were out on our own when we were Tay's age. This was such a major difference from the way she was growing up. She lived in a high-rise apartment in the middle of a city: no way could she, at age five, run outside and play without the supervision of an adult. How was she going to learn to be independent? I worried about it constantly and tried to give her as much freedom as I could.

Taylor was the easiest child. She was never sick — I don't think she missed more than five days of school her entire life — and she was always happy. As she got older I wondered how I, of all people, had been so blessed. I didn't think I was a great mother, though Taylor knew I loved her, that I was her rock, and that she could always find me.

My colleagues used to tease me that Taylor was the only child on Earth. If she called me, I'd get on the phone right away. If I was out of the booth, someone would find me and I'd race back. I'd hang up on sources, put officials on hold, talk to her on deadline: "Hi, angel. What happened at school today?" "Nothing." Every day, the same conversation. And if she didn't call me, I'd call her. She had to know I was her mother.

More than anything, I was her social secretary. I prayed my bosses wouldn't find out how much time I spent organizing her social life with the endless arrangements. Carmen, the nanny, didn't drive, so there were the pickups and the dropoffs; who had to be where at what time to retrieve her from whose house and who was coming over to ours.

When I got home at night she'd act out what she'd seen on *Sesame Street*. She adored it. We gulped our laughs like Ernie, sang Joe Raposo's songs, and wondered what Mr. Snuffleupagus ate for dinner. I told a magazine that year, "Since I've had this child, there is no such thing as depression. I walk in the door and there is that smiling face. You can just see how sweet human beings are when they start out."

The interviewer asked how I balanced it all. "I think I'm exactly like any other woman with a five-year-old," I said. "Whether you work or not, Monday, Tuesday, Wednesday you think: 'Gosh, I'm terrific, I can handle anything.' Thursday and Friday you can't handle anything at all. Saturday and Sunday, you coast."

I BEGAN PLANNING for the new *Face the Nation*. The producer, Joan Barone, was asked to come up with a new format and proposals for four different shows. Sauter's only guidance, that the broadcast — temporarily called "Stall the Nation" — not be as Washington-centric as the competition, *This Week with David Brinkley* and *Meet the Press*.

Aaron, who had worked for several magazines, urged me to think of *Face* as if it were *Time* or *Newsweek*. "When there's an obvious story of the week," he said, "*Time* puts it on the cover. That's what you should do. If there's a big story that everyone's talking about, you should be talking about it on the air." But when it's not so obvious, the magazines rarely put a Washington or hard-news story on their cover. "Then they go way off the news into science or Hollywood or a social trend, and you should do the same."

That sounded right, and I thought it would appeal to Sauter. Joan was reluctant to stray too far from topics with a hard edge, but I relished the chance to expand the narrow band of issues I had covered for more than a decade. So Joan and I wrote up a proposal that included a mix: an interview with the secretary of state one week, dieting the next; a Senate heavyweight one Sunday, next week the contraceptive sponge.

BY SPRINGTIME the economy had begun to turn around. The president's new chief economic adviser, Martin Feldstein, acknowledged that it was the Federal Reserve Board's tight monetary policy that had brought down inflation and triggered the recovery, but that didn't deter the president from taking credit.

It seemed to boost his spirits, yet in May, back in Santa Barbara, we were immersed in conjecture over whether he would run again. A group of reporters invited Jim Baker to dinner at the San Ysidro Ranch, where Jack and Jackie Kennedy had gone on their honeymoon. Bill Plante, as usual, ordered a great wine. Over rack of lamb the chief of staff confided that Reagan hadn't informed him yet.

"Bet he doesn't run," I said.

"Bet he does," Baker shot back. "I'll bet any one of you 50 bucks he runs again."

All seven of us took him on. He was so astonished that the next day he ordered up a White House spin campaign to persuade the press that the president would run. After all, no power resides with lame ducks.

I bet Reagan wouldn't run again because I thought he didn't *like* being president. The job was so cerebral; there was so much paperwork, though obviously he'd found a way to get around that. Then there was the constant challenge to his precious ideology—from his own staff. When he'd give one of his rare interviews, he'd complain about being locked up in the White House as if it were a jail. Just recently, he'd expressed a yearning to go to a drugstore—just to browse. And I couldn't see Rawhide relishing four more years of the kind of press notices he'd been getting. The poverty rate had risen to 15 percent, the highest level in 17 years, and Reagan was taking the blame because of his reductions in food stamps and nutrition programs.

Yet, to avoid lame duckdom, Ed Rollins—a *Star Wars* R2D2 look-alike—and his team in the White House worked up a political concerto that certainly had the melody of a reelection campaign. The first movement: consolidating his core constituency in the West. Reagan flew to

Phoenix to shoot off a progun speech to the National Rifle Association and then continued on to Texas, home to a significant Chicano vote, to celebrate a Mexican holiday. Second movement: the South. Off we went to Miami to celebrate a Cuban holiday. If that wasn't a campaign, what was? Needless to say, the pictures were glorious.

The administration began governing by the polls, which showed the gender gap widening, so Reagan made new arms control proposals. Women liked that. The polls continued to reveal a compassion gap, so the president invited the participants in the Special Olympics for handicapped youth to the White House. There he was on CBS and the other nets amid those happy-faced athletes who just melted your heart. Polls showed that Reagan's budget cuts in education and the environment were unpopular, so he went to Kentucky and Kansas to promote vocational education, and he hired environmentalist Bill Ruckelshaus as the new EPA administrator. (This was the same Bill Ruckelshaus who had resigned from the Justice Department during Nixon's Saturday Night Massacre.) By mid-June I was pretty convinced I would lose the 50 bucks.

AARON AND I rented a big house in Nantucket for two weeks in July and filled it up with our friends. I love it there. The air is delicious with the smell of the ocean, and the routines of life are uncomplicated and unpretentious: riding bikes to town, shopping for fresh-grown vegetables on Main Street, reading the paper on a canvas sun chair in our backyard.

Taylor was getting a rare feel for old-fashioned family life: a mother home every day making lunch, picking up shells on the beach and stringing them into necklaces, just being there. We entered the sand castle contest on Jetties Beach: we made a Triceratops and were heartbroken when a dragon won.

That was the summer Aaron taught Taylor how to ride a bike. There was the inevitable spill and the split lip and ugly bruise on her chin. This would be bad enough, but two days later my parents arrived. Dolly, who never once hinted that I was a neglectful mother because I worked, lit into me that day: "How could you let a little girl ride off alone like that? She's only five!" "You moron" was left unsaid. Even with that I loved having Dolly and Lou there. We drove them all over our island so they could see why we kept coming back.

It took two weeks to get my metabolism down to a normal rate, and then it was time to leave.

IN THE CRONKITE ERA the *Evening News* had opened with a ticking off of the correspondents and their stories. The message: Walter had his horsemen, this was a team. Sauter had taken the ticking away. The show opened with a shot of Dan, just Dan sitting at the anchor desk. He was the managing editor and the star, more like the sun. The broadcast revolved around him and his personality more and more, and it was working: he was firmly in first place. So in August Roone Arledge answered the challenge by making Peter Jennings the lone anchorman at ABC; NBC dropped the team of Mudd and Brokaw. Like Dan, Tom would solo. Now there were three young, handsome men at the three helms.

And I was about to turn 42, the age past which newswomen weren't supposed to survive on television. Lots of men assumed that. But Pauline Frederick had been NBC's correspondent at the United Nations until she retired in 1974 at age 66; Aline Saarinen was still working as NBC's Paris bureau chief when she died at 58.

"Why Are There Still No Female Dan Rathers?" asked *TV Guide* on August 1, 1983. There I was on the cover holding a microphone, along with Judy Woodruff and Ann Garrels of ABC. The answer, according to the magazine, was that male dominance and subtle discrimination remained in the TV industry, not to mention the White House. In the article, Joan Barthel wrote that when I asked a tough but straightforward question at the daily White House briefing, Larry Speakes would get noticeably annoyed. When a man asked a similar question, he would joke with him. "When a press secretary's frustration level rises," I told her, "he strikes out at the women much more readily than at the men. Jody Powell did it, and now Larry does it. It's something that's talked about here quite often." I paused, thought about it and added, "Well, the women talk about it, the men joke about it."

The Christine Craft case caught my eye. She had sued her company, Metromedia, for sexual discrimination, claiming that their station KMBC-TV in Kansas City had demoted her from an anchor post because they considered her "too old, unattractive, and not deferential enough to men." In a tape played at the trial a man asks a focus group to watch Christine on the air. "Is she a mutt?" he asks. That seemed to clinch it. A federal jury in Kansas City awarded Craft $500,000 in damages. Asked to comment, I said, "She was treated outrageously." But Roone Arledge, the president of ABC News, said, "The criteria are different in television as long as your face is out there as your byline, and you are judged by all the cosmetic things that go into that." Dolly went along with Roone. "Don't be foolish," she lectured me. "Get a better haircut and stand up straight."

Truth is, I spent as much time as I could spare on my appearance. I got my hair done twice a week, and I bought and used enough makeup to open my own boutique. But our new boothmate at the White House, reporter Deborah Potter, was living through her own Chris Craftian crucible. Deborah, one of the few brunettes in television news, was a superb journalist and a fast writer, but Sauter and his number two, Ed Joyce, didn't think she was attractive enough.

Our bureau chief asked if I would talk to her, which I found difficult — Deborah was a proud person — but I did it. "What about a new hairdo?" I asked reluctantly. "Maybe you should pluck your eyebrows." I didn't dare suggest she become a blonde. This was hard; I loved Deborah and this was obviously painful for her, and embarrassing. She resisted any cosmetic changes: "If they don't like the way I look, well, they can . . ." But then the directive came down from Sauter and Joyce: no more television for Potter, only radio.

This whole episode, she would tell me years later, had set off her own decade of anger and rage. At the time it triggered a wave of outrage and protest in the bureau since she was one of the strongest reporters we had. We all began conspiring to sneak her onto the tube, especially Zee, who used Deborah on late-night feeds to the affiliates that the bosses never saw. Eventually Deborah succumbed. She changed her hair, went to a television coach, moved to the State Department, and got back on the air. All in all it was an ugly chapter that added to Washington's hostility toward Sauter and Joyce.

REAGAN WAS on his annual month's vacation at his ranch when a Soviet fighter shot down Korean Air Lines Flight 007 on September 1, after it had strayed into Soviet airspace; 269 people were killed, including 61 Americans. Secretary of State George Shultz called the speaker of the House, Tip O'Neill, to inform him of the incident and confided that the president didn't know yet; he was still asleep.[23] When Reagan was informed, his initial response was offhand. It wasn't until Mike Deaver saw the CBS broadcast the next night, with pictures of Rawhide horseback riding while the crisis escalated, that it was decided the president should return to the White House.

Fixed on the notion that the Soviets had done this deliberately, Reagan delivered a hard-hitting televised speech on September 5 in which he demanded that the Russians allow an international search for the bodies and pay compensation to the families of the victims. Recently I saw copies of the original draft of the speech and again was surprised at how much of it Reagan had written out in longhand himself — a full seven of the 11 pages — with echoes of the Evil Empire language: "They reveal that — yes, shooting down a plane, even one with hundreds of innocent men, women, children and babies is a part of their normal procedure. . . . Memories come back of Czechoslovakia, Hungary, Poland, the gassing of villages in Afghanistan."[24]

But when all was said and done, Reagan didn't approve any retaliatory actions. Truth be told, with all his bellicose rhetoric, in practice he responded calmly to provocation. In my close that night I said, "The White House is sensitive to charges that its reactions are wishy-washy and ineffective. But, said one official, 'You have to add to this the fact that the Soviets have already inflicted serious damage on themselves.' "

A few nights later I said that "polls done this week show overwhelming support for the president's handling of the incident. Even the harsh criticism from the far Right [which wanted military retaliation] is seen as a gift, aides saying it helps define Mr. Reagan as a moderate, coolheaded statesman."

I WAS IN MY OWN war. The ideas Joan Barone and I came up with for the new *Face* were approved by Sauter, but they were also leaked to Walter Cronkite, then a member of the CBS board of directors and an outspoken critic of Sauter's approach to the news. Cronkite took our contraceptive sponge proposal to the board and passed it around as an example of how Sauter intended to remold *Face the Nation*. Walter was quoted as telling the board, "He's ruining CBS News on every front."

Face the Nation dated back to 1954. Its premier broadcast with Senator Joseph McCarthy aired on the eve of the Senate debate that resulted in his censure. It was not a tradition to be trifled with, and now Sauter had to assure his bosses at Black Rock that *Face* would remain the venerable, hard-news broadcast it had always been. He called me and said the show would not get a new name after all—which was just as well. We had considered names such as "Universe" and "Eye on the Globe." "Let's start off with some traditional shows," Sauter said. "Once we persuade everyone we're serious, then we can start experimenting." Joan was relieved.

I called my two favorite interviewers. The first was Ted Koppel, the master inquisitor of *Nightline*. What I admired about Ted's technique was that he was challenging but polite, persistent but detached. I told myself not to even think of him as a competitor; he was on his own playing field. So with that in mind, I called and asked for his advice. "Don't ever sit in the same room with the person you're interviewing," he said. The guests on *Nightline* usually sat staring into a camera in one studio, while Koppel was in an adjacent studio, staring into his own camera. On TV you'd see the two of them on a split screen, side by side—though they were not really side by side—each looking straight out. "You can be tougher when you don't have to look into their eyes," he said. "It's much easier to interview that way." I thought that wouldn't be true with me. Too sterile.

Then I called Mike Wallace at *60 Minutes*. "Tape everything," he advised. "Never go live."

"But, Mike," I pointed out, "that's just what we do. *Face* is a live, spontaneous broadcast. It's the whole point."

173

"All I'm telling you is that you'll never get as much out of them live as you will if you tape them." Great advice, but not that helpful, since I would never be allowed to change the *Face* format that much.

Once the basic concept was approved, Sauter left Joan and me to get *Face* on the air on our own. We were flattered they thought we could do it, but wondered if the hands-off approach meant they really didn't care about *Face* all that much.

They didn't leave us entirely unsupervised—we were females, after all. To Joan's great chagrin, they brought in Jonathan Ward, a gentle man who read a lot and loved good music, hardly a grizzly out on a power grab, but, poor man, that's the impression we all had. No wonder he caused the very unsteadiness he was intended to prevent. In their paternalistic wisdom, our bosses bestowed on him the title Joan deserved: executive producer. What ensued was a struggle with Joan and Jon vying for my endorsement, my loyalty, my attention. And that added to my already impressive daily output of stomach acid. It was around this time that I started coming down with serious bouts of laryngitis. I wouldn't find out for years that they were caused by something called an esophageal reflux, in which roiling acids shoot up from the stomach into the esophagus. People like me who tell ourselves we can handle oceans of stress often discover that the tensions and strains have been stockpiled in various body pockets. Eventually they explode. Ten years later my reflux produced an ulcer. On my esophagus.

Jon concentrated on aesthetics: he designed a new set and graphics and chose new music. Joan, our associate producer, Karen Sughrue, and I worked on format and content. Within a short time, Jon decided to rule us from an office in New York. We rarely saw him and I cannot recall a single time when he disagreed with a decision Joan or I made.

Things had been going well for Joan in the late 1970s—she was good at her job at CBS and happy with her boyfriend, Michael Barone, a political analyst. But then she found a lump in her breast. After surgery, she and Michael got married and five healthy years later adopted Sarah, my godchild. But no sooner had Sarah arrived than the cancer metastasized. As we started the new *Face*, Joan was in a battle for her life.

Jon Ward had come up with a handsome set in soft blue-gray tones. Handsome but, as we would learn, impractical. There were really two sets: one for the one-on-one interview in the first half of the broadcast and a separate set with a semicircle of chairs for a group discussion in the second half. What that meant was that after the interview, I would have to politely but briskly dismiss the guest, unplug my mike, dash across the studio as the other guests were being ushered in, greet them, get us miked up, and calm down—all during a two-minute commercial.

We did a series of practice shows, one on obesity, for instance, to get the acrobatics down and to allow me to find my voice. Aaron had been advising me that at every great magazine, there was one dominating voice that gave it its personality. In my case, he meant not just on the air but in the selection of the stories. He said that I had to make sure the *Face* voice — taste, really — was mine.

I became fixated on the lighting. Friends in Hollywood and New York would say, "What? You don't have a lighting director? Unheard of." To the crew's horror, I took up the slack, fussing over the megabulbs every Sunday morning. I knew the crew thought I was a pain in the ass, but if I didn't fight for myself, I'd look like dreck. And I, not they, would have to answer to Dolly.

Even after weeks of preparation, our first show sneaked up on us. We decided to make Lebanon our issue. The old *Face* had been built around a single interview. We were going to have multiple guests discussing a single topic. President Reagan had sent U.S. Marines into Lebanon as peacekeepers, and we had booked the Lebanese president, Amin Gemayel, as our big, look-at-us headliner to discuss the civil war and the U.S. Marines caught in the middle. But at 5:30 Thursday evening, he canceled on us. It was three days before our debut. I went numb and stayed that way until the Monday after the show. Actually, I managed to be numb and panicky at the same time. Joan and Karen got on the phones and somehow persuaded the marine commandant, P. X. Kelley, to be our leadoff guest. Gemayel showed up on *This Week with David Brinkley*.

Sunday morning I got two dozen yellow roses with a card from my sweetheart that said, "Break a leg and all their hearts. Love, Aaron." If you were watching CBS at 10:30, September 18, 1983, then you saw me — eyes in a semipop, neck veins in a full pop — and you heard me say, "Lebanon is at war. This time a unit of a U.S. Marine brigade is caught in the cross fire." I was so nervous, my usual alto approached Tiny Tim range. "Four U.S. Marines have died in Lebanon, and Americans are asking why." P. X. Kelley, tall and ruddy-faced with ramrod posture, made one ask if looking the part was a criterion for the job of commandant. Speaking of parts: mine, as hostess, was to relax the guest. But on this day it was P. X. who reached over, patted my hand reassuringly, and said, "It'll be fine. You'll do great." With that, I got a cue that meant: Go!

"Are you personally concerned that we are getting into a situation that is so tangled we will not be able to get out gracefully?"

"That's something," he replied, "the administration and the government far above my pay grade is going to have to answer."

Kelley continued to duck and circumvent, but I was so grateful he'd

175

shown up, I didn't push. I would have to get over the idea that I was a "hostess" in the homey sense. If I didn't toughen up, this was going to be a Sunday-morning tea party.

The show was reviewed the next day as if I had opened on Broadway. Most of the articles dwelled on my limp style and failure to ask tough questions. The TV critic at *The Miami Herald*, Sandra Earley, was typical: "Stahl sank under the weight of the program. . . . CBS is asking Stahl to compete with Brinkley and his fine public-affairs program. The network seems to have set her up to fail." Good grief. How do performers ever survive the critics? Glue themselves together and go back out there again? I did get some buck-up letters. Mike Deaver wrote kindly, "I thought your opening show was great," and Mr. Class, George Herman, sent me a note signed, "Your friend and admirer." Flowers came in from my bosses: "Relax!" said the card. "You're a winner! Van and Ed."

From then on I worked at a maniacal pace: Monday through Friday at the White House, Saturday at *Face*. We'd order in Chinese, pull our chairs into a circle — Joan, Karen, and I — and strategize. We were determined that no one would ever again say I didn't pursue or follow up. We would try to guess what the newsmaker might say to various questions, then fashion comebacks. I never went on the air without a thorough blueprint. The trick, though, was not to stick with it but to use it as a backup security system that would leave me free to listen and point out when a question was ducked. Many officials actually took lessons in how to avoid answering, how to wriggle out from under tough questions. I can't count the times administration officials told me flat out that their goal in coming on *Face* was to escape without making one parenthetical phrase of news.

I WAS CONCENTRATING on getting *Face* on the air just as Taylor was starting first grade. In the middle of everything, Aaron and I went over to Sidwell Friends for a parent-teacher conference where we were told that Taylor was behind in reading. I mark that as the moment I grew up, the point in time I crossed the line from thinking of myself as somebody's daughter to being an adult. "What do you mean?" I asked, feeling woozy. Till then Taylor had been problem-free — the ultimately convenient child.

My mother-in-law, who had taught grade school for 30 years, told me not to overreact. I, of course, searched out tutors and specialists. "Every child has a built-in reading clock," she said. "They read when they're ready. Don't push her." But doing nothing was harder than hustling. Aaron's mother was right, of course. But Taylor had tutors anyway.

And piano lessons, which she hated. And ballet, which she loathed. And gymnastics which she liked. And pottery, which she loved. I thought if I kept her busy maybe she wouldn't notice that I wasn't there very much.

One morning as Aaron was getting ready to drive her to school, Tay blurted out that she had a paper on the red fox due that day. "What? You didn't write it?" I was raising my voice. "You simply didn't do it?"

Her sweet little face got red and sad. "No, Mummy."

So I felt bad. "Don't cry. We'll get it done in the car." Half dressed, I ran around the apartment looking for "R" and "F" in the encyclopedia and raced to the car. Aaron drove while I read, "The red fox is the most common fox in Canada and the northern United States." Taylor, in the backseat, took dictation. By the time we pulled up to Sidwell, the paper was done. We three were elated as if we'd won the four-by-400-meter relay at the NCAA track finals. But as we drove away, I told my husband, "Aaron, we're doing this all wrong. What kind of parents are we? What kind of lesson was that to teach her? That we'll do her work for her?"

"You've got it all wrong," Aaron said. "We've just given her one of the most valuable lessons she could ever learn."

"Now what could that be?" I asked.

"How to meet a deadline!"

FACE's most daunting challenge wasn't the interviewing, it was the booking. Not only did we have to convince top officials to be grilled at the height of a crisis, but we had to compete with two other Sunday shows for the same officials. Actually, we had to beg for guests, and beg we did. Frequently the White House would wait until late Friday to accept or reject our request, often squeezing out concessions in return for the appearance of, say, the secretary of state or the Treasury. "We'll let him do your show as long as no one with an opposing view appears." Or "He wants more time."

My being at the White House was an advantage. The press officers there had become the casting directors for the Sunday shows, so I often did the begging and bargaining in person. I was able to book Jim Baker for our October 16 show, called "Will Ronald Reagan Run Again?" It came as no surprise that Baker said, "In my personal opinion, he is going to run." I mentioned a possible opponent, Senator John Glenn. We had gotten a clip from the new movie *The Right Stuff* about Glenn the astronaut, which we ran in the middle of the Baker interview. "So, what do you think of celluloid heroes?" I asked. "How worried are you that this movie is going to turn John Glenn into a big national hero, if not a myth in the country."

"Well . . ." He seemed caught off balance. I thought: These guys are always so prepared, they know just what we're going to ask. But this time,

177

I had surprised the great Jim Baker. "I can't — for one thing, I can't believe that the voters are going to base their voting decision on a movie."

"You don't think Hollywood can create a president?" One of my all-time favorite questions.

"One reason a lot of people say [Reagan] is not going to run," I said, "is because when that Korean airliner went down . . . we got the impression that he would rather be at the ranch than come back here and deal with the issue. Is this not a factor?" I was thinking of how diligently Jimmy Carter had worked round the clock in a crisis, and, by contrast, how devil-may-care Reagan could be. There were times when it was shocking.

"No, but the fact of the matter is — the fact of the matter is, he did come back here, and he did deal with the issue, and he dealt with it very, very well."

"But his first instinct was to stay at the ranch." I was learning how to follow up.

"Well, I'd tend not to agree with that. I don't think that's an indication at all that the president is thinking in terms of not running."

I'd been doing the show for more than a month, and this was the first time I actually had fun. A few days later John Carmody, who wrote "The TV Column" in *The Washington Post* had this to say: "Dare we call this a 'Face' lift? Well, anyway, for the second time in the five weeks since Lesley Stahl took over as moderator, CBS' 'Face the Nation' finished first in the weekly Sunday morning public affairs race." It was *Face's* highest rating in almost two years.

For the next Sunday, we lined up Defense Secretary Caspar Weinberger to talk about the escalating violence in Lebanon, along with the Syrian ambassador, Rafic Jouejati. My phone rang at about 3 A.M. A truck bomb had exploded at the U.S. Marine barracks in Beirut, and more than 70 Americans were reported dead. The number would reach 241.

Joan, Karen, and I went into the bureau very early, relieved that we had lined up the perfect guests. ABC's *This Week* and NBC's *Meet the Press* must have been scrambling to match us. But our little bubble did the proverbial pop when I finally got through to David Gergen at the White House. "We're awfully sorry," he said, "but Cap's in a national security meeting in the Situation Room which we think will go on for several hours." I was discovering that live Sunday morning television was the twin brother of terrorism.

"But David, don't you think the American people are going to want some word from the administration? We're talking about the wanton murder of who knows how many Americans." I implored him to lean on Weinberger. "Let us set up a camera crew in the White House. All Cap would have to do is leave the meeting for ten minutes max. We'd carry him by microwave. Please ask him."

It was known that while Secretary of State George Shultz had pushed for the deployment of the marines in Lebanon, Weinberger had strenuously opposed it. It was characteristic of Reagan that when his Cabinet officers failed to reach a consensus, he would decide on a split-the-difference solution. The contingent of marines was so small that they were, in effect, sitting ducks.

Gergen called back with word that Weinberger was considering my proposal. "We'll send our crew right over." It was after nine o'clock, 90 minutes to air. It would take the cameraman at least an hour to set up.

As I worked on my questions, Joan positioned herself at the front door to greet our other guest and escort him into the makeup room. Wire service reports out of Beirut were laying the blame for the bombing on Syria, so we thought, even if Weinberger stiffs us, at least we'll have the Syrian ambassador, who, to our great relief, finally showed up. When he arrived he told Joan, "Oh, miss, I cannot stay. I only came by to apologize in person that I must not appear on your broadcast. This is not a good time. Please forgive." But as he bowed and begged Joan's pardon, she was gently guiding him back into makeup. He continued to protest, but somehow the self-effacing Joan eased him into the makeup chair, all the while sympathizing, understanding. "Well, Mr. Ambassador, you can tell Lesley all this yourself in just a few minutes."

Meanwhile, I was sitting alone in the studio, staring into the camera à la Ted Koppel, still not certain whether Weinberger would show up. David Gergen was with our crew in the Roosevelt Room, one flight up from the Situation Room, telling us that he "hoped" Cap could get away. "No guarantees."

Minutes before the red light went on, Secretary Weinberger eased into a chair in the Roosevelt Room. I almost wept. I asked about a U.S. military retaliation, pointing out that the president had recently said he would "not stand idly by and have our marines brutalized."

"That is part of the agenda this morning," said Weinberger. "[We're] trying our best to find out exactly who was responsible." He said that the "circumstantial evidence" pointed to Iran. Was Syria also involved? He said that the investigation was just beginning but again fingered Iran.

During the commercial the Syrian ambassador was ushered into the studio. "Ambassador Jouejati," I asked, "did your government have anything to do with this tragic bombing this morning?"

He put his hands together in the prayer position and arced forward in a slow bow so low that he almost touched my knees with his forehead. 179 This was done in silence. Finally, on the upswing, he made a long speech of condolence: "The marines are our brothers, and we regret that very, very, very deeply."

I eventually got to reask my is-Syria-involved question, which provoked a bout of petulance: "You have been asking Mr. Weinberger once and again is Syria responsible. . . . Syria is not interested in partitioning Lebanon."

After the show, we congratulated ourselves. We had talked the secretary of defense into an extraordinary middle-of-a-meeting appearance; Joan had persuaded a reluctant Syrian ambassador to participate. And we had pulled it off all by ourselves.

The next day, Monday, October 24, 1983, I was in the booth, writing a story on the president's determination to keep the marines in Beirut in order to demonstrate U.S. resolve and reliability. Around four in the afternoon Bill Plante got a tip: a contingent of marines was about to invade the Caribbean island of Grenada — the next morning. Bill went off to ask Speakes about it. Larry told him, "Preposterous. No. Absolutely not."

First thing the next morning, 1,900 marines invaded Grenada. The president was on a golf outing in Augusta, Georgia: To avoid the inevitable stories that he had either putted or slept his way through the crisis, the White House released photos of the president attending a 5 A.M. briefing in his pajamas and robe. Back at the White House, he explained the invasion as a mission to rescue Americans, including hundreds of medical students who were exposed to "great danger" from a "brutal group of leftist thugs" running the government. The White House said the action had been requested by other Caribbean nations to prevent a takeover by Cuba.

At our briefing that day a reporter quoted an administration source that one of the motivations for the Grenada operation was distracting the public from the fiasco in Beirut. Larry Speakes exploded — protesting too much, I thought. "I tell you what I would do. I'd go back to that source and I'd grab him right by the collar and jerk him up and say, 'You didn't give me the facts.' . . . That is a foolish and incomprehensible deduction."

I didn't think it was foolish. And Speakes, denying it, was unconvincing. Larry's credibility, which was not too sturdy to begin with, was deeply damaged by his apparent lie to Bill Plante the day before, when he'd said "preposterous."

SPEAKES: I think the question was more in terms of "Are U.S. Marines *in* Grenada?"
PLANTE: That was not the question.

Speakes was out of the loop, and we didn't trust him. One of the reporters called on Plante to repeat the precise question he'd asked Larry.

"Just for the record," said Bill, "the inquiry was, 'Are marines going to land on the island tomorrow morning?'" Speakes told us later that he had threaded Bill's inquiry back to Admiral John Poindexter, the new number two man on the National Security Council. Poindexter had told him, "Knock it down hard."

Obviously, a "no comment" to Bill would have been a signal that indeed there was some truth to the tip. But Larry could have said, "I can only tell you completely off the record and ask you not to report this." In most cases involving secret military action, news organizations agree not to report until after the operation is launched. He could have told Plante he'd check it out and then disappear. Anything but lie. As Bill Moyers, who had been Lyndon Johnson's press secretary, once said, "Censorship is acceptable, lying is not."

But censorship in Grenada was as much a source of grousing as the misleading. Reporters were being prevented from covering the Grenada invasion. "You're totally controlling the flow of information," I complained at the briefing, "as though this isn't an open and free democracy."

"Number one," said Speakes, "it's a very active situation in Grenada and the military is occupied in running that operation. When they're ready to [allow coverage], they will do it."

Someone pointed out that reporters had gone into combat with American forces beginning with the Revolutionary War. This issue, as much as any, had tempers flaring on both sides.

DONALDSON: What you're doing here is covering up an operation against another nation involving American troops and not allowing reporters in there to see what's happening.
SPEAKES: I'll tell you what I think we need to do. I think we need to really work on, all of us, restoring a little civility here.
STAHL: Don't censor us in here, either.

I wanted to smack him. How I hated it when Speakes assumed the role of comportment cop. I took it as an insult when he stood before us day after day, not knowing anything about anything.

REPORTERS DIDN'T GET into Grenada until after the fighting was over, and then the administration released its own videotapes of the operation without a single frame of combat footage. In its attempts to minimize the danger, the Pentagon came up with briefing language so cleansed, you hardly realized the soldiers were in a war zone. A military action was a "predawn vertical insertion"; nouns became verbs: tasking, absenting. When we protested the obfuscations, our lack of access, the managed news, the mangled syntax, the press got little public support.

The president delivered a speech on television, true to form blaming the Russians. Not only was Grenada "a Soviet-Cuban colony being readied as a major military bastion to export terror and undermine democracy" throughout Latin America, but the Beirut bombing had been carried out with Moscow's "direct support through a network of surrogates and terrorists." This speech — much of which he wrote himself — was one of Reagan's most effective, and I think it gets to the heart of the emotional grip he had on the American people.

I have a copy of Reagan's handwritten notes: "This past Sunday at 22 minutes after 6 Beirut time, with dawn just breaking, a truck, looking like a lot of other vehicles in the city, approached the airport on a busy main road. . . . At the wheel was a young man on a suicide mission." He took you there, to Beirut. "The first warning something was wrong came when the truck crashed through a series of barriers, including a chain-link fence and barbed-wire entanglements. The guards opened fire, but it was too late."

Most presidents lecture or plead or give you laundry lists. Reagan sketched out an adventure tale about Beirut, another about Grenada, and both were romantic allegories of gallantry and patriotic sacrifice. Grenada involved a big-screen Rambo rescue mission where American kids were saved from the Commies. You could just see Sylvester Stallone. This was Reagan's appeal: an idealistic, cinematic vision of American youth slaying the evil forces. He painted pictures of us that we liked and that we wanted so much to be true. So it wasn't just that he was an actor who read his lines well, he wrote them too. He sold us his pretty illusions through storytelling; it was his greatest gift.

Aaron, who was deep into books about the Civil War, told me that if Abraham Lincoln hadn't been such a fine writer, he might have gone down as the president too weak or too lacking in judgment to prevent a civil war, the "foolish" president who had led the nation into the bloodiest battle we ever fought. But he wrote the Gettysburg Address and the second Inaugural Address ("With malice toward none, with charity for all, . . . let us strive on to finish the work we are in, to bind up the nation's wounds") and thereby established the history and defined himself as our most principled leader.

Reagan did that with Grenada. Though evidence came to light that many of the U.S. casualties had been caused by friendly fire, that the medical students weren't really in danger, that the Soviets weren't actually intent on taking over the island, Reagan wrote the history as far as the public was concerned with his script about a magnificent rescue mission.

His poll ratings had been tumbling. He had taken a big hit after the Beirut bombing, but that speech changed everything.

Kathy Frankovic, director of polling at CBS News, told me that this speech marked the big switchover from his unpopularity of 1982–1983. "It was the breakthrough event that made him the invincible candidate," she said. The economic recovery was in full roar, but it wasn't until Reagan delivered that speech that the polls jumped, and they wouldn't slide back down until long after the 1984 election.

But while the president was soaring, his press secretary was floundering. The strains of the past few days were exacting such a toll that *The Washington Post* ran an article about his "testiness." For four straight days, Speakes bickered and browbeat in the briefings. It started as we reporters hounded him about Reagan's decision not to go to Dover Air Force Base to receive the coffins of the dead marines from Beirut and then about the continuing restriction of press coverage in Grenada. In defense, Speakes complained about some inaccurate reporting.

Bill Plante replied, "That's what the system's all about."

"Bum stories?" asked Speakes.

Plante shot back that one organization's inaccuracy was no reason "to keep us out of there. . . . The system is about our right to observe it for ourselves and be wrong."

> SPEAKES: I'll tell you what I want. Anybody who reports on this, I'd like you to report what Plante said, and I'd like—
> STAHL: We don't care what you'd like us to report.
> SPEAKES: I wish you wouldn't interrupt. . . . Let me tell you one thing, Lesley. I've about had enough of you.
> STAHL: Well, I've had enough of you telling me how to act.
> SPEAKES: Listen. Let me finish. I've had enough. If you can't be—not interrupt me back there—
> STAHL: Watch out, he's pointing his finger at me.
> SPEAKES: I sure am. Now you're the greatest violator of this thing—
> REPORTER: The Violator!
> SPEAKES [to Stahl]: I'm sick and tired of you. I am sick and tired of you. I am tired of you.

He damn near came apart. Can you just imagine what would have been said about his PMS if he were a woman?

Truth is, I was the least of his tormenters that day. Sam, Bill Plante, David Hoffman of *The Washington Post*, and others were challenging him in deep, angry voices. It was just easier for him to strike back at a female.

A WEEK LATER the president held a rally on the South Lawn, a welcome-home celebration for 490 of the medical students who'd been "rescued" from Grenada. The Reagans were turning the White House into a Hollywood soundstage, where little shows were being dramatized. This was a   183

Deaver-goes-all-out production with a band, waving flags, and young, cheering faces. To me it looked like a diversion to erase the memory of Beirut.

In my script that night, I included a quote from the president, who "shared the students' anger at skeptics who question the invasion and belittle the danger you were in." I wrote a close noting that flag-draped caskets were returning to Dover Air Force Base that very day from both Beirut and Grenada (18 Americans had died there), but there had been no mention of that at the White House. Any hint of failure or tragedy would be driven off by the sights and sounds of triumph. The close was rejected in New York, and I went wild. "They think your point is inappropriate," Zee explained.

I called one of the producers in New York, a friend, one of the serious "yesterday" types, Mark Harrington. "This is pretty unsubstantiated," he said. "Who specifically told you this?"

"This is my analysis of what's going on here. They're trying to create amnesia about the bad news of Lebanon, and I think we should report it." [25]

"We think you need to change it to something more neutral."

I argued but couldn't move him. Harrington would tell me later that they were still being subjected to a nightly diet of Sauter's "There she goes again. The country loves this guy. We should ease up." Another of the New York producers told me recently, "We felt: If Lesley does this, Van will be in here tearing our asses off afterward. He'd have notes, and he'd be complaining about your tags." Sauter said he wouldn't mind so much if my closing stand-ups were covered over with pictures.

I was ordered to rewrite a tag to the Grenada rally piece. Which I did since I had no choice:

> The president leaves on a one-week trip tomorrow for Japan and South Korea. Mr. Reagan expected to point to the Grenada operation as an example of U.S. resolve to fight the spread of communism.

I went home cross and choleric, packed, and the very next day left with Reagan for Asia, where I got laryngitis again.

AFTER A WHILE, when it wasn't my turn at the White House, I began taking Mondays and Tuesdays off. I would pick up Taylor at school, run errands, and sleep. There's no question that I had taken on too much. But I never once considered shedding either of my jobs: the White House or *Face*. I would just have to adjust, manage my time, figure it out. Meanwhile, I lost fifteen pounds.

We had collapsed our two *Face* sets into one and ironed out a few

184

more kinks, but still, every week was a booking agony. Whenever there wasn't one overwhelmingly obvious must-do issue, we would try to be offbeat. On November 20, while Brinkley and *Meet the Press* tackled arms control, we did a show on the Equal Rights Amendment with, among others, Phyllis Schlafly. A few days before the show I taped an interview with the conservative columnist Patrick Buchanan in his home. I asked him his views of modern American women.

"I don't think," he said, "they're endowed by human nature with the singleness of drive, the singleness of purpose, the fierce ambition to succeed, to succeed above anything in the competitive world of Western capitalism along with men. And for women there is an honorable and honored exit from the marketplace. There is a way you can drop out and become wife, mother, build a family as it were." Buchanan and I were seated on ottomans in his living room. I leaned back and fell onto the floor.

We ran the tape of Buchanan's quote in the show. "What do you think of that, Phyllis Schlafly?" I asked.

"I think he's absolutely right, and if we ever have a world in which women are in the workforce fully all their lives just like men, we will have a world in which the children are all in day care centers."

"I must say, I never thought you, Phyllis Schlafly, would say women are not endowed with ambition and drive." Karen Sughrue told me later that Schlafly's daughter, who was in the control room, began pounding the table with delight at my comment.

By then I was developing a reputation for toughness as an interviewer. My attitude was that public officials in our system are obliged to explain and justify their policies, decisions, and actions. So I was proud of being tenacious; I liked being called tough. But I was also called impolite, and that I didn't like. I told one critic, "The pressure of the clock is why so many interviewers get the reputation for being discourteous. The time is being eaten up [by the interviewees' filibustering] and you're still stuck on question two. It's a constant balancing act between moving it along and not being rude."

December 1983. By the time I found a few hours to do my Christmas shopping, all the Cabbage Patch dolls were sold out. Aaron and I drove to every toy store in the greater Washington metropolitan area until we finally found one.

THE FIRST SIGN that Reagan's reelection campaign had started in earnest was the president's sudden slam of the gears into reverse on Soviet policy. In what was billed as a major foreign affairs speech, he once again turned the issue into a little movie about an Ivan and Anya and a Jim and Sally who meet and discover all the things they have in common: "Ambitions and hobbies and what they wanted for their children and problems of making ends meet." On a dime the Evil Empire was transformed into a Peoria of folks like us. In my stand-up close that night on a snowy White House lawn, I said, "His main message: that he's not what all those Democrats have been saying about him. In fact, he's a peacemaker." Nancy Reagan, the grand impresario, had decided that her husband should go down in history for making peace with the Russians.

Another issue the president decided to run on was "reverse discrimination." He took up the cause of white men who complained they were facing racial and gender bias because of programs designed to benefit minorities and women. Until Reagan was president, the job of the Civil Rights Commission had been to act as the nation's conscience on race. As an independent commission, it had criticized every president since Eisenhower. But when it rebuked Reagan for not hiring more blacks and women, he fired the recalcitrant members.

During my years as a reporter, many of my colleagues and I had been accused of bias, of being closet liberals. I never saw myself as subscribing to anyone else's packet of political views, but I am human and on given issues did, of course, have opinions. Being a beat reporter at a television network meant that I was obliged to submerge those opinions, keep them out of my copy. This was (and is) a duty, a requirement of my job. It's something I, and all of us, work at—sifting out our views.

At CBS we also had filters, producers, and editors who acted as watchdogs. One night, Brian Healy, an *Evening News* producer, edited a script of mine about abortion: "If you say one side is 'pro-choice,'" he said, "you can't say the other side is 'anti-abortion.' You have to say 'pro-life.'" I wanted my reports to be balanced and impartial. I took pride in it, so it had never taken anything as strong as willpower to launder my opinions—until Reagan began reversing nearly 25 years of civil rights policy.

When I was growing up in the 1950s, one of my formative experiences was watching the battles to integrate southern schools on television. I was a sophomore in high school in September 1957, when President Eisenhower sent federal troops to Little Rock, Arkansas, to escort nine black kids my age to school. From that time I accepted civil rights as a moral cause, a matter of principle with no shades of gray. I was therefore perplexed by many of Reagan's actions on the issue.

I asked one of his more moderate aides, a longtime supporter of civil rights, "Does it bother you?" I remember I was struck that he made excuses for Reagan, rationalizations. "He's not a racist or anything like that," he said. "It's just that he doesn't grasp the realities of race relations in the 1970s and 1980s. He thinks American life is all about Ozzie and Harriet. It's a generational thing."

186

Our guest on *Face* on January 22 was Clarence Pendleton, the black, anti–affirmative action chairman of the Civil Rights Commission. He argued that there should be no special advantage accorded to "groups" because of past discrimination. He wanted to give benefits not to groups but to individuals. I asked, but he could not explain, how an individual would get the benefits without the affirmative action programs he and Reagan were trying to abolish. I asked, but he could not explain, how the Reagan administration planned to deal with black unemployment which was nearly 18 percent, more than double the overall rate. Or with the 35.6 percent of blacks below the poverty line (compared with 12 percent of whites).

The next day Reagan nominated Ed Meese to replace the retiring William French Smith as attorney general, which was in itself a blow to civil rights since Meese was an ardent opponent of affirmative action. But polls showed that the president's championing of a "color-blind" society and his fighting against "reverse discrimination" were popular with the so-called Reagan Democrats. It would be an issue that would help him win reelection.

On January 29, 1984, the president formally announced that he was running again. Fifty bucks gone, I thought (though I don't recall ever paying Baker). The date, we would later learn, had been chosen in accordance with Nancy's astrological consultations.

I WAS SITTING in the CBS booth at the White House when my friend the writer Gail Sheehy called from New York to tell me that she'd been seated next to Van Sauter at a dinner party the night before. "Did you know," she asked, "that he's a Reagan Republican?" He had made it clear in their conversation, she said, that he supported the president down the line.

I hadn't known. I had assumed that Sauter, like most of us in the business, kept his political beliefs as buried as he possibly could. I had also assumed that because Van was married to Kathleen Brown, daughter and sister of two Democratic governors of California, Pat Brown and Jerry Brown, that he, too, was a Democrat.

In September Van moved to Black Rock, the CBS headquarters, as the new executive vice president in charge of the News Division and CBS's five owned-and-operated television stations. With this move, he helped tear down the wall between CBS News and the corporation — we once called it the separation of church and state. No longer would news be exempt from the bottom-line imperatives that ruled the other divisions.

Sauter's consigliere and best friend, Ed Joyce, took over as president of CBS News, though he would have Sauter looking over his shoulder. While Van was an expansive, friendly, Whitmanesque character, Ed was more like Ezra Pound, wiry and cold. Ed lacked Van's gregariousness, rarely leaving the sanctuary of his office, so he persuaded Howard Stringer to come into management as his number two, to charm people for him.

That left an opening as executive producer of the *Evening News*. The job went to Lane Venardos, a more zealous adherent of the Sauter school of journalism than Stringer. Once he took over, my copy was watered down more than ever.

ON FEBRUARY 7, after the president and Mrs. Reagan were on their way to Santa Barbara for another vacation, the White House released a slip of paper late in the day, announcing plans to pull the marines out of Beirut. It was a full-blown retreat, a caving in; now the administration would do everything possible to distance the man who had sent the marines there in the first place from any connection to the embarrassing withdrawal. There were no Reagan sightings. No White House officials were available for comment. No one from the administration would appear on *Face* or Brinkley or *Meet the Press* to explain. The president went directly to his ranch and would not be seen in public for more than a week. While the president cleared brush and rode his horses, the Soviet leader, Yuri Andropov, died, but neither the vacuum in Moscow nor the crisis in Lebanon, where the U.S.-supported government was collapsing, was enough to pry Reagan from his ranch. In his first few years in office I had seen a virtue in having a president who didn't overreact to every provocation as Jimmy Carter had. But by 1984 I thought it wasn't so much wisdom on Reagan's part as laziness.

The irony was that Reagan climbed ever higher in the polls. The pullout of troops from Lebanon was taken as evidence that despite his gun-toting swagger, this was a cautious leader not too proud to walk away from a fight if it meant avoiding a Vietnam-like quagmire. The few times he did engage, he made sure it was against a small and weak adversary like Grenada.

THE CAMPAIGN OF 1984 was under way, and I got to cover both sides: the Republicans from the White House, the Democrats from the set at *Face the Nation*. A cast of Democrats — known as the Seven Dwarfs — jumped into the race, one being the Reverend Jesse Jackson — hardly a dwarf — who spoke in clever rhymes. I thought there was something healthy and cleansing about an intelligent black man running for the highest office. He would attract not just blacks and the poor; liberal suburbanites also backed him, and, as CBS correspondent Bob Faw reported, "Campuses have gone wild over him; a handful of union officials have defied their leadership to support him." Yet he and I were to develop a strained relationship. Early in the campaign when I interviewed Jackson at his headquarters, I asked a series of pointed questions about his liberal policy positions on economic issues and about his association with Yasser Arafat and Louis Farrakhan. When the camera was off, he bristled at me, "That was racist. Your questions were racist." Perhaps he was trying to chill me; instead he had me burning. "Are you saying I'm a racist?" I demanded. It was the deepest insult, and I let him know it. But he did not back off, insisting that he was not saying I was a racist but that my insinuations were. I stormed out.

A few weeks later, on February 13, *The Washington Post* reported that Jesse Jackson had referred to Jews as "Hymies" and New York as "Hymietown." A *Post* editorial called the words "disgusting" and demanded that Jackson apologize. The next Sunday I was broadcasting *Face* from Iowa (the caucuses were the next day) with Jesse Jackson. He flatly denied ever making the anti-Semitic remarks (though the story wouldn't die and eventually he apologized).

I went on to ask about "a story I heard": Had Jackson told former vice president Walter Mondale he would get out of the race only if Mondale recognized the PLO, the dreaded enemy of Israel and virtually every Jew in America? "Is that what you told Mondale?" I asked.

"No, no, I did not."

"If Mondale gets the nomination," I continued, "will you whole-heartedly support him?"

"Well, I expect to support him, but I think the conditions really must be met."

"Are they still a PLO recognition condition?"

"Oh, of course."

WALTER "FRITZ" MONDALE easily won the Iowa caucuses on February 20 with 49 percent and moved on to the New Hampshire primary one week later. And so did I, to interview presidential candidate Gary Hart on *Face*. This was a particularly frozen winter — local ice carvers made sculptures of all the candidates (reminding me of Winter Carnival at Dartmouth College). I was staying at the Sheraton Wayfarer in Manchester, a maze of buildings and wings with a waterfall — a perfect backdrop for our stand-ups.

The race was thinning down to a mano-a-mano match between, as columnist Murray Kempton put it, "Mondale, the husband type, and Hart, the boyfriend type." Senator Gary Hart was running as the avatar of a new generation — as my colleague Eric Engberg put it, "the first openly Yuppie candidate for president of the United States." My plan for the Hart interview was to start with questions about his disorganized campaign and move on to foreign policy issues, his area of expertise. But when I got back to my room Saturday night, I found an article by George Lardner of

189

The Washington Post slipped under my door by his *Post* colleague Marty Schram. He had circled several paragraphs about Gary Hart's real name and age.

The next morning on *Face* I asked Hart if he had changed his name "from Hartpence to Hart right after you finished college." I felt uncomfortable bringing it up, but I was sure he'd be ready with a quick explanation. I had questions on foreign policy I wanted to get to.

"It was to restore our name to what it originally was some long time ago." He said the decision had been his, his parents', and his wife's, "a collective decision on all of our parts."

"Your uncle Ralph Hartpence [says] that you wanted to do it because you wanted to get into politics."

"No, that — well." He was obviously unprepared for this. "That is not the case." The Lardner article said that Hart had feared that in politics he'd be haunted by his childhood nickname: "Hot Pants."

I asked about another issue in the Lardner article: that Hart was shaving a year off his age in the biographies distributed by his Senate office.

"No. I am exactly the same age as my birth record, which is 1936." I could practically touch his crankiness.

When the show ended, he stomped out, vowing he'd never appear on *Face* again!

I had not expected to ask so many questions about his name and age, but I felt obliged by his hesitancies to press on. When he didn't own up to the discrepancy about his age, I thought I had raised serious questions about his forthrightness. But this was 1984, and "character" issues were not yet a routine subject on Sunday-morning interview shows. We were expected to deal with more weighty issues. Some time later, Tom Shales, the TV critic at *The Washington Post*, would use that interview as an example of a new "gunslinger mentality . . . a new style of aggressive, more contentious and much more personal questioning [that] has grown increasingly popular with TV correspondents." Shales quoted a Hart aide as saying, "They don't ask these kinds of questions of Mondale." [26]

Hart may have felt abused, but two days later he trounced Mondale in the New Hampshire primary with a surprising 41 percent to Mondale's 29 percent. Jackson came in fourth. Someone who wasn't even running in the Democratic primary came in sixth with more than 5,000 write-ins: Ronald Reagan! [27]

When the campaign moved south, Mondale landed a bruising punch on Gary Hart during a March 11 debate in Atlanta, suggesting there was no there there: "When I hear your new ideas, I'm reminded of that [hamburger] ad, 'Where's the beef?' " Two days later, on Super Tuesday,

Hart won three of the five states, but Mondale was still considered the front-runner. (John the-celluloid-hero Glenn pulled out.)

At the White House the only concern was overconfidence. An old saying holds that a grueling primary season gets a candidate in shape for the general election. But in truth the grueling battles usually bloody a candidate, tainting and tarring him so thoroughly that he is damaged goods.

IN EARLY MARCH we booked Republican candidate Pat Robertson, the televangelist, on *Face the Nation*, where he declared that the United States "should be a Christian nation." When he said that polls showed Americans favored school prayer, I pointed out that polls also showed Americans favored legalized abortion and the Equal Rights Amendment.

Joan and I were quarreling. The booking headaches were of migraine proportions. Not only were we inviting four or five guests a show, we'd often start the week pursuing one subject, only to change direction late in the week. And I confess, I was demanding: "We need to get someone better." Or "Not him again!" But mainly Joan fought any idea that strayed off the hardest news story of the week. The bickering made me feel guilty: she was sick, and when I thought I upset her, I'd hate myself. Finally one day she burst into tears on the phone and told me she was leaving the show. She swore there were no hard feelings but that she wanted to work full-time on the campaign.

Not long after, she went into the hospital again. This time the cancer was in her liver. I kept promising her she would beat it. "You have to remain positive and fight. Be as feisty as you've ever been." She begged me to reassure her over and over, which I did as convincingly as I could.

I TOLD MY BOSSES I wanted Karen Sughrue to replace Joan, and after much debate, I got my way. Karen had two very distinctive characteristics: she was tall—5 feet, 10½ inches—and she was patient. She was also smart, quick, and fun. We rarely argued about the direction of the show, though we had some doozies over what questions to ask.

Karen was creative and eager to experiment with different formats: town meetings, mixing live and taped interviews, and traveling. We both assumed that we were free to plan our own shows as long as we stayed within budget. So we never thought twice about going to Egypt to interview Hosni Mubarak.

Over we went: Karen; our director, Bob Vitarelli; and I. We took off the whole week so we could do a little sightseeing (at our own expense): a camel ride around the Sphinx, a tour of the artifacts found in King Tut's tomb. Aaron joined us, and one day we took a side trip to Luxor. I had always wanted to see the tombs in the Valley of the Kings.

I sat down with Mubarak in his palace, in a grand, high-ceilinged room with gilded rococo moldings. The interview went well. It didn't make headlines, but he was a head of state, the Middle East was in the news, and he was plucky. We congratulated ourselves. Not only had we had a great time in Egypt, we'd put together a solid, important show. I should have realized I would be punished: whenever you have fun *and* congratulate yourself, ye shall suffer.

Back at the White House in a few days, I got a call from Karen. "Have you heard?" she asked in a shaky voice. "Ed Joyce went ape shit when he saw the show on Sunday. No one had bothered to tell him we were in Egypt. He turns on his TV and there we are — 'Welcome to *Face the Nation* from Cairo' — and he can't believe it."

"Didn't we tell him?"

"Well, everyone else knew. No, I didn't make a special call to him," she said. "It was in the paper, for Chrissake. Well, whoever should've told him didn't, and now he's tearing mad. He says nobody gives a shit about Hosni Mubarak, says it was stupid to go there and we can never travel abroad again. I think he wants to fire me."

Cavalierly I told Karen not to worry and called Howard Stringer, Ed Joyce's lieutenant. "Is it true? Is he really seething?"

"Oh, yes," said Howard in his sardonic Welsh way. "Fluids of rage are oozing out of him. Hot fluids." He was laughing. "Look, Lesley, he was blindsided." Howard told me he understood that our mandate from Sauter had been to try different things, and said he thought Van approved. Aha! I said to myself, we have two masters, Ed and Van. I calculated that the one in the big house, Black Rock, was the one I should care about.

"Karen's not in trouble, is she?"

"Don't worry. Ed will calm down."

He did — after I called and apologized. Not that I thought we'd done anything wrong, but I didn't want him to take it out on Karen. At any rate, we were forgiven, so much so that Karen and I thought it was time to "experiment" with the kind of subject matter Van Sauter had first discussed with me when he said he wanted a "new" kind of Sunday broadcast. After considering several ideas, we settled on a "trend" show on androgyny. I saw *Face* not as the front page of *The New York Times* but as *Time* magazine with "back-of-the-book" subjects such as sports, art, culture, and trends. I thought we had paid our dues in six months of hard subjects.

We called the July 8 show "The Feminizing of Society" — an issue Facing the Nation. Our guests were the rock singer Boy George and the Reverend Jerry Falwell of the Moral Majority. In the opening essay I said, "They call it gender blending or even gender ending — the merging of what we used to think of as distinctly male and female in our society —

and it's shocking to a great many of us. . . . One simply has to ask what's going on when you see male college students dabbing on a little rouge and eyeliner for a new look."

Boy George had on more than a little rouge. I had interviewed him in his recording studio in London. Boy's makeup was fastidious and as concealing as a geisha girl's, but he had the body of a truck driver, which I discovered when we posed for still photos and I put my arm around his back: steel muscles. Looking pale with his light bisque foundation and powder, he said, "All this kind of illusion that I'm promoting homosexuality is obvious rubbish. . . . You cannot promote homosexuality, okay? You can promote liberalness, but not homosexuality."

Falwell, who managed to tell us that his own wife is "very feminine," said, "When a man wants to be like a woman, it displays an unhappiness with who he is and how God made him."

If I hadn't realized that we were deviating from *Face*'s traditional path, Tom Shales reminded me in Monday's *Washington Post*: "*Face the Nation* turned into Sunday Morning Fever . . . criss-crossing real news with show biz news." He ended with the fact that on Brinkley they were discussing the Supreme Court's most recent attack on civil liberties. Oh, well . . .

Ed Joyce went into another one of his nuclear spirals. I was told, again by third parties, that he was burning with anger, but Van Sauter called me himself this time and said he had loved the show and not to worry about Mr. Shales.

TAYLOR SWEARS she never resented my being at the office as much as I was. She has told me she even considers it auspicious. I'm not sure that's a compliment. "If you didn't work, you'd be miserable, and we'd all be miserable," she said. I'm grateful that she feels that way. But more, I'm grateful that Aaron filled the vacuum, though I must say he was the most permissive parent ever.

Taylor wanted a chicken. All I could think of was the visit Lou had taken us on when I was a kid to his cousin's chicken farm in Sharon, Massachusetts. I can still smell the place and see all those pecking, cackling monsters. "Our apartment is just too small," I explained to Taylor. And thus began a test of wills.

When I was off to work, she went straight to Aaron, who never could and never did say no to her. "Dad, can we get a chicken?" Of course, said he.

So while I was struggling with Reagan's refusal to answer questions about his mining of the harbors around Nicaragua and scuffling over the White House's refusal to supply *Face* with a high-ranking guest for Sunday, I was negotiating with my six-year-old about a chicken. We agreed to launch an investigation, which mercifully culminated in a compromise: a parrot, a Kelly green male parrot we named Paley, after Bill.

NANCY REAGAN was always a force to be reckoned with. She wanted the public to think she was a Tammy Wynette kind of gal, an un-Rosalynn first lady who kept her nose out of issues. But Nancy Reagan's nose was deep into everything. Over the years I have grown to appreciate her, even admire her, but back then, I had little sympathy for the Imperial One.

As someone pointed out to me: first she picked the chief of staff, then she made him obedient. I was sitting in Jim Baker's big corner office one afternoon, on one of the couches in front of the fireplace. Our not-so-regular regular monthly meeting had been put off and put off until late in the day on Friday. But here I was, giving more information than I was getting. At 5:20 we both heard *Marine One*, the president's helicopter, land on the South Lawn. Baker looked at his watch and went pale. "What time do you have?" he asked. It was 5:20, all right. "Oh, my God." It was the one and only time I ever saw him flustered. He jumped up. "Just wait here. I'll be right back."

"What's wrong? Is there an emergency?"

"I think I may have missed the helicopter." He looked frazzled. "The president's leaving for Camp David any minute. Maybe I can still make it." With that he bolted out the door and ran through the Rose Garden, trying to catch the president before he left. I was sure he had a grave matter he had to discuss; maybe a political scandal was brewing, maybe a message had come in from the Soviets. I began to worry about my deadline. It was late. Would I break a big story?

A few minutes later Baker was back, all smiles. "Phew," he said, "I made it!"

"Well, tell me, what was so urgent?" I had my notebook open to a fresh page, a new pen in hand that wouldn't run out.

"Oh, I didn't have anything special to tell them," said Baker, his composure restored. "I just wanted them to see me standing there as they left for the weekend."

I was floored: the steady chief of staff intimidated by the mild-mannered Ronald Reagan? No kidding. I began to develop a theory that Reagan's aloofness created a low-grade fever of fear, and that was how he was able to overrule his staff. But then I told the Baker helicopter story to someone in the higher reaches of the White House, and he just laughed. "It wasn't Reagan Jim was afraid of," he chortled, "it was Nancy! Reagan wouldn't have noticed whether Jim was there or not. But Nancy—she expected things to be done just so."

Nancy and Ronnie were a salt-and-pepper set. He was as calm as a sunny day, she was a williwaw; he was sweet as Brie, she was sharp

194

cheddar; he was unpretentious as Chianti, she was Dom Perignon; he bore no grudges, she never forgot; he was the browser who liked window shopping, Nancy was the buyer. And what Nancy was buying in 1984 was détente with the Soviets. According to a White House official, "She thought this was the only thing between Ronnie and the Nobel Peace Prize. It would cap his career, and she really pushed it with him and with the staff."

She was also busy trying to diminish the power of the ideologues such as Ed Meese, who she thought were steering the president into one embarrassing fix after the next. Allied with the "pragmatists," Baker and Deaver, she waged war on the president's stubborn mind, trying to get him to lower the temperature of his support of the right-wing social agenda. She was the one, I was told, who made sure he did not attend the annual antiabortion rally across the street from the White House, speaking to the marchers only over the phone. No pictures.

A friend of Nancy Reagan's related a story about a dinner party the first lady had thrown in the summer of 1984, an intimate gathering of eight friends in the upstairs dining room of the residence. According to my source, Nancy called two or three of the guests before the dinner and said, "Ronnie trusts you. He listens to you." She explained that she'd been having a hard time getting through to him on toning down his rhetoric. She'd been begging him to stop bringing up his more conservative positions "just till the campaign's over." Why did he have to mention that he was against gun control? or abortion?

She plotted with her guests: "When I give you the signal, I want you to tell Ronnie how unpopular his position on abortion is and that he should stop talking about it." But when Nancy signaled, the conversation was so off the subject of the campaign that the guest balked. Nancy shot a long, glaring look, which the guest pretended not to notice. Finally Nancy interrupted another anecdote about Hollywood and said something like, "Ronnie, I think Mrs. X has something she wants to say, don't you dear?"

Poor Mrs. X was then compelled to argue that it would be the better side of prudence for the Gipper to cool it on abortion till after November.

As the president listened in cold silence, Nancy gestured to another guest to follow up, which he did dutifully, explaining that Mrs. X was right on. At which point Reagan did what my source said was unheard of: he snapped at his wife. "Nancy, I know you've put our friends up to this," he said sternly, "and I don't appreciate it. Not one bit." He let the guests know he wasn't happy with them either.

Said another source, "Nancy would drive him nuts, like a fly buzzing around him." And yet she could not yank him away from his core issues; he went on to bring up abortion throughout the campaign. You have to scratch your head. He was so passive and malleable and then, hey, he wasn't.

There's no question Nancy Reagan ran the studio, and did so more as time went by. In *Affairs of State*, about first couples, the historian Gil Troy argues that first ladies traditionally reach for power when their husbands are weak. Ronald Reagan certainly was that throughout the 1983 recession. And, says Troy, a first lady in that circumstance will be resented if not reviled, because in our system of democracy there is a reflexive resistance to any unelected force that tries to exercise control.

Another theory has it that Mrs. Reagan was so spooked by the assassination attempt that she sought more control as a way to protect her husband. One of the president's more perceptive advisers explained to me, "The woman's afraid of everything; it's her fears that propel her." So perhaps it was her fears for the president's life that motivated her. But I wonder whether she realized that her husband's faculties were failing. If she suspected the onset of Alzheimer's disease or something like it, did she move in to compensate as a way of keeping his impending decline a secret?

IN MAY the CBS Television Network held its annual affiliates meeting at the Century Plaza Hotel in Los Angeles. This was an unstinting affair, with a tour of Universal Studios for the spouses, a big lavish lunch by the pool, and a campaign roundtable by the News Division. Dan Rather moderated our panel discussion with Susan Spencer, Bruce Morton, Bob Schieffer, and me. I knew that most of the local stations were owned by right-leaning Republicans who thought Ronald Reagan walked on water, but it never occurred to me that I should censor my remarks. To my mind, I was being purely analytical when I remarked that Reagan was "hiding" from the press and ducking responsibility for his administration's actions. I added that nobody seemed to pay attention when he flip-flopped on the issues. Sitting at CEO Tom Wyman's table were my friends the songwriter Joe Raposo and Ed Gaylord, head of Gaylord Entertainment, which owned the Grand Ole Opry, a chain of newspapers in Oklahoma, and several television stations, including the CBS affiliate in Tampa. According to someone at the table, "As you started, Ed Gaylord put his head down and grumbled for the whole time you talked. 'Christ . . . Son of a bitch.' Then you said something about Reagan running his campaign from the Rose Garden, hiding from the public, and Ed had a roll in his hand. 'See what I mean about these fucking people,' he said and threw the roll, which hit his coffee, which drenched the guy sitting next to him. Old Ed got up, left the room, and didn't come back for the rest of the day, which I can tell you, Lesley, did not endear you to Tom Wyman or anyone else at Black Rock."

That night at the gala black-tie dinner a senior executive from Black Rock approached me and said, "Can't you lay off Reagan? You should just back off, you really should." I was shocked. That kind of overture was a clear violation of a fundamental ethic of our business, and particularly of CBS. There's a body of CBS literature on the subject, that the news operation must be unfettered by any business interests of the company. The principle went back to the creation of the corporation, when it was clear not that the journalists had to be protected but that the advertising department needed what they call in government "plausible deniability" when sponsors complained about the content of the news shows. It was a way for the CBS admen to say honestly, "I have nothing to do with what they say. They do their jobs, I do mine." Television needed this deniability more than the other media, because we were an industry regulated by the government, which made us vulnerable to political pressures in a way newspapers were not.

I suspected that the White House had instigated a campaign by the CBS affiliates to complain to Black Rock about my coverage. But David Gergen has assured me that never happened. So did a friend who was a top executive of CBS in the 1980s. He told me, "Many of the station owners complained to Sauter and Joyce about Lesley Stahl and even more so about Dan Rather, but they did it on their own, not because the White House asked them to." Some of the stations, like the one in San Diego, were so upset at Dan Rather, Bill Moyers, and me that they threatened to leave the network.

"Whenever an affiliate complained," my CBS friend said, "Tom Wyman would chew out Sauter." The News Division had been criticized in the Cronkite era too, but in those days Dick Salant would stand up and defend us. Sauter, said my friend, "would call you guys, 'those bozos' or he'd say, "Look, I'm doing my best. You can't imagine what it's like trying to control those people.' "

But as I discovered, Sauter's impetus to temper our coverage came even more from the fight to overturn the Financial Interest and Syndication, or "FinSyn," Rules. In his vendetta against the networks, Richard Nixon had had the FCC impose the rules, which denied the nets any revenue from reruns, leaving the Hollywood studios as the main beneficiaries. The FinSyn Rules had handicapped CBS, NBC, and ABC for 14 years; now the networks were trying to persuade Reagan's regulators as well as Congress to abrogate them — it was Black Rock's top priority — and CBS feared that my coverage of the White House would ruin everything.

Van Sauter was a soldier in the war. In his book *Prime Times, Bad Times*, Ed Joyce wrote, "Every time Van went in to lobby some congressman, it quickly turned into a litany of complaints about CBS News. What on earth was the President of CBS News doing at a lobbying lunch? Holy Shit."[28]

Wyman lobbied too, and, as my friend told me, "He hated the idea that he had to listen to some two-bit congressman beating him up because Lesley Stahl said something nasty. When he went to make nice, he had to put up with you goddamned people." The griping from Washington had been much worse during the Nixon administration, but the executives back then had felt they just had to bear it. Wyman didn't understand that it came with the territory.

When the networks lobbied the White House on the finsyn rules, David Gergen says, they were heavy-handed: "I thought they were threatening us. The guy at ABC came right out and said, 'Don't you understand how much power we have in our coverage?' " CBS was only slightly more subtle. "Using muscle," as Gergen put it, was not the most effective approach.

The syndication business was a golden goose, so the Hollywood studios, which were making millions from reruns, saw the network move as a serious threat and waged their own lobbying campaign. But they were much smarter than the nets; they sent Larry Hagman and Alan Alda to Congress and got Reagan's old friends to massage him. Bud Rifkin at Orion Pictures wrote to the president, reminding him of his screen test at Warner Brothers before urging him to side with Hollywood in the syndication battle. And it seems that Nancy was doing her part for Hollywood, too. In a March 8, 1983, letter Charlton Heston wrote, "Dear Mr. President: I hate to keep throwing paper at you, but Nancy said you wouldn't mind one more. . . . We're the good guys." He enclosed a long argument for keeping the syndication rules intact.[29]

In September 1983 the FCC made a preliminary ruling in favor of the nets. Reagan's old agent and friend MCA Chairman Lew Wasserman called personally to lobby the president. After that Reagan asked for a meeting with the FCC chairman, Mark Fowler, who then changed his mind. A few weeks later he announced that the FCC would delay any change in the rules.

Jack Valenti, who had spearheaded Hollywood's lobbying effort, wrote Reagan a thank-you note on November 18, 1983, which the president answered by hand: "You know, for a little while I felt like I was still Pres. of the Screen Actors Guild & it was a good feeling. Sincerely, RR."

The executives at Black Rock couldn't see what was wrong with expecting reporters to help them get legislation beneficial to the company — after all, we worked there too. They couldn't see it as a weakening of our independence that could lead to a loss of credibility. CBS News's sacred autonomy was breached, and I felt it in the constant pressure to tame my copy.

What was outrageous was the widely held opinion at Black Rock that the syndication battle had been lost because of CBS News' coverage.[30] That was nonsense. Reagan weighed in for his movie pals, which would have happened even if I had sent him a televised valentine every night on the air. Hollywood would keep the syndication rights — and all that money — for another ten years.

THERE WAS A LOT of criticism after the 1984 campaign that the media hadn't covered the issues, that we had concentrated our coverage on style rather than substance. That was in large measure true, but it was true because Reagan, as his campaign manager, Ed Rollins, admits, ran a feel-good campaign, "short on specifics and long on fuzzy thematics." There were no issues, he said, because, "the Reagan Administration was out of gas."[31]

What had happened was that many of the issues Reagan had championed were unpopular. He was out of sync with the public on the environment; focusing attention on taxes might shine a bright light on all the tax *increasing* he'd been up to; and, as his pollster Bob Teeter was discovering, Reagan's stand on abortion was suicidal. Teeter pored over his polls, perceiving again that Reagan was far more popular than his policies. So a campaign strategy was developed to market his personality, to emphasize *him,* while at the same time downplaying the issues.

Every effort was made to ensure a constant flow of content-free, positive visual images. If they managed to eclipse the competition, all the better. Which is what was happening in early June. Just as Gary Hart won the California primary and Mondale won New Jersey, Reagan went on a triumphal tour of Europe. As I said on the *Evening News:*

> When it comes to political one-upmanship, Ronald Reagan is a master. Upstage the winner of the California primary? Piece of cake: have lunch at Buckingham Palace with the Queen of England, meet with Britain's Prime Minister Thatcher, and pay tribute to the thousands who died on the beaches of Normandy.

While the president was in France, Michael Deaver produced his masterpiece: Reagan's commemoration of the 40th anniversary of D-Day from high atop the cliffs at Normandy — a filmmaker's Valhalla. Reagan gave one of his finest speeches, crafted by his new speechwriter, Peggy Noonan, who had recently been hired from CBS News. Ironically, she had written weekly radio scripts for Dan Rather, a man many in the Reagan White House saw as the Devil himself. But Peggy's conservative credentials were immaculate: she was a committed Reaganite.

She had also written radio scripts for me the one week I had anchored the *Evening News*, and so, when she moved from New York to Washington, we renewed our friendship. She would drop by our booth from time to time to kibitz and to ask me if Nancy Reagan thought her clothes were too schlumpy: "She looks at me funny."

On the site of the Normandy invasion, Reagan won the almost awed attention of the country when he read, "These are the boys of Pointe-du-Hoc," referring to the veterans sitting before him. "These are the men who took the cliffs. These are the champions who helped free a continent." The "boys," now in their 60s, wept.

I loved my job. I know I've said that before, but with all the annoyances, there were times like this when I stopped to live in the moment and say to myself, "Wow, kiddo, you are there. You are a witness, you lucky son of a gun. Just be still, slow the engine, and make sure you remember."

I MIGHT have even teared up a little at Normandy, but that was unusual. I had tried so hard to kill off my crying spasms, my internal quakes when things got hairy, that by now I had pretty much succeeded. When critics scraped me over, I simply flexed my well-developed I-don't-care muscle. When someone at the White House complained in an unpleasant decibel range, I'd turn some optic handle and dam up the water that had so easily flowed, back when Jody Powell yelled at me. I was being called a tough cookie, and through careful training, I was actually becoming one. And not always a pretty one.

Joan Barthel of *TV Guide* ran a picture of a sneering me in the June 30 issue with a line: "Her questions range from sharp to stinging." But it was Barthel's description of me as "difficult" that was the real stinger. Quoting me on the *Face* set one Sunday morning, she wrote, "She asked: 'Do I have enough rouge on?' A technician relayed the word that came through his headphones from the control room: 'They think so, Lesley.'

" 'Not on this monitor, I don't. And there's a shadow under my left eye.' " She portrayed me as one demanding bitch-monster. I cringed when I saw the mirror and suffered for days, hating myself and resolving to ease up, to remember the job was fun. Just when I thought I was inured to criticism and attacks, one would come along that would throw me off my pins.

REAGAN'S POLLSTER Richard Wirthlin was trying to sell the idea that the gender gap wasn't about women deserting Reagan but about men flocking *to* him. But the Reaganites were worried about the gap, which was brought on by the budget cuts and issues such as the arms race, the environment, and abortion. That's why Nancy was begging her husband to skirt those subjects.

On their side, the Democrats wanted to exploit the gap, but would Mondale go so far as to pick a woman as a running mate? It was the question in June, so naturally we did a *Face* on the subject (June 24) asking, "Madam Veep, is it time?" "CBS News did a poll," I told my guests, Congresswoman Patricia Schroeder and Bert Lance, then chairman of the Georgia Democratic Party, "showing as many men would be turned *off* by a woman on the ticket as women would be turned *on*, and they are the very men Mondale needs to vote for him, needs to woo back to the Democratic Party."

Pat Schroeder pointed out that the electorate was nearly 54 percent female: "Mondale can only benefit with a woman on the ticket." Bert Lance went the other way, arguing that a woman would weaken the ticket in the South.

But Mondale's team concluded that he couldn't beat Reagan unless he did something dramatic and unorthodox. So, defying advisers like Lance and many others, he chose Geraldine Ferraro, 48, as his running mate. She was a three-term congresswoman from Queens, someone even more liberal than he was.

I watched his televised announcement at the Minnesota statehouse on July 12 and must admit that, like most women I knew, I was filled with a sense of pride and even ownership. I surprised myself. And I prayed, "Geraldine, don't mess up, or we'll all get blamed." Mondale, never a sparkler on TV, said, "This is an exciting choice. . . . Let me say that again. This is an exciting choice." The need for a politician to be telegenic was so vital by 1984 that columnist Marquis Childs wrote, "Candidates no longer 'run' for office, they 'pose' for office."

The next day at her first news conference, Ferraro attacked Reagan's character: "The president walks around calling himself a good Christian. I don't for one minute believe it, because the policies are so terribly unfair." She never made a dent.

BACK IN WASHINGTON, I had lunch with Lee Atwater, one of Reagan's top campaign strategists. Lee had cut his teeth in the racially charged politics of South Carolina and still believed that the 30-year-old Republican "southern strategy" — exploiting the racial fears of white voters — was the key to victory not only in the South but also in the northern suburbs.[32] Atwater was the ultimate pragmatist, close to amoral in the pursuit of political victory — but likable, dammit. I enjoyed his company.

Atwater loved to analyze politics, and so did I; he was irreverent, even about Reagan; and he wanted me to know he was smart. In other words, he was a great source. "The primaries are taking a toll on Mondale," he said over a sandwich at Joe and Moe's on Connecticut Avenue. "His negatives have gone up." He said he was feeling better about the compassion issues. "We're neutralizing them with all the trips [Reagan's] taking. It's more exposure in a non–talking head way." He spelled it out for me: "Just put him on TV; it's all about looking warm. We gotta get him out of the limousines, get him out of the mansions and into the barns." Not a single word about a single issue ever passed his lips. "I'm only worried about two things," he told me, "white women and fat cats."

Reagan was definitely "out of the mansions" and getting on television with fuzzy slogans and pretty pictures, and he was bolstered by an improving economy that he took total credit for — which is, after all, a presidential perogative. An autoworker I interviewed in Detroit said, "He helped me get my job back." In Texas Reagan told a crowd, "It's the first administration since, well more than 20 years ago, that has reduced both unemployment and inflation in the same period of time." Even if Mondale had had the acting skills of Marlon Brando, he couldn't have beaten that.

I'VE SAID that my mother never made me feel guilty about not staying home with Taylor. That doesn't mean I didn't feel guilty. I went to her soccer games and every play she was in at school — the one where she was the giraffe in *Noah's Ark*, and then Hephaestus in *The Life of Odysseus*. Man, was she adorable. I didn't drive her to ceramics class or gymnastics, but I made sure, like an air traffic controller, that all her takeoffs and landings were smooth and on time. But in between I fretted that I wasn't a good parent. It ate into my mind, breaking in on me at work with a sharp whomp, out of nowhere.

I WAS in San Francisco for Walter Mondale's nomination as the Democrat's candidate for president. This was Van Sauter's first national political convention as a CBS executive, and he went all out. With his old pal Ed Joyce at his side again, he wheeled about the Moscone Center, throwing around his weight and CBS's money. He even took Lanny, CBS's New York shoe-shine man, to San Francisco. The correspondents, producers, and executives were all put up in the best hotels (I stayed at the Clift). Sauter spent much of the week dumping on the Washington staff and "pissing all over the process," as one of the producers put it, complaining about how "tedious and boring" the convention was.

This was the first year the networks decided not to broadcast the proceedings gavel to gavel, and with good reason. Conventions had become little more than staged rubber-stamping occasions rather than the unruly decision-making conclaves they had once been. But on July 23 we were criticized in *Newsweek* for "somehow undermin[ing] democracy itself."

As a measure of the times, the CBS floor correspondents were two girls and two boys: Diane Sawyer and me, Ed Bradley and Bob Schieffer.

There was also a measure of the times at the convention itself. I dashed around the rackety, stultifying indoor city as always, bumping into absurd-looking creatures wearing fruit hats, bird's-nest hats, tennis-shoe hats. What was unfamiliar were all the women — 50 percent of the delegates. Every time a speaker at the podium said, "Ferraro" or "ERA," there'd be a booming cheer, followed by the chant "Gerry, Gerry, Gerry!" There were whips roaming about representing the woman's caucus — this was all new. As Carol Bellamy in the New York delegation said, "We've moved from being the ladies' auxiliary to being the front line." There was something sisterly about the atmosphere that swept up anyone female, even an "impartial" reporter. I was getting that I'm-an-insider quiver again.

It was just a quiver, though. A group of the top political reporters held regular breakfasts at the conventions. When Linda Wertheimer tried to get an invitation, she was turned away: it was males only. So she organized a females-only group, and off we went to the same restaurant as the boys, sitting where they could see what we were up to. Linda had to be selective: women covering the campaign had reached a critical mass. Most of the barriers in political reporting were down. As Jane Mayer put it in *The Wall Street Journal*, it was at last a coed activity. The nets and the major newspapers were all assigning women to the campaigns, but the fight wasn't over. The men, wrote Mayer, were still joining the candidates at "male-exclusive" poker games and the racetrack. The male reporter may not get a story at the event, she said, but it "sure as hell gets the staff to return your phone calls faster." [33]

WHOEVER SAID POLITICS ISN'T ROMANTIC? The day after the convention ended, Zirinsky did the unusual: she took a day off. With nothing to do, she and Joe Peyronnin took a cable car to City Hall, where, it being Friday, they discovered they could get married for half price. Clutching a pile of CBS News convention sweatshirts in a bright yellow CBS shipping bag, she married Joe in a ceremony that lasted — she clocked it — three minutes, 28 seconds.

An hour or so later she kept a date with Jim Brooks, the Hollywood writer/director (*Terms of Endearment*) who was working on a movie about broadcast news. "What's it like on the road?" he asked. "Lots of sex?" She told him that everyone was too tired. "What about you?" he asked. "Me? Well," she said, "I just got married."

ON SATURDAY, July 21, I got up at 5 A.M. and drove for an hour and a half to Thurmont, Maryland, the closest town to Camp David. I met Maureen Reagan there at the Cozy Country Inn to tape an interview for *Face*. We had reserved the largest room the motel had. Before we started Maureen and I bonded by romping around on the billows of the Cozy's queen-size water bed, laughing ourselves to tears.

Maureen, an adviser to her father's campaign on women's issues, was a spirited interview, sassy and therefore great theater. She wouldn't take any guff from me, simply refusing to follow a line of questioning she didn't like. When I asked about the abortion issue, for instance, she said it was a personal, moral matter.

"But your father makes it an issue," I said.

"Well, *I* don't make it an issue," she responded emphatically. "It is simply that you'll have to talk to somebody else about that because this is something I just don't get involved in."

"Religion, then. That's becoming an issue with Geraldine Ferraro questioning your father's Christianity."

"Which I think was a very stupid thing to do."

Maureen, an avowed and dedicated feminist, was living in the White House, and while there is little evidence she was able to change her father's mind any more than anyone else had been able to change it, she had more success with Nancy. In time the onetime Dragon Lady and her stepdaughter would become kindred spirits.

WHY DO CHILDREN like to see movies over and over? I told Taylor she'd have to find someone else to take her to her seventh screening of *Return of the Jedi* when we were on vacation in Santa Barbara. I took her with me on the press plane, and that's when her romance with Sam Donaldson began. The two of them spent much of the flight in the aisle of the plane saber-dueling — with umbrellas! "Ah ha!" Sam mock growled. "I lasered you!" For years Taylor called him Darth Vader.

We were in Santa Barbara for another Reagan vacation, the slackness of which was broken on August 1, when the press was invited up to the ranch for a photo op. It was unusual, having us up to the sacred aerie. I'd been there just once before.

When the president was asked a straightforward question about arms control for outer-space weapons, he stood frozen and bewildered, unable to come up with an answer. He grunted and shrugged until finally Nancy, standing beside him, lowered her head and muttered sotto voce, "Doing everything we can." This was followed by an echo in exactly the same cadence: "We're doing everything we can." The marionette president. That night my piece showed the head of the studio acting as chief prompter. Suddenly we were dealing with the question of the president's altogetherness.

Mike Deaver made things worse when he admitted, in an interview with Chris Wallace on NBC, that yes, it was true: the president fell asleep during Cabinet meetings. In my follow-up report I quoted an official as saying, "A lot of people think you shouldn't fall asleep at work." The campaign persuaded Reagan to cut his usual monthlong vacation short lest it contribute to a new problem for Reagan: the age issue.

On the one hand, the White House worried about the age issue cropping up in the Democrats' political ads; on the other, they felt they couldn't have asked for an easier ticket to run against. Ed Rollins told me, "Mondale is perfect: a card-carrying liberal with the albatross of Jimmy Carter around his neck. It's a dream come true." Then, to everyone's surprise, the economy turned out to be the Republicans' best issue. Despite the gargantuan deficits, we had low inflation and a dramatic overall economic recovery, which allowed Reagan to recite his mantra about the bad-old-Carter-*Mondale* days in contrast to his Morning-in-America days.

I again anchored the pre–Republican National Convention *Face* from Dan's anchor booth. Our guest, Vice President Bush, was in Washington, where he watched my opening essay with a sound bite from Terry Dolan, head of the National Conservative Political Action Committee (NICPAC), that George Bush "really isn't a conservative." I went on to tick off Bush's impressive credentials: former head of the CIA, special representative to China, U.N. ambassador, chairman of the Republican Party, and the youngest navy pilot in World War II. So I was baffled when the vice president started the interview on a sour note: "Thank you for that unique introduction, Lesley."

"Unique in what sense?" I asked.

"You figure it out."

I moved on, asking if he thought the Republican platform — with the gold standard and its abortion litmus test on judges — was too conservative for him to run on. "Forget about it," he said flippantly. "I don't worry about it."

Right after the show we got a call from Washington. Bush was seething, not over any of my questions but over the lead-in essay. What had I said? I finally reached his press secretary, Marlin Fitzwater, who explained that what had Bush so out of joint was that we had used Terry Dolan to say he wasn't a real conservative. Bush had nothing but contempt for Dolan and NICPAC. I wrote to the vice president and got a handwritten note back, dated September 5, 1984: "You're right. I didn't go for the 'intro' shots etc, but you were direct and very fair."

Like most people who got to know him, I found Bush infectiously congenial. And like Terry Dolan, I assumed that if he ever got his own power, he would transmorph into a moderate eastern Republican. The only thing that gave me pause was that as vice president, he'd been invisible. He had faded away from the press: no backgrounders, no leaking — unusual for a vice president. And as far as I could tell, he was leaving no footprints on the inside either: no policy disagreements, no championing of issues he believed in.

THE REPUBLICAN NATIONAL CONVENTION started the next day in Dallas, which was unbearably hot and steamy. Everything was heavily air-conditioned at the downtown Convention Center, a stone's throw from Kennedy's grassy knoll. I was made to venture out in the soupy air several times a day to shuttle between the convention floor and our compound of trailers, which included a prefab mess hall, a mobile home for the correspondents, and another fancy one with couches for the executives. Each network had exactly what we had. And then hundreds of local stations crammed their own microwave trucks into the complex. Altogether there were more people in that temporary village than in Aaron's hometown of Spur, Texas.

Monday morning we had our usual strategy session in the correspondents' trailer with Dan and the floor correspondents, deciding that the big story here was that the ultraconservatives were hijacking the Republican Convention. So two minutes into our broadcast, Dan threw it to me. I introduced Maureen Reagan, who said she was very disappointed that the platform didn't endorse the Equal Rights Amendment — this from the president's daughter.

"Geraldine Ferraro," I said, "hounded by tax problems. Do you think she can survive?"

"I think she can survive," said Maureen, never one to equivocate. "I don't know in what shape."

By then Ferraro had released her and her husband's tax returns. The issue of their finances, already sapping the Mondale campaign, threatened to become the focus of the Republicans' prime-time convention. And so on August 21, day two in Dallas, Ferraro called a news conference and answered questions from 200 reporters before 38 television cameras for an hour and 40 minutes. "John did nothing wrong," she said about her husband's "borrowing" $175,000 from the funds of a wealthy 84-year-old widow whose estate he was overseeing. She took every question in a marathon so exhaustive that *Time* scrapped an article it had prepared about how Ferraro "Lets Down the Women of the Country" and instead put her on the cover with a caption: "Under pressure, Ferraro passes a vital test." The issue was put to rest for the duration of the campaign.[34]

REAGAN'S MORNING IN AMERICA campaign had a handsome leading man to star in the soft, hide-the-wrinkles, sunlit television vignettes. If Reagan's campaign was Technicolor, Mondale's was black and white. Some horrible infection was turning *his* photo ops into darkly lit tribulations. In the very kickoff of his campaign, at the Labor Day parade in New York, he marched so early, the crowds were nonexistent. Then there was the memorable TV shot of Geraldine Ferraro in Portland, Oregon, on September 5, holding an umbrella over Mondale while local candidate Barbara Roberts sat next to them, getting drenched.

Meanwhile Ferraro, a prochoice Catholic, was under constant attack from prolife protesters, who chanted "Baby killer" at every one of her rallies. Archbishop John O'Connor of New York campaigned against her, while the head of the nation's Roman Catholic bishops issued a statement that seemed to all but publicly endorse Ronald Reagan.[35] Mary McGrory summed up the frustration of the Mondale camp when she wrote about Ferraro in a column on September 25, "Here she is, a lifelong Roman Catholic, a product of Catholic schools and colleges, goes to Mass every Sunday. Yet the hierarchy of her church is acting like an arm of the Reagan re-election committee."[36] As McGrory pointed out, Reagan hardly ever went to church.

THE PRESIDENT STARTED TONING DOWN his Cold War rhetoric as Nancy had urged. He even began calling for arms control negotiations with the Soviets. Before long he was campaigning as the candidate of peace. In a stand-up close at a Reagan campaign event, I pointed out how clearly political his turnaround was, and that in case anyone had missed the point, he had uttered the word "peace" 23 times in his 20-minute speech. Zee was crash-cutting the story under the usual deadline pressure; I recorded the stander in front of the audience while Reagan was still speaking. I had to talk in what we call a golf tournament whisper, sounding like Ken Venturi on the 18th hole of the Masters.

When the piece aired that night, there was no stand-up. Lane Venardos in the fishbowl had chopped it off without telling us. He said it was flip. Zee cried. I raged.

If the Democrats had a chance of exploiting Reagan's flip-flop on arms control, the issue was lost when the White House announced on September 11 that he would soon meet with Soviet Foreign Minister Andrei Gromyko. I called it the September surprise: "Ronald Reagan was handed a plum by the Soviet Union five weeks before the election. . . . Walter Mondale got a big lesson today in incumbency politics."

Before the Reagan-Gromyko meeting in the Oval Office on September 28, the two men held a brief photo op. As I said that night, "President Reagan looked tense and uncomfortable. This was his first superpower meeting. Gromyko, the old veteran, was relaxed as he met with his ninth American president." I was told later that Reagan had been squirming with exaggerated discomfort. Once again he was being accommodating, while at the same time signaling in symbolic body language that he really didn't mean it. White House officials leaked the story that it was the first lady who had talked "the old man" into making an overture to the Soviets.

It turned out that Nancy's political instinct was right on target. The meeting was construed by the voters as a sign that Reagan's tough talking had brought the Soviets around.

READING FROM ATWATER'S no-limousines playbook, Reagan went campaigning in Nashville at the Grand Ole Opry. It was a photo op blowout, with balloons and country music stars Minnie Pearl and Roy Acuff, and a Grand Ole Opry finale with everyone singing "I'm proud to be an American. There ain't no doubt I love this place. God bless the U.S.A."

Zee and I lapped up the razzle-dazzle. But when New York rejected the piece — "There's no news here" — and cut it down to a sleek 20-second "Dan tell," Zee burst into tears again, and I hissed with fire again. It didn't help that Sam and NBC's Chris Wallace both got their pieces on the air that night. But this time, the fishbowl was right.

Dan and his team in New York had made an editorial decision by then that they weren't going to air campaign pieces unless the candidates made news. We were going out of the business of running their vapid photo ops, if that's all they were. We were the only network with a policy like that — and so it contributed to the White House's feeling that CBS was tilting its coverage away from Reagan, even though the policy hurt Mondale just as much.

ANOTHER SUICIDE BOMBER, the third in less than two years, drove into the U.S. Embassy Annex in Beirut, killing two more Americans. "The Reagan administration is on the defensive," I said on *Face* in late September, "under criticism for a serious failure of security." Apparently someone had left the iron gate that was supposed to protect the annex lying on the ground awaiting installation. When asked about that at a Q-and-A session, Reagan said, "Anyone who's ever had their kitchen done over knows that it never gets done as soon as you wish it would." The remark, flippant and inappropriate, was roundly criticized.

Had Reagan stumbled? Dan asked me the question on an 11:30 P.M. election special. "Gaffes usually roll off his back," I replied. "Don't forget, he told that joke about bombing the Russians just a few weeks ago, and we've all forgotten that by now. It's very conceivable that the mistake, as you call it, will disappear, as all the other mistakes have in the Ronald Reagan presidency."

"Let the record show," said Dan coldly, "I asked the question of *whether* it was a mistake." I felt terrible.

208

☐

AND THEN we went to Bowling Green State University in Bowling Green, Ohio. "Inside the gym," I reported, "the capacity crowd of 5,000 cheered thunderously for the president, expressing something close to adoration." These were college kids wild with excitement over this old man. I was so surprised by the intensity that I kept scanning the stage to see if some rock star was up there drawing their attention.

"Answering Mondale's charge that he's isolated," I said, the president took questions. When a student asked about peace with the Soviets, Reagan responded, "The people of Russia want peace; we know that we want it. We want it because peace in America is such an attractive way to live that a war is a terrible interruption." No one seemed to think that was an absurd answer. They cheered as if he were Michael Jackson doing his moon walk. It didn't make sense on the surface, but here was this new generation craving the we-can-win optimism and patriotism that their Vietnam-era parents had disdained. They seemed to crave the images of young heroic Americans he talked of in his speeches, which were, in a way, remakes of the propaganda films he had worked on during World War II. Ronald Reagan at 73 was their idol, and I was standing in the midst of their adulation.

TAYLOR HAD STARTED second grade, and Aaron was writing his second movie, *Perfect*, based on two of his *Rolling Stone* articles: one about the health club dating scene, the other about the car manufacturer John DeLorean. I was in Washington for a brief respite from the campaign in late September when Diane Sawyer and her boyfriend, Richard Holbrooke, invited us to dinner. Aaron and I liked them both. Holbrooke, a talented foreign policy analyst and former assistant secretary of state, had a shrewd and inventive mind and a boundless capacity for friendship. Diane was one of the few newswomen I knew who projected an air of softness. But she was sharp and sparklingly smart, with an appealing carelessness about her beauty. She had just joined *60 Minutes*. I was not going to let it bother me that she and not I had gotten the best job in TV news — though I had to tamp down an occasional pang of envy.

I had never aspired to Dan's chair, but *60 Minutes* — that was different. I had thought it was the obvious next step. But now it was probably out of the question. They'd never take two women, never. Thank goodness I wasn't tired of my job.

IN EARLY OCTOBER the *Evening News* asked me to put together a piece summing up the Reagan campaign to that point. It turned out to be a much discussed report with a curious resonance.

The piece started benignly enough: "How does Ronald Reagan use television? Brilliantly. He's been criticized as the rich man's president,

209

but the TV pictures say it isn't so." *Evening News* producer Janet Leissner put the piece together, using pictures of Reagan picnicking with ordinary folks; you saw him surrounded by black kids, you saw him with farmers in a field. And you saw him in the midst of happy flag-waving supporters. "At 73," I said, "Mr. Reagan could have an age problem, but the TV pictures say it isn't so." You saw him pumping iron, tossing a football.

"The orchestration of television coverage absorbs the White House. Their goal? To emphasize the president's greatest asset, which his aides say is his personality. They provide pictures of him *looking* like a leader . . . confident, with his Marlboro Man walk . . . a good family man." Over my track Janet edited in shots of him receiving the Olympic torch from a runner.

I turned to the question of issues, making the point that Reagan was trying to create amnesia about many of his policies. "Mr. Reagan tries to counter the memory of an unpopular issue with a carefully chosen back-drop that actually contradicts the president's policy. Look at the handi-capped Olympics, or the opening ceremony of an old-age home. No hint that he tried to cut the budgets for the disabled or for federally subsidized housing for the elderly." Here you saw him at campaign events with the ever-present oversized American flag behind him, the worshiping crowds waving the little flags, the big brass band, the bunting, and the balloons. With the sun always hitting him just right, he was handing out medals to handicapped athletes or cutting the ribbon on a new nursing home in Buffalo, daring you to remember that he'd tried to cut the funds for nursing home construction.

"Time and again," I said in the piece, "the president — with uncanny skill — shifts the focus from the details of an unpopular issue to a popular subject: himself. Take education. He responds at a briefing about an inner-city school's dilapidated conditions with a personal story."

REAGAN: In our high school gymnasium, in my day, there were a few places on the floor that you couldn't try for a basket because the beams holding the ceiling up interfered.

"President Reagan is accused of running a campaign in which he highlights the images and hides from the issues. But there's no evidence that the charge will hurt him because when the people see the president on television, he makes them feel good: about America, about themselves, and about him."

I knew the piece would have an impact, if only because it was so long: five minutes and 40 seconds, practically a documentary in *Evening News* terms. I worried that my sources at the White House would be angry enough to freeze me out. Lane Venardos, the executive producer, was worried too. He went over that script more intensely than any he can remember. He told Marty Schram at *The Washington Post,* "I know I'm going to take a lot of flak for this. The phones will ring off the hook, and Larry Speakes . . . will be on the phone with this one." I bet he was thinking Sauter would be on the phone too.

No sooner had it aired than my phone rang. It was Dick Darman, and I thought: Here it comes. He was calling from Jim Baker's office, where they had watched the piece with Mike Deaver and Margaret Tutwiler, Baker's assistant. "Way to go, kiddo," Darman said, a lilt in his voice. "What a great story! We loved it." The others shouted out, "Yeah, Stahl, that was marvelous!"

"Excuse me?" Were they joking?

"No, no, we really loved it. Five minutes of free media. We owe you big time."

"Why are you so happy? Didn't you hear what I said?"

"Nobody heard what you said."

Did I hear him right? "Come again?"

"You guys in Televisionland haven't figured it out, have you? When the pictures are powerful and emotional, they override if not completely drown out the sound. Lesley, I mean it, nobody heard you."

I knew instantly he was telling me something important. I knew from my own viewing that what he said was true. So I began repeating the story. "Did you realize this?" I asked the producers in Washington, the producers in New York, other reporters. No one had grasped it. Finally, Marty Schram took a copy of my piece to an audience at the Smithsonian Institution. I was in the room when he showed about a hundred people the story without my track: just the pictures and sound of Reagan. "What is that?" he asked. And just about everyone said it was an ad for Reagan's Morning in America reelection campaign. Of course, the pictures were similar to the ones in his commercials — flags, happy faces.

Marty ran the piece again with my track. And most of the audience thought it was either an ad for the Reagan campaign or a very positive news story. Only a handful heard what I said.

The pictures were so evocative — we're talking about pictures with Reagan in the shining center — that all the viewers were absorbed. Unlike reading or listening to the radio, with television we "learn" with two of our senses together, and apparently the eye is dominant. When we watch television, we get an emotional reaction: the information doesn't always go directly to the thinking part of our brains but to the gut. It's all about impressions, and the White House understood that.

So did Van Sauter. Maybe not as precisely, probably more instinctively, but that's what his "moments" were all about. Dan Rather once

211

described "moments" for *Esquire* magazine: "When somebody watches something and feels it, smells it and knows it." No wonder Sauter wanted my "tough" stand-ups covered by pictures.

What happened in the early 1980s to television news and to American politics was like a loud crack in a chemistry lab when a scientist mixes two dynamic compounds together. CBS put Van Sauter with his "moments" in charge at the same time the White House gave Mike Deaver real power. *Kaboom!* The chemical reaction was explosive. Partly for political reasons, mainly in the pursuit of ratings, the two forces ended up working in concert. But Richard Darman argues that it was less a manipulation than a collaboration, that we were "co-conspirators" in seeking to get on the air.

Deaver echoes Darman. He says he orchestrated his "movies" because he knew that's what we wanted, suggesting that the networks started the whole chain reaction. But Deaver was anything but reactive. He wrote in his book *Behind the Scenes*, "Unless you can find a visual that explains your message, you can't make it stick."[37] He carried his obsession with putting Reagan in photogenic settings to extremes, even scheduling photo-op lunches in the White House garden despite the president's allergy to flowers.

By late 1984 the Sauter-Deaver effect had so taken hold that, as Meg Greenfield would put it in *The Washington Post*, the "seamless visual projections . . . had come somehow to be seen as synonymous with the act of governing itself." We had arrived at "the age of presentation as leadership."[38] And Dan Rather understood that intuitively. That's why he implemented the no-vapid-photo-op policy. What an irony that in my piece I had tried to blow the whistle and had ended up allowing the White House to "produce" a full quarter of our show.

ALL OF THIS worked against Walter Mondale. By early October he was lagging so far behind in the polls (Reagan had a whopping 26-point lead in the CBS News/*New York Times* poll) that whatever chance he had left was riding on two debates. I was there for the first one in Louisville, Kentucky, watching on television in the pressroom. I saw what the public saw, which was a stunning role reversal. There was Mondale, confidently in control, while the Great Communicator kept losing his train of thought, groping for words. "The system is still where it was with regard to the . . . uh . . . the . . . uh . . . the . . . uh . . . the . . . uh." The synapses finally connected: "progressivity." Reagan's closing soliloquy made little sense. He summed up, admitting, "I'm all confused now." No matter what the Reagan team spoon-fed us, both the press and the public saw clearly that Mondale had won.

Throughout the campaign, the president had avoided answering questions about the issues. In fact, he avoided answering questions about anything. We complained constantly about his inaccessibility and about the White House using the Secret Service to shield him from reporters. Larry Speakes took to stepping in front of Reagan to physically block him from approaching us. A joke among the reporters was "Covering Reagan means having to say you never saw him." It was no accident that the debate was the one time Reagan stumbled in the campaign. It was the one time he was forced to answer questions and deal with issues.

The next morning, op-ed columns were filled with speculation about Reagan's fitness for office. The White House's greatest and perhaps only fear — the age issue — was rearing up. Deaver and Company knew that people watching television make their political judgments emotionally, and their gut feeling from the televised debate had to be: That's one befuddled old man.

Live by a strategy based on television, die by it. The night after the debate I did a report on the president's campaign trip to North Carolina and made much of a sagging hot-air balloon, a perfect metaphor for "the deflated spirits in the Reagan camp." The following day *The Wall Street Journal* ran an article pointing out that 10 percent of people at age 75 suffer from senile dementia and that Reagan's mother had had it.

"There seems to be a *Two Faces of Eve* quality to the reaction around here," I said on a late-night election special from the White House. "On the one hand, you have obvious concern, almost panic, over the age issue. He stammered and stuttered through the debate. The other face," I said, "is one of utter and sheer confidence beneath that. Someone said to me today — someone high up in the campaign: 'We have built an electoral fortress in the South and West. We can withstand anything in this campaign — any mistake, anything at all, and still win.' That's confidence!"

Rather said, "This is not to be challenging, but in fairness, is it fair to say that the president stuttered and stammered through the [debate]?"

"Well, he seemed to lose his place," I pointed out, surprised by Dan's question. "He'd lose his thoughts. There were a couple of times when the word he was searching for wouldn't come to mind. Also, on the closing statement, Dan, I'm told that two different closing statements were written for him and neither one came to him. As you recall, he threw out a lot of numbers at the end. His closing statement didn't come together."

Rather seemed put out with me. I didn't know why.

The White House staff tried to resurrect the old standard: "Oh, Reagan's been like that for years. He was the same way when he was governor of California." But they couldn't mask their concern. Out campaigning on October 10, they did everything they could to present Reagan as vigorous. "Today, a show of stamina," I said in my report, "the president walking when normally he would take his limousine."

I had the two campaign managers, Bob Beckel and Ed Rollins, on *Face* the following Sunday.

> ROLLINS: Ronald Reagan gets measured against Ronald Reagan. He's like Babe Ruth. Every time he went to bat, people expected him to hit a home run. I think he hit a triple.
> BECKEL: It's a good analogy, because what happened to Ronald Reagan on Sunday is that Ronald Reagan got off script, and him off script is like Babe Ruth without a bat.

The Democrats did what they could to keep the age issue alive. But by the second debate in Kansas City, Reagan had regained all the yardage he'd lost in Louisville, despite two weeks of negative reporting. The strong medicine of nightly pictures on television of a spry, energetic campaigner and continuing reports of a strong economy had knocked out the pesky bacteria.

But the Reagan campaign was taking no chances. On the eve of the second debate, Lee Atwater wrote a memo on what to do "If We Lose the Kansas City Debate":

> Create a fog machine. Obscure the result: shift the emphasis to Mondale, drive up his negative rating.
> Points to make:
> • The capacity to endure a 90-minute TV debate has nothing to do with the capacity to govern the Nation.
> • The debate seems to have become a forum for the press to display its arrogance.
> There is of course an irony in the above counter-strategy. The media will notice that for the first time we are minimizing the importance of television.[39]

Expectations for Reagan were so low for the second debate that all the president needed to do, as Ed Rollins put it, "was stay on his feet for 90 minutes without slobbering." But he did better than that, delivering a slay-the-dragon line. Looking over at the 56-year-old Mondale, he said, "I will not make age an issue in this campaign. I am not going to exploit for political purposes my opponent's youth and inexperience." With that one line, Reagan smote the age issue. It just went away.

My job in Kansas City was once again to corral the spin doctors.[40]

214

This time Nancy Reagan showed up, and we swarmed her like ants around a cookie crumb. "What about Mondale's charge that the president is incompetent?" she was asked.

"After a while you get used to hearing that from the other side, but it's not true."

Lyn Nofziger asserted that this had been Mondale's last shot; it was all over. It was so all over that two weeks later on election night Rather declared Reagan the winner at 8:01 Eastern Time.

I was in charge of the contests for the House. "This is the great drama of the night," I said. "Can Ronald Reagan pick up enough Republicans and conservative Democrats to give him a working majority in the House of Representatives? Dan, if the president's party can pick up 26 new seats, he probably will have that ideological majority."

As the evening progressed, it became clear that there were no presidential coattails; the "Reagan Democrats" were splitting their votes. At the end of the evening, at 2 A.M., I summed up: "In the House only 14 seats changed. . . . Our exit polls show the voters don't want to see spending cuts for the poor. They like the nuclear freeze. Only 24 percent say they want to see abortion illegal. The numbers suggest that what the voters like is the status quo. They like Ronald Reagan in the White House, but they like to see Democrats in Congress checking that the Reagan Revolution doesn't go too far."

But meanwhile Reagan had a landslide of historic proportions. He won 59 percent of the vote, carrying 49 states—all but Mondale's home state of Minnesota and Washington, D.C. Even the gender gap shrank. Reagan got 55 percent of the women's vote, as opposed to 64 percent of men's. But he all but eliminated the gap with married women (with 60 percent of their vote), who liked his values and his happy marriage. As my friend Dotty Lynch, the pollster, explained it to me, in an era when the public craved upbeat optimism, "very few of Mondale's messages were positive." His greatest stroke had been selecting Geraldine Ferraro: "That played into the new mood: all things are possible. Life is getting better for everyone." But then, Dotty said, the Mondale campaign had grown fearful that the Democratic Party was becoming "feminized." So Ferraro had not been highlighted in those terms.

The election was about rewarding a president when the economy is sturdy, but even more it was about personality—a personality made for television. What the cameras did not catch in one of the most tightly controlled campaigns ever was the part of Reagan's character that allowed him to detach himself from the rigors of his job. With their genius for TV packaging, his handlers were able to keep that side of Reagan off TV, even as they put all his attractive qualities on: his grace and poise. He was normal, and that was reassuring. He was steady, a man of conviction who never took actions that scared us. And he had the power of sweetness. Television magnified it all.

Like a besotted woman, the entire country ran off with the dashing cowboy, even if he was 73. It was romance.

PART FOUR

NANCY AND RONNIE

RIGHT AFTER the election we asked the president when his next news conference would be. "Look," he said with a mischievous smile, "I won. I don't have to subject myself." Could he become even more inaccessible?

I was back in my cell at the White House, feeling like the little man on *The Ed Sullivan Show* who ran back and forth twirling wobbly glass plates on top of long poles. My wobblers were the White House, *Face the Nation*, Aaron and Taylor. I wasn't unhappy; there wasn't time. And besides, I was beginning to master the beat. This would be my seventh year in that place, and I was finally clicking into my pace and my voice. No more pathetic calls to my producers — well, only every now and then.

There was still the quickening of nerves at deadline, when it was time to slap on makeup and someone was in the ladies' room. I can still hear my bang on the door and my chirpy little reminder to Maureen Santini of the AP or Andrea Mitchell of NBC: "I'm on deadline, dear, ha ha." The three nets, the two wires, CNN, NPR, *USA Today*, the Baltimore *Sun*, and *The Washington Post* all assigned women full-time to the White House, and there was still just one bathroom for all of us — one small room with a lock.

The real reason I was able to keep those glass plates in the air was Aaron's devotion to Taylor. Aaron loved Taylor the way Merlin the magician loved Vivien the Lady of the Lake. Merlin knew that if he taught Vivien magic, she would maneuver him into a tower and imprison him there forever, but he didn't care because he loved her so much. That was Aaron with Taylor.

Aaron says it started at childbirth. Because I had a cesarean, he was the first one to diaper and feed Taylor in the hospital. And it didn't hurt that she looked exactly like him. Whatever the reason, I had never seen anything like it. He was working out of an office in our apartment but never got annoyed when she interrupted his work. He would go with her to the dreaded park whenever she asked and would take her and five or six friends to hockey games at the Capital Center or to Chuck E. Cheese. And he always volunteered for field trips with her class. Starting in third grade, he went on all the camping trips, managed to keep up on the bicycle tour, and videotaped every game and play she was ever in. After a while Tay signed him up without asking. It was a given that her dad would come along. She knew that he never said no. If he were to write a Guide to Child Rearing, he would outline the Aaron Latham three-step method to fatherhood: (1) Whenever possible, use the answer "Okay." (2) Or use the alternative answer: "Anything you want." (3) If all else fails, try the surefire sum-up statement: "If you're too busy, I'll do it."

It wasn't that I had to wear a sign around the house that said, "Hello, I'm one of your parents too," though occasionally I heard myself apologizing for not being there more, rationalizing, "Look, honey, a little of me goes a long way!"

"Did you ever resent that I wasn't home more with Taylor?" I asked my husband recently. "Did you think, 'She's not doing her share'?"

"Never. I mean it," he said. "I guess a pattern was set that first day in the hospital that I was the primary care giver. It sounds pretty Pollyanna-ish, but I liked it." Can you believe I gave this dear man only one child? It hurts just to write this down. He should have had a battalion.

JIM BAKER was a trim 54, with graying temples and patrician good looks. I have a soft spot for plodders, and that he was: a diligent and disciplined man who studied hard, plotted his moves, and prepared almost as much as I did. And he had a sense of fun about him, a twinkle. I liked him very much. Of course I did. It was part of his plan to charm the CBS correspondent. It was said that Jim Baker was a genius at manipulating the press. It was not because of any direct input into what we might say on the air, as he actually did very little to steer me about Reagan. What he worked on was how we felt about *him* so that, when the time came, we would give him the benefit of the doubt. This is the tricky part of covering a beat: it's hard to slice someone you like. As Henry Kissinger had before him, Baker wooed the press with that foolproof method: flattery. He'd quiz me about what I thought of a certain policy, then ask, "How do you think it'll play, Lesley?" Jim Baker had a golden press.

Now, after nearly four years as chief of staff, Baker was aching for a change. Back in October 1983 he had asked to be the national security adviser, but after agreeing, President Reagan had yielded to opposition from Ed Meese and reneged. Now Baker's urge to move on was even stronger. He'd been bruised by Nancy's open disapproval of him after Reagan's poor showing in the debate in Louisville (she had blamed him for "overbriefing" Ronnie), and he resented that the Reagans treated him as little more than "staff." When Treasury Secretary Donald Regan heard that Baker was itching to leave, he proposed that they swap jobs. Regan, 66, a bull of a man, had come to Washington after making multimillions running Merrill Lynch in New York, where he was accustomed to snapping out orders and seeing results. He was bored after four years at the slow-moving Treasury and looked at the chief of staff's job as more powerful and center stage.

But it was inconceivable that Reagan would ever let Baker go. After all, he had engineered the most successful presidential term in more than 20 years. Not only did Reagan get his major goals enacted (tax cuts, military budget increases), he had won a second term resoundingly, in no small measure due to Baker's stewardship. Yet Reagan signed on to the swap without a flicker of hesitation. I was told that Baker was crushed that the president had agreed to his leaving so blithely. But if Baker was hurt, Don Regan was surprised that Reagan hadn't asked a single question. What the chief of staff–to–be didn't realize was that the deal had been greased. Mike Deaver, the go-between, had finally won Nancy Reagan's approval. I've been told she resisted the change but was finally persuaded "with a degree of anger." Don Regan didn't know that Mrs. Reagan's okay was a prerequisite. He didn't get her — or grasp her influence. This was his first mistake. His second was not appreciating how submissive Reagan could be.

When the story broke that Reagan had acquiesced to the swap so carelessly, it touched off a new discussion about the disengaged president. I asked an old Reagan hand to explain the man to me. "You know," he replied, "we completely changed him for public consumption. The guy you saw was not the real Reagan."

"Oh?" I said. "And what exactly did you change?"

"We made him seem an activist, when in fact he was probably the most passive man to ever occupy the Oval Office." He told me a story from the 1980 campaign. The Reagans had begun to worry that Carter would make it an issue that he and Nancy never went to church. So, one Sunday a stop at an Episcopal church in northern Virginia was added to their schedule. On the way, Nancy leaned over to Deaver and said, "Mike, I hope they don't take communion, because I've never done that. I'm sure I'll make a big mistake and the press will write all about it."

Mike assured her that seven-year-olds take communion, and he began to walk her through the ritual. "What was that, Mike?" Reagan asked.

"Ronnie," said Nancy, "when we get in the church, just do whatever I do."

As communion began, Nancy grabbed Mike's arm and whispered, "You didn't tell me they drink from the same cup. I can't do this." Mike assured her that it was permissible to take the wafer in her hand and dunk it. "It's okay. It'll be fine."

"What was that, Mike?" Reagan spoke for the second time.

"Just do whatever I do," Nancy told him.

When it was her turn, Mrs. Reagan took the wafer, then watched in horror as it slipped from her fingers into the bowl. The priest recognized the distress signal on her taut face and quickly moved the chalice over to Mr. Reagan, who took a wafer smartly and with a flourish plopped it into the wine. Doing exactly as he'd been told, he beamed at the congregation.

"That defined the man," said the former aide, quoting someone who had said, "Reagan was a willow tree who called himself an oak and made you believe it." But in fact Reagan was Janus-like, apt to yield, though also capable of sticking to his guns when he really cared. Here was the elusiveness of his power: he was easily piloted, *except* when he was stubborn. Just when you were sure he was a cipher, a hologram, he'd cling to his Star Wars or a tax cut. Kathy Frankovic, the CBS pollster, told me that his popularity derived from the consistency this stubbornness provided and from the sense people had that he did what he said he would do. He said he would cut taxes and he did. He said he would increase military spending and he did. He said he would cut social programs, and at least he tried to. This gave Reagan the image of a straight shooter, the guy who came in from the West on his horse: the Hollywood-cowboy savior.

IT IS FAIR to say that the day Reagan agreed to the Baker-Regan switch was the day his White House lost its magic. The first-term team of Baker, Darman, Deaver, and Gergen understood what this president could and could not do. They knew Reagan had a great store of common sense, but they also knew he was ill informed. Issues had to be explained to him at a simple level, often with pictures or videos. The president rarely asked questions. In meetings, Bill Clark or Mike Deaver had often jumped in with the basics — What does that mean? or Explain that more slowly — in order to get answers out in front of the president.

Don Regan knew none of this. And there was no one left to explain it to him. Bill Clark was gone and Deaver was leaving as well, saying he could no longer live on $100,000 a year. Meese was about to become the attorney general, and Baker was taking Darman, with his knack for damage control, to Treasury. Now the only one who understood how Ronnie functioned or how to protect him was Nancy.

JANUARY 20, 1985. My guests on *Face the Nation* were George and Barbara Bush. We had worked for weeks to convince them that this was a good idea — appearing together to launch the second Reagan-Bush administration. One person who never had to struggle with a bad press was Barbara Bush. Even when she had seemed to call Geraldine Ferraro a bitch during the campaign, everyone forgave Bar. I think the quality the American people like most in a first lady is honesty. That's why Betty Ford, with her outspokenness, was so popular, and why Barbara would be. I think Mrs. Bush agreed to the interview because she wanted to apologize for having called Geraldine Ferraro a "bitch," but her husband kept interrupting her. He didn't have her ear for what played with the public.

I asked Mrs. Bush if she was looking forward to her husband's running for president. "After the campaign you just went through when

222

Mr. Bush was lampooned and criticized — he himself called it 'an ugly campaign' — are you anxious to get into that again?"

Mrs. Bush, with her she-looks-older-than-George white hair and her unchic, un-Nancy blue dress, hesitated, then said slowly, "Well, one would hope if I got into it, I'd be better behaved."

"Look, it wasn't that bad," the vice president jumped in. "We won 49 states."

Mrs. Bush tried again to apologize: "I wouldn't do anything differently except one thing."

"The one comment?" I asked, dancing around the B-word.

"Yes, I would never say that, or mean it or think it. So I would never — I'll be more careful. And that's too bad."

I'm thinking, isn't she terrific, when Bush interrupts again: "Not if that's picked up by a group and tried to make look like a character flaw, or a change in image or something." He wanted to blame someone; she wanted to say she was sorry.

I WAS STRUCK at how much of Reagan's foreign policy was run by Democrats (with the significant exception of the moderate Republican George Shultz, one of the more forceful and influential secretaries of state). These "neocons" roosted in strategic positions within the Reagan administration, usually at number two or three in rank: Richard Perle who had served on Scoop Jackson's Senate staff was at the Pentagon pushing a tough arms policy; Elliott Abrams from Daniel Patrick Moynihan's Senate staff had gone to the State Department, where he fathered the movements to fight the Soviet-backed insurgents in Central America; and Jeane Kirkpatrick at the United Nations kept up her rat-a-tats of indictments of Soviet misbehavior.[1] They had more influence over Reagan's anti-Communist agenda than the Reaganites did.

The president, meanwhile, was having it both ways on arms control. He was engaging in arms talks with the Soviets but obstinately refusing to compromise on SDI. On January 6 I had asked Henry Kissinger on *Face* about this. "I do not think," Kissinger said, "we should begin the negotiations by making a concession."

The next Sunday I asked Caspar Weinberger, "Is [SDI] totally non-negotiable?"

He indicated that it was by announcing plans to begin testing antisatellite missiles in March: "I am ruling out the possibility of giving up a strategic defense either in the research stage or, if it becomes feasible, in the deployable stage." Bingo. Monday-morning headlines.

JOAN BARONE had been in the hospital, but now she was home, and she was dying. The cancer had metastasized to her brain. What I loved about her was her honesty: she was scared and admitted it. So Aaron and I and many others went over to the house almost every day, partly to give Michael and little Sarah a respite. Finally, after a difficult last week when I don't think she ever slept, Joan, just 38 years old, died on March 11. It was unbearably sad.

My grieving for Joan broke through the wall of self-control I had been plastering together. I had been so successful that I began to worry about my disappearing emotions, which had been tamped down to the depth of an index card. I'd even lost all interest in being seductive. My urge to flirt — once so central, an identity mark, the way I knew I was alive — was gone. Now I didn't flirt at all.

I began mourning for me. Had I lost me because I was a mother? Was it age? Or was it simply that female sexuality and power were incongruous? Psychiatrist Anna Fells told me that the workplace "crushes female sexuality." Women have to be pretty and feminine but not sexy. This bind, she said, makes us angry, because we can never get it right: either we're too sexy or we're not sexy enough.

Nancy Reagan found a balance between power and ladyness (though not sexiness). We ended up accepting her influence because she emphasized her wifely devotion and was willing to let her marriage define her (not an acceptable solution for your average feminist). She looked unquestionably feminine in her soft, lovely clothes. And Ronnie helped by costarring with her in little ogling playlets that said: we still flirt with each other. Still, she was a force, and the public came to accept it. Her age probably helped. Age makes women less threatening.

Her influence was most public in March 1985, when the Kremlin introduced its new Soviet leader, 54-year-old Mikhail Gorbachev. I reported that the president had written to Gorbachev, inviting him to a summit meeting in the United States. Nancy let it be known that she had been behind the overture.

Nancy Reagan was no less contradictory than her husband. "She's the most timid person I've ever met," one White House official told me. Yet another described her as "the opposite of Ronnie, definite and insistent," and that was the face the public began to see more and more. In early 1985 she went on television to declare: "My husband *is not* disengaged." No longer demure (the "gaze" was gone, "because it was kind of ridiculed," she said), she spoke on the *CBS Morning News* on January 21 about the Baker-Regan swap: "Maybe this will quiet once and for all the people who keep saying, 'Well, Ronald Reagan doesn't run the government. . . . Now maybe they'll realize that all this time it's Ronald Reagan who has run the government." That's not exactly how things turned out.

Mrs. Reagan started the second term with glorious ratings, 71 percent according to the CBS News poll. Reagan lagged ten points behind.

One reason, I thought, was that she was increasingly seen as a moderating influence. There were pictures of Nancy sitting on the lap of Mr. T, the star of NBC's *The A-Team*. The first lady, that chummy with a large black man wearing lots of gold chains? It was marvelous, and an antidote to her husband's weak record on civil rights. She even publicly disagreed with her Ronnie on abortion: she said she had an open mind about it in cases of rape. And it was no secret that she had been active in nudging out the ideological Reaganites, such as Bill Clark. She was such a force against the conservatives that one of them referred to her as "the Dominatrix."

Still, she didn't make it easy to like her. As a White House reporter, I kept hearing tales of her heavy-handedness with the president's aides. One of them confided, "She scolds the president in front of us." She was either the fawning wife who had given up everything for her man (the feminists' bête noire) or an éminence grise, pulling the strings backstage. Only now do I see that, like many other women in positions of influence, she was struggling to find a balance.

Another example of this women's quandary was Jeane Kirkpatrick, who was about to leave her post as the U.S. ambassador at the United Nations. She gave me a farewell interview on *Face the Nation* on February 17, 1985. "What is all this business I keep reading," I asked, "about the sniping at you, about these factions developing against you?" Anonymous government sources were spreading stories that she was "erratic" and "bitchy." Some of my own trusted sources told me, "She flies off the handle, loses it" in national security meetings. "They say you're temperamental."

"They don't even know me, is my response. . . . It is a classical sexist charge."

"Yes, I'll go with that," I said. Even the conservative columnist William Buckley agreed. "If you are in the market for examples of male chauvinism," he wrote, "watch when they use the word 'temperamental.' They are usually talking about either Arturo Toscanini or a woman."[2]

"But were there temper tantrums?" I asked. "Did you throw temper tantrums?"

"Oh, never. Oh my gosh, no."

Even Jeane Kirkpatrick had trouble finding that balance between femaleness and wielding power.

I CALLED JENNIFER HERSHBERG, Mrs. Reagan's press secretary, and pitched an interview with the first lady. I noted that her antidrug campaign was not getting much network coverage, that she seemed to be coming into her own, and that I wanted to show the "new Nancy" to the public. When Jennifer ran my request past Mrs. Reagan, to my surprise she said yes. So every few days I would follow her out of Washington for a speech

225

against drug abuse. She was a hesitant, uncomfortable speaker, but she exuded sincerity, and the audiences, often young people, responded. As always she wore the most gorgeous clothes: a white Adolfo jacket with black piping over a red V-neck dress or a chic Bill Blass tweed suit.

On the day we were scheduled to film Mrs. Reagan at her staff meeting, my phone rang at 6:30 A.M. It was Robin Weir, my hairdresser and Nancy's as well. "Can't see you this morning. Sorry." Whenever Mrs. Reagan called Robin, even at the last minute, he would drop everything: women in his shop with wet heads, hairdos in midtease, and now me. It was part of his agreement with the White House. In exchange, he was the most famous hairdresser in Washington. To my frustration, Robin honored the other half of his agreement: coiffeur-client privilege. He never once gave me a story.

The point of the profile was to show the fun-loving, relaxed woman behind the first lady's mask, to catch the *real* Nancy with her easy laugh. Maybe I could get her to tell a joke. As we were setting up in the Map Room (used as the Situation Room by Roosevelt during World War II, and also the scene of President Clinton's videotaped grand jury testimony on August 17, 1998), James Rosebush, Mrs. Reagan's chief of staff, came to check on the lighting. I pleaded with him to urge her to be herself, explain that there was no reason for her to tense up.

But the minute the cameras rolled, I knew I was in trouble. Mrs. Reagan looked beautiful in a royal blue silk dress with a cowl neck, but she was tighter than a clenched fist, with an artificial smile that made her seem as natural as NutraSweet. I stopped the interview at one point, hoping the break would give her a chance to find herself. No such luck. Almost everything she said seemed to be recited from memory.

"Do you think you've changed in the White House?"

"I'm still the same person. If you say, have I grown? Yes, I think I have. I think I don't know how anybody could be in this position and not grow." She'd said that before, in those words.

An interview that isn't going well is like trying to sail with no wind. I tacked left in search of a question that would unlock her stiffness. Then right, casting about for a way to lull her wariness. I was becalmed (though far from calm). Still, our story came out fairly well. We pegged it to the opening of the First Ladies Conference on Drug Abuse on April 24:

STAHL: She has traveled to 44 cities, sticking with the drug issue against the advice of her media experts, who said it was too depressing.

The piece was mostly complimentary, though I did mention that the White House staff was "afraid of her" and that feminists criticized her for not using her position "to promote women's issues."

226

NANCY: I have the best of two worlds. I had a career which I loved, I enjoyed, and then I met the man I wanted to marry and I gave it up. Well, now that, it seems to me, is the whole idea of women. You have a choice of what you want to do.

A scent of feminism — more like eau de toilette than the real thing — but Nancy did support the notion that women participate as equals at work and in politics. Could it be that the president's daughter Maureen, with her outspoken feminism, was rubbing off on her stepmother? I had a theory that Maureen, who had moved into the White House, was one of the reasons the first lady was becoming more of her own person. Nancy Reagan would tell you that Maureen had zero influence on her. In fact, she bristled at the mere suggestion, but I was not alone in this view.[3]

CHANGE THE DIRECTOR and the whole character of the movie changes. And that's just what happened to *The Reagan Years*. Sweet Ronnie of the first term became Dirty Harry, with a newly contentious approach to Congress and the press. Before, it would have been out of character for him to tell off a group of governors, but now he did just that when they complained about his plan to cut funds for state and local governments. Don Regan, with his combative personality, got the credit and the blame for this image metamorphosis. But I thought it was due more to Patrick Buchanan, the former Nixon speechwriter who was now head of Reagan's Communications Office. Buchanan was a pugnacious, hard-line conservative with a soft voice. It was hard to reconcile the easy-to-laugh, almost gentle Pat you'd meet in his office with the public persona: the unbending Pat, a man allergic to the concept of compromise.

It's usually the one with the zeal who steers the boat, which Buchanan did by spiking up the speeches that remained at the heart of Reagan's leadership. On the possibility of Congress raising taxes, he had the president do an imitation of the leathery Clint Eastwood: "Go ahead, make my day." Then there was his description of the contras as "the moral equal of our Founding Fathers." The contras were the rebel force trying to overthrow the Marxist Sandinista government in Nicaragua. Reagan was having trouble persuading the public and Congress to support the contras, which he said was necessary in order to contain the spread of communism.

I was once seated next to the Sandinista leader, Daniel Ortega, at a dinner party in New York. And all I could think was: How on earth did he get ten people, no less a whole country, to follow *him?* When you think of revolutionaries who have overthrown entrenched regimes, you think of the dash of Castro in his sexy fatigues, you think of the presence of Zapata, you think of the fire and spiritual air of Mao Tse-tung. Yet

227

here was an almost frail, bashful man. When he got up to speak, he had the charisma of lima beans. This phlegmatic man next to me — with his limp handshake and dull eyes — was Reagan's Minotaur?

BITBURG WOULD BE A FIRETRAP, and Nancy Reagan knew it. She begged her husband not to go. But he got stubborn.

You could see the catastrophe coming from the first day. It was April 11, Reagan was on vacation at his ranch, and Larry Speakes told us at a briefing at the Sheraton that during the president's trip to West Germany (as well as France, Italy, Spain, and Portugal) in May, he planned to lay a wreath at a military cemetery in Bitburg where the soldiers who had fought the Allies in World War II were buried. In my story that night I ran a sound bite of a Holocaust survivor: "[The visit to Bitburg] is an absolute outrage. He is aligning himself with all those elements who would have wished that Hitler had succeeded."

Over the next several days my pieces from Santa Barbara were litanies of complaints from Jewish groups, Protestant churches, the VFW, and politicians of all persuasions. A Republican congressman said, "I really have to wonder if the new crew in the White House has gone bonkers." It became clear that Don Regan, chief of staff for just two months, had yet to set up a mechanism for damage control. So when the big bomb dropped — the news that 49 Waffen SS Nazi troops were buried at Bitburg — it was not the staff that took the fall; it was the president himself. That had never happened in his first term.

Reagan justified the visit by claiming that German soldiers "were victims, just as surely as the victims in the concentration camps." Whoa. Not a good idea. Said an aide, "Oh my God," and he was right. Reagan's remark so incensed the writer and Holocaust survivor Elie Wiesel that he embarrassed the president by publicly chastising him during a ceremony at the White House. With our cameras rolling, Wiesel faced Reagan and implored him "to find another way, another site. . . . That place, Mr. President, is not your place. Your place is with the victims of the SS." I was in the room. It was breathtaking. Reagan was distraught.

Eighty-two Senators, 257 congressmen, and 100 Christian church leaders called on the president to drop the Bitburg visit. On the other side was Patrick Buchanan, who kept urging Reagan not to cave in. Jewish leaders were invited to the White House for a calm-the-waters session. Marvin Kalb reported on NBC that, according to participants at the meeting, Buchanan wrote over and over in his notebook: "Succumbing to the pressure of the Jews."

The denunciations grew, but Reagan seemed unfazed with his uncanny ability to block out criticism. An official on the NSC told me about a working lunch to discuss the trip: despite the protests, "Reagan was in fine fettle, emitting dangerous quips" as if he hadn't a care in the world. His advisers spent hours every week in search of jokes, often raunchy ones, to tell the president. At that lunch, Jim Baker asked, "What's the difference between a moose and Lawrence Welk's orchestra?" Answer: "The orchestra has the horns in the back and the asshole up front." The table in the Roosevelt Room vibrated from all the pounding. It was as if the gathering storm over Bitburg didn't exist.

Two weeks later the speechwriter Ken Khachigian met with Reagan to discuss what he should say at Bitburg and at the Bergen-Belsen concentration camp. According to Khachigian's handwritten notes, Reagan told him, "Out of these ashes, came something good. . . . I find myself thinking, 'But we killed these people. Are we holding a grudge?' "[4] That same day the president got a letter from the Dutch prime minister "urgently" requesting that he cancel the visit to Bitburg: "This is shocking to many of those in our country who have been subjected to the most gruesome repression and persecution by fascism."

A few days later, on April 28, when I asked Don Regan on *Face* if the president was anguished over Bitburg, what I heard was bitterness: "The president feels that being a friend, as he is to Jews everywhere — he's worked hard to get them out of the Soviet Union and the like — to have this now overshadow a state visit to Germany is distressing."

It has been reported that at Nancy Reagan's urging, the president did try to cancel the Bitburg stop, but German Chancellor Helmut Kohl was insistent, and Reagan backed down.

When we got to Germany, it was cold and drizzly. According to *People* magazine Nancy arrived "with 19 suitcases containing three umbrellas, a mink, 15 pairs of shoes, 16 handbags, six cashmere pullovers, 21 daytime dresses, and 11 evening gowns."[5] My colleague Jackie Adams was told that Mrs. Reagan would send swatches of her clothes along with the advance team for major trips to make sure her suits and dresses "worked" against the backdrops.

The visit to Bitburg was on May 5. The cemetery was hardly the storm-trooper bleakness I'd pictured. It was lush with flowers, which I saw on a television screen because it was Sunday and I was at our makeshift studio at the Cologne airport getting ready for *Face*. What I saw was a perfunctory wreath laying lasting a total of eight minutes. This was Mike Deaver's swan song. For the first time, the master of camera angles put the camera platform behind a clump of trees so that we could barely see a thing. However, our enterprising CBS cameraman Kurt Hoeffle bought a fancy $1,000 tripod and with it managed somehow to get a shot of the SS graves.

With our guest, George Shultz, sitting next to me at the airport, I noted that there were several demonstrations against the visit around the United States. Some 250,000 rallied in New York alone.

> STAHL: The president apparently told Chancellor Kohl he was sorry that there had been a flare-up of anti-German sentiment in the United States.
> SHULTZ: The president never apologizes for America, let me assure you.
> STAHL: Somebody read me — an American note taker wrote that down — that he apologized.
> SHULTZ: Well, he didn't apologize.

I also interviewed Simon Wiesenthal, the much admired Nazi hunter, a sturdy 76-year-old with a holy aura. "Do you think the German people need this symbol of reconciliation?" I asked him.

"No," he said, "they absolutely don't need it. . . . Sixty percent of the Germans are born after the war, another ten percent were small children. They are absolutely different."

One of the president's aides told me that on the way out of Bitburg, a group of 40 to 50 young Germans mooned the president and Mrs. Reagan as their bullet-proof limo sailed by. "Well," said Reagan later with a smile, "I saw these people on the hill beside the road, and suddenly they opened their jaws!"

Bitburg exposed the weakness of Reagan's new team, with its willingness to let him bear the weight of the criticism, and it identified Pat Buchanan as a force that had to be reined in. But as I would learn, Buchanan got blamed for things he didn't do.

THE PRESIDENT'S SPEECHWRITERS were known to be more royal than Reagan. As a White House aide said, "They see themselves as the only worthy receptacles of the Reagan wine, the only toilers in the vineyard who should be trusted with the bottling process. The problem is, every now and then they become the process itself."

In the first term, the speechwriters had reported to Richard Darman, who had cleansed their first drafts of scripture. My friend Peggy Noonan once explained her method of speech writing to me: "It was obvious that to get anything sensible said, you had to overload. There were times when I would write a whole speech with 'red meat,' but I'd really layer it thick in the fourth paragraph. I would know that in staffing they would fixate on that and leave the rest."

"Did Darman destroy your speeches?" I asked.

230

"No, but he made them weaker, less pointed."

Darman understood how central the speeches were to Reagan's

image and always left in enough "red meat" to convey that Reagan was consistent on his core issues — and tough.

Once again, the new Regan team was unaware of the "system." So when Peggy was assigned a major foreign policy address for the president to deliver at the European Parliament in Strasbourg three days after Bitburg, she wrote Evil Empire Revisited, full of chili peppers about the loathsome Commies, and then she did what she always did: she sent it out for "staffing."

Unlike Darman, Buchanan sent her draft on virtually intact. No one in the State Department or the NSC had seen anything like this before. So when National Security Adviser Robert "Bud" McFarlane read the speech, he assumed that Buchanan had added the red-hot touches, and he exploded. A former lieutenant colonel in the marines and military assistant to Henry Kissinger, McFarlane was a man of uninterrupted taciturnity whose face seemed incapable of expression. He had been almost obsequious with Jim Baker, but now he was screeching, accusing Buchanan of deliberately radiating the speech with strident anti-Communist invective "more suitable for the American Legion in Philadelphia than the European Parliament." Buchanan was stunned. He had no idea what had gone wrong.

The criticism wounded Noonan's authorial pride, so she fired off a deliciously insulting memo to the "know-nothingniks" at State and NSC: "If they'd been around in the Kennedy years, he would have gone to Berlin and said, 'I am a citizen from the German city of Berlin.'"

Meanwhile the speech, 24 hours away, had yet to reach the president. In those last hours Bud McFarlane rewrote it, watering it down so much that the TelePrompTer going on the fritz made more news. As did the hecklers. "What about Nicaragua?" they hooted. Reagan always won with hecklers. This time he looked out at the audience and said, "They haven't been there [to Nicaragua]. I have." Which wasn't true.

In due course, Nancy Reagan complained to Don Regan about the speech-writing operation. Within a few weeks Buchanan was demoted: another conservative reined in by the first lady.

TAYLOR WAS IN THE THIRD GRADE. At her own insistence, she was growing her hair, which was straight, lushly auburn, and halfway down her back. I remembered my own straight, mousy hair at that age. Shirley Temple ringlets had been *the* look, so Dolly had sent me to Aunt Freda's every few months for permanents. Aunt Freda was my dad's aunt, and while she made me luscious cupcakes, I hated the pungent, drippy lotions and tight curlers and especially how I looked afterward. That's why I let Tay do what she wanted with her hair. The tutor was a different matter. Tay did not want to go to the tutor, but she was having a hard time learning to read, so after school on Mondays and Thursdays she worked with Mrs. Rigby. On Wednesdays she took piano lessons, which she kept begging me to stop. Tuesday was tap dancing and Saturday mornings, gymnastics. Was I replicating my own hectic life?

One of her school projects that year involved Aaron and me. Each set of parents was called upon to deliver a "roots report" to the class. Since I knew very little about my roots, I had to investigate, which wasn't that easy. All four of my grandparents had come to the United States from Poland around the turn of the century, but they had never talked about themselves as children. The only relative of that generation still alive and lucid was Aunt Adele, another of my father's aunts. I called her one afternoon and got her to reminisce.

My grandfather, Heinach, came from Włodawa, Poland, a small village in the forest not far from Warsaw, she told me. His father died young, so it was left to my great-grandmother to support their five boys and three girls, which she did by running a small farm and a store in the woods. My grandfather and his brothers were lumberjacks, but they were also musical. Nathan, the eldest, had a real violin; the others carved their own horns, fiddles, and drums. With their cousins they formed an orchestra in the middle of the forest.

Nathan and my grandfather had to walk to town for their violin lessons. One night, on the long walk home, Nathan was beaten up by a group of older boys, who smashed his violin into a hundred pieces. For weeks, after work and after studies, Nathan stayed up late and piece by piece glued his violin back together.

The third-graders at Sidwell Friends seemed to like my story. At least they stayed awake. Then it was Aaron's turn. He told about his family crossing the country in a covered wagon, all the way from Virginia to west Texas, finally settling in Spur, where both men and women wore guns and resolved disputes by shooting each other. Aaron told the class about his uncle Hool, who was riding home one night when his horse stalled. Hool got furious at that old animal and threatened him. When the horse still wouldn't move, he took out his six-shooter and blasted him between the ears. Old Paint keeled over . . . onto Hool. Who remained trapped under a ton of horse with a broken leg for two days until finally someone rode by and saved his life. Aaron said, "My Uncle Hool wasn't quite as smart as a fence post." That was the tale the third grade voted the best story.

When husbands of working women are happy, working women are happy. It's axiomatic. The year 1985 was a good one for us. For the second time in his life, Aaron became the object of a Hollywood bidding war, with one studio after the next upping the price till finally Columbia bought "Perfect." And so Aaron again moved to Los Angeles to write a

232

screenplay with his friend the director Jim Bridges. They set up tables facing each other in a bungalow on the lot of the old Laird Studio, where David O. Selznick had made *Gone with the Wind* and Charlie Chaplin had made *Modern Times*.

Aaron had an Osborne I, the first so-called portable computer, a big, clunky machine that was too heavy for me to carry. Portable! Jim was so intrigued by it that they eventually wrote the computer into the screenplay. I think it was the first movie in which a PC became part of the plot.

In the original version, the star was a sedentary reporter who falls in love with a health club goddess. Jamie Lee Curtis, with the best body in the world, was everyone's first choice. They'd been thinking Dustin Hoffman for the reporter, but John Travolta, then the antithesis of out-of-shape, wanted to work with Aaron and Jim again. The script was rewritten; the reporter got pecs! If Travolta wanted in, he was in.

Aaron came home every weekend except for the few times Taylor and I went out there. On one of those trips Bridges put Taylor in a scene as a model in a fashion show at the health club. Travolta kept trying to hug her. She's probably the only woman in America who ever rebuffed him.

THE MIDDLE EAST was sapping Reagan of his Irish luck with one act of terrorism after the next: bombings followed by hijackings followed by kidnappings. On the third Sunday in March I reported on *Face* that Terry Anderson, chief Middle East correspondent of the Associated Press, had been taken hostage in Beirut.

Three months later, on June 14, TWA Flight 847 to Rome was hijacked by Lebanese Shiites, who showed they meant business by killing a U.S. Navy diver, Robert Stethem, 23, and dumping his body onto the tarmac. The gunmen said they would not release their 39 hostages until Israel released more than 700 Shiite prisoners.

The networks would again be accused of "providing a platform for terrorism" when we interviewed the families of the hostages. Columnist George Will called the close-ups of anxious hostage mothers and wives the "pornography of grief."[6] But in this case, we had not pursued the families (for a change); they had come after us. Almost immediately, they began issuing statements, showing up at the State Department, offering themselves for debates and interviews. They figured out that if they humanized and personalized the hostages — turned them into sons and fathers — it was less likely they would be abandoned and sacrificed to the war on terrorism. An official on the NSC staff called me and pleaded, "All the publicity you're giving the families is making it difficult for the president, who gets very emotional when he sees these mothers and wives."

"But if families in a democracy don't have access to the media, the way the government does," I asked him, "how can they exercise their right to pressure the government not to treat the hostages as expendable?"

The criticism about our putting hostage families on TV was heated but not nearly as intense as when we put the hostages themselves on. Edwin Diamond wrote in *The Media Show* that we simply couldn't "pass up the good pictures" — and, I dare to add, the good emotion, the "moments."

ABC got the first scoop "moment" on June 19, when correspondent Charles Glass came up with an exclusive interview with the TWA pilot aboard the plane. Smiling rigidly, Captain Testrake said the crew was being treated fine. He was speaking from the window of the cockpit with a gun held to his head. Far from treating this questioning at gunpoint with indignation, as we should have, we at CBS were crestfallen that we'd been beaten.

Predictably, Israel felt the heat, and on June 23 Defense Minister Yitzhak Rabin chose *Face* to announce a token gesture: Israel would release 31 of the 700 Shiite prisoners.

STAHL: Did the U.S. in any way ask you to take this action? Did they ask you for a gesture?
RABIN: The 31? No, not at all . . . not asked. It was not even hinted.

Diplomatic shading.

FACE'S AUDIENCE in this period was close to 1.5 million larger than normal. In fact, the hijacking story was increasing the ratings of all the news shows. Which encouraged us to maintain the intensity of the coverage. Which produced more criticism. Yet with all the complaining about our coverage, there was no indication the president was suffering politically, as I pointed out on the air in late June: "During the crisis his popularity and the support for his actions, as reflected in the polls, have actually grown." As with Jimmy Carter in the beginning of his hostage crisis, the country rallied behind the president.

But with Carter's experience as a guide, the Reagan White House made sure the hostages did not linger in captivity. On the 17th day, a Sunday, they were set free while *Face* was on the air. "The American hostages are on their way to freedom," I reported. "They're traveling in a convoy to Damascus before flying off to Frankfurt." My guest, Vice President Bush, joined us via satellite from Paris, "taking an oath" that there had been no "deal" to win the release.

234

STAHL: I know this is a delicate time, but have the avenues for retaliating at this point been pretty much closed off? Here Syria has now been so helpful. We've always talked about them being involved in some of these acts of terrorism in the past.

BUSH: Lesley, let me ask you to take the question back because I'm not going to answer it. I hope you'll understand . . .

I think: I can't just drop this. It's the question everyone in the country wants to hear. I worry about seeming to badger, but I'm live; no time to second-guess. I asked why the president had "threatened retaliation on Friday when the release seemed imminent." I'd put him in a tight spot. I knew it.

He lapsed into Bushspeak about not wanting to "escalate a rhetorical output about what we might or might not do as the United States of America down the road." Then I couldn't resist:

STAHL: Would you like to apologize to Jimmy Carter for some of the statements you made about his "pussy footing around" when he was waiting and hoping that he could bring those hostages, those Iranian hostages, home safely?

BUSH: Well, no. And again, I don't want to get into that. This isn't the time to finger point or to try to say whether we did it better than Jimmy Carter, worse than Jimmy Carter, or something of that nature. I'm sorry, I view this with too much solemnity to get into that.

The administration continued to deny publicly that any deals had been made; but it was later learned that the Reagan team had leaned on the Israelis, who, after the Americans were safely home, released the 700 Shiite prisoners in stages.[7]

In *Turmoil and Triumph: My Years as Secretary of State,* George Shultz wrote that "the most effective tactic we used [to resove the crisis] was silence." Reagan put a lid on comments by U.S. officials. "The relative silence created a threatening aura that astounded the world's observers and the terrorists. . . . Silence can instill fear."[8]

At a congressional hearing examining the TV coverage in late July, family members testified that the extensive exposure might have ensured the safety of the hostages and had possibly hastened their release. Ironically, it was Jody Powell who rang the loudest bell defending the networks. He testified that the coverage had not undermined foreign policy in either the TWA or his own Iranian hostage crisis. "What the coverage did in both cases was to increase pressure on the White House," he said, "but presidents are big boys, responsible for their own actions, and blaming the press for policy problems cannot be a way out." Yo, Jody.

The major critic was Fred Friendly — champion of the First Amendment. He said he had been disgusted by the networks' "unseemly . . .

haphazard frenzy of competition." He even accused us of "probably advancing the cause of terrorism."

A few years later, Friendly illustrated his point in a PBS seminar on terrorism in which a group of jurists, government officials, and journalists —I among them—were put into a hypothetical hijacking predicament and called on to make instant decisions under pressure. We sat around a U-shaped table as the moderator, Arthur Miller of Harvard Law School, laid out the crisis: the hijacking of an airliner much like TWA 847. Among those around the table were CIA Director William Casey, playing himself; Sir Kenneth Newman, head of Scotland Yard; and Peter Jennings, the anchorman. I was there as the reporter on the scene.

At a critical moment Miller turned to me: "Miss Stahl." He paused to let me jolt up as he knew I would in that intimidating company. "The plane is on the tarmac, and you have been invited on board for some exclusive interviews. Do you go?"

"Yes." I don't hesitate.

"Are you sure?"

"Oh, yes." At which point Miller says that the terrorist leader orders me to keep the camera rolling while he executes one of the Americans on board "as an example."

The glow on my face goes out like a match in wind. I'm on that plane and my heart is beating and I have to decide *now* what to say to this murderer in whose hands I have so carelessly placed myself. I pause, and pause some more trying to find a way out. Finally, I say I will tell the cameraman to stop rolling. Maybe that will discourage the killing.

With that Miller springs at me, building the tension in the room and true terror in my heart. If I don't keep the camera going and tape the hostage execution, he will shoot my cameraman.

I can hardly breathe. I am in the throes of real fear, with all the bodily manifestations of a panic attack. Peter Jennings tries to rescue me, but Miller quiets him. I am on the hot seat, holding the fate of two men. I can't choose, I cannot, but Miller just waits until finally I say, "I'm sitting here thinking I don't want to be a reporter any more when this is over if these are the kinds of choices we have to make."

On July 13, 1985, the president had surgery to remove a polyp from his colon. The surgeon, Dr. Dale Oller, briefed us: "There was no sign of cancer whatsoever."

The White House press corps crammed into an amphitheater at Bethesda Naval Hospital, where Larry Speakes called our skeptical questions "catty." He told us to "go fly a kite" when we pressed about why we couldn't have more interviews with the doctors.

A few days after the operation we were on the air live with a briefing

about the results of the biopsy. I was sitting in the front row when
Dr. Oller said, "The villous adenoma confined to the cecum of the
bowel within the radical, or the right hemicolectomy specimen contained
adenocarcinoma confined within the muscle of the bowel wall, such that
there was no evidence of spread of the cancer within the villous adenoma
to the pericolic fat, vessels, fifteen lymph nodes — many sections of those
— and the nerves."

I'm taking notes as if I got it. Dr. Oller went on: "The president
continues his superlative recovery, and when asked how he felt about this,
well, he says, 'I'm glad that that's all out.' " He chuckled.

Then Dr. Steven Rosenberg of the National Cancer Institute at the
National Institutes of Health got up: "The president has cancer." He kept
talking: "There's no evidence it has spread." I stopped taking notes. The
president has cancer. Here was a maze of distorted clauses and twisted
confusions, and then, so suddenly and jarringly, the jumble turns into a
sound bite of staggering clarity.

I asked the first question: "Will he have to be on any kind of medication? Chemotherapy? Radiation? Anything like that?" My voice quavered.
Zirinsky told me later I had sounded upset. I was surprised the news had
shaken me as deeply as it had.

"It's my feeling," said Dr. Rosenberg matter-of-factly, "that no further
therapy is indicated at this time. . . . Given all the pathologic findings in
the president's case, in most cases [the cancer] would not return."

Dr. Oller was back at the microphone. I wondered if Nancy had
instructed him to be cheery and up-tempo. "The president has been out
of bed today. He's read the majority of the day. He's ebullient, in excellent
spirits."

We reporters continued to complain about access, because that is
the nature of the beast. Truth be told, the White House released more
information about Reagan's operation than had been disclosed during
other presidential hospitalizations.

As we struggled to tell the story of the president's cancer, a subplot
was brewing over the jurisdiction of authority at the White House. That
night I reported that "the true lines of power will flow up to one man,
Chief of Staff Regan. He'll be in charge of decisions, paperwork, the
president's schedule, and he'll determine what is said to the public about
the president's condition." In other words: Who is this guy usurping the
power, anyway? Who elected him? What about the vice president?

Don Regan was about to get a drubbing. There was an outcry when
it was learned that Margaret Thatcher had called to wish the president a
quick recovery and the call had been routed to Regan — not to the vice
president, who, by appearing to accept his upstaging by Regan so pas- 237
sively, came off as acquiescent.

But at the time, far more attention was paid to the bigfooting Don Regan. I marveled at Washington's periodic blood hunts. Victims of this ritual like to blame the press. What I saw with Regan, and with many others, was a strong character who was not liked by the body politic whose immune system kicks in to surround and destroy the intruding force. When Regan appeared to grab for too much power, the antibody army mobilized, bit and chewed, and then offered morsels to the circling press corps.

You have to feel sorry for the guy. He got blamed for expropriating presidential powers, and then we learned it was Nancy, after all, who had been the wizard behind the curtain. It was she who had instructed that Regan would be Ronnie's *only* official visitor and that he would receive no phone calls — no calls at all.[9]

President Reagan left the hospital on July 20, looking remarkably fit. As I reported in a news special from the hospital, "He looks wonderful." His recuperative powers must have been helped along by his ability never to accept anything negative. "I never had cancer. I had something inside of me," he said, "that had cancer in it, and it was removed."

On the same day Reagan was released from the hospital, *The New York Times* ran a picture of Manuel Garcia posing on his stoop with a group of friends and relatives. Garcia was a 35-year-old Puerto Rican auto mechanic from Milwaukee who also had cancer. After chemotherapy, when all his hair fell out, he was embarrassed. To express solidarity and love, Manuel's brother Julio shaved his head, then two of Manuel's sons shaved, and then 50 friends shaved. In the picture Manuel was in the center, looking just like all the other bald guys seated around him.

I saw that picture the same day I learned that none of Reagan's children had been to visit him in the hospital. Under Mrs. Reagan's direction, they hadn't even talked to him on the phone. And there was Manuel surrounded by a sea of loving Humpty-Dumpty heads — which I understood. Reagan. He was a bafflement.

As THE REAGANS LEFT for an extralong summer vacation at the ranch, Aaron, Taylor, and I went back to Nantucket. Aaron let Taylor, now eight, drive the jeep a few times. She almost knocked down the garage.

We rented a huge house and invited our friends up for weekends. The house was lived-in with wicker tables and big soft couches. It had five bedrooms, but we stuffed more couples in by renting cots and putting people up in the living room, over the garage, and in a little artists' studio. We stuffed ourselves on mammoth lobster banquets and took wild drives along the beaches in four-wheel-drive jeeps. And we instituted a regular whiffle-ball game in our yard, where every Sunday someone or other pulled a muscle somewhere between home plate and first base. We old farts in our mid-40s were simply not used to running that fast.

WITH THE FIGHT against the Hollywood studios for syndication revenues lost, newsmagazines were one of the few ways networks could produce and own their own shows. *Dallas*, which was not owned by CBS, still cost the network something like $1 million an episode.[10] A newsmagazine cost one third as much. In those days Don Hewitt estimated that *60 Minutes* made $70 million a year for CBS, roughly one fourth of the network's profits.

Inspired by the moneymaking muscle of *60 Minutes*, ABC News had developed *20/20*, NBC News was starting its own magazine, *American Almanac*, with Roger Mudd as anchor, and CBS News was launching its second magazine, *West 57th*. Because they were competing in prime time with sitcoms, these shows brought news closer to entertainment than it had ever been. Some argue that *60 Minutes* invented "infotainment," and that may be. But *West 57th* was the great leap forward.

Patterned loosely on *60 Minutes*, *West 57th* had a team of correspondents all under 40. The promos emphasized how hip they were. One of the producers called the show "Yup to the Minute." There was a lot of grumbling around CBS News about the softness of *West 57th* with its profiles of rock stars and starlets. So naturally, the old battle between the yesterday and today people flared anew. I was at war within myself over *West 57th*. One side of me resented these young reporters leapfrogging over us veteran vineyard stompers. How come they got into prime time? It isn't that I wanted to do that kind of broadcast, but I wanted at least to be asked. How come my package, with all the years of political, economic, military, health, you-name-it journalism, wasn't considered for this obvious wave of the future? But then I would get ashamed. How could I, of all people, begrudge the newcomers? Wasn't this exactly the way Dan Schorr had felt about me?

Andy Lack, the executive producer of *West 57th*—shrewd, savvy and young himself at 38—began leaking stories that his broadcast was "with it," unlike *60 Minutes*, which was fading into old age. The line was that if the tired old Mike and Morley Show gets any tireder, it could be replaced by the hipper, cooler knockoff.

Don Hewitt, 62, took all this personally. *60 Minutes* was his baby: he had created it, he produced it, and he was convinced that Andy Lack was trying to sabotage it. And so he struck back, telling Sally Bedell Smith of *The New York Times* (August 15) that at *60 Minutes* "we play major-league baseball; that doesn't mean there isn't room for the minor league." Andy Rooney was less subtle but more succinct; he merely called *West 57th* "trash journalism."

239

While the turmoil between the generations churned internally, CBS was attacked from without. Our economics correspondent, Ray Brady, reported on April 17 that Ted Turner, the owner of CNN, was about to launch a hostile takeover bid for CBS. Earlier in the year Senator Jesse Helms, convinced of our liberal bias, had sent a letter to a million conservatives asking them to buy CBS stock and "become Dan Rather's boss." This effort fizzled. But it suggested that CBS was, as they say, in play.

After telling reporters that the way to respond to a raider was "to reflexively bite their ankle," CBS CEO Tom Wyman reared up and bit, taking steps that some analysts considered a foolish overreaction to the Turner threat. *Newsweek* said that his offering in junk bonds ($5.4 billion in stock and debt securities, no cash) "bordered on the preposterous." Yet Wyman bought back 21 percent of CBS stock at $32 a share over the selling price and in the process took on a debt of nearly a billion dollars. In early August Turner caved in, so Wyman won. Some victory. To pay off the huge debt, Wyman sold CBS's toy business; KMOX in St. Louis, which CBS had owned for 30 years; and its one-third stake in the film studio Tri-Star. After all that, he plunged into a severe cost-cutting drive.

As part of that drive, CBS News was told to eliminate 74 jobs, one out of ten. The Washington Bureau had already been traumatized by the firing in August of Supreme Court correspondent Fred Graham (he was later reinstated). Now this new wave of layoffs would be made worse by the insensitive way it was handled by Sauter and Joyce. Those on the hit list were notified on Thursday, September 19, that they were terminated and told they had to be out of the building by the close of business the next day. And by the way, don't ever come back. If an office-door key was not turned in, the lock was changed. Some of those given 24 hours to clear out were CBS veterans of 20 years.

We learned that Sauter had not even argued against these firing-squad dismissals. His loyalties belonged not to the News Division but to Black Rock.

REAGAN'S RACIAL POLICIES were perplexing. Beyond his attempt to protect tax subsidies for racist private schools and his fight against renewal of the Voting Rights Act, Reagan named one of the most outspoken critics of civil rights legislation, William Bradford Reynolds, as the head of the Civil Rights Division of the Justice Department. Then came his policy on apartheid in South Africa, "constructive engagement," which favored quiet diplomacy over sanctions. South African Archbishop Desmond Tutu called the policy "immoral, evil, and totally un-Christian" and told

Reagan in an Oval Office meeting in December that he believed it had "worsened the situation of blacks in South Africa."

Now, in late August 1985, calls for sanctions accelerated. Still Reagan refused, telling an interviewer that the South Africans "have eliminated the segregation that we once had in our own country, the type of thing where hotels and restaurants and places of entertainment and so forth were segregated. That has all been eliminated."[11] Which, of course, was not true. That night I was made to report what the president had said, without correction or comment.

These are the kinds of dilemmas reporters often face: What is "unfair"? Is it unfair to say that smoking causes cancer? That cigarettes kill? The tobacco companies said it was. Was it unfair to say that "Reaganomics" didn't work? I saw much of what would be labeled "editorializing" as a matter of straightforward reporting. This time I just caved in. I was tired of arguing over my copy and fighting an urge to ask for a new assignment. Leaving the White House, the top beat, would not be the wisest career move.

David Broder wrote an article in *The Washington Post* arguing that "Reagan . . . has never accepted the reality of racism. Just plain won't recognize it."[12] What did that mean? I'd heard such analysis before, that there was an America of Reagan's imagination, a place where race problems did not exist and everyone knew his place. Now he was transposing this idyll to South Africa?

POLLS IN THE FALL OF 1985 showed less than half the people — 44 percent — believing the country was moving in the right direction. As much as the public loved him personally — Reagan's personal popularity was as high as 65 percent[13] — I watched eyes glazing over as he pressed his issues, especially his number one priority, tax reform. The president had the public by the heart but not the mind. He was not helped by the huge budget deficit, the sluggish productivity rate, the compounding national debt, and the decline in the value of the dollar.

But as a friend once explained to me, if the American people have a choice between a politician who is smart and one who is lucky, they'll go with lucky every time. And Reagan was their man. Just as his second term was turning into a country called Disaster, back roared his good fortune. It came in the form of a crisis, which meant I was working round the clock, putting aside my desire to leave. Just when you have time to contemplate how you feel, wham! — a story breaks that blots up every second of your life.

October. Another Palestinian terrorist hijacking. This time it was the

Achille Lauro, an Italian cruise liner filled with American and European tourists.

STAHL: At the White House, no threats, no harsh words — only signs of frustration, President Reagan calling the hijacking "the most ridiculous thing."

The next day 69-year-old Leon Klinghoffer of New York, a passenger on the *Achille Lauro*, was murdered in his wheelchair and thrown overboard. The hijackers fled to Egypt, where President Hosni Mubarak, one of our closest allies in the Middle East, let them go free.

The notion that the United States was too big and powerful to act had taken hold. So when the navy sprang into action on October 10, everyone was surprised. U.S. fighter jets intercepted an Egyptian plane carrying the hijackers from Egypt to Tunisia and diverted it to Italy. Dan Rather said it all that night: "The day the U.S. took terror, captured it, and cut it down to size."

STAHL: At the White House aides called it "hitting the jackpot in Sicily, the best two days the president has had in a long time."
REAGAN: These young Americans sent a message to terrorists everywhere. The message: You can run, but you can't hide.

Reagan, thumb up, said, "We did this all by our little selves." With not a single casualty, U.S. airpower and technology worked flawlessly. His free fall under Don Regan was reversed with a startle, like a bungee jump. Back came the luster. And once again Reagan was able to explain the operation as a parable where the shining knights of the U.S. Navy Round Table slayed the dragon. There was one catch: the mastermind of the seajacking, Muhammed Abul Abbas, Yasser Arafat's confrere, escaped. On Sunday the 13th we had FBI Director William Webster on *Face*. He said that the Italians had had him in custody, then let him go.

WEBSTER: He's a moving horse . . . operating under an Iraqi diplomatic passport.
STAHL: Do we know precisely where he is right now?
WEBSTER: I think there're reasons to believe he's in the PLO Embassy in Belgrade.

Muhammed Abul Abbas was convicted for the Klinghoffer murder in absentia. He was never captured.[14]

242 CBS WAS A COMPANY on edge. The network had ranked number one for six straight years, but now NBC was running past us with hit sitcoms such

as *The Cosby Show, Cheers,* and *The Golden Girls.* We were getting stodgy.

With more layoffs, morale was lower than ever in the News Division. Amid the turmoil, Don Hewitt, a man of perpetual motion and hydraulic insistence, hatched one of his more daring ideas: he would buy CBS News. His purpose: to free us of the dreaded Sauter and Joyce. He put together an inside consortium of big-name "yesterday's people" (Dan Rather, Diane Sawyer, Mike Wallace, Morley Safer, and Bill Moyers) and in mid-October decided it was time to see Gene Jankowski, Tom Wyman's number two at Black Rock. The plan was to make a formal offer to purchase the News Division. Don asked Dan Rather if he'd come along to the meeting.

Rather begged off, explaining that he was having lunch with me. "Take her another time," said Hewitt. But Dan insisted on keeping our long-standing date. I met him at a French restaurant in the Parker Meridien Hotel. We were discussing the Reagan White House when Hewitt appeared, squeezed in next to me on the banquette, and without preamble started to describe the scheme I knew nothing about. He said he'd asked Lew Wasserman of MCA/Universal for advice. "Lew said, 'You're crazy, Don, they'll never sell you CBS News. You'll make a fool of yourself.' Lew paused, then added, 'If they say yes, call me.'" We laughed.

Hewitt had tried to find Jankowski, who was out of town. He had eventually reached him by phone. "Look, you're selling CBS anyway," Don told him. "Why not break CBS News off and sell it to us?" He said that at first Jankowski had thought he was joking. When he'd realized it was a serious offer, Don said, "The first words out of his mouth were 'You're out of your mind. No one is going to sell it to you.' He turned us down flat." Don said that since that plan had failed, they would have to think of another way to get rid of Sauter and Joyce: "They're ruining CBS."

Within a few weeks half of Hewitt's hopes were realized. Ed Joyce was out, sent up to some nondescript job at Black Rock. But far from out, Van Sauter was back, reinstated as president of CBS News.

Meanwhile, CBS was in financial trouble. Its net income for 1985 had plunged in one year from $212.4 million to $27.4 million.[15] Loew's had been buying up CBS stock. The question was: Was its chairman, Larry Tisch, trying to save CBS from outside raiders, or was he another Ted Turner, a raider himself? Tisch claimed that he had no intention of seeking control of the network, but he was refusing to sign anything that would prevent him from buying more stock — which he subsequently did, acquiring 12 percent of CBS stock by the end of the year. At that point Wyman invited him to join the CBS board. Once there, according to

Ken Auletta's *Three Blind Mice,* Tisch complained about the heft of the correspondents' contracts in the News Division.

ON THE EVE of Reagan's first summit with the Soviets, he had them running scared. On *Face,* *Time*'s bureau chief, Strobe Talbott, praised Reagan's brilliant use of "a nonexistent defense program," Star Wars, to frighten the Soviets into making arms control concessions. Fear of SDI, it was said, had propelled Gorbachev to propose cutting the two countries' stocks of nuclear weapons by 50 percent.

Here's one way to look at the history of arms control: During the Johnson administration the United States learned to MIRV, that is, to put multiple independently targetable warheads on a single missile. In response the Soviets entered serious arms talks (SALT I), urging us not to develop MIRVs. We rejected that and began MIRVing our missiles. Within a couple of years the Soviets also began MIRVing their missiles. Then the United States developed the cruise missile, a radar-equipped unmanned flying bomb that guides itself to a target. Once again, the Soviets entered arms talks (SALT II) to urge us not to build the cruise, and again we refused. So within a few years they had their own cruise missiles.

And now there was Star Wars. It was hard to read Reagan, as usual. Did he want the "defensive" SDI because, as he said, it would free the world of nuclear weapons? Did he want it because he thought it would ensure U.S. military superiority over the Soviets? Did he want it to beggar the Soviet Union? Did he want SDI as a bargaining chip? Or did he want Star Wars, as Aaron kept saying, because the movie had been a big hit?

The president had spent his public career distrusting the Soviets and fighting against arms control treaties. Now he was asking for a summit. It was like a movie. A mystery. Would he sign an arms control treaty with the Evil Empire? Reagan was inscrutable, the mark indeed of a skilled negotiator.

The president went into intensive training for the summit. Videos of Gorbachev were prepared — the best way to "educate" Reagan. On November 17, the Sunday before the summit began, I was in Geneva with Don Regan as my guest on *Face.* What I didn't know was that the broadcast went out without pictures. All the viewers saw was a sign, apologizing. Yet we had one of our highest ratings. People at CBS were scratching their heads; close to three million people were in effect *watching* radio.

The glitch was at first explained to me as an equipment failure at a ground station in Medley, England. I later learned that the foul-up had actually been caused by CBS's newly mandated cost cutting. We had not

244

been allowed to buy a backup satellite, always considered a necessity. That saved us all of $9,000.

A news blackout was imposed on the first day of the Geneva summit when the two leaders held a private meeting with only their interpreters. We would later learn that Reagan told Gorbachev that the world would have to come together to ward off an invasion from outer space, an idea he apparently got from the 1951 film *The Day the Earth Stood Still.*

With little news about the main event, the press concentrated on the first ladies, who were not getting along. First ladies always got along — or at least said they did. So this was news. The buildup to their get-together didn't help. European newspapers ran "Style Wars" headlines, with Raisa Gorbachev, 53, described as the first fashion-conscious Soviet first lady; Nancy, 62, was just overstyled. It was noted that she had traveled with her West Coast hairdresser, Mr. Julius of Los Angeles, who managed to go public with a bitchy take on Mrs. Gorbachev's hair: "It looks like it has a freeway or a grand canal coming down the middle of it." [16]

Mrs. Reagan hosted their first meeting, an afternoon tea, after which she let it leak that there was no love lost between them. With her doctorate in sociology, Raisa had lectured Nancy on the glories of Marxism-Leninism. How delicious, we thought, to cover a global Cold War catfight.

For me day two of the summit started with an early-morning pool assignment at the Soviet Mission compound. When Gorbachev arrived, I shouted the one sentence I remembered from my year of Russian in high school: "*Dobroye utro, uchitelnitsa,*" which translates "Good morning, lady teacher." Gorbachev stopped and smiled at me. Oh boy, I thought, it worked. But when I then asked (in English) about U.S.-Soviet relations, he walked off.

My pool went inside for a photo op of the first formal session. The two leaders sat opposite each other with six aides each around an oval table. Reagan looked pasty — he often did in the morning — and shuffled his papers. "Can you give us any hint about atmosphere, mood, anything, Mr. President?" I asked.

"No reporting until the meeting is over," he said.

I continued asking questions, and Gorbachev answered (through a translator), "We have a very wide-range discussion of everything in a frank, businesslike, and I think responsible way."

"No table pounding?" I asked.

Gorbachev smiled widely for the cameras. "This is not going to happen today or tomorrow or in the future." This was a man who knew how to play on the world stage and flatter a reporter as well. As the pool was asked to leave, he quipped that I should be awarded a medal for "most curiosity." "Perhaps," he said, "the medal should be financed by both sides."

At the end of the summit I reported that while the two leaders had clearly established a good chemistry, "there was no progress on arms control, human rights, or regional issues." But, said the president, "We cleared the air."

Meanwhile, Don Regan was in hot water again. Before the trip, he'd remarked that women would be more interested in Nancy and Raisa than in the summit. He explained that women were "not going to understand throw weights or what is happening in Afghanistan or what is happening in human rights." Naturally, women's groups protested, and Mrs. Reagan (a budding feminist?) made her displeasure known. When he was our guest again on *Face* on November 24, I asked about his comments.

> REGAN: I don't think most women are interested in the nitty-gritty of what is happening in the Geneva armament talks, but—
> STAHL: Are most men?
> REGAN: No. Most people, let's put it that way.
> STAHL: Well then, why did you separate—
> REGAN: That was—I misspoke, very frankly, and when I misspoke apparently it was a beaut.
> STAHL: That's an apology?
> REGAN: That's an apology to those who feel offended. My own wife wasn't offended, by the way.
> STAHL: A lot of women told me to "go get" you today.
> REGAN: Well, I'll tell you this: that was not my intent to have at them.

FROM WHERE I SAT, women were making dramatic progress. There had been a number of promotions under Sauter and Joyce. CBS's bureau chief in war-torn Beirut was Lucy Spiegel; the bureau chief in Paris was Jennifer Siebens; in Dallas there was Kathy Moore and in Atlanta, Sharon Houston. In Washington, the assignment editor was Susan Morrison. In New York Joan Richmond was vice president and director of special events. Twenty-four percent of CBS's on-air reporters were women.

My colleagues at ABC, however, were complaining that promises made about promoting women there were not being kept. This tweaked the interest of Phil Donahue, who invited a group of newswomen from each network onto his show to debate the issue. Phil didn't dance around; his opening question was "Well, are you ornaments?"

Connie Chung, then at NBC, replied, "I have a serious problem with the fact that we have to sit here and all become Mrs. Whiner. I mean, we're all complaining. I get so tired of hearing it, you know. I get tired of my own self." The audience applauded.

"I'm sorry, Connie," said Carole Simpson, one of the ABC women who had complained, "I really can't let you say that. I don't consider myself a whiner because I go to my employers."

"No?" Connie was unusually combative. "It sounds like it."

"I'm going to get fired by some man for saying this," I interrupted, "but the best producers at CBS News are women." The audience applauded again. This was not the smartest thing I've ever said. For days after the show, I got grief from the male producers at CBS.

When Phil asked, "Can you get anywhere if you're plain?" the audience sang out in a chorus, "No!"

"All the women in television news are not beauty queens," I said. "And I'll tell you a secret, we're all wearing ten pounds of makeup and we're all slaves to our hair."

We were seated around a table, each of us with a lavalier mike pinned to our blouse, with Phil at the head like a father at dinner. He wanted to know if we thought we would last. "Like, do you see yourselves with careers like Walter Cronkite, Eric Sevareid, when you are 60 or 65?"

"When I started," I said, "the line was: women will not last past 30. Then it was: women will not last past 40. Now it's 50. Phil, we'll outlive them all."

"But there are some women over 50 who are having a very tough time in this business," said Rita Flynn of ABC.

"And so are men over 50," added Mary Alice Williams of CNN.

Hear, hear! What was happening to women in television was also happening to the men. Men were actually facing more age discrimination because of their sheer numbers. As for the lovely-to-look-at meter, it would be hard to convince me that it isn't just as important today for a man to be a looker in TV news as a woman, Peter Jennings being just one example. Look at them. They're all gorgeous: Rather, Brokaw, Stone Phillips, Brian Williams, Mike Wallace.

JIM BROOKS, the Hollywood writer and director, was following Susan Zirinsky around. He was writing a movie about broadcast news with a female White House producer as his central character. We were in Santa Barbara again, and Jim was with us, sitting quietly at a table in the corner of our edit room, taking notes in a small, black notebook and mumbling into a tape recorder. Every time Zee called someone "pookie," he'd scribble; when the editor spoke about "feeds," he'd scribble. I would tell Zee, "I need three minutes to futz with my hair." She would shoot back, "Helmet to go!" and he'd scribble. At first it was disconcerting, but soon he was just another member of our little family, so we unself-consciously carried on our usual banter.

One day Brooks asked me to lunch. We went to one of those places with an open brick oven in the middle of the restaurant and ordered blackened swordfish with eggplant (I never did like all that healthy California cooking). "I wanted to talk to you purely and simply as a friend," he began. This did not sound promising. "I want to warn you."

Jim explained that *West 57th* was the future of television news and that I, sticking to the old-fashioned way of reporting, was going to be left behind. He mentioned one particular report on *West 57th* about a hospital emergency room in which the reporter, John Ferrugia, had thrust himself into the action, becoming an integral part of the story.

"Jim, that is precisely what I was taught journalists are *not* supposed to do: change the story, get involved. We're supposed to be impartial observers, merely recorders of events."

"That's oldthink," he said. "Look, I'm not criticizing you, but I think you should know that your bosses consider your stiff, look-into-the-camera style as 'yesterday,' and I'd hate to see you left in the dust."

My throat closed up. I couldn't eat; I could barely talk. Under Rather and Sauter, there was an A-list of reporters, and then the everybody-else list. The A team got on the *Evening News* regularly, the others hardly at all, which caused friction among the troops. But up to this minute I had assumed I was in the A basket, still a "comer" in spite of the tinkering with my copy. Jim was warning me that I was on the verge of being a has-been. I couldn't get to my hotel room fast enough.

I thought about little else for weeks. I couldn't see a way to become a bona fide "today" person from the White House. Not that I wanted to beam my way up to a *West 57th* type — I really didn't like that show. But I thought if I could cover something other than Geneva summits and the gross national product, I could loosen up. Show some humanity. And besides, I wasn't enjoying Reagan II.

After fretting and hashing it out with Aaron, I called Sauter: "Van, I've hit the wall at the White House. It's been seven years, and while I thought I'd never get bored, my time has come. You have to get me out of here."

With all the arguing over my scripts and with Jim Brooks's signal, I was sure Van would simply say, "Okay, kiddo." But he didn't. He asked if I was absolutely sure. "Has something happened recently? Was there an incident?" I assured him I was just burned out.

"Here's what I want you to do," he said. "Think on it. Sleep on it. I want you to reconsider. Take a few months. Then if you still feel the same, we'll talk."

"Months?" I asked, astonished.

"Months."

248   On December 12, 1985, the plane transporting troops home from duty in the Middle East crashed in Gander, Newfoundland. All aboard were

killed. Five days later a memorial service was held in a hangar at Fort Campbell in Kentucky.

I was up on a scaffolding in the back, straining to hear as the com- mander in chief spoke to the families of the 248 soldiers who had died only an hour or so before they were due home for Christmas.

> REAGAN: I know there are no words that can make your pain less or make your sorrow less painful. . . . As a poet said of other young soldiers in another war, "They will never grow old. They will always be young."

Everyone was teary-eyed, even the cynics up on the press platform. And then something extraordinary happened. The president and Mrs. Reagan stepped down from the dais and walked among the mourners, stopping to touch, to embrace, to say something comforting.

> STAHL: The president and Mrs. Reagan spent about an hour talking with each and every family member here, an estimated 350.

There was Mrs. Reagan with her caring eyes, which Garry Wills called "indefatigably understanding." [17] She held sobbing wives, touched a picture of a son. The president hugged a black man. In her book *What I Saw at the Revolution*, Peggy Noonan said that the grieving in the hangar "released the nation from a style of mourning that had dominated since the '60s — the stoicism mania, begun by the Kennedys as they buried their husbands and fathers, blank-faced, dry-eyed and dignified. It set a style the middle class adopted." The Reagans did just what presidents and first ladies should do: they gave us the cathartic release we needed; they gave us permission to cry at our funerals again and bare our grief.

ON JANUARY 19 I had the first televised interview in the United States with Corazón Aquino, 52, who was running against the dictator, Ferdinand Marcos, for the presidency of the Philippines. She had been a housewife until her husband, Benigno, a longtime opponent of Marcos, was assassinated in 1983. [18]

> MRS. AQUINO: I wish to categorically state that I am not a Communist, and I have not been a Communist, and I will never be a Communist.

The charge that she was "deep red" was at the heart of the Marcos campaign. So was "Cory's" gender.

> STAHL: Mr. Marcos says the Philippines is not ready for a woman president.
> AQUINO: If Mr. Marcos had seen my rallies, he would know how enthu-

siastic all of them are, and sex is no longer the issue here. It is a matter of credibility.

JANUARY 28, 1986. On the day of Reagan's State of the Union Address, the anchormen were invited to a series of briefings at the White House, which were to culminate with a Q-and-A session over lunch with the president. Peter Jennings, Tom Brokaw, and CNN's Bernie Shaw were there, but for some reason Dan couldn't make it, so I went in his place.

We were sitting around the large oblong table in the Roosevelt Room, waiting for the president. Don Regan sat at one end, Pat Buchanan at the other, and Teddy Roosevelt looked down over my shoulder. As Vice Admiral John Poindexter, the new national security adviser, began his presentation, an aide brought in a note for Regan. He read it, looked up, and interrupted: "I'm very sorry to have to tell you, the space shuttle *Challenger* has blown up."

Peter, Tom, and Bernie dashed off, sending in reporters from their White House teams. Regan had a big-screen TV wheeled in so we could watch the excruciating reruns of the deadly tufts of smoke divide into two separate arcs in the sky. We watched over and over as we waited to see if the president was going to go ahead with his speech.

At one o'clock Reagan poked his head in: "Well, I'm sure we all realize there's a little change in the procedure." He stood in the doorway. Ever gracious, he'd come to apologize for not joining us as scheduled. "I'd looked forward to coming in here and having a little session with you and some briefing, but in view of the tragedy that has befallen us, I don't think we'll do that."

He hesitated, which gave us an opening. "Mr. President," I asked, "can you give us your comments on the tragedy so that we can tell the American people your thoughts?"

"Well, what can you say?" He moved into the room. Without his cue cards, he spoke movingly. "It's a horrible thing that all of us have witnessed and actually seen it take place. And I just can't rid myself of the thought of the sacrifice and the families that have been watching this also." It was Reagan who had pushed the idea of having citizens aboard the space shuttle. Christa McAuliffe, a teacher, had been aboard with the six astronauts. One of my colleagues asked the president if he was having second thoughts.

"Well, they're all citizens," he said sadly. "And I don't think anyone's ever been on there that isn't a volunteer. I know I've heard many times— reasons why they or someone like them should not be included in flights of this kind. So, no, that is the last frontier and the most important frontier."

250

He said he was determined to go ahead with his speech that night.

"You can't stop governing the nation because of a tragedy of this kind." I was seeing a fiber I had not expected. Reagan was even more certain when asked if he feared a public backlash against the space program. "I shouldn't think so. You know, we have accidents in every line of transportation, and we don't do away with those things. They've probably got a better safety record than we have out on the highways."

Finally, Reagan was asked to say something to the children. Because of the first teacher in space, classrooms all across the country were watching the liftoff on television. "We've always known that there are pioneers that give their lives out there on the frontier," he said. "And now this has happened. It probably is more of a shock to all of us because of the fact that we see it happen now and, thanks to the media, not just hearing about it as if something that happened miles away. . . . Life does go on, and you don't back up and quit some worthwhile endeavor because of tragedy."

As I took notes, racing to keep up with him, I thought of how many times Reagan had faced challenges as president and had come through. We made fun of him and I myself thought he was slipping mentally, but not that day. That day, that time, he was magnificent.

I ran to the lawn. CBS and Dan Rather had been on the air with a special report, and I repeated as much as I could of what the president had told us.

By *Evening News* time, Reagan had changed his mind about delivering his State of the Union speech, which was supposed to be upbeat. Instead, he once again led the nation in communal mourning. Just two weeks after the crash in Newfoundland, he was on television again, binding us together in sadness and shock. To the families he said, "Your loved ones were daring and brave, and they had that special grace, that special spirit, that says, 'Give me a challenge and I'll meet it with joy.'" A president who doesn't understand the power of words simply can't lead.

A week later Reagan turned 75. "Seventy-five," he said, "is only 24 Celsius!"

PERFECT opened, and I gave Aaron a screening party. The stars, John Travolta, Jamie Lee Curtis, and Marilu Henner, came, as did Dolly and Lou and half the White House. It was a great celebration at a health club in the suburbs. I danced with John. Bethesda Fever.

Columbia Pictures spent that first weekend doing exit polls, which, according to the experts, showed that Travolta, the man who had personified the 1970s, was marooned in the 1980s. Based on the surveys, the studio decided to kill its expensive promotion campaign. The TV spots were pulled, newspaper ads scrubbed. When the movie was not the big hit everyone had expected, Aaron slumped into a depression.

251

Columbia was one of the first studios to use exit polling at movies. The studio was owned by Coca-Cola, which relied heavily on focus groups for its product development. In fact, Coca-Cola had just come out with its sweeter "New Coke," which, polling had shown, young people would like more than the old "classic," real thing Coke. So much for polling. New Coke was a fizzle, but so was *Perfect*, and that fizzled enthusiasm for what Aaron had thought would be his next movie, based on another magazine article about after-hours speakeasies.

My husband turned into a man with dark days and nights. He would pull himself together for Taylor, but otherwise he receded into a state of semireclusiveness. I went out alone, or, if I managed to drag him to a party, he often walked out, stranding me. I knew how sad he was, and I often blamed myself. Had I caused this? Was my success making his life worse? But he didn't want to talk about his problems, and I didn't want to add to them by insisting.

ED MEESE had a peculiar way of interpreting constitutional rights. "You don't have many suspects who are innocent of a crime. That's contradictory," he told *U.S. News & World Report* in an interview on October 14, 1985. "If a person is innocent of a crime, then he is not a suspect." [19] This from the new attorney general, the country's chief law enforcement officer.

When Meese gave his first televised interview as attorney general to *Face the Nation* on March 24, 1985, we were thrilled. One of my first questions was about his campaign to challenge affirmative action: "You're writing letters to communities urging them to go into court, isn't that true?"

"No," he replied. Then he conceded, "Only those cases where the Justice Department is party to those decrees." Which was the same as saying yes. Only he'd said no. Certain politicians deal with reporters by challenging the premise of every question, hoping to avoid answering directly. The champion premise challenger was Ed Meese, who kept insisting, despite the evidence, that he wasn't trying to get rid of affirmative action programs.

"How do you make up, then, for past discrimination?" I asked.

"You go out and have training programs. You have an outreach program."

"But you cut the funds for training programs."

"No, not at all. Not at all."

"Yes, the Reagan administration —"

"No," he interrupted.

"— is cutting back on training programs." It was.

Although I found his evasiveness infuriating, he was the attorney general, so we asked for a return appearance ten months later, on February 9, 1986. This would be the single most frustrating and enraging live interview of my eight years as host of *Face the Nation*.

Before the show I had been leaked an internal administration study of affirmative action in the workplace, which contradicted Meese's contention that it was forcing companies out of business because they were required to hire a specific number of minorities under a quota system. I asked about his plan to water down the program.

> STAHL: Why don't you . . . admit that most people in the country don't want this to change?
> MEESE: Well, first of all, Ms. Stahl, you're absolutely wrong. I don't want to weaken the affirmative action rules.

I thought of *Blume in Love*, a movie in which George Segal's wife (Susan Anspach) catches him in their bedroom with another woman. As the wife screeches in outrage, the other woman gets dressed and leaves, and Segal tells the wife she's crazy, that she didn't see what she saw. Ed Meese was George Segal: "No one in this administration wants to weaken the affirmative action rules." Exasperated, I held up the study I had been leaked.

> STAHL: This is a government study, a Reagan administration study, that says that these affirmative action rules are not being used as quotas. . . .
> MEESE: . . . Every time I meet with business organizations, they come in to see me and say: spare us from what is happening when these government inspectors have imposed on them what amount to quotas.
> STAHL: But you have a government study that says it's not being done.
> MEESE: This is the study done by the same people that have been imposing the quotas over the years.
> STAHL: The Labor Department? The *Reagan* Labor Department? They did a study with figures and statistics. [I held it up]
> MEESE: No, no.
> STAHL: Yes, they did!

I didn't know how to deal with this. Meese denied the validity of the Labor Department study, denied the stiff opposition he faced in Congress and the administration. My frustration showed on the air. Karen told me later that Mrs. Meese, in the greenroom, had been in such a rage at me that she'd had to be restrained from storming the studio. I never requested an interview with him again.

CORAZÓN "CORY" AQUINO beat Ferdinand Marcos in the Philippine election on February 7, yet Marcos, still in control, declared himself the winner. Aquino responded by announcing a program of nonviolent resistance to bring him down. I spent much of February covering President Reagan's refusal to criticize Marcos's abrogation of the election. "Administration sources," I reported, "say the president doesn't want to abandon Marcos the way Jimmy Carter abandoned the shah of Iran."

When I interviewed Marcos in mid-February on *Face*, he first denied that his party had engaged in voting fraud or violence in the campaign. I pressed him.

MARCOS: Now, hold on. I may admit to some. As usual, the two parties engaged in fraud and violence. To what extent? We say they are guilty of the more massive fraud and violence.
STAHL: Would you consider giving Mrs. Aquino a Cabinet post?
MARCOS: She wouldn't know how to run it.

Talking to him over a satellite as I had with Aquino a month earlier, I asked if there were any circumstance that would cause him to step down. He gave me a you're-such-a-dumb-blond look and dismissed the question. "That's ridiculous. That's foolish. Why should I step down?"

Over the next week, crowds of Filipinos, tens of thousands, moved into the streets in a peaceful "citizens' revolt" to protest against Marcos. Reagan was confronted with a chorus of calls to change course: to abandon his pals Ferdinand and Imelda. For some reason Reagan admired Marcos, whom he and Nancy had visited in 1969.[20] Over the years Imelda had sent Nancy evening gowns: three in 1981, four in 1982, two more in 1985 — most of them beaded, sequined, or rhinestoned. As far as I could tell, Mrs. Reagan never wore them.[21]

Under severe pressure from Congress, from commentators, and from powerful voices within his administration, Reagan finally succumbed on February 24, calling on Marcos to step aside, offering him "a Baby Doc exit" from the Philippines where he could go into exile with a lot of his loot.

But it was not until Mrs. Aquino was being sworn in as president that Ferdinand and Imelda hopped onto a U.S. government plane and fled to Hawaii with all the money they could carry, which turned out to be a bundle — "valued by customs officials at well beyond $30 million," I reported, "including suitcase after suitcase filled with jewelry . . . and 22 crates of Philippine pesos worth $1.1 million."

Left behind at their palace in Manila were 3,000 pairs of Imelda's shoes with hundreds of matching handbags, and 500 black bras.

254 THE YEAR 1986 was the centennial anniversary of the Statue of Liberty, and there was a big Fourth of July celebration in New York. It was a good

time for the president—and the country. The economic recovery was spawning a roaring stock market; we had single-digit mortgage rates and low inflation, just 3 to 4 percent, thanks in large part to Paul Volcker at the Fed and the luck of collapsing oil prices. Reaganites said that the improving economy was due to Reaganomics; others said it was classic Keynesian deficit spending—if you borrowed the way the U.S. government borrowed in those days, you would be booming too. Much of the borrowing was needed to finance the military buildup.[22]

But the country was enjoying a refreshed spirit of pride and patriotism, and Reagan deserved full credit for that. Once again, a president's personality. On the Fourth of July Reagan transmitted his infectious optimism when he joined the parade of tall ships in New York Harbor, acting as if he were going steady with the Statue of Liberty. The president was up on the gun turret of the battleship U.S.S. *John F. Kennedy,* and I was right beneath him. I was Zelig. I remember thinking that in our special report some red, white, and blue enthusiasm on my part wouldn't be inappropriate, though I may have gotten a touch treacly about it.

> STAHL: I feel compelled to say something on behalf of those of us whose grandparents came here at the turn of the century. My grandfather, who didn't know his own birthday, chose the Fourth of July. It's quite emotional, sailing past the Statue of Liberty today and seeing that torch lighted.
> DAN: Lesley, you mentioned your grandparents. They came from what country?
> STAHL: They came from Poland. My grandfather loved this country with an emotion that people who are born here don't understand. They really appreciated liberty and freedom. He talked to us about that all the time.
> DAN: We could all do worse than to do so.

THE MOOD of the Fourth was broken by one of Reagan's most resounding defeats in the Congress. It was over South Africa, where Archbishop Desmond Tutu was calling for broad economic sanctions to protest apartheid, and this time even conservative Republicans such as Newt Gingrich opposed Reagan's policy. Bob Dole came on *Face* to suggest that the policy of constructive engagement had to go.

Obstinately, Reagan called the drive for sanctions "an emotional clamor" in a televised speech on July 22—a speech that bombed—and he called for *more* business ties to South Africa. As I said in a report, "Even Secretary of State Shultz favored compromise on the sanctions, but conservatives at the White House like Patrick Buchanan won out." Reagan was denounced as "the president of apartheid"; *Newsweek* called this his "worst setback in foreign policy." The bill to establish stiff sanctions passed Congress. When Reagan vetoed it, Republican Richard Lugar led the fight to override his veto, which passed in both the House and Senate.[23]

CBS TOOK ANOTHER body blow. With our audience siphoning off to CNN and HBO, profits were sinking. A new round of cutbacks was ordered, and this time 90 newspeople were laid off on July 17 — "Doomsday." George Herman — among other fine reporters — was forced out. The downsizings changed our sense of who we were, and the troops raged at "the collaborator," Van Sauter.

Television critics, meanwhile, were writing that the Murrow aura was evaporating under the softening and "terminal trivializing" of the *Evening News*. Rather took the criticism to heart and decided he wanted to toughen the news again. Overriding Van Sauter, he replaced his executive producer, Lane Venardos, with Tom Bettag, a yesterday type and one of my favorite producers.[24]

This did not dissuade me from wanting to leave the White House, though. My months of reconsidering a move were up, and I began negotiating with Sauter for a new assignment. He offered me the weekend anchor job I had wanted. Everyone thought I would take it, but I decided I couldn't walk away from *Face*. Finally Sauter, Tom Bettag, and I agreed that I would be the national affairs correspondent, a roving reporter for the *Evening News*. I looked forward to taking a few days to research a subject, sleeping on a script overnight, mulling, pondering, weighing. I had become a quick-sketch artist. Now I would try to be a painter.

"I would like to acknowledge the end of an era." On July 31, Larry Speakes, in the briefing room, announced my imminent departure from the White House. "Lesley works the telephones probably better than anybody I've ever seen," he said. "She's tough but fair."

Sam started wisecracking. "I like this," I said. "You be quiet." [laughter]

And then it was my last day. As was the custom for a departing correspondent, I was to get a farewell audience with the president. Aaron and Taylor were invited to join me.

We were expecting a little good-bye present from the president in the way of a story. A hole was reserved for me in the *Evening News* lineup. But on the way to the Oval Office, Larry took my arm and guided me to a corner in the hallway: "Look, no questions. No questions at all, about anything. Those are the ground rules. And I swear, if you even try, I'll shoot you on the spot. And you'll be out of there faster than you can think."

"Larry, this is outrageous. Everyone gets a going-away story. You wouldn't dare tell *The New York Times* reporter he couldn't ask a question."

"You're not goin' in there," Larry said, "till you give me your word."

If Aaron and Taylor had not been there, I would have told him to go shove it. "Okay, okay," I said, making sure to leave the impression that this was a disgraceful injustice.

With Larry leading the way, Aaron, Taylor, and I entered the Oval Office. Standing in front of a Remington sculpture of a rearing horse, the president looked stiff and waxy. My anger subsided. I had a story.

Reagan was as shriveled as a kumquat. He was so frail, his skin so paper-thin, I could almost see the sunlight through the back of his withered neck. His bony hands were dotted with age spots, one bleeding into another. His eyes were coated. Larry introduced us, but he had to shout. Had Reagan turned off his hearing aid?

"Mr. President!" he bellowed. "This is Lesley Stahl." He said it slowly. "Of CBS, and her husband, Aaron Latham."

Reagan didn't seem to know who I was. He gave me a distant look with those milky eyes and shook my hand weakly. Oh, my, he's gonzo, I thought. I have to go out on the lawn tonight and tell my countrymen that the president of the United States is a doddering space cadet. My heart began to hammer with the import. As the White House photographer snapped pictures of us — because this was a photo op — I was aware of the delicacy with which I would have to write my script. But I was quite sure of my diagnosis.

Larry was shouting again, instructing the president to hand us some souvenirs. Cuff links, a White House tie tack. I felt the necessity to fill the silence. "This is my daughter, Mr. President," I said. "Taylor. She's eight." He barely responded but for a little head tilt.

Click. Click. More pictures. A flash. "When I covered Jimmy Carter," I said, "Taylor used to tell everyone that the president worked for her mommy. But from the day you moved in here, she began saying, 'My mommy works for the president.' " I wasn't above a little massaging. Was he so out of it that he couldn't appreciate a sweet story that reflected well on him? Guess so. His pupils didn't even dilate. Nothing. No reaction.

"You know, sir, I've covered the White House more years than you've been here. After I'm out a few weeks, I'll write you and tell you if there's life after this place." Again, only a modest acknowledgment that I was there.

This was painful. How had he deteriorated so quickly? I had seen him just the week before. There were more mementos. More photos. And then Larry was shouting, "Sir, Lesley's husband, Aaron, writes for Hollywood. He's a screenwriter out there. Wrote a couple pictures for John Travolta."

As Reagan turned his head to find Aaron, the glaze in his eyes
cleared, the freckles on his hands faded, the skin on the back of his neck
tightened, and color came to his cheeks. Clark Kent. "Aaron, who did
you work with?" he asked, jaunty and alive.

He pulled Aaron away from me and walked him over to the yellow
couches to discuss a movie idea he had in which he would star, not as
himself, not as the president.

I was left over by the Remington, clearly cut out of this and too
astonished to move. "Sir, it's time for them to leave," said Larry. We'd
been budgeted for ten minutes. But the president brushed him off. He
wanted to talk Hollywood. Five minutes later Larry became insistent. As
the president shook my hand to say good-bye, he said, "Lesley, you don't
have to write me. I was governor of California for eight years, so I already
know what it'll be like when I leave here." He was beaming, as engaged
as he'd been disengaged ten minutes before. "The first night Nancy and I
were back in our own home," he said grinning, "we were invited to a big,
fancy party. Well, we got all dressed up, went out, got in the backseat of
our car, and waited!" We all roared. I could see that Aaron, who had been
railing for years at this man and his policies, was a puddle. Reagan had
cast a spell. My husband was enchanted.

Somehow Larry managed to ease us out of the Oval Office, but
Reagan called out, "Taylor, Taylor!" He was heading toward us down the
hallway. When he caught up he said, "Taylor, I can't let you leave without
telling you the truth." She was looking up at a tall, robust figure. "Taylor,
I worked for your mother too."

As a transition from the White House beat to my new job as national
affairs correspondent, I decided to try to cleanse my pores of all the
poisons and resentments that had built up over the last couple of years.
In August 1986 Aaron, Taylor, and I went on safari in Kenya.

I bought a fancy camera with zoom and telescopic lenses. My friend
Herb Allen said, "Go out and buy ten times more film than you imagine
you'd ever shoot, and double that." Then Aaron and I went to Banana
Republic and bought everything they had in khaki. "Looking good," Herb
had said, "is part of the fun."

So off we went to the bush, in the care of Ker and Downey, the safari
company made famous by the patronage of the British Royal Family. With
my aversion to all things outdoors, I was relieved when I was zipped into
a tent our first night roughing it. The tent had electricity (for my hair
dryer), carpets, fluffy pillows, and a French Provincial commode. The
camp came with a refrigerator, a cook, a laundry man, and someone who
brought us hot water for our outdoor shower. The princess in me rejoiced.

The trip had a taking-the-waters, restorative effect on Aaron and me.

We had been so engrossed in raising Taylor and in our own grievances that we'd lost all but a flimsy connective strand between us. Here, under that big, pretty sky, in that soothing rhythm of life, we began to relax back toward each other. He was looking sexy out there on the savanna in his Finch-Hatton hat and photographer's vest with the 23 pockets. The gloom that had darkened his eyes lifted, and I recognized that laugh I hadn't heard in years.

The escape was not complete, however. Though I had intended to leave Washington and CBS behind, I saw reflections of them every day. There was the male gazelle-anchorman. He had fought his way to the top, but the other males were circling, threatening to invade his territory and take over. He was on constant vigil, sleepless with worry.

The most startling thing we saw was hundreds of gnus crossing the Mara River. Gnus are rumpled, funny-looking mooselike antelopes that follow their "president" up and down cliffs to a suicidal death. At the end of the day, gnu bodies were all over the river, while many others had been caught and eaten by lions who waited for them as they climbed up exhausted out of the water. And all these poor creatures had done was follow their leader blindly.

One day we drove alongside a huge family of elephants on a plodding hike to a mud bath. We were amid a matriarchy: every member of the herd a female, except for the babies. The males are loners who show up for sex — and leave. Imagine that.

The safari was full of surprises like that, and delights. On Taylor's ninth birthday we took a boat ride through a bird sanctuary at Lake Bogoria. Our guide, Derek Dames, clapped loudly, and a wide, pink sheet turned into thousands of flapping flamingos. We went hot-air ballooning, taking a silent journey over the tops of the animals, and met Anna Merz, who was raising Samia, a baby rhinoceros. The single best thing we did was go horseback riding with giraffes and zebras. They bolt if a human is on foot. But if you're in a saddle, they assume you're part of the horse, and they accept you.

But then came the night of terror. As we were pursuing a large pack of wild dogs out on a hunt, the Land Rover got stuck between two boulders, Scylla and Charybdis to us. Derek's attempt at winching produced one uprooted tree, which seemed to provoke the gods into dumping a furious thunderstorm on our path, turning it into a mud lake. By then it was dark. I was given the job of directing the flashlight ("torch" to Derek). I hugged Taylor, begging her not to leave the car, but there was no holding her back. "This is better than anything Tom Sawyer ever did," she said excitedly. She joined Aaron and Derek out in the rain trying to jack up the car, which had sunk into the mud. And all the while the flashlight shook as I listened to the night growls and hoots, monkey screeches and bush rustlings. I was convinced we were all going to die out there with all those hungry animals.

We winched our way through the boulders, but the "path" had been washed away, so that as we inched through the vines, we soon sank again and had to winch again. After several hours I burst into tears: "We're not going to make it."

"Aw, Mom." It is a painful thing when your nine-year-old tosses you a derisive snort. "The worst that'll happen," Derek assured me, "is that we'll sleep here in the car." With that, Derek took a tea break from our third winching, Aaron gave me a patronizing hug, and Taylor teased me for the rest of the trip. But in my soul I knew I had, like one of Iron John's heroes, gone deep into the wilderness, fought off the demons . . . and triumphed. You may laugh, but that night is the one and only time I ever thought I was going to die, the only time I faced, at least in my mind, mortal danger. I was giddy with survival. Derek, on the other hand, nearly fell apart that night. He left us for close to an hour to walk among the flamingos. By safari-guide standards, there is no pride in getting your clients lost on a cold, dark night. It was left to Aaron to read the maps and finally devise an exit strategy. "Let's turn around and retrace our own tracks," he said. And after winching one more time, that's how we finally made it back to camp by 4 A.M.

As I watched my husband heal in Africa and rediscovered his quirky humor and kindness, I wondered just how debilitating the gaseous toxicity of Washington had been. Aaron had never liked it there. If you're not in politics or reporting on it, you can become an alien, with all the discomfort that implies. He had stayed on account of me. That he was thriving in this quiet place added to my guilt. Because when the safari was over, we went back to Washington, the other — in many ways more savage — jungle.

MY FIRST STORY as national affairs correspondent ran on September 2, 1986. The subject was Ronald Reagan's War on Drugs: "There are more drugs, more available than ever before," I began. "The administration has tried to cut the force of customs inspectors, [did] slash the budget for drug education, [and wants] more cuts in the treatment area." It was left as I wrote it, in keeping with the Rather-Bettag regime's emphasis on hard news.

Washington stories were "in" again. We were getting three or four reports on a night, and no one was softening my copy. Sauter's attempts at tabloidizing the *Evening News* hit a stone wall. Rather decided he wanted to return to a more serious broadcast, and he was now, it seemed, more powerful than his boss.

But then strange things began happening. On Monday, September

1, Dan had signed off the broadcast with his usual "Good night" and added, "Courage." Explaining that he liked the word, he ignored his producers' advice and used it two more nights.[25] But then on Thursday he did not say "Courage." Oh, no. He said "*Coraje.*" Spanish. Over at NBC, Bryant Gumbel poked fun at Dan on the *Today* show, trying out his own sign-offs: "Valor," "Hot dogs," "Mazel tov." Under mocking assault, Dan stopped.

This came at a time of great stress for all of us. Large numbers at CBS News were openly rooting for Larry Tisch to take over the company. And why not? Tisch had been publicly declaring his love of "hard news." We paid no attention to the warnings that he was a bottom-line kind of guy with a record of merciless cost cutting. We were too busy being lulled by his signals, as Mike Wallace put it, "that he was on our side." Tisch told *The New York Times,* "Whether the news loses money or makes money is secondary to what we put on the air. I can't picture any point at which profit becomes the main thought in deciding on a news program."[26]

So on September 10, when the CBS board ousted Tom Wyman and named Larry Tisch acting CEO, we newsies celebrated. Someone warned that moving on to Tisch could be like replacing the shah with Khomeini, but we weren't listening. Especially on Tisch's first day at Black Rock, when he fired Van Sauter. The producers at the *Evening News* broke into song: "Ding-dong, the wicked witch is dead." Howard Stringer was named acting president of CBS News.

By the time Tisch came to the Washington Bureau a week later, I was — we were all — his grateful subjects. A dinner was arranged in the back room at Il Giardino on 21st Street. All the reporters came to meet our savior, a short, bald, pinkish man. "Oh," he said, starstruck, "Robert Schackne. I can hardly believe I'm actually meeting you." Correspondent Robert Schackne had been demoted to Rather's B-list. Tisch knew and loved Phil Jones, and Lem Tucker, and me. Message delivered: here was a besotted news junkie.

We sat around a big table, tossing him softball questions about his plans. He told us, "I'm not cutting News," and said he wanted to restore our luster, make us the great hard-news organization we had been. Between the clams marinara and the lathered flattery, we lapped and lapped.

AT THE WHITE HOUSE stories had fallen into my lap; now I not only had to forage for an idea, I had to make sure I wasn't stepping into anyone else's precinct. If I did a story about Congress, I knew I would suffer a week of cold stares from Bob Schieffer, and the same with the other beat reporters. They were all determined to keep me from becoming a bigfoot.

The worst of it, though, was that I was losing my visibility. If, by chance, I ever forgot that I had not been on the air for a week, I would get a comforting call from Dolly: "Where the hell have you been? You're disappearing."

I'm afraid I wasn't suffering my loss of visibility in silence. Everyone, it seems, knew I was unhappy. At the White House I had averaged three stories a week. My second report as national affairs correspondent ran two weeks after the first.

I had *Face*, though, where I was still able to cover the lead stories. We did several broadcasts on the Soviets' arrest of Nicholas Daniloff, a reporter with *U.S. News & World Report*. When President Reagan agreed to swap him for Gennadi Zakharov, a Russian spy, the conservatives howled that the deal was "Carteresque" (the highest form of insult). Reagan denied it was a swap.

One Sunday my guest was Yitzhak Shamir, who was about to become prime minister of Israel. This was his first major American television interview, and his spokesman, Avi Posner, made it clear that they were nervous about it. "His English isn't that good, and he's had very little practice on television," Avi said. He asked if we would tape the interview ahead of time. Sure, we said.

So we went to New York on Saturday and set up at the Regency Hotel (which Larry Tisch owned). Avi, who was fluttering around the suite like the mother of the bride, said, "Make everything ready so he doesn't have to sit there while you adjust the lights."

Everything was in order when Shamir arrived. But when he sank into the wingback chair, a terrible thing happened. He became Eloise, his feet dangling several inches off the floor. How were we to know he was that short? Naturally, we had to change chairs, which meant we had to relight. This was a calamity, made worse by the pacing and fidgeting of Avi Posner.

Apologizing to Shamir for the delay, I explained, "Showbiz!"

Shamir smiled warmly. "Good Shabbas to you too."

Was his English that bad? Now I was the nervous one. But as it turned out, Shamir was blunt and feisty, an interviewer's dream, and perfectly understandable. "Will you build more settlements?" I asked.

"For me the important thing is not the establishment of new settlements. The important thing is the increase of the Israeli population in these areas. . . . We want to have our population in all parts of the land of Israel." It isn't every day you interview a head of state who doesn't mince words.

"But it's occupied territory," I pointed out.

"It's not occupied territories; it's not occupied territories," he insisted.

He was a straight shooter, no flourishes, no evasions. Obviously his television handlers hadn't gotten their hands on him yet. I liked the interview. He did too.

WHILE I WAS UNHAPPY about the pace of my new assignment, there was an up side. The daily panics were gone, and I had more time for Taylor, a fourth-grader now. She was tall with beautiful hair almost long enough for her to sit on, and she was still perpetually sunny. This was a year in school with more and more homework for her — and for us. She read *The Old Man and the Sea* and learned to multiply and divide. She loved her teacher, Pete Peterson, who assigned a major report on something of local interest. "I'm going to do it on Maryland shellfish," she told Aaron and me one morning as we drove her to school.

"Are you kidding?" said Aaron. "Shellfish? That's boring. Why not the Washington Redskins?" Poor Tay. She argued for crabs, but Aaron was insistent, so she caved. But then when it came time to write the thing, he went out of town. That left me. On football. I suggested she become a reporter and interview people about the team. So she called Shirley Povich, *The Washington Post's* renowned sportswriter (he lived in our building) and Jack Kent Cooke, owner of the Redskins. She decorated her report with pennants and pictures of Art Monk and Ricky Sanders making their magical midair catches. It was a triumph, if I do say so. She not only got an A, but she became a devoted and knowledgeable fan.

Someone asked me how we disciplined Taylor. It struck me that we never did. She was never bad enough. Then I remembered that the only time I had ever been punished was when I fought with my brother. Tay had no one to fight with. That year we asked her if she wanted a brother or sister. She was adamant: no.

I WAS IN REYKJAVÍK in mid-October with the rest of the press corps for a Reagan-Gorbachev summit meeting. Nancy Reagan, told there was an agreement that the wives were staying home, did not accompany her husband. So it came as an unpleasant surprise when Raisa Gorbachev showed up and became the center of world attention. I did a piece about her "looking like a candidate for world office: visiting schools, posing with the prime minister." When asked about Mrs. Reagan's absence, Raisa suggested — with her flair for getting in Nancy's craw — "Maybe she is sick." Back in Washington Nancy was asked how she felt. "I feel fine," she said archly.

The next day, Sunday, the superpower meeting dragged on way past its scheduled time. It was not till the extended meeting finally broke up that the press realized it had turned into a disaster, the first sign of which was President Reagan's face. He walked out with Gorbachev, both of them grim and thin-lipped. I was watching on TV in our make-do *Face* studio, amazed at the rawness of emotion. There was George Shultz near tears, conveying a picture of smashed hopes. The deal had been right there, almost done, he said, except that the president would not compromise on SDI. "We are deeply disappointed at this outcome," he said.[27] Star Wars was added to the core of issues over which the usually willowy Reagan would not bend.

As the president drove off in his limousine, Don Regan would tell me later, "he was deeply in despair, but we decided we had to turn this around." Within an hour Reagan was at the U.S. Embassy in Reykjavík, telling jokes and insisting the meeting had been a success: Act I of the remaking of Reykjavík, as only Ronald Reagan could do it.

Back in Washington, the president went on television on October 13 and told the American people he could not bring himself to leave the United States unprotected. He wrote most of the speech himself, discarding the speechwriter's draft. When I saw a copy of his handwritten original, I was again struck by Reagan's lucidity. How to reconcile the apparent sharpness of mind here with the dullness at other times? "We are no longer talking about arms control; we are talking about arms reductions, possibly even the complete elimination of ballistic missiles from the face of the earth."

A week later Don Regan was on *Face*. "Apparently Mr. Reagan inadvertently agreed at some point during these talks to eliminate *all* strategic nuclear weapons on both sides," I said.

"What happened," explained the chief of staff, "was that after we put our final proposal on the table, they said, 'Why ballistic missiles?' That's what Gorbachev said. And he said, 'Why not everything?' And the president said, 'Well, if that's what you want to talk about, all right.' But at that point they launched into a discussion of SDI and the proposals to kill it, so they never went back to that. So it just came up momentarily, wasn't thrashed out. . . ."

"There are those who say: Thank goodness it fell through, because you were going down a path that would have . . . put us at a military disadvantage [in conventional weapons]."

"Just a minute." His eyes flashed. "We won't be at a disadvantage. Just listen to me for a minute. What has happened is, we would have at least ten years and probably longer than that in which to build up our conventional weapons to at least have equality which is what we would want. . . . Reagan is a man of peace, he is a man who wants to see a nuclear-free world."

264   While most of the critics were appalled that Reagan had refused deep arms reductions in order to preserve Star Wars, the military was

appalled that the president had even considered the elimination of *all* intermediate- and short-range nuclear weapons. That would have left the NATO countries at a disadvantage compared with the Warsaw Pact's large conventional force. Apparently John Poindexter was so aghast, he tried to persuade the president he hadn't done that. According to Jane Mayer and Doyle McManus in *Landslide*, Reagan said, " 'But John, I did agree to that.' 'No,' persisted Poindexter, 'you couldn't have.' 'John,' said the president, 'I was there, and I did.' "

Then, a few months later, Gorbachev came back to offer many of the same reductions without the SDI quid pro quo. What had looked like disaster was actually a turning point in U.S.-Soviet relations. Reagan had struck a rapport with Gorbachev that eventually led to the end of the Cold War, proving once again how central personal chemistry is to history.[28]

TISCH SHOWED his frugal colors early on by shutting down the executive dining rooms at Black Rock and banning company-paid birthday parties. Next to go was the medical department. Then CBS's contribution to the United Way. Before long Tisch was doing what everyone had feared from Ted Turner: he began disassembling the company. He said he wouldn't sell the publishing group; then he did. It was the same with the records division, as much a part of CBS's identity as radio and television. He stripped us down to bare bones, just as the other networks were expanding. So many people were let go that being fired came to be called "being Tisched." At News, however, we still felt protected, screened off.

By November, after exposing Tisch to his charm and humor, Howard Stringer was named president of News, and almost immediately he took the Tisches on a tour of the CBS News bureaus. In London, the entire staff of 65 showed up to meet the new boss. It was a strategic blunder.

Tisch should have walked into a bustling newsroom where a lean crew was operating full tilt, too busy to schmooze up the boss. Instead, no one was working and they were all complaining, "None of us ever get on the air." He must have thought he was in the middle of a Cecil B. DeMille extravaganza: You mean we pay all these extras full time? Similar scenes occurred in Paris and Rome.

When the boss got back to New York, he looked at News' $300 million budget, which had more than tripled in eight years, and called for a chopping block.

AS WE REPORTED the results on election night, we became aware of a stranger lurking on the set. He turned out to be the man from Coopers &

Lybrand, an accounting firm that Tisch had hired to do a top-to-bottom analysis of the entire company — including News.

The Republicans had had little to run on in the 1986 campaign. Reagan had already cut taxes (and was stealthily raising them); he had already reformed the tax code,[29] rearmed the country, and defeated communism. There was little left to his agenda.

I was back in the circle with Dan, Bob Schieffer, Bruce Morton, and Mike Wallace. At one point Rather asked me how women were doing in the governors' races. Not well. Not well at all. "Of the nine running," I said, "only one has won so far: Kay Orr of Nebraska, and her opponent was a woman. The women candidates were all experienced, Dan. They were all competent, they were all politicians who came up through the ranks. We expected we'd have a better showing." Oops! Did I say "we"?

"We can almost guarantee," I said, "that what President Reagan will talk about tomorrow are the statehouses and not the Senate races." The Republicans picked up eight new governors; but the president had campaigned for 16 Senate candidates, yet the Republicans lost their majority in the Senate. As *Time* said, "The Teflon President seemed to have Teflon coattails." But this was only a scratch compared to what came next.

EVERY PRESIDENT in my adult lifetime who won a second term ended up being involved in a whopper of a scandal. Reagan's giving arms to Iran was so explosive, it in effect ended his presidency prematurely.

Right before the election, the Lebanese magazine *Al-Shiraa* broke the story that former National Security Adviser Robert McFarlane (accompanied by Marine Lieutenant Colonel Oliver North of the NSC staff) had flown to Tehran that May with a planeload of weapons, a Bible inscribed by President Reagan, and a cake decorated with a brass key — "to open U.S.-Iran relations" and negotiate the release of seven U.S. hostages held by Shiite terrorists in Lebanon. But Reagan himself had signed a law banning arms sales to terrorist nations such as Iran.[30]

I did the first of many *Face the Nations* on the scandal on November 9, when Democratic Senator Patrick Leahy, vice chairman of the Intelligence Committee, clarified the issue: "Colonel Oliver North and others were running their own CIA, State Department, Defense Department out of the White House without anybody looking over their shoulder."

Republican Orrin Hatch, also a member of the Senate Intelligence Committee, responded, "It was an attempt to bolster the moderates [in Iran]."[31]

The president broke his silence on November 13 in a televised speech in which he dug a hole for himself by admitting that he had sent "defensive weapons" to Iran, but so few they "could easily fit into a single cargo plane.

266

... We did not — repeat — did not trade weapons or anything else for hostages nor will we." So, as with Daniloff, the swap had not been a swap.

As the White House tried to explain, Don Regan wounded himself by telling *The New York Times*, "Some of us are like a shovel brigade that follows a parade down Main Street cleaning up." Nancy Reagan seethed at this not-so-subtle shot at her Ronnie.[32]

Mrs. Reagan had a bag of punishments for those she felt were lacking in loyalty. If she couldn't get them fired, she might frost them at official functions. In the case of one senior official she found insufficiently effusive about the president at a congressional hearing, she denied him privileges to the White House tennis court.

THE WHITE HOUSE needed some credibility, so they all but forced a reluctant George Shultz to appear on *Face* on November 16. It was a miscalculation, since it was well known that the secretary of state had opposed the Iran initiative. Naturally, I asked him why, and found myself in the midst of what *Washington Post* critic Tom Shales would call "the bombshell appearance." When the interview was over, Shultz would have half the Republican Party and most of the White House furious at him, including the vice president and the president's protector in chief, the first lady.

"We need to, of course, respond [to terrorism]," said Shultz, "and among our responses is our denial of arms shipments to Iran. That policy remains our policy. It is in effect, and there it is."

Holy moly, I thought, what does that mean? We sent arms, but we have a policy not to send arms? Was he slapping the wrist of the president on national TV?

"I don't want to badger you," I said, "but you are not answering my question."

"Well, no, you can badger me."

"Okay, good."

"The basic truth is that we continue to have a very firm arms embargo, and we continue to — "

This was like looking at modern art. "It's like Daniloff," I said. "You try to tell us that a swap wasn't a swap; you are trying to tell us that we have a policy of not sending arms when we have sent arms directly. . . . How can you look at the American people and tell them that?"

As Shultz went on in his circuitous way, it became clear that he was not going to fall on his sword for the president. He left the unmistakable impression that he did not approve of Reagan's actions. This was the 267 secretary of state in open defiance, a public embarrassment.

We had budgeted Shultz for two segments of seven minutes each. I had been getting "cut" signals from the floor manager, but I thought we were on a roll and decided there was nothing wrong with an eight- or even nine-minute segment followed by a shorter one. "Did you ever consider resigning over this?"

"Oh, I talked to the president. I serve at his pleasure. And anything that I have to say on that subject I'd just say to him."

Shultz seemed to get bolder as the interview went on, at one point remarking, "It isn't the right thing for governments to trade arms or anything else for hostages just because it encourages taking more."

Now the cuer was gesticulating wildly and Karen was in my ear begging, "Lesley, cut. We have to break."

"Will there be any more arms shipments to Iran either directly by the United States or through any third parties?" I pressed on.

"Under the circumstances of Iran's war with Iraq, its pursuit of terrorism, its association with those holding our hostages, I would certainly say, *as far as I'm concerned*, no."

Karen screeched at me, "Wrap this up! Now!" I thought: So, it'll be an 11-minute segment followed by three minutes. What's the big deal? Shultz and I were locked in a special place, the two of us tense as cats, aware we were doing something big and maybe dangerous: he going public as secretary of state with his lack of confidence in the president; I getting the interview of my career. I had one more question I had to ask: "Do you have the authority to speak for the entire administration?"

His eyes were braced on mine. With a strange, hard-to-read smile (was it the expression one wears as one jumps off a cliff?) he said firmly, "No." He had decided that no matter what, he was not going to lie.

"On that note," I said as calmly as I could, "we'll take a short break. We'll be back after this message.

Both of us were drained. "I think we have another five minutes," I said, wanting to reach out and touch his hand. "What should we discuss when we come back?"

"Anything you want."

Karen was back in my ear: "Come back? Are you kidding? We have run completely out of time. If you had gone on one more second, the CBS computer would have cut you off."

We usually allowed wire service photographers into the studio after the show to take pictures of the guest, but Shultz asked if I would mind if he slipped out. "I never should have come on," he said. He thought he would surely be fired. He looked pale, and I felt bad. Had I pushed too hard? I told his aide, "I hope he's okay."

Late that afternoon I got a call at home from Kay Graham, chairman and CEO of *The Washington Post*. "George and I played tennis today," she said. "Lesley, he has no hard feelings toward you. None at all. He wanted me to tell you that."

With the interview as the lead story in almost every newspaper the next morning, "the White House blinked," as Shultz wrote in his book *Turmoil and Triumph: My Years as Secretary of State.* Larry Speakes issued the very statement Shultz had been demanding: there would be no more arms deals with Iran, and the secretary *did* speak for the administration on this issue.

As NATIONAL AFFAIRS CORRESPONDENT I was now doing the off-lead scandal story. Partly because of the new Bettag-Rather resolve, partly because of Reagan's sagging polls (the press is always emboldened by unpopularity), I was on the air with one prickly report after the next. I said that Reagan's foreign policy was "marked by confusion and inconsistency." I spoke of "a sense that [Reagan] is making policy for emotional reasons," and used critical soundbites such as "The emperor has no clothes."

At the same time, the emperor became a figure of fun. Robin Williams played Reagan at a news conference on *Saturday Night Live.* His staff was prompting him through his hearing aid, but due to some radio interference, he tells the press corps the latest traffic report. Ridicule, as Jimmy Carter had discovered, is the scourge of politics.

Things got worse. As I noted on *Face*, that "small cargo plane" of "defensive" weapons "turns out to have contained 2,000 TOW antitank missiles and 235 Hawk antiaircraft missiles." This was a significant *offensive* capability.

Then there was another first: the president delivered the bad news himself (Jim Baker would never have let this happen). On November 25 Reagan appeared uncharacteristically bleak in the Briefing Room and dropped the second shoe, revealing that Iran had been overcharged for the weapons and the profits diverted to the contras. National Security Adviser John Poindexter resigned; NSC staffer Oliver North was fired. Attorney General Meese had investigated. "The president knew nothing about it," Meese announced. This is when, it is believed, the cover-up began in earnest.

While the Reagans were on their December vacation in California, Don Regan explained, "I was never briefed thoroughly on all of this. Does the bank president know whether a teller in the bank is fiddling around with the books? No." Someone was quoted in *The Washington Post* anonymously, "Big take-charge Marine ducks the minute the flak comes in." This is when Nancy Reagan began urging Reagan to fire the chief of staff. She became so persistent that the mild-mannered Rawhide snapped and told her, "Get off my goddamn back!"[33] So she resorted to a stealthier tactic: leaking. And she sent an emissary to George Bush to ask him to encourage Regan to resign. The vice president said no. According to some of her allies, Nancy never forgave him.

Mrs. Reagan also inspired others to go public. "There's an ancient and cruel ritual under way in Washington," I reported in mid-December, "where the powers that be gang up to publicly persuade someone he's unwanted and ought to go."

> SENATOR RICHARD LUGAR (R., Indiana): I believe that the current chief of staff . . . ought to be replaced.
> STAHL: As resignation rituals go, the Dump Don Regan campaign is a classic.
> JODY POWELL: The common mode of operation is not with a stiletto, but with a sledgehammer. . . .
> DAVID GERGEN: The drumbeat is so loud, there are cameras parked outside a guy's house, his family feels imprisoned, and the only way out is to leave.
> STAHL: But instead of forcing him out, the public pressure has gotten Regan's dander up and made him determined not to leave under a cloud. So if it comes, the final whack may have to be delivered by the president.

The president was careening between two contrary positions on Iran-contra: claiming ignorance and defending his actions. He told *Time* that Oliver North was "a national hero" and dismissed the furor as nothing more than "a Beltway bloodletting." When a Gallup Poll registered the largest one-month decline in popularity ever recorded for a president (from 67 percent to 46 percent), Reagan appointed a commission under former Senator John Tower to investigate. On *Face* Senator Dole asked the obvious: Why didn't Reagan just call Poindexter and North and say, "Tell me what happened so I can tell the American people"? Then Pat Buchanan was let loose. "If he ripped off the ayatollah and took $30 million and gave it to the contras," he said, "then God bless Colonel North."

"How can a White House official of your stature be out there publicly suggesting that it's okay to break the law if it's for a good cause, or for any reason?" I asked Buchanan on *Face.*

"I think their motivation in trying to help the contras contain communism in Central America is the highest of motives. I think the motives of Ollie North are commendable."

"The ends justify the means?"

"The ends do not justify the means," he said, "but the ends in this regard, do we not agree, are noble: to stop communism in Central America. . . ."

270   "I've heard that you were disappointed with the president for sending arms to the regime in Tehran," I said.

"Listen, I support the president of the United States." Then he began lacing into *The Washington Post*.

I broke in: "It's diversionary on your part to go blame the press, blame the liberals, blame the Democrats, blame the Republican establishment."

"Lesley, let me ask you: What does Ben Bradlee, the editor of *The Washington Post*, mean when he says, 'This is the most fun we've had since Watergate'? What does he mean by that?"

"I think you're trying to divert attention . . ."

"I think Ed Meese and Ronald Reagan deserve the Pulitzer [*sic*] Prize."

THE GOVERNMENT was paralyzed. On top of the Tower Commission, the Senate set up a select committee headed by Senator Daniel Inouye of Hawaii to look into the Iran arms deal; the House chose Congressman Lee Hamilton of Indiana to head a similar committee; under the Ethics in Government Act passed after Watergate, a special panel of three federal judges appointed an independent counsel, Lawrence Walsh, to investigate the scandal; the Justice Department was already investigating the attorney general; everyone you can think of was calling on the chief of staff to resign; and CIA Director William Casey was in the hospital with a brain tumor.

While I was snooping around the congressional committees, I was leaked an important story, not by a staffer but by a member of Congress, someone I trusted completely. When I went on the air on January 15 with what he told me, I touched off a thermonuclear reaction.

Here's what I said: that CIA Director William Casey was emerging as "a key actor" in the diversion of money to the contras. I quoted a congressional source as saying that Oliver North's computer tapes showed that there had been many meetings and phone calls between North and Casey during the period under investigation. In his congressional testimony, Casey had denied having any knowledge of the diversion before early October. "But a member of Congress told CBS News that while there is no *one* document proving Casey's knowledge, the cumulative evidence shows that, quote, 'Casey had to know and had a central role.'" Casey remained hospitalized, I said, following brain surgery last month.

Within an hour, the wires were dinging with bulletins. The CIA, which as a matter of policy never comments on news stories, was blasting us, denouncing the report as "totally untrue" and a "disgrace to journalism." The CIA spokesman, George Lauder, was on the record attacking not me but Dan. "Dan Rather should be ashamed to report slanderous conclusions from information from an anonymous source and admit he has no proof to support what he says. It is garbage journalism."

I called my source and asked if I had gotten anything wrong. He reassured me that what I had said was accurate. I told him that, given the severity of the CIA response, I would have to reveal his identity to my boss. He understood. When I told the bureau chief who he was, CBS decided to stand by the story.

Dan called me the next morning and said he would like to develop a second-day angle on the Casey story, so I worked on getting more confirmation, as did other CBS reporters. Because the CIA had gone after him so personally, Rather did the report that night, first repeating what I had said, then adding, "The story's accuracy was confirmed by another member of Congress, three senior officials of the Reagan administration, and another Reagan administration source close to the CIA."

I NEEDED A BREAK from Iran-contra. Karen and I liked to do one sports show a year, and this was the perfect time: January 1987.

> Welcome to *Face the Nation*. I'm Lesley Stahl, reporting from the Rose Bowl in Pasadena. Super Bowl XXI, climaxing one of the most bone-cracking, shoulder-smashing, tendon-tearing seasons in the history of professional football. Violence in football: Is it getting out of hand?

I had flown out to California to interview CBS sportscaster John Madden, who so disliked flying that he drove from game to game every week, often crossing the country in a Winnebago. I was a big fan. He made the games so accessible. Am I revealing too much about my interest in sports if I confess that my favorite Madden play-by-plays are about the tailgate parties?

So there I am interviewing this giant with paws as big as the Goodyear blimp about how terrible it is that football is violent. "When you get big, strong, fast guys running into each other," he says as if I'm an idiot, "that's a violent act." I know he's thinking: What am I doing here? Get me out. When I ask about all the injuries, he says, "The guys are just bigger and stronger, and when those guys run into each other, that's a collision." He's shifting around as though this is torture. And when I ask why the sport has to be so bloody, he starts speaking slowly as if I'm from Tashkent. "See, football is a contact sport. That's the game. That's what it is."

IN EARLY 1987 a collection of Aaron's magazine articles was published in a book called *Perfect Pieces*. I gave him a party at the Bristol Hotel, where, along with Judge Sirica and Jack Kent Cooke, the guests included the stars of *Broadcast News*, the movie Jim Brooks had been writing in Santa Barbara and would soon direct. He had cast Holly Hunter to play a television news producer exactly like Susan Zirinsky: they even looked alike. The actors had each spent time in the Washington CBS newsroom observing, though one day I saw Albert Brooks helping Zee with a script. Hey, why not?

Jim Brooks even wrote in a part for a brassy White House correspondent — me. He cast the beautiful Lois Chiles, whose credits included the role of Holly Goodhead in the James Bond movie *Moonraker* and who, I would discover, was dating CBS founder Bill Paley. She began following me out on interviews, on stand-ups, and eventually on lunch dates. She watched me make phone calls, talk to my producers, cajole my sources. At first it was irritating and inhibiting, but I got to like Lois . . . and the attention.

Wanting to morph into Lesley Stahl, she went to get her dark, curly hair straightened and bleached, but, alas, the hairdresser turned it the color of Cheez Whiz and she had to go to some hair hospital for rehab. Once the shooting began, Lois showed up wearing a pen jutting out from behind her right ear (as I always did). Finally, as I heard the story, Brooks hollered, "Get that goddammed pen outta your ear! It's in every friggin' shot, and it's driving me nuts!"

"But, Jim," implored Lois, "it would destroy my sense of the character, her essence." Reduced to a ballpoint pen.

I loved the movie. Jim satirized what he had told me in Santa Barbara about the disturbing trend toward celebrity newsies — reporters who feel they have to be actors. And he captured Zirinsky, the way she shuttled between hyperworkaholism and crying jags. Above all, *Broadcast News* was hilarious. There was only one thing wrong: Lois's part was cut and cut until finally we were just a cameo. I looked great, though.

THE TOWER COMMISSION REPORT was a thunderbolt. Issued on February 26, it said, in effect, that while there was no evidence the president had known of the diversion of funds to the contras, he was, well, doddering.[34] He forgot meetings he had attended and key decisions he had made; moreover, it concluded that his team of advisers had lied constantly to Congress and the public.

The president had first told the Tower panel that he had approved the arms sales to Iran in advance; then he changed that and said he had not. Finally he wrote a letter to the board saying, "I don't remember — period." The president admitted he could not remember if he authorized shipping arms to Iran and then could not remember if he remembered. Would the center hold? My piece that night asked the question: Can the president recover? And pretty much concluded: no.

The Tower panel placed much of the blame for "the chaos" in the White House on the chief of staff. And so finally the president agreed to replace Don Regan, who learned about that from a TV report. Regan was so incensed, he "blew a gasket," as an eyewitness reported, and stormed out of the White House for good. Mrs. Reagan was said to be ecstatic.

In our special Bob Schieffer made the observation that Don Regan thought he could run the White House like a business: "Put in a chain of command, tell people what to do, and if they didn't do it, fire 'em." He compared Regan to Jimmy Carter, who had thought he could manage the government "like a hardware store, by keeping a close eye on the books, always reading the fine print." Schieffer said both men had found out that politics can't be run like a store. For one thing, no business ever had a roomful of reporters watching every single move. "But Regan committed the ultimate business sin," said Bob. "He got crosswise of the boss's wife."

Rather asked me, "What *about* Nancy Reagan?"

"She spent days building support for her Oust Don Regan campaign," I said. "She lobbied, she phoned, and she succeeded."

THE IMPLICATIONS of the Tower Commission's conclusions were devastating. If the president couldn't remember making such a momentous decision, you had to wonder: What could he remember? Comedian Mark Russell sang, "What does he know and does he know he knows it?"

On *Face* I asked Tower Commission member Edmund Muskie about it: "You described the president as 'forgetful, unaware, didn't understand.' Are you worried," I asked, "about his judgment, about his ability to govern?"

"I guess you state it more strongly than I would be inclined to for this reason," he answered. "In the interest of the country, he's got to recover as much as he can of what he has lost."

The panel had called on President Reagan to get more involved in his job. "Do you think he is capable of doing that?" I asked.

"One wonders whether, after a lifetime doing business as he has, whether or not he can really come to grips with the responsibilities of his office. We were all appalled by the absence of the kind of alertness and vigilance to his job and to these policies that one expects of a president."

The president's first response to the Tower Commission was a 13-minute speech on March 4, 1987, in which he acknowledged that the Iran-contra affair had been "a mistake," though he was careful not to say he was the one who had made it.[35]

He penciled in a few changes in speechwriter Landon Parvin's draft. Parvin had written, "I've paid a price for this silence in terms of your trust and confidence, but I have simply believed that the truth should not be rushed."

Reagan crossed out the end of the sentence and scribbled in: "Since

November I've told you all I know about this." He crossed that out and started again: "In November I told you everything I knew about this situation. Since then I've waited as have you to learn the complete story." That too was crossed out. His final attempt: "I have had to wait, as you have, for the complete story."

Someone else was editing as well. This person changed Parvin's line "I approved it, I just don't remember when" to: "I did approve it; I can't say specifically when." The change is less significant than who made it. I am hardly a penmanship expert, but I do have a few samples of Nancy Reagan's handwriting.

WILLIAM SAFIRE excoriated Nancy Reagan in his *New York Times* column for her "power-hungry . . . coup" in ousting Don Regan. He said the first lady was making the president "appear wimpish and helpless by the political interference of his wife."

Fred Barnes wrote a similar column in *The New Republic*. "Fred," I said on *Face*, "you have been going after that woman for doing what everyone in this town wanted done, which is to have Don Regan leave the White House. Why are you picking on her? . . . As a woman I feel there's a hint of sexism in it."

"That's what my wife says," he said with an uncomfortable chuckle, "but in my defense, let me say that Nancy Reagan has overstepped the normal bounds for first ladies in doing something that she couldn't get her husband to do."

Elizabeth Drew of *The New Yorker* jumped in, agreeing with Fred: "It's not that she advised her husband, it's not that she pushed him to do things; she went public, she became a player in this town. And in doing that made her husband look weaker."

"But on the other hand," I said, "no one else was doing it—"

"A lot of people were doing it," said Elizabeth.

"They weren't being effective," I said, "and they weren't willing to stick their necks out and really get in there and push."

"But she has to pay the price for making her husband, at a time he was trying to show he was in command, look like he wasn't in command," Fred argued. "That's the price. It was a high price."

"But was it worth it?" I asked.

"Well, they've gotten a euphoria with [Howard] Baker in now," said Fred. (Baker, the former senator from Tennessee and cochair of the Senate Watergate committee, was the new White House chief of staff.) "Let's see what happens."

I got a short handwritten note from Mrs. Reagan: "I just saw *Face the Nation* yesterday and wanted to thank you for coming to my defense. I really appreciated it! Nancy Reagan."

The "gazer" ended up as one of the most powerful first ladies we ever had.

IRAN-CONTRA was draining the Reagan presidency. Larry Tisch was doing the same to CBS News. Not all of it was Tisch's doing. There had been drastic upheavals in our business since I arrived. There had been three competing networks in 1972; now we were contending with CNN and independent stations that liked to pit our newscasts against sitcoms or game shows. On top of that, technology was doing us in. Satellites and microwaves meant that our local affiliates were able to run footage of the big stories (footage we supplied them) in their own local newscasts. By the time viewers saw it again on the *Evening News*, it seemed wilted. We were becoming redundant.

With that as context, Larry Tisch, the man who had promised not to touch News, pounced. On March 6 he announced the biggest cutback in our history: 215 people were fired, including 14 on-air reporters such as Fred Graham (this time for good), economics correspondent Jane Bryant Quinn in New York, Jim McManus in Atlanta, and Ike Pappas in Washington, who had risked his life for CBS in Vietnam. We had called the last cutback "Doomsday." There was no catchword for this gash into our bloodstream and bone structure. Tisch also closed down three bureaus: Seattle, Warsaw, and Bangkok. Chicago, once a thriving bureau covering the Midwest, was pared down to two correspondents, Paris to one, Germany to a camera crew.

The troops were depressed and angry; several were brave enough to attack Tisch personally. Andy Rooney of *60 Minutes* called him "heartless"; correspondent Lem Tucker told Tom Shales, Tisch "looked us all in the eye and obviously lied when he said this wasn't going to happen."

No longer a worldwide news-gathering organization blanketing the world with our own people, we reporters sat helpless at the shrinking of the reach, the depth, and the cachet of CBS News. As we grieved, CBS stock soared.

AFTER A DROUGHT of four months, Reagan finally held a news conference, and he looked great. With Don Regan and Pat Buchanan gone, so were the edge and the hostility, and *Time* said flat out that he didn't appear "senile." It was another one of the man's mysterious resurrections. On *Face* Tom Shales analyzed the performance as "presidential and televisionary at the same time." Reagan, he said, was president of Televisionland, "this other kingdom that exists between Americans and their TV sets."

276 Meanwhile Iran-contra-gate seemed to have initiated an age of scandal. There was "Pearlygate," the scandal that brought down television

evangelist Jim Bakker. And then there was the philandering scandal of Gary Hart, who was running again for the Democratic nomination for president. At a news conference in New Hampshire where Hart was campaigning, Paul Taylor of *The Washington Post* asked him what was then an extraordinary question:

> TAYLOR: Have you ever committed adultery?
> HART: I do not have to answer that question.

But then he was caught red-handed with a woman not his wife. When reports of relationships with yet other women began to surface, Hart got out of the race on May 8 with a bitter rebuke of a system that "reduces the press of this nation to hunters." He seemed to forget he had invited the hunt.[36]

"When someone runs for president," I asked my guests on *Face* two days later, "they know they are in a fishbowl. Shouldn't it be that way, a time of testing?"

Congressman Robert Torricelli of New Jersey, a Hart supporter, said, "The rules have changed. . . . We have turned a new corner. . . . I think there is going to be a price in American politics for it."

"I must say personally," I said, "I don't think I could ever confront a candidate and ask him a question like that: Have you ever committed adultery?" Words I would eat.

David Broder of *The Washington Post* said, "I think we in the press have learned that we have to ask the hard questions of candidates because . . . we have seen a succession of presidents break their trust with the American people."

The Hart scandal was not so much about a man caught cheating on his wife as about imprudence. Here was someone having an affair in the midst of a campaign with the national press swarming all around, a thrill seeker who liked skating on the edge. Better to learn this before he became president. The parallels to Bill Clinton's Monica Lewinsky scandal ten years later are eerie.

Over that weekend Aaron and I had dinner with Sam and Jan Donaldson and the actor Kirk Douglas and his wife, Anne. "There's a big difference between being an actor and being a politician," said Kirk, as handsome and sexy in his early 70s as he had been when he'd played Spartacus. "I changed my name," he said, "which was a good thing for an actor, and I lied about my age, which was expected. But the *best* thing that could happen would be to be accused of having an affair!"

Kirk was writing his first novel, *Dance with the Devil*; Sam was writing his memoir. "We always tell more of the truth about ourselves in fiction," said Kirk.

THE SENATE SELECT COMMITTEE on Iran Contra began its hearings on May 5, 1987. One of the star witnesses was Robert McFarlane, who contradicted the Tower Commission portrait of Reagan as a dazed and befuddled figure. McFarlane's Reagan was the engaged instigator. He testified that the president had approved a plan to use U.S. drug agents to ransom the hostages in Lebanon and that he had personally talked to the king of Saudi Arabia about sending $2 million a month to the contras. By the end of McFarlane's powerful testimony, the president conceded his active participation regarding the contras, but he went on to insist that the Boland Amendment forbidding aid, including arms transfers, to the contras[37] did not apply to him. So the new line was: I did it, but it wasn't illegal.

I was intrigued by McFarlane's testimony that if he had told the president they were violating the Boland Amendment, "Casey, Weinberger, and Jeane Kirkpatrick would have called me a Commie." I raised this point on *Face* with Fred Barnes.

"No one could even go in and tell the president [that funneling aid to the contras] was wrong," I said.

"Your assumption is that it was wrong," said Fred. "I think the president believes, and so do most people at the White House, that the Boland—"

I was getting a cut cue, so I interrupted: "Yes, but Fred, why all the secrecy if they didn't think it was wrong?"

"Well, that's a good point."

WE KEPT HEARING horror stories about the effects of the CBS budget cuts. Some of those left in the reduced bureaus had not had a day off in months. Only Bert Quint, not even with a camera crew, went with the pope to Chile. And we were getting beat. To make matters worse, Rather's new hard-edged approach was a ratings bomb. In the summer of 1987 the *Evening News* sank into third place.

It was being said that CBS News President Howard Stringer was trying to weaken Rather's clout. Sauter had given Dan the keys to the kingdom; now it was time to take them back. Instead of challenging Rather's influence over his broadcast, though, Stringer decided to set up other power centers, to diversify CBS News' resources. He extended the life of *West 57th*, and put into motion another prime-time magazine called *48 Hours* that started with an enterprising inside look at Gorbachev's Soviet Union. Stringer sent nine correspondents, including me, and a crew of 50, to spend a week behind the lifting Iron Curtain. He called the project "Seven Days in May."

Gorbachev wanted to prove that his glasnost openness was real, so he gave us the first peek inside an office of a Politburo member (Boris Yeltsin's, as it turned out), the first televised tour of a Soviet warship, the first report of an arrest and interrogation of a pusher in a country that had never admitted to having a drug problem. Even the first taping of the birth of a baby. That was my story.

I was sent to Tbilisi, the capital of Georgia in the southwestern part of the Soviet Union. Unlike Moscow, Tbilisi was clogged with traffic, the markets bulging with fruits and meats, the buildings painted in soft yellows and pinks like the towns along the Italian Riviera. I was told that the Georgians had a thriving underground capitalist economy.

By the time I got there, my producer, George Osterkampf, had found a family through which we would tell the story of Soviet medicine. This was my first stab at a *60 Minutes*–style piece, working in a foreign country, out of touch with the office. Our family was the Chachkianis. Mother and Father Yuppies: Maryka and Timori were both doctors, as was Grandpa Vanno.

We asked an American doctor to screen our footage and tell us just *how* out of date Soviet medicine was. "They're back in the 1950s," he said. At Grandpa Vanno's clinic hypodermic needles were washed and dropped into boiling water. Nothing was disposable. Maryka worked in an overstaffed emergency cardiac care unit: five doctors for every three patients. Our American doctor described a laser-therapy gadget as "witchcraft." Where they did have new, sophisticated equipment, it often broke down, and there was no way to get it repaired.

When we asked to record the birth of a baby, the head of the hospital shook his head and said, "If you were Soviet TV asking, we'd kick your butts right out of here." But he was under orders to give us free access. I was horrified to see three or four women in the delivery room at a time, each watching in fear as she waited her turn.

I ended up producing three stories: one on Soviet medicine, one on life in prosperous Georgia, and a third on a Communist Wedding Palace that looked just like a church.

I had wondered for some time why I had never been considered for *60 Minutes*. Before the trip to Tbilisi I'd asked a friend of Don Hewitt's to find out for me. Back came the message: Don thinks you're too stiff, not warm enough, not "human," one-dimensional, too Washington. He doesn't think you have the range to do the variety of stories he likes. Much as I had enjoyed my reporting in the Soviet Union, it was clear I would never work at *60 Minutes*.

THE IRAN-CONTRA HEARINGS were a soap opera with a handsome hero named Ollie whose medals gleamed from his marine uniform. On the stand Oliver North said that he had never carried out a single act without first seeking approval from his superiors. "I was not a loose cannon on the gun deck of state." But in his testimony he shot off one

explosion after the next: He told of five memos he had written for the president's approval of the arms sales to Iran and the diversion of profits to the contras. "I assumed the president was aware . . . and had approved it."

Of particular interest to me, he revealed that CIA Director Casey had been at the heart of it all. That night, July 8, in my off-lead story, I recounted North's testimony that "Director Casey had specific and detailed knowledge [of Iran-contra], because I briefed him frequently in detail." He also testified, as I reported, that Casey was the one who had authorized the diversion of funds to the contras and who had made day-to-day decisions such as who should run the secret airdrops, the "off-the-books, off-the-shelf operation." Vindication!

Over the next five days North boasted that he had shredded documents in the presence of Justice Department officials, that he had lied to Congress and prepared false and misleading documents. He didn't duck, didn't equivocate, didn't apologize.

The chairman and vice chairman of the Iran Contra Committee, Senators Daniel Inouye of Hawaii and Warren Rudman of New Hampshire, were our guests on *Face* that Sunday, July 12:

> INOUYE: The most depressing thing I've heard all week long was that if the cause is right, you may do anything: cheat, lie, manipulate, mislead.
> RUDMAN: Now, I'm going to tell you, Lesley, that in a democracy, if you carry this to its logical extreme, you don't *have* a democracy any more.

The hearings were heading toward the next, pivotal witness, John Poindexter. Inouye said, "There's an important document in which [Poindexter] says: 'I briefed the president, the president agrees on the use of these residuals . . . for other purposes.'" It sounded like a smoking gun, so I asked Inouye if I'd heard right. He leaned over to Rudman for back-up: "You saw it. . . . We all saw it."

Face made headlines all over the country. But at the hearings Poindexter claimed that he alone had authorized the diversion of funds to the contras, that he had kept the president in the dark in order to "provide some future deniability. . . . The buck stops here with me."

MEANWHILE, another stream of allegations, indictments, and trials of the president's friends and former aides went on in the background. We called it the "sleaze factor" or, as I titled one of my pieces, "Reagan's Rogues' Gallery." In addition to a probe into Attorney General Meese's improper dealings with the defense contractor Wedtech,[38] Michael

Deaver, then in PR, and Lyn Nofziger were both prosecuted for influence peddling (Lyn's conviction was overturned on appeal).

It was in this atmosphere that British Prime Minister Margaret Thatcher came to Washington. White House officials were telling us that the usually optimistic Ronald Reagan had become despondent and depressed. The British press wrote that Thatcher was coming to bolster the president, buck him up, and help improve his image. To our delight, she accepted our invitation to *Face,* on the condition we tape the interview on Saturday at a location convenient to the airport. We found a large, ornate room in the Capitol, but one with no separate enclosure for a makeup table. When she arrived, I apologized, "Hope you don't mind that we had to set the table up right here in the middle of the room."

Mind? She loved it. Her entourage of male advisers, most of them strikingly handsome, elbowed in to get closer as she primped at the mirror. Her features were far more delicate than I'd realized from television. She wore a well-made soft gray couture suit with a stark white V-necked collar. The assembly at the mirror was like a levee in the boudoir, with the prime minister fussing over her lipstick and hair and laughing coquettishly with her boys.

Had power become an aphrodisiac for *her* too, the one we called the "stern nurse"? As I watched, the word "foxy" came to mind. My, my, is the prime minister a vamp? She flirts with Reagan, I thought. Of course! And probably with Gorbachev. Who would have thought that the flinty Margaret Thatcher, with that silly handbag and gruff manner on television, had found the key to blending her power with her female sexuality?

But I put those thoughts away because I had already planned my own stern-nurse interview. I started by mentioning a report that on the day McFarlane and North were in Tehran with a planeload of weapons to trade for hostages, the Reagan administration had been assuring her government that no such deal was in the works. "What about trust?" I asked Thatcher.

She disliked the question. Her eyes daggered mine as she refused to answer: "I won't comment, it would be discourteous of me. You may go on asking the same question in a hundred different ways and you will still get the same answer."

I stuck with my game plan and asked again. And then I looked apologetic — this pains me to ask — but I ask: "Are you saddened by what's happened?"

Thatcher was poised, confident. "No. I think you are taking far too downbeat a view." She perched on the edge of her chair, leaned in, and began scolding me: "Cheer up! America's a strong country with a great president, a great people, and a great future."

I smiled. "Lighten up — is that what you're telling us?"

"Cheer up! Be more upbeat." There was no return smile.

I called her a "cheerleader" and repeated that the United States' credibility had been damaged. The nanny in her emerged with a two-minute lecture that, not to beat around the bush, demolished me by seeming to question my love of country. "Why are you doing your level best to put the worst foot forward? Why?" she asked. "America is a great country. . . . I beg of you, you should have as much faith in America as I have."

I was down on the mat, bloodied, but labored on, asking whether the president was depressed.

"He's fine. He's fine. . . . Aren't you pleased?"

I said I was and thanked her.

"Delighted."

I didn't think Thatcher was really angry at me. I felt that she saw this as a game, one she knew she was winning. But later that day, the press officer at the British Embassy called Karen to say I had gotten that wrong. Mrs. Thatcher was livid to the point that his job was on the line for setting up such an unpleasant session.

But then the mail started — stacks and bundlesful, all of it like this:

From a man in Seven Fountains, Virginia: "[Your] carping criticisms wrapped in gloom and doom . . . does [sic] not serve the national interest."

From Washington, D.C.: "We applauded when Mrs. Thatcher chopped you into bits."

From Fort Lauderdale: "You may be successful in intimidating our spineless [sic] Senators and Congressmen who are always conscious of their next election, but you fell flat on your behind using that strategy on confident Mrs. Thatcher."

A Mailgram from Ellicott City, Maryland, called me "a perverse and bigoted mental midget." Another from Los Angeles called me "lizard-lips." And my favorite, from San Francisco: "On that Thatcher segment: I loved you both. What a life."

It seems that Mrs. Thatcher got her own bagsful of mail, and hers was mostly positive. In fact, she got so many letters complimenting her performance that she changed her mind about the interview. I wrote her a thank-you note (as I did most of my guests) and got back, handwritten: "Please don't worry about the number of critical letters. In politics we get far more than that! And like you, we just carry on. Every good wish." That from the prime minister who had chewed me up, stomped on me, and left me in tatters.

And then the Iran-contra hearings were over. The public, so eager to make allowances for the president, clung to Poindexter's testimony of "deniability" and lost interest. As the neoconservative writer and editor of

The Public Interest, Irving Kristol, said of Reagan, "The Force is with him."

And so his personal ratings began to recover. But even with the Force, Reagan would never be the same. His great assets, his integrity and invincibility — his hero quality — were diminished.

DAN RATHER was in the news. He was anchoring his broadcast on September 11, 1987, on location in Miami because the pope was there. Word came down that because a tennis match at the U.S. Open was running late, CBS Sports would have to eat into the *Evening News'* time slot. Rather got angry and walked off the set, causing the network to "go to black" for a full six minutes, an eternity of dead air.

We were all afraid Tisch would fire him, but in the end Dan expressed his regret and Tisch accepted his explanation, and for good reason. There was simply no one better than Dan Rather at synthesizing and making sense of a fast-breaking news story. There was no one better on election night. These are the measures of an anchor — not whether he or she can read the TelePrompTer well. The truth is, no one could have stepped in for Dan. No one came close in what counted, and no one was being groomed for his place.

REAGAN NOMINATED an ultraconservative, Robert Bork, to the Supreme Court. Bork, the man who had carried out Nixon's order to fire Archibald Cox after the Saturday Night Massacre. The Democrats did an effective job of portraying his views as scary, but in truth, Bork had the same views as Ronald Reagan and Oliver North. So why weren't they scary too? It had to be the wrapping, the package. Reagan had his sweet nature and that cello voice; North had his boyish optimism and handsome face; and Bork had pointy eyebrows, a Star Trek goatee, and a dour mien. His looks seemed to fit with the Democrats' he's-not-one-of-us pitch. He simply wasn't telegenic, and that's what did him in more than anything. He was such an unappealing witness that the Democrats at his confirmation hearing were able to draw blood over his insistence that there is no constitutional right to privacy. Liberals conjured up government agents barging into bedrooms in the middle of the night.

They did more; they got a Hollywood actor with as much likability as Ronald Reagan to make a TV ad. Gregory Peck, who had played the principled father in *To Kill a Mockingbird*, looked straight into the camera and said of Bork, "He doesn't believe the Constitution protects your right to privacy." I did a piece saying that this had driven Reagan up the wall.

THE CHARACTER ISSUE became *the* story of the 1988 election.[39] Gary Hart 283
was forced out of the campaign because he womanized, then Joseph

Biden because he plagiarized. Then the Reverend Pat Robertson got hammered for having had sex before he was married. And I was in the thick of it, one of the morality marshals.

Senator Joseph Biden was accused of plagiarizing a speech by the British Labour politician Neil Kinnock. On September 16, Dan asked me in a "chat," "Lesley, exactly what is this all about?"

"Well," I answered, "it's about whether, when you hear Joseph Biden speaking, you are hearing an echo of the past. In many cases you are." I ticked off examples where Biden had lifted without attribution the words of Bobby Kennedy and Hubert Humphrey, then closed with a scoop: "When he was in law school, he was brought up on charges of plagiarism." Exactly one week from the initial story, Biden bowed out of the race.

The next to go, five days later, was Congresswoman Patricia Schroeder of Colorado. There was no scandal this time, but what happened caused a minor brouhaha. She wept as she announced that she would not run for president. This was seen as evidence she was unfit: women are too emotional, too unstable. Sadly, this reinforced what I was hearing in the office about studies of TV reporters: that women still registered lower scores than men in "authority." We were not as credible as men, though women tended to rate higher on "likability."[40]

I needed a lesson in likability. Case in point: my interview in early October with Mario Cuomo, the governor of New York, who was doing his Hamlet number, agonizing over whether he should enter the race. So far, the answer was no. Now he was coming on *Face*, and to prepare I called some of my reporter friends in New York. One of them said, "If you really want to get his goat, ask him about the rumors that he's staying out because of some kind of Mob ties."

Karen and I flew to Albany to tape the interview in the governor's office. Cuomo appeared to be in great discomfort from back pain and had propped a board in his chair for support. If his backache was in any way related to stress, I was not about to help. "There are theories out there about you that float around . . . that there is a skeleton in your closet," I said, "and therefore you *can't* run."

He said that he had run for governor twice and if there were anything to the rumors, it would have come out. I decided to pursue this: "Is there anything in your background or your family's background, moral, medical, legal, financial, educational background — law school, whatever — that could come up in a campaign that would embarrass you?"

"No, I don't — well, if you promise to accept my answer and not think I'm saying I'm St. Francis of Assisi, you know, no, I don't believe there is or you would have known about it."

That was a pretty flat denial. But — I can't explain why — I didn't drop it. "I know it infuriates you, doesn't it?"

"No, it doesn't," he said. "Do I look infuriated?"

"Oh, come on. Other reporters say, if you really want to get his goat, ask about the skeleton in the closet." Let me say it myself: I should never have asked the question, and certainly not that way.

Cuomo stayed cool. "Are you telling me you are asking me this to get my goat? That's very unkind of you."

A reporter has to have persistence and doggedness; but taste is also the mark of a good journalist. I lost all sense of taste that day. Believe it or not, I asked again. This was not my finest hour.

THE SENATE VOTED 58–42 against Bork for the Supreme Court. Reagan then nominated Douglas Ginsburg, a former Harvard Law School professor described as a "Borklet" for his conservative views. But he ran into trouble when it was revealed that he had smoked marijuana while he was a professor at Harvard Law School. On *Face* on November 8, I asked Ginsburg defender Orrin Hatch why he, of all people, thought it was okay that a pot smoker was teaching students the law. Hatch pointed out that it had happened a decade ago.

"But," I said, "he was a professor of the *law*."

"So what?" shouted Hatch. "I mean, I think that's — no, wait a minute, I . . . I think that's a factor to be considered."

Who was to blame for this moral McCarthyism? Richard Harwood of *The Washington Post* says that the baby boomers who had been wild in the 1960s turned self-righteous in the 1980s and set the tone. But what about the press's role? I don't want to let us off the hook. While I never thought adultery was a disqualification for office or that smoking pot in the 1960s meant a darn thing, there I was asking all those questions. And so were my colleagues. We were like that pack of dogs Aaron, Taylor, and I had chased after in Kenya.

IRAN-CONTRA was stale news.[41] Other events were intruding. Nancy Reagan was diagnosed with breast cancer; she had a mastectomy at Bethesda Naval Hospital. And on October 19 the stock market crashed more sharply than in 1929.

I was invited to join the United Nations Association as an observer on a trip to Moscow. Led by John Tower, our delegation of mostly former government officials[42] held meetings with officials of Gorbachev's government as well as "advisers" such as Evgeny Primakov and Georgi Arbatov and a lot of military brass decked out in medals and ribbons.

At one session around a long conference table Arbatov mentioned, "You in the U.S. depend for your self-image on us. If the Soviets are the 'Evil Empire,' then you tell yourselves, 'We must be the good empire.' If we Russians wear the black hat, you say, you must wear the white.

What we are doing now," he said, "is depriving you of your enemy. And when we do that, you will lose your sense of self. You will no longer know who you are; you will have an identity crisis." It dawned on me that Reagan's use of language — his defining the Soviets as "evil"— had had a profound resonance beyond the United States. But I found Arbatov's prediction unsettling.

Face producer Karen Sughrue was also in Moscow, setting up an interview for me with Andrei Sakharov. Gorbachev had only recently released him from his long exile of hunger strikes and illnesses in Gorki. The Soviet leader was courting this man, a highly decorated nuclear physicist who had become the country's leading human rights activist. Still, Sakharov insisted we meet him at a secret location in the dark of night and spirit him up to the apartment of our Moscow bureau chief, Joe Richey. Glasnost went only so far.

Sakharov was tall and frail with a sickly, sallow complexion. He seemed to wear a moral authority; I actually thought: saint, meaning he was unapproachable.

As I asked my first question (Joe Richey was interpreting), Sakharov produced a sheaf of papers from his jacket pocket and proceeded to read, head down, for five minutes.

I tried interrupting a few times, but he just plowed ahead. Finally breaking through, I explained gently that the format was questions and answers, not reading. He was taken aback. He had written out in long-hand ten pages of precisely what he wanted to say. So he continued to read.

Disaster. I tried again. Ahem. Excuse. Please, sir. What if we did both? You read a little, then answer a little? We had a negotiation in two languages. This was about as delicate as it gets: trying to nudge someone who had earned his holy aura by not giving in into compromising. I must have looked on the edge of weeping (wonder if the secret police ever thought of that), because he did agree, and so I had my Q and A with the great one.

GORBACHEV CAME TO WASHINGTON in December for a return summit. "Here's a stunner," I said on *Face* on the eve of the meeting, "Gorbachev's poll ratings in the U.S. are now almost as high as President Reagan's and higher than most of the presidential candidates'." Reagan commented, "I don't resent his popularity or anything else. Good Lord, I costarred with Errol Flynn once!"

While the men wrestled with throw-weighty matters, Nancy wrestled with Raisa, who kept up her annoying habit of lecturing Mrs. Reagan, this time on homelessness and racism in America. We had footage of Mrs. G. continually defying Nancy's request that she not talk to the press.

Raisa kept breaking loose to approach the cameras, as Nancy seethed in the background. In my piece that night, New York got me to add a line from a Mark Russell routine: "In fact, she's the first wife of a Russian leader to weigh less than he does!"

TV GUIDE gave me a Christmas present, declaring that I was the "toughest" of the Sunday-morning interviewers. Roderick Townley, asked to study the Sunday shows for bias, had concluded that I was not promoting a political agenda: "Essentially, she'll shoot anything that moves, on the left or on the right.... [She's] first and foremost, a watchdog... with perhaps a streak of pit bull somewhere in her ancestry." I wanted to frame it.

Tough or not, it was fortunate that when I interviewed Yasser Arafat in Tunisia on *Face* on January 17, 1988, we had to tape him early Sunday morning because he had a time conflict. Fortunate because we were able to leave much of his filibustering and our bickering on the edit room floor. We were on a satellite connection, both of us looking into the eye of a camera, so we were a little disoriented. But that didn't slow him down a bit. He punched out a tirade against Israel for a nonstop ten minutes, never allowing a single question. I would try, but we'd only end up talking over each other until I snapped and bellowed like a drill sergeant: "This is not a speech show, it's a Q-and-A show. You must let me ask you a question!"

He paused and said sweetly, "Oh, pardon, lady." And thus the interview began. Everything up to then was cut out. I asked why he, living in exile, wasn't encouraging a new, homegrown Palestinian leadership that the Israelis would be willing to deal with.

"Are you official spokesman for the Israeli government?" he inquired.

"Let's not attack the questioner, but let's answer it," I scolded. He seemed to accept the reprimand.

"The whole problem is not a new leadership or old leadership. The main point is the occupation, the continued occupation...."

"Would you offer a compromise to get to the [negotiating] table?" I asked.

"A compromise with whom? Are you authorized to speak by the Israeli leadership?"

"I don't think attacking me is going to get us anywhere."

"No, I am not attacking you," he said and thanked me sarcastically for the advice.

"Are you ready to accept Israel's right to exist?" I moved forward, trying to keep my frustration out of my voice and off my face. We were on a split screen, side by side, he in Tunis, I in Washington, he in his trademark headdress, I in my blond bouffant. 287

"Are they ready to accept my right to have my political rights and human rights? Ask them. . . . If they will accept, I will accept."

"Why don't you take the first step?"

"Not to forget that we are under their occupation, we are the victims."

"You say you want to have lasting peace, but you will not say Israel has a right to exist. How can they live in lasting peace if you won't make that statement?"

"Why, they are afraid from the Palestinians?"

"I think they are."

"They are occupying the Palestinians now."

We were a good 40 minutes into our interview by now, and he was actually talking to me.

"Mr. Arafat, the stalemate of your people living in those camps: Do you not see the need for any kind of conciliation, small steps, to get your people out of those conditions?"

He may have softened his voice, but he was uncompromising: "From one slavery to another new slavery? What they are — why? We are human beings, we are human beings too." This was said plaintively.

If we had done our usual "live" interview, all the public would have heard was his initial unilluminating rant.

THE 1988 CAMPAIGN

This tube is gospel! This tube is the ultimate revelation! This tube can make or break presidents, popes, and prime ministers! This tube is the most awesome goddamned force in the whole godless world!

— The anchorman in *Network*

By the beginning of 1988, the campaign was well under way. George Bush was frantically contending with his "wimp" image; the Reverend Pat Robertson was activating a phalanx of Christian soldiers for the Iowa caucuses; Senator Al Gore of Tennessee was grappling with Yuppies who were offended by his wife, Tipper's, campaign against offensive rock lyrics; and on *Face* Michael Dukakis ducked ten questions on whether he'd raise taxes. Most of the candidates were refusing to get specific about the issues. And if they were pressed, they often fought back with media bashing. Media bashing was the thing to do in 1988. For that reason it was unfortunate when Dan Rather did not get to tape his interview with George Bush (as I did with Arafat).

Bush had never given a full accounting of his role in Iran-contra. He routinely refused to grant interviews, claiming he had already answered all the questions — which he had not come close to doing. When the *Evening News* requested an interview, Bush agreed on condition that it be live. Print reporters edit interviews as a matter of course, but politicians prefer to be live on television because it gives them the option of meandering, digressing, diverting, rambling, anything to eat up time and get around the tough questions.

Bush was primed for the interview. He watched Rather's five-minute tee-up piece from his Capitol Hill office. When it ended, up he came on camera, jabbing and taunting. Bush would later claim he had been ambushed by Dan's single-minded focus on Iran-contra, but Bush's media man, Roger Ailes, told me they had been tipped off about it "by someone in the CBS newsroom. We knew what Dan was going to do."

Whenever Rather opened his mouth, Bush would interrupt to protest and complain. He simply wouldn't let Dan get off a question. Every time he'd start anew, Bush would jump in, and then they would talk on top of each other.

Rather started: "You have said that if you had known this was an arms-for-hostages swap—"

Bush broke in: "Yes."

"That you would have opposed it."

"Exactly," said Bush.

"You also said that you did not know—"

"May I answer that?"

"That wasn't a question," said Rather. "It was a statement."

"It was a statement, and I'll answer it."

"Let me ask the question if I may first," said Rather. "I don't want to be argumentative, Mr. Vice President, bu—"

"You do. Dan, this is not a great night. . . ."

I was watching with Zirinsky in our Iowa edit room. "Oh, no," I gulped. "This isn't happening," she moaned. It was like watching a parachute not open. The more Bush whiffled, the more Rather watched the clock, knowing that each interruption meant he was closer to a shutout —an interview without a single coherent answer.

Bush and Rather were talking via satellite. One effect of communicating in cyberspace, I'm told, is a tendency to "flame." It's easier to hurl insults when there's no eye contact.

"Mr. Vice President," said Rather, "these questions are—"

As he'd been prepped to do, Bush interrupted again to land his coup de grâce, a line he'd rehearsed with Ailes. "I don't think it's fair to judge a whole career, it's not fair to judge my whole career by a rehash on Iran. How would you like it if I judged your career by those seven [sic] minutes when you walked off the set in New York [sic]? Would you like that?" Bush smiled, in control.

"Mr. Vice President, you made us hypocrites in the face of the world."

Bettag got into Dan's ear: *Wrap*. But Bush goaded him: "Fire on another one!"

Dan went on: "Are you willing to go to a news conference before the Iowa caucuses, answer questions from all comers?"

"I've been to 86 conferences since March," said Bush, evading yet another question.

"I gather," said an exasperated Rather, "that the answer is no." With that he abruptly ended the interview. "Thank you very much for being with us, Mr. Vice President. We'll be back with more news in a moment."

When Zee and I, who had clutched each other, unraveled, we looked around. The Iowa newsroom was a morgue. The consensus then in Des Moines was that this would hurt Dan. But when someone called Bettag in New York, he was elated. "Great television!" he said.

I was then summoned. "Call on line three." It was Mary Martin, the CBS producer with Bush in Washington. "You're not going to believe this, Stahl, but George Bush just called you a pussy." When the interview was over, Bush, obviously pumped high on testosterone, had turned to his staff and the CBS crew, including Mary Martin, to say, "The bastard didn't lay a glove on me," adding that Rather made "Lesley Stahl look like a pussy."

According to Mary, Ailes, who had been cuing Bush through the interview, had warned him that his microphone was still on, but the veep had kept going: "I'm really upset. You can tell your goddamned network that if they want to talk to me, raise their hands at a press conference. No more Mr. Inside stuff." He was "like a warrior with his foot on his enemy's neck," Richard Ben Cramer wrote in his book *What It Takes*. Bush was "whooping to the heavens." He was the Great Dan Slayer! Lee Atwater told a reporter, "I guarantee you, this'll play stronger than grits in the South." Pete Teeley, the campaign spokesman, said this would put an end to all the "wimp bullshit."[43]

But first Bush had to overcome "pussy." Naturally, the rival Dole camp pounced, calling the remark about me crude and sexist. Pete Teeley called me and said, "Lesley, he meant pussycat. Really."

Bush felt he needed to make a public apology for his postgame, locker-room vulgarities. "If I had known the microphone was on," he said at a news conference in South Dakota, "I wouldn't have done it." That's an apology?

So is press bashing an effective campaign tool? In 1988 they were all taking potshots at us: Bush, Hart, Robertson, Jackson. But it rarely worked. Roger Ailes once wrote, "Hostility is a no-win strategy with the press. They have the last word." But in the Bush-Rather case, it seemed to have been Bush's magic potion; suddenly, he was muscle-bound. As Walter Shapiro of *Time* said on *Face* on January 31, "This was the introduction of the I-can-lick-any-guy-on-the-block, totally manufactured Charles-Atlas-course George Bush." He was a guy we had never seen before.

There was another benefit for Bush. Dan Rather was red meat to the right-wing crowd, which had never forgiven him for his reporting on Nixon. Dan bashing was a winner for Bush, who was still trying to earn his conservative spurs.

AN OLD FRIEND from Boston, Carl Covitz, was Reagan's undersecretary of housing. He called one day and asked if I would like to speak to the "Number Twos Club," explaining that the number twos in the Reagan Cabinet — the deputy secretaries — met on a regular basis with George Bush, the ultimate number two, presiding. From time to time, Carl explained, the twos invited guest speakers to breakfast, and he wondered if I'd come and talk about television coverage of the campaign.

We gathered at 7 A.M. in a small dining room off the White House mess. Seated at the middle of a rectangular mahogany table, I was introduced one by one to Robert Gates, deputy director of the CIA; Arnold Burns, deputy attorney general; Mimi Dawson, deputy director of transportation; seventeen in all. Everyone showed except the campaigning George Bush.

Over scrambled eggs and fresh fruit, I talked about the primacy of pictures in TV coverage. They were all pretty relaxed, asking tough questions but without acrimony. Just as it was time to leave, I said I had a question: "Why do so many people in the Reagan administration hate CBS so intensely?"[44]

"Everyone knows CBS is biased," said one of the twos. "You're all liberals. You're out to get us."

"No, no, that's not it," a second number two interrupted. "It's because of that snarling Dan Rather. He's the reason."

A third spoke up. "Let me tell you a story that I think will illuminate things." Sitting across from me, he spoke softly: "One day last year I went to see Pat Buchanan — he was still working in the White House. 'Pat,' I said, 'I want you to meet a new friend of mine, Van Gordon Sauter.'" He explained that he and his wife had gotten to know Van and his wife, Kathleen, socially. He told Pat that Van was a solid Reaganite who saw eye to eye with conservatives on the issues. "'Pat, you'd love this guy. He's just like you.' I told him that, and then I said, 'This guy's running CBS News, and his best friend is Dan Rather — they go fishing together every weekend. Pat — the guy running CBS is one of us! And he's closer to Dan Rather than anyone. I want to arrange for the two of you to get to know one another.'"

The number two paused and looked around the table. He said he 291 had expected Pat to be pleased, to jump at the chance to meet Van. Pat was, after all, the director of communications. But instead, he said, "Pat stared hard at me and said, 'I never want you to tell this to anyone else, do you understand? This must never get past this office. I don't want to know this man, and I don't want anyone else to know him either.' "

"What did he mean?" I asked. "Why didn't he want to meet him?"

He said, in effect, that now that Reagan was making friends with Gorbachev, the conservatives were losing the Communists as an adversary. They couldn't afford to lose their other great whipping boy, Dan Rather. Ed Rollins would later tell me, "Rather? He was our greatest foil."

Buchanan probably knew what Georgi Arbatov knew: that often countries — or, in this case, political parties — are defined by their enemies.

THE AUDIENCES for the three nightly network news shows were declining. Howard Stringer thought that if network news were to survive, we would have to move beyond the evening news. He became the first News president to develop multiple shows in prime time. In 1988 CBS had three: 60 Minutes, West 57th, and 48 Hours. (ABC had one, NBC none.) Because of Stringer's strategy, News was hiring again; our budget was growing.

Things were not going well, however, on the entertainment side of the network. For the first time ever, CBS dipped into third place in 1988, a serious matter since each rating point in prime time was worth about $100 million. All the nets were losing audience. With VCRs and cable in more than half the households by 1988, the network share in prime time was just 68 percent, down from 92 percent ten years before. Consequently, the ratings war became more intense and affected News more than ever.

This meant that despite Stringer's new prime-time shows, the campaign budget was put on a diet. Trying to save money, CBS sent "the kids" out on the candidates' buses during the primaries instead of reporters. The kids were a group of young, generally inexperienced, low-paid junior producers and desk assistants. If anything important happened, the kids would call in and CBS would dispatch a reporter to the scene as quickly as possible.

My role in the campaign was "issues" correspondent. I did a piece on the farm economy and then one on how the economy affects incumbents. The vice president was strong in New Hampshire, where the economy was soaring, but faltering in Iowa, where farmers were selling off their assets.

The Reverend Pat Robertson did not run as well as expected in Iowa. On Face right before the New Hampshire primary, I asked about his goal of a Christian nation, his faith healing, and his stated belief in Armageddon. I quoted one of his earlier remarks: "The second coming of Christ will come in some great, dramatic nuclear war between the United States and the Soviet Union." But he responded, "No, I don't believe that."

I was surprised. "Am I mistaken that you predicted the end of the world in 1982?"

"No way," said Robertson.

"I read that."

Robertson retreated: "Some of that was written during the Carter administration, and you will excuse me for having a certain degree of pessimism during that period."

One of my pieces, on February 16, was on campaign money. "All but a few candidates are already broke," I reported. "You have to have an airplane, a staff, phones, advance men." Only Governor Michael Dukakis of Massachusetts (he'd raised $11.5 million) and Bush (with $20 million) had enough to open offices and buy TV time in the 172 media markets in the coming all-important Super Tuesday states.

One candidate whose money had all but run out was Bruce Babbitt, the former Democratic governor of Arizona. He was flying around New Hampshire in a single-engine prop with barely enough room for him, his wife, Hattie, and a couple of aides.

I was assigned to follow him for two days and put together a package for 48 Hours. What a decent, lope-along politician. But what an anachronism. In an age when candidates avoided the tough issues and told the voters pretty much what they wanted to hear, Babbitt was spooning out medicine: "We're going to have to raise taxes." He was humorous in the style of Will Rogers but gawky and twitchy in the style of Ichabod Crane —a media expert's nightmare.

So there I am, crammed into his plane, riding backward with my right knee in between the candidate's lanky legs. I spend all my energy making sure we never touch. Ray Bribiesca, the cameraman, is next to me, leaning back because if the camera is too close, you get a fish-eye effect. Hattie is opposite Ray.

I try interviewing Babbitt about the issues, the difficulty of raising money, his opponents. Then the bumps start and I get queasy. And then I get sick and start vomiting into one of those little bags. I'm leaning over my knee—and by extension Babbitt's long legs. He is so flustered that he keeps on talking. I'm barfing . . . and he keeps going on about the environment and taxes. Finally, and I mean finally, Hattie (the very one to whom Babbitt would be caught whispering on camera, "Hattie, I'm horny") touched his arm and said, "Dear, I think you can stop talking now." Later, in a private moment—private except for the camera—Babbitt's gloom about his prospects spilled out and he all but admitted that his candidacy was done. "Might you try again in '92?" I

293

asked. "No, I don't want to be the Harold Stassen of the Democratic Party."

WE WERE ALL in a state of despair. Tony Streuli, who had just been promoted from radio to television, was running our newsroom in Manchester and doing a good job of it. I had worked with him for years in the Washington Bureau. Funny, smart, compulsive like the rest of us, a solid newsman, a good kid. Everyone liked him. Tony, 42, went to his room late one night and never woke up.

HAVING LOST to Dole in Iowa, Bush was desperate in New Hampshire. Peggy Noonan flew in to write speeches that would turn him from awkward prepster to appealing regular guy; the image makers dressed him in a rugged-man parka and had him drive a big 18-wheel truck. Even though the "drive" was in a parking lot, it was one of those photo ops that, astonishingly, worked. And then Dole helped by refusing to sign a no-new-taxes pledge, a death warrant in taxophobic New Hampshire. But what may have helped Bush the most was a negative ad inspired by Ailes, a maestro of the genre. It was called "the straddle ad," and it accused Dole of flip-flopping on the issues. On primary night, I did a report on how, even in this rural, walk-door-to-door state, television, and particularly campaign ads on TV, had become the fundamental way to campaign. Bush, better at it than Dole, won by nine points. As expected, Dukakis won on the Democratic side.

THE RACE MOVED south for Super Tuesday: March 8, 1988, 16 states with a hoard of 1,307 delegates. Southern Democrats had thought up Super Tuesday as a way of inoculating the party against a liberal nominee. As the candidates moved south, they adjusted with designer rhetoric — new slogans for the more conservative audience. But that produced, as I reported, charges of slip-sliding on the issues.

> STAHL: More than taxes and the deficit, more than the contras and the Communists, the issue in the South is consistency. . . . The candidates are terrified of being caught with their contradictions showing.

To make matters interesting, polls had Jesse Jackson poised to win as many as six states in the south. So much for the antiliberal toxin. In fact, it took so much money to run in 16 states (with 500 TV stations) at once that only someone with momentum out of the "liberal" battlefields of Iowa and New Hampshire could raise enough. On the Republican side, the only candidate with the resources to fight all across the South was the vice president, who was able to put $3 million into a regionwide ad campaign. As Richard Ben Cramer put it, "There were ad images of Bush-with-Reagan, Bush-with-soldiers, Bush-with-grandchildren, Bush-with-ocean, Bush-with-farmland, Bush-with-flags."

Because the territory was so vast, the campaign was run almost entirely on television, often with answer ads. One Monday night Bush ran an ad during *Matlock* walloping Dole, who answered on Thursday with an ad on *Wheel of Fortune*. One tactic was to produce a sizzle ad. If it sizzled enough, it would run as a news story, and then the campaign would not have to buy airtime.

Watching the ads was often as close as the network reporters ever got to the candidates. Avoiding us was a major strategy. They all did it, preferring interviews with local anchormen. One day I watched Richard Gephardt chat by satellite with ten local anchors back-to-back for about an hour and a half. These were often live, chummy, "patty-cake" interviews. Local anchormen depend on their likability for ratings.

Bush was making such a point of avoiding the national reporters that it became an issue. He was zipping through the South, escaping without having to say what he would do as president or what he had done as vice president.

I was on the set for our Super Tuesday prime-time coverage. Dan came on at 8 P.M. and introduced the "team": Bob Schieffer on the Republicans, Bruce Morton on the Democrats, Lesley Stahl on poll analysis, as well as *60 Minutes* men Ed Bradley and Mike Wallace and commentators William Safire and Roger Rosenblatt. As the night wore on Dan reported that Bush had beaten Dole in 16 states; Dukakis, Jackson, and Gore had carved up the Democratic vote. I offered stories from the polling desk on the black vote, the labor vote, the women's vote, the suburban vote. But never once did Dan throw it to me. He signed off at ten. I had not been on at all.

I was devastated. Some of the producers told me that Dan was down on me. But why? I was told that he had heard how argumentative I was over my scripts. "You're always fighting their changes. That kind of complaint — she's a pain in the ass — bleeds up." My head hurt. Then someone close to Dan pulled me aside. "He prefers Bob Schieffer; he's more comfortable with him. He doesn't think you're crisp."

I went to my hotel room and suffered. I had always seen my trajectory at CBS as upward. The advice from *Broadcast News* director Jim Brooks had been a warning, an alarm bell, but this was the fire itself, an unmistakable setback. I seemed to be sinking. At least in Dan's eyes, and that meant everything, since I worked for the *Evening News*.

My producers suggested I try using basketball metaphors. Then, to cheer me up, they began joking I should come up with some "crisp"

Texasisms to make Dan feel more "comfortable" with me. How's about: "Candidate Q looks like he's been rode hard, put in the stable wet, then sent on an overnight train to the glue factory." This was so pathetic. I was miserable.

Gary Hart was miserable too. He had reentered the race and was now pulling out—for a second time. When a reporter asked how he would make a living, he slid into his charm act: "It's none of your business." I was a little worried about what I was going to do in the future myself.

A FEW DAYS after Bob Dole got trounced on Super Tuesday, I reported that his campaign was calling around the country for advice on how the candidate could "bow out gracefully without looking like a quitter." In one of our on-air chats, Dan asked me what Dole's options were. I said he was being advised to "set up a shell operation just to keep his campaign officially alive," so that if Bush were to be felled by the expected Iran-contra indictments, he could jump back in. I tried so hard to be "crisp," I was nervous for the first time in years. Was my career a shell?

Dole pulled most of his ads off the air and came on *Face*. He was at his rapier-witty best, but the camera read it as bitterness, the very darkness he'd spent the race trying to camouflage. "Is it true," I asked, "that you really have a strong, personal dislike for George Bush? Has it come to the point of hatred between the two of you?"

"Oh, no," he said with a withering glance. "I do believe he's sort of had a charmed life in politics. He's gotten quite a ways without ever really doing very much. But maybe that's a key to success, one I hadn't thought of." Funny, yet snide. Not the best way to make people like you. I haven't decided which is more important to political success: a strong economy or likability. One or the other, and the guy's got a leg up. With both the public will forgive a pol almost anything.

Dukakis was working on his likability. Called dull once too often, he began playing his trumpet and dancing to show he had élan—and also to raise money at Greek events. After Super Tuesday I did a report saying that money was pouring into his campaign mostly from Greek Americans and Jews (his wife, Kitty, was half Jewish). "He's raised $20 million," I said, "nearly as much as all the other Democrats combined—a war chest so fat, it almost looks Republican."

THE TENACIOUS MEDIA REPORTER Gail Shister of *The Philadelphia Inquirer* called to ask me about Rather's heavyweight bout with Bush. I defended Dan and pointed out how hard it is to do live television: "There are no rules, no road maps. You're on your own. It's like a bullfighting arena."

I admitted to Shister that I was frustrated at not getting on the air as much as I used to and changed the subject to *Face* and our all-woman staff. "We are all compulsive," I said, "and driven in similar ways. Nobody puts anyone else down for working too hard." I didn't tell her that on Saturdays we often stopped everything to watch Elsa Klensch's fashion shows on CNN.

"The definition of female has to change," I said, which led her to ask for a comment about the network newswomen posing provocatively in various magazines. Diane Sawyer had gone first in September 1987 on the cover of *Vanity Fair*, bare-shouldered and sexy. You can't imagine the uproar. "Pure cheesecake," sniped one TV critic; others carped that celebrity was creeping dangerously into the world of serious journalism. I had called Diane to comfort her, but she said she wasn't upset, which I found astounding, given the onslaught of criticism — even from her colleagues. She had a pile of angry mail from women saying, "You let our side down." Diane told me she had wanted to break through "that little Dresden-glass image, all of us pretending we didn't want to be girls." Other newswomen began posing, including Maria Shriver in *Vanity Fair* and Meredith Vieira in *Esquire*. Andrea Mitchell of NBC went on ABC's *Good Morning America*, wringing her hands that all the peeks up skirts and down bosoms were going to erode our credibility, that the glamour flashing would impugn our reputations as serious journalists. But Vieira said, "I don't think that making it in this business means having to hide who you are. I think we have earned the right to play by *our* rules, not the rules established by men." There are two sexes, she said defiantly. Deal with it.

I told Shister, "I want the women's movement to encourage and applaud femininity and the public expression of it among professional women. I want the symbols to change." But much as I agreed with Diane and Meredith and longed to show up in plunging necklines and diaphanous organza, I was afraid it *would* hurt my credibility. There was a difference between a political reporter in the trenches, I told myself, and an anchorwoman.

The provocative pictures were a dramatic turning point in the journey away from the old Murrow-boy journalists of the men's club past. Along the path we all got blow-dried and made up, even the men, who began wearing sexy safari-jacket "costumes." But these pictures were a watershed, because the women not only survived the criticism, they all went on to thrive — and soar. My antennae had not picked up how important celebrity and glamour had become to success in my business.

AFTER LARRY SPEAKES left the White House on February 1, 1987, he came out with a memoir, *Speaking Out*, one of the most vicious to date.[45]

What was it about sweet Reagan that inspired such sourness and betrayal? Speakes wrote that getting Reagan ready for a news conference was "like reinventing the wheel." He confessed that he had made up quotes for Reagan, whose real words were often "very tentative and stilted." During the crisis of the downing of the Korean Air Lines plane, he had put some of George Shultz's words into Reagan's mouth "since the president had had almost nothing to say."

Speakes wrote a chapter on the White House press corps. Sam, whom he called "Shoot from the Lip," was the brightest, but—there was always a slice—"he didn't work terribly hard." Chris Wallace was "a bit slow on the uptake." And me? I was the "most tenacious," but "I always thought she got where she was because she was blond and attractive and female . . . she too often took a simplistic approach to the news." Dan Rather came to my defense. He said you can never trust a reporter who's praised by a press secretary. With his credibility blemished by his confession of fabricated quotes, Larry Speakes (blond himself) lost his $400,000-a-year job as chief spokesman for Merrill Lynch.

No sooner had the parade sweepers cleaned up after the Speakes book than another pachyderm charged. Don Regan's memoir, *For the Record,* was a grudge book, dedicated to getting back at Nancy. He portrayed the president as a near cipher, controlled by his scheming, astrology-addicted wife. He revealed her efforts to keep abortion out of the president's speeches, quoting her as saying, "I don't give a damn about the right-to-lifers." I remember thinking: In a hundred years who's ever going to believe the country was being run by these people?

On May 15 I asked Don Regan on *Face* why he had written a kiss-and-tell book. "If you expect loyalty from your subordinates," he replied, "you have to be loyal to them."

"You say in your book that you had to glean what [Reagan's] policy was, sometimes from his body language. You draw a portrait of a man who didn't study policy, didn't understand policy."

He said that what counted was the end product. "What's the bottom line of the Reagan administration? It's a great record."

"Bottom line?" I asked. "Largest deficit in history, largest debtor nation, can't afford to fix the housing emergency or the drug crisis."

"Oh, come on, now, Lesley," he came back, "that's Mike Dukakis's argument. What you've got to think about is 16 million more jobs,[46] a country with the greatest increase in its GNP for the longest period of time."

"But based on borrowing," I argued. "I don't remember reading that you admit you made any mistakes. Did you?"

298   "I think one was becoming chief of staff."

□

May 1988. Reagan was on his way to Moscow for his fourth meeting with Gorbachev. Lou Cannon wrote that George Shultz had coached the president for the summit by using stage direction terms and telling him what to do "in the scene." Some of the aides on *Air Force One* were concerned. Reagan seemed more unprepared and remote than ever. They were treating him less like an actor than a child, repeating instructions over and over. But as happened frequently, just when they were certain he had something like Alzheimer's, Reagan pulled himself together. In Moscow he made more than two dozen appearances, including speeches and negotiations, and — as far as I can determine — faltered only twice, though they were doozies. First he fell asleep during Gorbachev's toast at a state dinner in the Kremlin.

Then the exhausted president met with the foreign minister of Japan, who was also in Moscow. Each time Reagan's eyelids closed, according to an eyewitness, Shultz said loudly, "Who would like coffee?" Within minutes a waiter arrived with what was described to me as Valvoline-strength java for the president, who would rebound to wakefulness, but only momentarily. After a second round of coffee, Reagan was drooping again. So Shultz looked at his watch and told the Japanese foreign minister, "Oh, my, we have to catch a plane!" Catch *Air Force One*? But it worked. Everyone got up, then watched in horror as Reagan shook hands and said, "Well, Mr. Foreign Minister, it sure has been a pleasure" — to the interpreter.

Polls in the spring of 1988 showed Bush first ten, then 16 points behind Dukakis, who was banging away about Meese (under investigation for possible violations of federal conflict-of-interest rules, but refusing to resign)[47] and Bush's connections with "drug-running Panamanian dictators" (Manuel Noriega was refusing to leave Panama). The vice president added Noriega to the list of questions he would not answer.

There was a sense of inevitability about Dukakis, a consensus that Bush — with Iran-contra and the lingering wimp label — couldn't win. His team calculated that a public endorsement from Reagan would help, and they began planning a big gala where Reagan would pass the baton. George and Barbara thought their loyalty had earned this. But Nancy kept finding ways to keep it from happening. Finally in May Reagan promised to do the deed. Endorsement Night! The balloons were there, the flags, the crowd. But once again, Bush was all but cellophane. It had to be the most halfhearted endorsement of all time. Reagan spoke mostly about himself then ended with a short, perfunctory "next president of the United States" remark, mispronouncing Bush's name, rhyming it with blush.

I took particular notice that Barbara Bush was wearing red that night.

There the four of them stood at the head table holding hands, arms raised in the air: Barbara, then George, Ronnie, and Nancy, also in red. The only one not smiling was the first lady. To my knowledge this was the first Barbara-in-red sighting in seven years. She wore the color from then on.

LEE ATWATER was a wreck. Nothing was working. George Bush, with an overall negative rating of 40 percent, was in hopeless shape with women. He made Reagan's gender gap look like a crack in the sidewalk. Of even more concern, the Reagan Democrats were shifting to Dukakis. Atwater was in search of one of the so-called wedge issues he was famous for — gun control, crime, school prayer, racial quotas — that would recapture those northern white Democrats.

In late May, the campaign videotaped a focus group in suburban Paramus, New Jersey, and Lee leaked the tape to me for a report.

> ATWATER: We had two groups of 20 Democrats who supported Reagan in 1984 and were supporting Dukakis in '88. [August 12]

On the tape you heard the moderator tell the group about Dukakis's prisoner furlough program in Massachusetts, where a first-degree murderer, Willie Horton, a black man out on leave from prison, had raped a white woman in Maryland and stabbed her fiancé.

> WOMAN IN GROUP: He favors a policy of giving weekend furloughs to convicted felons for good behavior?
> MAN: No, that'd be bad. That'd be awful. I'd like to know why he would —
> ATWATER: After that, between 40 and 60 percent of these people changed over to Bush.

Lee had found his issue: "If I can make Willie Horton a household name, we win the election."[48] Republican candidates had been keeping their coalitions alive by playing the race card ever since the 1960s. But I was convinced that George Bush would never do this. I thought he would refuse, on principle. I was wrong.[49]

TAYLOR WAS COMING to the end of fifth grade, which marked the beginning of my second education. She had spent several months working on a report on Texas, including a profile of Sam Houston. When all the maps with oil wells were colored in and the charts of farm products were pasted together and the reports on governors and football teams were compiled, we helped Tay put it together in a big, oversized scrapbook because her teacher, Mrs. Levin, had invited the parents for a showing of the class projects. I took the day off, convinced Taylor would be the only kid with both parents in attendance. Boy, was I wrong. Every single child had at least two parents show up — in many cases, four. When mothers work, both parents tend to be more attentive. At least that was my observation.

TAYLOR WENT TO CAMP in New Hampshire for the month of July, and I went out full-time on the campaign trail, and then to Atlanta for the Democratic National Convention. On a preview show I mentioned Dukakis's main problem: Jesse Jackson, who was making it clear he wanted to be his running mate. But then he learned from a group of reporters that Dukakis had already picked Senator Lloyd Bentsen of Texas, a conservative Democrat. Obviously furious, Jackson came on *Face*, which we broadcast from Rather's booth overlooking the convention floor. To get up there, you had to climb a steep, narrow staircase. Special gels were coating the windows to keep the bright lights from all the other TV booths from shining into our set.

Jackson was in great form. Saucy, confident, and mischievous, he made it clear that he would challenge Dukakis: "This is the delegates' convention. They will determine . . . who the vice president will be."

"Every poll shows that you would hurt Dukakis as a running mate," I said. "Why did you keep upping the ante when it was clear he wasn't going to ask you?"

"It wasn't clear to me."

"Can you afford to have them lose and you be blamed? Can you afford to let them win without you? Some people in the party," I went on, "think what you are doing is forcing [Dukakis] to publicly make concessions to you and that that weakens him before the American people." (The next day *The Boston Globe* would say that Jackson had been "mugged on the Sunday show.")

"Putting Bentsen on the ticket," he said, "is a public appeal or a deal for the conservative wing. It has a place, as we seek to broaden. But when you broaden in that direction, it must be balanced in the other direction."

That evening CBS threw a big cocktail party at the Ritz-Carlton in Atlanta with an ice sculpture centerpiece that spelled out C-B-S. The room was filled with reporters, pols, and Hollywood types. I dragged Aaron with me only to have some schmuck start waving his finger in his face about his interview with Sid Sheinberg, president of MCA, in *Manhattan, Inc.* Using what has been called his "aggressively silent" interviewing technique, Aaron had encouraged Sheinberg to insult just about every other studio executive in Hollywood, starting with Michael Eisner at Disney. The article that had caused a West Coast earthquake was now producing aftershocks in Atlanta.

The convention opened the next night. It was exciting to be on the floor when keynoter Ann Richards, the salty Texas state treasurer known for her '60s beehive and merciless wit, whooped out her taunting rebuke of "poor George" with the crowd gobbling it up like ribs and black-eyed peas — especially the women. But the Bushes would remember her speech with vengeance in their hearts. They would use it to justify their own vicious attacks on Dukakis. "Poor George" — she stretched out the words with a comic's timing and cadence — "he can't help it. He was born with a silver foot in his mouth!"

I was reliving Super Tuesday. I was one of the four floor correspondents, but I could barely get on the air. And the few times I did, Rather either repeated what I had said or corrected it. Dolly and Lou were both asking, "What's Rather got against you?" I felt flattened.

Still, I roamed the range, listening as the little-known governor of Arkansas, Bill Clinton, gave a numbingly endless nominating address and watching Jesse Jackson deftly change course. After threatening to disrupt the convention, he exhorted his supporters to find "common ground" with Dukakis. And on the final night Zorba the Clerk, as the Duke was being called, entered the hall like Rocky and delivered a surprisingly strong acceptance speech, after which Dan tossed it to me. "He told us he is not the cold, dry person we've been watching over these campaign months," I said. "He had emotion, he had heart, and I must tell you, Dan, I am surprised." There was no correction. I felt like Rocky myself.

THE NEXT SUNDAY, Lee Atwater complained on *Face* that the Democrats were obscuring the issues. "You'd think they were Republicans!" he said.

I repeated one of Bush's recent lines about how far apart Dukakis and Bentsen were ideologically and suggested that in 1980 you could have said the same of Reagan and Bush.

"I was very heavily involved in that campaign, Lesley, and there was hardly any disagreement between Bush and Reagan."

"Voodoo economics stands out in my mind for starters," I said.

"Well, that is the one gag line of that campaign."

"Also ERA."

"No, let's talk issues, let's talk issues. You can name two or three. On every basic issue, Dukakis and Bentsen are apart."

I always appreciated the "operatives" who loved the sport, and that was Lee. His biographer, John Brady, wrote in *Bad Boy* that Lee's drive came from "survivor's guilt." His three-year-old brother had been burned to death in a kitchen accident. Aaron, whose 21-year-old sister, Sharon, was killed by two drag racers, has written about survivor's guilt. He discovered a surprising number of writers and artists with brothers or sisters who had died young: van Gogh, Charlotte Brontë, Gustav Mahler, Ludwig van Beethoven, Jack Kerouac — the list goes on. Aaron says that mourning for a sibling is often expressed in an artistic surge. I guess Lee poured his creative surge into the dark arts.

HOWARD STRINGER was promoted to president of the Broadcast Group, meaning he was now running the CBS Television Network. His replacement at News was David Burke, 52, who had been lured away from ABC. I was delighted, not the least because my friends at ABC were bereft at the loss. As Roone Arledge's right-hand man, Burke had been their patron saint of hard news, the one who had shaped their News Division into a serious competitor and had stood up to their new bottom-line owners at Capital Cities. Did Larry Tisch know this?

In *Three Blind Mice* Ken Auletta wrote that David Burke had a convert's zeal about news. He had come into our business out of politics: three years as Ted Kennedy's chief of staff in the Senate and three more years as assistant to Governor Hugh Carey of New York. He reminded me of my friends in Boston with his rich Brookline accent and his love of politics. I was immediately comfortable with him, as I often am with shy, starched, formal men.

A MID-AUGUST CBS News/*New York Times* poll on the eve of the Republican Convention at the Superdome in New Orleans showed Dukakis ahead by 17 points. I set up shop in CBS's trailer city, where I stayed put since I didn't want to find out what that humidity would do to my hair.

Bush's choice of a running mate was the only point of interest at the convention. Was George Bush secure enough to choose Bob Dole? Would Dole be able to serve as a loyal number two, or would he snipe for four years?

My guest on the preconvention *Face* was George W. Bush, the vice president's eldest son, who was playing a central role in the campaign. "Can you name an issue that your father has cared consistently about," I asked, "that he fought for in the Reagan administration, that he stood up for, and that he would continue as president to stand up for?"

"Peace through strength," he answered.

"But that's a slogan," I said. What did George Bush stand for? Even for his son, it was hard to say.

The son said he found it "refreshing" when his dad made verbal gaffes. The veep misquoted, of all things, the Pledge of Allegiance ("And to the liberty for which it stands"). "He is not so programmed," said his son, "and so mechanical that he's got aides writing every little script line and that there is this rigidity about him." Had I heard correctly? Was that a strike at the Gipper? I wondered what the Bushes said about the Reagans around the dining table.

303

I asked who would be his father's running mate. "Lesley, I wish I could help you scoop this story again for your second straight consecutive convention. [Lovely touch. Maybe, I mused, he should think about going into politics himself!] I don't know. I bombarded Big Boy with all my suggestions."

"Big Boy?"

"Well, Dad, of course." He smiled.

I asked if Dan Quayle would be the one. He said I shouldn't forget Kemp, Dole, or Governor of California George Deukmejian. This was a chance for Candidate Bush to make every known Republican think he was being considered.

I GOT OFF to a much better start in New Orleans than I had in Atlanta, with Rather coming to me early in the evening: "The names are Kemp, Dole, Simpson, Domenici, Quayle. The list goes on and on. One of Bush's problems is there's no one candidate who gives him a guaranteed block of votes — no big state or clear constituency."

I'd been picking up the name Dan Quayle on the floor and offered an interview. "Stand by," I was told, which I did with Quayle at my side in the Indiana delegation for a good 20 minutes. When they finally threw it to me, I asked the inevitable: "Why do you want to be vice president?"

"The only way I'd want to be vice president," he said nervously, "is if George Bush wants me to be vice president, because it's so doggone important that he be elected the next president of the United States. If he thinks I can help him, so be it." This was a chance for Quayle to make a good impression. Bush's campaign team — Jim Baker, the new campaign manager; Lee Atwater, who had stayed on; and Roger Ailes — watched with disdain.

"They say you would help with the gender gap," I said.

"Well, there's no doubt about that," said Quayle. "In the end the polls and everything show that I have done very well. I do not have the so-called gender gap. Hopefully we'll be able to carry that over to the rest of the country. Who knows?"

I spent the next day in a CBS trailer with Diane Sawyer, both of us trying to crack the who's-the-veep secret. Yet even though we called everyone we'd ever known, we were beaten. NBC broke the news that Bush was choosing the young senator from Indiana.

I watched Bush's announcement on television in the trailer with several other CBS reporters, as Quayle leaped onto the podium in a fit of hyperactivity that made you want to shout "Get that boy some Ritalin!" He bounced around, flapped his arms, and crawled up Bush's back. "My God," someone in the trailer laughed, "he's humping the vice president!"

304

"Believe me," said the running-mate-to-be, "we will win because America cannot afford to lose!" He grabbed Bush's shoulder, startling the man, and went on, "Let's go get 'em!" Bush had a look of "What have I done?"

That night Rather opened our convention with the news of the Quayle choice, saying, "A thunderbolt has hit the Superdome, and the lightning has yet to subside." Then he tossed it right to me. I didn't know why, but things were definitely different. Behind me the Indiana delegates were cheering as I looked straight into the camera, trying to ignore them. "Why did Bush choose him? First off, Dan Quayle is conservative, someone to activate the right. Second, he's a proven vote getter with women. We don't know if that's because of his good looks, but it is a move to deal with the gender gap. Third, he's 41, so it's an appeal to young voters. Lastly, he's a midwesterner, and they're hoping he will appeal to farmers and blue-collar workers. But in our survey, Dan, we found only two delegates in this entire convention hall who listed Quayle as their first choice for vice president."

Later in the evening I found Senator Pete Domenici of New Mexico and put him on the spot: "There's a charge already from the Democrats," I said, "that [Quayle's] a lightweight."

"No, not at all." What did I expect him to say?

Then Bill Plante reported that even "some of the political pros inside the Bush campaign" were calling him a lightweight. Ed Rollins said that Quayle "gets you nothing: nothing in California, no blue-collar voters. You can't send a wealthy scratch golfer in to work the blue-collar neighborhoods." This was what NASA would have called a flawed launching.

I found Bush's son Neil. "I understand there was a family meeting a week ago to make a decision about the vice president," I said. "How many voted for Quayle?"

"One person," he answered. Those were Quayle's odds: 12-to-one.

By the third day of the convention Quayle was mired in reports that despite his enthusiastic support for the Vietnam War, he had avoided the draft by joining the National Guard. He made matters worse by explaining, "I did not know in 1969 that I would be in this room today, I'll confess." It began to seem that every time Quayle opened his mouth he made things worse. I reported that while some of the delegates were discussing dumping him, campaign operatives were arguing that it would be too damaging to Bush since this had been his first presidential decision.

Peggy Noonan proved she was the best speechwriter in the country. Bush's acceptance speech was a knockout: "Read my lips! No new taxes!" It was one of many memorable lines. Bush drew a graceful, self-deprecating self-portrait: "[I] hold my charisma in check." The best line was: "I may sometimes be a little awkward. . . . I am a quiet man. But I hear the quiet people others don't."

Bush also differentiated himself from Reagan: "We need a new harmony among the races. . . . I want a kinder, gentler nation." This did not stop him from bringing up Willie Horton.

THE NEXT DAY Quayle held his first news conference as candidate in his hometown of Huntington, Indiana. As the questions grew contentious — Why had he asked his parents to help him get into the National Guard? What executive experience did he have? — a crowd of supporters began booing the press. It came close to a mob scene.

On Sunday on *Face* I asked Craig Fuller, Bush's chief of staff, if the campaign had deliberately set the press up as "the villain in this whole Quayle controversy."

"Listen, this campaign is not going to set the press up." With a straight face.

"Why hold news conferences with the crowds applauding and booing and so forth? Is that something you intend to continue?"

"No, it's a false charge. Our people made an effort in Indiana to quiet the crowd down."

"You loved it, come on," I said.

After just two days on the campaign trail, the Bush campaign sent Dan Quayle back to Washington for coaching or, as some reporters called it, "vice president school."

DUKAKIS HAD BECOME COMPLACENT, gravely miscalculating the potency of Bush's message: that the Duke was a man who let murderers out of jail and wouldn't let little kids say the Pledge of Allegiance (Dukakis had vetoed a bill in Massachusetts that would have required teachers to lead the pledge in classrooms). Bush had achieved the usual convention "bounce" in the polls; then, with his message and Dukakis's failure to fight back, he kept on rising.

The 1988 campaign saw the most extensive use of horse-race polling ever. The candidates polled constantly, and the major newspapers and networks did as well. With the electorate as the object of scrutiny, the leaders would become the followers.

There was heated debate in journalistic circles about the pros and cons of reporting the polls. The argument against was that they can be a self-fulfilling prophecy. Declaring the election over before it's held tells people: Why bother to vote? The counterargument, as Ted Koppel once put it: "If there were no polls by the networks, we would go back to the sort of Stone Age days of politics when the only people who really did the polls were the two campaigns. And they would tell everyone, 'We're ahead,' and we'd have no way of checking."

Rather was against reporting the polls and had been making his views clear at CBS for months. I got caught in the middle when I was assigned to report on our September poll, which showed Bush up by eight points. I was in New York that day so I could "chat" with Dan about the numbers, live on the set.

The poll was not particularly complicated, so I was finished early and decided to visit Joan Richmond, a no-nonsense producer who had for years run our Special Events Unit. Now, as number two to David Burke, she was the highest-ranking woman in news at any of the networks. As we chewed over the campaign, she smashed out one cigarette after the next into an overflowing, plate-sized ashtray. We were talking about Dukakis when Rather poked his head in.

"Look, I was just leaving," I said getting up.

"No, please stay, Lesley," Dan said. "What I have to say involves you too." He sat down. "I've decided we're not going to report the poll tonight."

Joan took a long puff. "I think we have to discuss this with David," she said, explaining that Burke was over at Black Rock. "Dan," she implored, "let me try to reach him so we can talk this through."

Rather was pleasant but firm, reminding her that he was the managing editor.

Joan explained that this was a major decision, since "as you know, Dan," we spent a fortune on these polls with *The New York Times*. "I'm sure they'll have a big front-page story tomorrow."

Dan told Joan he was merely notifying her of his decision, not looking for an okay. Again agreeably, he said he had to get back to the fishbowl, and off he went.

The published lineup still listed "Stahl/Poll" as the lead, but I asked Tom Bettag, "Since you're dropping my piece, can I go home?" It was about an hour to air.

"Please don't," he said. "Just hang around. Be available." I found an empty office and waited till 6:25, when Bettag boomed out "Lesley, hurry. We need you on the set. You're the lead."

I slid into the chair next to Dan with one minute to go. As I collected myself, he stared at me. "I know exactly what you did."

"Five seconds to air!" boomed Jimmy Wall, the stage manager.

Dan melted into his warm "Good evening. Eight weeks before American voters choose a new president . . ." He read his lines about the poll, then turned to me: "Lesley?"

"Dan," I said, "in that poll Bush is maintaining the significant lead he captured over Dukakis after the Republican convention." The director rolled the tape with the rest of my piece about the poll, which showed that Bush's message about Dukakis being soft on defense and unpatriotic was registering. While it ran, Dan turned to me and said again, "I know what you did, and I don't appreciate it one bit."

"What did I do?"

"You know what you did." Our "chat" on camera was pretty short. "Almost a quarter in the poll say their preference could change, Dan."

"Lesley. We shall see." And he moved on.

I unhooked my mike and left for the airport, baffled. What *had* I done?

Dan would not return my calls, I couldn't get my story ideas approved, couldn't get an assignment. When I called Tom Bettag to find out what was wrong, he advised me to be patient: "This will pass." But what was "it"? He said he wasn't sure.

There was one advantage. With little to do, I would leave work early to watch Taylor scrimmage. She was playing football for a second year. My daughter, number 92, was left guard on the sixth-grade team. She wore shoulder pads and cleats, wiped streaks of greasepaint under her eyes, popped in a mouth guard, and, towering over many of the boys, ran out on the field and smashed and got smashed. Sure, I'm a feminist, but even I thought this was pushing things. Aaron, on the other hand, had encouraged her to go out for the only violent sport her Quaker school offered. Taylor and two other girls were among the biggest on the team. And besides, Aaron kept assuring me, kids in sixth grade can't do much damage to each other, but how did he know? Despite my misgivings, I supported Taylor. It was, after all, adventurous and trailblazing. It's an odd thing to admire an 11-year-old, but I did.

After her practice I would take her shopping or out for ice cream. It was in our car that I found out she wasn't crazy about her new teacher. "He's not teaching us." This was something I had not heard before. She had complained the year before, when Mrs. Levin had piled on too much work; now she was missing the challenge.

One of those afternoons I took Taylor shopping for a new dress. I was treading very gently on her tastes, especially when I found a little green taffeta number with puffy sleeves that would have been perfect except for the fact that she despised it. "Just try it," I begged, fighting with the automatic trigger in me that wanted to go off: "This is what we're buying, period!" It was hell to disarm. Well, Taylor tried it on, and we bought it. But it hung in her closet, undisturbed, till we gave it away five years later.

308   I was an outcast at work for a week. Then my phone rang while I was at home in the kitchen. It was Dan. "I owe you an apology," he said

explaining that the day of the poll he had thought I had gone over his head to David Burke. "Now I know it wasn't you."

"Dan, I would never do that," I said quietly.

It was over. The Stahl-Rather relationship was at the center of my world, every little slight — every big one — a debacle, a desolation. It was impossible to consider that he wasn't just as consumed by it. When I finally asked him years later whether he had resented me, disliked my work, found me irritating, he said he had no idea what I was talking about. "Look, Lesley, you have to realize that this was one of my most difficult periods. I was contending with what had happened in Miami and with the Bush interview — CBS stations had complained. I was trying to walk the line." In both cases Dan had seen his actions as championing the prerogatives of news: in one case protesting the encroachment of a sports event onto the sacredness of our territory; in the other doing what reporters are supposed to do, which is ask tough questions. But still, he had been taking a pounding from his critics.

The pressure and frustration were increased when the local CBS station in New York had moved the *Evening News* from 7 P.M. to 6:30. They put *Win, Lose or Draw* on at 7 — a game show, because it made more money than news. "When that happened," Dan would say, "I knew the tide had turned against news . . . the signal goes out to our affiliates that they too can move the news to any time they damn well please."[50] In some cities we were moved to 4:30 in the afternoon. Who's home at 4:30? "Death Valley," said Rather.

It wasn't that we did not know by then that there was a new ethic at CBS — that going for the buck was the first, second, and third priority. But with each hit of evidence, it hurt anew. And it hurt Dan the most.

But at the time, all I could do was fret about the deteriorating dynamic between Dan and me. I was easygoing, I knew that. I would just have to work on being more cooperative and on sharpening my delivery.

IT IS OFTEN the case in campaigns that one side gets all the breaks and then suddenly the tide turns, as if Poseidon were directing the flow. For whatever reason, the gods had turned against Dukakis. He couldn't do anything right.

To illustrate that he wasn't "squishy soft" on defense, the Duke put on a large green helmet, climbed into the turret, and drove around in an M-1 battle tank for the cameras. That Sunday in Jack Kent Cooke's box at the Redskins' game, Jim Baker could not contain his joy, telling Aaron that Dukakis in the tank was a gift from heaven: "He looks just like Snoopy!" The Bush campaign quickly produced ads making the Duke look like an idiot in that tank, while Bush himself issued the helpful hint "If the tank doesn't fit, he shouldn't wear it."

Why did the ride in the tank bomb while Bush's equally preposterous ride in New Hampshire in the 18-wheeler had succeeded? Our *Face* editor, Ed Danko, put together a rock video of the two candidates in their photo ops that said it all. In each picture of Bush, he was smiling and visibly enjoying himself; in every picture of Dukakis, he looked miserable. The expression on his face said: "Get me out of here." You could sense the voters asking: Do I want to look at that dour face for the next four years?

I WAS PRETTY SURE NOTHING momentous was going to happen in the debates. Both candidates were drilled and tutored on everything from how to smile to how to chop their hands for emphasis to dropping in scripted gag lines. Debates were just another carefully rehearsed made-for-TV show. (But then, what is the presidency, anyway?)

After lengthy negotiations between the two campaigns that resulted in a safe, tightly controlled format, the first Bush-Dukakis debate was held Sunday night, September 25, in Winston-Salem, North Carolina. Dukakis's handlers told him to avoid sounding arrogant and to reach out to the middle class with some specific proposals. "I think it's time that when you get a job in this country," he said, "it came with health insurance."

Bush's objective was to keep Dukakis cornered on the left. He quoted the Duke: " 'I am a card-carrying member of the ACLU.' That was what he said. He is out there on — out of the mainstream."

The Quayle-Bentsen debate in Omaha on October 5 was not nearly as predictable. It was held in the same hall where Randy "Macho Man" Savage and Andre the Giant had held their big wrestling match. As I said on the air, "It was not so much a debate as an oral exam for Dan Quayle on his qualifications. He had trouble answering what he would do if he became president."

QUAYLE: First, I'd — first, I'd say a prayer for myself and for the country that I'm about to lead.

He made you think we'd need it. The debate "moment" came when Quayle explained that he had "as much experience in the Congress as Jack Kennedy did when he sought the presidency."

"Senator," said Bentsen, smooth as calfskin, "I served with Jack Kennedy. I knew Jack Kennedy. Jack Kennedy was a friend of mine. Senator, you're no Jack Kennedy." I wonder if Andre the Giant had had as easy a time with "Macho Man." A CBS News poll showed Bentsen the winner, two-to-one.

I was with the spinners again. Jim Baker couldn't hide his opinion

310

of Quayle. "When you think about what might have happened," he said, "we have to be pretty happy."

Humiliated by the campaign "handlers," who described their job as "potty training" him, Quayle sent the Bush people who had been "schooling" him packing. From now on, he said, "There's not going to be any more handler stories because I'm the handler . . . I am Doctor Spin." Soon thereafter he met his match in Suzi Chong, an 11-year-old reporter with *Children's Express*. She asked if he would deny a young girl an abortion if she'd been raped by her father. (Why didn't I think of that question?) "My answer would be yes," said Quayle.

"So," said Suzi, bolder than I, "although you're not actually killing me, you would sacrifice my prospects for the future for that baby."

THE SECOND presidential debate in Los Angeles and the race were over after the first question. The moderator, Bernie Shaw of CNN, caused a stir in the pressroom where I was watching on television. His question was so sensationally raw, we all gasped. "Governor, if Kitty Dukakis were raped and murdered," Shaw asked, "would you favor an irrevocable death penalty for the killer?"

Ignoring the part about his wife being raped and murdered, Dukakis answered without a trace of emotion: "No, I don't, Bernard — and I think you know that I've opposed the death penalty during all of my life; I don't see any evidence that it's a deterrent. I think there are better and more effective ways to deal with violent crime." The answer fed the "ice man," he's-not-one-of-us image the Republicans had so carefully nourished. Bush acted more upset about the thought of Dukakis's wife being raped than Dukakis had. "I do believe," he said, "that some crimes are so heinous, so brutal, so outrageous, I do believe in the death penalty, and I think it is a deterrent."

The next day Lee Atwater told me that an important part of their debate strategy had been to "humanize" Bush. "We wanted him to appear more *real*." Bush was told not to look directly into the camera but to make eye contact with people in the audience, even wave at someone in the middle of an answer. "We told him to relate because it will make you more of a human person." Dukakis, looking straight into the camera, reinforced the image of ice-man coldness.

The Bush team had plotted it all out. Lee pointed out that the day before the debate "we sent [Bush] off to jog." "That night," he drawled, "you saw our man on the *Evening News* running in a sea of people, sweating, looking real and relating. And Michael Dukakis went out and threw a baseball. But you couldn't see who he was throwing it to. He was just one cold, lonely dude."

That night Rather was anchoring from a small studio in our Los

Angeles Bureau. The space was so tight, I had to climb over Dan and squeeze in next to him for our "chat." I started my piece live: "Dan, in politics as in poker, the winners tell jokes, the losers say 'deal.' Bush and his handlers are telling jokes; Dukakis and his handlers are emphasizing there are still 25 days before election day. . . . The Republican strategy last night was to humanize Bush, deprogram him."

Dan asked about the Bush humanizing efforts.

"[His people] told him not to look into the camera," I said. The minute I started, I knew I was heading into a pit. I was describing exactly what anchormen do, but I couldn't stop the slide. "You know, when you look directly into a camera, you are cold — ah, apparently — they have determined." It was one of those moments in life when you see the ax falling in slow motion.

"Bad news for anchormen, Lesley," said Dan.

"We have a lot to learn from this." I tried to keep from choking. "Michael Dukakis kept talking right into the camera, and according to the Bush people, that makes you look programmed, Dan." (Can you believe I said that?) "They're masters at television symbols and imagery. And according to our poll, it worked."

"Do you believe it?" Dan asked.

"Yeah, I think I do, actually."

"Thanks, Lesley."

I had to climb back over him to get out. And I had thought my poker analogy was so good.

My relationship with Dan was complicated. I respected him and had affection for him going back many years. Aaron, a fellow Texan, was crazy about Dan and his wife, Jean, as was I. We'd all been friends since Watergate and managed, somehow, to keep what was happening at work from leaching into our friendship. And now I had embarrassed him. This time it was my fault, clearly, and I felt terrible.

Two weeks after the debate our guest on *Face* was Kitty Dukakis. She had admitted a year before that she'd been addicted to diet pills for 26 years. Now she was "clean" and composed.

"Why did it take so long for Michael Dukakis to come out swinging?" I asked. "There's a rule in politics: you don't leave negative ads unanswered." Which the Dukakis campaign had done.

"He just . . . underestimated how vitriolic, how vicious, how negative those false attacks were," she said, clear-eyed and confident. "Michael's never been a candidate for national office before, and part of it is a learning experience."

"What about *your* gut?" I asked.

"My gut? I am a fighter, and my gut said I wanted Michael to respond to those false charges. They were so untrue." Viewers might have wondered: Why isn't *she* running?

"The man you've seen on television since Labor Day: is that the same man you know?"

"Sure it is," she smiled. "Michael's a first-generation American, and oftentimes they are brought up not to display their emotions in public."

"You're passionate," I said.

"But I'm a second-generation American, and that's different."

Two weeks later our guest was Barbara Bush. These interviews with the candidates' wives made you proud to be a woman in 1988. Poised, intelligent, strong, authentic, passionate, take-no-guff-from-anyone, proud yet gentle — both of them.

By early November, when I interviewed Mrs. Bush, Dukakis was at last sound biting and attacking, and he'd begun to climb in the polls. *"The Wall Street Journal* poll says it's tightened to just five points," I told Mrs. Bush — in blue. "Are you worried?"

"No. I'm really proud of George and the stability. . . . I don't feel confident, I don't feel tired, I don't feel discouraged; I feel great, just as you should feel just about now."

"You said stability. What did you mean?"

"I think George, for 14 or 15 months, has had an enormous amount of criticism, heckling, whatever, and he's been stable and strong. He's been the leader of our camp all along."

Mrs. Bush had brought along her daughter, Dorothy LeBlond, and her second son, Jeb. I turned to him: "Sixty-two percent think this has been a more negative campaign than ever before, and more people blame your father for it. Do you think if he wins this is going to hurt his ability to lead?"

"Well, first of all, my dad has a great ability to heal wounds. . . . We've been called racist, a liar, you know, every name — Hitler."

Dorothy jumped in: "Wimp. . . . What really hurts me is when my father is called a racist, a Hitler, silly, pathetic. These are words I've heard from the other side."

"At the Democratic convention," said Jeb, "[Jimmy Carter] called my father 'silly and effeminate.' And other people got up there, and the rowdier the comment about George Bush, the bigger the applause line."

In her book *Barbara Bush: A Memoir*, Mrs. Bush wrote, "I'm not sure Lesley knew what hit her." What hit me was the gush of the Bush family's hurt and bitterness. The currency of campaigning is brutal, and the "negativity" of 1988 was especially cruel. We want our candidates to be thick-skinned, show they can take a punch, that they're resilient. But who ever said their wives and children don't suffer?

Later I wrote to thank them for appearing and got back a handwritten note from Barbara Bush, dated November 30, 1988: "Doro, Jeb and I were honored to be on 'Face.' We were also very flattered. All through the campaign I kept wishing my Dad was alive. He wouldn't believe the whole thing! I know you are going to be surprised by George. He is all I say and much much more. Again, thanks for your letter. Warmly, Barbara Bush."

BUSH'S REVOLVING-DOOR or turnstile TV spot graphically criticizing Dukakis's prisoner furlough program was becoming a cause célèbre. A CBS News/*New York Times* poll showed that it had the biggest impact of any ad in the campaign, effective because it was symbolic of the larger case Bush was trying to make about Dukakis: that he was a capital-L Liberal. But the ad had racial overtones and, as I reported, it was inaccurate.

I grilled Jim Baker, the campaign manager, about the ad on *Face* ten days before the election. "While the announcer says Dukakis let first-degree murderers out," I said, "the screen says '268 escaped,' clearly suggesting that 268 first-degree murderers escaped. In truth, only four *murderers* escaped. Two hundred sixty-eight is the number of all prisoners. Why have you not corrected that?"

"It is off the air," said Baker, "but I don't admit it's incorrect."

"You don't admit that saying 268 escaped while the announcers say 'murderers' is misleading?"

"I do not admit that this is misleading. No ad is run that is not checked by legal and by the research people for accuracy with respect to the facts."

"I'll tell you something," I said. "As a television reporter, if I say something and put some words up on the screen that conflict, that's inaccurate."

"Well, we make our judgments with respect to that," he said coldly, "and you can make yours. . . . We think it's very appropriate because it speaks to values and judgment."

Baker left the studio angry.

I WENT to Cotton Plant, Arkansas, to see why Dukakis was faring so poorly in the South even though the economy had suffered in the Reagan years. Bill Clinton was one of the few southern governors sticking his chin out for Dukakis. A big, friendly St. Bernard of a man, Clinton was eager to talk politics with me and my producer. But I thought that if this was Dukakis's most ardent supporter in the South, he didn't stand a chance. I asked Clinton to explain Dukakis's problem. "It's the way people perceive his value system," he said. "People won't vote for an alien. It'd be

314

like asking them to vote for somebody from another country for president."

I made it back to Washington for Halloween. Aaron rented a huge van so he could take Taylor and six friends to Georgetown for the annual parade. All the girls were dressed as fairy princesses. All except Taylor. She was a refrigerator.

THE RACE NARROWED in many of the large states (New York, New Jersey, Ohio, Illinois), but the CBS News/*New York Times* poll a few days before the election gave Bush an overall eight-point lead. In the final days, both candidates went on exhausting cross-country trips with the same strategy: attack, attack, attack. Bush kept Quayle off the air and out of his ads. One Democrat told me, "If Bush wins, it's because Willie Horton is better known to the American people than Dan Quayle."

The consensus among the Democrats was summed up by Bob Slagle, chairman of the Texas Democratic Party: "Dukakis made a mistake in trying to fight by Marquis of Queensberry rules when the other guy kept hitting below the belt for ten straight rounds." But Bush had done far more than just beat Dukakis in the attack department; he bested him in every aspect of the television game. The Bush people had figured out that to get "free media," that is, exposure on the evening news, they had to master the nine-second sound bite. We were packing so much into each story, the candidates really did get little more than staccato message bursts on the air. But rather than sit around moaning that "this is no way to cover an election," the Bush people had mastered it. They worked at sharpening and polishing the candidate's lines, donating a pithy zinger we couldn't resist: "Dukakis favors furloughs for murderers." *Bam!* And it was only three seconds.

Forget the issues. It was all slogans. And they did everything to make sure we used the sound bite they wanted us to (the message of the day). Nothing was left to the unpredictability of a news conference. They didn't hold them. It wasn't until the Dukakis people finally caught on that their candidate began to pull up in the race: "We're on your side." "He's riding on easy street, we want to improve life on Main Street." They had finally gotten the Bush-is-elitist message into short bursts — but too late.

It wasn't just the sound bites. The Bush people had reduced their campaign to a language of symbols. When Bush went to a flag factory and said "The Pledge of Allegiance," everyone knew he meant "Dukakis isn't patriotic." When he said, "prison furloughs," everyone knew he meant "Dukakis is soft on crime." As Larry Sabato, professor of political science at the University of Virginia, said on *Face*, "The Pledge of Allegiance, the furlough issue, the ACLU — all of these symbolic issues say that Dukakis is out of the mainstream. That he is liberal, doesn't share our values. . . . They fuse together: the symbols, the flag, the images, the words. It all fits together." And symbols can't be analyzed, torn apart, questioned by reporters.

We knew the Bush campaign was staging their events as commercials that we ran for free. We discussed simply not airing the "message of the day." But our election producer, Brian Healy, said that that would be arrogant, that we did have a responsibility to tell people what the candidates were saying, even if it was mush. If it was inaccurate or distorted, we had to say it was, but to stop reporting what they were saying would have been tantamount to censorship.

CBS NEWS PRESIDENT David Burke called. "We'd like you to cover the transition," he said. He wanted me to return to a beat, the incoming president. It was well known that I was unhappy with my ill-defined role as national affairs correspondent.

There was only one hesitation: "David, what does Dan think of this? I'm not sure he'd go for it."

"Dan's on board," he said.

A few days later I got a note from Dan: "Lesley. Just to pass along a welcome and so that you'll know how glad we all are that you're here. Dan."

ON THE MORNING of November 8, 1988, I went with a group from CBS to the Degas exhibit at the Metropolitan Museum of Art in New York. There's not much to do on election day until the exit polls start coming in. Then we start getting calls from the campaigns asking for data.

Rather was at his best that night in every way — as Tom Shales wrote, "fielding correspondents, interviewees and the flood of data with finesse" — and doing what he could to build drama when there really wasn't any. From the start, our map quickly filled in with blotches of Bush red, soon a huge swath across the South. "George Bush is sweeping the South like a tornedo through a trailer park," said Dan. In Florida, "where the flamingos fly, George Bush has taken off." In Georgia, Bush went through Dukakis's hopes "like a jackknife through peaches." He was on.

Bob Schieffer, up in the drum to Dan's left, was in charge of the Republicans; Bruce Morton, to his right, reported on the Democrats; and I sat directly opposite Dan, reporting on the governors and the House of Representatives. Because of Dan's welcome, I was more relaxed, telling about the Socialist elected to the House from Vermont, the first woman ever reelected to a third term as governor, and Evan Bayh, a Democrat, winning as governor of Dan Quayle's home state of Indiana. Man, was I crisp!

We called it for Bush at 9:17. Then what to do? Dan turned to me and asked why Bush had won. "Because he defined Dukakis. The big word wasn't the L-word, liberal, it was the W-word, weakness. George Bush had the label himself in the beginning, but he cast it off and transferred it to Dukakis, who became weak on crime, weak on defense, weak on patriotism." Bush had performed a miraculous political resurrection. He had altered perceptions of himself by realizing that in the age of television, politics is Kabuki, a theatre of visual illusions.

At one point in the evening Dan announced that I would be covering the transition and asked what Bush's Cabinet would look like. "It'll be more Nixonian than Reaganesque," I reported, "with centrists and pragmatists rather than ideologues." Jim Baker to State, Richard Thornburgh as attorney general, Nicholas Brady at Treasury, John Tower to the Pentagon. I predicted he would name one or two Democrats (I was wrong there). Dan asked about a black. "More likely an Hispanic," I said. My final contribution: "Dan, barbecue and pork rinds are in. The country will be run by an oligarchy of Texans: Bush, Baker, Jim Wright."

Bush had beaten Dukakis by a 54-to-46-percent margin. Voter turnout was just 50 percent, the lowest in more than 60 years.

WAS THIS THE END of the Reagan era? Or would the Bush administration be a continuation, the third Reagan term? It was *the* question during the transition.

One thing was for sure, these were two very different animals, Bush and Reagan. I began to reflect, as everyone did, on the Gipper. What an enigmatic force. He had managed to change the agenda, alter the American conversation — what we wanted, what we thought our goals were. He demonstrated that government could work (even as he bashed it and sought to dismantle it). What confounded me and many other Reagan watchers was that he did what he did as a man prone to delusion. He continually presented a false self. As Steven Weisman of *The New York Times* said, "He wasn't a cowboy, he wasn't a war hero, he wasn't a family man. Reagan was a mysterious combination of fakery and authenticity."

He was a rare politician who sailed by a fixed star and never called for sacrifice.[51] Political writer Richard Reeves called it Reagan's "stubborn integrity." "He risked his presidency for his most unpopular beliefs," says Reeves, "staying the economic course in 1982 and refusing to yield to demands for a nuclear freeze."

Reagan had three main accomplishments. One was as a truly gifted negotiator. He took pride in this, and with justification. He stood down the unions, and he stood down the Soviets.

The second was the unleashing of a new force of entrepreneurship in the country. But it is not clear that Reagan and his deregulation policies were as responsible for this as the mugging American corporations received in the 1970s, which spurred them to retool and downsize in the 1980s — a painful process we at the TV networks were hardly immune to.

With all the positive economic news, Reagan did not lift our standard of living, except for the trickle up to the already wealthy. During his time in office there was a shocking increase in female poverty: 13 million women living in poverty, the vast majority of them white and the sole supporters of their children.

The third was that Reagan lifted our spirits, no small attainment for a leader, even if he did so by painting a mythic picture of 1980s America as shining and triumphant. In the real America, despite his "family values" rhetoric, there was more greed, more sex and violence in our movies and on TV, more AIDS, more divorce, and an increase in the number of single-parent families.

Reagan made us feel good about ourselves, even as his hot-button rhetoric seemed to invite religious hatreds (he ignited the religious right) and racial intolerance. As Garry Wills said in *The New York Times Magazine*, "His amiable being — the sheer niceness and normality of the man . . . seem to immunize him from the poisonous implications of some of his own opinions."[52]

You cannot look back on the Reagan years and not wonder if the president had Alzheimer's even then. We will never know for sure. There are those who were close to him who like to say, "Oh, he was always like that, even when he was governor of California: unprepared, bored in briefings, ignorant of the substance of the issues." But others who were also close say that there was a marked difference, especially in the last two years. They talk about his little vacations from the scene when he would be there, yet not be there. They were concerned, and yet Reagan always seemed to recover. I had seen it in the Oval Office with Aaron and Taylor that day in 1986. White House officials tell me they saw the same glazed-over, spaced-out Reagan that we saw many times. If he was pulling these disappearing acts, who was making the decisions? On what was he basing the decisions he did make?

I had come *that* close to reporting that Reagan was senile. I had had every intention of telling the American people what I had observed in the Oval Office. But then I wondered: What *had* I seen? I recently asked gerontologist Dr. Robert Butler at Mount Sinai Hospital in New York about Alzheimer's. There are two chief forms of dementia, he told me. One is classical Alzheimer's, where there is a steady destruction of the brain cells. The other kind is episodic, involving small, repeated strokes and circulatory changes, which he described as "a heart attack in the brain." With this vascular kind, he said, "you see breakthroughs of in-

318

sights, intervals of lucidity." On average, he said, it's a nine-year disease, but it can go much faster, or last 18 years.

When I asked if he thought Reagan had had either kind when he was president, Dr. Butler said he couldn't make a diagnosis because he had never examined him, but that in truth, no one could make a real diagnosis of Alzheimer's until after death.

"What about the early symptoms of Alzheimer's?" I asked.

"It comes in stages. One could go back and forth in a shuttling, episodic slide. It might start with confusion about money, paying the bills, fumbling with change. They can't calculate the right amount. A president doesn't have to do that."

He went on: "In the beginning, there are lapses in attention span, in the formulating of speech: in language and concepts." But, I thought, Reagan was rewriting his speeches with clarity and color throughout this time.

"With dementia, people retain the earlier memories better. Maybe that's why he kept telling the jokes and the anecdotes. That's what he remembered." Was that what the harping on the Hollywood stories was all about?

"He didn't hold many news conferences," I noted, "but it's hard to believe he could pull off even one if he had it, and let's not forget that second debate with Mondale. He came roaring back."

"The disease has its ragged edges," said Dr. Butler. "You can pump it out—neurotransmitters—particularly for an actor with repeated re-hearsals. Patients with it," he said, "maintain a social facade. There are those who are brilliant in disguising it, even to those around them. Judg-ment," he explained, "is one of the last things to go."

Then he told about a new finding: that dementia may be triggered by major surgery in people over 70. He told me of recent studies showing that anesthesia has a profound effect on the elderly and that coronary bypass surgery can produce "severe neurological complications, including deterioration of memory, concentration or other intellectual functions similar to Alzheimer's disease." Dr. Butler said that after Reagan had been shot, he had had chest surgery that could have — he stressed again, he had never examined him — but could have had a major, permanent effect.

"By the way," said Dr. Butler, "the support system makes a big difference."

"Reagan had a very protective wife," I pointed out.

"Yes." He smiled.

Did Nancy suspect? Did she know and help him disguise it? Were there any parallels with Edith and Woodrow Wilson? I asked historian Doris Kearns Goodwin, who said she felt there was a stronger connection with FDR. Starting in 1944, after he was diagnosed with congestive heart failure, she said, "Roosevelt would occasionally blank out, his eyes would assume a glassy look, his mouth would droop, and he'd forget what he was talking about. People around him knew something was wrong, but then he'd bounce right back." Even though Roosevelt's doctors said he was in excellent condition, the rumors about his health were rife. Two senators, old friends of his, insisted on seeing him, to check. The first one came out of the Oval Office declaring that the president was funny, charming, alert, just like old times. There was nothing to worry about. The second senator went in a minute later, and Roosevelt had no idea who he was.

The people around FDR, said Goodwin, closed their eyes to his lack of focus and lapses in lucidity. They put more store in his rebounds because they had a vested interest in his surviving. Was this also true of Reagan's aides?

"Was he senile?" I asked one of his chief advisers.

"Maybe there were symptoms," he conceded, "though I say that in hindsight. He would come to life for the cameras. He was on/off, on/off."

When I told him about our meeting with Reagan in the Oval Office, he smiled. "I saw that come-to-life phenomenon many times. His eyes would brighten, blood would rush to his cheeks in a nanosecond." But then he said, "Look, my first meeting with him: he fell asleep, and that was before he was shot."

I asked Peggy Noonan, who admitted that even though she had been his favorite speechwriter, she had rarely seen him. "He was a distracted man, shy, never surly. He could always ignite the engines."

"Alzheimer's?" I asked.

"People with Alzheimer's don't take down the Soviet Union."

Jim Rentschler of his NSC staff told me emphatically, "Reagan wasn't out of it. The stereotype that he was just a man with a script was total bull. He had a steely inner core with three to four concepts that he would bounce his feelings and sentimentality off." He said he was sure Reagan did not have Alzheimer's. "No. At Cabinet meetings when he'd get that dull look in his eye, I always thought it was a sign of mental health. Great mental hygiene."

Another former aide said, "Reagan was selectively engaged. When he didn't care, he'd float. At Cabinet meetings, he'd check out. But when he cared, he'd get deeply in."

"When you heard he had Alzheimer's, what did you think?"

"That explains a lot," he said. "He tuned out — a lot."

"Did anyone back then ever say, 'This just isn't right'?"

"People didn't talk about it," he said. "People treated him with very special care. You had to explain things in elemental terms, but because he was so likable, everyone had so much personal regard for him—everyone protected him."

"Didn't you whisper around the water cooler that the president was zoned out? And that the public had a right to know?"

"No. He was treated with a reverence because of his personal qualities, especially after he was shot. The shooting transformed him . . . inside and outside the White House. We all became very solicitous. He was intellectually vacant, but I never felt the country was in any danger."

The people who had been close to him late in his second term, in 1988, suggested that there had been more symptoms. One told me that his eyelids had seemed incapable of staying open in any meeting after lunch. Another left the impression that he had worried every day about whether Reagan grasped what was going on. His staff never knew whether they were going to confront a with-it or out-of-it man when they entered the Oval Office.

"Did you ever think about the 25th Amendment?" I asked an official who saw him regularly in 1988. "Did you ever think you had a duty to question his mental health and viability?"

"Well, you could never be 100 percent sure about him, because he always recovered. He always came to life."

"Didn't you ever discuss it—what was obviously clear to many of you?"

"No. You have to understand, we all loved him."

Whatever was going on—Alzheimer's or something else—Reagan held on to his good common sense ("Judgment is the last to go") and was able to "break through" when he really had to. I'm convinced that Nancy Reagan suspected something and many on the staff did as well, and they chose to protect him and keep silent. The president's doctor, Burton Lee, was quoted in USA Today on November 29, 1996, as saying that late in his second term, "it was noticeable that there was something wrong there, but we figured it was just the natural aging process. Nancy was going to protect him and she did. She kept him further and further out of the flow." I now believe they covered up his condition; and many continued to as they wrote their memoirs.

But then the public knew something wasn't right. There were all sorts of signs. We all looked the other way.

When Reagan had a competent and steady staff, things ran smoothly, if not always brilliantly. And a great deal of the credit for that goes to Nancy Reagan, who, I suspect, did far more than we'll ever know to hold him, the White House, and by extension the country together. We'll never know exactly what Mrs. Reagan did, because she has chosen, as always, to protect her husband's image, which I think she will to the end. But I am quite certain we owe her considerable thanks.

PART FIVE

GEORGE AND BARBARA BUSH

Sign on wall of Michael Boskin of President George Bush's Council of Economic Advisers:

> To be is to do: *Descartes*
> To do is to be: *Sartre*
> Do be do be do: *Sinatra!!*

It was a coup getting an interview with the vice president-elect. Dan Quayle had been under wraps since the election, recovering from the mauling he had endured during the campaign. He liked to blame alternately his handlers and the reporters, none of whom, he must have noticed, had made him say that the Holocaust had been "an obscene period in our nation's history" or "The real question for 1988 is whether we're going to go forward to tomorrow or past to the — to the back!" Senator John Kerry of Massachusetts joked, "The Secret Service is under orders that if Bush is shot to shoot Quayle."[1]

It was mid-January but warm enough to walk over to Quayle's office in Lafayette Square. My producers, Janet Leissner and Brian Healy, and I mapped out a line of questioning along the way: I would concentrate on foreign policy since that's what I had pitched to his staff, but I would have to ask about his lack of experience and what appeared to be the president-elect's eagerness to pretend his running mate didn't exist.

Quayle comported himself well in the interview. There was no blaze of genius, but except for his irritating use of the third-person "Dan Quayle," he was boggle- and botch-free, even when I got personal: "Do you concede there is a public perception that you are not prepared to be president?"

"No, I do not concede that. I am prepared," he said. "I've proven people wrong in the past; and . . . I'm gonna prove a lot of people wrong in the future."

Sitting there knee to knee with him, I saw no trace of the trademark stare of terror that had so often betrayed him during the campaign. His press secretary, David Beckwith, a former *Time* reporter and friend, didn't hide his relief. If the veep-to-be could get through a televised interview without a single mulligan, all would be well. I'm not going to lie about it: we on our side were bereft. I was supposedly shooting fish in a barrel — and I had missed. How could we tell the *Evening News* that Quayle had been so disciplined that there was not a shred of news, not a single flub?

Back at the bureau, as I wrote a script, Janet screened the videotape, and pretty soon I heard laughter from her edit room: "Lesley, this is great stuff!" "What do you mean you got nothing?" My colleagues were patting me on the back.

There it was, filling the screen: the very stare I had not seen in person, the Quayle freeze of fear. Somehow the camera had reached behind his mask, yanked out his insecurities, and magnified them. His lack of confidence was so evident on the TV screen that it changed the sense of what he was saying.

The camera has an emotional life of its own. It adored Ronald Reagan and John F. Kennedy. It shuddered at Bob Dole and Dan Quayle. Quayle's real enemy was the camera lens.

DAVID BURKE summoned me to New York. "It's no secret you've been unhappy as national affairs correspondent," he told me starchily. That was hardly something I could deny. And yet when he said, "We'd like you to go back to the White House," I thought: Curse the day. I saw all the possibilities of misery and defeat.

"Why would I?" I asked, arguing limply. I was not his first choice. A friend told me, "David had his heart set on a blonde at the White House: Diane. But when he asked her to leave *60 Minutes*, she was insulted." The friend also confided that Dan Rather was against my going back.

"Not true," Burke said. "Not true. He has complained that you aren't always responsive to his questions on the air, but he's on board." Burke said he wanted to showcase me and would be my patron saint.

Soon my reluctance gave way to a stronger sense of salvation. I had not found the formula to life without a news beat. Once I acquiesced, Burke told me excitedly of his plans for Bush's Inauguration. "We'll be on the air all day. I want you to shine. I want you to be a big presence for us."

I thought of Jim Brooks's advice about abandoning the old detached style and insinuating myself into my stories. This was Sam Donaldson's contribution to White House reportage: his booming questions were often as much a part of the story as the answer or nonanswer. Sam was the costar.

We had traveled from "Don't smile" to "Get into the story." But how to be more *in* the story without being *part* of the story? Where is the tipping point? Do you end up covering yourself? I went back to my old beat without knowing the answers.

BY INAUGURATION DAY, I had studied more than I had for final exams in college. Bush's record, Barbara's background, the new Cabinet, the five living kids, the ten grandkids, and Poppy's brothers, Bucky, Pressy, and Jonathan. I was out on the lawn in my Klondike coat and boots.

For my first appearance at 9 A.M., I had to tell Dan's producers what

I planned to say. I wanted to mention that Bush was the first president since Kennedy to go to the White House from another house in Washington: "He's just moving in from around the corner instead of across the country." Moreover, he was a known commodity: "We'll be deprived of that phase of discovery as when we learned that JFK was a speed reader or that Jimmy Carter's aides scurried to get married because of the boss's born-again righteousness."

As I waited to go on, Bush's affable press secretary, Marlin Fitzwater, came trotting out of the White House. "Lesley, a little welcome-back scoop," he said with a chuckle. I had known Marlin for years. He had been in Reagan's press office as number two to Larry Speakes. I liked him a lot, especially when he was overcome with blushing. Poor man, he would turn the colors of rouge pots, soft peach to burnt ginger.

The "scoop" was a charming little story about Bush coming into the White House early to wheel his chair from behind his desk in the vice president's office himself, through the corridors of the West Wing and into the Oval Office. Not a stop-the-presses bell ringer but fresh and fun. So when Dan tossed me a question about how Bush wasn't moving here from out of state, I said, "Dan, first let me tell you what Marlin Fitzwater just passed on." As I would discover, this was not "responsive" to Dan's question and definitely not appreciated. Which resulted in my being frozen on the White House lawn in a state of perpetual standby. They were always coming to me next, but they never actually came. Not all morning. And only once in the afternoon when I snared the president's son Neil for an interview.

This was not a good beginning.

MONDAY, JANUARY 23, 1989. It was Mary the nanny's day off, so I had to get Tay ready for school, including pulling her hair back into a ponytail, which produced a meet-the-day domestic donnybrook—just what I needed on my first official day back at the White House. We had crimped her hair the night before, so everything was thick and wavy and painfully hard to squeeze into the ponytail holder.

I had butterflies. My new partner, Wyatt Andrews, fresh from a tour as our bureau chief in Moscow, beat me in for Bush's first day. So did Bush. As I said in my piece, "Reagan moseyed in at 9:15; Bush got in at 7:20. By 8:20 he'd had breakfast with Quayle, a CIA briefing, a meeting with his top aides, and he'd sworn in his White House staff. He's wearing us out." And he was just getting started.

STAHL: In his first statement to the public on his first working day, President Bush sounded a lot like Ronald Reagan, not the moderate he's tried to be since the election. Speaking by telephone over loud-

speakers, Mr. Bush gave antiabortion demonstrators an emotional message of support.

BUSH: I think . . . *Roe versus Wade* was wrong and should be overturned.
I promise you that the president hears you now and stands with you in
a cause that must be won.

This surprised me because during his transition, I had thought that
George Bush was unveiling his true self, finally coming home to the
moderate, northeastern WASP his daddy had raised him to be. Everywhere I had looked I had seen signs of it and its corollary: that deep down
he was the *un*-Reagan. Bush's grandchildren were everywhere; Reagan
hadn't even known his. It had seemed to me that the nouveau, self-made,
blare-it-from-the-monuments wealth of the Nancy-Ronnie era got a private "yuck" from the subdued 63-year-old Yankee Barbara Bush. Why else
would she so proudly confess that *her* pearls were fakes, worn to cover up
the wrinkles in her neck? "My mail tells me a lot of fat, white-haired,
wrinkled ladies are tickled pink [with me]," she said.[2]

Bush had dropped all the campaigning business about liking pork
rinds and country music and had come out of his preppy closet, revealing
his sprawling mansion in Kennebunkport, Maine, with all its chintz and
Cigarette boats and other accoutrements of the WASP life style. And his
ratings had gone up. As Alessandra Stanley wrote in *The New Republic*,
"Now the pendulum has swung away from the Hollywood . . . make-
believe glamour. . . . After eight years America yearned for better breed-
ing."[3]

But Bush held a 45-minute news conference and remembered our
names, unlike Reagan. He answered two-part questions without having to
use five-by-nine-inch index cards. Instead of lopin' along with the tum-
blin' tumbleweed like Reagan, this man sprang and darted and flitted and
arced across the television screen. No inner calm here! But somehow it
made him likable, if not lovable.

Bush was sending conflicting signals: a strong antiabortion statement
one day, announcement of a centrist Cabinet the next. His new national
security adviser, Brent Scowcroft, was a protégé of Henry Kissinger, Luci-
fer himself to the Right since détente. If ever there was a signal that Bush
was siding with the pragmatists over the ideologues, this was it. When he
announced Scowcroft, he made a point of saying in his clipped Bushspeak, "Keep me informed." A reporter asked, "Postmidnight, does he
wake you up?" "Wake me, shake me, and wake me," Bush replied. Trans-
lation: I'm not Reagan.

I was seated on Scowcroft's left at a dinner party. Margaret Tutwiler,
the new spokesperson at the State Department, was on his right. Someone
at the table said, "History will find that Ronald Reagan was the worst

president we've ever had. He neglected our problems: drugs, the home-less, our bridges are falling down."

"He was much worse in foreign policy," Scowcroft replied, causing Margaret to exhale several perplexed wheezes. But he went on, "We'll be damned lucky if we pull ourselves out of the mess he created for us in Europe. He gave up the weapons we need and kept the ones we don't."

History would prove that Scowcroft was mistaken, but at the moment Margaret's eyes were bulging. "I'm sorry," she sputtered. "I believe in loyalty, and I worked for him."

Those who believed that Bush would continue along Reagan's con-servative pathway pointed as evidence to his choice of the devoutly con-servative John Sununu as his chief of staff. But I had thought Sununu was more a statement of Bush's independence from his pal Jim Baker. Baker had strongly objected to the former governor of New Hampshire.

If Bush's actions were unclear at first, I chalked it up to the loss of identity any vice president would experience after eight years of "cooper-ating."[4] I believed that he intended to undo the excesses of Reaganology, even though he had been there at the Crusade and had brought back many of his fellow Crusaders to help him unravel what they had wrought. More than half his Cabinet members were recycled from the Reagan years: Richard Darman, the new budget director, and Jim Baker, the new secretary of state, to name two. One analyst said, "There are more retreads here than in Akron, Ohio!" But most of them were pragmatists.

One who wasn't a retread was John Tower, nominated for secretary of defense, a mistake that would consume Bush's first 40 days in office. Tower, strutting about in Turnbull and Asser–like splendor, was shorter than most of Taylor's girlfriends. Sharp-tongued and prickly, he was not well liked by his former colleagues on the Senate Armed Services Com-mittee, where he had served for 19 years, "a time," as I reported, "when defense spending soared from $48 billion to $220 billion a year." In that time he had managed to accumulate a squadron of detractors, who ea-gerly leaked one story after the next about his personal misconduct. He told me himself on *Face* on Christmas Day 1989, "I discovered, much to my dismay, that not everybody loves me."

In fact, Tower had built up such ill will that there were few in Washington who came to his defense when stories about his drinking, womanizing, and coziness with defense contractors began to surface. "Just to clear the air," I said, "there are apparently charges of drinking. Do you drink?"

"Only in moderation," he said. He had come on specifically to answer these questions. "I'm only a wine drinker. I don't drink spirits."

"There are a lot of charges of womanizing," I pressed on, embar-rassed. I actually had a sense of foreboding, as if I were walking down an unsafe street, cheapening myself by discussing the tawdriness of his life. I could feel it happening, the toppling of another barrier to bad taste on television.

"I was faithful to my second wife."

"You do have a reputation — not that reputations are always correct — of being a ladies' man."

"Well, Lesley, I traveled all the way to the Soviet Union with you. Did I behave as a gentleman?"

He'd gotten me. "You did indeed; you led a delegation, and it went swimmingly well, that's true."

Bush made it clear he was going to stick by Tower no matter what, having learned from the campaign, when he had refused to jettison Quayle and watched his wimp image recede.

I was at my White House post on February 7, working the phones, concentrating on the Hill, a nest of Tower's enemies. I found a press secretary who told me in a conspiratorial whisper, "I hear Sam Nunn [chairman of the Senate Armed Services Committee] is, as we speak, at the White House in a secret meeting with the president."

"Why's he here?" I asked.

"To tell Bush he's against the Tower nomination. If Nunn votes against the guy, he's probably dead. And Lesley, you didn't hear any of this from this office." A story! A terrific story. I felt like Ernest Hemingway finding the Greater Kudu.

I reached a source in Nunn's office who refused to confirm the story but danced around enough to convince me it was true. I called the office: "Rome, I think we've got a big one for tonight." Rome Hartman, a grown-up version of Christopher Robin, was the new White House producer. He had come aboard when Zee had been promoted to senior producer in charge of the *Evening News* in Washington. I'd thought there could never be anyone as organized or efficient as Zee, but here was Rome, 34 and a magician. He could do everything all at once at high speed.

I started writing a script as Rome dispatched a camera crew to see if we could get a picture of Nunn's car leaving the White House, which we had to do without arousing the curiosity of the other networks. For the same reason, I wandered nonchalantly, without any hint of urgency, up to Fitzwater's office. But I was waylaid when Wyatt, who thought we spoiled Taylor, came running after me: "Your daughter's on the phone."

School was just out, and Taylor, in sixth grade now, wanted to throw a party. "You know how you're going to have my room painted? Can I have my friends over to paint it some wild color before the real painters come?"

"We'll discuss this tonight." This was curious: my mother's voice coming out of my mouth.

I started writing my script and was interrupted again when Dolly called, just to chat. From grade school, Dolly had tried to instill in me the hard lessons she had learned, one of which was: you can't trust anyone. But especially you can't trust other women. So, naturally, trust became my motto, the core of my rules to live by. While I found myself abiding by my mother's wishes in so many other ways, there was always this one big rebellion: I not only trusted people in general, I especially trusted other women.

I eased my mother off the phone, and Taylor called again. "I'm on deadline, honey," I told her, straining to sound patient.

"But, Mom, if you say yes, then I can start inviting kids. Mom, I want to have boys too."

"Boys? How many?"

"Six, eight, whatever you say. Please say yes. *Please.*"

"Well, how much of a mess are you going to make?"

"We'll clean it all up."

I looked at my watch. It was late, and I hadn't yet reached anyone from the White House. "I surrender. You can have your party."

I finished the script, recorded the middle section, and — Taylor. "Can it be from one in the afternoon to ten at night?" "Yes." Anything you want.

Then on my way to Marlin's again, in the corridor outside the Cabinet Room, I bumped into John Sununu. Who better to ask than the chief of staff? "Governor, I'm told Senator Nunn was here today informing the president he's now against the Tower nomination."

"Not true. Where do you get these stories, Lesley?" He was playful.

"Are you denying that Nunn was here?" I was in my don't-be-cute-with-me mode. "You're telling me he did not warn the president that he's opposed and that Bush should consider withdrawing Tower's name?"

"It's not what happened. You got a bum steer."

I raced back to the booth and called my original source: "Sununu says it's not true."

"Well, I'm telling you it is true. All of it. Nunn told Bush he'll vote no on Tower and urged Bush to dump the guy. Call Sam yourself."

Taylor called again. My rule about always taking her calls no matter what was facing a mighty test. But I have this theory that working mothers are afraid of their kids. I took the call and found myself talking to her best friend, Lauren. "I'm the only one brave enough to ask," Lauren said. "You know Tay's painting party? Can boys sleep over too?"

"No!"

Lauren passed the phone to Zoe, who begged.

"No. No means no means no!"

I put in a call to Sam Nunn's office and told his press secretary what Sununu had said. "I'll get the senator to call you back," he said. It was 6:20; I had to get out to the lawn. I was the lead. Cameraman Al Bargamian set up a phone outside, so I got in position and waited with a nervous pounding for Nunn to call me back. With just two minutes to air (was I living some movie?), the phone rang: "This is Sam Nunn."

"Thank God," I said.

"Lesley, Sununu was not exactly telling you the truth." And he gave me the story himself.

STAHL: Dan, Senator Nunn expressed his misgivings personally to President Bush today in a secret Oval Office meeting. The sources say Nunn's concerns include those new allegations of drinking but are not limited to them. And there are signs that other Democrats on the committee share Nunn's concerns.

No wonder I had come to a stage where I doubted almost everything White House officials said. While I had rarely encountered such outright, unnuanced untruthfulness as Sununu's, I had grown to be wary of what officials told me on the record. There was some general assumption that "off the record" was where truth lived, and therefore "on the record" was the opposite.

The irony was that I had become the great *un*truster. After all my resolutions, after my big Dolly defiance, even in this I was ending up being just what my mother wanted me to be.

AS THE SHOWDOWN VOTE in the Senate approached, Old Iron Pants, as his old Senate colleagues called Tower, appeared on *Face* for a second time on March 5, 1989, in a last-ditch effort to save his nomination. Taylor came with me. It was the first time she watched the show from the control room.

Tower was tense as we sat in the studio listening to excerpts from the bitter Senate debate, with flying charges of conflicts of interest, wenching, and alcohol.

SENATOR HOLLINGS: It says in the FBI reports . . . these are the words: crocked, bombed, sloshed, stoned, comatose. Too much of that.

I leaned forward, "It must hurt."

332   "No!" Tower snapped. Then he paused. "Oh, well, it isn't pleasant hearing those things said about you, but I'm tough and I can take it."

I was more disquieted, I thought, than he was. He quibbled over the term "alcohol abuse," saying he was not "alcohol dependent" nor "do I have chronic alcoholism. I only drink wine," and he repeated his pledge not to drink again.

"You told *The Washington Post* you're still drinking."

"I still have a sip of wine now and then," he said. "Once confirmed, I'll give it up altogether."

"Why don't you stop now as an act of good faith?"

"Why should I?" he growled twice. "Why should I?"

"Because of the appearance," I answered.

"Look," he purred, "it's so little that it doesn't really matter."

This was sticky stuff. It got stickier when I brought up his congressional testimony about breaking a promise he'd made his second wife to stop drinking. His answer was so personal, I was mortified. "I could make the case that my second wife broke some undertakings to me. And actually the primary reason for our breakup was a matter of incompatibility — her attitude toward my children, for example — "

This was unbearable. I cut him off, all but begging him to desist: "I'm not trying to ask about your personal relationship with your wife."

Charles Paul Freund would write in *The Washington Post* two days later that this was all a tactic carefully calculated by Tower to give the press more intimacy than we could stand. It was "the rhetorical equivalent of what the Russians did to Napoleon: They retreated and waited for winter," wrote Freund, who added that my cutting Tower off was "the first sign of snow." If it was a tactic, it didn't work. Tower was more like Napoleon, trapped by his own devices. The next day Marlin Fitzwater said, "John Tower is the only man who's ever made Lesley Stahl look like a sympathetic character."

Tower went down to defeat on March 9, when the Senate voted against him, 53–47. Bush quickly nominated Dick Cheney, longtime congressman from Wyoming and former White House chief of staff for President Ford. He sailed through Congress, where he was respected and liked.

A few weeks later Taylor had the painting party. She and her friends were throwing buckets of color against the walls, with each toss layering and darkening till the shade was a putrid deep khaki. The kids all had dark green-brown linings along their fingernails and in the corners of their eyes. Oily paint was oozing and squishing, and everyone's hair was coated with an ugly glop. And they were all bellowing at top volume. What could possibly be more fun . . . more uninhibited and disgusting? But all I could think was: What will their mothers say if it doesn't come out? "Everyone," I drill-sergeanted, "into the showers."

333

The paint washed off. And boys slept over.

□

DIANE SAWYER announced that she was leaving *60 Minutes* and going to ABC News, a devastating blow to CBS. We thought the hemorrhaging had been staunched. Now this.

Within a few days I was asked to record 20 TV spots called "Presidential Minutes" to air in prime time. They replaced the ones Diane had recorded. I was the OB—the other blonde.

IF JIMMY CARTER'S FRAME OF REFERENCE was the small town and Ronald Reagan's the big screen, George Bush's was the locker room. This president saw the world not in terms of issues or even values but in terms of personal relationships. What counted was comradeship and loyalty. He had stuck with Tower not from conviction but because of this code. You rarely if ever saw him do that with an idea or a principle. No windmill tilting for this president, though he did have a political signpost that read: don't rile up the Right.

Bush was tested after a bloody massacre of children in a schoolyard in Stockton, California. A gunman sprayed them with a legally imported, Chinese-made semiautomatic AK-47, killing five and wounding 30. When he watched my report, Aaron was so appalled by Bush's continued opposition to a ban on these military assault weapons that he began harping and lecturing me on how immoral and unconscionable this "ersatz Texan" was.

My usually reticent husband began complaining about Bush at a dinner party thrown by Jodie Allen, the editor of *The Washington Post's* Sunday Outlook section. "He doesn't stand for anything," said Aaron. "He makes Reagan look better and better." Everyone at the party was criticizing Bush, including Senator Al Gore, who was drawing pictures of greenhouse gases on a napkin.

IN THE FALL of 1989 Aaron started coaching Taylor's basketball team, part of the Montgomery County girls' league. He had never coached before, so he studied videotapes and talked to his dad, Clyde, almost every night, sketching out plays on yellow legal pads that his father had taught his players when he'd coached Texas high school basketball in the 1940s, 1950s, and 1960s.

I've always wanted Aaron to write a movie about his team, an interracial power machine. In addition to Taylor, there was Makay Woods, the fastest, and Kyra Taylor-Grossman, a gifted athlete with an impala's spring and a Magic Johnson dribble. The tallest was Theresa Ann, who played with the same doggedness as her father, the former New York Knicks star Senator Bill Bradley. But the soul of the team was Jillian Cutler, who had cerebral palsy. Here was a child who, after 11 operations, ran up and down the court, albeit in a stiff, jerky gallop. I sat next to her father at the first game and saw him weep.

Bill Bradley came to every game and never intruded except the one time the referee didn't show and Bill, much to Theresa's embarrassment, was called upon to substitute. Then there was the father with the Abe Lincoln beard who hollered in plays and other annoying instructions from the bleachers.

Aaron never missed a practice or a game no matter how blue, how down, how despairing he was. Despite all the public service announcements on television and all the articles in magazines about the telltale signs of clinical depression, I didn't recognize them in my own husband. He was in the grip of the disease, but I was either too busy, too self-absorbed, or too irritated with him to put it all together. But you could go down the list of symptoms for depression and check off one after the next for Aaron. He was sleeping away most days, locking himself in the den. How many times I called from the White House booth and he wouldn't answer the phone. A cold fear would take me: "Is he all right? Is he — is he alive?"

"Aaron, please see a doctor. You need a shrink."

"I don't need one. I'm fine." He was dead set against psychiatry. All that hokum. I felt helpless, afraid, and at the same time furious at him. So many times he'd agreed to come with me to a party like the one at the Chinese Embassy. He wouldn't tell me until we were 30 minutes late, "I'm not going. I just can't. They only want you anyway."

I commuted back and forth between "This misery of his is all my fault, I'm suffocating him" and "How can he do this to me?"

I HAD VOLUNTEERED in mid-March to give a group of eight Sidwell students a tour of the White House pressroom. To my surprise, Bruce Zanka, one of Fitzwater's assistants in the press office, took us out to the South Lawn to watch the president leave for a speech across town. Before I knew it, POTUS was heading our way. "Hey, guys." That's the way this POTUS talked. "I used to jog on your track over at Sidwell." He was loose and lanky. "So, what are you doin' here?"

"We're studying broadcast news!"

"Well, you've found the right person to explain that with Lesley." I grinned. "I wish I could stay and chat some more with you guys, but I'm late for my speech." And he was gone. How Asimov was that? Like an extraterrestrial landing and takeoff. We rubbed our eyes: Had that really happened? I explained to the kids, "No one ever gets to see the president like that. Not even me." How would I explain to Aaron how hard it was not to like George Bush? The public felt the same way. He had a 70 percent approval rating. 335

I did a piece on Bush's first 100 days, asking: Why is he so popular? "Anyone can be," said Congressman Bill Gray, chairman of the House Budget Committee, "if they don't make tough decisions that call for sacrifice." John Sununu explained it this way: "It's because he's the guy next door. If they had a problem, he's the kind of next-door neighbor they would go to to try and get it solved."

"The problem is," said conservative operative David Keene on *Face*, "once you convince folks that you're just like their next-door neighbor, they look across the fence and say, 'You know, that fellow couldn't solve the problem, and I'm not sure the president can either.'"

But Bush's friendliness, his over-the-fence regular guyness was, indeed, what the White House was selling. And the fact that he was nothing like Ronald Reagan. Television had been Reagan's best friend. Bush treated it like an unwelcome relative — except when it came to televised news conferences, where Bush showed off his un-Reaganesque ability to get through them without making mistakes. He met more often with the press in his first 100 days than Reagan had in his last two years. He held both full-fledged news conferences and less formal, impromptu sessions. Plus he called reporters on the phone, asked them to jog with him and have lunch with him. He was so accessible that Tom Meyer of the *San Francisco Chronicle* drew a cartoon of Bush in my bedroom pointing at me as if at a news conference: "Miss Stahl?" In bed in curlers, I say, "I know it's crazy, but I almost miss the days when he was less accessible. . . ." Still, most of this access was reserved for print reporters. Tom DeFrank at *Newsweek* told me, "He calls you guys in TV land 'breathless wonders.'"

I was in the pool for one of Bush's impromptu get-togethers on April 20. Nine of us were arrayed in a semicircle around him on lawn chairs and ottomans, on the patio outside the Oval Office. He was so reluctant about television, I had to beg him to wear a lavaliere microphone: "Sir, couldn't we please clip a mike onto your tie? We're outside, and the sound won't be good."

"Maybe I want it that way!" he said.

We *were* breathless, each of us fighting to get off our own question — just as in the big news conferences. Except it was fun being that close, knee to knee. Bush wanted to assess his first 100 days in office. Responding to recent press coverage, he said in essence, "I have too done things!" I kept thinking: He's good-looking, and he's not saying anything.

This White House had a plan to shift the emphasis from network coverage, away from the Reagan obsession with camera angles. No longer would timetables be adjusted to network deadlines. It went beyond that. They acted as if television didn't matter. Bush went on a trip to eight cities in three days. Neither he (nor I) got a single moment of airtime. The Reagan people would have been upset; the Bushies sloughed it off.

Columnist Gerald Seib remarked in *The Wall Street Journal* that television reporters who had complained about "the cynical, manipulative Reagan presidency" were now complaining about the "unpackaged Bush presidency." I'm guilty. I was astonished at how sloppily Bush's events were thrown together and how many opportunities the president lost to promote his antidrug or his literacy messages just because cameras weren't in good positions or one couldn't hear what was said. In the pressroom we debated whether Bush had real contempt for television news or whether he felt he wasn't articulate, so he didn't want to come out and play. Whichever, he couldn't avoid us.

An explosion in a gun turret on the battleship *Iowa* had resulted in one of the country's worst peacetime military tragedies. Forty-two had been killed.[5] Bush attended the memorial service at the Norfolk, Virginia, Naval Air Station on April 24, 1989. I started my piece with music.

> STAHL: President Bush, for the first time our leader in mourning. . . . There were prayers for Eric Casey and Gary Fisk, for Jose Luis Martinez and Otis Moses and Tung Thanh Adams.

The president said later that the Bush family was not very good at this sort of thing and confessed that he had asked President Reagan, "How do you do it?" But Bush was wrong; he, rough around the edges, and Mrs. Bush had done very well.

DOLLY CALLED the White House booth, worried because my brother, Jeff, was home sick with no voice. "He won't go see the doctor." He had had a small malignant tumor removed from his left vocal cord in 1985. Now every time he got a cold, we all panicked.

At four o'clock we were escorted out to the South Lawn to see the First Family helicopter off to Camp David. Bush came bounding, leaping, flapping out of the Oval Office, running awkwardly like a spruce goose across the grass.

I was working on a piece about how the Bush administration was unfocused. Bush had said he lacked "the vision thing"; what he seemed now to lack was the passion to *do* things. I was beginning to think I had erred in thinking he wanted to undo the Reagan agenda.

A few days later Bush held an unexpected news conference at 11 in the morning. As we waited, I chatted with Rather on the air, standing on a camera box in the front of the pressroom. John Cochran of NBC, ABC's Brit Hume, and CNN's Charles Bierbauer were doing the same. One of the print reporters yelled out, "They look like Mount Rushmore!" I was telling Dan what to expect. Unbeknownst to me, the president was behind me, making faces into the camera.

He had come armed with documents to refute my piece: "We are not adrift. There is not malaise!" He went on, "I would simply resist the clamor that nothing seems to be bubbling around, that nothing is happening. A lot is happening — not all of it good, but a lot is happening."

That night I noted Bush's habit of commenting on the state of his inner calmness. "I still feel relaxed," he had said, insisting that his negative reviews hadn't rattled him. A few weeks back he had told Helen Thomas and me, "I'm calmer now than I used to be," which he said in a tone of "isn't this a miracle?"[6] Why was this man always checking on his level of composure? One got the feeling he was fearful of how he would act when the stress level went way up. I wondered about that myself when Bush gave an interview to CBS Sports about golf. "I can't putt," he said, "and because I know I can't, I clutch every time . . . making it even worse."

IF BUSH CLUTCHED, his anchor was nearby. Barbara Bush was strong. I once told one of their friends the story about Nancy Reagan's tile man and the red dress. "I'll bet George told Barbara to just swallow it," I said.

"Oh, no," said the friend. "Barbara's tough. Much tougher than George. He hasn't told her to swallow it or do anything else in 20 years!"

I was pleased to be one of eight reporters (four TV and four print) whom Barbara Bush invited to lunch at the end of April. No cameras were allowed, but it was on the record. Mrs. Bush wore a white dress with black polka dots and puffy sleeves. Very stylish. She had lost close to twenty-five pounds and looked beautiful.

We were up on the second floor of the living quarters in a charming private dining room that Jackie Kennedy had decorated with wallpaper depicting Revolutionary War battles and bluish green curtains draped back with a flowing valance and fringed tassles. Over artichokes stuffed with salmon mousse, Mrs. Bush revealed that George often called her from the Oval Office just to say hi. She could see into the Oval Office from the Truman Balcony, where she would occasionally poke out to wave to him. The historian Gil Troy says that most First Family marriages improve in the White House.[7] No wonder: first ladies get to keep their eyes on their men — at last! (Though it obviously didn't work that way for Hillary Rodham Clinton.)

As Mrs. Bush described their early-morning strolls together around the South Lawn, a glow came over her and a girlish grin crept up. One of the print reporters, a young woman, asked exactly what I was thinking: "Mrs. Bush, are you finding that the White House is a romantic place?"

The mood broke. Barbara flashed her eyes. "That's a dumb question. If you'd been in Washington for the last eight years, you'd know that

338

George and I have always been close." This was the side of the first lady the public never saw. The young reporter was humiliated.

I jumped in to spell my colleague. "I kind of like that question," I said, smiling to take the edge off.

"You would," snapped the first lady. She was frosty, and I felt the sting.

The first 100 days? we asked. "George doesn't react," she answered, "he acts. He's the most stable, the most sensible person I know." I found her barometric readings of his moods as curious as his.

Veal scaloppine with Hungarian spaetzle. The food was great. Dessert: honey ice cream on cake piled with strawberries and whipped cream. "At night, in bed, the pillow talk?" brave Jim Mickleshevsky of NBC asked. "Do you discuss abortion?" Barbara Bush had let it be known that she tilted prochoice.

"None of your business." She glowered at Jim.

She was most impressive when she talked about parenting. Working moms shouldn't come home "too tired," she said. I felt a pang. "People are going to have to reevaluate their lives a little and put their children first." Mrs. Bush complained that parents weren't monitoring what their kids were watching on television. "Just saying, 'Shut up and go watch TV' is not good enough."

Then she took us on a tour of the living quarters. In eight years of covering that place, I had never had such a day. She walked us through Reagan's old workout room, now transformed into a grandchild's bedroom. We got a history lesson in the Lincoln Bedroom, where old Abe had signed the Emancipation Proclamation. Teddy Roosevelt's huge hand-carved bed, with its arched headboard, makes the room seem like a chapel. President Bush set up his own office right there, as FDR had done. George's toy soldiers decorated the mantelpiece, and in the corner was a big toy chest for the grandchildren.

I called Joe Peyronnin, now a vice president in New York — David Burke's number two — and proposed a prime-time special: Mrs. Bush's Tour of the White House with Lesley Stahl. Joe told me to check with Marlin Fitzwater.

I went immediately, but on the way — smack, there he was, right in front of me: POTUS. By the Rose Garden, heading home. "It's you!" I said, astonished to see the president alone except for his Secret Service escorts.

"Lesley!" he said, just as surprised to see me. It was providence, I thought, and I decided to put the request directly to him. He said that Barbara had also enjoyed lunch. "No, really, she did," as if neither one of them believed it.

"The tour was such a treat. Don't you think the American people should go on it?" I asked. "Wouldn't Mrs. Bush like to show everyone the Lincoln Bedroom?"

The president seemed interested. "Why don't you call Barbara?" he suggested, offering to put in a good word.

I tried asking about this issue and that, but he wouldn't bite. "I don't know anything," he said. "You know much more than I do." And off he went along the colonnade.

Peyronnin said the network would not give up an hour for a tour of the White House but that it might be incorporated into a *48 Hours* show. So that's what I proposed to the White House. A Barbara Bush/Lesley Stahl tour as part of a CBS News hour.

There was a hitch: Dan Rather anchored *48 Hours.* A few days later, when I asked Marlin if there was any response to my request, he said, "Never if it involves Rather. You and Kuralt — we'd consider it. But never Rather."

Dan had told me he was convinced that Bush and Company were out to destroy him, that they were going after him; investigating him in his hometown and elsewhere, looking for dirt.

MY REAL LIFE was stretched with stress. Aaron wasn't answering the phone. I was often frantic. Tay got braces. "Honey, wear your headgear" was our nightly sign-off. "What's French kissing?" she asked one night. A few days later a boy called Taylor but didn't leave his name. Her face lit up, and off she raced to her room for a full round of giggly who-could-it-have-been calls to her friends.

I turned to Aaron. I could see the pain in his glassy eyes. "I want to sleep for the rest of my life," he moaned.

"You could learn from Taylor," I said.

"I know. When she's out of gear," he said, "just riding along in neutral, she's happy."

"And you?" I asked.

"I'm unhappy."

"And me?"

"You're never out of gear."

EARLY MAY: Marlin was meeting with his staff and I was staking him out when — again: there was Bush. Right next to me: Mr. President. "What about Panama?" I asked. Manuel Noriega was being accused of fraud and manipulation in the recent elections. "What are you going to do, sir? I have to say *something* tonight. Don't make me say you're being cautious."

"Won't be rushed," he said. What about military force? I told him I knew he'd just met with Secretary of Defense Cheney and CIA Director

Bill Webster. We had exclusive pictures of them arriving at the White House. You cannot imagine how worked up we get over pictures of the comings and goings of cars.

"Cautious," he said. And off he went.

Bush had put his best friend, Jim Baker, at the State Department, signaling that his major interest would be foreign affairs. And his goal would be preserving the status quo. This produced a cautious—as Bush often called it, "prudent"—foreign policy, in the Kissinger balance-of-power mold. It meant that the administration was slow to accept change, as when Gorbachev agreed to stop shipping arms to Nicaragua. Instead of welcoming the overture, Fitzwater called Gorbachev a "drugstore cowboy" and questioned his credibility: "We're very leery of their intentions. We see a very strong pattern of public relations gambits." Sununu's aide Ed Rogers told me, "Gorby's trying to make Bush follow. For those who want him to be 'hip, trendy, and boutiquish,' he won't. He doesn't want to react."

I had recently gone to a conference where politicians from Western Europe were expressing trust in Gorbachev, a feeling that "the threat is gone," and a deep resentment toward Bush. They seemed to believe Bush had a vested interest in keeping the Cold War going.

I wrote a piece for the *Evening News* on May 24, asking why Bush was so unlike the Gorbachev-trusting Reagan, and ran a string of sound bites as evidence of the administration's wary approach.

> BAKER: We think it's important to look for deeds rather than just words.
> SCOWCROFT: I don't think we ought to oversell what's happening.
> BUSH: We're looking for reality versus rhetoric.
> STAHL: When détente crumbled in the 1970s, Mr. Bush and his top advisers, then working for Gerald Ford, felt a personal sense of betrayal. Richard Cheney was Ford's chief of staff; Brent Scowcroft, his national security adviser; James Baker, his campaign manager; and George Bush, his CIA director.

The next day, I spoke to a high-level official in the State Department on background. "You got it wrong last night," he said. "The lesson they learned from the Ford years was less about détente than about politics. They were mauled by the right wing over détente, and the deeper, indelible lesson was: never let anyone stand to your right." He said that Baker and Bush had learned this not in Ford's 1976 campaign but in Bush's own 1980 campaign, when Reagan had clobbered him; for Scowcroft it had also been 1980, when he had watched Kissinger's career go down the tubes for the same reason. That's how Bush had won the presidency. Atwater had told him, "Don't let any candidate get to your right." It had worked, and now they were applying the same standard to foreign policy.

Another official in the administration added this assessment: "The key problem is that Jim Baker didn't play chess. If ever there was a need for chess players, it's now." Israel was battling the Palestinian *intifada*, the Chinese were battering students in Tiananmen Square, and Gorbachev was trying to manage the collapse of the Soviet empire. All of this, all at once. And Bush was dealing with it like the Dutch boy and the dike.

I wondered if, beyond his fears of the Right, Bush's need to keep checking on his own inner calm had something to do with his wariness. Was he projecting some personal fear of chaos to the world outside? Go slow, don't trip off the very turmoil I'm guarding against within. What so many in the West saw as an exciting, global explosion of democracy, he saw as a breakup of the old order, the end of stability.

DAN RATHER was the only anchorman who went to Beijing to cover Gorbachev's state visit in mid-May. While Rather was there, the students went on a hunger strike in Tiananmen Square to protest the lack of freedoms, and workers began to join them. The government reacted by imposing martial law, and Rather was the right man in the right place.

I was in Kennebunkport with the president, where we got pictures of Mrs. Bush lambasting him because the Secret Service had torn up her garden in order to build a helipad.

I was getting ready for a "chat" with Dan on *48 Hours*, which he was anchoring from Beijing. My producer, Rome Hartman, had picked a pretty spot outside near the ocean, but it was freezing. "Look," I pointed out in a what-are-you-doing-to-me tone, "I'll be shivering, my eyes will water, my nose will dribble. Doesn't indoors make more sense?"

When Dan came to me, I was — outside. I said the White House was relieved it was Gorbachev and not Bush who had been in China when the student protests started. "How could the leader of the Free World not have endorsed the cries for liberty?" I asked rhetorically. "How could he *not* have walked among the hunger strikers? Yet it would have been an excruciating decision for George Bush, Deng's old friend." My nose dribbled.

Bush wasn't saying a word about the student protest or the government's order to fire on the protesters in Tiananmen Square if they didn't leave. What the White House did say was "Things are in a state of flux; we're waiting to see what happens." That Sunday I interviewed Democratic Senator Christopher Dodd on *Face*: "How deeply we are moved as Americans when we watch a model, a six-foot replica of the Statue of Liberty," he said. "I would like to think the president might be able to express views that only a president can, expessing the feelings of the American public that would reach those students in China . . . that

342

we really care and what you're doing is something we profoundly agree with."

But Bush would not.

LEE ATWATER and I had lunch together fairly regularly. Bush had chosen him to be chairman of the Republican Party, and now the "ambassador of negativity" and I were having sandwiches at the Monocle on Capitol Hill. There was something intense and strange about Lee that day. He was wild-eyed, explaining how he was in charge and how much Bush relied on him.

"We've just completed a series of focus groups," he was telling me. They had divided the baby boomers into every conceivable subgroup: by income, education, region, even age. They were trying to see what, if anything, unified this huge bulge in the population. "Nothin'. They have absolutely nothin' in common with each other, except for one thing. Lesley, the only thing that ties these folks together is that they hate phoniness on television." He called it the "baloney aversion." "Look, bull permeates everything. People see it in the double-talk, they see it everywhere, across the board." He mentioned politics, religion, and everything on television: commercials, sitcoms, and the news.

"Start watching," he said. "You'll start seeing ads with more 'real' people. No more big announcer voices. And shows like *Roseanne* will be more popular than shows like *Cosby*, 'cause she's authentic. Real life."

He said he had told Bush, " 'Just be real and they'll love you.' I told him, I said, 'Goofy, clumsy, that's okay. They'll believe that. Bad syntax, don't worry about it.' " Bad syntax was Bush's middle name. Timothy Noah of *The Wall Street Journal* compared his lack of pronouns and mixed metaphors to call waiting: "Bush is always putting one half-finished thought on hold to take up the next one." "Please don't ask me to do that which I've just said I'm not going to do, because you're burning up time; the meter is running through the sand on you, and I am now filibustering." Not to mention the malapropisms. During the campaign he spoke of having "sex" with Reagan (he meant "success") and of liking the "Star Banner Spangled." He had all the signs of dyslexia, which is probably why he preferred meetings and phone calls to memos and white papers.

Atwater stared at me: "There's something in here for you too. You gotta be more real. Less hair spray. Loosen up. Move around. Those stiff, static shots — they won't buy it." Echoes of Jim Brooks.

"How am I going to be loosey-goosey telling the public about arms control proposals and student protests in China?"

"Find a way," Lee said. "Find a way."

343

□

AFTER MONTHS of criticism over his reticence in foreign policy, George Bush suprised the world. At the end of May he went to a NATO meeting in Brussels and proposed a major reduction in U.S. and Soviet conventional force levels in Europe. Until then it was Gorbachev who'd been enchanting European public opinion with a series of disarmament offers. Now the headlines were announcing, "Bush unifies NATO." There was a swagger in the Bush camp.

Standing in a pretty little square in Bonn with a yellow post office behind us, Dan asked me if Bush's new position was a flip-flop. "Up to now George Bush has seemed to be fighting the end of the Cold War," I said. "What he did in this initiative was acknowledge that those days are over. The era of dismantling is upon us. He went beyond just recognizing that. He told the Europeans he wanted to lead in this new era, and that's just what they wanted to hear from him."

Many of the CBS people on the trip, including Dan, were strung out. They had not had a rest since China, but we all plunged on. The next day, the press pool choppered to Mainz, West Germany, in a marine CH-46 helicopter, many of us dozing along the sides on canvas benches with military-style seat belts and earplugs. The door was open, admitting a cold, hard wind.

In Mainz, Bush challenged Gorbachev to tear down the Berlin Wall. "That wall stands as a monument to the failure of communism. It must come down — now. . . . Let Europe be whole and free." In my script that night I called George Bush "the conqueror."

When I interviewed John Sununu the next day in London at the American Embassy, he came bounding in like a little boy who had just pitched a no-hitter at Little League: "Loved you last night. George the conqueror. Good stuff."

"Has Bush put Gorbachev on the defensive?" I asked.

"The shoe is on the other foot," he said. "Print it."

When we got home, we learned that our correspondent in Los Angeles, Terry Drinkwater, had died. He had suffered from the same kind of larynx cancer as my brother, Jeff.

WE WERE no sooner home in early June than the Chinese army began its assault on the prodemocracy student protesters in Tiananmen Square. CBS News owned this story. Because Rather had been there, we had swarms of reporters and producers in place. This allowed us to run new footage on *Face* of China's People's Liberation Army opening fire on the people in the square, shooting with automatic rifles, beating, and crushing hundreds of students and others who had been peacefully demonstrating.

344

Our guest was Senator Jesse Helms of North Carolina, who spoke for the right wing, which so intimidated Bush: "Lesley, we need to stand with these young people who are trying to achieve freedom."

"The Bush administration says they don't want to undermine 17 years of diplomacy just because of one weekend," I said.

"This is the trouble: make a deal, get along. You just can't make a deal with a Communist government anywhere in the world. Every time we've tried it, we've been taken to the cleaners — and so has freedom."

For the next several days, we at the White House watched the horror of Tiananmen on television. But wherever there was a TV on in an official's office, it was tuned not to CBS, ABC, or NBC but to CNN. This was when I realized that I was no longer top dog as I had been through the Carter and Reagan years, when the clocks, as I used to say, were set to Cronkite and then Rather time. With Bush's fixation on foreign affairs, this White House paid heed to what the other world leaders watched. There was no deadline; now we had the round-the-clock CNN vigil. When I wanted to speak to an official, I found myself in line after the CNN correspondents. If Bush wanted to send a message, he wanted it to resonate globally. This was disconcerting for those of us with only a national reach. My power as a network correspondent at the White House was wasting away.

BUSH HELD a prime-time news conference on June 8 in the middle of the Tiananmen crackdown. He was torn between the need to condemn the violence and, as he kept repeating, the importance of "preserving the relationship" with China. I asked how it was possible to retain normalcy when the Chinese leadership had ordered the killings. He ducked: "The question is so hypothetical." When I pressed, he admitted it would be difficult to do so but stressed again that maintaining ties was the goal.

I raced to the lawn. Rather said, "He seems to be straddling the fence."

"That's not my impression," I said, contradicting Dan.

"Are you saying he doesn't care about what's happening to the students?"

"No, the president said he deplores the violence against them, but above everything he wants to find a way to keep the ties." Then I worried. Maybe I should have agreed that he was straddling the fence. That's what the wires were saying.

The next morning Fitzwater knocked me out of my socks. "You made a valiant effort with Dan last night," he said. "He was so unfair to Bush. He tried to paint the president as someone who didn't care about the students. You tried, Lesley."

Of course, that is not at all what had happened. Quite the reverse. But as I was wondering if they blamed Dan for everything I said, Marlin pulled out a newspaper article on how CBS had been four times more negative about Bush than ABC or NBC, with some examples of my work. Running down the side margin was a note from Bush to Marlin on how disappointed he was to read this. "We like Leslie [sic] Stahl. Rather's another story." He had written that he had expected Rather to go after him, "but that Leslie has is a surprise. What happened to that pussy?" Once again, Bush must have meant pussycat—or did he?

The White House may have been glued to CNN, but our coverage was excellent. On Sunday, June 11, correspondent Bob Simon said on *Face*, "If Vietnam was the first televised war, this is turning into the first televised reign of terror."

When the Chinese executed the first three demonstrators, there was no comment from George Bush.

"GEORGEUM BUSHUM!" That's what the crowds at the Lenin Shipyard in Gdańsk were shouting. Poland in July; my first visit to the country my grandparents had come from.

Here, as with China, Bush would demonstrate his don't-tip-the-apple-cart approach to world affairs. I chatted with Rather every night, analyzing the day's events. What I focused on was the president's legitimizing of General Wojciech Jaruzelski, the strong-arm Communist leader. Bush seemed to go out of his way to praise this man, who had imposed martial law and locked up the Solidarity leadership. Inexplicably, Bush called him "a reformer," a "man of courage."

Because I was traveling in the presidential bubble, I hardly saw the two cities we visited, Warsaw and Gdańsk. After one and a half days with little sleep and no sightseeing at all, we flew on to Budapest, where my dad had taken me in 1973 on one of his business trips. Then the buildings had still been pockmarked with bullet holes from the 1956 uprising. The pockmarks were gone now, and the stores were filled with consumer goods. The Hungarians were much better off than the Poles. I attributed that to their history of entrepreneurship before the Communists had taken over. The Poles (with help from their friendly neighborhood Germans) had killed off their tradesmen, the Jews, in the 1940s.

Here again, Bush advertised his willingness to work with the reform Communists. What appealed to him was the slow, gradual pace of reform, and if that meant endorsing the Communist Party, so be it. He bought into Kissinger's theory that the division of Europe was a positive stabilizing force.

346   There has been, of course, a long history of U.S. presidents supporting antidemocratic regimes in the name of stability: Batista in Cuba,

Somoza in Nicaragua, Pinochet, Marcos, Saddam Hussein. In many of those cases, the goal had been to prevent a Communist takeover. Now here was Bush seeming to prop up the very system we had fought so long to defeat.

CBS had hired László, a young Hungarian student who spoke perfect English, to help us with logistics. I pulled him aside and asked how he thought Bush was playing with his countrymen. "Oh, they love Boosh."

"But he's sucking up to the Communists," I said. "The people don't like that, do they?"

He explained that it was not communism per se that the Hungarian people objected to, it was the Russians. "We all hate the Russians." He said that when he was growing up, taking Russian had been mandatory in all the schools. "But no one learned it. No one in my country, after 12 years of study, can speak a word of Russian!" We both laughed. "Except for me," he said. "I speak fluent Russian. I learned it."

"How come?" I asked.

"Because my father told me not to." There really is a universal human nature.

That next Sunday on *Face*, I put it to Brent Scowcroft: "This is a new policy, accepting the Communists despite their past actions. I mean, the tiger and his spots. They're still Communists. . . . Why are we endorsing them?"

"Because what the president is trying to do now is encourage them on the reform path . . . not to accelerate the process, not to get out of control and cause a backlash either domestically or on the part of the Soviet Union."

The problem was that the mechanisms for repression had not been dismantled and could therefore be utilized as in China, with the United States ending up looking like a chump. In the case of China, I said, "there was a very mild condemnation. What is the message to Poland and Hungary about what we would do if they crack down again? Isn't the message: 'We wouldn't do anything'?"

"I think the message is really that it is important that economic reform not get too far out in front of political reform . . . the two need to be in some balance and move forward together in order for it to be successful." When the show was over, Scowcroft said, "You were tough."

Aaron was in Europe too. *The New York Times* travel section had sent him to St. Tropez, and now he was in Paris with me on Bastille Day. The concierge got us a dinner reservation by telling the restaurant, "*Monsieur Latam, le plus grand homme!*" We went to Pré Catelan in the Bois de Boulogne and clogged our arteries with sautéed foie gras, lobster in a dangerous cream sauce, and almond soufflé, then walked back along the Champs-Élysées, which was crowded with Parisians all looking up at the fireworks spouting out like candy-cane volcanoes over the Arc de Triomphe. It was like the old days: just the two of us having fun. Aaron seemed to lose his demons whenever he left Washington.

MY NEGOTIATIONS for a new contract brought with it the usual ego blandishments. Joe Peyronnin mass-mailed a computer message: "From here on Lesley Stahl will be known as CHIEF White House Correspondent." The technical term for that is contract foreplay; the supposition: the longer the title, the smaller the raise.

A week later Dan called me "chief white house correspondent" for the first time. He led to me, saying I was with the president. "Actually, Dan, I'm on the lawn. He's inside holding a series of meetings with his national security advisers." Oops. I goofed—again. Everyone was livid at me because I had contradicted Dan. Bettag said, "It made me wince." "It was off the cuff," I argued, "impromptu." I was told I was "insensitive to other people's feelings. You never think how Dan's gonna feel." I called Dan and apologized.

I had to redo the piece anyway, because I had—speak of impromptu —transposed two words. Instead of what I intended: "The president cut his trip short," I said, "The president cut his shit trop." When Dan led to me for my redo, I was no longer *chief.*

My agent, Jim Griffin, was to have his first meeting with David Burke about my contract. "Do you want to leave CBS?" he asked. I told him I didn't want to, but I would. Negotiations are devastating exercises; you confront what your bosses *really* think of you. They make you see yourself as others do. This particular negotiation was excruciating, especially when the opening money offer was considerably less than I had expected. And Burke didn't offer any additional assignments, no new directions. He did say he would change *Face the Nation* to *Face the Nation with Lesley Stahl.*

CBS didn't see me as a "star," but I often had the impression George Bush did. I was *his* celebrity, dressing up the entourage. One night after Marlin had put on a lid, Jack Nishimura, our radio tech, came crashing back to the booth: "Hurry, hurry. Bush is in the briefing room." I went galloping out like a Lippizaner.

"Get outta here, Lesley," said Bush with his big Charlie Brown gash of a grin. Cameras were everywhere, but I was the only reporter. "Lesley, come meet my friend Bobby Brown [head of the American Baseball League]. Barbara, come say hi to Lesley." Mrs. Bush appeared in an aqua dress with white polka dots and huge plastic earrings. "These are my Texas Ranger earrings," she said, holding them out with her fingertips for me and the cameras. They were iridescent purple with pink polka dots. "Aren't they great?"

"And with the polka dots, they match!" I said.

"Oh!" She laughed. "And here's Millie" — her dog, her true love. It was hilarious. This was in the midst of a hostage crisis in Lebanon. Where's the tension? I thought as they left for a baseball game. I heard the helicopter taking off.

Aaron picked me up, deep in his depression. I didn't tell him how much fun I had just had with the man he so disparaged.

I LEFT FOR VACATION with my negotiations up in the air. We were going on another safari. This time I bought hiking boots, rain gear, and batting gloves.

My brother, Jeff, and his son, Matthew, were with us. Jeff had left behind an unfinished real estate deal and spent much of his time trying to make phone calls — not easily done from the bush. Every day Derek, our guide, would try to patch Jeff through to Boston. Sometimes it actually worked.

Never were two people more different than Jeff and me. From the beginning, as Dolly loved to remind us, I had been outgoing, hard-driving; he, the introvert, accepting and sweet-natured like my dad. No sister ever had a dearer brother with a weirder sense of humor, though you had to listen carefully, because he was shy. Now in Africa he was making me laugh with his Ionesco sense of the absurd. Here he was in the jungle, trying to consummate a deal for some high-tech high-rise, throwing around a million here and a million there. I laughed, but I also worried. His voice was gravelly. Why was he so hoarse?

This trip would be different from the last one. Aaron had decided to write a book about African safaris, so instead of just meandering around as we had before, he wanted to see specific things: a cheetah, a bull elephant charge, and especially a kill. So we set out each day with a mission.

I had decided by August 1989, in my 48th year, that I had already had the best day of my life. Even with the little annoyances of my job, I was on a pretty even keel. There were no more deep despairs but no rapturous highs either. This was OK. I was not the least bit unhappy. Maybe a little wistful, concerned about a degree of numbness, but I thought this was what "middle age" was all about.

Then we went to Rwanda to see the mountain gorillas, Dian Fossey's gorillas in the mist. This was why I had bought the hiking boots and batting gloves. Derek said he hoped we were in shape for a grueling climb. "Do you think we can do this?" Aaron asked the night before. "No."

When we got to the base of the mountain, we were put in a group of eight. "How old are these children?" asked the head of the Mountain Gorilla Project, pointing to 12-year-old Taylor and ten-year-old Matthew. "Fifteen," we lied. Anyone younger was barred from contact with the gorillas to protect them from human childhood diseases.

Taylor passed, but even though we had put glasses on Matthew and draped our most expensive camera around his neck, they pulled him out of the group. Jeff stayed behind with him.

Off we went, Aaron, Taylor, and I. Not off but up. I was assigned a sherpa just for me, which I thought was silly. What did I need my own sherpa for? As it turned out, I needed him to keep me from quitting. We started our climb through a templelike bamboo forest. The sun came through in sharp, spiritual spikes. When we broke into a clearing, climbing more steeply, there were nettles everywhere. That's why the gloves. By now my sherpa was carrying my backpack and my camera. Taylor was at the front of the line, jaunting along as we tracked the gorillas. Aaron and I were at the back, huffing. Every now and then our French-speaking Rwandan guide, François, hollered out gleefully, "*Merde!*" and pointed out a mound only King Kong could have left. This was good. It meant we were on the trail.

Soon we were in a thicket of underbrush so impenetrable that François had to cut holes with a machete for us to crawl through. Imagine, on our hands and knees slithering through mud or squeezing through nettles. Imagine me, Ms. Bruno Magli. I couldn't believe I was doing what I was doing. We'd been at it for two hours when I announced I would not take another step. I was finished. My sherpa got behind me and gently but firmly kept moving me along. A young Rwandan was climbing just ahead of me, barefoot, with a refrigerator balanced on his head.

After two and a half hours, we were walking on a mattress of bamboo, then climbing straight up, at a 45-degree angle. My sherpa was either pulling me up or cupping his hands on my buns and hoisting me. He simply would not let me stop. And believe me, I was insisting.

"Soft *merde!*" This exciting news at the three-hour mark. I, who never exercised, I, totally out of shape, was beyond exhaustion, near tears when we were hushed in French and reminded not to use cameras with flashes.

And there they were: two baby gorillas frolicking like any four-year-olds. We snapped and stared. We were right there, *in* their lives, in the middle of their open-air house. And then the silverback, the patriarch, seemed to welcome us, as three females kept grooming him. The guides called him Ndume, which they told us meant "powerful" in Swahili. Ndume had lost a hand, probably in a battle. We were told to bow, to keep our heads lower than his, as in *The King and I*. I was crouched down, staring up into his eyes, and he was staring right back.

We spent one hour in their world, watching them tumble and wrestle, nurse their babies, swing in the trees, forage for food — vines, leaves, berries — and just commune in small groups. At one point everyone in our group began scratching wildly. We had all sat in a red ant nest. I had the creatures biting me everywhere: behind my knees, in my bra, down my back. We had to take off our clothes and kill the critters on each other!

But we went right back to the gorillas and spent our time amid them, so close that a female reached out to touch me. When I went to reciprocate, the guide hit my arm with a stick. "*Non, madame. C'est interdit.*"

My exhaustion was gone. Everything was gone except a total body and mind exhilaration, a joy so strong and complete I wanted to laugh and cry and sing and fly. It came partly from the almost religious experience of being among those magnificent creatures who were so hospitable and gentle with us. It came also from my beating the elements. I had somehow endured.

What I decided that day with the gorillas in Rwanda was that the best day of your life may not have happened yet. No matter what you think.

IT TOOK EXACTLY three days for the African calm to turn to Washington angst. It had to be a record turnaround time, instigated by my trip to the suburban mall at Tysons Corner to buy Taylor a party dress. She hated all the dresses, all the skirts, all the blouses. We schlepped from Nordstrom to Bloomie's to a dozen boutiques. Finally, after arguing against it, she consented to try on a tuxedo with a red vest. She looked great. Under duress from me — she could tell I was unraveling — she also consented to try on a red dress. She looked beautiful. "I hate it. I despise it. I'll never wear it. Never." Okay.

This was all about *my* impatience. Taylor was still as sunny as ever, with few signs of the seventh-grade rebellion syndrome that my poor mother had suffered through with me. I was prepared to help my daughter traverse the ragged agonies of adolescence, based on my own miseries in junior high. I never dreamed I would be spared.

IN ONE of my occasional meetings with John Sununu, we discussed the country's deteriorating educational system. In a recent test 20 percent of 12-year-olds had been unable to identify the United States on a map. I argued that you couldn't fix things without money, and he told me I was wrong. "Money isn't everything" had become the president's motivating domestic policy. All the energy and the brains of his administration went not into finding solutions to problems but finding arguments for *not* spending money.

On *Face* in early October Governor Mario Cuomo of New York was agitated about this very point:

> CUOMO: [The President] found $166 billion for savings and loans, but for drugs, there's no money. Day care, there is no money. . . . They came up with $600 million for SDI. Where did they find it? . . . Drugs is a national problem. Education is a national problem.

But when I asked Governor Cuomo if "these are issues worth raising taxes for," he ducked. In 1989, no one wanted to use the R-word.

The C-word was another matter. In mid-September Bush proposed a *cut* in the capital gains tax. I was told this was phase one of a "master plan." Phase one: fight for a capital gains tax *cut* in order to win the trust of the conservatives (again, don't rile up the Right) and ensure only muted criticism in phase two, a Bush cave-in on a tax increase in his second year. How could you not get a little cynical?

ZIRINSKY WAS BEING promoted from her job running the *Evening News* in Washington to producer in the fishbowl in New York. Her husband, Joe, was there; it made sense. I sent her a note: "Don't blow it." She knew what I meant: have a child. I had often lectured her on this subject, assuring her, "You'll love the stress."

What her move meant was that I was also losing my White House producer, since Rome was being promoted to Zee's job. This was all very painful. I had finally come to believe I had cracked the White House reporter's code and could now do the job with a minimum of panic. Much of that I owed to Rome, who made me eat my words about women making better producers. I relied on his solid news instincts and rapid responses. He was one of the strongest all-around producers at CBS News.

NBC's Jim Mickleshevsky was in the White House booth next to ours. He called Rome to congratulate him, and I hollered over, "Ask him how much he's going to miss me."

"He says half a tick's ass."

MY DAD CALLED in late September. Jeff was in the hospital: "They found something." Another tumor on his larynx. It had not spread, but the doctor removed all but half of one vocal cord. I called his wife, Paula, and said, "We have to find a device to boost Jeff's voice. Let's call AT&T and get a voice enhancer for his phones. And we'll do research on what

352

else is out there." I needed to contain this into a manageable project, narrow the focus.

AARON WAS ALWAYS showing me how to parent. He would explain, "It doesn't matter who teaches a child, a teacher or a parent, just as long as she learns." For years it had been Aaron who had sat with Taylor doing math and English. When people ask me, "How did you do it?"—that's how. But now she was taking current events. One night a week she and I would go out to eat (me cook?) and read a week's worth of *Washington Posts* together.

This was the year she started at the Beaux and Belles Dancing School on Saturday nights. I wanted her to be a real belle, which is why, when she put on a big, bulky black shirt over a big, bulky black skirt, I said, "You know, honey, I have the perfect blouse! It's my black-and-white polka dot with the baby-doll sleeves." Aaron sat silent.

"Don't you like what I'm wearing?"

"No, no, I like it. It's just that I think you would look *even* better in my blouse. Just try it."

She looked at herself in polka dots in the mirror, glumly. "You look *great!*" I said. She was miserable and slumped off to her room.

"Why did you do that?" Aaron asked.

"What? You saw how much better she looks in my blouse than that baggy, formless thing she had on."

"What matters?" he asked. "How *you* think she looks, or how *she* thinks she looks?"

First off, I hate when he's so wise. Second, the epiphany: I was being Dolly in a way I had always promised myself I wouldn't be. "Tay," I summoned her. "You know, you're right. You look much better in that black shirt. I don't know what I was thinking." She brightened and changed, and then, afraid we'd get lost, we left early for the dance and had to drive around the block 37 times.

When she got home, she was sparkling; she had danced all night.

THE SYNDICATED SHOW *Hard Copy* went on the air in the fall of 1989. Like its older siblings, *Inside Edition* and *A Current Affair*, it was a tabloid show that in format and style looked like a network news broadcast. The lines between these tabloid-style shows and us were blurring, and it wasn't just how we looked. More and more we were covering their subject, the world of personality. The private lives of famous people were becoming our territory too, as the competition for ratings heated up. The networks' overall share of the audience was down to 67 percent. In homes with cable it was just 56 percent.

This meant more belt-tightening. Our bureau chief, Barbara Cohen, threw a dinner for the Washington correspondents to tell us we were going to have to do with less: more work with fewer producers. And, she said, David Burke wanted us to come in early and be live on the *Morning News.* "Live on the *Morning News,*" said Rita Braver, "dead on the *Evening News.*"

PRESIDENT BUSH had been encouraging the military in Panama to overthrow Manuel Noriega whom he called a "thug." When a group of Panamanian generals staged a coup that failed, Jesse Helms beat up on Bush for not sending in the marines to help. A few days later Frank Sesno of CNN reported that John Sununu was blaming Defense Secretary Dick Cheney for the administration's "weak-kneed, do-nothing" reaction. I raced up to Fitzwater's office so fast, he was still frozen in front of the TV set listening to Sesno. With me in the room, he phoned Sununu — who denied the story — and then Sesno. "Sununu says you're flat wrong and that you're an asshole."

Back in the booth, I got a call from Sununu's aide Ed Rogers. "It's bullshit!" he yelled, "One hundred percent turd pieces of shit." I gathered this was a denial. I left the story alone, though I believed it.

Then on Sunday, on *Meet the Press,* Secretary of State Jim Baker disassociated himself from the Panama policy. "It was George Bush who made this decision," he said. The same guy who had said, "It was George Bush who made the decision to pick Dan Quayle." Cheney, on *Face,* had referred to "our" decision.

I GOT A TIP: Larry Tisch was at the White House, meeting with John Sununu. I worked it like a story, learning that Sununu had spent most of the time complaining about Rather. I was told that Sununu had praised me: "John bragged on y'all, said you have to fight Dan just to let you be fair. He wanted to show Larry that we're not anti-CBS, just anti-Dan." I began to agree with Rather that the White House might well have a blueprint for destroying him.

That night Aaron and I got into bed to watch the World Series from San Francisco on ABC. But the game never began. That was the night of the San Francisco earthquake (7.1 on the Richter scale) when the ground rumbled in waves with such force that buildings toppled and major roadways buckled. ABC Sports was on the air live. We were not. Some of my colleagues at CBS think this was a devastating turning point for us, that after the earthquake, people began to think: Maybe it's ABC and not CBS we should turn to when there's a crisis.

Bush, who had felt the sting of the critics when he was nearly invisible during Hurricane Hugo in September, decided not to make that mistake again. He was all over the earthquake. At an early-morning photo op the next day he said he cared; then later, at a midday photo op, he cared again. The following morning we left Andrews Air Force Base at 6 A.M. so he could care in San Francisco.

I was walking along with the president as he toured the rubble under the collapsed freeway. We could look up and see cars still hanging over the precipice. I was broadcasting live over a cell phone — a wholly new piece of equipment — commenting on the eeriness under the listing and cracked roadway with its wire entrails dangling down. Bush shook hands with rescue workers, and I was on the air with a blow-by-blow: "The president, as you can see, is chatting with a row of hard hats." Dan corrected me: "I don't call them hard hats, Lesley. I call them heroes."

We went on a helicopter tour over the Bay Bridge. The quake had severed electrical lines and gas mains, fueling several fires. At least 59 people had died, and thousands had been left homeless. I tried to slow down and quiet my engine: "This is worth remembering, old kid," I told myself. I was in the bubble of the rescue operation, *inside.* Don't forget this. Don't forget how much it looks like Beirut under siege and how hard it is not to get emotional.

When I got home, I was summoned to New York for a contract meeting with David Burke. "I'm putting you in the rotation as one of Dan's substitutes." I grinned. "You'll anchor the *Evening News* three, four times a year." Something substantial at last.

NOVEMBER 9. The Berlin Wall began coming down. At Gorbachev's urging, the East German government opened the border for free travel, and a flood poured through into West Berlin. The president decided to speak about this on camera, so an Oval Office "tight pool" was organized. It was my turn to be the lone broadcaster. Bush was at his desk, a map of Germany spread out before him. Jim Baker sat to his left, Scowcroft and Sununu to his right. This would be the president's first comment on the coming down of the odious Wall, communism's most sinister symbol, the very wall he and Reagan had nudged Gorbachev to destroy. But Bush, with what looked like a frown, sat there so limply, he actually listed in his chair. And his voice, instead of expressing the excitement of the moment, whined. We poolers were standing in a knot, the still photographers clicking and weaving around us. "You don't seem very elated," I said.

"I'm very pleased," Bush answered in a gray tone. "I'm not an emotional guy."

"Well, how elated are you?" I asked.

"I'm very pleased, and I've been very pleased with a lot of other developments, and as I've told you, I think the United States' part of this, which is not related to this development today particularly, is being handled in a proper fashion."

Bush was missing a characteristic essential for a president, an emotional ignition key. He couldn't seem to light up to these surges of human freedom, to ring out with appropriate poetry in times of crisis or exaltation. He was trying to send Gorbachev a message that the president of the United States was not going to gloat over his defeat—but what about a message to the American people? What about expressing *our* communal joy? This was an echo of Tiananmen, when he had been busy sending signals to Deng instead of expressing outrage. I thought Bush's assuring the Soviets was the right approach, but surely there was a way to satisfy the soul without threatening Gorbachev. Reagan would have found it.

I raced out to the lawn for a special report, but there was no camera. Cal Marlin came running . . . plugging in, heating up, planting tripod legs. A frantic hookup. When Cal was on-line, Rather tossed it to me, saying, "Bush just sat there like a hunk of liver."

I tried to explain the policy of prudence, the fear of inciting a backlash. "He doesn't want to be a beacon of democracy like past presidents," I said.

"What!" said Dan. "A president of the United States not wanting to be a beacon of democracy?"

I explained again Bush's desire to see things move forward slowly without chaos and send a signal to Gorbachev that the United States would not rub it in.

Pascal Taillandier, the White House correspondent for Agence France-Presse, was up with Fitzwater. He told me that Bush had come tearing into Marlin's office, blurting out, "Those jerks—saying I'm not a beacon of democracy!"

Five minutes later Marlin called me in the booth: "George Bush is so a beacon of democracy! He's just trying to avoid creating a backlash."

"That's what I said, Marlin."

"I know," he said soothingly. "It's that Dan. He keeps pushing you." Of course, "beacon of democracy" had been my phrase.

Fitzwater reminded me of Eeyore. He was a virtuoso worrier who let me know he was as uncomfortable as I was with the simmering feud between the men we worked for. We chatted, exchanged ideas several times a day. He needed my feedback—part of any White House press secretary's job is to gauge the mood of the network correspondents and warn his boss; and, like any beat reporter, part of my job was staying plugged in in order not to be beaten. So even though we each owed our first allegiance and loyalty to Bush and Rather respectively, we resided in a strange middle corridor.

356   Tom Brokaw was in Berlin, Rather was in New York. Our bad luck. NBC's broadcast was spectacular, with Tom near the Brandenburg Gate

as West Germans pulled East Germans over the wall. Dan had scooped everyone in Tiananmen; now Tom was beating everyone in Berlin.

By Sunday the Berliners were dismantling the wall and West German Chancellor Helmut Kohl was already saying, "One nation; we belong together." But, as I pointed out on *Face*, the prospect of a united Germany was sending panic waves through the Western world. Margaret Thatcher was especially alarmed. She flew to Washington two weeks later, on November 24, and went to Camp David to persuade Bush to help her put the brakes on German reunification. She arrived in a helicopter that whipped up a huge snow drift, which floated in the air until it got right on top of me — then fell on my head. Wet ice. On my *hair*. I was there to see Maggie and George get into a golf cart and drive off. Yet Thatcher was never as successful at manipulating Bush as she had been with Reagan.

BUSH FINALLY DECIDED to offer Gorbachev a public endorsement by meeting him at an impromptu summit in Malta in early December. The central issue was to be Eastern Europe. As I put it:

> STAHL: Eastern Europe is moving like a raging bull at a speed no one on Earth anticipated. Mr. Bush and Mr. Gorbachev are like two men at a rodeo. The key question is, can they stay on the bull, ride him, and tame him? Are the superpowers powerful enough to control events that are moving so rapidly?

For CBS, the summit in Malta was an opportunity to recover ground we had lost in San Francisco and Berlin. So we showed up in force with more than 100 reporters, producers, and technicians. Despite the budget cuts, we spent a fortune on this one story — more than $1 million. We brought "flyaway" portable satellite dishes and microwave "hops" to transmit the signals from the Russian cruiser *Slava* and the USS *Belknap* anchored in Marsaxlokk Bay.[8] Bush wanted a summit at sea. This was no easy technological feat: we had to relay signals from the ships, up to a church bell tower, and across the island to our newsroom at the Excelsior Hotel in Valletta. It was right out of the movie *Back to the Future*.

I did my first report, a bulletin, live from the newsroom, standing next to Rather in front of an open window. The wind was wild, a storm so strenuous — winds up to 60 miles an hour — you had to wonder how Bush and Company slept out on the USS *Belknap*, how the hell they were going to survive the inevitable seasickness. Having the summit on naval ships was Bush's way of keeping the press away.

We had brought along our high-powered camera with the extender

357

lens, so the next day we got extraordinary pictures of Bush's launch trying to get back from the Slava to the *Belknap* after the morning session. The storm was now producing waves of 12 feet. Bush's small launch was swamped and pitching about. "They can't dock!" Zirinsky boomed out. She was running the newsroom. "Great pictures." You could see POTUS drenched by the hurling waves, Secret Service agents holding him. You had to wonder about the president's judgment.

We taped the *Evening News* in front of the open window. I was "chatting" with Dan about how the storm had forced Bush to cancel the afternoon session and the dinner; how he was stuck out on the *Belknap*, a hostage. As I talked, a blast of wind lifted my hair—I had to reach up and hold on. Said Dan: "Make no mistake, this wind would drive Sinbad the Sailor or Lord Nelson to cover."

Because of the storm, CNN was on the air almost constantly with the story, as it had been with Tiananmen, the San Francisco earthquake, and the fall of the Berlin Wall. This opened a new chapter not only in television news but in world diplomacy—and politics, for that matter. With each technological advance, the time for making news judgments was getting shorter. Time for checking out sources and thinking through the coverage was shrinking to no time. The same could be said for the world leaders.

When I interviewed Jim Baker for *Face*, he said they had all worn a scopolamine patch behind their ears and so no one had succumbed to seasickness. I asked how concerned he was about the conservatives back home criticizing Bush for offering the Soviets trade concessions before the human rights issues had been resolved. "They don't have open, free travel. There are still dissidents in jail," I pointed out.

"We did focus on human rights today." Baker was reeking with confidence.

I called home as the wind howled like Heathcliff on the moors. Taylor said she'd had one of her best days ever. Skating, movies, three boys were over. And I'd missed it.

We flew directly to Brussels for a NATO meeting. Bush worked the room as if he were in Iowa, shaking hands with aides and aides' aides. At a news conference, Maureen Santini of the Associated Press showed she had real *cojones*. "Weren't you hotdogging when you were out on the launch submerged by the waves and spray?"

"Hotdogging?" said Bush. "No!" He laughed. "Well, you know, these charismatic, macho, visionary guys, they'll do anything." I found that so disarmingly funny, I threw my head back and laughed so hard, I slid out of my chair onto the floor. Oh, God. At NATO. Embarrassing. I picked myself up and prayed no one had seen me.

358

WE TOOK a short vacation to Paradise Island in the Bahamas. Taylor and Aaron went scuba diving; I went to the pool, where I covered my hair with a scarf and smeared zinc all over my face. A man who recognized me stood over me on my chaise and told me loudly how much he enjoyed *Face*. I fled to our room.

When Aaron and Tay got back from their deep-sea dive, they brought a videotape. There they were like stars of a *National Geographic* special, with tanks on their backs and huge flipper feet. When they squirted Cheez Whiz out of a little pouch, they were swarmed by hundreds of lovely zebra fish and flatfish, and football fish made passes at them. They were both effervescing like the bubbles gurgling up from the tanks.

On our second day there, the United States invaded Panama. "We have decapitated the beast," announced General Colin Powell, chairman of the Joint Chiefs of Staff; but Noriega had not been captured. I flew home, leaving the scuba divers behind.

Bush held a news conference. CBS and ABC split the screen. As you watched Bush on one side, you saw on the other side four body bags arriving at Dover Air Force Base, the first U.S. servicemen killed in Panama. The White House went nuts: "Outrageous! Unfair!" Fitzwater protested. The TV-conscious Reagan White House would have known when those body bags were coming home and scheduled their news conference accordingly.

As I reported, the White House wanted Noriega "to go to a third country and disappear." A trial in the United States could turn into a "nightmare" since he had been on the CIA's payroll when Bush was CIA director. But they couldn't find a third country "where he wouldn't end up at some villa with a shortwave radio, trying to whip up support and foment revolution back in Panama." There was no choice but to take him into custody.

Noriega sought sanctuary in the Vatican Embassy in Panama City, where he stayed holed up for two weeks until finally, on January 3, he was arrested and flown to Miami for trial. CBS broke the story. One of Scowcroft's staffmen told me, "We never thought we'd get him. We thought he'd go down fighting or that he'd sneak away with his money." In my story I said that after months of Noriega bashing, the White House was suddenly clamming up lest it prejudice the case. The president had been calling him a "thug" and a "narcoterrorist."

After his news conference on the Noriega capture, Bush said he had "a housekeeping matter" to bring up and gave me a long, cold stare. He wanted to discuss the split-screen coverage of "slain soldiers—and me goofing around." He was furious. "If you ever do that again, tell me so I

359

can stop the news conference." Rather followed the news conference by explaining that the coffins' arrival home had been long scheduled and suggested that the White House had known that.

Now the White House was even more unhappy with Dan. Nor were they pleased with me. In my report that night I said that Bush was imposing a gag order on the Noriega case, "which is convenient since he is sure to be hounded by questions which he can now continue to duck with a good excuse."

On Saturday we taped an interview with Sununu for *Face*. As we sat in the studio while the lights were adjusted, he unloaded: "I don't know what you people think you're doing. You are self-destructing. What Rather said after the news conference — " He shook his head. "The reason Rather's ratings are sinking is because he's so damned negative about Bush." Dan had slipped into third place. Then Sununu added, "And you, your bit about the gag order." We were both on mikes. Everyone in the control room was listening. "Gag order," he said, "connotes cover-up. It's pejorative, unfair." A short pause. "Bush said to me, 'I have a love-hate relationship with her. I love her, then she does something like this.' I just don't know."

Karen was in my ear: "I don't want you to be affected by this psychological warfare he's pulling on you. Don't let it affect our interview." I nodded.

I questioned Sununu about Bush's secret, if not deceptive, diplomacy. "While the president said no contact with China, he was sending two high-level missions there. Credibility problem?"

"I think if you look very carefully at what was said and what was done, there's a consistency."

"You're saying that the American people have to look at the fine print?" I asked. "You're saying every time he speaks, we have to question his language?"

"No, I don't think so, Lesley. The president feels he has to be able to communicate with leaders in particular circumstances — and he's going to continue to communicate in that personalized way."

"Does he keep secrets about foreign policy from you?"

Sununu dodged that one, changed the subject, and turned combative: "Until I came down here, I never gave an interview on an off-the-record basis. And yet the desire of the press to keep things secret, to keep sources secret, the fact that they want people to talk so that they can put things in the paper without identifying who it is, I found astounding." Who was he kidding?

360   WEST 57TH, the show Jim Brooks had urged me to watch and learn from, was taken off the air. With all its glitz and new-style journalism, it faded

while the wrinkled old *60 Minutes* with its *tick-tick-tick* and its antique values flourished. *60 Minutes* hired two of the *West 57th* reporters, Meredith Vieira, 35, and Steve Kroft, 43, to replace Diane. Don Hewitt never even looked my way. My friends at the ladies' lunch asked if I cared. I lied and said I didn't.

Linda Wertheimer said, "Do you realize that we're the vanguard of the baby-boom women? They are right behind us. Everything we do is setting the path for this giant bulge of women in the workplace." She paused, making sure she had our attention. "What will it be like when 50 percent of the American workforce has menopause? Think about it!" We thought. "Imagine the Kleenex supply!" someone said. "Imagine the market in fans!"

Women were making progress in a ragged way. Look at the world stage, and you saw them running countries from Britain to Pakistan, the Philippines to Lithuania, Nicaragua to Iceland. How come we in the enlightened U.S.A. couldn't produce a viable woman candidate for high office?

There was the same lopsided headway in network news. Even though women had outnumbered men in journalism schools for the past 12 years, at NBC and ABC they were still complaining about having second-tier status. But at CBS, in Washington particularly, we seemed to be taking over. Our bureau chief was Barbara Cohen, her deputy was Mary Martin, Susan Zirinsky had headed up the *Evening News* in Washington, Lucy Spiegel ran the *Morning News*, Deborah Johnson *Nightwatch*, Karen Sughrue *Face*, and, most incredible of all, Darcy Antonellis was chief of technical operations. We were the Land of the Amazons. Rita Braver said, "No one around here's ever going to say, 'That's an awful big job for a little girl.' "

We were still considered bitches, though, still looked on as shrill and a half-dozen euphemisms for ball busters. When I persisted, I was badgering; when Sam persisted, he was pursuing. Would we ever get past it? Slowly. Very slowly. Still, prime-time television was beginning to look like the CBS Washington Bureau, with all-female shows such as *Designing Women*, *The Golden Girls*, and *Kate & Allie*. And *Newsweek* put *Murphy Brown* on its cover.[9] All these TV women, and not a simp in the lot. They all worked, all had an edge; they lost their tempers, they cried; they were bitches, but they were accepted.

ANN WEXLER, my friend who had worked in the Carter White House, had her 60th birthday party at the Cosmos Club. One of the toasters noted how much times had changed: "The Berlin Wall comes down, communism is dying, Ivana and Donald get divorced, and women are having 60th birthday parties."

□

BUSH'S URGE to carry out his policies through personal relationships reached new heights over the hostages. Eight Americans were still being held captive in Lebanon.

Rome called me with an unconfirmed tip that an Iranian official had phoned Brent Scowcroft to say that Hashemi Rafsanjani, the Iranian leader, wanted to talk to Bush. And then it happened: they spoke! The president tried to enlist Rafsanjani's help in winning the hostages' release. I told Fitzwater.

"Did you get this from Iran?" he asked.

"I don't know," I said.

"I'll get back to you." I got excited.

A few hours later he summoned me to his office. "A month ago, an Iranian got through to Scowcroft," he started. My heart was racing, this was great. "We checked out the contact through various methods . . ." I was taking down every word. Would this be the biggest story I ever broke?

"So Bush called the number and spoke with the man. Rafsanjani. Then further checks were made." Wait. What? "In our judgment . . . we decided it was all a hoax."

A hoax? After swallowing my disappointment, I asked for more specifics. What had Bush said on the call? It was still a nifty story.

I called Tom Bettag in the fishbowl and said I'd like to tell the hoax story just the way Marlin had told it to me: with a real surprise kicker, a punch line. "Yes!" he agreed and later improved my script. I had written, "A man claiming to be an Iranian government official . . ." Bettag thought I was giving away too much and changed it to "A man who identified himself as an Iranian government official."

"What this shows, Dan," I said, "is that if Rafsanjani were to call the White House, the president would take the call. Truth is, he's been trying to establish just that kind of direct contact for a long time. It's the Iranians who haven't been interested."

The wires picked it up: "CBS News reports Bush in a hoax with an imposter." The few reporters still around congratulated me. I felt sensational.

The next day Rafsanjani ridiculed Bush from the pulpit. But Fitzwater denied the hoax was an embarrassment, saying that the president wanted the American people, and especially the hostage families, to know he was willing to follow any lead to get the hostages out.

But the jokes flew: Bush might have a future hosting a game show. Something like 20 Questions: President Bush takes phone calls from around the world, then guesses who he's talking to.

□

THE PEACE DIVIDEND — would we ever get one? — was heating up as an issue. On February 4 I suggested to Defense Secretary Cheney on *Face*, "If you cut out the B-2 stealth bomber, everyone could get health benefits; if you cancel the Trident-2 submarine missiles, public education could be saved."

"The reason we are here today where we can talk about the collapse of communism . . . in part has been the success of our strategic deterrent for over 40 years."

"But communism has collapsed."

"It has not yet collapsed," Cheney contradicted me. "There are still 380,000 Soviet troops in East Germany."

President Bush went on a cross-country campaign to fight the move for massive defense cuts, dragging the press corps around until we begged for mercy. After the hazy, lazy days of Ronald Reagan, this felt like a death march. We started with a 6 A.M. takeoff from Andrews Air Force Base and found ourselves in a war by midmorning California time. We raced up a hill in humvees and, like Pierre in *War and Peace*, watched from a hill as the army staged a simulated battle in the Mojave Desert. The "United States" fought the "Red Brigade" in armored vehicles that looked like the Soviet real thing. Gorbachev was chairing a meeting in Moscow right then about ending the Communist Party's monopoly of power, and here was Bush battling to build strategic weapons to fight the Soviets.

We jumped back into our humvees and went down into the battle itself. The president's doctor, Burton Lee, told me, "If you have hemorrhoids, like Brent Scowcroft, that humvee ride was so rough it probably cured 'em. But if you didn't have them, like the president, you might now!"

The next day Bush took us to the Lawrence Livermore National Laboratory in northern California to promote Reagan's SDI. I sat in a mound of grease on the press helicopter, then stood in a shower of mud splatter from Bush's chopper. "He's here on the warpath," I wrote, "while Gorbachev is promoting democracy." I called it his "we're-not-ready-to-let-down-our-guard message."

From Livermore we went to the Strategic Air Command, where the president, in an Eisenhower jacket and baseball cap, got into the cockpit of a B-1 bomber. He spoke to SAC troops by radio: "For you missile crews," he said, "the pointy end is up." The Bush White House was catching on. This was like a Deaver "moment."

THERE WERE NO BREATHERS in early 1990, as one momentous event bumped up against the next. I was in the Oval Office pool when President Bush admitted he had been caught by surprise when Gorbachev suddenly reversed himself and accepted a plan to speed German reunification. "Changes are goin' on so fast there that it's hard to keep up with them all," he said. Gorbachev had even gone so far as to stop fighting the idea of a united Germany in NATO.

"We're dealing with historic change," said the president. "I'm beginning to be very elated about this and — " Looking right at me, he smiled. I smiled back. He pointed at me. I pointed back. Everyone laughed. "Seriously," he said, "it's . . . it's very, very fast." Later Fitzwater told me that Bush often asked his aides after news conferences, "Do you think Lesley thought I was elated enough?" It was a running joke: "Will Lesley say I was emotional enough?"

This would be one of his great achievements, German reunification, and it was bold. Mitterrand and Thatcher opposed it. But Bush kept pushing. Richard Holbrooke, who would later serve as U.S. ambassador to Germany, told me, "This was Bush's brilliant move. The wall came down, all Eastern Europe was in an uproar. Then Bush backed unification and the transition was peaceful. There was stability, after all."

Gorbachev, on the other hand, didn't grasp that his empire depended on maintaining a strong position in Eastern Europe. He ended up destroying what he wanted to save, killing off communism without intending to.

DAN QUAYLE was our guest on *Face* in early March. He showed up with a full deck of aides, among them David Beckwith and Bill Kristol, his chief of staff. "What are you going to do?" Quayle asked me.

"Skewer you!" I grinned. "Or will you skewer me? I'll bet you've got a real plan."

I asked about the Republicans' new policy on abortion: "You say everybody can be in the Republican Party. Are you saying now that abortion is not murder?"

"I'm saying that the Republican Party stands by its platform. We're not going to change our prolife position, but we're going to recognize that the tent is bigger than just being prolife."

"If the tent's big, and you accept them, why isn't that prochoice?" I asked.

"Because our position . . . is firm, and we're not going to change it."

"Do you concede the inconsistency of accepting people who disagree with you and then turning around and saying abortion is murder and it should be made illegal across the land?"

"No, I don't see any inconsistency."

When I asked the obligatory question about his approval ratings — then up to 16 percent — he came up with a little dig: "Would I like to

364

have higher ratings? Of course. I'm sure you'd like to have higher ratings on this show." So he did have a plan.

That night I went alone to the annual election party thrown by the CBS News political editor, Marty Plissner, and bet that the 1992 race would be Richard Gephardt–Dianne Feinstein versus George Bush–unknown.

AARON, so bright after Africa, was back in the dark corners of depression. I was troubled that I was not doing more to help him, but if I tried, he would just shut down. He simply would not see a doctor. When I pushed too much, he made me feel I was punishing him. He drove me to work one day, and I lectured my heart out: "You have to get out of the house. Exercise. Call people." He acted as though I was cutting his skin with a sharp razor.

But no matter how much he was suffering, he still managed to coach Tay's basketball team. That year they won the championship.

IT SEEMED as if everyone around Bush was getting sick. Lee Atwater was in the hospital with a brain tumor; Barbara Bush was taking radiation treatments for Graves' disease, a thyroid condition; and now the president was diagnosed with glaucoma, which he tried to minimize — no president wants to appear unhealthy. "The vision thing," he cracked. Aaron laughed at the irony: "The cure for glaucoma is marijuana!" Others joked that Bush had gotten it because he hated broccoli. His mother had made him eat it, he had explained, and now that he was president of the United States, he wasn't going to eat it anymore.

As president, Bush was so much fun, so normal and gemütlich, you wanted him to be what you wanted him to be. Then when he wasn't, there was a sense of betrayal, as when he neglected the country's domestic needs. Standing by his no-new-taxes pledge had a ripple effect, making it hard for governors and mayors to raise the money they needed to fix their problems. Then came the issue of global warming. Instead of admitting there was a problem, Bush called for more research to see if the greenhouse effect was real. In a piece in mid-April I called it Bush's "let's-check-the-price-tag policy." I was told that Chief of Staff Sununu had been so incensed at my story, he had called Larry Tisch. What had Tisch said? I asked. That he had not seen the piece but would look into it.

Mary Martin, our deputy bureau chief, got a call from Tisch for some "fact finding" later that day. "What was in Lesley's piece last night? We stand by it, don't we?" he asked. "Yes, of course," Mary said. "Oh, of course," Tisch said.

A week later a friend told me over lunch that Bush had recently

365

complained to him: "Lesley Stahl, she's always tough on me." The president also let on that Sununu had called Larry Tisch to complain about Dan's story on the price-tag policy.

"About Dan?" I asked. "But it was *my* story they hated. It's part of their effort to get rid of Dan."

I remembered a conversation I'd had with a White House official a few days before. "The best way to 'get Dan,'" he had said, "is not Sununu's approach of calling Tisch directly. It's better to plant negative thoughts about Dan with people Tisch respects and listens to." Bush had done just that with my friend who happened to be someone Tisch turned to for adivce.

I made some calls around the White House. One of my sources used the words "the project." "What project? The project to get rid of Rather?" I asked.

"We want you to be the anchor." What? That echoed something Fitzwater had said to me a while back: "You're good at anchoring. You get that job, and CBS gets an interview with Bush like that." He snapped his fingers and chortled. I had thought it was a joke. Now I wondered. Maybe there was a real "project" to get Rather fired.

I WAS GOING to New York to substitute-anchor the *Evening News*. When I kissed Aaron good-bye, he had a pink, soupy look in his eyes. I called him before the broadcast, but there was no answer and I got a pang of panic. I had begun to fear he might take his own life.

Earlier in the day I had shared a cab with Mike Wallace. "How's Aaron?" he asked.

"He's depressed," I said, not really thinking about Mike's well-publicized bout with the disease.

"What's he doing about it?" he asked.

"He won't see a doctor."

"Well, make him," he demanded.

"I can't. He's a grown man. He's adamant," I said.

Mike grabbed me by the shoulders and began shaking me. "Listen, you," he said sternly, emotionally, piercing my eyes with his gaze, "you find a way. Whatever it takes, you get him to a doctor. You must not let this man suffer another minute. Do you understand? Not another minute. Find a way." My eyes burned with tears. Why hadn't I come to this on my own?

Aaron has an expression: "So suddenly, there's God." [10] Well, that's what happened. There was God, the very next day. I was back in the White House booth, looking for the producer assigned to work with me. "He's gone to his psychiatrist for his depression pills," I was told. What? What do you mean?

With everything that had been written about depression, I still had not fully realized that Aaron could be helped with a pill. I look back at my ignorance, my neglect, and want to weep. "I need your help," I told the producer when he got back. Within a half hour I was on the phone with his doctor. "Would you see my husband as an emergency patient?" I burst into tears. She said she would. Now I had to do what Mike Wallace said: I had to find a way to get Aaron there.

That night I told him it wasn't real shrinking; it was pharmacology: "You have a physiological problem, a chemical imbalance. Please try this. Please." I thought I would have to claw and scrape and beg. But my sweet suffering husband looked out through his foggy eyes and said yes, he'd go. So suddenly, there was God.

Or so I thought. The doctor said his symptoms were those of "classic depression" and put him on medication that, I learned, takes several weeks to kick in. One night during that time, Aaron was in such despair he stayed out all night in the rain. I was so scared, I sat up in a frenzy. Should I call the police? The hospitals? A friend?

When he came home at 6 A.M., shivering and soaked, I called his doctor. "My husband's in crisis," I cried. She assured me he would get better in time.

IN MID-MAY I ran into Mike Wallace again. This time he asked if I would be interested in joining 60 Minutes. After I caught my breath, I told him, "Don doesn't want me." Mike seemed surprised. He said he'd find out.

I was in the White House booth when Mike called: "It was true a few years ago that Don didn't want you. Now he does. We all think it would be wonderful."

"I'm bowled over," I said. This was so unexpected, so heaven-sent. "I don't want to sound overanxious, but I'm very interested."

Then Mike called back. Hewitt had chewed him out for calling me. "David Burke will think we're cooking things up behind his back and go wild. David sees you at the White House, period. Don't say a word to anyone," urged Mike. "Just wait. We're going to work on it. Be patient." I thought, this'll never happen.

I WAS ON Late Night with David Letterman on NBC. Before my turn, I waited in the green room with La Toya Jackson, who had a python wrapped around her torso. One of Letterman's producers had interviewed me ahead of time, but Dave tossed the crib sheet away and asked mischievously about Bush calling me a pussy. "Bush called you a name, didn't he?" I laughed nervously. "Dan Rather makes Lesley Stahl look like a mmm-hmm," said Dave.

"Are you going to say the word?" I asked. No, said Dave, who prodded me into revealing, "He called me a pussycat." I paused. Letterman gave me a comic's come-on-there's-more look. "Except," I said, "he left off the 'cat.' " The audience loved it. "The word was printed in *The Boston Globe*," I said, "and my mother called to say, 'Wasn't that nice of George Bush.' " The audience laughed again. "You have great teeth," Dave said with a smile, "and you smell good too."

Afterward he offered me a magnum of red wine. "I don't drink," I said. He leaned over and whispered, "I had to stop too."

WHEN I GOT HOME the next day, Aaron — who had been on an antidepressant for a month — was out. I noticed an unopened letter from his editor. He had submitted his book on Africa nearly a month before. What if she didn't like it? I was so worried, I called her. The book needs a lot of work, she said.

When Aaron got home he read the letter and went quietly to the den. As he told me later, "I went off to be alone and let the darkness take me, the inevitable plunge into the pit. So I sat on the couch, and felt myself begin the usual slide. But something extraordinary happened. I hit a floor. It was physical, something solid was preventing my submersion into the misery. I could *feel* it, at first sure this floor would give way. But it didn't. It wouldn't. So I got up and joined you and Taylor."

I was sure I wouldn't see him until the next day. But he showed up in the kitchen and had dinner with us as if the letter were no big deal. And the next day he sat at his computer and rewrote his book in one long gush.

I'm not sure what triggered Aaron's depression, but once it took hold, I am sure it changed his chemistry to such an extent that he was incapable of pulling himself up out of that pit. The pills saved his life — and I don't say that lightly. They saved mine too.

BARBARA BUSH SPOKE at the Wellesley College commencement on June 1, 1990. She had left Smith College early to marry George Bush. Now 100 seniors were protesting her appearance; a wife is not a good role model, they said.

I listened to Mrs. Bush's address in our booth — CBS ran it live — and thought she struck just the right tone. Her message was about tolerance for the different paths people take. She said she wondered if her successor was in the audience, "someone to preside over the White House as the president's spouse. Well, I wish *him* well!" A whoop went up in the press room.

Responding to a question about his wife, the president said the American people love her "because she's comfortable with who she is." I wrote him a personal note that I handed to Fitzwater for back-channel delivery: "You were right about Mrs. Bush. I'm a feminist, and for me there's nothing more feminist than being true to yourself." I got a reply: "Love your note. Hang in. George Bush."

I WAS SUMMONED to New York to participate in a news panel at a radio advertisers' lunch where I was asked about Bush's prudence. "He's hamstrung by his connection and allegiance to Reagan," I said. "To be bold would mean a sharp break with the past, which he can't do without repudiating Reagan."

Despite his being prudent and hamstrung, George Bush was popular, with approval ratings higher than any president since Kennedy. Part of it was because his first 18 months in office had been consumed with foreign issues, which, through experience and instinct, suited him. But now he was being sucked into a season of domestic issues, such as the savings and loan scandal, known around town as "bubonic banking." Bush took the S and L crisis particularly hard since it involved so many Republicans, but more so because it ensnared his son Neil.

But Bush's real nemesis was not the S and L crisis, it was his campaign pledge not to increase taxes. In late June a source on the Hill told me that in secret budget talks with the White House, the Democrats had issued an ultimatum: if the president didn't say publicly that he was willing to raise taxes, the negotiations would collapse. Within a few hours the White House put out a piece of paper with the president saying, among other things, "Because of the growing deficit, a budget package requires tax revenue increases." On the air that night I said, "Not only is he abandoning his own most politically potent campaign pledge, he's reversing ten years of Republican catechism on taxes."

Next came the howls: "turncoat," "double-crosser," "two-timer." I went on the air holding up the headline in the *New York Post*: "Read my lips: I lied." Bush was refusing to repeat the words on the printed statement out loud, until finally he acknowledged at a news conference that he was doing *it* because the economy demanded it. But he wouldn't say specifically that "it" was — raising taxes.

With some encouragement from the White House I grilled Senate Majority Leader George Mitchell on *Face* on July 1. "The president has obviously done the ultimate," I said. "He's really suffering. Isn't it your turn to tell us what magnitude of spending cuts you're talking about and take some of the heat, some kind of equivalent risk to show good faith, to balance this out?"

"We've already done that," said Mitchell, hanging the president out to dry. "We've indicated we accept the president's conclusion that taxes are necessary."

KAREN SUGHRUE had become the indispensable executive producer. I relied on her drive and judgment, not to mention her good nature and friendship. So I was shaken by her announcement that she was getting married, which came out of the blue. "To whom?" I asked. Not only did Karen marry Pat Sullivan, an ABC News producer who worked in Germany, she actually went off and lived with him. In Berlin. She left me. I kept telling her how happy I was for her; I was miserable for me.

Karen's last show focused on Soviet relations, with Defense Secretary Cheney and Gorbachev's spokesman, Gennadi Gerasimov, live from Moscow over satellite. Zirinsky was there, acting as our producer. She chose the perfect Moscow backdrop, the Cathedral of St. Basil in Red Square, with its brightly colored onion domes. But it started raining, so Gerasimov opened his huge umbrella, which blocked out St. Basil. As our show began, the light drizzle turned into Noah's own downpour. You could hear the pounding. When I asked Gerasimov about a letter Gorbachev had recently sent Bush, the rain pellets echoed like bullets on the umbrella, syncopating with a *plink-plink-plink* on the pavement. And the wind. He was fighting with the umbrella so strenuously, I thought he might take off like Mary Poppins. All the while, Gerasimov kept answering questions about the letter. Karen, usually unflappable, was having an embolism in my ear: Wrap. Dump it. Pull the plug. But the Cheney interview was on tape, meaning we had to fill up an allotted amount of time with Gerasimov, so I let him prattle on as if his hair weren't standing straight up, as if his coat weren't flapping like a large crane taking off, as if his umbrella weren't fighting him like a sumo wrestler. Zirinsky said I made history: the first *Face* interview that was funnier than Al Franken on *Saturday Night Live*. What a swan song for Karen.

THREE DAYS after Justice William Brennan, the great liberal mainstay of the Supreme Court, announced that he was resigning, Rita Braver called to say she was hearing that Bush had already chosen a replacement. It would be his first appointment to the Court. I called everyone I could think of in the White House. No one would talk, a definite sign that something was up. A staff person on the Senate Judiciary Committee told me that Bush was leaning toward Edith Jones of Texas, a judge of the U.S. Court of Appeals, 5th Circuit, and first choice of the right-to-lifers. I started researching her.

At 4:30, the pressroom loudspeaker boomed, "The president will be in the briefing room at five to announce his choice for the Supreme Court. His candidate will be with him."

370   I called the bureau's emergency line and asked for all the information we had on Edith Jones. Then I called Mary Matalin at the Republi-

can National Committee. I told her secretary, "It's an emergency." When Mary picked up, I said, "You can't let me go on the air and not know who it is. I'll look like a jerk."

"It's not Ken Starr," she said, wanting to be helpful. Starr, Bush's solicitor general, had been widely mentioned. "I can't tell you any more." One of the CBS deskmen called: "It's not Edith Jones. She's in her office in Houston." Rita called again: "I think it's Clarence Thomas." I began scribbling down info about him. It was 4:45. I had to get in my position in the front of the pressroom so I could chat with Dan before the president appeared. I began slapping on makeup. The phone rang. It was Mary Matalin: "It's David Souter." "Who's he?" The phone went dead.

I called it in and raced up to my seat. By the time I got there, Rita had it confirmed. Rather went on the air for a brief special report and broke the Souter story at 4:50. Afterward, I heard Dan in my ear: "This is great! Did we beat everyone?" We had.

I stood up on the Mt. Rushmore box and asked my print colleagues for help. Ann Devroy of *The Washington Post* and David Lauter of the *Los Angeles Times* fed me some facts about Souter: a judge from New Hampshire, a Sununu man.

When we went on the air, Dan came right to me. I had just enough on David Souter to describe him sketchily. And then there they were, Bush and his nominee, a man in near shock. We would later learn that Souter had been brought to town from New Hampshire the night before to meet Bush for the first time. After a 45-minute chat starting at 1:30 that afternoon, Bush had made a list of his pluses and minuses on a yellow legal pad and then offered him the job at 4:15. They raced out with the announcement at 5:00. The man hadn't changed, hadn't shaved, hadn't collected himself.

And there he was in a full-scale White House news conference, during which the president bobbed and weaved over Souter's stand on abortion. One of Souter's strongest selling points was that his position on *Roe v. Wade* was unknown. I had just said in my preannouncement ad libs with Dan that Souter was antiabortion. I'd gotten carried away with his ties to Sununu. I had broken the rule: never assume.

The president was annoyed by our questions: "You might think the whole nomination had something to do with abortion." He insisted he had chosen Souter for his intelligence and not to appease his conservative base, which was still furious with him for breaking his no-new-tax pledge.

I started writing my script at 5:30, still exhilarated by the chase to break the story. Souter was 50; Bush had appointed him to the U.S. Court of Appeals two months before. I called an old friend from my days of covering New Hampshire politics for the TV station in Boston and learned that Souter was a bachelor. He had had a big love affair many years back, had been jilted, and had never gotten over it. (My girlfriends and I decided that only a 50-year-old male, unmarried and living in the wilderness with his mother, could have no known position on abortion.)

With all the attention on the abortion question and his need to find a nominee who would not offend either wing of his own party, President Bush must have wondered: How had he done it? How had Ronald Reagan held the Republican Party together, with its Yuppies and the religious Right, its supply-siders and Wall Street conservatives? The Republican tent was splitting at the seams. On abortion, it was civil war. Bush needed a Supreme Court choice who would not rip the tent in half, especially as key prochoice Republicans were running that year. Now that he was concentrating on domestic issues, Bush's poll numbers were sinking.

MARTY PLISSNER, our CBS News political editor, wanted to discuss the incredible shrinking sound bite or, as we called them, SOTs — sounds on tape. We met for lunch at the Hay-Adams. He said that in 1968 the average bite had been 42 seconds long; by 1990 it was down to ten. "The academics say this means we're more shallow," he said, "but in 1968 the 40-second bite was the whole piece, with just a short top and close." Marty said that because of technology, our "element patrols" were gathering sound pops from all around the world, so we were now able to include three or four ten-second bites in one piece with opposing views, analysis, context.

Marty said he had been comparing the television stories of 1968 and now, and after slogging his way through all the pyrotechnics, sexy graphics, and snappier pacing, we were, in the end, doing a better job. No longer did we do simple here-they-come-there-they-go pieces. We ended our lunch, ready to battle the academics.

AARON, on antidepressants, was a new person. Usually taciturn, often glum, he would now tell Hollywood stories at parties like the one about Greta Garbo and Montgomery Clift arguing over who was lonelier. "Monty," said Aaron, "told Greta, 'I'm so lonely, my apartment has just one plate.'

" 'I'm so lonely,' Greta one-upped him, 'I eat alone every night — out of a can.' "

Only a few weeks before, I'd been living in fear. Now Aaron was the man I had married, with his depths of kindness, his sparkle back. It was a miracle.

372   AUGUST 2, 1990. I woke to the news that Iraq had invaded Kuwait. The Cold War had just ended, and the very first thing we did — was go to war.

Bush's first public comments were tentative. Asked if the United States would intervene, he hesitated: "I'm not contemplating such action." And then he flew off to Aspen, Colorado, to meet with Margaret Thatcher. What the eye saw were wildflower gardens and snowcapped mountains; what the feet contended with were mud and horse dung. Maggie, the one the Iraqis called "a hag whose mind has been invaded by the Devil," had trouble maneuvering in her heels. So did I.

Bush made a desultory statement about Iraq, emitting traces of his old wimpy self. Her Ironness, on the other hand, belted out a ringing condemnation of Iraqi leader Saddam Hussein.[11] But belying his cautious public posture, Bush, who had always insisted that economic sanctions didn't work, decided to organize an economic embargo. In an early-morning meeting, the president had overriden his foreign policy team, whose advice — with the exception of Scowcroft's — was, in so many words: too bad about Kuwait, but it's just a gas station.[12] It was President Bush who had asked the right question: "What happens if we do nothing?" And the answer soon became clear: Iraq would go after Saudi Arabia next, and more than half the world's oil supplies would come under Saddam's control.

My long-awaited one-month vacation was to start that Sunday. We canceled our trip, and instead I took Taylor with me to see the president's helicopter land on the White House lawn and hear his ultimatum: "This will not stand, this aggression against Kuwait." It sounded like a threat of military action. I wrote a two-minute story for *60 Minutes* that Bush was putting together a military blockade.

It was widely said that Saddam had invaded after taking George Bush's measure by observing his appeasement of China during Tiananmen and concluding that this American president would not resist an Iraqi move on Kuwait. But Iraq was threatening a vital U.S. interest, the oil supply. The man who had been a "hunk of liver" when the Berlin Wall came down would transmorph into sizzling red meat.

One of his inner circle called to tell me that Bush was "really in command," deciding policy, then employing his "Rolodex diplomacy" — getting on the phone and pushing it with foreign leaders. He planned and implemented a painstaking process of coalition building. "He's cajoling, persuading, changing the world. And he's so calm," the source said. Less than a week after the invasion, the president announced that the United States was sending troops to Saudi Arabia. In all the years I covered the White House, I cannot recall having so much admiration for a president.

Rather was anchoring from Amman, Jordan, and he reported on the self-indulgent lifestyle of the Kuwaitis. With a large audience of reporters in his office, Marlin Fitzwater let loose: "Dan's pulling for the wrong side. What's he up to? Doesn't he know how bad he looks? You guys have pictures in your own library of Saddam cutting off someone's ear." Marlin kept going: "This isn't a threat or anything. I'm just telling you, Dan's hanging himself." I was told that Sununu called Larry Tisch with the same message.

AT A NEWS CONFERENCE, Bush warned Saddam not to use his chemical weapons: "That would be intolerable and would be dealt with very, very severely." Lane Venardos, now head of the CBS Special Events Unit, whispered to me that Saddam had been killed. When Bush called on me I said, "Mr. President, I'm being told in my ear that there is a rumor out of Jidda that Saddam Hussein is dead."

The room buzzed. "I have not heard any of that," he said. The session ended quickly.

I called Lane and asked where his "rumor" had come from: "I can't find it on the wires." He said, "Monte Carlo Radio," and added, "It's not true." I got nothing but grief from my colleagues. At least ten reporters asked Marlin, "Is Saddam dead?" He answered, "There's a report from Jidda: Lesley's gone." This was only the beginning of this new-age war that would be so influenced by televised on-the-run reporting and diplomacy.

The last thing this White House wanted was Bush appearing to be held hostage by Iraq. They had Jimmy Carter's example to learn from. So the president went on vacation to Kennebunkport. If he could go on his holiday, I could go on mine.

NO SOONER had we arrived in Nantucket than the office called: CBS News President David Burke had been fired. After just two years, he was out, and Eric Ober, 48, whose experience was mainly in local news, was in.

We had rented a lovely little cottage on the bay that we again filled up with our friends. One day, as we were piling into Jeeps to go off to the beach for a picnic, the phone rang. It was Eric Ober. "How would you like to take on *Nightline?*" he bubbled. He said he had a plan: "We go on the air at 11:30 every night with Persian Gulf specials, and then we never relinquish the slot. The network," he said, "has given me the green light to try it — with Charles Kuralt and Lesley Stahl." Ober said my role would be hard-hitting interviews in Washington, while Charles would do well-written packages out of New York. I said yes right away.

"We start tonight," said Eric, "if Dan, who's in Baghdad, gets an interview with Saddam." We were to launch the show with Rather's exclusive. Ober asked me to call him in one hour. If they needed me, they would send in a charter and fly me to Washington.

I had one more day in the sun. Rather got his interview on August

29, and I dashed home to a nightmare. Lane Venardos, our executive producer, had spent several days accumulating producers in New York but hadn't bothered to assign anyone in Washington. Karen Sughrue had not yet left for Berlin, so I called and begged her to come in and help us launch the thing.

Rather got the first television interview with Saddam by sitting tight in the region for 23 days. When it came to pass, Dan asked tough questions about Saddam's stockpile of poison gas and the American hostages he denied he was holding. Kuwait, Saddam said, was part of Iraq, a "province."

Nothing had been done to book any guests since we had no bookers. So Karen and I got on the phone, finally landing Senators Joseph Biden and Richard Lugar. Not the kind of central players you'd expect for the debut of a new broadcast.

We led our first show with Rather's interview, followed by my interview with Rather about Saddam. "He's tough . . . with tattoos on his arm representing his manhood. . . . He thinks he's the one who has Bush backed into a corner." Responding to my question, Dan related how Saddam's bodyguards had separated him from his crew and taken him off alone to do the interview, using an Iraqi cameraman. It must have been frightening. And still Dan hadn't pulled his punches.

After the show there was a postmortem with the producers. Venardos's critique was about style. For instance, he thought there had been too little communication between Kuralt and me. Charles and I had agreed that we hated forced chitchat between anchors. So there hadn't been any chat at all. I was so dazzled to be working with Kuralt, grateful to be given the chance to grow, that I had that everything's-right-with-the-world feeling you get once every ten or 12 years.

Any fool should have known that a cold shower was on its way. It arrived the next morning when Lane asked on a New York–Washington conference call who my guest would be that night. Only then did it dawn on me that I would have to come up with guests to interview *every* night — not to mention for *Face* on Sundays.

After a day of rushed phone calling, we finally landed the Iraqi ambassador to Washington, Mohammed al-Mashat. Lane sent me a rundown: "Iraqi Amb 4 mins." I called: "We need eight minutes at the least." Lane said we would never do eight minutes. "Never. It would bring the show to a halt." I said that in that case I did not want to do the show.

I phoned Ober and found out how steely he could be. I said I was disturbed that such a fundamental format decision had been made without any input from me. He said, "Lane is the executive producer." I said, "I don't want to be superficial." He backed Lane but said, "There are no

375

rules; we can negotiate." This was no easygoing conversation. I said again I didn't want to do the show if my role would be doing four-minute *Morning News* interviews: "That's not how you sold it to me."

In the late afternoon Lane called. The four minutes for al-Mashat was up to five. I was still insisting on eight. When we hit the air, I got six.

Saddam was holding hundreds of Americans and other Westerners hostage, planting them at strategic locations the United States might bomb. After trying to elicit information about the condition of the hostages, I threw off any pretense of impartiality: "Is there any wonder . . . the American people see this as an act of unbelievable inhumanity and view your leader, Saddam, as a monster?"

"Well, I'm sorry to say," the ambassador responded, "we feel it is most inhumane what you have done to us by denying us food and denying our children milk. This is the most inhumane." He was referring to the U.S. economic sanctions.

The ambassador and I went back and forth like that until the six minutes were up, when he stormed off swearing he'd never do our show again.

Don Hewitt called: "You jumped right off the screen. You're the next Mike Wallace."

"You're just looking for an old fart to come aboard," I laughed.

"You can't be an old fart at *60 Minutes* till you're 72," he said.

When the war was over, I would be going back to the White House, where I was in the tumble cycle, coming back round and round: the yearly budget, the summits with the Soviets, the hothouse competition, the sucking up to my sources after a swipe at the president. *60 Minutes* was the answer, of course, but I told myself not to get my hopes up.

CHARLES KURALT was the best writer and best reader in TV news. But with all his informality and warmth on the air, most people confronted a wall when they tried to get close to him. Our being in different cities made it hard to develop a rapport. When I saw him in New York, I asked what he wanted me to call him on the air. I'd been saying "Charles," but it felt stiff and formal. He said he didn't care. "Are you sure? Is Charlie okay?" Yes, he smiled. Really? "Yes, some people even call me Chuck." So I called him Charlie, and Lane phoned after the show and said, "Call him Charles. That's what he prefers, but he'd never tell you that."

I confided in Diane Sawyer that I was having trouble establishing a chemistry with Kuralt. She had been his partner on the *Morning News* for a year and a half. "It's his rhythm," she explained. "It's so stylized and idiosyncratic, no one can mesh with it." She said she had also called him Charlie on the air and gotten a note from their executive producer, Shad Northshield. "On the whole, Charles is better."

BUSH HAD TALKED to more than 60 world leaders, building his coalition. Now, as I was reporting, he was asking Gorbachev for a summit so together they could send Saddam a video message: the superpowers are united against you. This was the first time in 45 years that the United States and the Soviet Union would be on the same side of a major world dispute.

Rather went to the Bush-Gorbachev summit in Helsinki, Finland, straight from his reporting in the Middle East, looking relaxed. I flew in from Washington and got a hug. I was there to interview Secretary of State Jim Baker for *Face*. "This man, Saddam Hussein," I said, "has taken American citizens and put them at military installations and God knows what other kinds of places — to use them as human shields."

"It's outrageous. It violates any standard of international norms," said Baker. "This is the first crisis of the post–Cold War era, and we simply cannot fail to succeed."

ON THE PRESS PLANE HOME, I read Aaron's rewritten Africa book, *The Frozen Leopard*, now a personal journey of recovery and healing, a brilliant, poetic, self-revealing tale of two safaris: one in Africa, the other through Aaron's soul. Aaron was working now as if he were making up for lost time. He had already begun his next project, a screenplay for Sam Goldwyn, Jr., about college football.

I flew home to a continuing battle over the 11:30 broadcast. I would come to realize that Eric Ober, with his local-station experience, was pulling the strings. I sensed a preference for short, tabloid-style pieces and lots of arguing. Lane said that "heated conflict" was an Ober mandate. Now Ober, my seventh CBS News president, was in Washington to meet the correspondents, and I was surprised at how easygoing and funny he was. Still he complained that we at CBS News were too reluctant to discuss cosmetics, "the delivery side of our mission." One of our finest correspondents, Bob Simon, he said, needed voice lessons. Eyes met in horror. "Guess it's time for my face-lift!" I hollered out. "No!" said Ober. "Older is more authoritative. People want their news from older-looking people." Thanks.

I still didn't have a producer for *Showdown in the Gulf*, the 11:30 show. I asked Lane about Janet Leissner, one of the best producers on the *Evening News*. The next day Janet Leissner was assigned as our senior producer in charge of Washington. She was smart, editorially strong, and experienced, and she wanted the job. I was overjoyed.

But I had no say in what I covered. At the White House and at *Face*, I participated in the decision making. Lane saw me as the greenhorn I was my first month as White House correspondent, and he treated me that way: dictating, not collaborating, not asking my opinion. I chose to take this as an insult. I knew Lane was *asking* Charles, not *telling* him, what his role was, so now I had to fight an impulse to scream, "Sexism!"

What a cabbage head. I could be so wise with my friends, stategizing about how they should act with *their* colleagues and bosses. But I was out of focus with myself. Blurred vision. No vision. I was caught up in a tyranny of resentment. Is this a girl thing? Or do we all, men and women, succumb to the darkest demons in us when our status is disputed? My agent, Jim Griffin, advised me to get my flies with honey. I was incapable of doing so. As I waged this war of my own making, I morphed into a scold. Trust me, I lived up to all the "bitch" whispers as I left the room.

Meanwhile, I was still covering the White House as well as moderating *Face* and anchoring the 11:30 specials, for which Janet Leissner was putting together a staff of young bookers and producers.[13] I must have been a total loon to think I could do all three jobs, but saying "I can't" seemed worse than driving myself into the ground.

Joe Peyronnin called me at the White House on September 13 with our 11:30 ratings. The first show had had a presentable 5.1, but after two weeks we had slipped to 2.8. "We need 3.0 to make money," he said. "By the way, kiddo, can you do it all? The White House, *Face*, and the specials?" I stopped for a minute and then admitted I was crumbling. He called back and offered me a leave of absence from the White House.

By late September George Bush was sending 150,000 U.S. troops to the desert of Saudi Arabia (with the prospect of doubling or tripling the numbers) to join soldiers from more than 20 other nations. The president hoped the show of force would convince Saddam to withdraw from Kuwait.

On September 28, the president met with the emir of Kuwait, Sheik Jaber al-Ahmed al-Sabah, who recounted tales of widespread looting, of Iraqis going into hospitals and taking old people off life-support systems so the machines could be sent to Baghdad. Bush said, "Iraq will fail. Kuwait, free Kuwait will endure." It was the last White House piece I did for three months.

OBER HAD PERSUADED the network to approve our specials as a regular nightly show, at least until the end of the year. Aaron proposed that we call it *Taps*, but Lane said that sounded like a funeral. Howard Stringer liked *Double Exposure*, but I thought that when anything didn't work the critics would say, "Out of focus." We settled on *America Tonight*.

From our first broadcast in late August, the 11:30 news specials had been exclusively about the Gulf War. On October 1 *America Tonight* debuted as a whole new show with a wider portfolio. At nine that night I got a call from Ted Koppel. "Good luck," he said, "but not too much of it." Classy.

"Here we begin something new," Kuralt said. That's how he started. "In this half hour each night we'll try to cast some light into dark corners of big questions. Are we about to have a war? Are we about to have a recession? And to poke around in some other corners too, to find out what's going on in America tonight. We hope to have some insights, have some arguments, and have some fun." But no one had thought through what we were about. Ober had said, "Don't overthink it. Not having a set format or concept will lead to creativity." We had doubts. Our only mandate was "Be different from *Nightline*."

It was no surprise, then, that our *America Tonight* debut was a clutter, a little of this and a little of that. I moderated a debate on the Gulf War between Richard Perle, who advocated a let's-attack-now policy, and former Secretary of the Navy James Webb, whose position was "Why so fast?" Eric had said he wanted a "stable of arguers." You knew as the clock ticked toward midnight on that first show that the wind was not with us. And the critics were not kind. Howard Rosenberg said in the *Los Angeles Times* that we looked like "an unearthed stiff" and that the program had "a mood of musty *déjà vu*."

The good thing about daily journalism is that you get another chance every day, and we did better on Tuesday. We booked the House GOP whip, Newt Gingrich, who was fast becoming George Bush's antagonist. Newt, the bomb thrower, had brought down Speaker of the House Jim Wright. Now he was aiming his grenade launcher at the head of his own party, leading the fight against Bush's budget agreement.[14] The post-Reagan ideological fight in the Republican Party was raging. And no matter how much Bush pandered to the Right (this was why George Will had called him a "lapdog"),[15] it still and always saw him as an enemy.

The White House, meanwhile, saw Gingrich as a man who wanted to "destroy the temple." So Richard Darman refused to come on our show with Newt, as did half a dozen Republican senators. I called Fitzwater and asked for help. "Naw, we want to leave Newt out there debating himself." "You're leaving this to me?" I asked. "Yes! Go get 'em, bulldog."

We finally booked Carol Cox, a feisty redheaded budget expert, a real match for Newt on the subject of taxes. The debate crackled — so much so that Lane let it run an extra 30 seconds. Everything ran smoothly. Charles did a nifty piece on the humvee as the new military jeep. "Great show!" boomed Lane in my ear. I bounded into the control room on a high. Everyone was elated.

But then producers began calling from around the country, dispatched by Venardos to work on stories for me, including some I had no interest in: women reporters in sports locker rooms, how police treat victims of rape. I wanted to stick with the budget, which, because of Gingrich's assault, had Bush shilly-shallying on what the Democrats thought he had agreed to: raising taxes on millionaires. He had recently reversed himself four times. At one point while the president was jogging, reporters asked him to clarify his stand, and he blurted out, "Read my hips." As he swerved this way and that on taxes, there was one steady-as-she-goes trend: his approval ratings went straight down, plunging 20 points in just a few weeks.

I called Lane and argued, "We'll look foolish ignoring the budget."

"Look, I'm the executive producer and this is my call, not yours."

"But we will be wrong," I shot back. "How come Charles gets to do what he wants, but I don't?" This was a mistake, and I knew it the minute I said it. Bad form.

When we went on the air, the budget debate was still on in the House; if the package was voted down, it would be a mammoth story. *Nightline* did the budget. I did five minutes on rape.

The next day Ann Reingold, one of *America Tonight*'s New York producers, said, "Lane wants you to do a segment on condoms in the New York City schools."

"We'd look like idiots doing that instead of this big budget story," I protested.

"Funny, that's what Charles said when we tried to get him to do the segment."

Gingrich won the battle in the House to defeat the president's deficit-cutting budget. It was a great story. Eventually, though, the Democratic Congress and the Bush White House agreed on a package that did pass. It raised taxes, cut spending, and imposed fiscal discipline with a new "pay-as-you-go" rule that required Congress to make budget cuts before passing tax cuts.

AMERICA TONIGHT was like a child with colic. Instead of using honey to remedy the problems, I grumbled and bellyached. My friend Brian Healy sent me a note: "Colleague dearest." But it wasn't until Aaron weighed in that I began to take stock. I came home late, as usual, close to 1 A.M. "Wasn't that segment they made me do just dreadful?" I grouched.

"I knew you would say that," he said, disappointed. "That's all you do, is complain. You think if you interview a kid or an ordinary citizen, you look bad. Well, you're wrong. The show was great. Why don't you just back off." I felt like a crushed can. Every now and then Aaron, who was usually nonjudgmental, would cut through with such clarity, it was like electric shock treatment. He was, though it was hard for me to admit it, simply . . . right. After his little lecture, I was left with bouts of remorse at how I had been acting. From then on, the "war" was one within me, to silence the anger in my head, which had become my Other Person. A

380

presence, a being. Someone told me the opposite of happiness isn't always depression; sometimes it's anger.

I tried. I spoke up on the morning conference call as sweetly as I could: "I think our opening segments have been too disjointed. Shouldn't Charles and I do a one-two on the same issue?" Lane said he didn't disagree and suggested we both do something on oil prices that night. After that we settled into a rhythm. I'd do a lead segment on the surtax on millionaires followed by Charles's interview with Ross Perot (who said millionaires did not mind the surtax). Charles would write a piece about the troop deployments to Saudi Arabia, and I'd follow up by asking Les Aspin to explain the game plan.

The show improved. We were finding our voice, and New York began to treat us country mice in Washington more like partners than underlings.

CBS WAS THE ONLY NETWORK to put on a full two-hour election night show. I was assigned the governors' races, which turned into the best story of the night: Lawton Chiles, the Democrat, won in Florida even though his opponent had made an issue of his taking antidepression pills, and Ann Richards won in Texas. Dan said the Texas race had been "so nasty it would gag a buzzard!"

Aaron watched election night from his room at Penn State. He was working on his movie for Sam Goldwyn, living in the football dorm with the players. He said, "I've never felt this good. Never." His doctor had told him that some people get depressed all over again, thinking about all the years they wasted by not going on medicine earlier. I told him it was never wasted for a writer.

BUSH WAITED until after the election to announce a massive buildup of U.S. troops in Saudi Arabia, to 430,000. With those numbers, an attack on Iraq could be launched by January 15, the deadline set by the United Nations for Saddam to withdraw from Kuwait.

My guest on *America Tonight* on November 8, 1990, was again the Iraqi ambassador, al-Mashat. My attempts to ask a question were turned aside until I finally bulled my way in: "First you invaded Kuwait. You also have taken American hostages. You are not allowing food and water in to our embassy, and you have raped and pillaged the country of Kuwait. My question to you is: Is your country prepared to take on the biggest and most powerful military force in the world?"

"You have blockaded the country without any authorization," he said. "Does that not move you a little bit?"

"Are you prepared to take on the most powerful —"

"No, we don't want — we want peace."

"Are you going to pull out of Kuwait?"

"We are asking to negotiate. . . . Why you sacrifice American boys for nothing? What are you going to gain? You will gain ashes. It is not an American business. It is an Arab business and United Nations business."

"But you took hostages and pillaged the country."

"We didn't."

"Human shields. Don't say you didn't."

"We will never surrender, never capitulate."

As he stomped off, al-Mashat said, "Ted Koppel would not interrupt. I will never do this show again!" Again. Don Hewitt called to say nice things.

It was as if George Bush had been preparing his whole life for this crisis. One of his advisers remarked that all the jobs he had held were coming together. He had been CIA director, so he knew which department to call for the best intelligence; he'd been U.N. ambassador, so he was receptive to the notion of using that body (even though he had disparaged Dukakis during the campaign as an "internationalist"). It was because of the many personal relationships Bush had so carefully nourished over the years that he was able to persuade 26 nations to send troops to join his coalition. Reagan had been the cowboy hero who liked to ride alone; Bush liked to do things in concert, so, as it was said, he rounded up a posse.

JANET LEISSNER came up with an idea for *America Tonight*: "Let's go home with a senator and televise a town meeting with him on Iraq." We chose Democrat Bob Kerrey of Nebraska, a veteran who had lost a leg in Vietnam and was now opposing Bush's war.

Lane, several producers, Charles, and I were in Omaha the afternoon of the event, November 29, going over the format, when the phone rang. Kerrey was pulling out. He was objecting to our having invited Hal Daub, a former Republican congressman from that area. Either we cancel out Daub, we were told, or we lose Kerrey. It was three hours to air.

We lost Kerrey. Charles and I, up on a stage, took turns asking questions, but mostly we let the assembled citizens debate the war. Some agreed with Bush: "What about the country's honor? Our credibility?" Others had kids over there: "They've sent 55,000 body bags over to bring our children home in." A priest said, "That royal family [in Kuwait] isn't worth one drop of our blood, but we have to support our troops." A businessman called for patience; but a mother said her son, a marine, was a hostage, "a guest" in Baghdad. She did not want to give up her son, but *he* thought the principle, standing up to naked aggression, was worth dying for.

They were raw and honest and genuine, and they all cared deeply. What you learned was that the country was divided. Bush had not yet done the work of bully-pulpit convincing that he needed to.

When the 60 minutes were up, the audience gathered around us. It was too soon to end, there was so much more to say, so we stayed there on the stage and kept up our discussion without the forced rancor of a manufactured debate with a "stable of arguers." This show made us a team. Charles gave me a rose. I decided I liked him a lot. Not because of any personal relationship; we still had none. But I had come to respect his toughness, his doing what he wanted to do, on his own terms — and how, with that benign, folksy exterior, he managed to incite a kind of veneration through aloofness. Mostly I liked him because he was grounded in principle and integrity.

On the flight home, we sat together. I read three newspapers, underlining stories about the Persian Gulf, the White House, the budget, the president's poll numbers. Charles flipped through the lifestyle sections and did the crossword puzzle.

Several weeks later Bob Kerrey held his own town meeting in Omaha and because of his anti-Bush stance was booed.

I WENT TO A CONFERENCE in Washington of women journalists from around the world and was surprised by the seeping resentment toward American imperialism in journalism. An articulate woman from Zimbabwe complained that Africans were being force-fed CNN news with its American bias. "Why can't we have our own people telling us the news?" she asked. A woman from Nigeria ridiculed the idea that the American press was objective. "In none of your stories on the Persian Gulf," she said, "do you liken Saddam Hussein's takeover of Kuwait to the U.S. invasions of Panama or Grenada."

I left the conference pondering questions I had not put my mind to: When is the time for a journalist to show loyalty to her own country? Is war the time? Or now that news is globalized, is there ever a time? These were subjects we never talked over, never debated. We would have to as we moved forward in Desert Storm.

I HAD PROPOSED a series of interviews for *America Tonight* called "The Wise Men and Women," in which I would ask gray heads, in effect, "What's been pissing you off lately?" When I asked Bob Strauss, he answered that as a lover of Thoroughbred horse racing, he always wished he could "breed" our leaders, custom-design one president with *all* the right attributes. He said, "We always get them with some defect or other."

He waited to tell me his best anecdote until the camera was turned off. During his last meeting with LBJ, Johnson had summoned a local Lutheran preacher, who took a piece of paper from his lapel pocket and began to read: "Lyndon Johnson: a humble man, a man of the soil, a man of the people."

"No!" roared the Great One. He grabbed the paper, scratched out what the preacher had written, and penciled in his own thoughts: "Lyndon Johnson: statesman, world leader, powerful force for change."

"Yes, sir, fine," said the preacher.

Johnson died soon thereafter. At the funeral the preacher took a piece of paper out of his lapel pocket and read, "Lyndon Johnson: a humble man, a man of the soil, a man of the people."

"The moral of the story," said Strauss, "is, when you die, you're dead. So's all your power. So's everything. Somethin' to remember."

LARRY TISCH continued to close down what most of us reporters considered essential news bureaus, such as the one in Chicago. I thought that he was the reason I was having a recurring dream that CBS was crumbling. There was this big adobe wall with cracks and holes and sand sifting down. It was Tisch who was making all those holes, destroying Paley's mansion. He had sold off the building blocks of a communications company of the future: music, publishing, cable, and even interactive TV. CBS had had them all when Tisch took over — all the ingredients of a modern powerhouse. As one of his own assistants told me, "He was in over his head; he didn't know how to grow a company."

One of his executives said, "Because of arrogance and pride, he wouldn't listen to those who understood the television business far better than he." So he waved off his lieutenants at Black Rock and against their advice cut the compensation payments to the affiliates, the money a network pays its stations to carry programming. If ever there was a red-hot-poker-in-the-eye sure to drive off the best of the stations, that was it. At the least, it persuaded many of them *not* to carry *America Tonight* at 11:30 — or at any time.

THE BUILDUP in the Gulf was a preoccupying story on *America Tonight.* I interviewed Crown Prince Hassan of Jordan, a longtime U.S. ally now tilting toward Iraq. Prince Hassan used the interview to plead with President Bush to give a little on the Palestinian issue "so the Arabs can feel the U.S. is not irrationally pro-Israel." I asked Israeli Deputy Foreign Minister Benjamin Netanyahu about Saddam's threat that if Iraq were attacked, its first act of retaliation would be to bomb Tel Aviv. Netanyahu said that Israel would not stage a preemptive strike: "We will have to be dragged in."

One of the president's shrewdest moves in this buildup period was downplaying the American hostages. He never talked about them, never made demands about their safety, mindful of the trap Jimmy Carter had fallen into by allowing *his* hostages to consume his presidency. Bush's tactic paid off. The hostages were of so little value that Saddam released them in December.

One of my guest wise men, retired *New York Times* columnist James Reston, was critical of Bush's handling of the Persian Gulf buildup. He charged that the president was "continually issuing ultimatums that he can't live up to."

Scotty Reston had covered ten presidents. Who was the smartest? Carter. "Jimmy Carter was very smart and not a very good president, so that intelligence is not necessarily the test." The worst? Reagan. "The worst but the nicest. The most delightful fraud we've ever had." The best? Ike. "He knew it was so much easier to get into wars than to get out of them."

I remarked about those presidents who, in spite of their success, hadn't felt they'd "arrived" and sat in the White House still trying "to prove something to themselves and to the world."

"All these guys are beyond journalism," said Reston. "They're all psychological novels. How do you explain a guy like Nixon? He lived a life of pretense; tried to be a tough guy when he wasn't tough, tried to be vulgar when he wasn't really vulgar. The real Nixon was better than the phony Nixon, you see?"

"Is Bush trying to be what he isn't?"

"Bush is essentially a New England gentleman, but he's trying to overcome it."

I TOLD TAYLOR she could go to the mall with her friends, but then she was late and didn't call. Every mother's nightmare. She was out there somewhere in Washington, D.C., which, don't forget, was the homicide capital of the world. When she finally sauntered in, I told her, "No more malls, no more after-school running around. Tomorrow you come with me to work, you hear, missie." But instead of being dejected, she loved the whole idea. "I'm grounded!" I heard her bragging to her friends. This was a badge of being like all the other kids.

ERIC OBER got onto our *America Tonight* conference call in early December—we had been on the air for four months—and announced our cancellation after the end of the year, due to weak ratings. I was either relieved or disappointed, I didn't know which. "But if there's war," he said, "we're back with war specials every night at 11:30 with Charles and Lesley."

385

Later in the day, Ober called me. I thought he was going to thank me for the hard work, but instead he dumped ice chips on my head: I had been demanding and difficult. "If you ever go to 60 *Minutes*, Hewitt won't put up with it."

"I concede I'm difficult, but if I hadn't been difficult, this show wouldn't be as good as it became." What a dreadful thing to say. There's a reason for the expression "We're our own worst enemy." Eric went silent, then got off. I felt awful. I couldn't fall asleep that night. The next day I went in and did my job. Around 6 P.M. I got a dozen red roses from Ober.

We were contending with stations dropping us one by one. Charles sent us all invitations to a party "To celebrate a failure." And we kept going. As Congress began its debate on the Gulf War, we flew to Chapel Hill, North Carolina, for our second town meeting. I was on a medicine chest of pills: prednisone for laryngitis, an antibiotic, nose drops, Tylenol.

We assembled in the "parlor" of the Morehead Planetarium near the University of North Carolina. This was Charles's alma mater, so there was quite a fuss. The first person I met was Charles's brother, Wallace, with the big white beard. He owned a chain of country book stores and adored his brother.

As in Omaha, we booked the audience: mothers and wives of boys in the Saudi desert, reservists, preachers, a mayor, a businessman. "Should we go to war?" I asked. A man whose son had been killed in a car crash in Saudi Arabia stood up. "I'm not bitter," he said. "I support Bush. Getting Saddam out of Kuwait isn't enough. We should go after him and kill him."

Everyone in the room froze. No one wanted to contradict this man, who so clearly was in pain. There was a poignant silence. I mumbled my way to a segue: "Very emotional and I'm sure very difficult for you, sir." Another question, and soon people began jumping up. "Saddam's counting on our blinking," said a mother. "We can't blink." A farmer said, "We should exhaust patiently every possible, reasonable alternative to postpone the shooting indefinitely." An Episcopal priest from Raleigh asked, "What are we going to kill for?" This session was even more passionate than the one in Omaha. Some of the people were pointed, accusatory; some pleaded; some cried. At the end I blurted out, "This'll probably sound corny, but I'm so proud of my country."

COUNTRIES ABOUT TO ENTER a conflict used to communicate through their ambassadors or by secret cable. In 1990 President Bush and Saddam Hussein sent messages back and forth over television, which became a leveling factor. Television allowed a small-time tyrant such as Saddam to compete for public opinion on an equal footing with the leader of the Free World.

The press is always a factor in a crisis. But in Desert Storm globalized television became a force in the equation of war. What we did, where we went, how and when we broadcast became part of policy to a far greater extent than ever before. How would our pictures affect support for the war? After Vietnam, the Pentagon became convinced that strong public backing was a necessity for military action. Saddam's access to the airwaves was frustrating for the Bush administration, just as our airing the views of the hostages' families had been for the Carter and Reagan administrations. Television was weakening the hand of government by giving voice to the once voiceless.

CONGRESS FINISHED ITS DEBATE on a war resolution and voted to support Bush, though there was strong opposition. On Sunday on *Face* Sununu said, "I think it's unfortunate that there was . . . partisan opposition to the president's policy evident in the [congressional] debates. . . ."

"Are you suggesting [those negative votes] were political and not heartfelt?" I asked.

"No, I'm saying that the president received bipartisan support for his policy, and that's an important message to Hussein."

Of course he was questioning the patriotism of the Democrats who had voted against Bush. Samuel Johnson's scoundrel came to mind. In the makeup room I showed Sununu an article about Lee Atwater's having written to apologize to Michael Dukakis for the racist Willie Horton campaign.[16] Sununu's response was "Lee's sick. They shouldn't exploit him this way."

JANUARY 15. *America Tonight* was still on the air. The U.N. deadline for Saddam to withdraw from Kuwait was less than 13 hours away. Eric Ober got onto the *America Tonight* conference call and announced, "Our cancellation has been revoked indefinitely." Called upon to say something, Charles sounded glum. Most of us had come to see *America Tonight* as a burden, especially as we had struggled through the lame-duck shows of the past several weeks. Only Ober seemed triumphant.

The next day, I called Zirinsky, who was running the "War Desk." "We're on Def-con standby," she said. "Can't talk." There were rumbles all morning that this would be the day we would go to war, which would mean we'd go into 24-hour, round-the-clock coverage. "When it starts, we want you at the White House," Joe Peyronnin said. A courier was sent to my apartment to pick up my heavy-duty boots.

We stayed on alert all day. Then, as Rather was suggesting on the *Evening News* that an attack was imminent, the wires started pinging with a bulletin: "Flashes over Baghdad." Just then our CBS phone line to our reporter Alan Pizzey in Baghdad went dead.[17] Carin Pratt hollered over from *Face*, "Switch to CNN," which, I suspect, is what many CBS viewers did that night. CNN was reporting tracers in the skies over Baghdad. You could hear the U.S. bombs going off. The president had launched an air war over Iraq. The size of it was staggering.

I put on my boots and raced over to the White House in a heavy snowstorm. Fitzwater was briefing: Bush had learned of the attack he had approved from CNN and ABC. Fitzwater told us the president had invited Billy Graham to sleep over at the White House.

Bush went on air from the Oval Office at 9 P.M. It was a short, to-the-point speech, the most watched broadcast ever up to that point — 65 million households tuned in. I went on right after: "He said he had 'no choice.' He said, 'We will not fail. We will knock out Saddam's nuclear potential, chemical facilities, his entire military arsenal.' "

We were now on the air nonstop. David Martin at the Pentagon did a first-rate job, as did Bob Simon in Saudi Arabia, and Rather managed the bombardment of information brilliantly. But with no phone connection to Baghdad, we were being badly beaten by CNN which alone was able to keep its line open. CNN's live reports from inside an enemy capital were extraordinary. John Holliman: "Whoa! Holy cow! That was a large airburst that we saw." Bernie Shaw: "This feels like we're in the center of hell." Peter Arnett: "We're crouched behind a window in here . . . the antiaircraft is erupting again."[18]

We came in fourth — a stunning defeat. CNN was first. CBS affiliates in various parts of the country dropped our coverage that night to take CNN's. When I got home around 2 A.M., Aaron was up watching CNN.

DAY TWO. Colin Powell, chairman of the Joint Chiefs of Staff, and Defense Secretary Cheney briefed together. The air campaign was a success, they said. There had been 1,000 sorties, with no aerial resistance to the initial air attack, equivalent to an atomic bomb in payload (18,000 tons). And there were no reports of any U.S. casualties. The stock market soared.

I was back at the White House, where all the TV sets were tuned to CNN. There was still no Iraqi resistance, only sporadic and ineffective surface-to-air firings. I rushed to the lawn every now and then with tidbits: a report on Bush's attempts to dampen the country's euphoria; another on his remarks at a Cabinet meeting that there would be no pause, "no letup till Saddam surrenders." It was exhilarating to be working on the big story.

Wyatt went home. Bush went home. I was watching the news from the booth when, at 7:05 P.M., CBS correspondent Tom Fenton, on a phone line from Israel, came on with terrifying news: alarms and sirens were going off in Tel Aviv, and there had been hits. Iraqi Scud missiles were pelting Israel. This was disaster: now Israel would strike back.

I ran to Fitzwater's office. He had turned off his TVs and, with his hat and coat on, was giving CNN's Charles Bierbauer tomorrow's schedule. "We're reporting Scuds hitting Tel Aviv!" I sputtered. Marlin slouched and slowly put his briefcase down. "Can you find out anything?" I implored.

Marlin called the Situation Room. "I have some reporters with me. What do you know?" When he hung up he said, "They say they saw the TV report. They're checking." Other reporters began streaming back and joined us camping out around Marlin's office.

Tel Aviv had been hit. In Israel, newsmen were on camera speaking through gas masks. We watched CNN's reporters put masks on each other. ABC said it was a nerve gas attack. But that was wrong. At one point Rather went to Jim Jensen in Tel Aviv, the anchorman of WCBS in New York, who reported that Israel was retaliating. That too was wrong. CBS's Tom Fenton, ever solid, was cautious. When he was pressed, he resisted reporting anything he couldn't confirm.

Around ten, an exhausted Marlin Fitzwater posted a sheet of paper confirming that Iraq had sent missiles into Israel and Saudi Arabia. By then we had been on the air with pictures of the hits in Tel Aviv, which again was how the White House was getting much of its own information. The coverage of localized areas of damage was somewhat misleading. What we saw on television looked like Beirut. Buildings had been demolished. By some miracle, there had been only a handful of injuries.

I went on the air after midnight to describe the extraordinary if not desperate phone calling by Bush's foreign policy advisers to make sure the anti-Iraq alliance held together. I commented on the exceptional act of restraint on Israel's part in *not* retaliating. I also noted that antiwar protesters were camped across the street in Lafayette Park: "You can hear the drums and the shouts."

DAY THREE. Wyatt was rushed to the hospital with chest pains. We were terrified he had had a heart attack. Within an hour we learned he was okay, just dehydrated. He'd been working round the clock. Everyone was worn out, including the president, who looked drawn at a morning news conference. "Are we trying to kill Saddam?" I asked. "No one is being targeted," said Bush. I asked if Israeli jets had begun a retaliation the previous night that he had stopped. No, he said, but he hoped Israel would continue to hold its fire. That's what all of us were holding our breath about. If Israel struck back, it would hand Saddam a victory since the alliance would probably fall apart.

389

Throughout the day there were terrifying reports of more Scud attacks on Israel. Piercing sirens would go off, but then there would be all clears. As I said from the White House lawn, "When the false alarms go off in Israel, the tension here is higher than ever. Bush is off to Camp David while his team stays here, braced for another night of terror." Marlin made fun of my tension-higher-than-ever line. "Did I get it wrong?" I asked.

"Tension? C'mon," he said.

"Well, what would you say?" I asked.

"Our anxieties are evening out. We have an understanding with the Israelis."

I left the White House at around 9 P.M. and went to the bureau to get ready for *America Tonight*. This was to have been our last night; instead, it was another war show. We were all dead, but we had to move quickly, because I had an interview with Israel's Netanyahu at precisely 10:40, CBS's time on the "bird." Satellite bookings were very tight, with four nets vying for time. But then the sirens went off in Israel again, and everyone there was ordered into sealed rooms with gas masks on. Once again it was a false alarm, but it meant that Netanyahu was late. By the time he arrived we had just four minutes, but he was eloquent in describing the courage of his people in not striking back.

I was finally on my way home at 12:30 when the alarms went off in Israel again and Tom Fenton was saying "Four hits!" Four in Tel Aviv. I turned the car around and went back. Rather was on the air again, interviewing our military consultant, retired general George Crist, who said that it appeared that "the enemy has a far more sophisticated system than anyone imagined." I chilled. "If the Israelis do retaliate," I wondered on the air, "how can they do a better job of taking out the Scuds than the Americans?"

When I finally left at 2 A.M., M Street was blocked off by fire engines. A small white car, one of those Yugoslav minis, was in the middle of the street, right in front of the bureau. I grabbed a member of the D.C. bomb squad: "There are 50, 60 people inside working," I said, then dashed around the corner to a pay phone. I screamed to Janet, "Get out. Go out the back. *Now.*" When I got home, I kept calling the control room until finally Janet answered. There had been an all clear on the white Yugo. No bomb. It was after 3 A.M.

IRAQ KICKED OUT the foreign press on day four. A convoy of 110 foreigners drove to Amman, Jordan, praying the whole way. Everyone left but CNN.

U.S. planes were flying as many as 2,000 missions a day against Iraq. The Pentagon was providing us its videos of 2,000-pound, laser-guided "smart" bombs dropped by a stealth plane into a communications center

390

in Baghdad. In another scene a stealth bomber released a load and banked sharply, showing the bombs zapping a bunker into flames.

I watched our coverage in the bureau control room with Rome and Carin Pratt, the associate producer of *Face*. At a Pentagon briefing, Lieutenant General Thomas Kelly was saying, "We control the skies." Never before had the generals held daily televised briefings during a war. The briefings were aired live on CNN and at least in part on the networks. This had its downside, since the public was horrified to see how rude and irreverent we in the press could be. What business did some pipsqueak reporter have probing and pestering a four-star general during a war?

Often, the only way to pluck out information is to ask a lot of questions that may seem like nitpicking or sound uninformed (which they often are) or argumentative (which they also are). But this is what we do. As Bill Plante said, "The public watched us make the sausage, and they didn't like it." The news media became so unpopular that at one point 62 percent in a *Washington Post* poll said that the Allies should bomb a Baghdad hotel even if it were filled with Western reporters. More than 80 percent told the Gallup Poll that they approved of tight restrictions on the news media. On *Saturday Night Live* someone with a reporter's notebook asked someone in a general's uniform, "Are we planning an amphibious invasion of Kuwait? And if so, where exactly would that be?"

General Norman Schwarzkopf was the quarterback of the war. He had the build of a lineman and the presence of George Patton, perfect for the television age. He came on *Face* by satellite from U.S. headquarters in Dhahran with all the trappings of his military power: epaulets, bars, stars, stripes, flags, and khaki everywhere. We have cut Saddam's command and communications networks, he said; "in other words, Saddam is no longer communicating with his troops." I asked a *Saturday Night Live* question: "What does that mean?" He explained very patiently, "A lot of them aren't getting orders."

I took a break. Sunday afternoon at home, sitting on the bed, staring out. Aaron was watching the football play-offs, which were interrupted several times by bulletins: Scud attacks on Dhahran and on Riyadh proper. CBS correspondent Scott Pelley in Dhahran shouted through his gas mask. Patriot missiles were striking back; you could see the streaks in the sky.

This was breathtakingly new: a war fought in real time on television. Vietnam had been reported after the fact on film that had to be flown to New York and developed. The Gulf War was bombs going off and the wail of air-raid sirens filling us with terror in our living rooms. I can still see our reporters and cameramen standing up against that Scud sky.

DAY SIX. Bob Simon was missing. He had taken a four-wheel-drive land cruiser and with cameraman Roberto Alvarez, soundman Juan Caldera, and producer Peter Bluff had headed for the Iraqi border. By the time *America Tonight* went on the air, he was at least eight hours late. Bob had complained openly about the Pentagon's plans to restrict and "sanitize" press coverage. Reporters were not being permitted to go out and cover the war without military escorts. He had been quoted: "The brass is still convinced that the press had a lot to do with the political fallout from the [Vietnam] War, so they are trying to do what they can to prevent those things from happening again."[19]

Two days went by. No one heard from Simon or the others. I thought about them all the time. Morale at CBS could not have been lower; if anything happened to Bob, we would break. He was our best. When the Saudis found the van with the keys, $6,000, and TV equipment inside, we got desperately nervous.

I hadn't seen my daughter for a week. I insisted that I go home for dinner. Tay and I went out to Enzio's and talked about her being the stage manager at Sidwell's production of *South Pacific*, and directing her friends in *Blithe Spirit*. She said she wanted to work in Hollywood when she grew up. Like her dad.

CBS was contacting everyone in sight to ask for help in finding Bob and the crew: foreign diplomats, heads of state in the Middle East, everyone we interviewed. I worked at getting a message to Jordan's King Hussein. Richard Holbrooke was helping Bob's wife, Françoise, organize a campaign to find Bob.

At a book party we threw for Holbrooke on January 25 — he had coauthored the just-published Clark Clifford memoir — the only topic of conversation was the war. Bob Woodward, who was writing a book on the Pentagon, said that the main strategy was drawing the Republican Guards out of their bunkers. Dick Solomon, the assistant secretary for the Far East at the State Department, said that the Arab coalition was very shaky: "The more we bomb Iraq, the harder it'll be for any Muslim country to back us."

Pamela Harriman had lived through the London Blitz during World War II. "The bombing stiffened people for the fight," she said. "It made those of us at home part of the war. We saw ourselves as soldiers too." She told us about a woman who had been pulled out of the rubble of her bombed-out house. The rescue workers said, "Where's your husband?" "The coward's in France!"

We asked Senator Al Gore for his thoughts. After maintaining silence during the congressional debate, Gore had finally voted with the president. He said he thought the sanctions would have worked, but once Bush sent 400,000 troops, he couldn't vote to pull the plug. He was halting and defensive.

☐

WE WANTED TO HOLD ANOTHER *America Tonight* town meeting, but we canceled it because we couldn't find enough opposition to the war to make it interesting. *AT* was struggling. Many of our producers were diverted to war coverage. Not only were we stretched thin, we dared not ask anyone in the rest of the company for help: it was like asking them to give blood. Correspondents were already being called on to get up early for the *Morning News*; how could we ask them to stay late? We were orphans. I was wearing down, losing my edge. So when Howard Stringer called and said he was canceling the show after all, I was grateful. He said that our ratings were up 30 percent, but despite the good showing, he had already spent close to $20 million on an action series. "If I don't run these shows, we'll have to absorb more budget cuts to compensate for the loss." He didn't say exactly when we would be off the air. As long as there was war, there would be an *America Tonight*.

The Pentagon kept ladling out rosy accounts and then preventing reporters from independently checking on them. Some of the Pentagon's restrictions were legitimate, but others were infuriating, obviously put in place to keep public opinion on board — like the banning of pictures of caskets arriving at Dover Air Force Base or the cleansing of pool reports, changing the word "giddy" to describe a pilot's reaction to a hit, for instance, to "proud."

Coverage of the battlefield continued to be limited to pools controlled by military escorts. And many topics were off-limits, such as the number of Iraqi casualties, again to prevent a dip in public support.[20]

PETER ARNETT of CNN was the only reporter left broadcasting from Baghdad. He was operating under strict censorship, all his stories reviewed by the Iraqis. When Senator Alan Simpson, Republican from Wyoming, accused Arnett of being "an Iraqi sympathizer," it tripped off a volley of attacks by the press; we were all appalled at Simpson. It was obvious that Arnett was working in a dangerous milieu, that most of what he was allowed to see — mainly the damage caused by the Allied bombs — was being orchestrated by the Iraqis; but he was doing a valiant job of skirting around the Iraqi propaganda. Simpson's attack seemed more like a wacky tantrum than well-considered criticism. For there was a value in hearing from the other side, in keeping the lines of communication open, both for the American public and the White House. But when I asked Simpson on *America Tonight* on February 22, about his attack on Arnett, his eyes turned hard and icy. He spoke scathingly about all the smears he had suffered at the hands of reporters. He would remain bitter about it for years.

The press was facing questions about patriotism in a war with globalized communication. There were no rules written in a book somewhere. It was like my bounding up into the terrorists' plane in the Fred Friendly scenario: Oops, how did we get here? Now what am I going to do? If the other side in a war invites a news organization to come behind enemy lines, we go and worry later. I am sure that if CBS had been allowed to stay in Baghdad, we would have, and we would have aired the reports along with reminders that the stories had been subjected to Iraqi censorship. Which is just what CNN did.

By early February, the planning and pre-positioning for the ground war into Iraq were grinding on. Tanks were moving forward from the Saudi desert. One of our reporters there, Eric Engberg, said that the line of tanks was so long, you couldn't see from one end to the other. The thing the U.S. troops feared the most, he said, was that the Iraqis would use gas as they had in their war against Iran.

Bob Simon, Peter Bluff, and the crew were still missing.

I WAS IN NEW YORK on February 7, because Charles and I were anchoring our first *America Tonight* call-in show. We sat side by side at a drum-shaped desk in the studio, fielding questions from around the country — or at least that was the concept. To save money, we had hired the fledgling long-distance carrier MCI, which meant we were subjected to one glitch after another. For the first hour all the calls were from either Texas or New York. Charles or I answered the questions or sent them on to David Martin, who was standing by at the Pentagon, Tom Fenton in Tel Aviv, Eric Engberg in Dhahran, or General Crist and Mideast expert Fouad Ajami with us in the studio. Several callers complained that the press was undermining the war effort, though there was one man who said that antiwar views were not getting a fair hearing. I loved this: no four-minute cutoff time, no agonized afternoon of bookings, no essay writing. And as a TV show it worked.

The CBS brass agreed we would do more. And we did. Two weeks later, on the second one, 420,000 people called in. With all the annoyances, I came to see that *America Tonight* was allowing me to break out of the box I was in in Washington, to become three-dimensional and human.

The next day Peter Arnett of CNN reported that Bob Simon and the team were alive in a Baghdad prison.

DON HEWITT asked me to meet him for lunch at San Domenico on Central Park South. He wasted no time on preliminaries: "I hear you're difficult." I braced for a lecture. "Show me someone who isn't difficult," he said, "and I'll show you someone with no talent. I want you for *60 Minutes*." After all those months of patience, of my being too afraid to want it too much, here it was plunked down unceremoniously before me. He just said it.

So I said, "Oh, Don, I'm ecstatic!" Right? That's what anyone in my shoes should have said. But like a schlemiel, my first words were "Can I keep living in Washington?" My very first reaction. I'd been churning over the idea of moving Taylor to New York. It was corroding my upper GI tract. I could not do that to her.

"No, you have to move to New York." Then Hewitt said, "Well, maybe. I don't know." Clearly I had flummoxed him. He had been led to believe I was salivating for the job. So I went on to make it worse. "Can I keep doing *Face?*"

When I told my agent, Jim Griffin, what I'd said, he was incredulous. "Look, you don't want to go back to the White House, and here's an offer to be on the number one–rated show in the country." In other words, have you lost your mind?

I went to get my hair cut. When I reached Aaron and told him about the offer and the possibility of staying in Washington, he went wild. "It's my turn," he said. "I hate Washington, always have, and you know that."

"But Taylor," I said.

"The perfect time to move Taylor is in ninth grade."

"Well, if we move, you have to tell Tay it's *your* idea. If she thinks it's because of me, she'll never forgive me. But she'll accept it if it's you who wants to move." He agreed and begged me to call Hewitt before he got second thoughts.

So with the hair dryers blowing, I phoned Don. "Doing this from Washington won't work," I said. "I spoke to Aaron, and yes, we'll move to New York — and forget what I said about *Face*." Now I was jabbering with enthusiasm.

"Oh, great!" said Don. Then the cold shower: "Now I have to bring this to my war council, to Mike, Morley, Ed, and Steve."

"Huh?" Not a firm offer?

"But you have Mike and me," said Don. "Don't take this as an audition or anything, but maybe you should do some pieces to show us what they look like."

The following night at dinner I told Taylor, "*60 Minutes* might want me."

"We're not moving," she shot out. "We're not!"

I assured her that nothing was definite, there was no clear offer, and there was no point worrying until there was.

When Aaron went to the men's room, Tay asked, "What did you get Dad for tomorrow?"

"What's tomorrow?" I asked. Then I told her I'd owe her forever if she never told Aaron I'd *almost* forgotten our wedding anniversary. Married 14 years.

395

☐

ON FEBRUARY 15 Saddam Hussein offered a conditional pullout, but President Bush dismissed it as a "cruel hoax." The bombing continued. Three days later Iraqi Foreign Minister Tariq Aziz flew to Moscow to meet with Gorbachev. The Soviets were proposing a "peace plan," a face-saving way out for Saddam. I'd been told that Bush was livid at Gorbachev, but naturally Brent Scowcroft on *Face* was circumspect, repeating that the Soviets were on board with us, all the way.

After the show Scowcroft confided, "I'm nervous. Nervous Gorbachev will engineer a deal." It was obvious that the administration wanted to crush Saddam and dismantle his war machine, and the only way to do that was with a ground war. They didn't want the Soviets gumming that up. Scowcroft said that their biggest surprise had been the extent of Saddam's buildup and planning. He'd been getting ready for years, creating redundancy in his communications setup: cables and extra connections and lots of pontoon bridges.

"He wasn't planning on a war with us, was he?" I asked.

"Well, he was planning to take over the Gulf states, to become the dominant force in the Middle East. And we never saw it coming."

When he left the studio, I dashed over to Britches to buy Aaron a present. At home, Taylor made us an anniversary brunch. She set the table with our good china and silver and served us scrambled eggs, French toast, and cake.

ON FEBRUARY 22, after five weeks of aerial bombardment, Bush issued an ultimatum: Saddam, you have until noon tomorrow to leave Kuwait. Otherwise, the ground war will commence.

The next day, Saturday, Aaron and I watched the ground war begin on television. There were amazing logistical feats: fuel trucks, mobile hospitals, food caravans speeding through the desert, keeping up with the 100,000 troops dashing across Saudi Arabia and into southern Iraq. One of the pilots flying cover said it had looked like ants eating their way through a giant peanut butter sandwich.

Sheik Saud Nasir al-Sabah, the Kuwaiti ambassador to Washington, called our control room Sunday morning at eight. He had declined our invitation to appear on *Face*, but now, because the ground war was going so well — with thousands and thousands of Iraqis surrendering — he wished to be on. His eyes teared as he thanked the American people for helping free his country: "Let me say how deeply appreciative and grateful we are to this great nation." I should have asked if Kuwait would now recognize Israel but didn't.

396   DON HEWITT CALLED: "We want you to do a piece for us to see if you're happy with us and we're happy with you."

"You know my work," I said calmly as I bristled. "What does this mean?" He was vague. "Can I call you back?" I asked. I didn't want to say anything I'd regret. I phoned Eric Ober. "Do it," he said. "Just do it." He explained, "There's a general worry that you can't do stories outside the Beltway." He urged me to be smart for once, sit on my tongue, and "do whatever Don wants you to. Show him you're not difficult after all." With all the arguing I'd done with Ober, he turned out to be a wise friend.

I called Don back and said I wasn't happy about this: "You've seen my work for 20 years. *Face,* the White House, *America Tonight.* I don't like it, but I'll do it because I want the job."

THE GROUND WAR against Iraqi troops was brilliantly executed with lightning attacks and feints that threw the enemy, already "attrited" (one of the Pentagon's many sanitized euphemisms), into chaos. The truth was, the dreaded Iraqi Army was not any good. From the opening shot of the ground war, its soldiers fled. It was a rout; the air force didn't even go up for a fight. There were few American casualties, and then an Iraqi Scud hit a U.S. barracks in Dhahran, killing 28 Americans and injuring 89.

On the third day of the ground war CBS's Bob McKeown was the first reporter to get into Kuwait. He broadcast an emotional report on the liberation with ecstatically applauding Kuwaitis all around him. Dick Threlkeld, who had returned to CBS, was just outside Kuwait City, so far ahead of the troops that he and his crew accepted the surrender of six Iraqi solders. Betsy Aaron was in Baghdad. CBS was redeeming itself.

The Persian Gulf War was notable for many firsts, most of them involving technology. It was also the first war in which men and women were on an equal footing in war coverage. CBS sent not only correspondents Betsy Aaron, Susan Spencer, and Martha Teischner but also Mary Beth Toole, the soundman on the Threlkeld crew — and, of course, Zirinsky was running our command center in Dhahran.

Bush had managed the war with a sureness of touch that impressed even those who had initially opposed our going in. All the way through he kept up his tireless phone calling: to keep the Israelis from retaliating, the Soviets from rescuing Saddam, the Iranians from sponsoring terrorism, the Germans and French in line, and the Syrians on board. And at home he ran the PR effort like a quick-response political campaign. He went on television almost every day with upbeat, optimistic reports, as did the Pentagon. Their press strategy was to keep us in the dark so we couldn't contradict them.

I WAS in New York for another *America Tonight* call-in show on February 27. When I walked into Lane's office, Ann Reingold teased me about *60 Minutes:* "The hair apparent!"

We watched the liberation of Kuwait on the *Evening News,* and then Bush announced a temporary cease-fire. Desert Storm was over. U.S. planes would no longer pursue the retreating Republican Guards on what was being called "the highway of death." Colin Powell and James Baker argued that television pictures of U.S. forces slaughtering the fleeing Iraqis would look like a "turkey shoot" and disgust the American people. This was just what they had worked so hard to prevent. They wanted to control *all* the images with their own made-for-prime-time videos. So television would rescue Saddam by producing pictures of a slaughter that would prevent his own slaughter.

We haven't figured out how or why TV pictures have such a deep impact. I think it's possible that a powerful visual image makes an indelible imprint on our brain that must be like a photo album where a picture is glued in. And while we may not actually *see* the picture itself in our minds, the imprint remains to influence our judgment and our opinions. That's why the Reagan campaign vignettes were so powerful. And why these war pictures were so feared by the Bush administration.

There were strategic reasons why Bush stopped the war before Saddam was deposed, including a desire to maintain a balance of power in the region by keeping neighboring Iran in check. That required a relatively strong Iraq. Without Saddam, Iraq might well have imploded into civil war. The moderate Arab allies told Bush that the disintegration of Iraq would be the worst possible outcome. Not pursuing the war to Baghdad would come to be seen as a mistake, but that night there was jubilation at the victorious cease-fire. Our call-in was, once again, a great success. But we were still using MCI, and most of the calls were from Lubbock, Texas.

I was talking with my dad more frequently. I'd call home and find myself telling him, not Dolly, about my troubles. Since he had retired, he had time to schmooze, and I was discovering his wisdom. He was becoming my best friend. We'd talk politics, we'd talk the stock market, we'd talk human nature. He called me "Lez." No one ever called me "Lez" or "Les" or anything but "Lesley." Only Lou.

Soon my dad knew more about me than anyone but Aaron. I confided in him now because I didn't want to upset Dolly and because there was no one I trusted more. He confided in me too. It was as if we were contemporaries. And we worried together about Jeff.

Then our fears came to pass. My brother was back in the hospital. This time they took out his entire larynx. He would have no voice at all. We would now learn about his character and fortitude. I cannot recall my brother ever complaining.

He had two options, the doctors said. He could get a small portable machine with a magic wand. If he touched the wand to his throat as he vocalized, out would come monotonal, robotic speech, the sound that makes heads spin around to see who's talking like that. The alternative was to learn something called esophageal speech, where he would have to burp and push a few words out at a time. Neither sounded very appealing.

But operating on Aaron's so-suddenly-there's-God principle, Jeff's mother-in-law, Dorothy, tuned in to *Good Morning America*, and there was Dr. Nancy Snyderman with a report on a new larynx device that produced a real voice, a human voice, without burping. I called her that day, and she put Jeff in touch with the makers of the Blom-Singer valve. It would take months for Jeff to heal, but eventually he got a real voice, his own.

In the meantime, though, he was working on a real estate deal that was at a crucial stage. How could he negotiate without a voice? He turned to Lou, who, to everyone's surprise, was thoroughly enjoying retirement. He was traveling around the country fund-raising for MIT and a few other pet causes. And now here was my brother writing on slips of paper: "Dad, there's no one I trust but you. Will you come and be my voice?"

"But I don't know diddly about the real estate business."

"I'll teach you," wrote my brother to my father. So, at 77, Lou started a new career. He went in to Jeff's office every day and learned a whole new job. It makes me want to weep, my father working for my brother without a voice because he had cancer. My wonderful, sweet, lovely dad went to work every day until he died to help my brother make his real estate deals. I had always said I didn't have any heroes. Women don't, I thought. But now in 1991 I realized that Lou, who had become my friend, was my hero and that more than ever I wanted to be just like him.

COPIES OF JOHN CARMODY'S COLUMN in *The Washington Post* were faxed to me in New York. It said in so many words that Don Hewitt was firing Meredith Vieira because she was pregnant. Whoever writes the first press release gets to tell the story, and Meredith was doing that by getting to Carmody before anyone else. This would be a PR calamity for Don, and potentially for me. Technically I was replacing the retired Harry Reasoner, but now the press would write that I was taking Meredith's slot. Why can't anything ever go smoothly?

Meredith at 37 had everything. She was a talented reporter, she was beautiful, and she was well liked at CBS. I liked her a lot and in no way wanted to take her job. Now she was expecting her second child and telling Carmody, "I wanted to stay on. . . . I wish they could have shown some flexibility."

I put my head down and got out of the way. My attitude was "I have no dog in this fight." But my disappearing act didn't work. *The New York Times* said Don was replacing Meredith with Lesley Stahl, "an honorary man" — excuse me? And on March 28 the Washington *Times* said, "Stahl makes it with a workaholic image few mothers can match" and went on to scold me for never talking about my child: "She won't arrive at the office smelling of sour milk or peanut butter." They made it sound as if I were ashamed of being a mother. This scalded me deeply. I didn't talk about Taylor because Aaron and I had decided we had to protect her from publicity. Also, contrary to the Washington *Times'* implication, I always thought that being a mother would *help* my image, make me more likable. I didn't talk about Taylor because I didn't want to exploit her, use her to enhance my career.

The dustup made me stop and think about the trade-offs I had made. Those of us who had been hired back in 1972 had wanted to be seen as one of the guys. The men didn't ask for sick days to take care of their kids, so I hadn't either. It really wasn't till women came into the workforce in substantial numbers that we dared to ask. By 1990, 68 percent of women with kids worked; in other words, the two-career family was the norm. Women were finally emboldened by their numbers to talk about motherhood and ask for part-time arrangements.

But there were always going to be jobs where that just wasn't possible. In one interview Hewitt talked about how *60 Minutes* correspondents have to travel a good deal of the time. An integral part of the job, he said, was being away from home.

I spoke to Taylor about it. She said that among her friends, the kids of mothers who worked full-time were better adjusted. She assured me that she thought I had balanced the job and her just right. I'm one lucky daughter-of-a-gun.

WHEN THE WAR ENDED, Bush's popularity rating soared to 88 percent. The last time a president had scored that high was Harry Truman at the end of World War II. Like most Americans, I thought Bush had led the effort with sophistication and patience, even wisdom. He had turned the conflict from an American-Iraqi contest into one between the civilized world and a madman. It was a diplomatic and military tour de force. But within a short time, his image of resoluteness faded. As Bush turned back to domestic affairs, he reverted, as *Time* put it, to his old pattern of "deliberate drift." He was hurt too by the economy, which was then in a recession.

Reaganites will tell you that Bush's presidency failed because he never understood that leadership requires a strong sense of direction — and of course because he broke his promise on taxes. But we have had many successful presidents who have not had a strong sense of direction or an ideology. In fact, most presidents, including our most successful, veered away from their campaign slogans. They compromised, balanced, moved to the center. Even the king, Reagan himself, raised taxes — over and over.

Bush's losing a second term may have had more to do with his not becoming enough of a centrist. Instead, in several key ways he stuck to the Reagan course, perpetuating the trend toward income disparity and the atmosphere of greed; he even played the race card in his campaign. As for taxes, his downfall may have been due not so much to his breaking the no-new-taxes promise as *how* he broke it — what he said and how he acted when he said it. Right after he signed the bill to raise taxes, he vowed immediately never to do so again. He renewed his no-new-taxes pledge this way: "Congress will raise taxes over my dead veto . . . or live veto . . . or something like that." It comes back to performance on television. Reagan had been skillful both at slipping away from these things and at having it both ways. He would say, "I was forced into it, I *had* to do it." But Bush said, "I should not have done it." Bush probably would have gotten credit for the eventual reduction of the deficit — for including serious spending restraints in his budget package — if he had presented what he'd done as an act of courage. Then the voters would have seen him standing tall. Instead he ran from it and was diminished.

A key to George Bush, I thought, was the son-of-the-great-man syndrome, the son who can never compete with or live up to the force or heft of the father. Bush had actually fled his father, the great senator of principle, and went to Texas to make it on his own. But then when he went into politics, he did it by yoking onto powerful patrons, taking on the coloration of these new father figures. And so he flipped from a Goldwater conservative to a moderate Nixonian, from a critic of Reaganomics to one of its ardent defenders. When he finally hooked up with Reagan, he allowed himself to fade into his shadow. Perhaps that's what sons of great men do: find themselves another man of force and heft, latch on, and, as destiny would have it, suffer in the comparison.

President Bush, the Warrior King, gave a speech of triumph to a joint session of Congress and got 22 standing ovations. The pundits were saying he was invincible. But with the economy in recession, his popularity soon receded. By the 1992 election his job approval rating was down to 37 percent.

EARLY MARCH. A Saturday morning. Bob Simon, Peter Bluff, and the crew were released after being held in an Iraqi prison for two and a half months. I heard Bob on radio at 7 A.M., apologizing to his family for putting them through the pain. When I opened my *New York Times*, I read, "According to Don Hewitt, he has two candidates to replace Meredith Vieira: Lesley Stahl and Bob Simon." I went shopping.

Bob and the crew went to London, where a doctor examined them and said they were in good health. At a news conference Bob said he had obsessed about two things during his captivity. One was food; the other, that the Iraqis would find out he was Jewish and torture him. He told CBS he wanted to go home to Tel Aviv right away and write a book.

That's when Don called me from London: "This is going to happen, you're coming to *60 Minutes*." Was it me by default?

"I have to do something that I'm so afraid is going to make you angry," said Don. "You're going to be really upset with me. I hate to say this. We're getting along so well."

"What? You can say anything," I said. "What?"

"Don't be mad, okay?"

"What, already?"

"I hate your hair. You have to change it. It's too stiff. Too Nancy Reagan."

If I'd been younger, I would have chafed at the insult—how dare he! But I wasn't offended. "I stiffen it," I explained, laughing, "because I can't be futzing with it in the middle of everything at the White House. I don't have time. So I get up, tease it, spray, and forget it. But if you want me to change it, no problem, I'll change it."

He offered to take me to Frédéric Fekkai himself. It was settled. New hair.

A week later I got a call from a *60 Minutes* researcher. "You're going to Bucharest to adopt a baby. You're going next week." A platoon of happily rejuvenated molecules began marching around inside me.

At dinner I told Tay I was going to Romania and that I was going in a wig. That tickled her: "Mom, just like *Mission Impossible!*" "About going to *60 Minutes*," I said, "they haven't asked me yet. And the New York part isn't definite." Aaron broke in, "You know, Taylor, I've always wanted to live in New York." Before she could get upset, I assured her again: nothing was definite. If and when they ask me, I said, we can talk about it then. Now if it was in print and someone mentioned it to her, she wouldn't be fazed and feel betrayed. I went back to work thinking I had handled it well. Aaron said she had told him, "I'll take pills and jump off the balcony."

The day I flew to Bucharest, Don was quoted in the Carmody column as saying, "Lesley and I are living together before we get married!"

In Bucharest I was racked with anxiety attacks about Tay. Will I ever see her? How can I abandon her just as she's adjusting to a new school and a new city?

When I got home, Don called: "Let's do this. Let's wrap this thing up tomorrow!" Eric Ober called: "It's happening just the way I wanted it to. It's perfect: Don wants you, and we want you there." I ached about my daughter. But now I was on the moving train. I flew to New York. At 60 Minutes everyone greeted me warmly. Mike was there, which was surprising since he had had a pacemaker put in over the weekend. I got a big welcome hug, gingerly executed since he was in some discomfort. Ed Bradley hugged me too. They made me feel I was in the family.

It was definitely time to tell Taylor. We were on our way to Vail for her spring vacation, waiting in the airport lounge. "It's going to happen," I said. "You'll love New York," said Aaron, "I promise." She cried and sobbed and heaved. I myself had lived in that zone my entire 14th year, but this was unusual for Tay. Was I ruining her? Aaron and I kept exchanging looks of helplessness. I signaled, "Do something." He signaled back, "What?" As agreed, Aaron insisted it was his idea, his desire to leave Washington: "I've always hated it here."

Taylor fell asleep instantly on the plane. When she woke up, she offered me a deal: "I'll move to New York if I don't have to take piano lessons anymore."

"Deal," I said. She never cried about it again.

OUR LAST America Tonight broadcast was a call-in show from New York with General Thomas Kelly, the Pentagon briefer, in Washington, Bert Quint in Kuwait, Fouad Ajami with us in New York, and Bob Simon in Tel Aviv — his first TV appearance since his news conference — and the phones worked.

"It's finally time to play taps for America Tonight," I said in my farewell. "A show that was born because of the Gulf War. A show that evolved into a dialogue with the American people." I ended quoting Robert Frost's "Reluctance":

> Ah, when to the heart of man
>   Was it ever less than a treason
> To go with the drift of things,
>   To yield with a grace to reason,
> And bow and accept the end
>   Of a love or a season?

As the credits rolled, everyone came up on the podium and hugged Charles and me.

It was much harder to say good-bye to Face after eight years and 300 appearances. With everything I had done, those shows were my proudest work. I didn't "make news" every week, but I did get my teeth into a subject, explore it for 30 minutes, and at least try to achieve some depth. And the excitement of live TV is a kick. It was heady and hard, and I loved it.

"I'm going to miss this good old chair," I said in my good-bye broadcast. After thanking all the wonderful men and women I had worked with, the producers, the editors, and the crew, each by name, I said, "So long, and I'll see you on *60 Minutes*."

We had a farewell party, and the Brinkleyites came by: David, Sam, Cokie, and George.

SO WHAT HAD I LEARNED in 20 years in Washington? I learned that it's not only "the economy, stupid." It's also television, stupid. Television had become the center not only of campaigning and governing but also of diplomacy and decision making. I also learned to have enormous faith in our system. Democracy works. It even intrudes on the way the media functions. I came to see that the press is far more reactive than influential, far more reflective of public opinion than most people realize. Jimmy Carter wasn't unpopular because the media battered him; we battered him because he was unpopular. We had license. And Reagan got an easier press because the public loved him, which meant that our usual sources on the Hill — where they're mindful of the views of their constituents — dried up on us. The will of the people prevails even on the big, bad press!

As I packed up to leave Washington, I thought sadly of my ride on the decline of network news. Much of the erosion had been brought about by technological change, but deregulation had been the other factor. Deregulation was one of the few policies Jimmy Carter initiated that Ronald Reagan adopted and carried forward. In fact, he turned it into part of his free-market religion. In the old days, the Federal Communications Commission used to mandate that those of us who used the free airwaves broadcast a set amount of public service programming. To win "brownie points," in Don Hewitt's words, we put on hour-long documentaries and lots of other hard-boiled news shows. As Don told *The New York Times*, "We wanted to show the FCC we were good boys who deserved to have our licenses renewed."[21]

When *60 Minutes* came along, it showed that news could make money. After Reagan's deregulation, with no more pressure for brownie points, all the networks got into the prime-time game. Now, as Hewitt says, "You cannot do news on television *unless* you make money."

Deregulation brought us more stations, and technology brought us cable and even more stations, more competition. When there was a strong FCC and only three networks, we were encouraged to be the front page of *The New York Times*. Today, in the 300-channel universe, we compete with tractor pulling on ESPN, game shows on the independent channels, and *I Love Lucy* reruns on cable. To compete we eventually succumbed to wet-fingering like the politicians, relying on polls so we could give the public what they wanted.

Enter the blurring of hard news and tabloid news, where the concentration is on personalities. By the early 1990s we were covering O. J. Simpson and Princess Di as if they were Charles de Gaulle and Mao Tse-tung. The same pressures began intruding on political reporting, except there we called it "character" journalism. And the politicians have colluded with us ever since the days of the Sauter "moments."

With the falloff in audience, we also began to introduce more conflict into our reports. Actually, the drift toward hostility journalism developed out of the best of intentions. When we realized that the new technology allowed us to squeeze three or four sound bites into one piece, we began to look for "opposing views" to flesh out our reports. We thought of it as good journalism, but it had the unintended effect of exacerbating a public discourse of disputatiousness. Our bosses began asking for extreme views — a "stable of arguers" — in the hope that the audience would like the dueling. Soon we were searching for the most polarized views so we could get a real battle going.

Even with all these changes, and while other broadcasts have softened up their content, *The CBS Evening News* is still a place where you find solid, old-fashioned journalism. Dan Rather is first and above all a hard-news reporter who has managed to preserve his edge and the highest of standards.

And I was going to another grand institution of the old values. *60 Minutes*, with its unshakable ratings, had not felt the pressure to melt into an electronic grocery-store tabloid. No wet-fingering here. *60 Minutes* kept its lust for hard-edged investigations and jabbing interviews. Don Hewitt had invented the television magazine in 1968 and simply refused to change his tell-me-a-story format. Don says he decided back then to make the stories "reporter-oriented," which meant that I was going to be able to loosen up and practice a more personal style without compromising or selling out.

I would get questions about being the "only" female at *60 Minutes*. But nearly 40 percent of the producers — 11 out of 29 — were women (today it's down to 36 percent: 9 out of 25), and both Hewitt and I said publicly that we thought the next correspondent hired would be a woman. And, in fact, the next was Christiane Amanpour of CNN.

Don said he was afraid I was too Washington. "We're a repertory company," he told me at lunch at Café des Artistes. "Mike, Morley, each one of you has to play all the parts. One week you're Hamlet, the next Ophelia, the next Iago. I want you all to do it all." So one week I would profile Paul Newman at 70, the next investigate Medicare fraud, the next interview Yasser Arafat. Can you imagine after all those years of being straitjacketed into presidential issues what it was like to go out and cover any story I was interested in? It was a holiday. On my first day at *60 Minutes*, someone turned to me in the elevator and asked, "Going up to Paradise?"

Working with the very best in my business, I was floating. More than that, I was getting younger. Well, you'd get younger too if you worked with guys that old! Morley used to say, "We've reached the point where, if we do a story on Medicare, it's a conflict of interest!" Joking aside, there simply is not a better job or a better shop in all of television news — possibly in all of journalism.

THE ANGER I had lived with, that I thought was defining me, retired like a burned-out employee the minute I started at *60 Minutes* on April 2, 1991. I smiled all that day — so much my face hurt — and I haven't stopped yet eight years later.

So suddenly, there was God.

ACKNOWLEDGMENTS

The first person I wish to thank is my husband, Aaron Latham, for his wisdom, patience, and impeccable advice. I also thank my daughter, Taylor. When she was a senior in high school, I began to fret about the empty nest. What would I do when my only child left home? That was when I first thought about a book. It wasn't until she actually went off to college that I started discussing the idea in earnest: what would a book be about? Once I got going, Taylor teased me about my "replacement child." Now I'm wondering if I'm going to have to find a replacement for the book.

Reporting Live is my take on life in Washington from the wild Watergate years in the 1970s, when I was a cub reporter, to the tense days of the Persian Gulf War. In telling the story, I have tried to thread together several themes, one of which is about television: how TV has changed the presidency and how new technology and cable TV have transformed network news.

I'd like to acknowledge the journalists, network executives, colleagues, and friends who helped with this aspect of the book: Wyatt Andrews, Al Bargamian, Tom Bettag, Ed Bradley, Rita Braver, Lois Chiles, Judy Crichton, Mort Dean, Jed Duval, Eric Engberg, Ed Fouhy, Stanhope Gould, Fred Graham, Mark Harrington, Brian Healy, Don Hewitt, Kathleen Hall Jamieson, Ellen Kaden, Anthony Malara, Cal Marlin, Terry Martin, Joe Peyronnin, Bob Pierpoint, Bill Plante, David Poltrack, Deborah Potter, Dan Rather, Ann Reingold, Joan Richmond, Bill Small, Sandy Socolow, Susan Spencer, Howard Stringer, Richard Threlkeld, Lane Venardos, and Susan Zirinsky.

Special appreciation goes to the CBS News producers, editors, and cameramen who helped me during the twenty years I worked in Washington; the White House teams; the women at *Face the Nation* — Joan Barone, Carin Pratt, Millicent Adams, and Maryanna Spicer-Brooks; and Janet Leissner at *America Tonight.*

Another part of the story is the journey of one woman and many women. I owe special thanks to the following, whom I turned to for advice about this theme: Sylvia Chase, Eleanor Clift, Tish Emerson, Anna Fells, Ellen Goodman, Dotty Lynch, Cokie Roberts, Rozalind Rosenberg, Diane Sawyer, Gail Sheehy, Lynn Sherr, Gloria Steinem, Carol Tavris, Barbara Walters, Linda Wertheimer, and Kimba Woods.

I also write about the presidents I covered: Richard Nixon, the schemer; Jimmy Carter, the preacher; Ronald Reagan, the revolutionary; and George Bush, the warrior. In this category, I am grateful to the archivists at both the Jimmy Carter presidential library in Atlanta, Georgia, and the Ronald Reagan presidential library in Simi Valley, California (especially Diane Barrie).

I interviewed scores of White House officials, aides, pundits, pollsters, fellow journalists, and others to whom I am indebted: Bob Beckel, Dr. Robert Butler, Joseph Califano, Hodding Carter, Mike Deaver, Tom DeFrank, Tony Dolan, Sam Donaldson, Stuart Eizenstat, Susan Estrich, Marlin Fitzwater, Kathy Frankovic, Bob Gates, David Gergen, Hendrik Hertzberg, Drew Lewis, Johanna McGeary, Dick Moe, Terry O'Connell, Jody Powell, Howell Raines, Don Regan, Jim Rentschler, Nancy Reynolds, Ed Rollins, Maureen Santini, Ralph Schlosstein, Bob Sims, Sheila Tate, Margaret Tutwiler, Steven Weisman, Fred Wertheimer, Ann Wexler, Judy Woodruff, and Bob Woodward.

Great love to those friends who read the manuscript when it was more than 1,000 pages long, those who gave me copies of their notes and diaries, and those whose advice was especially helpful: Joan Cooney, Richard Darman, Clay Felker, Doris Kearns Goodwin, Jim Griffin, Rome Hartman, Richard Holbrooke, Jay Kernis, Eden Lipson, Peggy Noonan, Anna Quindlen, Carol Pearlberger, Karen Sughrue, Gil Troy, and those deep throats who wish to remain anonymous.

Finally, I wish to recognize the contribution of three diligent researchers, Mary Hammer, Dorothy Gannon, and Ethan Nelson, and Elizabeth Stein, who pulled everything together. I also wish to express my admiration and affection for my editor, Alice Mayhew.

Many of the quotations in this book, except where indicated, are reconstructions of conversations as I remember them, or as they were recounted to me by others.

NOTES

PART ONE: NIXON AND WATERGATE

1. *CBS News Special Report:* "Report from Vietnam by Walter Cronkite," February 27, 1968, 10–10:30 P.M. In his sum-up, which he called "an analysis that must be speculative, personal, subjective," Cronkite said, "We have been too often disappointed by the optimism of the American leaders, both in Vietnam and Washington, to have faith any longer in the silver linings they find in the darkest clouds. . . . It seems now more certain than ever that the bloody experience of Vietnam is to end in a stalemate. . . . It is increasingly clear to this reporter that the only rational way out then will be to negotiate."

2. David Halberstam, *The Powers That Be* (New York: Alfred A. Knopf, 1979), p. 657.

3. *CBS News Special:* "The Watergate Case: In the Courts and Before the Committee," July 26, 1973, 10–11 P.M. The "gossip" involved what Ehrlichman could not tell the committee for fear of endangering national security. Ehrlichman testified, "It deals with an extremely sensitive subject relating to another country." The "gossip" was that it involved breaking into a foreign embassy.

4. Finally, Solicitor General Robert Bork fired Cox.

5. Neil Postman, *Amusing Ourselves to Death: Public Discourse in the Age of Show Business* (New York: Viking, 1985), p. 102.

6. On July 12, 1974, 17 months after the hearings began, the Senate Watergate committee issued a final report, 2,217 pages long, laying out details of the scandal from the break-in to the enemies list, the "plumbers" unit in the White House, and the cover-up. But the committee avoided any judgment on Nixon's involvement, leaving that to the courts and the impeachment inquiry.

7. Michael J. Sandel, "Watergate Baby," *The New Republic*, October 26, 1998, p. 10.

8. According to a Roper Survey, 48 percent of respondents found television believable; 21 percent found newspapers believable ("Roper Survey," *The New York Times*, April 3, 1973, p. 87).

9. ARVN: Army of the Republic of Vietnam; KIAs: those killed in action; S and D: search and destroy; sappers: members of bomb disarmament squads.

10. Carter came in first; Jackson limped in third, behind Wallace.

PART TWO: JIMMY AND ROSALYNN CARTER

1. If your career at CBS took you through the morning neighborhood, you were in top-of-the-pack company. Walter Cronkite had been the morning anchor in 1954, followed by Jack Paar, Dick Van Dyke, Will Rogers Jr., Harry Reasoner (1961), Mike Wallace (1963–1966), and then John Hart (1970–1973).

2. After leaving the *Morning News*, Rudd became a general assignment

correspondent. Within two years he left CBS, joining the exodus to ABC News. He died in 1982 at the age of 71.

3. *The CBS Morning News*, February 15, 1978.

4. The *Evening News* is now 21 minutes long. In the early 1990s the network decided to add another minute of commercials, plus a 30-second promo.

5. The Sevareid profile ran on the *Morning News* on November 30, 1977.

6. Drummond Ayres, "The Importance of Being Rosalynn," *The New York Times Magazine*, June 3, 1979, p. 39.

7. *The CBS Morning News*, October 20, 1978.

8. The other women were Helen Thomas at UPI; Maureen Santini at AP; Judy Woodruff at NBC; Sam's number two, Ann Compton, at ABC; Lee Thornton, who was in the booth with me for CBS Radio; Johanna McGeary, who covered for *Time*; Eleanor Clift with *Newsweek*; and Philomena Jurey for National Public Radio.

9. Every White House resorts to blaming the press, but the Carterites succumbed so often that Hedley Donovan, a White House adviser who had been editor in chief of *Time*, sent Carter an "Eyes Only" memo (October 24, 1979) on "a reflex that blames the press first, and then asks only later, or maybe never, was there some Administration mistake here?" He said that the media had been blamed "six or eight times this morning for situations that need broader examination of who else might be at fault." The memo is on record at the Jimmy Carter Library in Atlanta, where I copied it through normal procedures.

10. *The CBS Evening News*, February 20, 1979.

11. Memorandum, Gerald Rafshoon to Jimmy Carter, July 10, 1979. Also copied at the Jimmy Carter Library.

12. Patricia A. Avery, "Rosalynn — Spearhead of Carter Campaign," *U.S. News & World Report*, November 5, 1979, p. 39.

13. Brock Adams at Transportation, James Schlesinger at Energy, Michael Blumenthal at Treasury, Patricia Harris at Housing and Urban Development, Attorney General Griffin Bell, and Joseph Califano at Health, Education and Welfare.

14. ABC News began a Monday–Thursday, 11:30 P.M. broadcast on the hostages anchored by Ted Koppel, who also counted the days of captivity. That show became *Nightline*.

15. Gallup Poll of December 11, 1979, as reported by the AP: 48 percent liked Carter and 40 percent liked Kennedy.

16. Donald Rothberg, Associated Press, September 22, 1980.

17. William Safire, "Essay: Stand-Up Savants," *The New York Times*, October 9, 1980, p. 35A.

PART THREE: RONALD AND NANCY REAGAN

1. Peter G. Bourne, *Jimmy Carter: A Comprehensive Biography from Plains to Postpresidency* (New York: A Lisa Drew Book/Scribner, 1997), p. 473.

2. Nancy Reagan with William Novak, *My Turn: The Memoir of Nancy Reagan* (New York: Random House, 1989), p. 240.

3. Bob Colacello, "Ronnie and Nancy," *Vanity Fair*, August 1998, p. 110: Nancy Reagan "detested Ed Meese and thought he was an idiot and too ideological and just not very capable."

4. According to *Time* magazine, Mrs. Reagan converted Amy Carter's bedroom into a spacious walk-in closet for her "extensive wardrobe." It measured ten

feet by 15 feet and held hundreds of dresses, "each one labeled with the occasions on which it was worn so Mrs. Reagan could avoid displaying it again in front of the same audience" (Ed Magnuson, "Why Mrs. Reagan Still Looks Like a Million," *Time*, October 24, 1988, p. 29).

5. Ron Rosenbaum, "The Man Who Married Dan Rather," *Esquire*, November 1982, p. 54.

6. Reaganomics involved a three-stage tax cut with a tightened money supply and cuts in federal spending for social programs, including health, food, housing, and education. The nation would undergo a severe recession, the worst since the Great Depression. Because of Paul Volcker's tight-money policy at the Federal Reserve Board, inflation fell to 4.3 percent, and by late 1984 unemployment fell back to 7.4 percent — just where it had been when Reagan took office.

7. United Press International, September 1, 1981.

8. Larry Speakes, *Speaking Out: The Reagan Presidency from Inside the White House* (New York: Charles Scribner's Sons, 1988), p. 114.

9. David Stockman, *The Triumph of Politics: Why the Reagan Revolution Failed* (New York: Harper & Row, 1986), p. 3.

10. Sauter spent his early career as a journalist. He was a newspaperman for nine years, Paris bureau chief of CBS News (1974–1976), the CBS censor (1976–1977), and the general manager of CBS's KNXT-TV in Los Angeles (1977–1980).

11. As Donald Regan wrote, "Every moment of every public appearance was scheduled, every word was scripted, every place where Reagan was expected to stand was chalked with toe marks. The President was always being prepared for a performance, and this had the inevitable effect of preserving him from confrontation and the genuine interplay of opinion, question, and argument that form the basis of decision" (Donald T. Regan, *For the Record: From Wall Street to Washington* [San Diego: Harcourt Brace Jovanovich, 1988], p. 248).

12. Lynn Langway with David T. Friendly, Diane Weathers, and Linda Prout, "Mrs. Reagan's Free Clothes," *Newsweek*, February 1, 1982, p. 59.

13. Six years later, *Time* reported that she hadn't stopped, that she kept borrowing designer dresses and never reported it as required (Jacob V. LaMar, "Nancy Reagan's 'Little Rule': The White House Contends That Her Borrowing Broke No Law," *Time*, October 31, 1988, p. 18).

14. Taxpayers earning under $10,000 a year lost an average $240 as a result of Reagan's 1981 tax cut, while those earning over $80,000 gained an average $15,130 (Congressional Budget Office press release, February 17, 1982).

15. Barbara Matusow, *The Evening Stars: The Making of the Network News Anchor* (Boston: Houghton Mifflin, 1983), p. 265. Rather's ratings fell apart during the last week of October 1981, when CBS was number two. In the first week of November, *The CBS Evening News* was third for the first time ever. The Cronkite show had gotten $40,000 for a 30-second commercial, $10,000 more than the other two networks' evening news shows. The price of a 30-second ad on the Rather show slid to $30,000 in this period.

16. Elaine Povich, "Reagan's Budget Totals Failed to Equal His Rhetoric," *Chicago Tribune*, January 10, 1989, p. 9C.

17. Peter Boyer, *Who Killed CBS?: The Undoing of America's Number One News Network* (New York: Random House, 1988), p. 140.

18. *The CBS Evening News*, November 30, 1981.

19. My producers during my tenure as White House correspondent were Lane Venardos, Joe Peyronnin, Susan Zirinsky, Rome Hartman, and Tom Metesky. The camera and sound men were usually Cal Marlin and Dan Radovsky, Al Bargamian and Chuck Violet.

20. Letter in the Ronald Reagan Presidential Library dated May 18, 1982.

21. Ronald Reagan, *An American Life* (New York: Simon & Schuster, 1990), p. 570.

22. As Larry Barrett concluded in his book *Gambling with History*, "To Reagan there is an element of human vendetta in the geopolitical contest" that began in the 1940s. Reagan told Barrett that he had gotten entangled in a union strike in which the Communist Party tried "to gain control of the picture business" (Laurence I. Barrett, *Gambling with History: Reagan in the White House* [New York: Doubleday, 1983], p. 58).

23. Thomas P. O'Neill, Jr., with William Novak, *Man of the House: The Life and Political Memoirs of Speaker Tip O'Neill* (New York: Random House, 1987), p. 361.

24. Documents were released in mid-1996 revealing the Soviets' mistaken belief that night that the KAL jetliner was an American RC-135 reconnaissance plane and that while the Reagan administration had released tapes of the pilot issuing a cold-blooded order to shoot without raising the question of the identity of the aircraft, other tapes that were withheld showed the Soviets making an attempt to ascertain whether the plane was military or not and even firing warning shots (Alvin A. Snyder, "Flight 007: The Rest of the Story: I Told the World the Soviets Shot It Down in Cold Blood, but I Was Wrong," *The Washington Post*, September 1, 1996, p. C2).

25. Tip O'Neill said that Grenada was "a mistake." He wrote, "The students were never in danger. . . . But more than 100 American troops were killed or wounded in that operation. As far as I can see, it was all because the White House wanted the country to forget about the tragedy in Beirut" (O'Neill, *Man*, pp. 366–367).

26. Tom Shales, "TV's New Game: Stalking the Candidates: The Contentious Interviews of '84," *The Washington Post*, May 5, 1984, p. C1.

27. The New Hampshire primary took place on February 28, 1984. The results of the Democratic primary were as follows: 1. Hart, 37,702 votes; 2. Mondale, 28,173; 3. Glenn, 12,088; 4. Jackson, 5,311; 5. McGovern, 5,217; 6. Reagan (write-in vote), 5,056 (Milly McLean, United Press International, February 29, 1984); 7. Hollings, 3,583; 8. Cranston, 2,136; 9. Askew, 1,025.

Gary Hart got 3,968 write-in votes in the GOP primary (UPI, February 29, 1984).

28. Ed Joyce, *Prime Times, Bad Times* (New York: Doubleday, 1988), p. 316.

29. Letters to Reagan from Rifkin and Heston were copied at the Ronald Reagan Presidential Library in Simi Valley, California.

30. Merrill Brown, "Wyman Seeking Better Reception for CBS on Hill," *The Washington Post*, May 13, 1984, p. G4. In an interview with the *Post* Wyman said that the work of CBS News "is not something that is enormously helpful because from time to time, if you're doing your job well, you are going to irritate people who have a different point of view." He said he wanted to see, as the *Post* put it, "programming begin to reflect the mood of the nation's political leadership."

Clay Felker, "A Corporate Finger in CBS News' Eye?" *Adweek*, August 1984, p. 1. Felker said that Wyman "seems to blame CBS News for his defeat [in the syndication fight] so far." He added that Wyman wanted "a weakening in the rigor and aggressiveness of CBS News."

31. Ed Rollins with Tom DeFrank, *Bare Knuckles and Back Rooms: My Life in American Politics* (New York: Broadway Books, 1996), p. 123.

32. Jack Bass (professor of journalism at the University of Mississippi), "End

of the Southern Strategy," *The New York Times*, January 12, 1991, p. 25: "The 30-year-old Republican 'Southern strategy' [is] based on the exploitation of racial fears." Barry Goldwater first articulated the policy in 1961 when he told Southern Republican leaders in Atlanta, 'We're not going to get the Negro vote as a bloc in 1964 or 1968, so we ought to go hunting where the ducks are.' He then spelled it out: 'I would not like to see my party assume it is the role of the Federal Government to enforce integration in the schools.' From there it was a straight line: Nixon's anti-busing stance, Reagan's 'welfare queen,' Bush's invocation of Willie Horton and his veto of the civil rights bill over the issue of quotas."

The Republican Party's recent record as the vehicle of white supremacy in the South began with the Goldwater campaign and reached its apex in Richard Nixon's "Southern strategy" in 1968 and 1972. Republicans appealed to Nixon Democrats (later Reagan Democrats) in the northern suburbs, many of them white ethnic voters who had left the cities to escape from blacks, with promises to crack down on welfare cheats and to bring law and order; the party also fought affirmative action (R. W. Apple, "Politics: The Issues," *The New York Times*, September 19, 1996, p. B11).

Thomas Edsall, "GOP Battler Lee Atwater Dies at 40: Leading Tactician of Party's Southern Strategy Victim of Brain Tumor," *The Washington Post*, March 30, 1991, p. A1: "To his critics . . . he was a symbol of the dark side of American politics. To them, his success in elevating a black-murderer-rapist named Willie Horton into a national figure used to crush the presidential bid of Michael Dukakis was a crude appeal to racism and the epitome of the negative campaign."

33. Jane Mayer, "The Girls on the Bus Move Past Tokenism on the Primary Trail," *The Wall Street Journal*, June 6, 1984, p. 1.

34. In her book *My Story*, Geraldine Ferraro says that after the news conference "the national press, anyway, stopped harassing me and started taking my candidacy more seriously" (Ferraro, *My Story* [New York: Bantam Books, 1985], p. 182).

35. The statement of the head of the nation's Roman Catholic bishops, James Malone, seemingly aimed directly at Ferraro, was that it is "not logically tenable" for politicians to assert they can separate their moral convictions from their public policy stances (Paul Taylor, "Morality, Policy Held Inseparable: Catholic Bishops Reject Stance of Ferraro, Cuomo," *The Washington Post*, August 10, 1984, p. A1).

36. Mary McGrory, "Natural: Ferraro's Performance Shows the Wit, Grit of a Born Politician," *The Washington Post*, September 25, 1984, p. A2.

37. Michael K. Deaver with Mickey Herskowitz, *Behind the Scenes* (New York: Morrow, 1987), p. 141.

38. Meg Greenfield, "Leadership by Presentation," *The Washington Post*, March 2, 1998, p. A17.

39. Peter Goldman and Tony Fuller, *The Quest for the Presidency, 1984* (New York: Bantam Books, 1985), pp. 434–438.

40. William Safire writes that the term "spin doctors" was coined after the first presidential debate of 1984 to describe Reagan's "phalanx of aides" who entered the pressroom to convince reporters that Reagan had beaten Mondale (William Safire, *Safire's New Political Dictionary: The Definitive Guide to the New Language of Politics* [New York: Random House, 1993], p. 736).

PART FOUR: Nancy and Ronnie

1. Jay Winik, *On the Brink: The Dramatic, Behind-the-Scenes Saga of the Reagan Era and the Men and Women Who Won the Cold War* (New York: Simon & Schuster, 1996), pp. 113–129, 598.

2. William F. Buckley, Jr., "Exit Jeane Kirkpatrick," *National Review*, December 28, 1984, vol. 36, p. 54.

3. Nancy Reynolds, Reagan's press secretary when he was governor of California, told me in April 1985, "I think [Maureen] has had a remarkable influence [on both Reagans]. Maureen has brought hundreds of Republican women officeholders to Washington to meet with the president. Of course, you're not going to change people overnight, but I think she has really made a difference in how they view women."

4. Ken Khachigian's notes on writing Reagan's remarks for Bitburg and Bergen-Belsen, Ronald Reagan Presidential Library, April 26, 1985. Reagan went on to say, "Should we say, 'All of these people have met the supreme judge and they will be judged by Him who has the only right to do that.' "

5. Andrea Chambers, "Doing Europe Right," *People*, May 20, 1985, p.90.

6. George Will, *This Week with David Brinkley*, June 23, 1985.

7. Edward Walsh, "Israel, US Reportedly Agree on Timing of Prisoner Release," *The Washington Post*, June 29, 1985, p. A20. In addition, George Bush had made a statement while in Bonn in which he all but publicly called on Israel to release the Shiite prisoners as a way to liberate the TWA hostages.

Behind the scenes, the U.S. gave private assurances to Syria that once the Americans were freed, Israel would begin the prompt release of the Shiites ("Israel to Free Its Prisoners in Stages," *Facts on File*, vol. 45, no. 2328, July 5, 1985).

Reagan both phoned and wrote to Syrian President Hafez Assad, allowing him to persuade the terrorists that they would see all the compatriots freed if they released the Americans first (Lou Cannon, *President Reagan: The Role of a Lifetime* [New York: Simon & Schuster, 1991, p. 607).

Improved relations with the Soviet Union were also a factor. According to various sources, the Soviets urged Assad to end the crisis.

And in *Turmoil and Triumph: My Years as Secretary of State* (New York: Charles Scribner's Sons, 1993, p. 665), George Shultz writes that Iran weighed in as well, leaning on Hezbollah to release *all* the TWA hostages.

According to Lou Cannon (p. 607), Reagan sent a message of thanks to Hashemi Rafsanjani, Speaker of the Iranian Parliament, for his help. As Cannon wrote, "By emphasizing Rafsanjani's role in their discussions with the president, [William] Casey and [Robert] McFarlane were also watering the seeds" of what would become the Iran-contra scandal.

8. Shultz, *Turmoil*, p. 668.

9. Walter Shapiro, "The Don and Nancy Show," *Newsweek*, July 29, 1985, p. 15.

10. Edwin Diamond, "The Great Magazine Race," *New York*, August 26, 1985, p. 34.

11. The president said this in a telephone interview on August 26, 1985. It aired on WSB in Atlanta, Georgia.

12. David Broder, "A President Who Flees Information," *The Washington Post*, September 1, 1985, p. C7.

13. Jack Nelson, "Desperately Needs Victory, Aides Say; Reagan Entering Critical Period of His Presidency," *Los Angeles Times*, September 9, 1985, p. 1:

"But while a number of polls show that Reagan has managed to retain popularity ratings in the 60% to 65% range, Americans oppose his policies on most domestic and foreign issues by substantial margins." The Louis Harris poll showed a 64 percent–34 percent negative rating for Reagan's handling of the deficit. He also got substantial negative ratings on defense spending, women's rights, nuclear arms, U.S.-Soviet relations, South Africa, and Central America.

14. Abul Abbas surfaced in the Gaza Strip in 1996, when he attended a meeting of the Palestinian National Council.

15. "Top 100 Eke Out 2.7% Ad Increase," *Advertising Age*, special issue, September 4, 1986, p. 3.

16. Stanley Meisler, "Reporter's Notebook," *Los Angeles Times*, November 21, 1985, part 1, p. 7.

17. Garry Wills, *Reagan's America: Innocents at Home* (New York: Doubleday, 1987), pp. 218–219.

18. Ending a three-year exile in the United States, Benigno Aquino returned to the Philippines on August 21, 1983. Upon his arrival at Manila International Airport, he was killed while in the custody of uniformed soldiers.

19. "Reagan Seeks Judges with Traditional Approach: Interview with Edwin Meese, Attorney General of the United States," *U.S. News & World Report*, October 14, 1985, p. 67.

20. One of the president's aides told me that Reagan had gotten it into his head that Marcos was a great World War II hero, one of the survivors of the Bataan death march. When I asked where he'd gotten the idea, the aides said, "From the movie! From *Bataan* with Robert Taylor. You know, the one with all those Filipinos in it. He just transposed." Actually, Marcos himself claimed to have been a Bataan hero and was decorated for it.

21. In October 1985 Imelda Marcos sent Mrs. Reagan two gowns estimated at $10,000: one a black velvet with a silver sequin and rhinestone phoenix, the other a red silk strapless dress with a rhinestone butterfly. They were put into the archives. (Sara Booth Conway, "The President's Presents: Annual List Exceeds $200,000 Worth," *The Washington Post*, March 7, 1986, p. D1).

22. During the first two years of his first administration, Reagan launched the most massive military buildup ever in peacetime, including the deployment of the new B-1 bomber and the MX long-range missile system.

23. Overridden by the House on September 29, 1986; by the Senate on October 2, 1986.

24. Lane Venardos was named head of Special Events, the unit that covers elections and crises.

25. Peter Boyer, *Who Killed CBS?: The Undoing of America's Number One News Network* (New York: Random House, 1988), p. 117: "What Sauter gave to Rather was *real* power—a voice in news policy, a direct say in story assignments and staffing, dominion over careers. . . . [Sauter] ceded a share of his presidency to his anchormen. . . . Rather attended management meetings; he was consulted on all hires; he was clued in to every aspect of the running of the operation."

26. Geraldine Fabrikant, "Tisch Rules Out Selling CBS Parts," *The New York Times*, September 15, 1986, section D, p. 1.

27. What we saw was crushing disbelief that after successfully using a nonexistent, dubious technology as a bargaining chip, Reagan refused to swap Star Wars for Gorbachev's offer of a massive, asymmetrical reduction in all Soviet nukes. George Shultz, it was said, had begged Reagan to make the deal.

28. One year later, the United States and USSR would sign the INF treaty

to eliminate medium- and short-range nuclear missiles in Europe and put an end to the superpower arms race.

29. This was the most significant tax-reform bill ever. It brought the top personal income tax rate down to 35 percent from 70 percent and closed a number of loopholes. It also included a $20-billion-a-year tax *increase* for corporations that was used to finance the tax cut for individuals. Democrats loved it, and Reagan seemed not to notice its departure from GOP doctrine.

30. *Facts on File*, vol. 46, no. 2398, November 7, 1986, pp. 825–826: "The White House is still refusing to comment" on the "swap of military equipment for American hostages." It was believed that Iran had leverage over Islamic Jihad and another terrorist outfit in Lebanon that together continued to hold the American hostages.

31. Patrick Buchanan was to have been on as well, but he canceled. I got a note explaining, "There was no way I could deal with Issue No. 1 on the show: The Iranian & Hostage Issue; as we are operating here under a vow of silence. . . . I owe you one. PB"

32. I wonder what she thought of Barry Goldwater's observation: "I think President Reagan has got his butt in a crack on this Iran thing."

33. Lou Cannon, "GOP Senators Ask President to Replace Regan, Casey," *The Washington Post*, December 6, 1986, p. A1.

34. A senior administration official told me that Reagan intuitively organized his staff so that several — say, three — aides would compete and argue with and rival one another. Out of that, decisions would "bubble up" to him; he would never reach down to grab for the power. "When he got Don Regan," said the aide, "he sank out of the picture through his own passivity."

35. According to the four-and-one-half-hour PBS documentary "Reagan: An American Story," when Howard Baker took over as chief of staff, he asked Nancy Reagan to help persuade the president to admit publicly that he had in fact traded arms for hostages — something he was continuing to deny. She was able to talk him into delivering the following lines:

> A few months ago, I told the American people I did not trade arms for hostages. My heart and my best intentions still tell me that's true, but the facts and the evidence tell me it is not. As the Tower board reported, what began as a strategic opening to Iran deteriorated, in its implementation, into trading arms for hostages. This runs counter to my own beliefs. . . . There are reasons why it happened, but no excuses. It was a mistake.

36. James Dickenson and Paul Taylor, "Newspaper Stakeout Infuriates Hart," *The Washington Post*, May 4, 1997, p. A1. Hart was quoted on the womanizing issue: "Follow me around. . . . I'm serious. If anybody wants to put a tail on me, go ahead. They'd be very bored."

37. The Boland Amendment, passed on December 22, 1982, barred the use of funds to overthrow the Sandinista government in Nicaragua or provoke fighting between Nicaragua and Honduras.

38. Meese was never indicted for violating the law over Wedtech. But the scandal induced his resignation as attorney general (Peter B. Levy, *Encyclopedia of the Reagan-Bush Years* [Westport, Connecticut: Greenwood Press, 1996], pp. 385–386).

39. Tom Wicker in "Character Above All," PBS, May 29, 1996: "Up until relatively modern times, people made a choice between Republicans and Democrats. And that's about all they knew. My father was a 'Yellow Dog Democrat.' And he would have never thought of voting for a Republican, didn't matter who

it was. So I think the question of trying to judge people's character, judge individuals and choose between them, has come about probably with radio and certainly with television, with modern times, so to speak. And it's fairly easy in a case like Gary Hart, who convicted himself almost."

40. Ken Auletta, *Three Blind Mice: How the TV Networks Lost Their Way* (New York: Random House, 1991), pp. 271–272.

41. The congressional committees on Iran-contra issued a final report on November 18, 1987, that blamed Reagan for not fulfilling his oath to "take care that the laws be faithfully executed."

42. Among the members of the delegation: Kissinger's old number two, Brent Scowcroft; Kenneth Damm of the State Department; and Ivan Selin of the Defense Department.

43. Donald Rothberg, "Bush Campaign Exploits Rather-Veep Confrontation," Associated Press, January 26, 1988, A.M. cycle.

44. The *Newsweek* issue of April 29, 1985, asked, "What makes CBS such a lightning rod?" "The real reason seems to lie in the network's history. CBS has a tradition of sticking its neck out on controversial stories." The magazine mentioned Murrow's reporting from Europe in the late 1930s and his commentary on Joseph McCarthy in the 1950s. Also noted: searing documentaries such as "Harvest of Shame," on migrant workers, and "The Selling of the Pentagon," on lobbying; Cronkite's reporting on Vietnam after the 1968 Tet offensive and on Watergate; Rather's clashes with Nixon. *Newsweek* said that in recent years "CBS stories have hurt liberals more often than conservatives," noting Roger Mudd's 1979 interview that ended Ted Kennedy's run for the presidency and Cronkite's constant reminder of the number of hostage days during the Carter administration (Jonathan Alter, "CBS as Lightning Rod," *Newsweek*, April 29, 1985, p. 56).

45. Larry Speakes left the White House at the height of the Iran-contra scandal because he was offered a job as senior vice president for communications at Merrill Lynch. His memoir was published in May 1988.

46. Economists Barry Bluestone and Bennett Harrison, "American Job Machine Has Begun to Sputter: Trend Is Toward Low-Wage Employment," *The Washington Post*, May 17, 1987, p. H2. They put the number of new jobs created from 1980 to 1987 at "almost 12 million," but they contended that two out of five of the new jobs "paid dismally poor wages," less than $7,400 a year.

47. Larry Margasak, "Thornburgh Asked to Pledge Full Meese Probe," Associated Press, July 13, 1988.

Meese was investigated by independent counsel James McKay for conflict-of-interest charges, including his assistance to Wedtech, a Bronx, New York, defense contractor; his actions in connection with a proposed $1 billion Iraqi oil pipeline project; and whether he took actions favorable to regional Bell telephone companies while he held $14,000 in telephone stock.

48. Marie Cocco, Saul Friedman, Ellis Henican, Susan Page, Gaylord Shaw, Patrick Sloyan, Myron Waldman, and Catharine Woodard, "Smears and Fears: The '88 Campaign," *Newsday*, November 6, 1988, p. 4.

49. Senator Bill Bradley went to the floor of the Senate to accuse Bush of using Willie Horton "to divide white and black voters and to appeal to fear." He said that Bush was "inflaming racial tensions." The Bush campaign itself never ran a "Willie Horton" ad; it was used by state operatives and independent groups. The Bush campaign did, however, run the "furlough-turnstyle" ad with its own racial stereotypes.

50. Claudia Dreifus, "The Survivor," *The New York Times Magazine*, September 10, 1995, p. 52.

51. Then again, who other than Winston Churchill ever called for sacrifice?

As my friend the historian Gil Troy pointed out, "LBJ, JFK, even FDR had not prepared the [country] for the sacrifices required to maintain a larger welfare state." Along with Reagan, they all "told Americans they could have their cake and eat it too."

52. Garry Wills, "Reagan's Legacy: It's His Party," *The New York Times Magazine*, August 11, 1996, p. 30.

PART FIVE: GEORGE AND BARBARA BUSH

1. "Kerry Kids About Shooting Quayle," United Press International, November 16, 1988.

2. Herbert Parmet finds hints in Bush's diaries of Bush recoiling from "the tacky ostentation" of the Reagan circle (Herbert Parmet, *George Bush: The Life of a Lone Star Yankee* [New York: A Lisa Drew Book/Scribner, 1997], p. 260).

3. Alessandra Stanley, "Presidency by Ralph Lauren," *The New Republic*, December 12, 1988, p. 18.

4. Finley Peter Dunne, aka Mr. Dooley, described being vice president of the United States as "a sort of disgrace, like writing anonymous letters" (Lance Morrow, "Caught in the Act of Soliloquy," *Time*, June 1, 1998, p. 98).

5. The Navy would conclude that an *Iowa* crewman, gunner's mate 2nd class Clayton Hartwig, had "most likely" triggered the explosion as an act of suicide ("FBI Doubts Iowa Blast Evidence," *Facts on File*, November 10, 1989, p. 837,G3).

6. White House pool report, February 24, 1989.

7. Gil Troy, *Affairs of State: The Rise and Rejection of the Presidential Couple Since World War II* (New York: The Free Press, 1997), p. 377.

8. Robert and Gerald Jay Goldberg, *Anchors: Brokaw, Jennings, Rather and the Evening News* (New York: Birch Lane Press, 1990), p. 349.

9. Harry Walters and Janet Hock, "Networking Women," *Newsweek*, March 13, 1989, p. 48.

10. Actually, he is paraphrasing Tennessee Williams. In *A Streetcar Named Desire*, Scene 6, Blanche says, "Sometimes — there's God — so quickly."

11. Margaret Thatcher chided him, "Remember, George, this is no time to go wobbly" (Margaret Thatcher, *Downing Street Years* [New York: HarperCollins, 1993], p. 824).

12. Dan Goodgame, "In the Gulf: Bold Vision," *Time*, January 7, 1991, p. 22.

13. The team of producers on the 11:30 Gulf War specials was Sarah Morton, Steve McCarthy, Dan Morris, Chris McHenry, and our secretary, Stacia Phillips.

14. One of my sources would quote Bush at the end of 1990 as saying, "Gingrich is our Heseltine," referring to the man who brought Margaret Thatcher down from within her own party in November 1990.

15. George Will, "Bush's Cupboard Is Bare," *The Washington Post*, January 31, 1986, p. A12: "The unpleasant sound Bush is emitting as he traipses from one conservative gathering to another is a thin, tinny 'arf' — the sound of a lapdog."

16. Atwater expressed regret. "In 1988, fighting Dukakis," he wrote in *Life* magazine, "I said that I 'would strip the bark off the little bastard' and 'make Willie Horton his running mate.' I am sorry for both statements: the first for its naked cruelty, the second because it makes me sound like a racist, which I am not" (Thomas Edsall, "GOP Battler Lee Atwater Dies at 40: Leading Tactician of

Party's Southern Strategy Victim of Brain Tumor," *The Washington Post*, March 30, 1991, p. A1).

17. Because of its commitment to 24-hour news, CNN was the only network that had booked a dedicated transmission line out of Baghdad, meaning that when the phone lines went down, only CNN had the capability of continuing to broadcast.

18. Richard Zoglin, "The Global Village: Live from the Middle East," *Time*, January 28, 1991, p. 69.

19. Brian Donlon, "Network Correspondents on the Front Line," *USA Today*, January 15, 1991, p. 3D.

20. 148 Americans died in combat, about a quarter from friendly fire.

21. Lawrie Mifflin, "An Old Hand's View of TV News: Not Good," *The New York Times*, March 22, 1998, p. 41-AR.

INDEX

Aaron, Betsy, 151, 397
ABC News:
  CBS reporters hired by, 136, 334
  female reporters at, 246, 334
  newsmagazine developed by, 239,
    292
  ratings position of, 159
  reporters for, 21
abortion, 163, 186, 191, 195, 215,
    328, 339, 364, 371–72
Abrams, Elliott, 223
Abul Abbas, Muhammed, 242
Abzug, Bella, 81–82
Achille Lauro, terrorist hijacking of,
    241–42
Acuff, Roy, 208
Adams, Jackie, 124, 155, 229
affirmative action programs:
  backlash against, 187
  in journalism, 11, 13, 15, 25
  Meese's efforts against, 252–
    253
Afghanistan, Soviet invasion of,
    107
Agnew, Spiro, 34, 50
Ailes, Roger, 289, 290, 294, 304
Ajami, Fouad, 394, 403
Allen, Herb, 258
Allen, Jodie, 334
Allen, Woody, 83, 138, 139
Alvarez, Roberto, 391
Alzheimer's disease, 317–21
Amadon, Greg, 138
Amanpour, Christiane, 405
American Almanac, 239
American Civil Liberties Union
    (ACLU), 310, 315
America Tonight, 378–85, 387, 390,
    392, 393, 394, 397, 403

Anderson, Terry, 233
Andrews, Wyatt, 327, 333, 388,
    389
Andropov, Yuri, 188
Angleton, James Jesus, 50
anonymous sources, 25–26, 43–44
Antonellis, Darcy, 361
apartheid, U.S. policy on, 240–41,
    255–56
Aquino, Benigno, 249
Aquino, Corazón, 249–50, 253–54
Arafat, Yasser, 189, 242, 287, 406
Arbatov, Georgi, 285, 292
Arledge, Roone, 136, 171, 303
arms race, 99, 244, 263–65
Armstrong, John, 14, 26
Armstrong, Scott, 27
Arnett, Peter, 388, 393, 394
Aspin, Les, 86–87, 381
Atwater, Lee, 201, 208, 214, 290
  apology to Dukakis from, 387
  illness of, 365, 387
  in 1988 Bush campaign, 300, 302,
    304, 311, 341
  on shift in journalistic style, 343
Auletta, Ken, 243, 303
Aziz, Tariq, 396
Azoff, Irving, 78, 97

Babbitt, Bruce, 293
Babbitt, Hattie, 293
Baker, Howard, 29, 41, 275
Baker, James A., III, 122, 220–21
  as Bush's campaign manager, 304,
    309, 310–11, 314
  as Bush's secretary of state, 317,
    329, 341–42, 354, 355, 358, 377,
    398

PICTURE CREDITS